The Renaissance
Discovery of Time

Harvard Studies in Comparative Literature
Founded by William Henry Schofield
31

The Renaissance
Discovery
of Time

Ricardo J. Quinones

Harvard University Press
Cambridge, Massachusetts
1972

In memory of my parents
Helen and Lawrence Quinones

Contents

Preface

An Associated Press dispatch from Arkansas City, Kansas, appearing in the Los Angeles *Times* (April 3, 1968) announced that members of the Chilocco Homemakers Club had bought a four-foot clock and placed it on top of one of the buildings of the Chilocco Indian School. The Homemakers were trying to encourage students, the report continues, to make use of the clock rather than the sun. The school superintendent was quoted as saying, "Reservation time means almost no time at all." This indifference to more precise and mechanical means of time-telling created difficulties for the Indians who had jobs or who needed to get anywhere "on time." In a chapter entitled, "The Voices of Time," E. T. Hall, in his *The Silent Language* (Garden City, N.Y.: Doubleday, 1959), recounts the measures that another superintendent took to make the Sioux Indians appreciate the value of time. Mr. Hall concludes, "He was right, of course. The Sioux could not adjust to European ways until they had learned the meaning of time." We ourselves can come to appreciate what a unique part of Western culture is our sense of time, when we see the stumbling block it presents to people of another inheritance. We segment time, we schedule time, and when it is thus segmented and scheduled, we regard it as an indispensable, precious commodity. This modern sense of time has its more immediate origins in that period of our history which, more than any other, has served to separate our values and responses from the rest of the world — the Renaissance. Arch-westerner Kipling's implied exhortation to "fill the unforgiving minute / With sixty seconds' worth of distance run," while nonsense to a contemporary Indian, would make perfect sense, in principle, to a Petrarch of the fourteenth century, and a Rabelais of the sixteenth century. They were only two of the writers who gave important expression to the new sense of time that was developing in the West. Petrarch made sure that he slept only six hours a day. Two hours he allotted to other "necessities," and the rest he was thus able to devote to his studies and writing: time was a precious thing, not to be wasted. Even more rigorous scheduling was involved in the educational regimen designed for that slumbering giant, Gargantua. Showing the close early relation between humanism and a sense of time, his new mentors so monitored his studies, "that not one hour of the day was lost." Although individual notions would undergo noticeable shifts and turns, still the basic conception of time in the West was given primary impetus by the men and society of the Renaissance.

Curiously enough, given this century's own fascination with time — the century of Proust and Mann and Joyce, of "West-Running Brook," "The Directive," and the *Four Quartets* — there exists no comprehensive and organic study of time in the literature of the Renaissance. This gap is more surprising when one considers how thoroughly the surrounding periods have been canvassed. For the classical, Christian, and modern notions of time there exist studies in abundance. One has only to look at the bibliography in the valuable and level-headed article by Arnaldo Momigliano, "Time in Ancient Historiography," *History and Theory,* Beiheft 6 (1966), to observe the wealth of available commentary on the Hellenic and Hebraic time senses. Very recently Jacqueline de Romilly's Messinger lectures at Cornell were published. Her *Time in Greek Tragedy* (Ithaca, N.Y.: Cornell University Press, 1968) is a work which could very well have served as prototype, in scope and purpose, of the kind of study I am attempting here. C. A. Patrides' very rich *The Phoenix and the Ladder: The Rise and Decline of the Christian View of History,* University of California English Studies, 29 (Berkeley: University of California Press, 1964) indicates how full has been the attention given the area of Christian eschatology, as does his *Milton and the Christian Tradition* (Oxford: Clarendon Press, 1966). Miltonists can find much of value in Oscar Cullmann's *Christ and Time,* translated by Floyd V. Filson (Philadelphia: Westminster Press, 1964). An expert summary of nineteenth-century attitudes toward time is Jerome Buckley's *The Triumph of Time* (Cambridge, Mass.: Harvard University Press, 1966). Even if we look at three recent anthologies, *Man and Time: Papers from the Eranos Yearbooks,* Bollingen Series 30 (New York: Pantheon, 1957), George Frazer's *The Voices of Time* (New York: Braziller, 1966), and Richard Gale's *The Philosophy of Time* (Garden City, N.Y.:

Doubleday, 1967), Renaissance spokesmen and even evidence are notably lacking.

I am of course not suggesting that the study of time in the literature of the Renaissance is virgin territory. There are valuable suggestions in Lewis Mumford's *Technics and Civilization* (New York: Harcourt Brace, 1934); in Sebastian de Grazia's *Of Time, Work, and Leisure* (New York: Twentieth Century Fund, 1962); in Hall's work mentioned above; in articles by Jacques LeGoff and E. P. Thompson, of which I make extensive use and to which I shall refer in my text; and also in Carlo Cipolla's *Clocks and Culture: 1300–1700* (New York: Walker, 1967). Suggestive pages in Alfred von Martin's *Sociology of the Renaissance* (London: Kegan Paul, Trench, Trubner, 1944), and Hans Baron's "Towards a Sociological Interpretation of the Renaissance," *The South Atlantic Quarterly,* 38 (1939), 427, are concerned with the new time valuations of bourgeois society and humanistic culture and bring us closer to our subject. Specifically dealing with literature are Paul Meissner's "Empirisches und ideelles Zeiterleben in der englischen Renaissance," *Anglia* 60 (1936), 165; a section of Douglas Bush's Claremont lectures of 1957, "Time and Man," reprinted in his *Prefaces to Renaissance Literature* (New York: Norton, 1965); and Erwin Stürzl's substantial *Der Zeitbegriff in der elisabethanischen Literatur: The Lackey of Eternity,* Wiener Beitrage zur englischen Philologie, 69 (1965); and of course Georges Poulet's studies are well known. There have also been some doctoral dissertations and numerous articles dealing with single authors. From art historians students of literature have had much to learn about the theme of time in the Renaissance; most prominently should be mentioned Erwin Panofsky's "Father Time," *Studies in Iconology* (New York: Oxford University Press, 1939), and the work of Samuel Chew, Rudolph Wittkower, and Fritz Saxl. But to say all this makes the lack of a comprehensive Renaissance time study even more surprising.

This study had its genesis in a doctoral dissertation, "Views of Time in Shakespeare," presented to the department of comparative literature at Harvard University in August 1963. I should be pleased if that department found its own liberality and encouragement justified herein. In its method this study blends the interests of comparative literature, thematics, and the history of ideas. I treat time as a theme, that is, a fairly recognizable constellation of attitudes and ideas, in relation to which I discuss some of the major literary figures of the Renaissance. As I utilize it, then, time is similar to what A. O. Lovejoy called a "unit-idea." To follow the course of such a concept can be of great importance historically: the method not only brings out similarities but also marks important divergences. It brings themes together on a common ground in order to distinguish them better. But above all thematics is an instrument of analysis and should not be confused with "general literature." E. R. Curtius once wrote that "all things are potent with unfathomed codes." Thematics, or the study in historical perspective of a particular configuration of ideas, can help to decode, or bring to attention, materials which might otherwise pass unnoticed. As one celebrated instance of this method I might point to A. O. Lovejoy's essay, "The Supposed Primitivism of Rousseau's *Discourse on Inequality,*" *Essays in the History of Ideas* (Baltimore, Md.: Johns Hopkins Press, 1948).

Underlying this approach is the desire on my part to be both analytical and historical; on the one hand to preserve the individual integrity of an author and on the other to draw the lines of continuity and change. These demands are not always easily reconciled. For a better solution to the problem of melding the interests of history and literary comment, the reader can refer to Harry Levin's much-praised *The Myth of the Golden Age in the Renaissance* (Bloomington, Ind.: Indiana University Press, 1969), which, if it had appeared earlier, would have been of great usefulness in the organizational strategy of this study but which nevertheless did appear in time for me to exploit its theme — the Renaissance counterpart of my own. In this study I have sought to immerse myself as deeply as possible in the particular qualities and individual evolution of particular writers, and this accounts for the length of some of the chapters. I have sought to avoid the kind of thematic study which is a simple listing of topics. Such organization, in addition to being anathema to literary discussion, sets the topic off in a timeless realm apart from the realities of man's changing nature. To a scholar who has followed the full course of a writer's development, his alternating currents of attraction, dismay and recoil, and then return, it is somewhat dissatisfying to come across a historical study which picks out one particular phase of his career and makes it typical. All of the men studied here went through more than one stage of growth — at one point committed to the public and ongoing world of time and history, later deeply disillusioned, and still later enjoying a return to their earlier commitments, although with a more personal and appropriate kind of style. The study of themes, in order to be valid, needs to consider an author's position in relation to the phases of his own evolution. But one does not want to stop there. Comparative literature, like archeological excavations, sends down parallel lines for the sake of a more significant yield. Stürzl's *Der Zeitbegriff in der elisabethanischen Literatur,* which I have found useful, includes a chapter on "Die Unsterblichkeit durch das Kind." But in no way does he indicate why this topic should have enjoyed a particular Elizabethan prestige. In fact, there is no mention of Italian bourgeois culture and civic humanism, of Ficino's commentary on Plato's *Symposium,* of Rabelais, nor of that critical transmitter of Renaissance Italian values to Tudor Englishmen, Erasmus, and his much publicized letter, translated as the "Epystle in laude and prayse of matrymony," which had a particularly fruitful career in England of the sixteenth century. Nor is there mention of the intermingling of children and time and the Renaissance concern for education. When such different phenomena recur persistently they seem to possess a greater than ordinary significance. Comparison tends to call for such elaboration; it leads to conceptual clarification.

One might say that there are two criteria which determine the worth of a theme. The first would be the question of what works of what authors it involves in discussion and to what extent it illuminates those works, and the second, a natural corollary of the first, would be the degree to which the theme seems to bring out the profile and essential dynamics of a historical period. When we consider time in the Renaissance we are obliged to deal with the most notable works of the greatest authors and are engaged, if we wish to pursue it to that level, with the very nature of the Renaissance and its most critical problems. I do not mean this in a casual sense, since in every writer the word "time" is employed and from every work one can deduce a "time sense." But time as a concept is essentially different in the *Purgatorio*; in Petrarch's *Rime,* his *Secretum,* his letters, or his *Trionfi*; in Spenser's *Complaint* volume and the much grander interludes, the *Bower of Bliss,* the *Garden of Adonis,* and the *Cantos of Mutabilitie*; in Shakespeare's sonnets and, in fact, almost all of his plays; in Milton's sonnets, his "On Time," *Lycidas,* and his three great later poems. In referring to the concept of time in these superior works, we allude to a palpable presence, an object of direct address. Furthermore, any attempt to understand them without some reference to time would be defective. To discuss time in these works is to face them centrally and to approach an understanding of the Renaissance in all its complexity.

The authors I have chosen are illustrious and illustrative. This thought reassures me when I wince at the notable names omitted or not given due attention. Time in the waning Middle Ages without Villon? In the Renaissance without Ariosto and Tasso, Ronsard and DuBellay, Donne and Herbert? . . . And the list expands. For personal reasons the neglect of the Spanish authors, in particular Cervantes, is embarrassing. But as soon as we begin to cite the authors not mentioned, and those only of the first rank, we begin to see the merits of limitation. As the book now stands, with this selected group of authors, acutely conscious of time in their most important works, studied in depth, it seems self-contained, it has clarity, point, development, and some comprehensiveness. We might argue for additional authors but not against any of those mentioned. And I am not aware of any way in which additional authors would substantially alter the argument or introduce new concepts of any significance. There might be other, but no grander spokesmen for the issues here delineated.

Mention of this study's necessary limitations brings me to a point about which students of comparative literature are rightly sensitive: how much our work is dependent upon that group of elite specialists who have made their life work the detailed study of a single author. If we studied Petrarch without Ernest Hatch Wilkins, Chaucer without Fred Robinson, Milton without Douglas Bush — how much harder our task would have been. Throughout this study, despite serious onslaughts of doubt and envy, I was saved only by reminding myself that my job was not to know all there was to know about the authors in question but to look at them from a single point of view. My additional stay was precisely the fact that I had such men of learning and insight, as well as others, to depend upon. My text and notes will make clear my indebtedness.

In several ways this study falls into two parts. Primarily I would have it considered a work of literary history and criticism. As much as I use literary evidence to illustrate developing notions of Renaissance time, even more I use time to illuminate works of literature. Yet, of all themes, time seems to involve man most readily in society and history, and, of all periods of grandeur, the Renaissance seems profoundly practical and equally profoundly antimetaphysical. Time, in its ethical imperative, and the Renaissance, in its drive toward practical cases, would seem to be interrelated. This would explain the fact that modern anthologies of time, primarily philosophical in focus, have little Renaissance representation, since such evidence would naturally be derived from the world of literature. While the main substance of each part of this work is literary, the introductory frames serve historical and semantic purposes. There, besides providing whatever background — economic, political, intellectual — that I think necessary, I also offer explanations of the ways I would like certain words understood. I indicate boundaries and introduce recurrent themes and their general implications, although as always in literary study, the individual readings and yields are most important. Quite naturally, where I am seeking a larger, supportive frame, I rely to a certain extent on major secondary works of interpretation; yet here I have chosen those that have direct bearing on my studies and whose results my own independent researches seem to corroborate. The other division in this work falls between the writers of the fourteenth and sixteenth centuries. The continuities between the two allow their inclusion in the same text; their differences insist on its separation into two parts.

On some technical matters I would like to add a few words. In line with the current trend that seeks to avoid excessive references and notes, I have tried to include as much information as possible in the text, including line or page citations for direct quotations. Occasionally, however, my notes tend to be large because of the particular problems of my procedure. Since I follow each of my authors in depth, I occasionally transect some lines of historical development, which have direct bearing on my text and for which there is useful bibliography. Where textual inclusion would have been inopportune, I have relegated these excursions to the notes. Since my notes are bibliographical, I have chosen to exclude a separate bibliography, referring the reader to the index, where sources can be cross-checked. In the text, I quote poetry in the original language, followed by prose trots. Prose — although in the Renaissance much prose, like that of Rabelais or of Montaigne, is as untranslatable as great poetry — I quote in extant translations, except in some instances where I use my own renderings of as yet untranslated material from Petrarch.

Various stipends have facilitated the completion of this study. My home institution, Claremont Men's College, was very generous, allowing me two summer grants and a sum to cover the expense of preparing the manuscript. In the summer of 1968 I was a Milton fellow at the William Andrews Clark Memorial Library in Los Angeles. During the tenure of that grant I was able to complete my chapter on Milton, which benefitted from the specialized criticisms of my fellow seminarists amid the particularly elegant surroundings. For the academic year 1968–69, I held a Younger Scholar fellowship from the National Endowment for the Humanities; without the release from teaching duties afforded by this grant I would not have been able to finish this study. As the country girds itself for another gloomy period of conservative retrenchment and financial belt-tightening I regret that such support might not be available for other younger scholars, who will be most in need of it.

The staff of Honnold Library of the Claremont colleges gave me patient help, as did Mrs. Wrigley of the Francis Bacon Foundation Library in Claremont. In relation to materials in this study, French Fogle, Robert W. Corrigan, Ralph Ross, and Geoffrey Strickland answered queries or were otherwise helpful. Early versions of the manuscript were read by Albert B. Friedman, Annette Smith, and Langdon Elsbree, and their interest was much appreciated. Professor Elsbree, as department chairman, was particularly helpful and considerate. Andrew Bongiorno, an always welcome visitor to Claremont, gave four chapters a very rigorous scrutiny; I have benefitted much from his concentrated attention. Dante della Terza wrote encouragements in regard to the chapter on Petrarch, and Douglas Bush, in a retirement that is purely nominal, submitted the chapter on Milton to his usual generous and accurate criticism. Herbert Weisinger was encouraging in regard to large sections of a rough manuscript. Walter Kaiser, chairman of the department of Comparative Literature at Harvard University and general editor of the Harvard Studies in Comparative Literature, read the manuscript in its entirety and offered helpful advice and queries. He further aided its publication by providing a most generous subvention from departmental funds. Harry Levin oversaw the inception of this study and assisted at its completion. When a very gangly and raw product descended upon his summer retreat, he saw its merits and offered useful criticisms and much-needed encouragement. Well beyond the call of duty, he has been a constant supporter. The argument of my text will give surer indications of the appreciation I have for the work of this man, who remains the scholar's scholar and the critic's critic.

My family has had to live with this project for too long. But my wife Laurel and our four children cannot really be thanked, since they are too closely connected with its ideas. In triumph and anxiety, they have made up its very world.

Claremont, California, May 1970
New York City, January 1971

Part One

Abbreviations

BHR	*Bibliothèque d'Humanisme et Renaissance*
ELH	*Journal of English Literary History*
JEGP	*Journal of English and Germanic Philology*
JHI	*Journal of the History of Ideas*
MLN	*Modern Language Notes*
MP	*Modern Philology*
PMLA	*Publications of the Modern Language Association of America*
PQ	*Philological Quarterly*
SP	*Studies in Philology*
SQ	*Shakespeare Quarterly*
UTQ	*University of Toronto Quarterly*

Chapter 1
The Setting

For the men of the Renaissance, time is a great discovery — the antagonist against which they plan and plot and war, and over which they hope to triumph. It is for the sake of such conquest that they separate themselves from a more easygoing world of restricted rhythms and patterns. Victory over time is the measure of their heroism; a need for special distinction, one which rises above the anonymity of the everyday, compels them to seek the arduous, the unusual. Their energy and their desire for learning they contrast with the sloth and the acquiescence in ignorance which they consider to characterize their predecessors and contemporaries. It is important to observe that for most of the writers discussed in this study, for Petrarch, for Rabelais, for Shakespeare, and for Milton, it is precisely this new sense of time, calling forth energetic, even heroic response, that they use to distinguish themselves and the leaders of their new age from the preceding age. For Petrarch, medieval neglect had allowed the cherished classics to suffer the ruins of time; for Rabelais, the energy of the new humanism is contrasted with Gothic torpor that only sleeps and feeds; for Shakespeare, the sense of effective management of time that Hal acquires sets him apart from the ruined monarchs, Henry VI or Richard II, who presume on the older conception of natural, unimpeded processes or on a premature sense of being, and Milton in the *Seventh Prolusion* and *Of Education* shows how much he is part of this same heroic humanism. In fact, a chief ingredient by which both Rabelais and Shakespeare form their ideal Renaissance prince is time. And precisely what is lacking in the older defective representatives is this sense of temporal urgency and the felt need to utilize one's time as vigorously as possible. Time is not an element that one divines in the men of the Renaissance: it is a force of their consciousness by which they themselves indicate the differences that set apart their new awareness of the world and their place in it from an older one. Time itself and temporal response are factors in distinguishing Renaissance from medieval.

Precisely the society to develop this new time sense was the growing commercial, capitalistic, and urban culture of the late Middle Ages and early Renaissance. The economic and social bases of the shift from the Middle Ages to the Renaissance have been comprehensively and expertly summarized by W. K. Ferguson, whose *Europe in Transition* is a modulated substantiation of the brilliant monograph, *The Renaissance*.[1] Italy, ideally situated as the *entrepôt* of the trade routes of East and West, was the pioneer in Western capitalism: "The history of early capitalism is to a very large extent the history of Italian commerce." (p. 97) According to Ferguson most of the capitalist business techniques were well established there before 1300, but it was the following century and a half that he chooses to call the "classic period" of early Italian capitalism. Of course, the more traditional and conservative ways of life were not overthrown instantly, if they were overthrown at all. Yet it is clear that a new dynamic had been introduced which, even according to our literary testimony, created tensions both in the developing society and, most keenly, in the minds and hearts of the writers. The medieval forms were relatively closed and local. The country manor and even the town guild traded freedom for security. Feudal society was a subsistence economy based on agriculture. Practically moneyless, it tended toward the barter system (although never quite reaching it). With the reopening of the trade routes, commerce and, in its wake, capitalism flourished. Enterprising spirits, the merchant-adventurers, whose questing spirit Dante captured brilliantly in his portrait of Ulysses, overstepped the former bounds and circumscriptions. Determined and daring, they insisted on the rewards of their risks. It was inevitable that their way of life and the life patterns of their brethren in the towns would involve markedly different time valuations. Marc Bloch has written that feudal society exhibited "une vaste indifférence au temps." [2] But in the new economy and society of the urban, commercial world a closer reading was given to time.

The mechanical clock, the instrument that fit their needs, providing a frame of some regularity and exactitude for the diversified activities of the city, first appeared, according to modern consensus, toward the end of the thirteenth century. Neither the sundial nor the clepsydra (the occasionally very elaborate timepiece powered by waterflow) could provide the regular time record that was needed. The sundial offered no reading when the sun was not shining, and the clepsydra was of no use in freezing temperatures. Beyond these timepieces, so reliant on the natural elements, a more uniform and undeviating means of measuring time was needed. This finally was provided by the mechanical clock and its ingenious use of the verge escapement and foliot. Such clocks could be very elaborate, and their great expense showed manifest civic pride. But in the history of "clocks and culture" what is new in the development of Western horology is the application of mechanics in a system of economic production.[3] Prior to their remarkable development in the course of the Renaissance, clocks were products of art and science but did not pass beyond the stage of the spectacular. In A.D. 807 an embassy from Haroun al Rashid to the Frankish court of Charlemagne excited the marvel of the courtiers with an elaborate water clock. But in the fourteenth century the development of the mechanical clock in the urban commercial centers of central and northern Italy, northern France, southern England, and Germany was an indication that the strong forward movement, the dynamic element, of society had passed from the East to the West.

More than coincidence, a causal relationship can be seen in the invention of the mechanical clock in the period of early capitalism. The interests of commerce themselves required more reliable timepieces (as well as a more aroused time consciousness). As Jacques LeGoff concludes, "Accurate measurement of time becomes more and more important for the success of business."[4] For instance, profits are dependent in crucial ways on time: the time taken for the transportation of goods from one place to another, the rise or fall in prices that occurs in the meantime, the amount of work time expended by employees, and their efficiency. Money, itself, in its fluctuating exchange values, also demands clearer conceptions of, and greater attention paid to, time. These are some of the early developments that look ahead to the world of "the Bourse when minutes and even seconds can make or unmake fortunes."[5] A new demand for exactitude is introduced by these commercial pressures.

Such developments, however, indicate more than mechanical and technical progress; as Gustav Bilfinger concludes, they show a transformation in the frame and life of a society. In his pioneer study, *Die mittelalterlichen Horen und die modernen Stunden,* Bilfinger discusses the patterns that had prevailed throughout the Middle Ages, when the

Church had regulated the comings and goings of daily bourgeois life. Mornings and evenings she rang the time of the Ave Maria prayer, thereby indicating the beginning and the end of the work day. Her bells announced the time of the mass and of the forenoon meal; they were rung to mark feasts and deaths, fairs and calls to defense. The Church provided the frame for all facets of city life. Given such a situation, Bilfinger asks "What interest could the Church have had to wish a change in such an order of things, where she was the absolute ruler [unbedingte Herrscherin]?" [6] In fact, it was to fill the needs of the growing bourgeois sector that the mechanical clock and its associated uniform and regular means of time computation were brought into being. In the course of the fourteenth century, the older way of temporal reckoning (Matins, Prima, Tertia, Sexta, Nona, Vespers, and Compline), which derived from the canonical hours of the monasteries, was replaced by an hourly system of time telling. The older means could no longer satisfy the multifarious needs of a bustling commercial city, whose many activities required a more regular and ordered frame of life. Here we anticipate, in mechanics, a primeval element of Renaissance time: it serves as an ordering and controlling force over rich variety.

Larger forces, involving ways of life, are at issue here. Bilfinger, looking beyond his subject, can see more than a transition from ancient to modern time calculation; he can see a shift from a religious to a secular point of view, from what LeGoff has called the "temps de l'Eglise" to the "temps du marchand." A religious containment attended the older temporal denominations. Florence, Dante tells us,

> dentro dalla cerchia antica,
> ond'ella toglie ancora e terza e nona,
> si stava in pace, sobria e pudica.

Florence, within her ancient circle from
which she still takes tierce and nones, abode
in peace, sober and chaste.

(*Par.* XV.97–99)

In his *Sociology of the Renaissance*, Alfred von Martin writes well of the broader implications of the time world of the new moneyed, commercial civilization. Feudalism was attached to the land and hence was conservative: its element was space. But money was a liberalizing force that required mobility. Nothing ventured, nothing gained, is proverbial among spokesmen for capitalism. In this new society time, motion, and money were intrinsic, all evidencing the greater need for man to achieve mastery and control over more aspects of his life: "In the Middle Ages power belonged to him who owned the soil, the feudal lord; but now Alberti could say that he who knew how to exploit money and time could make himself the master of all things." [7] Then, in words that echo the specific time concerns of Renaissance writers and poets, von Martin proceeds to describe more explicitly the new time sense and to contrast it in broad strokes with his notion of the medieval:

> The tempo of life was increased. Only now was formulated the new interpretation of time which saw it as a value, as something of utility. It was felt to be slipping away continuously — after the fourteenth century the clocks in the Italian cities struck all the twenty-four hours of the day. It was realized that time was always short and hence valuable, that one had to husband it and use it economically if one wanted to become "the master of all things." Such an attitude had been unknown to the Middle Ages; to them time was plentiful and there was no need to look upon it as something precious. It became so only when regarded from the point of view of the individual who could think in terms of the time measured out to him. It was scarce simply on account of natural limitations, and so everything from now on had to move quickly. For example, it became necessary to build quickly, as the patron was now building for himself. In the Middle Ages it was possible to spend tens and even hundreds of years on the completion of one building — a cathedral, a town hall or a castle . . . for life was the life of the community in which one generation quietly succeeds another. Men lived as part of an all embracing unity and thus life lasted long beyond its natural span. (p. 16)

For the Middle Ages time could be abundant, because behind the chances and changes of events man could sense a higher directing order. His life still had religious associations with the universe, his beginnings and his ends were in the hands of a providential and concerned divinity. Because of his faith he could then exist in an attitude of temporal ease. Neither time nor change appear to be critical, and hence there is no great worry about controlling the future. But for the new men of the Renaissance time was not plentiful but rare and precious. Since it was constantly slipping away, man must utilize available means of controlling it and, in some measure, ward off the termination it promoted. One must work as much as possible to see that events turn out favorably or, as in business, limit risk. But the problem here, as our writers sensed, is a psychological one — as most historical transformations are. One might logically argue that it need not be so, but nevertheless, the more of his own experience the individual managed to control, the more he mastered by his own skill, the less inclined he would be to let things be, to rely with patient trust in a providential Creator. But there are even more serious consequences here. While working to put more and more under the control of man, these new Renaissance developments also unleashed greater energies. Florence remained *sobria e pudica* within the old containments, but the new forces broke outside the old walls. And at the same time that new energies and desires were being aroused the older sources of satisfaction were losing their powers. Since the will is infinite the end must be tragic, our writers fear, because it will find no attainment fully capable of rendering satisfaction. *Cupidigia* for Dante, *concupiscentia* for Petrarch must go astray, since the only end commensurate with their power, the possibility of returning to God, has been destroyed by the very goals and ideals that aroused desire. Caught in between, it is no wonder that the Renaissance writers so dramatically conceive Hell and damnation, whether Dante's *Inferno,* Marlowe's *Dr. Faustus,* Shakespeare's *Richard III* and *Macbeth,* or Milton's Satan. The diabolic is impaled on its own boundless desire. It is no accident that the world of Renaissance literature is a world on the move, with great emphasis on will and desire, and that all of of these qualities are intimately connected with the changing temporal conceptions.

The chronological starting point of this study is Florence of the late thirteenth and early fourteenth centuries, that is, the society in which developed the first significant stirrings of what we could call, thinking of Dante, Petrarch, and Boccaccio, a poetic Renaissance. Proud in name and accomplishments, this mercantile and banking center provided a temporary coincidence between its energy and hopefulness and the higher heroic aspirations of the new writers. The walls of its public building, the Bargello, bear this inscription:

> Florence is full of all imaginable wealth
> She defeats her enemies in war and in civil strife,
> She enjoys the favor of fortune and has a powerful population;
> Successfully she fortifies and conquers castles,

> She reigns over the sea and the land and the whole world
> Under her leadership the whole of Tuscany enjoys happiness;
> Like Rome she is always triumphant . . .[8]

The world in which Dante grew up was that of a city flushed with victory. Through a series of encounters, the Guelphs had successfully established Florence as a city of burghers, ridding it forever of the threatening feudal landlords, the Ghibellines. Past good fortune led to anticipation of similar prospects in the future. The values of the citizenry were bourgeois, mercantile values. Yet however rational and confident, they did not feel their own endeavors to be at odds with their religious heritage. According to Millard Meiss, "though they remained deeply pious, they . . . believed with increasing assurance that they could enjoy themselves in this world without jeopardizing their chances in the next." [9] And it is in this sort of society and others like it that time became a crucial factor of consciousness. To be sure there were antecedents, but as of the fourteenth century, "le thème se précise, se dramatise." [10]

Not only in the case of great literature but also with the spokesmen for commonplace assumptions, time was an active part of moral exhortation. When we read the defenders of the seventeenth- and eighteenth-century "Protestant ethic" we can discern a remarkable conformity between their attitudes and those of these early burghers. In fact, one representative of the business mentality of early Florence, Paolo da Certaldo, has been called a fourteenth-century "Poor Richard." [11] Not only do we read in his book of maxims, *Il Libro di buoni costumi* (*Book of Good Habits*), "Chi troppo dorme tempo perde" ("Who sleeps too much loses time"), but even in more fundamental attitudes he reminds us of the circumspect, modest, yet reasonable and confident man to whom success belongs.[12] To be sure, there is a cosmic tremor in the background of his sensibility, as he reflects on the fragility of the human condition; there is also religious contempt for the "temporal goods" which can be taken from us by Fortune. (372) Paradoxically, however, such awareness leads not to despair but rather to its opposite: to conscious, determined effort. He advises his reader, "Always work toward and pursue gain. Do not say, 'I might be here today, but where will I be tomorrow . . .' You do not know the length of your life, nor what Fortune holds." (305) In a way that will become more prominent in the later Renaissance, uncertainty itself is cause for resolution and renewed diligence. Constant effort will eventually triumph, since, exhibiting the proverbial lore at which such a mind is adept, small raindrops wear down large rocks. (384) In the classic manner of Max Weber's thesis, he worships Christ but does not follow his ways. This is made clearer in another maxim, where he tells us of one Giovanni Chavaza, who, like King Lear, was scorned by the children to whom he gave all. From this experience he concludes, "He who abandons himself for others, will be destroyed by his madness." (304) Paolo da Certaldo's world is not that of the feudal grand gesture but rather that of bourgeois modesty, reasonableness, and practicality.

Almost naturally in his doctrine and in that of his many successors, procrastination is bad business. Maxims 17, 107, 254, 255, and 346 all warn against the dangers of delay. He quotes the proverb "Who wants to eat now must think of it before now," adding the conclusion, "You should not delay until the final moment when you can no longer." (107) "Provide, provide," is the cry uttered by Certaldo, which will continue to be heard whenever time is an object of address: "Foresight has much value and hindsight little. Therefore always be provident [sta proveduto] . . . and think that time passed can never be regained. Be diligent and provident in all your affairs, and keep from laziness as from the Devil himself or from any other enemy if you want to arrive at success." (346) Although Certaldo's purpose is mainly secular, woven through both thought and language are elements of Christian life and even demonology. The same mixture, with perhaps a different balance, is found in the work of Domenico Cavalca, a Pisan Dominican, who was a popular preacher in the fourteenth century.[13] His *Disciplina degli spirituali* uses as its text Paul's exhortation to the Galatians (6:9–10): "Therefore while we have time, let us do good to all men."

While thus far we have been emphasizing the large contributions to the new notion of time in the developing commercial centers of the Renaissance, this quotation should remind us — and there are others — that undeniably Christian thought yields more than one large tributary stream to the Renaissance discourse on time. While other exhortations from Christian tradition are gathered in Cavalca's chapters (see xix, xx, and xxi, whose respective titles reveal his argument: "Of Leisure and the Loss of Time," "What Reasons Lead Us to Conserve and to Keep an Account of Time," and "How Great a Vice It Is to Delay Doing Good Works"), he especially relies on the Gospels and Christ's concern with temporal vigilance. In Matthew 24, watchfulness is urged, since one does not know the hour of the Lord's coming. But perhaps the Gospels' most enduring temporal bequest derives from the subsequent chapter in Matthew, where Christ tells the parable of the talents. Its example of the servants' being called to account and the penalty inflicted on the niggardly servant who did not make use of his talent fits in with Renaissance activity and doctrine. The need for use and augmentation rather than idleness is the practical lesson of this parable, where indeed nothing ventured meant nothing gained, and where one could be punished for sins of omission as well as of commission.

A member of the preaching order, whose function was decidedly urban, Cavalca seems to have imbibed bourgeois values. He certainly uses his temporal sensitivity to reinforce a work consciousness. He shows impatience with the monastic orders and with those clergy who do not render services. Only the useful ones who say mass, or hear confessions, or preach, have the right to receive benefits. This attitude will clearly grow with the Renaissance, as will the consciousness of time. Cavalca is downright satirical, in a manner similar to Boccaccio's, of the contemplatives who forget that they are men and must also eat. If they want to eat, they must also work (his Italian text is another one that will recur in the Renaissance, the Pauline "Chi non vuole operare, non mangi"). The idle and do-nothing person is more than negligent; he is, after the parable of the talents, evil, since he scorns the gifts of God, among which Cavalca numbers time. "Therefore such a person will be called to account [sarà chiesta ragione] not only for the evil that he has committed, but also for the good that he has omitted." Citing the example of the talents and the barren tree Christ ordered destroyed, Cavalca concludes, "All of these examples show that the idle man [l'uomo ozioso] is in the danger of losing that good which he could have done, but he also incurs the wrath of God, and loses the time, and the talent that was given him so that he could add to it [il quale gli era stato dato afine, che con esso guadagnasse]." In the fourteenth century we find such intermingling of motives, the mixture of commercial impulse, which is almost intrinsic to the Renaissance concern with time, with biblical example and religious purpose.

To move from the more ordinary to the exceptional, Dante, Petrarch, and Boccaccio share their society's sense of energy and rejuvenation, as well as its most practical concerns with time. In them we find aroused energy and love of variety. They themselves were something of pioneers and acutely conscious of living in a new time, a time of poetic revival.[14] But they also could regard time as a precious commodity, an object worthy of scrupulous attention. This combination of forces was, as Hans Baron has noted, a disposition of humanism congenial to the tendencies of economic life: "The claims that man should wish for more than to fill his traditional station, that he should be a miser of his time and contemplate his life in the light of continuous progress and unlimited activity — these claims seemed to the men of the Renaissance a cultural as well as an economic need." [15] We must not forget that the men of this early, heroic age of modern capitalism have been heralded as pioneers, even *conquistadores*. For one writer, these chevaliers found their poet in Boccaccio, whose *Decameron* he has called "l'epopea mercantile," the merchant's epic.[16] Vittore Branca's thesis is that although Boccaccio's book of stories was written when the bottom had fallen out of Florentine optimism, during the depressed critical years of the 1340s, the years of bankruptcy, despotism, pestilence, and famine, still the basis of his book, and its subject, was precisely the earlier period of daring expansionism. Boccaccio's "libro del navigar mercantesco" imbibed and focused on the energies of this earlier period. Yet, Boccaccio is a case in point that this union had many submerged tensions and would reveal itself to be something of a misalliance.

Branca's phrase "l'epopea mercantile" is not mere hyperbole, nor is his reference to the "intraprendenza di quegli ulissidi degli scambi economici" ("the enterprise of these Ulysseses of trade"). It is precisely in the figure of Ulysses that Dante finds the energies of Florence worthy of epic address. *Inferno* XXVI, although its basic aim is to emphasize divergences, joins in summary testimony the movements of poet, city, and adventurer. The canto commences with an address to Florence. However much its economic expansionism is now the object of contemptuous and satirical reference, still Dante treats imaginatively and fairly the essential human desires represented by his city when he makes Ulysses their prestigious spokesman. When the master of human resourcefulness affirms that man is not a beast, that he was not meant to live and die domesticated, unadorned and unenlightened, he utters sentiments that will underlie the Renaissance war with time. From Dante to Petrarch and Rabelais, to Spenser and Shakespeare and Milton, only to sleep and feed is to be like a beast, and to meet a beast's end. Therefore, Ulysses exhorts his men in *carpe diem* fashion to use actively "questa tanto picciola vigilia dei nostri sensi" ("this so brief vigil to our senses"). Spirit and intellect, eager for knowledge and discovery, would leave behind the simpler routines of life, but his great fire ends in tragic self-destruction.

While obviously not doing justice to the subtlety and artistry of Ulysses' narrative, this discussion is enough to suggest the awe that Dante felt for this man of accomplishments, who seems to typify the greatness and tragedy of his own city, and also to suggest what will be one of the major themes of this book, the eventual separation of these major writers from an earlier, more vital identification with some of the larger ideals of their society. Ulysses' language, "picciola vigilia dei nostri sensi," indicates no comprehension of any larger direction or resolution to man's earthly passage — and this is what Dante required. How useful for our purposes, then that Dante should have transformed the traditional western voyage of Ulysses into the quest of modern Occidental man. As Ulysses moves to the West so does the strong movement of commerce and industry, science and technology, the clock and man's time consciousness, following their own "plus ultra" and leaving behind the Mediterranean world in which they were born. This study commences in the fourteenth century, when Europe begins to separate itself from most of the rest of the world. It terminates in the seventeenth century, when northern Europe moves into the post-Renaissance world, and southern Europe declines.

The Argument of Time

In the Renaissance time is part of a richly dramatic argument involving such new forces as children, secular education, and fame. It is for this reason that the more classic description of Renaissance temporal response, the Horatian *carpe diem,* or its variant *carpe florem,* motif, seems too limited in its horizons, too momentary, to encompass the larger relations of the individual to civilization and the race, those channels of continuity by which he sought to secure himself.

First, to deal with the nature of time rather than the means of response, the actual description of the processes of time in the Renaissance represents nothing new, although there is increased sense of urgency and a different emphasis on termination and final nothingness. In classical and Christian sources, in the Bible, Homer, Lucretius, and Ovid, life is seen as a process of natural succession, of comings and goings, of ripening and rot, of growth and decay. Ovid, using an image that Dante and Shakespeare would imitate, compares it to the movements of the waves:

> The tyme itself continually is fleeting like a brooke.
> For neyther brooke nor lygthsomme tyme can tarrye still. But looke
> As every wave dryves other foorth, and that that commes behynd
> Bothe thrusteth and is thrust itself: Even so the tymes by kynd
> Doo fly and follow bothe at once, and evermore renew.
> For that that was before is left, and streyght there dooth ensew
> Anoother that was never erst.[17]

For Augustine and for Boethius, this temporal exposure separates man from God. In these matters of time and eternity, they were the prime fashioners of the philosophic tradition of the Christian Middle Ages and of prime importance for the emergent poets of the fourteenth century. God's eternity is not merely one of superior duration to the time of man: it differs by virtue of the simplicity of its nature. Eternity is totally different from succession. In the compact rendering given by Boethius, "Aeternitatas igiture est interminabilis vitae tota simul et perfecta possessio" ("Eternity therefore is full possession of an endless life that is all one").[18] Impassioned prayer and philosophical awareness combine in Augustine's address to the Lord in the *Confessions* (XI.xiii): "Thou art the same, and thy years shall not fail. Thy years neither go nor come; whereas these years of ours do both go and come, that in their order they may all come. Thy years stand all at once, because they stand: nor are those that go thrust out by those that come, for they pass not away; but ours shall all be, when they shall be no more." [19] And in Augustine's commentaries on the Psalms (*Enarrationes in Psalmos*), we find an even more dramatic record of his awe at the notion of eternity, his terrible sense of human transience, and his thrill at the possibilities of spiritual renewal. In fact, rather than deriving from Plotinus, the first sentence of the quotation from the *Confessions* above is an exact quotation from the Psalms (101:28): "Tu autem idem ipse est, et anni tui non deficient." [20] It is this division between the life of God and the lives of men that Augustine is so deeply and passionately aware of, and that the writers of the Renaissance, the later ones as well as the early writers of the fourteenth century, will not ignore. The Latin verb (from the Psalms) is particularly revealing: "non deficient." Indeed, involvement in time is the great falling off and root deficiency for many of our writers. As we shall see, like *deficere* (*de + facio*), verbs of "undoing," primarily in Dante and Petrarch, are frequently used to describe the temporal process. And in Shakespeare, too, time is recorded by the withering of the flesh. Echoing the language of the Psalms, Augustine can cry out, "Ecce veteres posuisti dies meos" ("You have put old age into my days").[21] God's years neither come nor go (to return to the passage from the *Confessions*) but ours come "ut omnes veniunt." God's years stand together because they stand, "nec euntibus a venientibus excluduntur." Again the Latin verb is important; the process of our years involves "exclusion," even, in the typically vigorous English translation of William Watts in 1631, "thrusting out." [22]

Borrowing another English Renaissance phrase, I have called this process of time, to which classical, Christian, and Renaissance figures are so sensitive, *emulation*.[23] For two of our writers, Dante and Shakespeare, this essentially natural process contains vivid social truth: the life of man in society is also one of "exclusion" and "thrusting out." Emulation forms one of their basic and shared insights into human society and is descriptive of the drama and the contentiousness, the human will and the energy that are qualities of their work.

Yet to mention the names of Augustine and Boethius is also to recognize that even for the men of the fourteenth century a system of thought and belief was still available that seemed to transcend the painful facts of change and death. For example, to look at only the conventional consolation in Chaucer's *Knight's Tale,* two related forms of belief lead to acceptance of the sudden, unexpected death of Arcite.[24] First there is the recognition that change is part of the nature of things and that man must have in readiness a prior attitude of alienation. The world is but a highway, Egeus reminds the sorrowing society, "And we been pilgrymes, passynge to and fro." (2847–2848) Fortune is by its nature unstable; one should not expect anything more. But his same conception of alienation is placed in a cosmic setting by Theseus, who sees a Prime Mover ordering all things to their better end. It is useless to strive, or gripe — "grucchen" — against this plan. Awareness of this order allows man his sense of stability within the dominant experience of change and alienation and accounts for the important image of the pilgrim, who, while unattached to the passing things along the road, is sure of his terminus.

These are the philosophical and theological bases of the attitude that allowed man to absorb the facts of change and emulation, those facts that cut like a knife across the high ideals of the Renaissance. Perhaps more an aspect of personality than a theological world view, there is another kind of consolation that is connected with the recurrent cycles of nature. It belongs to an endemic patience, a natural inclination to look at what continues and what abides. Man can weather the storm; even darkest February prepares the spring plowing. Ages old, this vision predated the medieval theological structure and would continue after it. One entertains no larger expectations, no fiery hopes. This vision is not heroic, nor is it tragic, because one knows that all will change. If we look to literature we can find some expression of this attitude in Chaucer, less in Spenser and, of course, in Montaigne. In art, there is the Book of Hours. But, as Panofsky has pointed out in his "Father Time" essay, a new element is introduced into the Renaissance iconography of time. Associated now with Saturn, time takes on a more menacing and destructive aspect. And on man's part the attitude becomes one of militancy, of the need to make response. New ideals emerge to form the arsenal of human possibility. Children, fame, fidelity in love, all those areas that lend continuance to human life are endorsed as hopeful responses to devouring time. This might explain why Chaucer's tone is rarely one of anger or protest at death and infidelity; whereas other writers, those who have a more fundamental commitment to the means and possibilities of temporal response, who show more faith in human means of transcending change, can only feel keen anger at the sad facts of mutability.

We can perhaps gain some needed perspective when we recall, with Jacqueline de Romilly, that Greek tragedy was born precisely when the consciousness of time became ripe and the idea of time important.[25] When man addresses time most vividly, the fact of change becomes most pressing. In the Renaissance, when time comes to be a precious, individual commodity through the effective use of which man can elevate his life and preserve his identity, then energies and possibilities are aroused that force abandonment of the older, contained universe and simple acquiescence. Exile in Dante, or the death of Laura for Petrarch, can be associated with deposition or forgetfulness in Shakespeare, or the loss of paradise for Milton, by the fact that, at the beginning, there had not been submissiven   ignation but rather larger hopes and dreams, involving human passion and commitment. Yet, these fourteenth-century writers still had spiritual solutions open to them that were not always available to most of the later writers, who seemed more exposed to the facts of human change and the single, irreducible and unalterable event. The very developments of Renaissance time, in support of Mlle de Romilly's thesis, seemed to lead toward tragedy. Unlike the audience of the *Knight's Tale,* King Lear is riveted to the simple fact, "Thou'lt come no more. Never, never, never, never, never."

"Laicization" has been one concept used with some success to describe the process of development in the Renaissance. It implies an adaption of religious forms and language for more secular purposes. The burghers of Florence, as Millard Meiss pointed out, saw no great discrepancy between their ideals, with their latent utilitarianism, and their religious heritage. Similarly, for most of the Renaissance the primary attractiveness of the emerging ideals of fame and progeny lay in the rapport between these secular goals and the religious concern for immortality. They were worldly matters that smacked of the spirit and seemed to direct the soul to higher things or, at least, to keep it from baser. Themselves imbued with eternity, they fitted into the religious picture and seemed to reconcile the here and the hereafter. Plato, in the *Laws,* explains why this might be so. Children represent man's "share in immortality": "A man shall marry between the ages of thirty and thirty-five, considering that the human race naturally partakes of immortality, of which all men have the greatest desire implanted in them; for the desire of every man that he may become famous and not lie in the grave without a name, is only the love of continuance. Now, mankind are coeval with all time, and are ever following, and will ever follow, the course of time; and so they are immortal, inasmuch as they leave children behind them, and partake of immortality in the unity of generation." [26] But this natural desire for continuity and self-perpetuation, which is instinctive, can be assumed and unexpressed, or it can be a vigorously pursued ideal. In the Renaissance war against time even a biological function like procreation could become a conscious ideal, energetically espoused. The Middle Ages tended to value the ongoing rhythms in which man participated; the Renaissance, the continuities that he himself effected. The problem here is not whether man always begot children — quite obviously he did — but whether he came to regard procreation as a valuable and even necessary way of countering time, and to locate great hopes in such a means. Ernst Cassirer, in remarks that are valuable for their understanding of cultural innovation and what it means, has emphasized that elements that had been submerged within a culture can become themselves cultural forces and conscious values.[27] In the Renaissance, progeny is one such value that emerges from silence and contends with the more sharply defined pressures of time.

Primarily in times of growth and optimism, the ways of succession seem especially valuable. Children, whether in Florence or in the Greek city-states of the fifth century, assume great importance. They are what one works for, and they seem to be worth the effort. Although the process was, to be sure, a slow one, and not without setbacks, still the developing bourgeois society of Florence at the end of the thirteenth century and the beginning of the fourteenth was the ideal milieu to foster the values of progeny and family. Chroniclers of the time praise that city's air as suited for generation, and the Florentine women for being prolific. Millard Meiss tells us that in paintings of the first half of the fourteenth century in Florence and Siena the theme of the Holy Family appears for the first time, along with other subjects that are "expressive of family sentiments, of the emotional bond between mother and child, mother and son, or husband and wife. They reflect burgher values and many of the paintings were commissioned by a married couple for their own private devotion. It is not surprising then that children should have become especially prominent." [28] Phillipe Ariès, whose book *Centuries of Childhood: A Social History of Family Life* is receiving wide discussion, can make the startling statement that the art of the Middle Ages was indifferent to children and that, beginning with the thirteenth and fourteenth centuries, a "new sensibility" is introduced, which led to "The Discovery of Childhood." His sociological findings are supported by the literary evidence that this study will present. [29]

Along with the new validity attributed to children as a means of response, the changed consciousness of time in the Renaissance also meant an alteration in the attitude toward lineage. Aristocratic devotion to lineage and inherited nobility of blood obviously predated the Renaissance and had its origin as far back as Roman society. But Dante, with whom this study commences, with his profound sense of the role of change in human affairs and of man's subjection to time, gives some indication of new bourgeois values when he insists that nobility must be more than an inheritance, that it will quickly pass away unless the individual himself struggles to maintain it. "O poca nostra nobiltà di sangue," he cries out in the opening lines of *Paradiso* XVI:

> Ben se' tu manto che tosto raccorce;
>   sì che, se non s'appon di dì in dìe,
>   lo tempo va dintorno con le force.

> O our poor nobility of blood. . . . Truly
> thou art a mantle that quickly shrinks,
> so that if we do not add to it day by day
> time goes round it with the shears. [30]

That man cannot simply rely on the store of the past is the lesson of change that figures even in the elevated atmosphere of the *Paradiso*. The same lesson can be learned from the disastrous ends of those of Shakespeare's kings who, in the histories, cling to the outmoded versions of temporal immunity. "Not all the water in the rough rude sea / Can wash the balm off an annointed king," Richard II's main defense, proves no adequate bulwark against the sea of historical change.

Dante's own insistence on effort and responsibilty, although in a larger context of divine comedy, of providence and grace and humility, represents a bourgeois transformation of the older notion that had placed nobility in the family line. Such transformations would continue and gather force in the Renaissance and are evident when the temporal realism of Bolingbroke and his son would replace the feudal attitudes of Richard II. Rather than look backward to an inheritance, men of the Renaissance would look forward to a continuity that is the product of aroused temporal awareness and their own active effort. Dante's poem is eloquent testimony that pride in the past, the glory of lineage, did not disappear, but would gradually be overshadowed by the hope in the future to which it was joined. Indeed, in the Renaissance, the aristocratic notion of line merges with the new interests in progeny and the more immediate family to become one of the great avenues of time-transcendence open to man. One has only to think ahead to Edmund Spenser's Garden of Adonis and to his *Epithalamion* to appreciate the large possibilities of that merger.

The theme of children is valuable because it is open to such variations not only between writers but also within the evolution of a single writer. Stoic and civic humanists will disagree over whether fame or children are superior investments for a man — and this will even amount to something of a *querelle*. And even among the civic humanists, those who endorse the values of the polis and generation, there can be sharp alterations. Dante, although a son of the city, lost faith in the ways of generation, and the *Commedia* is the great record of this major reorientation of values. The purely natural and human order does not make for a dignified and serene life, where man's desires for harmony and continuity are satisfied, but rather leads to hell. After the experience of the *Inferno*, Dante reverts to an older system of belief, one that looks with suspicion on the validity of generation:

> Rade volte risurge per li rami
> l'umana probitate; e questo vole
> quei che la dà, perchè da lui si chiami.

> Rarely does human worth rise through the
> branches, and this He wills who gives it, that
> it may be sought from Him.
>
> (*Purg.* VII.121–123)

Dante thus returns to the wisdom of the church, summarized by Augustine in his commentary on Psalm 38. "Thesaurizat," is his text, "et ignorat cui congregabit ea" ("He heapeth up riches, and knoweth not who shall gather them"). The man who looks to his progeny has not left his trust in a safe place. Do not, he exhorts, pile up store on earth, because you do not know who will gather it once you are gone. Instead, he repeats the counsel from Matthew (6:20), "Thesaurizate vobis thesaurum in coelo" ("But lay up for yourselves treasure in heaven").[31] As Dante's changed sentiments return him to such traditional attitudes, so they serve to alienate him from the goals of developing bourgeois society. This separation comes sharply into focus when his notion of the unreliability of succession is contrasted with that of the other exemplar of civic wisdom and caution, the prudent Paolo da Certaldo. "Take care," he tells the marrying man in maxim 91, "that your bride-to-be comes from good parents, and that her grandparents are also of good repute, because rarely [rade volte] does an evil girl come from good mother and grandmother."

But of course Dante rejects such plausible wisdom, just as he rejects the adult model it seeks to produce. He would favor backward steps, a retraction of the accumulated wisdom that shapes maturity. The ideal age is not that of the adult but that of the child. The longer it stays in the world, the more the soul, which came innocent from God, is infected with the world's ways. Dante's interest shifts from progeny to childhood, from sources of continuity and the notions of development implied to sources of individual salvation. Although their divergences are fundamental, his notion of childhood and that of the nineteenth-century poets and novelists have more in common with each other than they have with the historical confidence in natural generation and social development displayed by the men of the Renaissance. The higher Dante proceeds in his journey toward the vision of God, the more he recovers the innocence and the purity of the child and the more Beatrice becomes the Mother. Such were the little children that Christ suffered to come to him. But, as we shall see, the conception that developed in the Renaissance was one which treated children as sources of continuity, and consequently, as objects of education, so that they might fulfill their adult functions all the more honorably. Both Rabelais and Shakespeare have in mind the education of a prince for the role of successful and adult leadership.

These goals of the developing Renaissance society ran counter to the medieval neglect of children, as they did the medieval neglect of time. In fact, the way the new time sense enters into Renaissance educational change (a core part of this study) provides substantial contrast between medieval notions of time and learning and those introduced by Petrarch and his humanist successors. Even when we consider so advanced and formidable an intellect as John of Salisbury, the evidence is clear that in his attitudes toward the materials studied, the amount of time spent, and the arrangement of the courses of study he differs profoundly from Renaissance humanists more alerted to the pressures of time.

Through his love of learning and his taste and capacity for diligent study, John rose above the rudimentary skills taught by the schools and put them to higher uses and purposes. Consequently, he scorns the attacks of twelfth-century educational reformers on the time spent in what they regarded as the futile arts of grammar and logic. In his *Metalogicon,* he reviles their aims and motives and lampoons them as mercilessly as Rabelais does the educational system of which John himself was the great representative. We know of Cornificius (the derogative pseudonym given by John to the reformers in general whom he attacks) and "his" arguments only from John's recapitulation and response, yet it is clear that the assaults on grammar and logic that Cornificius represents anticipate the arguments of a long line of Renaissance writers and educators who desired theory more alive to the experiences of society and who wanted the subject matter of education to relate to the human condition. In a startling proof of the separation that existed between the twelfth-century renascence and the values and ideals of the Renaissance, John of Salisbury has more in common with the Gothic methods that Rabelais caricatured, while Cornificius evidently would not have been at all uncomfortable with Rabelais' new program.

To be sure, John of Salisbury attacks sophistry and the abuse of dialectics in vain dispute, and he also laments the waste of time spent in "gambling, hunting and like frivolous pastimes," but when it comes to logic and grammar he was quite unperturbed by the long years he had spent in their study — a nonchalance from which the subsequent age would notably defect. A temporal easiness, worthy of admiration, attends his account of his scholastic career. "When still a youth" he went to Paris for his studies; he does not give us his age, nor the year — it was simply one year after the death of Henry I. After about four years' training in dialectic (where he became adept at pointing out "topics, rules and other elementary principles"), he spent three years studying grammar with William of Conches, and although it is hard to determine — a revealing sidelight — he must by then have been twenty years old. "Nor," he tells us "will I ever regret the time thus spent." Subsequently he became a student of Richard l'Evêque, with whom, while advancing in the quadrivium, he also reviewed all that he had studied under his other teachers, including rhetoric. At the end of John of Salisbury's account of studies and teachers, he sums the total: "Thus engaged in diverse studies near twelve years passed by me" ("Sic fere duodecennium mihi elapsum est diversiis studiis occupato").[32] The original Latin phrase is important because it provides one of those rare instances of cultural confrontation, which, however unrelated, still reveal striking differences. In a letter of 1351, whose subject is the preciousness of time, Petrarch can maintain, "non elapsa sunt tempora sed erepta." [33] Time did not slip by him; it was torn from him. And thus he expresses a summary Renaissance consciousness and sense of belligerency toward time, which is all the more impressive since he is in context expressing his relative youthful indifference to it.

In his *Metalogicon* John of Salisbury denies that this was wasted time, and he scorns the "professors of the arts [who] were promising to impart the whole of philosophy in less than three or even two years." Yet, several centuries later, and even throughout the Renaissance, educational reformers will be saying very much the same thing: more interesting materials can be better taught in shorter period of time. This combination of forces, the need for new material and the felt pressures of time, would increase the attention the Renaissance paid to rational programs of study. There was much repetition in John of Salisbury's account of his education, and Ariès has declared that the medieval cycle of courses lacked "gradation" — that is, an arrangement of studies to fit the age and development of the student.[34] When education had to fulfill the needs of the emergent laity, such temporal casualness was to be avoided. Not only must the student spend less time on less useful material but the briefer period allotted to his studies must be put to better use. The need to exploit the available moments to the fullest and to see that no time is wasted accounts for the greater Renaissance interest in scheduling — an interest that extended to the materials of education as well as to the hours of the individual life.

While they were at odds on the value of progeny as a source of perpetuation, stoic and civic humanists were united, at least in significant parts of their individual development, on the value of fame. This is the other great means of personal extension and another thread I shall carry through this study to see what thematic coloring it acquires. As with the other lines of this study, our starting point centers around Florence, central and northern Italy of the late thirteenth and early fourteenth century. "Here again," to quote Burckhardt, "as in all essential points, the first witness to be called is Dante," [35] Although Brunetto Latini evidently first encouraged Dante in his quest for fame, it is in the *Commedia* that the epoch-making voice declares, "Onorate l'altissimo poeta." The poet thus honored himself does not suffer from the loss of interest in self-perpetuation that is so noticeable in the lower reaches of Hell. The Roman spur of fame is still active when, in canto XXIV, Virgil rouses Dante:

> "Omai convien che tu così ti spoltre,"
>   disse 'l maestro "chè, seggendo in piuma,
>   in fama non si vien, nè sotto coltre;
> sanza la qual chi sua vita consuma,
>   cotal vestigio in terra di sè lasica,
>   qual fummo in aere ed in acqua la schiuma."

> "Now must thou cast off all sloth," said the Master,
> "for sitting on down or under blankets none comes
> to fame, and without it he that consumes his life
> leaves such trace of himself on earth as smoke
> in air or foam on the water."
>
> $(46-51)$

He then urges his disciple to rise up and conquer all fatigue with the power of soul that overcomes all obstacles. This passage, along with the one quoted earlier from *Paradiso* XVI, clearly justifies the prominence given to Dante in the first part of this study.

As Burckhardt is right in his insistence on the desire for fame as a new and important factor in delineating Renaissance energy and spirit, so is he right in seeing a large part of that inspiration as coming from Rome, and Italy's relations with its Latin past: "The Roman authors, who were now zealously studied, are filled and saturated with the conception of fame, and . . . their subject itself — the universal empire of Rome — stood as a permanent ideal before the mind of the Italians. From henceforth all the aspirations and achievements of the people were governed by a moral postulate, which was still unknown elsewhere in Europe." (p. 87) As the spirit of the classics returned — so preeminently embodied in Dante's Virgil — so did the custom of the laureatation and the great concern with the fame and glory that poetry and art confer. In this revival Petrarch is perhaps of greater historical importance than Dante. He reproduces the Latin sentences on time, and in his "Coronation Oration" and elsewhere, Roman boasts of the triumph of their art over time are the jewels with which he studs his commentaries. From Petrarch, fanning throughout Europe to the belated renascences of other nations, this faith in the permanence of great poetry and the undying glory it confers will spread. Immortality through verse for poet and subject — this was the generating force and *apologia* that filled the "springtides" of Renaissance poetry, the *Pléïade* in France and the young writers of Elizabethan England. In all three periods we find young poets moved by the same spark, and, moreover, defending their art by its power to transcend time.

Burckhardt saw in the desire for fame a distinctive part of the Renaissance mentality. Yet his vision is not as simple as his detractors would imagine. He can also see within the quest for fame evidence of a "boundless ambition and thirst after greatness, regardless of all means and consequences." His own nineteenth-century preoccupation with the creative and destructive energies of the human will brings him close to the imagination of the Renaissance writers. The desire to be "somebody" — at any cost — can be a diabolic principle: "In more than one remarkable and dreadful undertaking the motive assigned by serious writers is the burning desire to achieve something great and memorable. This motive is not a mere extreme case of ordinary vanity, but something daemonic, involving a surrender of the will, the use of any means, however atrocious, and even an indifference to success itself." (p. 93) Both Dante and Montaigne will lament, in the disordered time of civil war, that every peasant wants to be a Marcellus. And one can imagine the fascinated horror with which Shakespeare followed the devilish courses of characters like Richard III, Iago, or Macbeth. As he separates himself from them, he senses in their energies some desperation, some final suicidal thrust (which Burckhardt sees as a strange disregard for the outcome itself):

> March on, join bravely, let us to't pell-mell,
> If not to heaven, then hand in hand to hell.
> (*Richard III*, v.iii.313–314)

This diabolic transformation of the frustrated or misguided desire to be "somebody" will result, as the Roumanian expatriate essayist E. M. Cioran tells us, in paradise lost: "It is hard to believe that [man] would have sacrificed Paradise out of the simple desire to know good and evil; but on the other hand we can perfectly well imagine him risking everything to be somebody. Let us rewrite *Genesis*: if man squandered his initial happiness, it was not so much from a taste for knowledge as a thirst for fame." [36]

For better or worse, the quest for fame was one of the fundamental impulses that drove the aspiring Renaissance mind to separate itself from the earlier world of simpler being. The English title of Cioran's essay, "The Ambiguity of Fame," could well serve as the heading for the Renaissance attitude. All of the writers we are concerned with here were of several minds about fame. In many it was an ardent, early faith, the reward of their great achievement. But for the more religious writers, Dante and Petrarch, Spenser and Milton, the desire for fame had to undergo a harsh subordination to purely religious priorities before it could be restored to its former validity. They sensed the need for a higher trust and support in the hazardous world of time. But this is precisely the usefulness of so important a theme — not only does it serve to distinguish one writer from another but it also marks, like the theme of progeny, stages within the evolution of an individual writer.

Briefly to fit this thematic material into the frame of historical suggestion, it is clear that in the fourteenth century vital interests in progeny and a preoccupation with fame emerged; so, too, a new awareness of time as a pressure and as a destructive force became part of literature. In that century, too, the mechanical clock came clearly into view — the city clocks began ringing each of the twenty-four hours, as "the tempo of everyday life increased." In their energy and activism, in their sense of the shortness of life and the need to utilize that time profitably, poet-humanists and the bourgeois elements of society formed a united front against the temporal nonchalance of the older scholastic and feudal institutions. As we shall see, this particular conjunction helps to account for the problem and paradox of time in the Renaissance. It will also explain later developments. In the course of the seventeenth century the themes of children and fame would cease to be important literary preoccupations (thus helping us to close off the lengthy period of our cultural past under consideration). This does not mean that children or family declined as interests to the developing society; on the contrary, as Ariès has concluded, they would only become more solidly entrenched as values with the triumph of the middle class. But rather than providing the thrill of continuity, the illumination of some victory wrested from time, progeny would be absorbed in family and become an object of common piety. Similarly, fame would lose some of its transcendent appeal: the buoyant optimism and hopefulness of the Renaissance would subside, and more modest and practical considerations prevail. Yet, at this very time, the minute hand was added to the clock. Obviously a parting of the ways had come about. Poet and society, after having shared similar energies and optimism, however uneasy the alliance, were revealed to be actually following different gods, looking in different directions. We witness a separation between a more subdued and chastened literature, still cherishing its past, and the forward-moving energies of a modernizing society.

Being

Time is the element of Western man. But yet, that period of history, the Renaissance, which witnessed the establishment of time, also saw in its major writers a critical disillusionment with the rewards and pursuits within the temporal realm. Like Ruskin, they could conclude that a man's "glory is not at all in going, but in being." [37] This study, which began as an investigation of the theme of time, and which emphasizes its fundamental importance in the makeup of the Renaissance mind, reaches the further judgment that for these aspiring men reliance on the ways of succession was too vicarious and insecure unless the individual himself possessed a sense of fulfillment. Their hopefulness in man's powers and the continuities that he can create to add to his own existence are frustrated by man's natural limitations and the disasters of his society. Trust in fame implies a temporal confidence that one would be allowed to live long enough to accomplish meritorious works; hope in generation implies a society in which it is worth while to raise children. But, for the writers with whom we deal, experiences of civil war, pestilence, or just the sheer uncertainty as to how children turn out (they are not, in *King Lear,* for instance, the protective enclave against man's emulative tendencies that they had been in the histories) all work to shatter any kind of long-range consolation that the individual might take in his own progeny. Then there were all the arguments brought over from Macrobius and Boethius on the actual pettiness of fame, moralizings on its shadowy insufficiency. And if a man were to die before the great works were accomplished, how would fame be his? In these particular thematic concerns, one can see how the Renaissance had encountered realities against which its newly liberated sense of possibility could do little.

In his attempts to manage time, Renaissance man strives to achieve by means of process what eternity possesses in stasis. Even Plato could say that man shared in immortality through children or fame. Yet, beyond this, it would seem that man's greater desire is to savor the present wholeness and being that he has always conceived to be the properties of divinity. Of course, as long as man is involved in time this is impossible. Yet in the works we shall study two ways emerge by which man's experience can break through the condition of change and simulate the qualities of being. A sense of presentness and a sense of contraction are recurring means by which the writers we shall study attest to their experience of wholeness. These two elements recur in sufficiently similar and dissimilar ways to provide very practical thematic material. Dante's *Paradiso* is literally an approximation of God's presentness. But even Montaigne, on a decidedly less lofty plane, will sense the lines of his own life coming together in the fullness of the present moment, where past and future are annihilated. By analogy with eternity, the present is not merely the moment at hand; it is summary and all-embracing, compressing in the depth of its vision a completed and rounded-out picture of human existence.

The attitude of "readiness" provides another access to being. Alienated from the promised securities and relationships of society, man comes to know an "orphanhood in time." [38] The sheer unknowability of what is to come, the long shadow of death — such realities as these can daunt the more optimistic Renaissance faith. Yet the point is reached where fear and anxiety over these imponderables are discarded. This is frequently expressed as a condition of readiness, whereby man, whether in Dante or Petrarch, in Montaigne or Shakespeare or Milton, moves forward with a sense of completeness and trust into the unresolved and the terrible.

Chapter 2
Dante

Time and the City

Io, che al divino dall'umano,
   all'eterno dal tempo era venuto,
   e di Fiorenza in popol giusto e sano . . .

I, who had come to the divine from the
human, to the eternal from time, and from
Florence to a people just and sane . . .
                                    (*Par.* XXXI.37–39)[1]

Dante's *Commedia* depicts and foretells, as he himself admits, the most painful separation from all those things that he had held most dear. That is exile's first shaft: "Tu lascerai ogni cosa diletta / più caramente." With eager faith and naive confidence he had yielded himself to the communal ideals and rewards that his city had offered. The city of Florence, its people, their strengths and optimism had most engaged his affections. It was because he had, in his way, most innocently committed himself to his time that exile hit him the hardest. This is his admission to Cacciaguida after the latter more clearly draws for him his future prospects:

Ben veggio, padre mio, sì come sprona
   lo tempo verso me, per colpo darmi
   tal, ch'è più grave a chi più s'abbandona.

> I see well, my father, how time spurs towards me to
> deal me such a blow as falls most heavily on him that
> is most heedless.
>
> (*Par.* XVII.106–108)

Dislodged from his nest, Dante was forced to come upon a more universal meaning for his existence. His habit of affections had to be those of a pilgrim, with true citizenship reserved only for the end of the journey. An exchange in the *Purgatorio* makes this point. In canto XIII, Dante, coming toward a group being punished for envy, inquires if there be any among them from the land of the Latins, or Italy. The response (94–96) contains a correction:

> O frate mio, ciascuna è cittadina
> d'una vera città; ma tu vuo' dire
> che vivesse in Italia peregrina.

> O my brother, we are every one citizens of one
> true city; but thou wouldst say, any that lived in
> Italy a pilgrim.

Clearly, the city remains the dimension of the *Commedia,* while its earthly rejection is the poem's essential theme.

More than any other philosopher standing behind Dante, Augustine represented these complex loyalties. He occupies, we remember, a choice position in the *Commedia*: as high as canto XXXII of the *Paradiso,* just below John the Baptist, at the next fold of the rose, reside Benedict, Francis, and Augustine. Such honored placement is warranted not only by the great role he played in the construction of the Christian edifice but also, and more to the point, by his importance in Dante's own spiritual biography. The historical role of each was to witness the demise of a secular order. Virgil's attribution of "imperium sine fine" to the earthly Rome was misplaced; Beatrice could well be echoing Augustine when she instructs Dante that he will only a "brief time" remain in the garden of the earthly paradise, but will be 'forever [sanza fine] a citizen of that Rome of which Christ is Roman." (*Purg.* XXXII. 100–102) Yet, despite its radical defects — its subjection to change and its existence in time — the city, rightly understood and rightly functioning, is not totally debased nor totally condemned by Augustine or Dante. Within its confines man can achieve a peace which, though of

a lower order than that of the heavenly city, still permits an existence
that is reliable enough and one that represents a great improvement
over any other kind of earthly life. But in Augustine's as well as in
Dante's vision, there is one large precondition to the felicity of man's
life among men. This could be simply called "right focus." The predominance of spiritual priorities, a basic attachment to the goods of
the heavenly city as against the goods of the earthly city, must be clearly
established and observed before such peace can be achieved. But if
these other priorities are neglected the city will come to ruin. Thus
Augustine in the *City of God* (XV.4) completes the argument that we
have been summarizing: "But there are higher goods that belong to
the city above, in which victory will be untroubled in everlasting and
ultimate peace. If these goods are neglected while others are so coveted
that they are either believed to be the only goods or are cherished more
than the goods that are believed to be higher, then the inevitable consequence will be new misery and more and more added to the old
[et quae inerat augeatur]." [2]

In Dante's time these essential preconditions, this "right focus,"
have been neglected and abused, and he himself stands as a spokesman
for misguided mankind when he confesses to Beatrice, the representative
of these higher goods, that "presenti cose"

> col falso lor piacer volser miei passi,
> tosto che 'l vostro viso si nascose.

> Present things with their false pleasure
> turned my steps as soon as your face was hid.
> (*Purg.* XXXI.34–36)

Frequently for the men of the fourteenth century, life is described in
terms of falseness and deception. Beatrice in Canto XXX accuses Dante
of "following after false images of good which fulfill no promise." Such
liability for disappointment belongs to the increased expectations and
aroused energies that the development of Renaissance society would
promote. At the heart of Dante's animated universe and literally at
the center of his *Commedia* (*Purg.* XVI–XVIII) is his sense of man
as a creature of force and desire. Consequently, the great need is to
"set love in order," for "neither Creator nor creature . . . was ever
without love." Derived from their Maker these remarkable energies
seek their return to the fulfillment they had known. But the danger ex-

ists that false objects would be placed in front of them, objects that are incapable of fully satisfying their needs. Such are Dante's "present things," which, because they do not last and because they cannot be shared, not only fail to satisfy man's desires but also pit him in competitive strife with his neighbor. While Dante's psychology has obvious roots in traditional views of the individual and the cosmos it is clear that the new moneyed economy and its wide-ranging acquisitive energies lend new urgency and dramatic focus to the problem.

The mad pursuit of these perishable and strife-producing present goods provides the social corollary to the natural role of emulation in Dante's universe.[3] Like Shakespeare's his world is on the move, bristling with competitive energies, all seeking their place. The temporal principle of emulative replacement not only holds true in nature, or in questions of reputation (*Purg.* XI.91–103) or language (*Par.* XXVI. 124–130), but works its way into the heart of the city, destroying that peace it was the function of the commune to insure and protect. One of its victims, Guido del Duca, reflecting on his own sin of envy, can cry out, "O race of men, why do you set your hearts where needs must be exclusion of partnership?" (*Purg.* XIV.86–87) The importance of the phrase is underlined in the next canto, when Dante asks Virgil what the former leader of Romagna meant by "exclusion" and by "partnership." Virgil's response (XV.49–57) reveals a fundamental preoccupation on the part of Dante, one which will be crucial for this study of time:

> Perchè s'appuntano i vostri disiri
>   dove per compagnia parte si scema,
>   invidia move il mantaco a' sospiri.
> Ma se l'amor della spera suprema
>   torcesse in suso il disiderio vostro,
>   non vi sarebbe al petto quella tema;
> chè, per quanti si dice più lì "nostro,"
>   tanto possiede più di ben ciascuno,
>   e più di caritate arde in quel chiostro.

> It is because your desires are fixed where
> the part is lessened by sharing that envy
> blows the bellows to your sighs; but if the
> love of the highest sphere bent upward your
> longing, that fear would not be in your breast.

> For there, the more they are who say "ours" the
> more of good does each possess and the more of
> charity burns in that cloister.

The loss of this higher vision converts the city into Hell, dividing Dante, like his modern American successors, between his awareness of the city as an ideal and his experience of it as the jungle it has always been. Indeed, for Augustine the earthly city was defective from its very origins: "The first founder of the earthly city [Cain] was consequently a fratricide; for, overcome by envy, he slew his own brother, who was a citizen of the eternal city sojourning upon this earth [civem civitatis aeternae in hac terra peregrinantem]. No wonder then that this first example or, as the Greeks call it, archetype was followed by a copy of its own likeness long afterwards at the foundation of the city that was destined to be the capital of this earthly city." (XV.5) Romulus and Remus stand in the line of Cain and Abel and summarize the emulation that Augustine saw to be so persistent a pattern in the earthly city. And such fratricide was the real pattern of the near century of civil war that marred the communal life of Dante's experience. Since the early thirteenth century, Florence itself, torn between the exits and entrances of Guelph and Ghibelline, and after them, White and Black, seemed unable to break the pattern of strife that amounted to something like an original taint.[4]

While Dante's great achievement is his ability to fit the facts of his personal history into the enduring patterns of Christian myth, it must be stressed here that pattern does not mean necessity. The inability of the earthly city to fulfill its legitimate functions derives from historical causes, causes that amount to what could be called a second fall.[5] This was the special significance of the conflict between church and state in the Middle Ages, a conflict of which Dante's poem is one great record. The two institutions whose purposes were to limit desire and establish right focus had failed to do so. When the church involved itself in the things that were Caesar's, the secular arm was frustrated and the spiritual power tainted. Men no longer entertained a vision of the heavenly city because of the obvious discredit into which its representatives had fallen. The political adventures of the church stymied the empire, with the result that, in the absence of any firm secular power, desire was misdirected and aggressiveness uncontrolled.

But if these calamities are historical, they are therefore reversible, should their causes be identified and corrected. Dante never relinquished this historical faith, a faith that has its roots in the order of God's creation and his providential intent. Dante was all too typical of his age, which, as Gerhart B. Ladner reminds us, "sometimes forgot that all terrestrial order is relative," and "failed to remember that Augustine had conceived of the *Civitas Dei* as *peregrinans*." [6] To be sure, Dante's moral invective against the perpetrators of his country's harm was not relaxed to any noticeable degree. Exile itself can only serve to make more intensive the attachment to the place from which one has been evicted. What brought Dante to replace his notion of citizenship with one of pilgrimage was his extraordinary awareness of the role of time and change in putting an end to all earthly orders and institutions. From the perspective of Paradise (XXVI.124–142), Adam will inform Dante that it was not sin (as Milton and Augustine believed) — the sin attending the tower of Babel — that occasioned the diversity of tongues, but that even in his own lifetime the word for God had changed. Nothing human is durable, no product of hand or mind, because our tastes as well as our works are subject to the changes of time. It is natural that man speaks, but more particular determinations are the results of changing pleasure. And this is the way it should be, "chè l'uso de' mortali è come fronda / in ramo, che sen va e altra vene" ("for the usage of mortals is like a leaf on a branch, which goes and another comes"). [7] The very processes that brought a word in, now take it out, and it must, as in the emulative world of nature, cede place to what is new. *Si volet usus.*

Families, cities, and nations are subject to the same process. Fresh blood grows old and watches new blood come to take its place; but the pattern repeats itself when the young power, decaying, finds itself threatened by the same process of supplantation. In its relation to social change the role of time is subsumed under the concept of *Fortuna,* a concept that has theological implications for Dante. As Virgil explains in *Inferno* VII, these processes of change do not occur by chance. Fortune is really a regularly functioning minister of God; hence she is blessed. Of necessity earthly goods change so rapidly, because so quickly come new people who would try their hand. Fortune must move quickly in order to keep up with the incoming waves of people and generations. Cacciaguida, even in Paradise, can speak soberly of the new blood that has altered the old life of Florence. But if the general principle of emulative replacement is true in nature, and in the rise and fall of cities, why should not Florence be included in this pattern? Since cities themselves have disappeared, Dante should not be surprised to learn how family lines have been undone ("come le schiatte si disfanno"). With the equanimity that the paradisal vision represents, even the despised new people become part of Fortune's blessed dominion:

> E come 'l volger del ciel della luna
> cuopre e discuopre i liti sanza posa,
> così fa di Fiorenza la Fortuna.

> And as the turning of the moon's heaven covers
> and lays bare the shores unceasingly, so Fortune
> does with Florence.
>
> (*Par.* XVI.82–84)

A higher process of providential control dominates the emulative place-taking for which nature is the pattern and society the unfortunate reality. The plot of the *Commedia,* and its theme, is the drama of Dante's passage away from present things, the record of his disengagement from the events of the earthly city in their discrete and self-contained significance to the perception of this higher order directing all. The perception of this order absorbs the sting of replacement and exile that was so personally bitter to Dante. His own attachments were in need of being relocated. Perhaps, then, Dante would not have been unprepared to learn the future prominence of the descendants of some of the despised new people, like the Medici or the Buonarroti.[8]

After glimpsing some of the essential conditions of time and of Florence and before we enter the dark and downward gyre of Hell, it might be well to have before us an image of Dante's sense of eternity and his understanding of a just and sane people. The first canto freed from the shadow of earth, *Paradiso* X, has that discreet power and poetic control which we too often neglect in our avoidance of the *Commedia*'s third cantica. Not only does this canto show the ideals that animate Dante's vision of time and eternity, but for our purposes it is especially illustrative, since its contexts are the cosmic and mechanical measurements of time. Its location is the sun, "whose light measures time for us." It begins with the justification of God's direction of the planets and their dependent seasonal changes and closes with the celebrated (and disputed) simile of the clock. Man's sense of time both as physical passage and as emulation forms some of the substance of this canto. But while rooted through observation and simile in time, Canto X breathes an air of time transcendence. Cosmic and human time measurements are only the limits of this canto; in reality time is still subordinate to the spiritual coordinates of eternity: permanence and concord. Neither the planets nor the clock are final referents, since each points to another spiritual order, of which it is a model of exhortation or an example. Each attests to the principles that govern the universe and ought to govern the community of men; they are physical instances of spiritual possibilities. For this reason the reader is urged to raise his sights to the order of the planets, so that he might taste of the "ineffable power" guiding the movements.

The heavens move as Dante's witness to cosmic order, an order which does not eradicate energy but rather harmonizes it. The path of the sun, the ecliptic, which cuts obliquely through the celestial equator, thus producing the change of seasons, is not placid, but rather striking (l'un moto e l'altro si percuote," 9). For an Englishman the seasons' differences therein created might be regarded as Adam's penalty, but for Dante it becomes the play of the weather. The difficulties of such vicissitudes are absorbed in the sense of the directing order and its satisfaction of the multiple demands that rise up from the earth. If we think back to Dante's defense of fortune's transmutations ("Sì spesso vien chi vicenda consegue," *Inf.* VII.90) we see that his rationale for the change of seasons is similar. The sun moves obliquely, altering the seasons, in order to "satisfy the world which calls for them" ("per sodisfare al mondo che li chiama," 15). The world is peopled by new energies, all desiring the sun, and God's design brings an operational order to these divergent needs. The vision of the populations of the world all clamoring for their place in the sun is remarkable, yet typical of Dante. Through the fusing power of his imagination, this spare phrase yields an expanded suggestiveness: beyond the physical sun it is really their cravings for the spiritual Son that they would satisfy.

Dante celebrates his arrival in the sphere of the great minister of time, but the precise moment does not register, since he is led from one level to another by Beatrice in a way beyond any temporal measurement ("che l'atto suo per tempo non si sporge," 28–39). The movement from physical to spiritual is part of the plot of this canto, in which Dante proceeds from contemplation of the natural order, the circle of the heavens, to communion with the spiritual order. In the circle of the sun is lodged Dante's pantheon of Western philosophers, his founders of the Middle Ages. And if the deity seems to have had skill in according the diverse physical energies, Dante performs a minor miracle in converting wrangling disputation into music, a faculty meeting into higher song and dance.

The vision of paradise, while respecting the individual energies of each, brings together in a single picture the rival and even hostile personalities of the past. All are conjoined, all do their share, in the total vision of God.

> Tal era quivi la quarta famiglia
>   del'alto Padre, che sempre la sazia,
>   mostrando come spira e come figlia.

> Such was there the fourth family of the Father on high,
> who ever satisfies it, showing how He breathes forth
> and how begets.

$$(49-51)$$

It is important here that faculty should be converted into family. In small and in large, the great image of the concord of rival energies is the family. It is for this reason that Canto X opens with praise of the Trinity, and that it is by looking upon the processes of breathing forth and begetting of the "alto Padre" that this philosophical family is always satisfied. As we shall see later, the image of the father, son, and holy spirit will be valuable in Dante's conception of poetic tradition, where the great goal is also the victory over the forces of emulation in time and in man. Just as significant, therefore, are Augustine's prototypes of the emulative struggle within the earthly city: Cain and Abel. As the victory over emulation is described in processes of the family, so the confirmation of that principle of division has its keenest expression in the breakup of the family, when brothers divide. One can judge then how formative of Dante's vision of the world was his experience in the Florence of civil war, where brother took opposite side from brother.

Rather than the brutalized conflicts of Florence, Canto X shows a world where all delight in their just position and where each is content to find his true identity as part of the larger processes of God's providence and universe. Rather than linear questing, the path of Ulysses, desire is gathered in and being is rounded out. Twelve philosophers form a garland, a wreath, a crown. They indicate the twelve hours of the clock but also the number of Christ's original disciples. From the circle it is Aquinas who first speaks, indicating for Dante who are the "plants which bloom in the garland which surrounds with looks of love the fair lady who strengthens thee for heaven." At the heart of the temporal is the spiritual, just as the basis of the vision of paradise must be the larger capacities of a Beatrice. A just generosity and an eager mutuality of sharing so infuse the spirits in paradise that Aquinas would be as little moved to deny Dante's need for knowledge as the river to fail to flow to the sea. The love that moves nature inspires him, and gladly would he teach.

The simile of the clock with which Dante closes Canto X is admired and debated.[9] But for our purposes it does not matter whether the clock he had in mind was mechanically powered or not. It is clear that the importance of the clock lies in the regulation it brings to different energies, and as such it is similar to the spiritual concord that is at the heart of this canto and especially dear to Dante, since it suggests the way the city itself ought to have been operating, were it fulfilling its ideal functions. Time and energy are not dissolved, individual natures are not eradicated, but rather through the very parts themselves harmony is sought. God's overriding plan sends the sun striking across the movement of the equator, various people clamor for their sun and their fortune; so, too, like these larger energies, the clock "draws and drives [tira e urge]" its wheels and levers to produce the sweet music that summons the world to worship Christ. As throughout this canto, the end of time, its directing principle and its telos, is spirit. Some historical development can be marked when it is observed that here, in the early days of temporal awareness, the clock can serve to summarize the spiritual possibilities of the universe, while in the seventeenth century, with a Descartes or a Kepler, the universe resembles the mechanical plan of the clock. For Dante, the clock is also the complete circle, representing the harmony that occurs where "joy becomes eternal [dove gioir s'insempra]." We return to the great motive forces in the *Commedia* — things that can be shared and things that last.

Dante clearly endorses no progression into some indeterminate future — hence the disaster of Ulysses, his dissatisfaction, and the destructive competitiveness that results. In contrast to that forward pursuit, Dante values containment, and Canto X bring together two major representations of that order, the Trinity and the circle. Georges Poulet correctly perceives the relation between the two in his discussion of Dante in *The Metamorphoses of the Circle*: "If God as the Father begets an image of Himself, who is the Son, the love that has made Him create this image of himself, returns it to him identical. The Father reflects Himself in the Son, the Son reflects Himself in the Father, and this reciprocity of love is nothing more nor less than the third person of the Trinity, the Holy Ghost. The cycle is complete. The infinite activity that binds the three Persons constitutes an immense sphere, at every point of which the same plenitude can be found." [10]

The opening lines of Canto X reinforces this connection:

> Guardando nel suo Figlio con l'Amore
>   che l'uno e l'altro etternalmente spira,
>   lo primo ed ineffabile Valore,
> quanto per mente e per loco si gira
>   con tant'ordine fè, ch'esser non puote
>   sanza gustar di lui chi ciò rimira.

> Looking on His Son with the Love which the One and
> the Other eternally breathe forth, the primal and
> ineffable Power made with such order all that resolves
> in mind or space that he who contemplates it cannot
> but taste of Him.

The ordering power of the Trinity assures the circling heavens. The cosmic order inspires peace and satisfaction, a taste of the Godhead, just as the Trinity itself brings satisfaction to that circle of philosophers who contemplate its mystery: "how [the Father] breathes forth and how begets." The peace that Dante desires is to be had not in some open future but rather in the perception of a pattern.

While emphasizing the patterns that contain, delimit, and subsume, Dante must also find room for expansion, variety, and historical particularity. The circle, that image of containment which yet encompasses multiple points, serves Dante's purpose. "For Dante," Poulet perceives, "as for most of the thinkers of his time . . . the position occupied by the central point of the circle represents not only the unity and fixity of duration but the multiplicity of simultaneous rapports that it holds with the peripheral and mobile duration of creatures." (xiv) Hence the coincidence of the circle and the Trinity: the passage from center to sphere, and back again, that concourse of communication, is most fully suggested by the Incarnation. In the beginning was the word, but the word entered into the flesh of history. Indeed, the very value of Erich Auerbach's figural contribution lies in the way he applies ontology to history.[11] *Imitatio cristi* was a pattern to follow for St. Bernard of Clairvaux and his Cistercian followers. But Dante's later presentation gives the Christian pattern a specific historical context. Even in a homely and unwholesome way (the rejection of the earthly father in the marketplace of Assisi and the marriage to poverty) the events of St. Francis' life, as Dante presents them in *Paradiso* XI, inform the pattern he was fulfilling. For Dante — and this will only grow in the course of the Renaissance — a new historical reality infuses the forms of the past. Stylistically as well as thematically, then, Dante's poem is filled with those present things whose spiritual sufficiency he denied. And even when he describes paradise, its values are those of the city as it was meant to be — full of many colors and divergent energies, yet all concordant. In fact, the paradisal vision itself might be called precisely this contentment and harmonization of individual natures through the vision of God's will and lastingness.

But in history, by virtue of the second historical fall, these ideals of the city have been vitiated. Rather than imitating the heavenly city, the earthly city seems closer to the land of Diis. Within its walls its citizens, like rats, gnaw each other, as Guido del Duca laments. Succession is no longer a realm of realization consonant with timeless eternity, but rather its opposite — opposite to such an extent that even the natural possibilities available to man for perpetuating himself are perverted and turned against their very lifegiving sources. Rather than progression or even continuity in time, history means decline and termination. Progeny and fame, those two major means of continuity, lose their efficacy and cease to be positive powers. Nevertheless, their importance for Dante can be measured by the fact that it is in the violation and degradation of these values of succession that Dante shows the depth to which a culture can decline whose sight is only fixed on "present things."

Inferno: Fame and Children

Although Virgil is introduced in Canto I of the *Inferno* as the author of the epic poem whose hero, like Dante, was forced to leave his native city and live in exile, still the city that he goes on to found is not the heavenly city of Dante's discovery but rather the supreme representative of all earthly cities, Rome. The *Aeneid* is the poem of history *par excellence*. Its dimensions are within historical time, and its consolations, and some might say triumphs, are located in the continuities of civilization. The great public poem, finding mission in government, history, and tradition, it shows none of the personal illumination of being that Christ's followers discovered in his life and teachings. Even earthly means of grace — heroism and love — are shed in Aeneas' moral journey. The poem could rightly be called a classical farewell to arms.

Being a poem of history it is only natural that the *Aeneid* should extol the ways of succession and that in it the link of generation is crucial. Tempest-tossed, suffering from the acute enmity of the world's forces, shunted and exiled, Aeneas finally succeeds in imposing a human order on the forces of chaos without and within. Powers of endurance, tenacity, and forbearance finally succeed in giving root to a new civilization. It is important that Dante introduces Virgil as the man who wrote of that "giusto / figliuol d'Anchise," acknowledging the great familial and communal *pietas* that binds Virgilian society. But these are mainly consolatory writs, hardly leading to any time-transcendent sense of fulfillment. And this is as it should be, since history proceeds by succession and cannot escape from the past nor yet possess the future. Historical man is a creature of known suffering and postponed realization. He sacrifices his own present for a suprapersonal ideal of historical continuity and achievement: these are the costs of empire and history. Aeneas, after all, will die three years after having reached the fabled area destined for the triumphs of his race. We could borrow Rilke's phrase (as it was used by Rossiter to describe the limitations of Shakespeare's men of history) and say that Aeneas as prototypic historical man is "verwirrt mit Wircklichkeit," a bondsman of reality.[12] The continuity of civilization, of name and fame, and the generative link which embodies the future hope, are his main resources. But in a world of disorder and chaos these are consolations not to be scoffed at. In fact, in the dialectic of the historical work, they can assume an inspirational potency — but never fulfillment.

Graduated values are important to Dante. If, on the one hand, he senses that the *Aeneid*'s great lack is the personal sense of being that Christianity offered, he still regards its values as standards in relation to which deviations from the merely natural and historical can be criticized. In canto XIX of the *Inferno* the simoniacal clergy are excoriated in the figures of their papal leaders, who, though nominal Christians, fall short even of the Roman ideal. Instead of sparing the vanquished and laying low the proud ("parcere subiectis e debellare superbos"), they rather trample on the good and exalt the wicked. However insufficient the natural and the historical might be, mankind even under the Christian dispensation has means of perverting both and converting them into their hellish opposites. This is what happens to children and fame in the *Inferno*. Here again the famous Ulysses canto is summary: not merely because it vitiates the threads of continuity — children and fame — but also because of the implied standards against which such action is measured.

There is much that Dante finds personally appealing in this intellectual adventurer who chucked all, who resented the progressive stultification of the spirit in the rounds of domesticity.[13] Like Dante, Ulysses was a traveler, a spiritual freebooter, searching out the ways of men, knowledge, and experience "delli vizi umani e del valore." Men were meant not to live like brutes but to follow virtue. Burning within Ulysses is the fire that leads him in the direction of the mountain of Purgatory (although he does not know it). Dante sympathetically understands the source of his movement and its misdirection. Not provided with commensurate objects in extension, this fire turns against its source and is destructive. This free-lancer is merely footloose, and his questing is open-ended, issuing nowhere, finding no peace or satisfaction for his burning restlessness. Ulysses is not a model to follow but a tragedy to avoid. Looking down on the spirit of Ulysses, whose spirit is consumed by the very greatness which animates it, Dante records a note of self-warning. Then he sorrowed and now,

> e ora mi ridoglio
> quando drizzo la mente a ciò ch' io vidi,
> e più lo 'ngegno affreno ch' i' non soglio,
> perchè non corra che virtù nol guidi;
> sì che, se stella bona o migilior cosa
> m' ha dato 'l ben, ch' io stessi nol m' invidi.

> I grieve anew when I turn my mind to what I saw,
> and more than I am wont I curb my powers lest they run
> where virtue does not guide them, so that, if favouring
> star or something better have granted me such boon, I
> may not grudge it to myself.
>
> (XXVI.19–24)

To be blessed overmuch, as Yeats recognized in the case of tragic beauty, can be an unsettling experience. And the problems of exceptional promise and talent (the joined cases of Ulysses and Dante) are crucial for the form that divine comedy took in the fourteenth century. It is important that these are not the dramas of Everyman but rather the stories of those who sought an extra-special distinction, who felt that life required a more than usual effort and valor. Against the "picciola vigilia / de' nostri sensi" — the brief vigil left to their lives — Ulysses' entire speech, calculated endeavor that it is, urges his men to go down in style, to rush wide-eyed and unflinching into the final abyss.

The heroism of their end would be consonant with the valued conception of their lives. But Dante avoids such tragedy when he discovers in the world values and ideals which seem to answer, while controlling, his great needs.

Consequently the perspective of the canto befits comedy — it is the survivor's perspective — and Ulysses' characterization is imbedded in a context that is largely ironic. Ulysses' account of his travels begins not with any direction toward Troy, or desire to return home, but rather with his year-long delay with Circe. Furthermore, it was not Ulysses who gave the place a name but Aeneas, that founder of civilization. In Dante's scheme this is clear evidence that Ulysses' passing leads to no kind of continuity. Further, those links of generation and continuity, father, child and wife, have no hold on his spirit, avid for new experience:

> Quando
> mi diparti' da Circe, che sottrasse
>   me più d'un anno là presso a Gaeta,
>   prima che sì Enea la nomasse,
> nè dolcezza di figlio, nè la pièta
>   del vecchio padre, nè 'l debito amore
>   lo qual dovea Penelopè far lieta,
> vincer poter dentro da me l'ardore
>   ch' i' ebbi a divenir del mondo esperto,
>   e delli vizi umani e del valore.

> When I parted from Circe, who held me more than a
> year near Gaeta before Aeneas so named it, not fond-
> ness for a son, nor duty to an aged father, nor the
> love I owed Penelope which should have gladdened
> her, could conquer within me the passion I had to
> gain experience of the world and of the vices and
> the worth of men.

(XXVI.90–99)

The contrast with first presentation of Virgil ("giusto figluol d'Anchise") in Canto I is clear: neither city nor family could hold him.

Ulysses' mad flight has neither historical nor transcendent possibilities. So much is now made clear by the two extended similes with which Dante hedges and ironically comments upon Ulysses' story. Looking down upon the flickering flames of the false counsellors, Dante likens himself to a peasant sitting on a hill during a midsummer evening and watching the fireflies in the valley below where he labors:

> Quante il villan ch'al poggio si riposa,
>   nel tempo che colui che 'l mondo schiara
>   la faccia sua a noi tien meno ascosa,
> come la mosca cede a la zanzara,
>   vede lucciole giù per la vallea,
>   forse colà dov' e' vendemmia ed ara.

> As many as the fire-flies which the peasant, resting
> on the hill — in the season when he that lights the
> world least hides his face from us and at the hour
> when the fly gives place to the gnat — sees along the
> valley below, in the fields, perhaps, where he gathers
> the grapes and tills.
>
> (XXVI.25–30)

This scene of the pensive peasant contrasts in its closed frame with the unbounded search of Ulysses. It has a settled and rooted quality that is alien to Ulysses; within natural limitations, contentment, satisfaction, and even strength are possible. Despite the prospect of change, the peasant is an instance of calm: his labor all takes place under the eye of reassuring cosmic forces. This is a tableau (more fairly rendered, perhaps, than in Rabelais), of the medieval sense of being which the more aspirant Renaissance figures, as they experience their perilous freedom, will envy. Its security within change is an ideal toward which — or back to which — they will look. Its importance is underlined for us by Dante when his own vagrant genius realizes the need for taking hold, "following the lonely way among the rocks and splinters of the ridge, the foot made no speed without the hand." (16–18) It is on hands and knees that one must occasionally maneuver in this large world of dangerous inner and outer forces, where a man of Ulysses' grandeur is destroyed. And later, when to get a better — more curious — view, Dante stands up, he would have easily fallen into the pit of Ulysses, "s' io non avessi un ronchion preso" ("if I had not taken hold of a rock"). Such stability of place obviously not only finds favor with Dante but within the natural order is a valued necessity, preparatory for that peace and community which are the highest offerings of the earthly city.

The other simile immediately following this sees in the fire a more divine principle, contrasting as much with the low flame of succession as it does with the destructive fires of Ulysses' intellect. Rather than Roman and historical, its vision is Biblical and transcendent:

> E qual colui che si vengiò con li orsi
>   vide 'l carro d'Elia al dipartire,
>   quando i cavalli al cielo erti levorsi,
> che nol potea sì con li occhi seguire,
>   ch'el vedesse altro che la fiamma sola,
>   sì come nuvoletta, in su salire . . .

> And as he that was avenged by the bears saw the
> chariot of Elijah at his departure when the horses
> reared and rose to heaven, who could not follow it
> with his eyes so as to see anything but the flame
> alone like a little cloud mounting up . . .

(34–39)

So Dante saw only the flames, the sinners within being concealed. But again the simile offers an ironic commentary by way of contrast to Ulysses' fate. The fire burning within all of us can persist in nature, destroy itself, or rise to heaven; Roman, Greek, and Christian dispositions of the flame are here presented, in dramatic commentary one upon the other. We live or die, consumed by fire or fire, T. S. Eliot would write. And as in *Little Gidding,* the tongues of Ulysses' destructive fire are constrasted with a divine, redeeming fire.

Modern experience and classical myth converge and inform each other, when Florence and Ulysses, representing directionless energies, both stand as tutelary figures over the borders of hell's deepest reaches, over the land of deceit, fraud, and treachery. Like Ulysses, Florence beats her wings over the sea. She has embarked on a mad flight of acquisitiveness and economic expansion. The spread of her name is notorious: there are thirty-two Florentines in hell, four in purgatory, and but two in paradise. She, like Ulysses, is consumed by activities with no moral end or merit. Ulysses, for his part, is identified with the familial (Cain-Abel) strife of the earthly city when the bifurcated flame that holds him and Diomede (pointedly, even allies are separated) seems to Dante to "suger della pira / dov' Eteòcle col fratel fu miso" ("to rise from the pyre where Eteocles was laid with his brother"). Sheer intellectual energy and agility, the divided flame of "science sans conscience," seems to result in the fratricidal conflict that spells for Augustine and for Dante the radical defeat of the earthly city, for which Thebes, with its curious family histories, stands as emblem. (This also explains the importance of Statius, the author of the *Thebaid,* as another epic model for Dante.) Both Florence and Ulysses are markedly opposed to the right functioning of the earthly city. Dante's Ulysses carries with him none of the seeds of Roman civilization, the familial loyalties, the giving of name, and the fixity of place. And Florence's infamy, her pursuit of expansion by whatever means, remarkably differs from the honorable fame sought by the few just men of the classical world who are enregistered in *Inferno* IV.

Fame, be it remembered, as a fundamentally natural impulse toward self-continuation and time transcendence is not necessarily alien to a Christian setting. After due sifting of ends and means, fame, as we shall see, is majestically reintroduced into the *Divine Comedy.* Our first impression, but Dante's final position, occurs in *Inferno* II, when Virgil, the apostle of Rome soon to embark on a mission of grace, is greeted by Beatrice, his close Christian relation:

> O anima cortese mantovana,
> > di cui la fama ancor nel mondo dura,
> > e durerà quanto 'l mondo lontana.

> O courteous Mantuan soul, whose fame still endures
> in the world and shall endure as long as the world lasts.
> > (58–60)

A seal is placed on this obviously favorable address when, two cantos later, Dante has it explained to him that some pagan souls receive special treatment in hell, since

> L'onrata nominanza
> che di lor suona su nella tua vita,
> grazia acquista nel ciel che sì li avanza.

> Their honourable fame, which resounds in thy life
> above, gains favour in Heaven which thus advances them.
> > (76–78)

This explanation is affirmed by the exhortation that follows, "Onorate l'altissimo poeta . . ." In fact, among the virtuous pagans the word "honor" or its derivatives is used eight times. Florence's falling-off from the dimensions of even the earthly city is stressed by the shame rather than the honor brought by her citizens ("tu in grande orranza non ne sali").

Augustine has several relevant discriminations to make in his discussion of fame or glory in Book V (12–14) of *The City of God*. The first and most elementary is his distinction between those who sought honor by virtuous means and those who sought it by any means. And although the Romans built the temples of virtue and of honor in close proximity, still such an alliance was only practiced by a few moral aristocrats. This attachment to honor, however virtuous, is linked by Augustine with the limited goals of the earthly city (justifying, incidentally, this study's emphasis): "since those Romans were in an earthly city, and had before them, as the end of all the offices undertaken in its behalf, its safety, and a kingdom, not in heaven, but in earth — not in the sphere of eternal life, but in the sphere of demise and succession, where the dead are succeeded by the dying — what else but glory should they love, by which they wished even after death to live in the mouths of their admirers?" [14] Given this rationale, whereby even the virtues of the earthly city are imperfect, Augustine's priorities are clear. Higher than the honor sought by the ways of virtue is the unsolicited renown that is simply a byproduct of one's love of the good. Augustine's supporting quotations indicate that what he is espousing is Christian virtue, summarized by St. Paul, whom he quotes: "For this is our glory, the testimony of our conscience." Consequently, however valuable the love of glory — it restrains vice and incites toward virtue — those who follow such desire, and seek human praise, "are not indeed yet holy, but only less base." Whether fame is the last infirmity of a noble mind or the last stirring of something valuable in an otherwise defective code of values is a moot point. What is clear is that a similar code of priorities must be learned by Dante when he enters the realm of misplaced affections.

Dante is the Christian chronicler of the fall of Florence, as Augustine had been that of Rome's demise. The *Commedia*, particularly in the *Inferno,* is a gallery of portraits and a roster of names. To have a name is to be part of a community. Especially is this true of Florence, so proud in its family histories and its code of civic honor and achievement. As Dante severs himself from the earlier expectations of the earthly city, so too, with equal steps, he releases himself from the fixation on name and fame, the proper recompense of those who live in the sphere of succession. But this process of dissociation is more painful and arduous in Dante than in Augustine. Dante after all was a living son of a community; his eager, youthful mind — as the *Commedia* suggests — took fire at the myths, stories, and names of his city's past. More than in Augustine, firmly held assumptions, even unconscious reverences, are being raked over. Dante's very life and loyalties must be rooted up. Dante meets Ciacco, Farinata, Brunetto Latini, Iacopo Rusticucci, Tegghiaio Aldobrandi, and Guido Guerra in hell. Of these men it might be said that they associated fame with public virtue. All being, at least as Dante dramatizes them, honorably inspired men, none was outwardly vicious. They were "worthy" and set their minds to "ben far." But they were all essentially marred heroes and imperfect exemplars. As Dante comes to reject his city, so he rejects the fathers of that city, not for their utter worthlessness but for their insufficiency. He must pass beyond these men and their inner spiritual defeats if he is to resolve the problems of the will and control those beasts that threatened his progress.

Dante's first encounter with a Florentine in hell occurs in Canto VI, where he meets Ciacco, damned through gluttony to the loss of his spiritual identity. A psychological realism completely of this world shows through this other-worldly meeting (another instance of the mimetic functioning that Auerbach perceives in the poem). Dante, fresh on the road, still new to his condition as a pilgrim and consequently still retaining his strong Florentine attachments and identity, is filled with curiosity about events and names of his home town. Although he is in the middle of life's journey, still there is a boyish faith and innocence (qualities which, misdirected now, will be saving features later on) in the first inquiries he makes about the personalities (most of them just mentioned) that loom so large in his youthful imagination. These men whom Dante meets in the first half of hell still have some glimmer of their former possibilities about them, some holdover which, if it does not make them virtuous, at least makes them less base. Ciacco initiates his exchange with Dante by asking civilly to be recognized, and he terminates it by making that oft-to-be-heard and pathetic attempt to retain some hold upon the living:

> Ma quando tu sarai nel dolce mondo,
>   priegoti ch'alla mente altrui mi rechi.

> But when thou shalt be in the sweet world, I
>   pray thee bring me to men's memory.
>   (88–89)

Nevertheless, however friendly at first these meetings are, they all seem to end on a note of disquiet, even of bitterness. Ciacco's closing words are strangely final: "I tell thee no more nor answer thee again," giving us in anticipation a suggestion that the ultimate condition of hell is one of silence. And from this we may come to realize that it is only through Dante's art and memory, through the exigencies of communicating meaning, that these creatures have momentarily been brought to life. At length, they all relapse as Ciacco does, "to the level of the other blind." True realization intrudes upon the former hospitable welcome. Looking askance and bowing his head, Ciacco could hardly be said to have uttered a farewell, or a valediction; rather in closing he suggests the lingering malaise that attends all of these eagerly awaited renewals of acquaintance. Dante's being in life and hope and the necessary return of the infernal souls to their real condition, once the temporary reprieve is terminated, are all too evident. From Virgil's explanation of Ciacco's final unsettling gesture, we learn some of the truth about hell:

> Più non si desta
> di qua dal suon dell'angelica tromba,
> quando verrà la nimica podèsta:
> ciascun rivederà la trista tomba,
> ripiglierà sua carne e sua figura,
> udrià que ch' in etterno rimbomba.

> He wakes no more till the sounding of the angel's
> trumpet, when the adverse Judge shall come; each shall
> find again the sad tomb and take again his flesh and
> form and hear that which echoes in eternity.

> (94–99)

"Tromba," "tomba," "rimbomba" are all resonating words which in their echoing effects summarize the sentence the damned will always hear. While the sonic extensions emphasize eternity's vast stretches, the real horror is in the sameness of the activity. There was some hint of this condition when Dante first entered the land of the gluttonous:

> Io sono al terzo cerchio, della piova
> etterna, maladetta, fredda e greve;
> regola e qualità mai non l'è nova.

> I am in the third circle, of eternal, accursed rain,
> cold and heavy, never changing its measure or its kind.
>
> (7–9)

Although he had divested himself of hope when he entered hell, Dante still retains one essential for improvement, and that is time, with the possibilities of change. The damned, on the other hand, can only look forward to a horrid sameness. Farinata, another of the great figures about whom Dante inquires, explains that their ability to forecast, if cryptically, what will happen, is only a temporary dispensation to be revoked after the day of judgment:

> Però comprender puoi che tutta morta
> fia nostra conoscenza da qual punto
> che del futuro fia chiusa la porta.

> Thou canst understand, therefore, that all
> our knowledge will be dead from the moment
> the door of the future is closed.
>
> (X.106–108)

The state of hell is a terrible changelessness, when all man will have in front of him are regrettable memories — his knowledge is dead — that are the more bitter when contrasted with their prior possibilities. And if the future is closed, so is the door to future fame. In Dante's scale of values it can be a bitter consolation (see Ciacco's hard "valediction") if man himself does not possess, to return to the phrase of St. Paul, "the peace of righteousness."

But we must not underestimate the passion and faith of Dante's local attachments. In the *Inferno* name and fame seem fragile indeed, and even pathetic, when measured by the spectral shadow of eternity. But after the process of purgation in the *Paradiso,* these same present things are revitalized. And even in the *Inferno,* there is something grand in the way Farinata assumes the position of a single just man for the sake of Florence.

> Ma fu' io solo, là dove sofferto
> fu per ciascun di torre via Fiorenza,
> colui che la difesi a viso aperto.

But there I was alone where all agreed to make an
end of Florence, the one man to defend her before them
all.

(91–93)

For the sake of his city he was willing to risk a position of singleness, something he was not able to do for his soul. As an exemplar of civic devotion Farinata is immense, but as a model for exile he is deficient, being totally confined within the dimensions of the earthly city. It pains him more than the "bed" in which he is suffering, however disdainfully, that his people have not been able to recover from their last exile (his Ghibelline party was finally and irrecoverably driven out in 1265). Although exiled, his frame of reference is always Florence. By Dante's Tuscan speech he is immediately stirred and for this reason engages him in conversation. Dante is a son of that "nobil patria" to which Farinata was perhaps "troppo molesto." But Dante is physically frightened by the superb figure and for refuge draws closer to Virgil, a better model in exile and recovery. Scornfully, having recognized in Dante some family trait, and before he can answer, Farinata demands, "Chi fuor li maggior tui?" ("Who were thy ancestors?") The ensuing exchange encapsules the history of conflict and exile of Guelph and Ghibelline, which so damaged Florence in the thirteen century. It is important to note how quickly the concern for the "simple speech" of a son of the noble fatherland converts itself into a resurrection and re-enactment of the civic strife of that city. The factious emulation that tore their city apart continues to divide two compatriots meeting in the lonely ways of hell. What should be the basis of reunion turns out to be the cause of separation: and this is the way it must be, Dante implies, when the beginning, middle, and end deal only with Florence, as they do for Farinata.

This encounter with Farinata is another step on the way to Dante's severance of his ties with Florence, and ultimately with the expectations of the earthly city. When we think of Farinata's total identification with the earthly city, his placement among the Epicureans immediately becomes clear. He refers by name to two other Ghibellines suffering with him, the Emperor Frederick and Cardinal Ottaviano. This Ghibelline gathering in Canto X suggests that their political hostility to the Papacy may, in part, have been based upon a disregard for the spiritual resources of the soul. Ottaviano is noted for his quip, "If I have a soul I have lost mine a thousand times for the Ghibellines." [15] This perspective also explains the exchange with Cavalcante, who, significantly enough, just as Farinata is only concerned with people in relation to Florence, is only brought to life by curiosity over his son, Guido Cavalcante, and then disappointingly drops back to silence when, from Dante's hesitation, he gathers that his boy is dead. His anxious questioning is at once beautiful and pathetic as he asks why Dante referred to Guido in the past tense: "non viv'elli ancora?" / non fiere li occhi suoi il dolce lome?" ("Lives he not still? Strikes not the sweet light on his eyes?") From the sheer physical quality of his son's bright eyes the elder Cavalcante himself derived his life. In his son's apparent death, he has no more reason for existence — and indeed there is just such a finality in his final position: "supin ricadde e più non parve fora" ("he fell back again and was seen no more").

All characters in Canto X are circumscribed by the dimensions and expectations of the earthly city. None entertains any ulterior source for reference. Of the two states of exile, from the earthly and from the heavenly city, they are more concerned with the disappointments of the former and thus never escape. But Dante is more concerned with recovering his lost heavenly city. Troubled by Farinata's dire reference to the future and the unreturning exile of Dante's party, the White Guelphs, Dante turns to his "saggio" Virgil, who encourages him to wait for Beatrice. From her Dante will learn of his life's journey — "di tua vita il viaggio." The phrasing itself suggests the absence of any postponed vicarious dependencies — on the fortunes of party or city, on the successes of offspring. To know of the voyage of one's life suggests a rounding off into completion, a contentedness in wholeness and sufficiency, a perception of the providence and meaning of one's own journey.

Evidence of the close and active Florentine civic life abounds in Dante's poem. One form it takes is the solicitude and care that the older men have in providing for the education and careers of their younger townsmen. This, as we have seen, represents the new paideutic function introduced by early bourgeois culture. It is no accident, then, that one of the great themes of the *Commedia* is the relation between teacher and student. Ever in search of the master-father, Dante, the student, very willingly acknowledges his indebtedness to the fatherly Brunetto Latini (who twice previously had referred to Dante as "my son"):

> chè 'n la mente m'è fitta, e or m'accora,
> la cara e buona imagine paterna
> di voi quando nel mondo ad ora ad ora

m'insegnavate come l'uom s'etterna:
  e quant'io l'abbia in grado, mentr'io vivo
  convien che nella mia lingua si scerna.

for in my memory is fixed, and now goes to my heart,
the dear and kind paternal image of you when many a
time in the world you taught me how man makes himself
immortal; and how much I am grateful for it my tongue,
while I live, must needs declare.

(XV.82–87)

More will be added shortly about the immortalizing functions of Latini's teaching. From the physical drama of the piece, however, Dante
has already expressed his reservations about the suitability of Latini as
a model to follow. In fact, the great achievement of the canto is its atmosphere of restraint, the tacit but nevertheless clear awareness, shared
by each, that the positions of teacher and student have been reversed.

Only once and inadvertently does Dante's shock at their changed
positions show itself, and that is his very first question of surprise, "Siete
voi qui, ser Brunetto?" Throughout the canto, however, it is mainly the
dramatic means of Dante the author that clarifies the moral truth of the
encounter. Dante, the student, perhaps remembering their old situation,
would gladly sit and talk with Brunetto. But the teacher is no longer a
model of rest or stasis, but only an instance of restlessness. Dramatically
enough, he cannot sit still, but must keep moving. Further, it is Brunetto who must leave the line of his progression in order to keep up
with Dante. The student would preserve the semblance of the old relationship, and treat him with the reverence and just acknowledgment
which are his due. But the reversal of roles is clear: Brunetto is on the
level below Dante. For the student to follow the master in his moral life
would be a descent rather than ascension:

I' non osava scender della strada
  per andar par di lui; ma 'l capo chino
  tenea com' uom che reverente vada.

I durst not descend from the track to go on his level,
but I kept my head bent down as one that walks with
reverence.

(43–45)

An essential notion of the community, a kind of secular paideia, where the young are fostered by the old, prepared for life and given standards of conduct, is here drastically subverted. Rather than serving as objects of inspiration and assistance, the models that his city provides require restraint in Dante. Rather than freedom of development its representatives produce tension and hidden rivalries. Dante has acquired other masters who will satisfy his needs. Significantly sparing of Brunetto's feelings, he refers to Virgil, his new teacher, not by name but rather as "this one" who met him when he was lost, and is now leading Dante home, not to Florence, but to a better life ("E reducemi a ca per questo calle"), where again the journey in progress suggests not unknown exploration, but rather a return to what was given. Brunetto's insights into the future and the moral equipment he would lend Dante to cope with his exile are corrected rather than confirmed by the younger man, who breaks through his deferential reserve and speaks for once from conscience. He has not been Virgil's student for nothing, and when Brunetto alludes to the blow of exile that fortune is preparing, Dante, bringing together the lessons of Cantos VII and X, professes his readiness for whatever Fortune will. (88–93) While it is always hazardous to speculate about orthographic differences, especially given the uncertain early manuscript condition of the *Commedia,* still it is perhaps indicative that when Latini refers to "fortuna" it is twice used in lower case, but in Dante's usage it is capitalized.[16] For Brunetto "fortuna" is more of a pagan concept, indicating chance or a particular human destiny. For Dante it is on its way to becoming a religious concept which in its blessedness and relation to his own life will be glossed for him, not by his earthly teacher Brunetto, but by his heavenly instructress, Beatrice, to whom Virgil is leading him.

From this it is obvious that the eternity promised by Brunetto and the stirrings it awoke in the young Dante were not necessarily the same as that which Dante is on his way to recovering. "S'etternare" is reflexive, and emphasizes that man makes himself immortal, while the whole purpose of Dante's journey is to commit himself to the divine forces of the universe that redeem him. Brunetto's insight into Dante's future is concerned with the "onor" that is reserved for him, and his final words call attention to the literary work by which he would survive:

> sieti raccomandato il mio Tesoro
> nel qual io vivo ancora, e più non cheggio.

> Let my *Treasure,* in which I yet live, be commended
> to thee; and I ask no more.
>
> (XV.119–120)

This final phrase clarifies the scope of Brunetto's vision, and the meaning of the phrase "s'etternare." It indicates that Brunetto Latini was dedicated not to the ends of the heavenly city, but, as with his use of the word *fortuna,* was still bounded by the limits of man's earthly existence. His vision engages no transcendence but is limited to the ways of succession: he asks for no more than the after-life of his book. And, to be sure, there is a great deal of courage both in the affirmation of his work and in the persistency with which he moves on — and Dante registers both justly. In good and bad Brunetto is surprising. His qualities draw out of Dante a valedictory image which seems to congratulate the spirit of Brunetto, but more exactly, rests on his essential ambiguity, the difference between his appearance and his reality.

> Poi si rivolse, e parve di coloro
>   che corrono a Verona il drappo verde
>   per la campagna; e parve di costoro
> quelli che vince, non colui che perde.

> Then he turned about and seemed like one of those
>   that run for the green cloth in the field of Verona,
>   and he seemed not the loser among them, but the winner.
>
> (121–124)

Brunetto is one of Dante's marred heroes, admired up to a limit but also defective. His story is a major revelation in Dante's separation from the means of continuity sought within the earthly city.

The stupendous individual figures of the *Inferno* are so overwhelming that the groups of individuals tend to be neglected. Such is the case of the Florentines about whom Dante inquired from Ciacco. They too are in the bolgia of the homosexuals, but are overshadowed by Brunetto Latini. Still this encounter with Guido Guerra, Tegghiaio Aldobrandi, and Iacopo Rusticucci is every bit as significant and even perhaps more emotionally powerful than the subtle dramatic masterpiece, Canto XV. Importantly enough, they too recognize Dante by his Florentine dress and rush toward him. Virgil indicates his respect for these men and their public values by observing that, had he known who they were, he would have thought it more fitting for Dante to go to them. Within the limits of the earthly city, fame is still exchange current: forming a ring about him they implore Dante to identify himself, at least out of respect for their fame ("la fama nostra"). They have hit upon the right fellow townsmen, for only too willingly would Dante converse with them. They are the heroes of his past, the myths of his consciousness. It was at the mention of their names that his young imagination took fire. And above all, he is the son who remembers and who keeps (and who continues to keep) them alive:

> Di vostra terra sono, e sempre mai
> l'ovra di voi e li onorati nomi
> con affezion ritrassi e ascoltai.

> I am of your city and your deeds and honoured names
> I have always recounted and heard with affection.
>
> (XVI.58–60)

So compelling is the encounter and so overwhelming is Dante's sadness at seeing his heroes thus terribly changed that if there had been protection against the fire he would have hurled himself among them, and Virgil, significantly, would have allowed it. (46–51) But another reality intervenes to limit the affection of remembrance and compassion. The responsibility of individual salvation and the attendant sense of justice and his own moral integrity prevent this selfless but destructive commitment to his early loyalties. In no place does Dante make more clearly understood the seriousness with which he believed that man must love the creator before the creature, and in few places does he show how painfully the lesson is learned. To cast his lot with theirs when other posibilities present themselves, to throw himself blindly and tearfully into what was, would be a nostalgic suicide, a self-abandonment and rejection of the positive ideals and goals he feels are available to him. The world for Dante, no less than for us, would be unbearable were there no intellectual justice. To stay with them, rather than moving on, would be an abidcation of his own lights, his own vision of moral excellence, and Dante himself would be the immolated victim.

As Dante enters the larger world of universal time, so he has for his protection more perfect models of conduct, and other names. Because their attachments are all within the confines of the earthly city, the men of his city whom he meets in hell are deficient models for the son of their city who is seeking to cope with a more important exile. Their offerings do not lead him out of the radical alienation and exile of hell.

Presenting Dante with small means to beat the beast that threatened him at the opening of the poem, these civic exemplars offer no possible peace of righteousness for his own disquiet. In fact they all show a restlessness typical of the earthly city. And if they were men of honor, still their allegiance to the earthly city and their resulting restlessness connect them with the public restlessness and disorder of those who lower down in hell bring about social chaos through dishonorable deceit and treachery. In the moral realism attendant upon Dante's larger historical consciousness these virtuous public men are marred not only in themselves, but in the disasters toward which, beyond themselves, their public allegiances tend. For Dante, historical man, without any transcendent reference, must necessarily experience decline. The topography of hell is instructive: those Florentines of public virtue are on a descending slope which is continuous with and derives from Satan.

As we descend into hell, not only is this restlessness directed outward to destroy that very earthly city to which these honorable men committed themselves, but the desire and the rewards of fame undergo a remarkable change. A process of reticence accompanies the growth of sin, until in a true reversal typical of hell (and anticipated by Ciacco), we reach something like Iago's final silence, "Demand me nothing. What you know, you know. From this time forth I never will speak word," or Goneril's "Ask me not what I know," followed by her portentous exit. Earthly fame that had derived from God's trumpeting glory becomes the total opposite of itself. Such are the ironic justicers that threaten man's unwary reliances, and such is the process of decline that seems intrinsic to his history in the earthly city.

Roughly in the first half of the *Inferno,* the offer of keeping a man's name alive is a means of procuring a life story. Virgil can use such means to elicit response from Piero delle Vigne:

> Ma dilli chi tu fosti, sì che 'n vece
>   d'alcun'ammenda tua fama rinfreshchi
>   nel mondo su, dove tornar li lece.

> But tell him who thou wast, so that, for some amends,
>   he may revive thy fame in the world above, where he
>   is permitted to return.

(XIII.52–54)

This "dolce dir" (sweet talk) so pleases the suicide that he tells his memorable story. But when we come to Canto XVIII and the first

pocket of those whose vice led to others' harm, there is greater resistance
to having one's story told. Of course the house rules of *Inferno* insist
that willy-nilly the agonists' fortunes and defects must be revealed. But
nevertheless as we descend the unwillingness to tell is increased, and
there is a greater need for Dante to pry loose their names and their
stories.[17] In Canto XVIII, one Alessio Interminei of Lucca (not otherwise known) shuns the glare of Dante's light, and is indignant that he
should be singled out from the others in the filth. In Canto XIX,
Boniface's name (he is still alive) is released inadvertently, and his
predecessor Nicholas, the spokesman for the offense of simony, is never
named, although he too recounts his failings in an allusive way. In Canto
XXIV Vanni Fucci suffers more than at his own death because he is
seen and is obliged to tell his story to Dante. Canto XXVI opens as we
have already indicated with Dante's condemnation of Florence's undiscriminating pursuit of fame, which does not bring "honor." And in
Canto XXVII, encountering Guido da Montefeltro, ever the political
fox, Dante asks him to identify himself "se 'l nome tuo nel mondo tegna
fronte" ("if thy name would keep its place in the world"). In his response, crisp with the subjunctives of the politician's discourse, Guido
outwits himself just as he did with the devil, who surprisingly was a
"logician":

> S' i' credesse che mia risposta fosse
>   a persona che mai tornasse al mondo,
>   questa fiamma starìa sanza più scosse;
> ma però che già mai di questo fondo
>   non tornò vivo alcun, s' i' odo il vero,
>   sanza tema d'infamia ti rispondo.

> If I thought my answer were to one who would ever
> return to the world, this flame should stay without
> another movement; but since none ever returned alive
> from this depth, if what I hear is true, I answer thee
> without fear of infamy.

> (61–66)

As he descends, Dante does not have to rely on the individual sinner
to reveal himself and his fault; there are others who will do it for him.
But rather than simply accepting such identification, the person named
takes it meanly. Now, as the code of the underworld breaks down, it is
treacherous to name names. And this betrayal results in mutual vilifica-

tion. Witness Master Adam, the counterfeiter, who in the bolgia of falsi-
fiers (Canto XXX) identifies Potiphar's wife and the Greek Sinon,
deceiver of the Trojans, and is struck by one of those whom he names.
(100–102) Master Adam replies with his free hand, and there then en-
sues a duet of accusations and betrayals, a street scene of fishwifery,
from which Virgil has to call back Dante's curiosity with a reprimand.

And in the Ninth Circle where treachery is punished, the case of
Bocca degli Alberti provides us with our summary example of the processes of change which fame and name undergo in the *Inferno*. Significantly enough in the Antenora, where treachery to country and cause is
punished, the angered soul of Bocca meets Dante's query with a coun-
ter-question of identity, to which Dante answers:

> Vivo son io, e caro esser ti pote,
>   fu mia risposta, se dimandi fama,
>   ch' io metta il nome tuo tra l'altre note.

> I am alive, was my reply, and it may be worth much
> to thee, if thou ask for fame, that I note thy name
> among the rest.
>   (XXXII.91–93)

But Dante is still a novice in his belief that such hardened sinners have
the same interest in the life-furthering impulse of fame. A sullen isolation, as bitter as the response, is all that is desired in this dead-end sector
of human experience:

> Del contrario ho io brama;
>   lèvati quinci e non mi dar più lagna,
>   chè mal sai lusinghar per questa lama.

> What I crave for is the opposite. Take thyself
> hence and do not vex me further, for thou ill knowest
> how to flatter in this depth.
>   (94–96)

The rules of the land have changed. We are far from the positive dimension of the earthly city, and its rewards of fame. In the realm of Antenora, the individual is single, and name and fame, those once-valued
means of human continuity, those antidotes to annihilation and total
oblivion, are no longer desired. Instead, anonymity and nothingness are

preferred. The life impulse here is totally frustrated, and all consciousness or trace of having lived would gladly be obliterated.

Progeny, that other source of human continuity, encounters a similar defeat in the *Inferno*. As the resounding note of the human impulse for fame is converted into dead silence, the life impulse of procreation is turned against itself and rather than progression suffers a reversion. This is the way it must be in the realm where all hope is lost and the door of the future is closed. Fame and children are part of the historical realm of succession: they both look to the future with hope. But the faculty of hell is memory, which looks at the hopeless present from the recollection of ruined past possibility. The means of hope are fundamentally antithetical to the ways of hell, and their defeat and perversion are indications that a total concentration on the earthly city leads eventually to the defeat of that sphere's very rewards and sources. The earthly city, by itself, in history must be self-defeating.

Children are one of the present things that occupy the attention of the earthly city. It is for his children that man labors. Cavalcante, totally within the sphere of the secular and disregarding the dimension of soul, comes to life only to inquire about the bright eyes of his brilliant son. And when he mistakenly conceives that his boy is dead he relapses as if there were nothing else of interest for himself. Like the reliance on fame, the total dependency on children within the earthly city is dramatized as a source of self-disappointment. But we must remember that this link of generation, like fame itself, does have a value. And as Virgil represented the quality of honorable fame, he too, through his *Aeneid,* dramatized the importance of generation for historical continuity. As we descend in hell this natural reliance does not rebound against the soul that singlemindedly depends upon its consolations; rather it is an ideal through the perversion of which the decay of the earthly city is measured. It is significant that the final spectacle among the makers of discord in Canto XXVIII should be the tremendous figure of Bertran de Born, who set the son against his father, Henry II of England. As J. D. Sinclair points out, there is a connection between the false counsellors of Cantos XXVI and XXVII and the makers of discord. Over all looms the presiding genius of Ulysses: the heirs of his agile counsel are Curio, who uttered the Machiavellian maxim before Machiavelli, ' 'l fornito / sempre con danno l'attender offerse" ("one prepared always loses by delay"), and Mosca, who voiced the summary tag of political cunning, "Capo ha cosa fatta" ("A thing done has an end") — each leading to the civil wars in

Rome and in Florence. Rome and Florence again are the examples, and at a decisive moment the false counsel of a rootless intellect incites the discord which ruins a community. The crowning piece in this progression is the punishment of Bertran. He confesses that, a latter day Achitophel, he urged the son to rebel against the father. His punishment bespeaks the offense:

> Perch'io parti' così giunte persone,
>   partito porto il mio cerebro, lasso!,
>   dal suo principio ch'è in questo troncone.
> Così s'osserva in me lo contrapasso.

> Because I parted those so joined I carry my brain, alas,
> parted from its root in this trunk; thus is observed
> in me the retribution.

(XXVIII.139–142)

Breaking that great father-son bond is in effect separating the head from the body, the mind from its larger locations in cosmos and community. The principles of continuity are disrupted, and man is locked in a singleness typical of hell:

> Di sè facea a sè stesso lucerna,
>   ed eran due in uno e uno in due:
>   com'esser può, quei sa che sì governa.

> Of itself it made for itself a lamp, and they were two
> in one and one in two: how it can be He knows who so
> ordains.

(124–126)

The unity of father and son in the human race and in the cosmos is verbally recollected here to express the magnitude of Bertran's offense. This description of his punishment emphasizes, as it will do for Satan, what a travesty of important principles his actions represent. Under the reign of Satan, the father-son link does not simulate the accord of God the Father and God the Son; rather it is converted into a cruel parodic opposite.[18] Time is not the moving image of eternity, and man cannot base his expectations on the order of succession. It is highly significant, then, for our thesis that the great encounter before Dante meets the Evil

One himself should be the Ugolino episode. This provides climactic evidence that the way to salvation does not lie within the normal patterns of time. But the importance of the father-son link for Dante is thereby attested: its violation serves as final persuasion.

In Canto XXXIII we hear the story of Ugolino, a Pisan political leader of Dante's young manhood, and his four sons, who where imprisoned and finally left to starve to death. The horror and the pity we experience at the narration of the sons' slow deaths in the presence of their helpless father is given larger scope when considered in the light of the dramatization of the ways of succession thus far revealed in the *Inferno*. This crucial and pivotal conceptual value attributed to the father-son link is supported by the freedom with which Dante dealt with the apparent historical fact for the sake of his artistic vision. The four people who historically died with Ugolino were not all his sons: two were grandsons; and they were not all children: three were adults. But Dante makes them all the Count's children. As in Shakespeare, such interpolations reveal fundamental preoccupations.

Whereas normally (throughout Shakespeare, for example) the resemblance of the child to the parent is a pleasurable recognition of continuance and a modest denial of death, when Ugolino looks into his sons' faces, the bitter truth of his own death and decay is only confirmed:

> Come un poco di raggio si fu messo
> > nel doloroso carcere, e io scorsi
> > per quattro visi il mio aspetto stesso,
> ambo le man per lo dolor mi morsi.

> As soon as a little ray made its way into the doleful
> prison and I discerned in four faces my own look, I
> bit both hands for grief.

$$(55-58)$$

The bright light of day, rather than shining through the keen illumination of the young Cavalcante's eyes, reveals death's heads instead. And when one of the boys sees his father gnawing his knuckles, thinking he does it out of hunger, he offers him their flesh to eat:

> Padre, assai ci fia men doglia,
> se tu mangi do noi: tu ne vestisti
> queste misere carni, e tu le spoglia.

> Father, it will be far less pain for us if thou eat
> of us. Thou didst clothe us with this wretched flesh
> and do thou strip us of it.
>
> (61–63)

The children would offer consolation to the father not by continuing his physical existence, but by returning the miserable flesh to its origin. The theme is reversion and reversal in time, not progression. Death is not countered, but affirmed. Rather than human community and triumphant continuity, man is reduced to the level of bestial appetite. This brutalization of the natural sources of life and consolation works its corruption into the father's bereavement and the form his sorrow takes. His eternity in hell is spent gnawing on the head of the man responsible for the brutal imprisonment and savage deaths, and he is consumed by an insatiable and impotent lust for revenge.[19] Even the legitimate outlet of sorrow is defiled. This is the way of the world, and the way the world leads in Dante's *Commedia,* back to the valley of death. Far from transcending time, the concentration on the present and the earthly city perverts those very natural means of human interpretation. In order to survive and preserve their efficacy, these present concerns must be reconstituted through the vision of God.

Divine Comedy, Succession and Decline

In the *Inferno,* naturally enough, there are no broad perspectives of temporal development. The state of hell is single and disjoined, and the mind of the sinner is so absorbed in its own past that there is little interest in perceiving sequential connections between events in history. When we come to the *Purgatorio* and gain a higher position in the mind's progressive liberation, more and more connections are made in time. Larger visions come under Dante's mounting purview. In the *Inferno* he was the compassionate and terror-struck novice. In his involvement he had little capacity for any kind of overview. The presentation itself led to a kind of disjunctiveness, without any strict historical rapport. In the *Inferno,* with few exceptions, rather than historical development Dante saw moral patterns transcending history. All sin and misery derived from and duplicated that dread Original who turned such beauty into such bruitishness. In the *Purgatorio,* although Dante is practically effecting his release from the hold of the earthly city, still his upward climb allows for a backward vision of the hell he is leaving behind.

Larger historical patterns and developments are the subject of his increased illumination.

From the confident city life into which he was born, and out of the power of his own talents, Dante acquired a strong natural faith in the time-transcending ways of succession — fame, name, and progeny — which later events forced him to deny. In hell he saw the violations of the ideal of generation and the dangers and even pathos of fame. In purgatory he meets with rulers who seem to have hoped too much and worked too single-mindedly for the sake of their heirs. Their life passions were almost totally absorbed in their line. And yet their line was the greatest source of their disappointment. Sordello's survey in *Purgatorio* VII of the royal houses of his time leads to the conclusion we have already regarded as summary:

> Rade volte risurge per li rami
> l'umana probitate; e questo vole
> quei che la dà, perchè da lui si chiami.

> Rarely does human worth rise through the branches,
> and this He wills who gives it, that it may be sought
> from Him.
>
> (121–123)

The ruling figures of the great European houses of the past generation have occasion now for a broader historical vision than they allowed themselves during their embroilments. The atmosphere is one of pensive sadness at the passingness of the things for which they labored, at the now apparent fruitlessness of their quarrels and the general unworthiness of their heirs. Their declined children are not necessarily punishment, no real retributive nemesis, but rather God's way of reminding them of the surer spiritual resources that they had neglected. These monarchs now turn away from life's uncertainties, from the things that so absorbed their attention, to participate in the harmony made possible by such release. Almost invariably they are considered superior to their children. Ottocar of Bohemia is better than his son Wenceslaus, "cui lussuria e ozio pasce" ("who battens on wantonness and ease"). The father and father-in-law of Philip IV of France, who becomes the *bête noire* of Dante's poem, now are sorrowed by their successor's activities. They know his foul and vicious life, "e quindi viene il duol che sì li lancia" ("and from this comes the grief that so pierces them"). Two enemies in life, Peter of Aragon and Charles of Sicily whom he had defeated and succeeded, now accord well, singing together. A portion of their union derives from their common fate: neither had great luck in his heir. In Canto VIII Dante meets Currado Malaspina, who asks news of the area where he was once great (Valdimagra). Here in purgatory he purifies the love which he bore to his own ("a miei portai l'amor che qui raffina"). All were devoted to their own line; and it is on the inscrutabilities of succession, beyond human powers or responsibility, that they now reflect.

In hell, children were mainly ideals whose loss was an indication of the bankruptcy of the natural order. In purgatory it is from the hope in their promise that man must divest himself. One might say that the forced estrangement of hell is chosen in purgatory for the sake of a more certain reliance on God. The times are so degenerate that natural means of succession are no longer desired, and in the ascent to the vision of God Dante meets many fellow travelers who act as guides in the most painful of separations. In Canto XIV Guido del Duca (upon whose phrase "exclusion of partnership" we earlier relied) recites for Dante the decline of his province of Romangna. (Typically enough, for Dante, the canto is introduced by a picture of Tuscany's decay: the more Tuscan flavor the Arno acquires on the way to the sea, the worse it becomes, terminating, as in hell itself, with the foxes of Pisa.) A poison seems to have invaded his homeland, and instead of the honorable families there are now corrupt scions. He introduces Rinier da Calboli,

> Questi è Rinier; questi è 'l pregio e l'onore
>   della casa da Calboli, ove nullo
>   fatto s'è reda del suo valore.

> This is Rinier, this is the boast and honour of the
> house of Calboli, where none since has made himself
> heir to his worth.
>
> (88–90)

A curse of bastardization seems to be working on procreation, so that succession is no longer increase and the natural is no longer desirable:

> Ben fa Bagnacaval, che non refiglia;
>   e mal fa Castrocaro, e peggio Conio
>   che di figliar tai conti più s'impiglia.

Bagnacavallo does well that breeds no more, and
Castrocaro ill, and Conio worse that still troubles
to breed such counts.

$$(115–117)$$

Given Dante's values, Guido's outburst is memorable: "Ben fa Bag-
nacaval, che non refiglia." Together with Sordello's lines which Chaucer
twice translated ("Rade volte risurge per li rami / l'umana probitate
. . ."), it serves as a landmark, indicating the more spiritualized medieval conception, which is suspicious of the ways of succession, and to
which the earlier Renaissance writers can cling, or revert, in the face
of life's obscurities. Those who have departed without heirs are fortunate,
since in the overturned state, the future, rather than bright perpetuation
of name and fame, would only mean taint and notoriety:

> O Ugolin de' Fantolin, sicuro
>   è il nome tuo, da che più non s'aspetta
>   chi far lo possa, tralignando, oscuro.

> O Ugolin de' Fantolini, thy name is safe, for no more
> are looked for who might blacken it by degeneracy.

$$(121–123)$$

The time is out of joint and there shall be no more children. But this
disruption is not a natural or original fall, but rather an historical one.
Once Romagna, like Florence, was thriving, and Dante can point to
quite specific historical causes for its decay. In Canto XVI of the *Purgatorio,* Marco Lombardo dismisses the notion of an inevitable decline.
Valor and courtesy once reigned in Romagna until the Emperor Frederick met with Papal opposition in the early thirteenth century. The
Church's competition with the temporal ruler precipitated the confusion
of values, the concentration on present things, which spelled ruin for
the area. In Florence's case, also, there are well known historical causes
working to bring its decline from the once admirable commune of the
early twelfth century. New people and fast money broke the bounds
of order and moderation. Within the old walls where its people could
still be circumscribed by religious order, responsive to the bells sum-
moning them to morning and noon services, Florence was peaceful,
sober, and chaste. But as they expanded beyond these walls and wealth

increased, virtue declined. And in Canto XX when Hugh Capet surveys his line, he has only regret at the "evil tree" of which he was the root, a tree which overshadows all of Christendom "sì che buon frutto rado se ne schianta" ("so that good fruit is rarely gathered there"). Territorial expansion and the "gift" of Provence turned out to be means of undoing.

Thus it becomes clear that no facet of succession, whether it be the life of a city or the smaller familial or larger dynastic line, guarantees a stable continuance. This is God's plan, lifting and lowering, quickening and killing, and this is the dramatic, spiritual world, where the wealthy are brought down and the poor are raised, to which Dante rises from the expectations of succession. After the dissolution of the Carolingian line it was from lowly stock, "the son of a butcher of Paris," that the next great French dynasty arose, only, in Dante's mind, to become corrupt through growth. A pattern close to tragic emerges in the life lines of families and dynasties. The Capetians in acquiring wealth and power introduced principles of their own undoing. This nemesis within wealth, like the disappointment within the line, is a means of distracting man from his reliance on the order of succession. It is part of God's providence that there should be few securities and many surprises in the world. Look at the business of Bethlehem. And this is the way it must be in divine comedy, where man must pride himself not on his own resources but rather on their source.

Dante points to quite explicit historical causes as he traces the decline of cities. But beyond blame there is the sad spectre of mutability, bringing to an end all the once flourishing centers of human affection and activity. Time, in its length, is this great force of disintegration, scattering and burying what was integral, compact, and prominent. Nowhere do we get a greater impression of the *Commedia* as a book of names than in the registers of the dead which Dante reads over and preserves.[20] Guido tells Dante,

> Non ti maravigliar s' io piango, Tosco,
>   quando rimembro con Guido da Prata
>   Ugolin d'Azzo, che vivetter nosco,
> Federigo Tignoso e sua brigata,
>   la casa Traversara e li Anastagi
>   (e l'una gente e l'altre è diretata),
> le donne e' cavalier, li affanni e li agi
>   che ne 'nvogliava amore e cortesia
>   là dove i cuor son fatti sì malvagi."

Do not marvel Tuscan if I weep when I remember Guido
da Prata and Ugolin d'Azzo, who lived among us, Federico
Tignoso and his company, the Traversaro house and the
Anastagi — the one family and the other now without an
heir — the ladies and the knights, the toils and the
sports to which we were moved by love and courtesy
where hearts have now grown so wicked.

(XIV.103–111)

And particularly when he approaches home the rhetoric of mutability
rises as Dante litanies once prominent Florentine names, now buried
in time. Again he is warned not to be surprised if the names of once
proud people are no longer extant, since cities themselves have disappeared. So it is with human things: they all have their deaths. This is
not the product of the second fall, but rather the radical consequence
of the first fall, of being involved in time and succession,

> per che non dee parer mirabil cosa
>   ciò ch'io dirò delli alti Fiorentini
>   onde è la fama nel tempo nascosa.

> It should not therefore seem a marvelous thing that
> I have to tell of the great Florentines whose fame is
> hid by time.

(*Par.* XVI.85–87)

This is Cacciaguida's preface to his recitation of the names he once
knew, and which his great-great-grandson, a true historian, has revived.
He saw the Ughi, the Catellini, Filippi, Greci, Ormanni and Alberichi
— "illustrious citizens already in decline." Time and arrogance, change
and sin have done their work on Florence. Dante's picture of Florence's
decline seems to oscillate between the larger vision of inevitable death
for all human things and the moral indignation at the human faults
which seem to bring ruin to the things he cares for most deeply. Caring
and not caring: these are the great motives which Dante must harmonize.

The pattern for the fall of the earthly cities is recurrently Rome: as
Florence tried to rise higher than Rome so it will fall lower. But else-
where in the *Paradiso* the great pattern of decline is taken from the
Bible. A single just man with surprisingly humble beginnings finds favor

with God, who forms a covenant with him and his followers. For a time people observe the covenant, only eventually to fall away from the original inspiration. The fire is brought back, the pact re-established, but man repeats the pattern of defection. For Dante the history of the Christian religious orders is similarly one of periodic *renovatii,* where privileged men, yet humble, consumed by a vision of divinity for a time, give new directions to humanity. The ages of Peter, Benedict, Bernard, and finally Francis and Dominic in the early thirteenth century represent for Dante the great periods of religious revival. But each as he appears in the *Commedia,* either through himself, or through his spokesman, only reflects on the decadence which followed. "O buon principio," Peter cries out, at the culmination of a speech of righteous anger (XXVII. 40–66), "a che vil fine / convien che tu caschi!" ("O fair beginning, to what base end must thou fall!")

As with the earthly city, quite specific moral and historical causes are at the root of religious decline. Benedict clearly indicates them:

> Pier cominciò sanz'oro e sanz'argento,
>   e io con orazione e con digiuno,
>   e Francisco umilmente il suo convento.
> E se guardi il principio di ciascuno,
>   poscia riguardi là dov' è trascorso,
>   tu vederai del bianco fatto bruno.

> Peter began his fellowship without gold or silver,
> and I mine with prayer and fasting, and Francis his with
> humility; and if thou look at the starting-point of each,
> then look again whither it has strayed, thou shalt see
> it become dark from white.
>
> (XXII.88–93)

Benedict lashes the corruption that has attended the accumulation of Church revenues. Usury itself is not as offensive as such abuse, where rather than for the needs of the poor, money goes to relatives and mistresses, nepotism and concubinage. (79–84) Damian, reflecting on the decline of the monastic orders, sees the cloisters empty of contemplative men. Called from the monastery he came to the cardinalate, where things are going from bad to worse. (XXI.124–126) Peter and Paul went barefoot and hungry, while the modern churchmen are princes and fat cats. In the wake of the Franciscan evangelical and social gospel, Dante celebrates the marriage of Christ to the soil and to poverty and simplicity.[21] Like Chaucer he would have the parson brother to the plough-man. But he has an equally fervent appreciation of the intellectual fire of a Dominic, who is likewise of the Lord in his scorn for petty gain. In *Paradiso* XII, the Franciscan Bonaventure lauds his love of the "true manna." Dominic was one of the great vintners called by the Lord to prune his vineyard — "which soon withers if the keeper is at fault."

Unlike the natural order where decomposition is organic and neces-sary, the human order has the capacity for true development. Yet, how-ever much this might ideally be the case, in reality the materials which the spiritual vinedresser has to tend show an alacrity in decay. High things cannot maintain themselves in the realm of succession. And, although in Benedict's vision monastic decline can be attributed to specific his-torical and moral causes, still his narration is prefaced by a larger vision of imperfection, a greater, all too human susceptibility to fallings-off. Man's own flesh and mortality subvert the great beginnings.

> La carne de' mortali è tanto blanda,
>   che giù non basta buon cominciamento
>   dal nascer della quercia al far la ghianda.

> So soft is mortal flesh that a good beginning
> below does not last from the springing of the
> oak to the bearing of the acorn.
>   (XXII.85–87)

Indeed, in Canto XXVII, following the preceding canto's interview with Adam, and his vision of mutability, Beatrice shows, as Benedict did, the pattern of decay to be much more fundamentally present in human life:

> Ben fiorisce nelli uomini il volere;
>   ma la pioggia continua converte
>   in bozzacchioni le susine vere.

> The will blossoms well in man, but the continual rain
> turns the sound plums to withered.
>   (124–126)

The phrase "pioggia continua" is highly suggestive. In existence itself, there is a weight that drags down all of man's attempts at rising. The sheer barrage of daily living washes out the firmness and color of the early bud. Only in our wills do we fruit and flower. It is not man's way to be constant in his direction and purpose, to bring early promise to fruition, to preserve the fire and fervor of his original setting-out. Human development, rather than producing a satisfactory adulthood, seems only to result in moral decay. Faith and innocence are found only in children, but they flee even before puberty. In the material awkwardness and imperfections of childhood there was a kind of abstinence, but with the coming of facility, the tongue is not as continent. Lisping, he loved his mother; but when his speech is perfect, the grown man longs to see her buried. (127–135) Things were once united, runs an essential myth of Dante's consciousness, but existence has separated and scattered them. In history and in the individual human life the spiritual unity of the early family falls apart. The weight of existence, the "pioggia continua," seems too heavy for its preservation. The very condition of man, the nature of his existence, does not promise continuance; rather, it requires remarkable effort and grace to overcome its dead weight and battery of change.

Existence without essence is ruinous for Dante. Consequently, he turns to the idea of the Trinity in the universe to replace the disintegrated ideal of family he found at home. The vision of God renders perfect that which is otherwise defective and perishable. (XXXIII.105) Only then, united by the vision of that love, do present things assume coherence and form, have significance, become, in fact, a book, a rational, purposive and enduring accomplishment:

> Nel suo profondo vidi che s' interna,
>   legato con amore in un volume,
>   ciò che per l'universo si squaderna.

> In its depth I saw that it contained, bound by love
> in one volume, that which is scattered in leaves through
> the universe.
>   (XXXIII.85–87)

The opposite of this universal integrity is summarized in that remarkably suggestive verb, *squadernarsi*, a verb of "undoing" so important for Dante.[22] This verb is all the more suggestive in the context of Dante's notions of time and human development. In Canto XXVII of the *Paradiso*, Dante is asked to observe how time originates in the swiftly moving crystalline sphere. There it has its roots which, developing down through the other planetary spheres, appear to man as the leaves of time. Man sees the leaves but they are really part of a system of growth and order that is nested in the Godhead. *Squadernarsi* is thus a valued term in Dante's lexicon because without the sense of the higher order and purpose, only the disparate leaves of time are seen. This is the consequence of concentration on present things: man will lose his sense of a cosmos and of his place in it, and instead will come to see himself only as the insignificant passing leaves. This higher vision contrasts, as Canto XXVIII commences, with the "vita presente dei miseri mortali," just as its notion of growth and connection contrasts with Beatrice's description of the reality of human decadence. Certainly the phrase "ciò che per l'universo si squaderna" raises the spectre of an incredibly vast space and time where man's accomplishments seem as insignificant as the leaves. And this is the impression we had in our descent through the *Inferno,* how fragile and soon to be forgotten were all these loyalties, great men and names. How quickly the waters close over them. The final impression was one of a terrible, inhuman silence, another derivation of the scattered leaves, since, taken out of their essential forms, in the course of time the leaves will be illegible, unread, ignored and even unknown. To save himself, man must separate himself from succession and time and discover the "universal form of this complex." Only by sensing a creator does the creature assume valid proportions. It is essentially to redeem present things from the vast time that he imagines and its physical, moral, and social consequences that Dante enjoins their utter rejection until they can be reconstituted from the vision of God. Then all of his people come back again as part of a divine comedy and a book. Although he momentarily denied them, Dante was ever the true unforgetting son, the "giusto figliuol," of the names he cherished in his old city.

Purgatory

The Temporal Fire

In the *Inferno,* where there is no hope, time is dead, and its denizens are unchangeably tied to the past. Their freedom has been lost and they ceaselessly rehearse in action and memory the great sadness of their straying. For Dante, as for Shakespeare, hell is tedious, and, as in Milton, its hours are irksome. In paradise, too, there is a lack of freedom, but it comes from the fulfillment and total satisfaction found in God's will. Both *Inferno* and *Paradiso* are monochronistic: the damned eternally limited to the past, and the saved eternally partaking of the bounty of God's present. They are the eternal fires, but in purgatory burns the "temporal foco," and only in this realm is time as an active presence consistently addressed.

Purgatory is the time of hope, which looks and works toward some realizable goal, some manageable end. Emphasis is placed on effective activity: this is the realm where souls purge themselves. Consequently, in the *Purgatorio* the preciousness of time is felt. Forese Donati is obliged to terminate his meeting with Dante, "chè 'l tempo è caro / in questo regno" ("for time is precious in this realm"); it is a commodity not to be squandered, as people who have wasted and abused their spiritual potentials try to make amends. We might take as another motto of purgatory a phrase which more specifically refers to the restitution required of the late penitents, but which could just as well serve to characterize the entire ascent: in this land "tempo per tempo si ristora" ("through time, time is restored"). This purgatorial experience, under the shadow of time, is one of high seriousness and earnest labor, of little allowance for distractions from the primary task of returning to God. But it is also a realm of possibility, where the spiral topography summarizes spiritual motives: ascent and return. Despite its severity, our first impression of purgatory is one of uplift. After the stultifying constrictions of hell, Dante raises his poetic sails to run better waters. Poetry, which in its decorous suitability to the material it treated was rough and cragged in the *Inferno,* now resurges and Dante's vision too will enlarge in scope and illumination. Hell was monochromatic as well as monochronistic — "aura sanza tempo tinta." (II.29) There is no coloring brought to that gloomy landscape through the processes of daily or seasonal change — it is without time: "regola e qualità mai non l'è nova" ("never changing its measure or its kind," VI.9). Purgatory reflects new dawnings, new possibilities. Being the realm of time, it is also the realm of change, and where there is change there is still the possibility of hope. Dante delights again in the

> Dolce color d'oriental zaffiro,
>   che s'accoglieva nel sereno aspetto
>   del mezzo puro insino al primo giro,
> alli occhi miei ricominciò diletto,
>   tosto ch' io usci' fuor dell'aura morta.

> The sweet hue of the oriental sapphire which was
> gathering in the serene face of the heavens from the

clear zenith to the first circle gladdened my eyes
again as soon as I passed out of the dead air.

(I.13–17)

And turning in the other direction, he observes the four stars "non viste mai fuor ch'alla prima gente" ("never seen before but by the first people," 24). Dante's return to the road he had lost is given cosmic and mythic extension: it is joined with the reawakened blessings of the changeful natural world and associated with the return of the race to the terrestrial paradise.

It is important for the larger associations of this book that the *Purgatorio,* where time as a pressure is keenly experienced, should also be the place where Dante is concerned to delineate the ideal functioning of the human community, to show church and state in their true and legitimate operations. Time, to be sure, is transcended and even reversed in purgatory, where the Garden is regained. But the Garden in Dante is only reached through labor and history. Only after the Law comes the deliverance. So despite its lyrical resources, the *Purgatorio* is deeply imbedded in history.

As we shall see in other writers of the Renaissance — Petrarch, Spenser, and Shakespeare — historical construction and historical values are closely involved with a sense of time's urgency; they form a part of the temporal configuration that we have called the argument of time. Although there are very radical divergences, in the *Purgatorio* we see important recurring elements of the argument.

The Argument of Time

In the *Inferno,* Dante was primarily an observer. Although he occasionally took an active hand, mainly his way was one of avoidance and restraint. In the *Purgatorio,* he must pass from observation to empathic practice. Rather than models to avoid he finds models to follow: a new paideia emerges. He must commit his will to a particular mode of conduct. And if Kierkegaard's terminology can be of any use, we could say that Dante must pass from the aesthetic to the ethical, from diffusion and fragmentation to commitment and identity. He must close the contradiction in himself and submit himself to a particular moral code and personal unity. In Dante, as in Petrarch and Shakespeare, the prime agent of conversion from the aesthetic to the ethical is time, and the great embodiment of the time-sense and the representative of the Law is the father figure.[23]

Another common characteristic of this constellation of forces and issues that surrounds the argument of time is the painful exclusions and rejections it requires. In the *Inferno* the means of the earthly city — progeny and fame — were unnaturally turned against themselves. But in the *Purgatorio* these qualities of purely human time-transcendence must be voluntarily rejected for the sake of a higher ideal. Christ, we must remember, brought a sword to the normal human relationships. Larger ideals must also pass a rigorous and cutting scrutiny. Art and poetry, remembrance, lines of continuity abound in the growing illumination of the *Purgatorio*. But all of these ideals and higher resources, lyrical though they be, must pass under the hard eye of the porter of purgatory, Cato. The road to renewal is not an easy one, for individual man, like the race, must pass through the Law and the ethical before he arrives at his freedom. And the ethical is prohibitive and necessitates painful exclusions. Here in the *Purgatorio,* as in Shakespeare's second tetralogy (to glance ahead), the ethical and the temporal lead to an infamous rejection — this being one of the few things that Virgil and Falstaff could have in common.

Yet, in Dante's theocentric world, where the conflict arises between purely human means of transcendence and the perfection and permanence sought in God, the situation is more complicated than in Shakespeare's secular histories where the choice must be made between law and license. This is why the *Purgatorio* is Dante's greatest drama: the forces he must reject are not debased or even socially dangerous, but are themselves expressions of man's higher resources. Yet, such humanism, it would appear, mainly because it does seem so lofty and high-minded a substitute, is all the more to be feared as detracting from an absolute reliance on God.

Once we grant this radical importance of theocentrism in Dante and its absence in Shakespeare, we can safely discern another similarity in their uses of history. Each sees history as repudiating any premature possession of being. And in each, such precocious sense of timelessness is shown to be rudely interrupted by man's involvement in time and his consequent need for vigilance and labor. Purgatorial experience would appear to be time's natural habitat. There the individual must forsake his multiple identities, his premature sense of being, and his dangerous habits of procrastination — all facets of aestheticism; there he must learn with new urgency the preciousness of time as he commits himself to a definite moral code and identity, as he proceeds from potential beings to willed action.

If the realm of the ethical involves the cognizance of time, the father figure is the great instructor in each. The ethical is superior to aestheticism, in that the self-concern of the fancy and willfulness is replaced by a more objective vision of the self, a vision that goes beyond self-conception and potential being toward actual performance. The ethical rests upon disabusing the young person of his notions of immunity and converting him to a serious concern with his perishability. Time is the principle of reality that serves this purpose, and the experienced father is the natural figure to perform the educational function, as Augustine does for Petrarch, and as Bolingbroke does for Hal by providing him with an objective picture of the way his actions are interpreted. For Dante, hell provided some such object lesson, wherein he witnessed the terrible consequences of actions and ideas to which he had been committed. We recall his dead faint at the recognition of the fate toward which the service of love could lead in the Paolo-Francesca episode. In the *Purgatorio,* where active measures of improvement are sought, it is important that the first personnage encountered should be Cato,

> un veglio solo,
> degno di tanta reverenza in vista,
> che più non dee a padre alcun figliuolo.

> an old man alone, worthy by his looks of so great
> reverence that no son owes more to a father.

(I.31–33)

And it is typical of the kind of experience he represents that Cato should confront Virgil and Dante with a concern about the laws. Their coming from hell is so unusual that he demands by what right or privilege they appear. "Son le leggi d'abisso così rotte?" ("Are the laws of the abyss thus broken?" I.46) Beatrice too shows some of this same legal strictness when, before she allows Dante to pass on to the salutary waters, she insists first on his public confession — otherwise the laws of God would be broken ("Alto fato di Dio sarebbe rotto," XXX. 142).

In two crucial ways Cato shows that the normal means of time-transcendence, memory and art, are by themselves insufficient. In purgatory Virgil is confronted by a new order where former strategies no longer succeed. We recall that until we approached the lower reaches of hell, the desire to keep one's name alive was an effective means of eliciting information. Virgil, in seeking permission to lead

Dante through purgatory, associates himself with Cato's wife Marcia (they are together in limbo):

> per lo suo amore adunque a noi ti piega.
> Lasciane andar per li tuoi sette regni:
>   grazie riporterò di te a lei,
>   se d'esser mentovato là giù degni.

> For her love, then, do thou incline to us; allow us
> to go through thy seven kingdoms. I will report to her
>   thy kindness, if thou deign to be spoken of there below.
>
> (I.81–84)

But the law's unmitigated strictness does not bend. When he was alive she pleased his eyes, but now higher objects and laws occupy his attention. This preliminary rejection of course prepares us for the larger and more painful one of Virgil, an anticipation increased by Virgil's emphasis on their common location. They may be in the softest spot of hell, but they have not known the illumination of the spirit. Cato is not responsive now to the pleasures of the eye. But if it is the heavenly lady that incites Dante's voyage, there is no need of these other means of transcendence. And in a verbal approximation of Bocca degli Alberti's words, Cato replies "non c'è mestier lusinghe" — there's no need for flattery with such sponsorship. Bocca told Dante that he "ill knows how to flatter in this depth." And indeed a kind of hardness informs both responses, the one possessed by a bitter hopelessness and the other by a toughness needed to realize the vision of hope. Incidentally, this is not the only occasion where the conditions of hell are approximated by the exiles of purgatory for the sake of a higher ideal.

Then, like any father, Cato urges Dante to wash up before his new appointment. But this cleansing is baptismal, as Dante on the shores of the new life washes away the remnants of the old. The sea trembles with sanctity and beauty. In lonely isolation Dante again tries out the ascent toward transcendence. But the climb at the beginning of the *Inferno* was premature and ill prepared; it was not a passage through life and history, but rather an avoidance of realities. It boded only superficial transcendence, marred by profound contradictions. Now after seeing the consequences of actions in hell, Dante humbly and lowly girds himself for the strenuous climb. He kneels and makes his vow before the priest-father Virgil. It is from such prostration and humble beginnings that Christian transcendence follows.

oh maraviglia! chè qual elli scelse
l'umile pianta, cotal si rinacque
subitamente là onde l'avelse.

O marvel! for as was the lowly plant he chose such
did it spring up again immediately in the place where
he had plucked it.

(134–135)

Humility is endless, another poet would say, who, similarly embracing
the Christian tradition, would believe that salvation comes not through
the affirmation of the self but rather through its divestment, and that
it is from such dispossession that new possibilities and beginnings arise.

Purgatory, the realm of time, sadly registers the perishability of the
body and the withering of the flesh, all that transience which Dante
seeks to hold and fasten securely. The angel who leads the newly ar-
rived boatload of souls comes beating "etterne penne, / che non si
mutan come mortal pelo" ("eternal pinions which do not change like
mortal plumage [or skin]," II.35–36). Against the mortal processes of
"undoing" Dante seeks out renewal. The plant of humility flourishes
again just as before. When in the earthly paradise the griffin-Christ
touches the barren tree of terrestrial life, "s'innovò la pianta, / che
prima avea la ramora sì sole" ("the tree was renewed which before had
its branches so bare," XXXII.59–60). And at the conclusion of the
Purgatorio, it is Dante himself who has been remade:

Io ritornai dalla santissima onda
rifatto sì come piante novelle
rinovellate di novella fronda,
puro e disposto a salire alle stelle.

From the most holy waters I came forth again remade,
even as new plants renewed with new leaves, pure and
ready to mount to the stars.

(XXXIII.142–145)

Paradise is, of course, the realm of such changelessness, where things
are never undone:

In questa quinta soglia
dell'albero che vive nella cima

> e frutta sempre e mai non perde foglia,
> spiriti son beati.

> In this fifth lodgement of the tree which lives from
> the top and is always in fruit and never sheds its
> leaves are blessed spirits.
>
> *(Par.* XVIII.28–31)

This spiritual tree differs from the physical tree of earthly life that is subject to despoliation and only revives at the touch of Christ. The Tree of Life is properly located in the *Purgatorio,* where forces of spiritual renewal war with the powers of decay and decline. Purgatory is the land where fidelity and remembrance are pitted against the sheer weight of mortality. Consequently, despite its stern rigors, the mode of purgatory is lyrical.

When old friends meet, the spirit is still somewhat triumphant over bodily alterations, and Casella can tell Dante, "Così com'io t'amai / nel mortal corpo, così t'amo sciolta" ("Even as I loved thee in my mortal flesh, so do I love thee freed," 87–88). It is this mixture of decay and memory which typifies Purgatory and, in a play so involved with those two forces, serves to explain the *oltratomba* location of Hamlet's father.

Old friends will gladly stand and talk. Neither is overendowed with the sense of urgency required in the purgatorial experience. In fact, before the mountain proper, procrastination seems to have been the rule for the late penitents. The new souls, upon seeing Dante alive, fixed their eyes on this prodigy, "quasi obliando d'ire a farsi bella" ("as if forgetting to go and make themselves fair," II.75). Rebuke is implied and dereliction from true purpose. These are the tensions that exist in purgatory: not between good and evil, but between essential and lesser means of transcendence.

Art is one of these lesser means. Dante, remembering the songs of Casella, asks him to play and sing again.

> Se nuova legge non ti toglie
> memoria o uso all'amoroso canto
> che mi solea quetar tutte mie voglie,
> di ciò ti piaccia consolare alquanto
> l'anima mia, che, con la mia persona
> venendo qui, è affannata tanto!

> If a new law does not take from thee memory or practice
> of the songs of love which used to quiet all my longings,

may it please thee to refresh my soul with them for a
while, which is so spent coming here with my body!

(106–111)

The effect of Casella's singing "Love that discourses to me in my mind"
was so overwhelming that all of the listeners, Dante and Virgil included,
feel transported. They all "parevan sì contenti, / come a nessun tocasse
altro la mente" ("seemed as content as if nothing else touched the mind
of any," 116–117). But in the question as well as in the nature of the
reaction, the attentive reader has been alerted to the danger signals
that Dante has raised. The aesthetic sense of rapture threatens to divert
the soul from its search for salvation. It is not art that provides the essential satisfaction for longings, which gives the soul its peace, and
true relief from the vesture of decay, but rather the vision of God. One
persistent psychological feature of fourteenth-century literature is the
palinode; and Dante here, as well as other instances throughout the
poem, deals with the superb attractiveness and ravishments of art, and
consequently, because of its very powers, with the dangers it holds for
the Christian soul seeking permanent satisfaction. The danger of this
purely human liberation and release is broken by the intervention of
the law:

> Noi eravam tutti fissi e attenti
>   alle sue note; ed ecco il veglio onesto
>   gridando: "Che è ciò, spiriti lenti?
> qual negligenza, quale stare è questo?
>   Correte al monte a spogliarvi lo scoglio
>   ch'esser non lascia a voi Dio manifesto."

> We were all rapt and attentive to his notes, when lo,
> the venerable old man, crying: "What is this, laggard
> spirits? What negligence, what delay is this? Haste
> to the mountain to strip you of this slough that allows
> not God to be manifest to you."

(118–123)

"Correte al monte," run to the mountain, he urges them; and in the
next canto, significantly enough, it is Virgil who especially feels the
rebuke of Cato, suggesting a classical over-readiness to accept aesthetic
gratification.

Still Virgil quickly becomes Cato's spokesman and Dantes' guide under the "new law." Loss of time is now important; the soul intent on

salvation must be wary of distractions that offer no certain time-transcendence. In Canto III Virgil asks directions for the slope of the mountain, adding, "chè perder tempo a chi più sa più spiace" ("for loss of time most grieves him that knows best," 78). And at the conclusion of Canto IV, he urges Dante on, "Vienne omai" ("Come now") with his sense of solar time; it is high noon where they are, and already dusk is covering the shores of Morocco. The reference serves to accentuate the steady and rapid passage of time. And when in the next canto Dante halts, startled by the amazement of the souls at the shadow that his body casts, Virgil scolds him,

> Perchè l'animo tuo tanto s'impiglia
>   disse 'l maestro che l'andare allenti?
>   che ti fa ciò che quivi si pispiglia?
> Vien dietro a me, e lascia dir le genti.

> Why is thy mind so entangled . . . that thou slackenest
> thy pace? What is it to thee what they whisper there?
> Come after me and let the people talk.

> (V.10–13)

We had already seen in *Inferno* XXVI and XXX that Dante's insatiable curiosity could be dangerous; and here he needs to be rebuked by Virgil, the representative of steadfastness, so that his alertness to what is around him does not become a source of constant distraction, squandering his energy and singlemindedness. In Canto VI, Virgil, after offering his explanation of intercession, defers to Beatrice for surer illumination. At the mention of her powers, "smiling in bliss," Dante himself lights up with eagerness, anticipating the more positive energies which she will inspire in him:

> Segnore, andiamo a maggior fretta,
>   chè già non m'affatico come dianzi,
>   e vedi omai che 'l poggio l'ombra getta.

> My Lord, let us make more haste, for now I do not
> weary as before, and see how the hill now casts its
> shadow.

> (49–51)

Dante, in a response that summarizes the directions of the *Purgatorio,* presses on to the ethical for the sake of the lyrical that is its destination.

He shoulders the responsibility of diligent effort, of working against the lengthening shadows of time, for the sake of the lightened smile of bliss. It is this goal and this eager relish that separates Dante's use of the ethical from Virgil's burdened seriousness in the *Aeneid*.

In Canto XII, to spur on Dante, who had been absorbed by the art work showing the debasement of the proud, Virgil reminds him: "pensa che questo dì mai non raggiorna" ("remember that today never dawns again," 84). Similarly in Canto XV, Dante, freeing himself with difficulty from the vivid representations of an angry mob and its saintly victim, acts like a somnambulant. Virgil impatiently asks him what is on his mind, not because he does not know, but rather to prod Dante on, the way one would prod "i pigri, lenti / ad usar lor vigilia quando riede" ("the sluggish who are slow to use their vigil [waking hours] when it returns," 137–138). And in Canto XVIII, the cry of the slothful is "Ratto, ratto che'l tempo non si perda / per poco amor" ("Haste, haste, lest time be lost for little love," 103–104).

The very important Cantos XXIII and XXIV — I shall treat them as a unit having as its center Dante's encounter with his old friend Forese Donati — begin with a renewed impression of the need to manage time. At the end of Canto XXII, a tree appeared in the way of the three travellers — Virgil, Statius and Dante — from which came voices attesting to the positive experiences of abstinence. As the next canto commences, Dante is still fixing his sight on the tree, "as he sometimes does who wastes his life after the birds" (the sport of hawking). To break this fixation, Virgil, "his more than father," urges him to go on, "chè 'l tempo che n'è imposto / più utilmente compartir si vuole" ("for the time appointed us must be put to better use").

In these two cantos, the pressures of time and its goal — individual salvation — are felt most poignantly. Personal destinies with all their separateness stand revealed, and at the end Forese must terminate their reunion and in so doing summarizes for us the sense of time's preciousness that is held in purgatory:

> Tu ti rimani omai; chè 'l tempo è caro
> in questo regno, sì ch'io perdo troppo
> venendo teco sì a paro a paro.

> Do thou remain now, for time is precious in this
> realm and I lose too much coming thus along with thee.
>
> (XXIV.91–93)

At their center these cantos are firm of faith and movement, but their atmosphere is undeniably saddened by the consciousness that in comparison with the need for salvation all other attachments are transitory and accidental. True, the joy of recognition in purgatory is strong, because it is here that Dante places his personal friends — Casella, Nino, and Forese. In hell there is only ambivalence and constraint in the encounters with people one once knew — Brunetto Latini is a case in point. And in paradise, there are mainly recognized saints and philosophers. The pleasure of meeting in purgatory is increased since, among the saved, old friends can reconstruct their friendships on a more enduring basis. When Forese, proceeding in the troop of penitents, spies Dante, he cries out "Qual grazia m'è questa?" Although his flesh is withered (the logic of the poem has it because of need to redress gluttony in life, but the poetry insists that it is the inevitable physical decline of time and age), still his voice — the tone of the spirit — reminds Dante of his old friend:

> Mai non l'avrei riconosciuto al viso;
>   ma nella voce sua mi fu palese
>   ciò che l'aspetto in sè avea conquiso.
> Questa favilla tutta mi raccese
>   mia conoscenza alla cangiata labbia,
>   e ravvisai la faccia di Forese.

> I should never have known him again by his looks, but
> in his voice was plain to me that which was destroyed in
> his aspect; that spark rekindled in me all my knowledge
> of the changed features and I recognized the face of
> Forese.
>
> (XXIII.42–48)

The single first name, emphatically placed as the concluding rhyme of a tercet, suggests the solid contentment and pleasure Dante has in a friend who has managed to save himself. Through all the withered flesh and the waste of years the essential personality still emerges intact.

But things have changed drastically since they knew one another as young men. And this aspect of changed relationships in their own lives and fates, in the lives of their friends, and in the places of their birth and growing up, accounts for the atmosphere of sadness. The first image that Dante uses to introduce the new group with whom Forese travels is that of a pilgrim ("come i peregrin pensosi fanno," 16). Pilgrimage is after all the primal Christian image, indicating a single direction toward a religious goal, with only passing attachments to things on the way. The decay of the flesh is another physical and vivid instance of life's transitoriness, one that Dante is especially sensitive to. Forese's features have "wasted away." The verb, interestingly enough, is one of "undoing," "sfogliarsi", which, like "squadernarsi," indicates a process of "unleaving," as in Hopkins' poem, "Spring and Fall: To a Young Child":

> Margaret, are you grieving
> Over Goldengrove unleaving?

This steady dissolution ("la pioggia continua") of what had been joined together, compact, sturdy, and brave, is a consistent way by which Dante describes the effect of time on man. This individual and natural undoing inherent in the organism takes on a broader social significance when it also describes the processes of disintegration in the community. The natural process of decay has a social correlative. Florence, too, is withering away in moral virtue and civic health: topless feminine attire seems to have become fashionable and will have to be condemned from the pulpit. And in the next canto, Dante expresses his own weariness of life, and his readiness to part for the other shore. Forese asks when they shall see one another again. Dante replies that he does not know, but it could not be soon enough,

> però che'l loco u'fui a viver posto,
>   di giorno in giorno più di ben si spolpa,
>   e a trista ruina par disposto.

> for the place where I have been put to live strips
> itself of good day by day and seems destined to woeful
> ruin.
>   (XXIV.79–81)

The Scartazzini-Vandelli commentary provides this helpful note: "spolparsi è immagine pittoresca del progressivo consumarsi e perdersi del bene." The processes of living engage one in this progressive wearing-out of what once was strong and flourishing. Although the conjunction is not necessary, this is equally true (because of historical reasons) for the civic life of Florence. But now rather than an intrinsic relationship with his beloved community, Dante only admits to an accidental one: Florence is the place where he was merely assigned to live as he takes up the true condition of exile and pilgrimage.

The Lyric of Memory

As we saw in Cato's rejection of Virgil's "lusinghe," the simple report of a name is no longer effective in the *Purgatorio*. Different preoccupations prevail among the souls intent on purifying themselves. In contrast with the large physical forces of time and nature, the endurance of a man's name seems a frail and short-lived consolation. Personal salvation is the supreme concern, and for this reason in purgatory the chastened and industrious souls are more eager that their names be remembered in prayers. Just as, for Dante, moral and spiritual communion transcends the separation in historical time, so an even more intense faith on his part is the possibility of a spiritual union that surmounts the physical barrier of existence and joins together the living and the dead. Manfredi, Belacqua, Jacopo da Cassero, Buonconte, La Pia, Nino Visconti, Sapia, Guido del Duca, Pope Adrian V, Hugh Capet, Forese Donati, Guido Guinizelli, and even Arnaut Daniel — an important part of the discourse of all these figures with Dante concerns a request for prayers, the fact that they are remembered, or their measured and just anger that they are forgotten. All of them acknowledge the Dantean faith, "chè qui per quei di là molto s'avanza" ("for much is gained here through those yonder," III.145).

It is this faith that death is not an insurmountable barrier which separates Dante from the historical Virgil, and of course Christianity from the classical world. Death as a finality is a fact at which the classical world, whose respect for the reality principle was very strong, did not rebel. To be sure, the consolations of cultural continuity were valued, and Aeneas — because of literary convention — can visit and converse with the dead, but mainly death is an implacable physical barrier. This is what Dante is referring to when he asks if there is a contradiction between Virgil's recognition of hard necessity and the requests and faith of the souls purging themselves.

Although he defers the resolution of Dante's doubt to Beatrice, Virgil — and Dante — already admits to the transcendence of the law by the fire of love. (VI.35–42) And here it is worth repeating that the whole point of the ethic of temporal urgency and strict justice — represented by Cato — is that spiritual salvation is possible; there is a continuing spiritual order with which the individual can communicate. Time is so urgent in the *Purgatorio* not because, as in Shakespeare's histories or in a classical ethic, it is irreversible, but because through the Christian dispensation time is subordinate, and hence reversible. Last-minute dying recourse to Christ or Mary redeems a Manfredi or a Buonconte. "Let the end try the man" is truer for Dante than it is for Shakespeare.

Because the benefits of intercession are so great, the defects of forgetfulness are all the more abhorred. For Dante, as for Shakespeare, oblivion is bestial. But it must be added that since those who are saddened by being neglected are ultimately sure of salvation, their censures are tempered. However, in Shakespeare, where theocentrism is not so evident and the goal of salvation not a dramatic force, fidelity and memory are fundamental ideals. Thus the horror and furious outrage (one can think of Hamlet, Troilius, and Lear) when these expectations are tragically broken.

From the *Purgatorio* we get an overwhelming sense of the fragility of human existence and the perishability of flesh. Coincidentally, it is in the dawning spiritual realm that some means are available to counter the horrors of annihilation. This is the realm of memory, and the heart revives as the spirit of those who were once dear is kept alive by faithful remembrance. But memory is not merely nostalgic in purgatory. In contrast to hell, a firm center of faith and possibility substantiates the aura of lyricism. Remembrance is validated in the powers of intercession, and both bespeak the human capacity for rising above present things.

Although the *Purgatorio* has little of the grotesque and contorted physical violence of the *Inferno,* the final agony of death is sharply felt. But even more important is this *cantica*'s picture of the body's fate when caught in the vast processes of the physical universe. Like Shakespeare, Milton, and T. S. Eliot, Dante, ever concerned with the preservation of the human spirit, is horrified at the prospects of death by water.

Two of the more impressive figures of the *Purgatorio* are Manfredi (III) and Buonconte (V), both Ghibelline enemies of Dante's Guelph party, and explicit reminders that God's mercy has a bit more latitude than our political animosities. Despite all appearances of an erring life, or even the Church's ban of excommunication, they were still received by the "bontà infinita," whose arms are always open to receive those who turn to him. (III.122–123) Insufficiently read in the mysteries and mercies of God's ways, the papal representative had the body of Manfredi removed from its hallowed burial place. Thus dislodged, Manfredi's bones are "now washed by the rain and driven by the wind." And in Buonconte's case there is an even more detailed description of physical annihilation.

Following his death, a good and a bad angel struggled over his remains, as they struggled over his father in *Inferno* XXVII, but with contrary results. The good angel took his immortal part, but the bad angel, angered at his loss, decided to work his revenge on the body. Dante then indulges in a pseudo-scientific description of the development of the storm, and in doing so emphasizes the large elemental forces:

> Ben sai come nell'aere si raccoglie
> quell'umido vapor che in acqua riede,
> tosto che sale dove 'l freddo il coglie.
> Giunse quel mal voler che pur mal chiede
> con lo'ntelletto, e mosse il fummo e 'l vento
> per la virtù che sua natura diede.
> Indi la valle, com 'l dì fu spento,
> da Pratomagno al gran giogo coperse
> di nebbia; e 'l ciel di sopra fece intento,
> sì che 'l pregno aere in acqua si converse:
> la pioggia cadde ed a' fossati venne
> di lei ciò che la terra non sofferse;
> e come ai rivi grandi si convenne,
> ver lo fiume real tanto veloce
> si ruinò, che nulla la ritenne.
> Lo corpo mio gelato in su la foce
> trovò l'Archian rubesto; e quel sospinse
> nell'Arno, e sciolse al mio petto la croce
> ch'i'fe' di me quando 'l dolor mi vinse:
> voltommi per le ripe e per lo fondo;
> poi di sua preda mi coperse e cinse.

Thou knowest well how there gathers in the air the moist vapour which changes to water again as soon as it rises where the cold condenses it. That evil will which seeks only evil he joined with intellect and by the power his nature gave he stirred the mists and the winds; then, when day was spent, he covered the valley from Pratomagno to the great range with cloud and so charged the sky overhead that the pregnant air was turned to water. The rain fell and that which the ground refused came to the gullies and gathering in great torrents poured headlong to the royal river with such speed that nothing stayed its course. The raging Archiano found my frozen body near its mouth and swept

it into the Arno and loosed on my breast the cross I
made of myself when pain overcame me. It rolled me along
the banks and over the bottom, then covered and swathed
me with its spoils.

(V.109–129)

This lengthy quotation is necessary to give the sense of movement
from the distant, unrelated stirring of the clouds to the raging river furi-
ously growing in scope and power as the passage itself progresses. Buonconte's frozen body is swept along in the rampage, and the physical sign
of his spiritual recovery, his arms crossed over his chest, is dissolved by
the flood. The passage, which reaches a fully crested rampage, subsides
into an even more ominous silence, as the once living figure of Buonconte, now part of the river's detritus, is slowly covered forever by its
debris. It is clear that for Dante these vast processes are of the devil's
party. To counter this final nothingness Dante wages his war against
time and searches for that which endures. It is also against such elemental powers that the subtle final words of Canto V, La Pia's "Remember me," must be registered.

In this context forgetfulness is all the more shameful because it yields
to disintegration, and refuses to take advantage of the Christian means
of resisting such processes. But in order to value prayerful remembrance
one must oneself be superior to present things. Buonconte moves with
"lowered head" and Nino Visconti burns with righteous zeal, not so
much for their own sake, but for what forgetfulness reveals about the
spiritual natures of those left behind. One of the rules of intercession is
that only the prayers of the virtuous, the innocent, those living in grace
are heard. To have forgotten is already a sign that the living are not
secure in their own hopes. Nino Visconti, in another encounter of friends
in purgatory (VIII), asks Dante to tell his daughter Giovanna to pray
for him, since his own wife has remarried and appears to have forgotten
him. And in a passage that could be taken from Shakespeare to describe
Gertrude or Cressida, Nino squares the general sex by his wife's rule:

> Per lei assai di lieve si comprende
>   quanto in femmina foco d'amor dura,
>   se l'occhio o'l tatto spesso non l'accende.

By her it is easy indeed to know how long love's fire
endures in woman if sight and touch do not often kindle
it.

(76–78)

"The present eye praises the present object" is a part of the all-too-human mechanism that Dante as well as Shakespeare resisted. The spiritual values of resistance depend upon transcending the present. But Dante is no outright misogynist. If like Shakespeare he has his Gertrudes and Cressidas, so too he has his Juliets and Hermiones and Desdemonas. Nevertheless, in his vision of moral decay, those who remember are more singly just then typical. Sapia's process of purification is helped by the "sante orazioni" of Pier Pettinaio (XIII.125–129), and Dante's other friend, Forese Donati, has moved more rapidly than his late repentance would otherwise allow because of the prayers of his widow, Nella.

True Succession

The powers and dimensions of art come under careful scrutiny in the *Purgatorio*. Aesthetic satisfaction can be dangerous if it is a deterrent to religious fulfillment, if it becomes an end in itself. The souls that are freshly come to the shores of purgatory, seeing Dante still in life, stare at him "quasi obliando d'ire a farsi belli." This phrase serves as prologue to one of the major dilemmas of the *Purgatorio:* Dante is well aware of the ravishing powers of art but he is also conscious of its temporary nature and sensitive to the horrors of moral contradiction if the soul itself is not an object of care. The purgatorial experience implies ethical effort: it is where one remakes oneself. It is no accident, then, that poets should, of all three levels, be most prominent in the *Purgatorio*. In their fragmentation and dilatoriness, their protean capacities for empathic recreation, their aesthetic distance from the moral will, it seems that they have need of the kind of ethical conversion required. From self-awareness they must proceed to actions that make the self whole.

Not only the poetic personality, but poetic and artistic descent are subject to Dante's mounting vision. In the *Purgatorio,* he dramatizes his own links with his modern and classical progenitors, delineates, as it were, his poetic genealogies, and in so doing, gives expression to his grand notion of the continuities of poetic tradition, which arises above emulation, replacement, and the whirligig of fame.

In Canto XI, on the cornice where pride is purged, Dante's own inflated pride in art and fame is reduced by Oderisi's account of the processes of generational succession and his long view of time. Based as it is on generations and vicissitudes of taste, artistic fame is one long chain of place-taking. Cimabue has ceded his place to Giotto, and the one Guido to the other, and perhaps even a third will come along to prevail in the public enthusiasm over Cavalcante. Any reliance on fame — here to be regarded as a kind of popular vogue — rather than transcending time is in fact a submission to its intrinsic processes of supplantation. But there is another process which does resist this temporal emulation, which more accurately reflects the indebtedness of one generation to the previous one, of student to master, and which takes the individual out of the present isolation and places him in relation to past and future. Part of Oderisi's discontent is the fact that Franco of Bologna, who replaced him, now has all the honor, "of which part is mine." While emulative time proceeds ungratefully, burying what went before, it is Dante's great desire to maintain these temporal connections. Ever desirous of a father-teacher, ever willing to record his indebtedness, even in hell, Dante acknowledges the "cara e buona imagine paterna" of Brunetto Latini. In fact, the line of poetic continuity traced by Dante serves the same function that family does. It resists emulation: the past is not excluded or overwhelmed, the master has some share in the honor of his student, and the student feels elevated by the lines of contact with the past. Like that of father and son, this is a legitimate and welcomed succession. And throughout the numerous encounters, the generational language of father and son will be constantly employed to express the integrity of this spiritual tradition. It is Francis Petrarch who provides a prose gloss in this instance, as in others, for what Dante has rendered dramatically. At the end of his *Familiares,* writing a brilliant letter to Homer, Petrarch advises him not to be miffed that his work has given rise to a host of imitators: "Even I, the least among men, not only rejoice, but, as if rejoicing were not sufficient, glory and boast that I am now held in such esteem that some (if some there be) hope to follow in my footsteps and to fashion as I have fashioned. Indeed, my joy would be the greater were my imitators such as ultimately to surpass me. . . . For if a father desires that the child of his flesh and blood be greater than himself, what should the author wish for the child of his intellect." [24]

This royal line of true poetic succession simulates for Dante as for Petrarch the relation of father and son. And it is of some consequence, then, that in the *Purgatorio* such a line should be traced. Cato is the reverent father, urging his sons to make right use of their time. And Virgil is Cato's spokesman in this time-consciousness. But when we come to poetic succession, although the instance is still parental, Virgil is "il più che padre," and "dolcissimo padre," indicating not only the severity of law but the liberation of spiritual paternity. Rather than temporal management, he is the father of inspiration. As Coleridge asked, "What is the right, the virtuous feeling, and consequent action when a man having long meditated and perceived a certain truth finds another, foreign writer, who has handled the same with an approximation to the truth, as he had previously conceived it?" To his own question he answered "Joy!" [25] This shock of recognition is the tremor of joy which distinguishes the elevated sense of poetic paternity from the serious business represented by Cato.

Innovation and continuity are two terms about which most discussion of the Renaissance, like other historical epochs, revolves. In Dante's dramatization of his own indebtedness both to the classical past and to his more immediate predecessors, we get some idea from the period's major spokesman (always a rewarding source) of what was new and what was received. Clear recognition goes to Guido Guinizelli in Canto XXVI — "the father of me and of others my betters, whoever have used sweet and graceful rhymes of love." In fact, the whole contemporary line of poetry with which Dante associates himself is only praised for its stylistic skill in the poetry of love. What they are lacking and what Dante found in the classical line of Virgil and Statius is the grand epic theme of history and society, of exile and return — lofty subjects in a commensurate style. Dante rises out of his own time to sing like Virgil of the gods and men, of man's relation to the great cosmic forces like time and death. It is this innovation in his own time for which Dante must receive credit, and it is this line or great cycle of literature, stretching to Chaucer, Spenser, and Milton and comprising the classics of the modern world, of which he is the true progenitor.[26] Guinizelli, for all his importance in Dante's development as a poet, cannot lead him to the sense of greatness that he feels, nor can he lead him to Beatrice. Guinizelli does not lead Dante through the fire.

Neither does Virgil, to be sure; but it is Virgil of all the poets who brings him closest to Beatrice. The honor, the fame, and the loftiness of the poetic ambitions that unite Virgil with the other classical writers serve as poetic models for Dante's own impulse to rise above present things. His elevated conception of poetry is on a scale, we could say, or part of a practice, of upward expectations which lead to better things. For this reason, Virgil is Beatrice's emissary, and the fame of the virtuous pagans has found favor with heaven. There is this thoroughfare of participation between the virtuous pagans and Christian ascent. This same "expansive power" of poetry is the spiritual cause of the purgatorial meeting between Virgil and Sordello. (VII) At the sole mention of "Mantua," Sordello abandons his reserve and surges toward Virgil — still unknown — to embrace his countryman. This ideal fondness and reverence for place that joins Sordello with the author of the *Georgics* breaks through the former's leonine and splendid isolation to establish an extrapersonal bond of connection. It is for such matters that can be shared and not diminished in the sharing, but rather enlarged, that Dante thirsts religiously.

Poetry shares in the same springs. In the realm of succession the continuity of poetic tradition satisfies two of Dante's deepest desires: his quest for permanence and a community of sharing. In such a tradition, one's merit is stable, constantly being revived through rediscovery so that while there is succession, there is no replacement. Rightfully, then, it is in the *Purgatorio,* the most temporal of books, that the true succession should be traced, joining together history and inspiration, time and lyricism.

Another ideal convocation, so typical of the many meetings between poets in the *Purgatorio,* brings together Virgil and Statius, with Dante tagging along. These magnificent scenes of wish-fulfillment (XXI–XXII) serve to intensify the drama of Virgil's rejection. As Dante did, Statius records his own indebtedness:

> Al mio ardor fuor seme le faville,
> che mi scaldar, della divina fiamma
> onde sono allumati più di mille;
> dell'Eneida dico, la qual mamma
> fummi e fummi nutrice poetando:
> sanz'essa non fermai peso di dramma.
> E per esser vivuto di là quando
> visse Virgilio, assenterei un sole
> più che non deggio al mio uscir di bando.

> The sparks that kindled the fire in me were from the
> divine flame from which more than a thousand have been
> lit — I mean the *Aeneid,* which was in poetry my mother
> and my nurse; without it I had not weighed a drachm,
> and to have lived yonder when Virgil lived I would have
> consented to a sun more than I was due before coming
> from banishment.
>
> (XXI.94–102)

The same parental relation exists between Statius and Virgil, who provided him poetic nurture, as exists between Dante and Virgil. It is no accident that Statius refers to the *Aeneid* as the "divina fiamma" and also perhaps some poetic justice that the adjective should have come to precede Dante's original title, *Commedia*. At the heart of Dante's heightened sense of poetry is that flame of life which is part of man as a creature of God, aspiring to return. In fact, within the composition of the line of poetic tradition we can see the cosmic principle of the Trinity: father, son, and "divina fiamma." This thoroughfare of participation between the lofty powers of poetry and the divine is reaffirmed when Statius, acting as Dante's surrogate, acknowledges, "Per te poeta fui, per te cristiano" ("Through thee I was poet, through thee Christian," 73). He thereby reinforces a pattern of relationships which Dante had dramatically worked out in the opening cantos of the *Inferno* and which, bereft of Virgil, he explicitly states. It was Virgil "a cui per mia salute die' mi" ("to whom I gave myself for my salvation," XXX. 51). When Virgil in the *Fourth Eclogue* sang of the return of the golden age and a new heaven-born race, his verse — well nigh inspired — so corresponded with the teachings of the Christians that Statius, secretly admiring their conduct and habits, made himself one of them. Christian writers, working in admiration of the ancients, frequently adduce instances of men whose faith was assisted by pagan writings. Petrarch will cite the cases of Augustine and Cicero, and could not we today cite the registers of belief that have been bolstered by a reading of *The Waste Land* (written when Eliot's religious conviction had not yet been clarified)? But it is this crucial intervention of Christ into history, which Virgil's verse inadvertently foretold, that most measures his limitations. That Virgil antedates Christ is not as important as the fact, evidenced by the sense of life gained from his work, that he shows none of the personal liberation and sense of being that Christ brought to man. Christ's descent into time provided man finally with a source and goal commensurate to his longings. Virgil — and Dante here is simply repeating the Latin poet's own image — is still longing for a redeemer, but instead must deal only with the consolations of fame and the continuities of civilization. In short, he is bound by history.[27]

And although the *Commedia* subordinates time to eternity and chronology to moral truth and spiritual affinity, still it is irreversible in its respect for historical fact. In the very first canto of the *Purgatorio* a foretaste was gained of the Law's implacability. Under the domination of the religiously ethical and the hard quest for salvation, Cato has no mind for those who dwell on the other side of the river. They are separated by a law and a historical fact whose workings Cato must uphold and Dante is at pains to understand. Through Virgil Dante was a poet and a Christian; a line of continuity was established which began in

history and led to being. Virgil was the "dolcissimo padre" to whom
for his salvation Dante gave himself. But the line was interrupted, the
student was saved, but not the teacher; the son, but not the father.
Virgil is a sacrificial victim. As Statius says in the splendid address which
Dante provides for him,

> Facesti come quei che va di notte,
>   che porta il lume dietro e sè non giova,
>   ma dopo sè fa le persone dotte.

> Thou didst like him that goes by night and carries
> the light behind him and does not help himself but
> makes wise those that follow.
>   (XXII.66–69)

With all his contribution to continuity, Virgil himself is a victim of replacement. He was one of the echelons of ascent, but the disjunction
caused by the intervention of Christ was so great as to qualitatively
separate those who came before from those who followed. Ironically,
Virgil and broader Roman matters were themselves victims of the legacy
of severity in judgment and justice that they left to Dante and the Christian West. This hardness would work to the tradition's disadvantage in
a later age when a Christian ethic, more humanitarian, would arise outside of the walls of orthodoxy, and mindful of the mysteries of God's
love, would read in the *Commedia* itself the possibility of a higher elevation for Virgil. With Romanticism, Virgil, like Falstaff, would enjoy
a better fate than the hard law of time and history could afford.

Paradise

Leah and Rachel

The *Purgatorio* contains "les années propédeutiques" in Dante's
pilgrimage. Its regime differs in its strictness from the liberation had
in paradise. In purgatory the labor is exerted by which paradise is
achieved; essentially its domain is under the Law. To be sure, there are
allowances: Cato, the last-minute penitents, and the powers of memory
and intercession. But in the purgatorial process memory is not only a
lyrical force; it is sternly fixed on the past, its failures and defeats. The
law-bound furies reign, exacting in their memory — and, as in the
Eumenides, providing an indication that purgation is under way. Not

only the penitents, but Dante, their common sufferer and open sharer, must not forget what once he was when the prelude to salvation is confession. Backward-looking, the *Purgatorio* would remind man of his humble origins, of his birth out of the shoreline of water and the land; forward-looking, it urges man on to his unconsummated but still realizable possibilities. These goals reinforce the reign of the religiously ethical in purgatory. Historical in scope, purgatory looks to the past and future, while in the present it requires labor. Paradise, of course, differs on all these counts. The past it looks to is not conscience-ridden; it needs no future since it already possesses God's bounty in the present, and its code is not work, but rather delight. Paradise is of course the sure realm of mind; its joys are in the highest order of the mind's perceptions, the totally redeemed spiritual continuities and the living presentness of great models to which one can commit oneself, even conjoin oneself, without reservation.

"Earnest of the eternal peace" of Paradise is had at the summit of purgatory (XXVIII–XXXIII) where Dante enters the "luogo eletto / all'umana natura per suo nido" ("the place set apart to the human kind for its nest"). It was this earthly paradise, Matilda informs Dante, and Virgil and Statius approvingly smile, that the pagan poets prefigured when they dreamed of an age of gold.[28] Here is represented the ideal functioning of earthly man:

> Qui fu innocente l'umana radice;
>   qui primavera sempre ed ogni frutto.

> Here the human root was innocent, here was lasting
> spring and every fruit.
>
> (XXVIII.142–143)

Experience here is not timeless, but the inner and outer conditions make it such that all of the heavy temporal implications of the fallen world are avoided. This is the world of "onesto riso e dolce gioco" ("honest mirth and sweet sport") that Adam and Eve in sinning exchanged for "tears and toil" ("in pianto ed in affanno"). Returned to innocence, man is freed from the inner pressures of sin and uncertainty which placed a screen between event and observation. In his new uprightness he is able to move in constant delight and appreciation of nature in all her multiplicity. Here is every fruit, every seed (some unknown to man), and Dante, on this side of the stream, gazes at the "great variety of fresh flowering boughs." The mountain is elevated above and hence freed from the perturbations and exhalations of the lower world. Man's mind here is as clear as the twin streams of water which produce innocence: the absence of painful memories and the remembrance of good works. Gone are the past hideousnesses at which the soul winces. Forthright and free, it looks upon the world and uses the things of the world for adornment.

Thus Leah in Dante's dream at the end of Canto XXVII anticipates Matilda. Dante dreams of her going through a meadow gathering flowers and singing: "per piacermi allo specchio qui m'adorno" ("to please me at the glass I here adorn myself"). Unlike her sister Rachel, who sits contemplatively in front of her mirror all day, completing an allegra-penserosa contrast, Leah's mode is active and her purview is that of man looking at himself in relation to the many things of the world. Matilda too is smiling, and justifies herself by referring the novice Dante to the ninety-second psalm, "Delectasti": "Thou, Lord, hast made me glad through thy work; I will triumph in the works of thy hands."

The earthly paradise is temperate; the season is always spring. And Dante is at pains to emphasize that here man is shielded from the hardships of change. One's first impression is of an "aura dolce" which,

> sanza mutamento
> avere in sè, mi ferià per la fronte
> non di più colpo che soave vento.

> A sweet air that was without change was striking on
> my brow with the force only of a gentle breeze.
>
> (XXVIII.7–9)

As Dante is on the verge of this "divina foresta spessa e viva" he realizes that its density does not obstruct illumination but rather tempers change. In this divine wood, Dante has again lost the point of his entrance — so thick was it with shade, "ombra perpetua." This shade, however, unlike that of the wood at the beginning of the *Commedia,* which prevented necessary illumination, serves as protection against the sun and moon, the great cosmic instances of time and change. There is in fact a strong anti-organic, anti-periodic bias in this seminary of all things (and hence significant contrasts can be made with Spenser's equivalent Garden of Adonis). Although two similes suggest sexual love (Venus and Hero and Leander), they are introduced to indicate their inferiority to the experience had here, and the basic simile for

Matilda singing and culling flowers is that of the virginal Proserpine before her fall and the underground days of winter. A fresh virginity of mind — its gaiety and delight which are distant from the heavy processes of growth and decay and seasonal change — personified by Matilda, and maintained by perpetual spring, are the provisions of the earthly paradise. Importantly, the water that feeds the springs of Lethe (forgetfulness of sin) and Eunoë (recollection of good deeds) is not restored by the normal processes, as Dante conceives them, of vaporization and condensation, processes which he so carefully described at work on the body of Buonconte. Rather its "constant and sure" flow is maintained by God's will.

Giving and taking, rising and falling, the sun and the moon, new days, first hours, exhalations and disturbances — free from all these processes, Dante looks for a spiritual renewal born of an intellectual delight, a gentle breeze, constant and sure. The Leah-Matilda line will take Dante thus far. But that hardly encompasses the experience of paradise, where there must be more concentration and contraction into God's being, where the soul upsurges at great discoveries. Perhaps for that experience it is not Leah but Rachel who is needed, anticipating Melancholia sitting in the midst of all the instruments of temporal measurement, but instead absorbed in the forms of her inner experience; not the gay eyes looking out onto the nature of the different things, but that inner, more religious pressure that is conducive to the paradise envisaged by Dante.

Man approaches the condition of being by simulating the nature of God in two important ways. God's dimension is one of presentness, but it is a presentness that encompasses all experience. He is the Alpha and the Omega, the beginning and the end, "il Punto / a cui tutti li tempi son presenti" ("the point to which all times are present," *Par.* XVII.17–18). Furthermore, when Dante looked into the eternal light he saw "sustanze e accidenti e lor costume, / quasi conflati insieme" ("substances and accidents and their relations as it were fused together," XXXIII.88–89). These two conditions — presentness and contraction — when regarded temporally are essential to the paradisal experience. Man loses his temporal anxiety, his fear and his fretting over past and future, and is totally content in God's present: whatever he sends is just. Wages and merit, in Justinian's phrase, are seen to be commensurate, and the souls' arrival at paradise occurs precisely when they have no further urge to climb, or need to cast themselves into the future. Moreover, everything they look upon from the past is blessed. Paradise is the way of seeing old things as part of the power, wisdom, and love of God.

Faults are understood in a richer context, having a purpose; they are reviewed under another dispensation and re-evaluated for the great things they lead to.

Vindication of the Self in God's Present

In the ninth canto of the *Paradiso,* Dante meets the living soul of Cunizza, the former mistress of Sordello and of other men at the court of her brother Ezzelino, the tyrant of an area north of Venice and whom Dante called a "firebrand." Again a family is notably separated in their final ends. Both Cunizza and Ezzelino represent the power of love, and both came from the same root, but in one the love was restored while in the other it was abused, and Dante has Ezzelino placed in *Inferno* XII with the violent. Cunizza's salvation is indicative of the way of seeing in paradise. Her past devotion to Venus is regarded in another light, and the energy of her sin, properly directed, is the cause of her salvation. She has come to consider the force that moved her to sexual love in a divine context:

> lietamente a me medesma indulgo
> la cagion di mia sorte, e non mi noia;
> che parrìa forse forte al vostro vulgo.

> I gladly pardon in myself the reason of my lot,
> and it does not grieve me, — which may seem strange,
> perhaps, to your crowd.
>
> (34–36)

In a religious context such benign self-excusal for a woman of pleasure might appear strange, and Dante explains the reason for her final serenity. She can forgive herself the lot because at the heart of her sexual drive was a beneficent principle which, properly used, has brought her to God.

Beside her is Folco, a troubador and lover whose ardent nature Dante considered happily redirected to a zealous attack on the Albigensians when he had become bishop of Toulouse. He too has given up remorse over his wayward past. Greater than Dido's or Hercules' passion was his misguided love, yet in Dante's paradise he does not repent. His explanation elaborates on his and Cunizza's cause of joy:

> Non però qui si pente, ma si ride,
> non della colpa, ch'a mente non torna,

> ma del valor ch'ordinò e provide.
> Qui si rimira nell'arte ch'adorna
>   cotanto effetto, e discernesi 'l bene
>   per che 'l mondo di su quel di giù torna.

> Yet here we do not repent; nay, we smile, not for our
> fault, which does not come back to mind, but for the
> Power which ordained and foresaw. Here we contemplate
> the art that makes beautiful the great result, and
> discern the good for which the world above wheels
> about the world below.

(103–108)

Both Cunizza and Folco have been enabled to see the good "ends" of their passionate natures. As they come to define themselves through the Godhead, their strayings have no place in the more fundamental recognition of pattern and purpose. In refining, but not razing, the power of their love, they associate themselves with its beneficent source. At once, this process is an act of identification with the greater powers and an act of self-definition. The joys of paradise derive from this justification of the earlier misdirected self.

It is only fitting, then, that cantos XV–XVII should have quite personal meaning for Dante himself, for in them the great present things, children, lineage, and fame, are reconstituted. These cantos form the actual center of the *Paradiso* and the personal center of Dante's pilgrimage. We can understand the meaning of divine comedy for Dante, when, ever in quest of a father, he discovers his poetic mission and inspiration from the real blood-founder of his house. Despite the melancholy recitation of the transience of once mighty Florentine names and the decline of Florence herself, these cantos breathe an air of exhilaration. And as we witness a justification of pride in descent, so, too, Dante is not only vindicated but even triumphant through qualities he had most cause to fear. His divine comedy enthrones not only general present things, but specific personal attributes. It is no accident that the only other reference to a member of Dante's family in the poem occurs in these same cantos, and that is to Dante's great-grandfather, who is purging himself of pride (where significantly fame and pride of house were deflated). It might be a family trait, and as such, penalized in purgatory, it flowers in paradise. There is some point in receiving inspiration from a spiritual father, a Virgil, but there is more astonishment when existence itself provides one with spiritual goals. When

Virgil, Dante's acquired mentor, brought Dante to the earthly paradise, he pronounced him "libero, dritto e sano." For all the merit of being "free, upright and whole," it is clear that these qualities are general without much specifically personal appropriateness. But there is something Dantesque when Cacciaguida bids him speak, "sicura, balda e lieta" ("confident, bold and joyful"). Just as the mention of Beatrice's name moves Dante through the fire in a way that Virgil's rational restraint never could, so Cacciaguida's words find greater native response and affinity in Dante. After all, despite the high theme and lofty language admired and imitated in Virgil, Dante's own qualities approximate more the stern language of the old crusader. We can appreciate, then, the pronomial stress when, after he looks into Beatrice's eyes, Dante thinks he has touched the depths of "*mia* grazia e del *mio* paradiso." (XV, 36) As in Spenser's cosmic comedy, *Epithalamion,* the poet's great service richly deserves this personal benefit.

Among the images of parent and child which give amplification to these cantos, one in particular should be singled out. It suggests that we were basically correct in locating with Virgil the dual concern with the child and with history. From within the cross, Cacciaguida reaches out to Dante as Anchises did to Aeneas in Elysium. And as if to underscore the link of Latinity Dante enchances the recognition by having Cacciaguida speak in the language of "*nostra* maggior musa":

> O sanguis meus, o superinfusa
> gratia Dei, sicut tibi cui
> bis unquam coeli ianua reclusa? [29]
>
> (XV.28–30)

There should be no mystery in this recourse to Latin, when the scene extols Roman roots of old Florence — roots that Dante shares, when the paradigm of the encounter derives from the *Aeneid* itself, and when it is the Roman virtue of familial *pietas* that finally returns in a Christian setting. At the very center of the *Paradiso* the physical and spiritual links of generation are reforged. The love for "sanguis meus" perverted in hell, stripped and refined in purgatory, is restored in the highest level of understanding, so that after hearing of the "così riposato, . . . così bello / viver dei cittadini" ("so peaceful and so fair a citizen's life," XV.130–131) in old Florence and of Cacciaguida's martyred death as a crusader, Dante the poet can begin the sixteenth canto with this exclamation:

O poca nostra nobiltà di sangue,
  se gloriar di te le gente fai
  qua giù dove l'affetto nostro langue,
mirabil cosa non mi sarà mai;
  chè là dove appetito non si torce,
  dico nel cielo, io me ne gloriai.

O our poor nobility of blood, if thou makest men
glory in thee here below, where our affections languish,
it will never be a thing for me to wonder at; for there,
where appetite is not warped, in Heaven itself, I
gloried in thee.

(1–6)

Despite all the hedgings, his instinctive pleasure in nobility of blood
receives paradisiacal approval, provided, as the subsequent terzina
stresses, nobility is added to by acts.

From Cacciaguida, Dante derives the inspiration and confidence
needed to add to the family name. In his need to be reassured he is
like Phaeton coming to Clymene to learn his true paternity. The image
is deliberate, since it also means to suggest Dante's own anxiety lest
he might be over-reaching. But Cacciaguida strengthens his courage
by telling him that his fame, from a party of one, shall outlast the punishment of his fellow citizens' perfidy: "s'infutura la tua vita / vie più
là che'l punir de lor perfidie." (XVII.98–99) They are the false parents,
the Phaedra; he is not the false son. And fame at last, after many
reroutings, is finally on the true road and restored in Paradise. Divine
comedy permits such great returns. Dante's original promptings and
ideals, which led to such difficulties and isolation, are heroically confirmed. Earlier Cunizza had referred to Folco:

Di questa luculenta e cara gioia
  del nostro cielo che più m'è propinqua,
  grande fama rimase; e pria che moia,
questo centesimo anno ancor s'incinqua:
  vedi se far si dee l'uomo eccellente,
  sì ch'altra vita la prima relinqua.

Of this brilliant and precious jewel of our heaven
that is beside me great fame was left, and before it
dies away this hundreth year will come again five times;

consider then if man should not make himself excel so
that the first life may leave another after it.

(IX.37–42)

Even with its temporal limitations (so heavily emphasized in the purgatorial period of crisis), still one great end of man is distinction of
merit and the extension of fame.[30]

Finally, unlike tragedy, divine comedy permits existence to confirm
essence. The drives and instincts which first caused the breakdown are
seen as the basis of recovery. After a tortuous process the first way of
seeing is restored and discovered to be right at least in its directions.
This is the nature of the *felix culpa* or fortunate fall and its relevance to
divine comedy. To recover after loss leads to a kind of jubilation greater
than where there was no loss at all. After the Law comes the glory,
and Dante's basically heroic conception of the world is confirmed when
his great attachments, children, name, and fame, return in the most
personal canto of the *Commedia.*

When we come to contraction, the vision of the unity of experience,
we see that there is a great difference between its purpose in divine
comedy and in Shakespearen tragedy. One's past, one's very birth,
rather than setting in action a series of relentless consequences that
destroy the individual, now initiates a life-giving pattern that leads to
salvation. The stars are not fatal, but rather auspicious; and contractions, rather than heralding death, mark fortunate occurrences.

There is, of course, some intimation of tragic contraction in the
Commedia, but that is mainly in the minds of the lovers, Paolo and
Francesca. For them love is a tragic principle, a mighty irresistible force.
Francesca's speech anaphoristically commences three periods with the
word "Love" — "Amor, ch'a nullo amato amar perdona." In their
book they read how love constrained Lancelot ("come amor lo strinse").
Not only does their account emphasize necessity, but their very presence
in the canto emphasizes contraction. Together they go, "insieme
vanno." And she had been seized with such a liking for Paolo that
even now it still possesses her, and he will never be divided from her
("questi, che mai da me non fià diviso"). The lovers have contracted
all experience to themselves; this principle, spiritually elevated in Donne,
is physically debased in Dante. Such a limitation deprives the soul of
its larger spiritual possibilities and frustrates the joy of comedy. Instead of leading to great and joyful discoveries, their contraction is
tragic, leading to a terrible perversion of what should be a life-seeking
force. As love brought them together, so love led them to a single

death ("Amor condusse noi ad una morte"). And for Dante, as for Shakespeare, there is something unnatural in love, the source of physical and spiritual life, leading to death. As Desdemona would say, "That death's unnatural that kills for loving." *Othello* to one side, however, not all the irony in Shakespeare's love tragedy reflects on the lovers. In Dante, on the other hand, the context of the canto reveals a double vision which prevents our total identification with the tragic rhythm and suffering of the agonists. We have instead what we have called a survivor's perspective, essential to comedy, and which suggests that other alternatives are possible than those immediately in sight. Deeply involved as Dante the pilgrim is for a variety of reasons in their lot, still he is a living reminder of other resources in love. Paolo and Francesca are looked at from a prospect of salvation and survival which are instances of other possibilities than the tragic necessity of contraction.

In Canto XXII of the *Paradiso,* Dante experiences one of those fortunate and joyous contractions, and here, typically enough, the contraction has strong personal meaning for his own existence. His ascent to the starry sphere and his passage out of the seven circling planets coincides with his own birth time. Existence again confirms essence, and real physical beginning is harmonious with true *telos.* His coming into time is sanctified in his passage outside of the realm of time and change and destiny. Contrary to what we have in Shakespearean tragedy, birth-time comes together, not with death-time as in the great final acts of *Hamlet* and *Julius Caesar,* but with the time of spiritual discovery. Dante expresses the same sense of personal vindication as he did in the Cacciaguida meeting when he rises under the sign of the Gemini:

> O gloriose stelle, o lume pregno
>   di gran virtù, dal quale io riconosco
>   tutto, qual che si sia, il mio ingegno,
> con voi nasceva e s'ascondeva vosco
>   quelli ch'è padre d'ogni mortal vita,
>   quand'io senti' di prima l'aere tosco;
> e poi, quando mi fu grazia largita
>   d'entrar nell'alta rota che vi gira,
>   la vostra region mi fu sortita.

> O glorious stars, O light pregnant with mighty power
> from which I acknowledge all my genius, whatever it
> be, with you was born and with you hidden he that is
> the father of each mortal life when I first tasted the

Tuscan air; and after, when grace was granted me to
enter into the high wheel that bears you round, your
region was assigned to me.

(112–120)

Such synchronization and collocations lend purpose and significance
to the universe. Spirit and idea heroically predominate, and multitudi-
nous existence is rounded out, given form and coherence. All disparate
and discontinuous things enjoy a coming together and an in-gathering,
of which the most important images, duplicating God's total presentness, would be the circle and the book. The book, we saw, warded off
the comedy of existence, and instead of the scattered leaves indicates a
unity bound with love and care. And the circle is the ideal contraction
without beginning or end, refuting all linear succession.

Millennial Hope and Imitation of Christ

As was clear from the inspired encounter with Cacciaguida, Dante's
greatest distance from our sad and furious world occurs when his sense
of the second historical fall converges with the original lapse, when
time is not seen to be a positive image of eternity. Lacking in necessity
though it may be, the pattern of historical decline is so overwhelming
that it reinforces the reality of the first fall. In such times, Dante's only
support is his faith in God's will, and his imitation of Christ. Yet images
of continuity and growth persist in the *Commedia,* suggesting Dante's
hopefulness for temporal affairs. While we see the leaves that fade,
they are actually part of a cosmic tree that has its roots in the crystalline sphere. Another image, in the earthly paradise (*Purg.* XXXII and
XXXIII), is the inverted Tree of Life that broadens as it rises. Far
from being an image of the world's disorder, the tree in its flourishing
reflects Dante's dream of a "world order, august, mighty, inviolable, a
tree of God's planting, a living thing rooted in the earth and reaching
high heavenward and wide-spreading." [31] In both instances, however,
visions of growth and development of continuity between time and
eternity are followed by graver impressions of man's historical decline.
Nevertheless, Dante's inveterate faith in the purposefulness of creation
revives; such setbacks are temporary, he feels, and the redeemer he so
ardently desires will one day come to set the world in its right order —
a formidable instance of how deeply run Dante's earlier commitments
to the ways of succession.

His own social disorientation was not free from the pursuit of the
millennium, which, as Norman Cohn has shown, was so much a part

of the revivalistic fervor of medieval society.[32] Pessimism in the present led to a revolutionary eschatology, to chiliasm, as the only means of alleviation. Indeed, as the *Commedia* proceeds and reflects more of the experience of Dante's later years, the great deliverer's arrival becomes more mystical and more deferred. Defeated in historical time, the basics of hope cannot be relinquished, but become apocalyptic. In *Purgatorio* XXXIII, Beatrice does not concede that the eagle of Rome will be long without an heir. "Stelle propinque" already foretell of a time when "five hundred, ten and five" sent by God will slay the harlot and the giant, the copulating monsters from Revelation that the Church and State have become. Although veiled, the hope is distinct for a redeemer relatively near at hand. In *Paradiso* XXVII, such a hero is farther removed. Now the force of revival will come in millennia — that is, by the time January will be removed from the winter months by the fifteen minutes the Julian calender loses annually. We return to the truth of Ladner's judgment that "the Middle Ages . . . sometimes forgot that all terrestrial order is relative." Dante's own expectations and tremendous commitments to the earthly city bring him dangerously close ("propinque stelle") to the fault of the divinators, those who "make the divine counsel subject to [their] will" ("che al giudicio divin passion porta"). So it is that Dante's unwillingness to abandon his hopes in the what Cullmann has called the redemptive line of history, whose providential course is traced by Justinian in *Paradiso* VI, introduces a strain of thought which could be alien to Piccarda's "nella sua volontade è nostra pace."

Although Milton was a practical revolutionary (or, at least for a while, of their party), he seemed to accept more willingly than Dante the end of the revolutionary eschatology. *Paradise Regained,* so to speak, more easily moves from the book of Daniel to second Isaiah, from the earthly paradise to the paradise within. But the same pattern of Christ that Milton specifically illustrates is the great operating spirit of the *Commedia.* In dealing with the religious writers of this study, we shall have occasion to return to the truth of Cullmann's observation: it is when God's lordship over time becomes most obscure that it is made visible again by the pattern of Christ.[33] The inevitable tension of Dante's allegiances is made manifest when the big, pennant-waving show of history, the flight of Justinian's eagle, is followed by the humble account of Romeo da Villanova, "persona umile e peregrina." After performing great services for his master, he was dismissed because of some slanderous accusations:

Indi partissi povero e vetusto;
   e se 'l mondo sapesse il cor ch'elli ebbe
   mendicando sua vita a frusto a frusto,
assai lo loda, e più lo loderebbe.

Romeo left there poor and old; and if the world knew
the heart he had, begging his bread by morsels, much
as it praises him it would praise him more.

(Par. VI.139–142)

Whether Boethius, Siger de Brabant, Cacciaguida, or Romeo da Villanova, it is with the exiles and the martyrs that Dante feels his greatest sense of identification. In their literal or figurative shedding of blood, they are the personal centers of the poem. Models in exile and pilgrimage — man's true condition for Dante in the earthly city — they are the single just men who transcend the hurt inflicted upon them. As they take up the burden of Christ they are, in their historical accessibility, the readier types to whom Dante turns when he is confronted with the mysteries of God's higher hand. This role of Christ as the paideutic model of imitation will last as long as the Renaissance, although other more secular types will threaten its hegemony. Christ will continue to represent (as he will for Milton, or as his type, Job, does for Petrarch), that inner faith, patience, and divine trust with which people of great heart move forward in a world that has been uprooted.

Chapter 3
Petrarch

Introduction

In the Renaissance discovery of time, as in so many other matters, Petrarch is a seminal mind, and of supreme historical importance. Not only is a sense of time derivable from his work, but time is directly and explicitly active as one of the great forces behind most, if not all, of his interests. In his *Rime,* time is a dramatic presence and an object of frequent address. In the two culminating sections the *Trionfi,* Petrarch states his final impassioned thoughts on the nature of time and the triumph of eternity. Not only in his poetry, but in his prose works, too, time is practically omnipresent. The useful index to the modern edition of his familiar letters can give a cursory impression of the frequency of temporal reference.[1] In fact, in the *Epistolae familiares* (as well as in the *Epistolae seniles*), large, important letters have time as their preponderant theme. If we ignore those letters where time is a passing reference or occupies only a few paragraphs, we still have *Fam.* I.3 ("de flore etatis instabilis"), XVI.11 ("quam cara res sit tempus"), XXI.12 ("de laxandis temporum angustiis sistendaque vite fuga"), XXIV.1 ("de inextimabili fuga temporis"), and the *Sen.* XV.1, also mainly on the use of time. The letters, of course, are works of familiar moral reflection, showing the development of Petrarch's life and thought. Yet not only they but also his more systematic prose contains throughout large sections whose concern is time. We can think of the "Coronation Oration," where temporal significance is basic to the symbolism of the laurel; the *Secretum,* too, is pivotal. In the *Life of Solitude* and in the great polemics of his later life, such as *Of His*

Own Ignorance (and That of Many Others) and the still untranslated *Contra eum qui maledixit Italie* — in all of these works private and public issues are critically influenced by Petrarch's sense of time. Time is the antagonist he would overcome in his pursuit of the laurel of fame and beauty; and in his rejection of those ways of succession, time is again part of the argument that exhorts him to look to more stable sources of reward. In his preference for Roman over Grecian things, for moral philosophy over speculative quibbles, the pressure of time is the force he feels: had he but world enough and time. And finally time is the awesome power that dwarfs all human accomplishment, and obliges Petrarch, in his quest for permanence, to look outside of time: *sine tempore vivete.* Our own researches abundantly confirm the conclusion of Fausto Montanari: "The passingness of earthly life under the pressure of Time is not . . . merely one among other themes in the work of Petrarch, it is a spiritual constant [una costante spirituale] present in every argument and behind every conception." [2]

Nor is this deep concern with time a late interest with Petrarch. Familiar letters I.3 and XXIV.1 tell us that time was the theme that precociously fired his heart as a young student. Latin utterances addressed to time were the passages he instinctively responded to, underlining them and noting them in the margins. Looking back from XXIV.1 he can say that what his fellow students and even teachers considered "somnia" — the themes of time's passingness and the coming of age and death — he took for living realities ("vera et pene presentia"). And in his search for words to say what a thing time is, he provides a lexicon of time's epithets: "I noted down not the verbal felicities but the substance of the thought — the distresses of this wretched life, its brevity, swiftness, haste, tumbling course, its hidden cheats, time's irrecoverability, the flower of life soon wasted, the fugitive beauty of a rosy face, the frantic flight of unreturning youth, the trickeries of stealthy age; and at the last the wrinkles, illnesses, sadness, toil, and the implacable cruelty of indomitable death." (Bishop, 201) Later (*Sen.* XII.1), even epithets suggesting the "race" of time or its "flight" appear inadequate, and Petrarch despairs of describing to the human understanding his conception of time's speed.

The above letter (XXIV.1) is both convenient and important: not only does it reveal Petrarch's obsession with time, it further shows that when the writers of the Renaissance antedated their confreres in the visual arts with their new sense of time's pressures and urgencies, they found the models for their address in the utterances of the great Roman writers. Nor is this connection between time and Rome accidental. The rising energy of young poets like Du Bellay and Spenser will respond to and exploit poetically the sonorous possibilities of these words but, like Petrarch, they will be more impressed by Rome as the great instance of a civilization's triumph over time. There is one other important connection. In these same letters Petrarch defends his practice of excerpting and culling sentences or memorable phrases. Indeed he does garner such treasures, but he values them more for what they say about life than for their eloquence. "Lego non ut eloquentior aut argutior sed ut melior fiam," he affirms in *Fam.* I.3. This penchant to move from time to questions of ethical reality is active not only in Dante and Petrarch, but in the other writers of the Renaissance as well. There is something involved in man's relations to time which urges him to take stock not of art and rhetoric but of living and acting better. If time is the great instrument of the ethical, Rome is again its historical exponent. We recall that in Dante's *Commedia* the great cantica of the ethical and the historical was the *Purgatorio*. The father-figure of this poem was Cato, the embodiment of the ethical life and a Roman, with the four virtues blazing from his face. This is the section where Dante is separated from the rapture of Casella's song, and urged, under the pressures of time, actively to purge himself. This will be for Petrarch, also, one great effect of his sensitivity to time. But in his inability to convert consciousness into willed action, we shall detect other important aspects of the argument of time.

The four familiar letters, I.3, XVI.11, XXI.12, and XXIV.1, can give us some idea of the scope of Petrarch's time-consciousness. On the one hand he is haunted by a remorseless, awesome, and all-too-imaginable time, a time of tens of thousands of years, the great "I am," which simply reduces to nothingness whatever is of significance in human life. But here the terror does not merely derive from great length, but rather from the ever-sameness of that vast extent. In I.3 and XXI.12 Petrarch describes the undeviating passage of time — an impression that he will continue to harbor even as late as the final *Triumphs* written in his last years. "All sublunary things," he writes in 1359, "as soon as they are born, hasten and are carried toward their ends with amazing speed. There is no intermission, no rest, nor is the flight lesser by night than by day. The diligent and the negligent move at one rate. . . . Do not think of a ship moving this way and that according to the various winds and waves — one unalterable speed is the course of life. There is no going back nor taking pause. We move forward through all tempests and whatever wind. Whether the course be easy or difficult, short or long, through all there is one constant velocity." The very early familiar letter, I.3 (1331), has the same thought and provides the further service of giving its source in Augustine's *City of God* (XIII.10): "our present life is nothing but a race toward the goal of death — a race in which no one is allowed either a brief pause or the slightest slackening of pace, but all are propelled with a uniform motion and driven along with no variation in the rate of progress." Throughout the course of Petrarch's writings, the Augustinian voice and conception of time will be formidable. With the exception of Seneca there is probably no other author whose temporal ideas exerted as full and abiding an influence. And it is to Seneca that we must look to account for Petrarch's other notion of time, so different from the Augustinian and yet strangely related to it. Within a time of such tremendous extent and moving with the same unalterable speed for everyone, great as well as small, Petrarch can still fit a more manageable kind of historical time, with which man can deal and within which his efforts and actions count for something. In fact, the rubric of the very letter (XXI.12) in which Petrarch utilizes the Augustinian conception, indicates that his main concern is with finding means of providing more time for himself: "de laxandis temporum angustiis sistendaque vite fuga." For this reason he schedules his day, and tries to cram as much activity as possible into his waking hours. From this attitude will develop the modern notions of time, and especially the temporal habits of the aroused humanists who imitated Petrarch. Within the order of civilization, Petrarch finds room for heroic time-transcendence through exceptional achievement. Time is here felt to be a great enemy, against which man must fight, the rewards of combat being a personal type of immortality through fame. The concept is Senecan and Augustinian, and it is around these opposite poles — confidence in the validity of his effort, and despair at the larger prospect — that Petrarch's spiritual evolution turned. Yet, strangely enough, it was by coming to terms with the Augustinian that Petrarch was able to dedicate himself as fully as he had always wanted to the maximum exploitation of his remaining days.

Petrarch was born in 1304, at the break of dawn on Monday, July 20, in the city of Arezzo on the Vico dell' Orto. (*Sen.* VIII.1) We have more precise information about his life than we have about that of any human being who lived before his time. This, as Ernest Hatch Wilkins reminds us in the preface to his *Life of Petrarch,* is a remarkable fact.[3] And as far as this study goes, we know more about Petrarch than we know about most of the men who lived after him. This is be-

cause he himself saw fit to make a record, or keep in consciousness, the temporal milestones of his existence. Petrarch maintained
throughout his life, not only in his letters and prose works, but also
in his poetry an attention nothing less than astounding to exactitude
in date. One will have to move many centuries into the future before
he will find poets and writers who note the time of composition so metic-
ulously and who make the date part of the position of the poem or treatise.

This keen attentiveness to dates is part of Petrarch's larger impulse
to bestow meaning on existence and to redeem distinctive human achievement. Time's terrible flow is undiscriminating and undistinguished; but
more than most people Petrarch is driven to tell the time — the impulse
can be as simple as that. When man marks off the years, months, days,
or minutes, he segments an otherwise undifferentiated terrain. Petrarch's
habit of mind, the distance he sets between himself and things, betrays
his need to see things in pattern, to gather them up in recollection, to
give them order, containment, and wholeness. Petrarch was married
to the order of consciousness, and he required his life to be an artistic
arrangement. In his two autobiographical pieces (his letter *To Posterity*
and *Sen.* X.2), we see his scholarly penchant for periodization as he
sorts out the events in his life and even remarks at one point how his
life at the time seemed to be divided into four-year periods ("sic tunc
vitam quaternario partiebar"). Given his type of mind, pattern might
somewhat predominate over record. Indeed, Petrarch is very much
aware (an awareness which old age will sharpen) that in the large run
of cosmic time all of these distinctions will be collapsed and all these
moments of importance shrink to practical nothingness, but in the more
hopeful moments of historical record man can wrest some meaning
from existence. More than simply telling time, the Petrarchan response
is heroic: as certain men rise out of the common lot by virtue of superior
talent or dedication, so, too, the normal flow of time can be set apart
and invested with special significance.

Petrarch's concern with dates proceeds generally in two ways. There
are dates that possess no intrinsic value in themselves, but only assume
value from the relationship they bear to Petrarch's own consciousness
or the work at hand. There are others which have value in themselves:
they are more or less significant past dates, and in their collocation with
present experience the individual feels himself enhanced. This feeling
is based on coincidence, and as we shall see, Petrarch is much given
to such perceptions. In the first kind of concern, he is more of a

recorder, laying down landmarks around which meaning clusters. In the second he sees in experience itself a significant rounding-out, an orderly completion.

In his *Rime* we find both kinds of procedures. That collection of poems, his most famous work, centering on his relations to Laura in life and death, is from one point of view an anniversary of Petrarch's aging. In these poems he goes "contando gli anni" and a loose chronology is one of the principles of their arrangement. Poems 30, 50, 60, 62, 79, 101, 107, 118, 122, 145, 212, 221, 271, and 364 mark off the years that Petrarch has wasted in his unhappy longing for Laura, and even after her death he records the years (278, 298, 359). Eleven years, ("Or volge, Signor mio, l'undecimo anno," s. 62), fourteen years, sixteen years ("Rimansi dietro il sestodecimo anno / de' miei sospiri," s. 118), seventeen years (s. 122), twenty years ("Così venti anni, grave e lungo affanno," s. 212): Petrarch is intently, agonizingly aware of the passage of time. In the *Rime,* such time registers are signals of rebuke: as Petrarch almost congenitally turns "a mirar gli anni," he is filled with regret at all the "perduti giorni." His own unhappiness in love sharpens his temporal awareness — fulfillment in love knowing no season, "nor clyme / Nor houres, dayes, months, which are the rags of time." But Petrarch's misfortune in love is only an organizing center for other areas of disappointment and anxiety — all of which intensify his awareness of the passing time and of the years that were being spent unprofitably. He was beset at certain periods of his life with feelings of guilt that he was squandering his talents, that in his over-ambitiousness he was commencing too many projects, none of which were completed. He felt a strong lack of "follow through" and character. His aging and lack of accomplishments contrasted strongly with his youthful promise, thus heightening the sense of waste and, with the falling markers of the years, his own deep sense of the limited amount of time left to him. Life was not open-ended for Petrarch: his consciousness of the certainty of death and the uncertain moment of its coming was acute. The threat of the last day looms large and is the third area that aggravates his sense of time and his fear of waste.

If the last day is always present to his mind, so also is the first day, the day he first met Laura:

> Mille trecento ventisette, a punto
> su l'ora prima il dì sesto d'aprile,
> nel laberinto intrai; né veggio ond'esca.

Thirteen hundred and twenty-seven, right
at the first hour of the morning on the
sixth day of April I entered into the laby-
rinth, and I do not know where I shall exit.
(s. 211)[4]

As he is with his birth into the world, so with his entrance into the confusion of adult life, with love the generating experience, Petrarch can be
precise as to the moment of initiation. But this critical date is more than
record: in two ways it enters into significant collocations. Emphasizing
the tensions that it was to create with his spiritual life, the day on which
Petrarch met Laura was Good Friday (s. 3). Born in religious competition, there seems something inescapable and inevitable in his love. The
ethos of necessity which such coincidence inspires is increased when
Laura dies twenty-one years later on the same day, at the same hour
(s. 336, and the *Triumph of Death,* 133–135). Such patterns of contraction will recur, especially in Shakespearean drama, whenever a tragic
ethos is invoked. In order to account for his own inability to transform
into effective action the imperatives of his consciousness, Petrarch has
recourse to the idea of necessity, a higher force that is compelling him
to pursue a course of action against his will. The sonnets abound in references to "sorte," "destino" — to fatal stars. Rather than mere sequence there is a pattern to events which controls Petrarch just as
strangely as its brings together his *innamoramento* and the Crucifixion,
the similar times of his falling in love and the death of Laura.[5]

Later in life Petrarch will come to reject such impressions of necessity. But in his early career, even with religious subjects, he enjoyed
perceiving or constructing such patterns of coincidence. In a letter to
Dionigi da Borgo San Sepolchro, *Fam.* IV.1 (better known for its subject matter, the ascent of Mont Ventoux), Petrarch enlists the *sortes
augustinianae.* Having reached, after much difficulty, the height of the
mountain, Petrarch randomly opens his copy of Augustine's *Confessions*
to a place that quite pointedly covers his own erratic wanderings in life.
This coincidence is heightened by the fact that the moment of this revelation came in 1336 when Petrarch was the same age, 32, as Augustine
had been when he experienced his conversion. It is no wonder, then,
that Petrarch tried in the letter to give the impression that it was written
immediately following the event.

Historically, Petrarch was well aware of "turning points." That seems
to be one recognized function of the historian, since he describes Thu-
cydides in the *Triumph of Fame* (III.55–56) as "he who well distin-

guishes the times." Thirteen forty-eight was a critical year for Italy and for Petrarch. The plague brought a rain of death which beat down the early flower of human possibilities. It would be no exaggeration to say that what exile meant for Dante the plague meant for Petrarch: a radical reminder of the liabilities in man's earthly existence and the insecurities of succession. This was the year, he writes in the preface to the *Seniles,* that through the death of so many friends robbed him of all solace in life. But rather than a sudden and single blow this pestilential year was only the beginning. It was the year "that we lamented" he writes in *Sen.* III.1, "but now I know this was only the beginning of our trouble, for this unprecedented and even, until our time, unheard of evil has not let up since then." Petrarch is writing in the third year since the fresh outbreaks of 1361, but it is really sixteen years since the beginning. As love was born on that sixth day of April in 1327, now death is the lesson learned on the same day, date, and time in 1348. Death is now triumphant. Whereas, earlier, time was told by the number of years since the fateful encounter with Laura, now 1348 and 1361 are the times of reckoning. Petrarch calculates the years of friendship that endured up to those dates, and he counts the years since his friends' deaths. Socrates, the coterie name he gives to the Flemish Ludwig Von Kempen, to whom the familiar letters were dedicated, died in 1361, as did Giovanni, Petrarch's illegitimate son. In *Sen.* I.3, he tells his friend Simonides (Francesco Nelli) that this is now thirty years that he has known Socrates; he met him seven years before the birth of his son. Three years later Simonides himself dies when Florence is again hard hit by pestilence. In lamenting the death of Laelius (the long-time friend, Lello di Pietro Stefano dei Tosetti), it is important for Petrarch to recall the years of their friendship: "This was the thirty-fourth year of our friendship, a time long when compared with the shortness of life, but brief for the heart's desire." (*Sen.* III.1)

Normally when we dash off a date at the top of a letter it means relatively little to us. We tend to be nonchalant about pinpointing temporal geography, mainly because such indications are readily available all around us. This is not the case with Petrarch: he spells out the dates (including the hour) with weight and deliberation, as if to stress the importance of taking one's bearings in time. In a letter of 1364 (*Sen.* IV.3), he can give the specific time of the arrival of the boat bringing news of the Venetian victory against the island of Crete. "It was, I believe, the sixth hour of June 4, this year 1364." The "when" of an event is an important part of its significance. And Petrarch, perhaps more than others, needed such anchors of stability. We must not forget that he was born into exile: *peregrinus ubique*. Dante, at least, had the inheritance of strong local attachments and identifications before he met exile and the condition of pilgrimage. But Petrarch was from birth cosmopolitan, and if later he tended to identify himself with Italy, and things Italian with Rome — forming *le cose nostre* — still he seems to have required the means of temporal location to help in the process. If not in space, then at least in time he would have his moorings.

Especially we sense this need in his letters and his prose works. In the epistle accompanying the major treatise *On his Own Ignorance (and That of Many Others)*, sent to his friend Donatus the grammarian, Petrarch appends the following notation: "Padua, on the thirteenth of January, from the bed of my pains, in the eleventh hour of night." The year, 1368, was unnecessary, since known to the recipient. And after the explicit of the treatise, he adds this note: "This little book was composed two years ago and written down by me elsewhere. I have re-written it, again with my own hand, and have brought it to an end at Arquà in the Euganean Hills, on the twenty-fifth of June of the year 1370, when the day was declining toward sunset." [6] Petrarch's time-consciousness is inevitably self-regarding. Scholar that he was, and distressed by the mangled condition of many of the classical texts that he was trying to rescue, and the uncertainties about their origins, it was inevitable that he should keep a weather-eye on posterity and try to keep clear the significant facts surrounding his own work. Fausto Montanari has well accounted for this impulse to such scrupulous temporal detail in Petrarch: "In the meticulousness with which he records on his papers . . . the minute circumstances surrounding all of his poetic activity we observe that subjective attachment [soggetivistico affetto] to every small detail of his own life, an attachment to the very hours and ever-fleeting minutes, which have been made infinitely precious by the irrecoverable flight of time. He would have loved to be able to translate all of his life into a perennial poetic fact [perenne fatto poetico] in order to rescue it from nothingness and to remain immortal in the memory and admiration of posterity." (pp. 12–13)

If he was concerned that posterity should know the details surrounding his life and works, so, too, he wrote to his classical predecessors, marking the differences that separated them. In these epistles, his datings assume a significant weightiness. He closes a letter to Cicero thus: "Written among the living, on the right bank of the Adige, in Verona, a city of Transpadane Italy, on the 16th of June, in the 1345th year of that Lord whom you did not know." (Bishop, 207) While such termination clearly separates Petrarch from his pre-Christian classical heroes, it also raises him above the very time that he so clearly marks, and elevates him to the level of civilization's continuing discourse.

Such communication was always inspiring for Petrarch. It is particularly in relation to the historical and traditional past that we see how ritualistic his sense of dates could be. The valediction to *Fam.* XXIV.7, addressed to Quintilian, claims to have been written "within the walls of my own city where I first became acquainted with thee, and on the very day of our becoming acquainted, on the seventh of December, in the 1350th year of Him whom thy master preferred to persecute rather than to profess." (Cosenza, 89) And perhaps his most important use of such temporal juxtaposition occurs in a letter to Urban V (in 1366) urging him to relocate the papacy in Rome: "I shall even use the day and the hour in which I am writing you as argument. This night, this very same hour, at which I am writing you with hope and faith and reverence were sanctified by the glorious martyrdom of Peter and Paul. Oh! if in this hour you were in the church of the principal of the Apostles — which is really the proper Church for you — and there you were able to participate in the singing of the divine offices, and at the matinals when Christ is praised, tell me what would be your supreme pleasure; with what sighs, with what tears, would you not beg that such a blessed night be prolonged?" In the father of humanism one can see the germ of sentiment that will render his later descendants loath to break with the traditions of Rome. Sanctity of place and time reinforce each other, and the individual is uplifted by the coincidence of his activities with a venerated past time. Or as Newman would later say, "To be deep in history is to cease to be a Protestant." [7]

But in his later years this seems to be the extent of Petrarch's willingness to posit a force in external dates themselves. In fact, later in life he will consistently refute the arguments of destiny and necessity that he had fostered in his own love poetry. Especially during the stressful years of the 1360s, Petrarch will denounce the popular reliance on astrology. One letter to Boccaccio (*Sen.* VIII.1) particularly lands on the notion that the year following a man's sixty-third birthday was the climacteric year, one of chaos and catastrophe. It was formed, interestingly enough, as the product of the seventh and ninth years, both known to be dangerous (a belief Petrarch accepts, *Sen.* VIII.8) — hence the sixty-third year must be multiply insidious. Petrarch rejects both astrology and such date-necessity from religious arguments. Such beliefs destroy free will, and more importantly they superstitiously challenge what ought to be the Christian's faith in God's lordship over time.

In this reallocation of trust, Petrarch's attitude toward the "present" also undergoes revision. His life goals had been futuristic. Now he feels great antipathy toward astrologers because they "disturb the present life and trouble it with lying fears of the future." In fact, Petrarch's praise of old age rests primarily on its own loss of grand schemes and high hopes for the future: "The young man wants to marry, have children, seek wealth, friendship, power and fame, enjoy his pleasures, reap honors and thinks to live a long time. But all of these things require much time. Since all of these hopes can be swept away by death, it must be that the fear of death possesses his life. But the old man has already turned his back on all of these things; . . . much securer in the proximity of death, he has nothing else close to his mind but to die well." (*Sen.* VIII.2) We have come here to a remarkable change in Petrarch's thought. From a young man trusting largely in this own energies and resources and looking to a future reward, he becomes the older man, confronted with the fact of death, who awaits patiently the divine will. For this Christian Stoic, death and the uncertainty of its "when," are the crucial psychological concerns. With David he can cry out in vain, "Notum fac mihi domine finem meum!" But all of his days, and that one above all others, he places at the disposal of the *rex seculorum* (Sen. VIII.1). And curiously enough, this total reliance on God, rather than diminishing Petrarch's tremendous activity, works a psychological release that makes him all the more eager and able to fill up the hours of his life.

Heroic Possibilities

"Ingentibus animis breve nichil optabile est." If there is one key to understanding Petrarch's essential motivation it is Ratio's advice to Gaudium and Spes in the first dialogue of the *De remediis utriusque fortune* (I.1: "De etate florida et spe vite longioris"): "to great-souled men nothing brief is worthy." And so it is that the proud passions of Petrarch's young manhood — love and fame — attract him by their powers of transcending time. Both, he protests to the doubting Augustine in the *Secretum,* have changed him from what he was. Both have raised his sights above the moribund material world of getting and spending. Even later in life, when he comes to experience the weaknesses of these attachments, it is only a goal of greater permanence that he will prefer to them. Love and fame are further allied for Petrarch in that, being objects of great merit, they require ardor, self-sacrifice, and struggle for their attainment. Instead of being easily accessible in the natural world, they are both lofty and available only to the most talented and the most dedicated. Petrarch, like many before and after, was haunted by the fascination of what was difficult. As he was born in exile and a stranger to every place, so in his lofty cultural aspirations and his idealization of love he was a stranger to his time. Searching for the rarest beauty and committed to an excellence that would endure — both connected in his mind — he separated himself in life as well as in art from the language and movements of the everyday and the mob.

Whether it is in his letter to Boccaccio (*Fam.* XXI.15), where he disclaims any jealousy of Dante, or the letter where he explains why he discarded his earlier purpose of writing in the vernacular (*Sen.* V.2), Petrarch was a man out of step with the conventional tastes and values of his day. And this was largely by choice and intention. The present time, as he tells us in his "Epistle to Posterity," has always displeased him; for this reason he has given himself over to the ancients and would have preferred to be born in another time. In the classical past he finds the examples of heroism and triumphs over time that he would make his own. The consortium of the dead seems to hold more reality for him than the living; consequently, he works to dissolve the boundaries between living and dead and to preserve the lines of communication with past greatness. In his correspondence with the past, life is lived at the desired level, far above the degraded present. Through reference to the example of the ancients, or quotations from their wisdom, experience is clarified and made firm; it is translated into the larger more relevant terms of universal experience. Thus classical analogy and quotation will come to be an intrinsic part of the humanistic frame of mind, thereby creating pressures which Petrarch himself felt. Through Augustine in the *Secretum* he will rebuke this aspect of himself, this need to hitch his wagon to a star, to show off his learning. But in *Fam.* VI.4 he will also feel that the practice is defensible, in that both writer and reader can measure their experience and intelligence against the culled wisdom of antiquity.

But there is a second, more personal reason for this defense: "I write for myself, and while I am writing I eagerly converse with our predecessors in the only way I can; and I gladly dismiss from mind the men with whom I am forced by an unkind fate to live. I exert all my mental powers to flee contemporaries and seek out the men of the past. As the sight of the former offends me, so the remembrance of the latter and their magnificent deeds and glorious names fill me with unthinkable, unspeakable joy. If this were generally known many would be stunned to learn that I am happier with the dead than with the living." (Bishop, 68) Solitude is delicious for such a soul, and provides the proper atmosphere for the kind of communication he wishes to enjoy with the past, the speculative distance he needs to insert between himself and the movement of his time. In solitude he knows life to be a shadow; he can withdraw from that which is fleeting and choose what is permanent. He can send back his memory, and range in spirit through all those who were great men ("gloriosi viri"), and thus forget the evil that is all around us, sometimes even within us.

The passage I am paraphrasing from *The Life of Solitude* rises in its fervor: "sometimes to rise, with thoughts that are lifted above yourself, to the ethereal region, to meditate on what goes on there and by meditation to inflame your desire, and in turn to encourage and admonish yourself with a fervent spirit as though with the power of burning words — these are not the least important fruits of the solitary life." [8] Always in Petrarch — and this is important to remember — his solitude and his transportation away from his time return to the fire and inspiration of present activity, to (as the above passage continues) "reading and writing, alternately finding employment and relief in each, to read what our forerunners have written and to write what later generations may wish to read, to pay to posterity the debt which we cannot pay to the dead for the gift of their writings, and yet not remain altogether ungrateful to the dead but to make their names more popular if they are but little known, to restore them if they have been forgotten, to dig them out if they have been buried in the ruins of time [senio abruta] and to hand them down to our grandchildren as objects of veneration, to carry them in the heart and as something sweet in the mouth, and finally, by cherishing, remembering, and celebrating their fame in every way, to pay them the homage that is due to their genius even though it is not commensurate with their greatness."

Obviously Petrarch is not a passive witness to ancient greatness. In the fourteenth century the *rinascimento dell' antichita* is connected with a *renaissance des lettres*. By looking backward, Petrarch was being original and active in the present. His concern will be repeated by many of his Renaissance heirs and will help to determine one of that epoch's most essential paradoxes: that though obviously arrière-garde, the Renaissance, at least in its pristine impulse, was also avant-garde. It was vigorously traditionalist and learnedly vital. Its guiding spirits sought to revive the sparks of communication, to reopen the channels of continuity. They sought the large discourse of civilization that would provide suitable room for their own heroic aspirations. The impulse and programs that we see in Petrarch (and also in Dante) will be prominently repeated by his poetic followers like Du Bellay and Ronsard and

Spenser in their belated national renascences. They are all engaged in
large-scale rescue work, redeeming from the past names and acts worthy
of greatness and fame, and in their own works similarly hoping to rise
above the present and elude the ruins of time. Their ardor contrasts with
the sloth — as they frequently described it — of the preceding age, that
allowed such classical greatness to fall into decay.[9]

Petrarch, while still rather young, did have his efforts and learning
recognized. On April 8, 1341, he was crowned with the laurel on the
Campidoglio in Rome, thus reviving the ancient practice that had fallen
into disuse. While Dante, we recall, had been offered the laurel, and
Albertino Mussato had in 1315 actually been crowned in Padua, it was
around Petrarch's coronation that most symbolic significance has clus-
tered.[10] His was the most memorable stage, though not the first, of a
process of reculturation that began in the fourteenth century. Perhaps
its Roman setting made it a purer act of revival, as Petrarch himself saw
in preferring the offer from Rome to the one from Paris (and incidentally setting up a dialectic and debate between French and Italian things
that would proceed with important implications throughout his life).
Petrarch wanted to "renew in the now aged Republic a beauteous custom of its flourishing youth." [11] Surely here, as with Dante of the *Commedia,* we are at the source of the poetic Renaissance: Petrarch is the
first poet, he himself maintains, since Statius to be so crowned. Not only
love for the *patria,* which for Petrarch is Rome, but also "affection and
reverence for those ancient poets of excellent genius" prompted his
choice. He quotes Cicero approvingly, "Our emotions are somehow
stirred in those places in which the feet of those whom we love and
admire have trodden." Petrarch feels himself enhanced by such historical
collocation, but he also derives from antiquity the spark of his present
endeavor. Ernest Hatch Wilkins, summarizing the historical significance
of the coronation, sees in it Petrarch's successful endeavor "to re-estab-
lish great cultural values in the position of high honor that they had
held in ancient Rome, and were to hold again, thanks largely to his
efforts, in the age that was to come." [12] Petrarch's backward perspective
clearly leads to activity in the present, and the communication through
example of poetry's high value to the future. In his letter of defense to
King Robert of Sicily (*Fam.* IV.7), Petrarch makes clear how much
this impulse transcends mere antiquarianism and leads to creative activity in the present.[13] The letter is written in reproof of the abusers of
history: *contra laudatores veterum semper presentia contemnentes.* Their
argument is one of historical decline (an argument Petrarch would later
have some use for, *Sen.* X.2, but never to the detriment of present ac-

complishment). Horace and Virgil are dead, great men have died, and so, a little while back, have the mediocre ones, and now we are faced with only the dregs. Petrarch's creative instincts are repulsed and horrified by this despair. He quotes to his advantage Plautus, who lamented before the advent of the Latin golden age: "in that time lived the flower of poets, but now they are no more." But in the carpings of his contemporaries Petrarch sees mere hostility, not lament: "they do not weep the end of learning (which in their heart of hearts they desire dead and buried); rather they seek to discourage their contemporaries whom they fear." But rather than disheartening him, their qualms only urge him on to become the kind of a man they believe only existed in the classical world, if at all. Such men are rare and few, Petrarch confesses, but there have been some. And he proceeds to the great utterance of his own personal hope and faith, one that is at the heart of the creativity of the Renaissance. There have been few such men, and who is to "deny us from being among these few? If the scarcity of such spirits frightened everyone, in a short time there would be not only few but none at all. Let us endeavor, let us hope, and perhaps it will be given to us to attain what we have sought. Virgil himself has said, 'they were able because they believed themselves capable.' We too, believe me, can, if we believe we can." The active encouragement, the collective imperative: *enitamur, speremus:* all are typical of the high possibilities envisioned by the men of the Renaissance at the outset. It is not hyperbolic to say that Petrarch heralds the dawn of a new era, because that is the way he and many of his followers felt. Like Bacon with his *New Atlantis,* Petrarch with the "'Coronation Oration" establishes himself as the high priest of a new science.

His "Oration" is one of the two keys to Petrarch's poetry, the other being the *Secretum.* It is an important statement of the desires for glory and fame that Petrarch acknowledges to be behind all great effort, and a valuable exposition, keeping the *Rime* in mind, of victories over time that are symbolized by several of the laurel's qualities. *Vicit amor patriae,* love of the Roman fatherland played an important part in Petrarch's decision to be crowned in Rome; it, together with the second half of the phrase, *laudumque immensa cupido,* "and the immense desire for praise," serves to explain the inner forces that move the aspiring poet to scorn delights and live laborious days, to leave behind, in the argument of sonnet 7, "la gola e l'sonno e l'oziose piume" the sleeping and the feeding, and try the arduous and lonely heights of Parnassus. "The desire for glory is innate not merely in the generality of men but in

greatest measure in those who are of some wisdom and some excellence."
(p. 1245) He quotes Ovid in anticipation of Milton, *et immensum gloria
calcar habet* . . . fame is the spur. From Ovid, Statius, Virgil, and
Lucan he quotes fiery professions of the permanence of their works and
their power to confer immortality. The laurel, in its own symbolic perdurability, is the fitting reward for poetic excellence. In its fragrance
the laurel represents the fame and glory that both Caesars and poets
desire. Among the other properties of the laurel is its ever-greenness. It
does not suffer the change of seasons. In its supposed immunity to lightning (although here the symbolism is forced more than usual) the laurel
is finally above the hazards of time, "for in the affairs of men what
thunderbolt is more terrible than the diuturnity of time, which consumes
all the works of men, all their possessions, all their fame? Rightly, therefore, since the laurel fears not the thunderbolt, is a crown of laurel given
to those whose glory fears not the ages that like a thunderbolt lay all
things low." (p. 1250) This faith of the "Oration" is reaffirmed throughout the *Rime,* where Petrarch asserts the after-life that his devotion to
the laurel will gain for him.

Of the two ways of self-perpetuation available to man in the realm
of succession, it should be clear that Petrarch places little faith in children. Late comes the tree that will provide shade for your descendants,
he will quote Virgil approvingly. Born into exile, his separation from an
actual community has its corollary in his preference for works of the
right hand over children of the right hand. This preference does not
necessarily grow out of the sentiment that one should not love too much
those things that one must fear to lose, although in *Fam.* XXIV.1, Petrarch declares it was the very uncertainties of life, and his special sen-
sitiveness to them, which prevented him from committing himself to
career and family, those things that occupied his more hopeful contemporaries. And later, especially in the *Seniles* (X.4) he can write genuinely
sorrowful letters over the deaths of children. But where Petrarch personally was concerned, the avoidance of family (I am not speaking of
his two illegitimate children, whom he acknowledged and provided for
dutifully) derived from the humanist's fears of involvements that would
compromise his freedom and leisure for writing and thinking. Nor was
this merely practical: his service to letters was in his mind a higher cause.
Another late letter (perhaps as late as 1373) makes this clear: "We
shall extend our name into the future, God willing, by intellect not
marriage, with the aid of books not children and through virtue not
wives. . . . You will not have a bright and long-lasting name, unless

you get it for yourself. This is the work of manhood, not women. How much fame would Plato and Aristotle, Homer and Virgil have today if they had thought to possess it through matrimony and offspring?" [14] Boccaccio would be repeating Petrarch's notions when, in his life of Dante, he would claim that Dante's involvements with love and politics made him a slave to fortune (thereby also anticipating Bacon's phrase, "He that hath wife and children hath given hostages to fortune"). The issues will be clarified, and the lines drawn when civic humanist Leonardo Bruni, in many ways an heir to Dante's involvement, will claim that it was this very public commitment on Dante's part that made him the great poet he was. [15] With this issue as only one index, the lines of Italian trecento and quattrocento humanism separate. Hans Baron's classical study, *The Crisis of the Early Italian Renaissance,* is a record of the larger implications of this division. [16] Likewise, Vittore Branca in his preface to Morelli's *Ricordi* separates the strands: "While Petrarch and Boccaccio deny the family as an obstacle to letters and culture, other Florentine humanists, from Salutati and Bruni to Palmieri and Alberti will argue the strict connection between culture and civic life, culminating in the theories of their greatest philosopher, Ficino: 'Remember that in governing the family with deep care you are developing yourself, you are becoming experienced and honored in the earthly republic and are making yourself worthy of the celestial.' " [17] A negative indication, if any is needed, of this connection between children and the city is contained in the very letter in which Petrarch advises against familial responsibilities for the man of letters. The first half of this letter is devoted to a vehement attack on the vices of the city, and praise of his correspondent's resolve to stay away from the city.

Dante is very much in evidence when, in a frequently reprinted letter to Boccaccio (*Fam.* XXI.15), Petrarch clarifies his attitude toward the great Florentine of the preceding generation, and disclaims any envy or jealousy of his attainment. As a matter of fact, he has only admiration for Dante's determination. In addition to being fellow exiles, Dante and Petrarch's father were united by similar qualities of mind and interests in study. However, "out of regard for his family" (Bishop, 178), Petrarch's father took on employment. But Dante neglected all else in his desire for fame. Neither exile, poverty, the attacks of his adversaries, "non amor coniugis, non natorum pietas" ("nor love of wife nor feeling for his sons") could deter Dante from the path he had set out on. One can see here obvious extratextual support for the evidence provided by *Inferno* XXVI itself that a good deal of Dante went into the creation of Ulysses. The difference here is that while Dante is aware of the rootlessness of such rejection, and its moral disorders, Petrarch, sensitive to his own distractedness, finds such singleness of purpose awesome.

Petrarch's tendency to avoid involvement, whether in family or society, has for our purposes another important corollary. His work is almost totally lacking in that sense of emulation that we find so strong in Dante and in Shakespeare. In a few places, especially in the *Triumph of Eternity,* Petrarch will emphasize the organic processes of replacement within succession, the growth and decay, the dying and giving birth, but we do not have in his work, either as substance or as quality, this sense of bristling conflict, of raw contention, of things meeting in "mere oppugnancy." [18] Petrarch sought a style more remote from the goings-on of his day, while Dante and Shakespeare held more dramatic mirrors up to the body of their times.

Idealized beauty in the person of Laura is the second power to which Petrarch commits himself. While their means are different — fame promising extension after death, through history, and love offering personal fulfillment and, as it were, the loss of any sense of incompleteness — both their ends are the same: a much-desired victory over time. The two are in fact linked as frequently in Petrarch as the play on the names "Laura" and "laurel." They are further associated by Augustine in the *Secretum* as the creatural powers that deter Petrarch from a primary reliance on God. And indeed it is interesting to note that just as Petrarch claimed to have first seen Laura on Good Friday, so the idea for his epic poem *Africa* came to him on Good Friday ("Epistle to Posterity," Bishop, 9–10). They are closely connected, as the vision of beauty provides poetic inspiration, which, transmitted into art, becomes the basis of personal fame.

Although Laura's beauty is the cause of his more lasting disquiet, during the rare moments when he is in her presence he senses a completion of all his human insufficiencies. All that is imperfect she makes perfect. Like Perdita's in *The Winter's Tale,* all her acts are queens. Sonnet 34 of the *Rime* is known for its miraculous conclusion. Petrarch urges Apollo, or the sun, with its warm rays to dispel the harmful vapors and cold that keep Laura ill and confined. If he would do this, then the two of them together, both lovers of the Laura-laurel, would be astonished:

> Sì vedrem poi per meraviglia insieme
> seder la Donna nostra sopra l'erba
> e far de le sue braccia a sé stessa ombra.

> We would then both marvel together to see
> our Lady sit upon the grass and provide
> of her own arms her own shade.

This picture of self-contained and self-collected sufficiency recalls one other quality that Petrarch saw in the laurel. Its shade, as he tells us in the "Coronation Oration," offers "a resting place for those who labor." Like the Garden it suggests, it provides man with ease from toil, a contemplative relief from time and history. But even this quality involves religious competition, since only the shade of Christ's tree was traditionally understood to offer man true repose.[19]

Laura's presence, while within nature and of nature, is hardly a part of the natural scene. She seems something special, self-involved and set apart. In sonnet 100, in enumerating the visibilia that recall his love for Laura, Petrarch mentions

> e 'l sasso ove a' gran dì pensosa siede
> Madonna e sola seco si ragiona . . .

> the stone, where in the season of longest
> days my Lady sits and alone with herself
> thinks . . .

The beatitude of the lady's self-communion contrasts with Petrarch's turmoil in isolation: wherever he goes he cannot escape "ch' Amor non venga sempre / ragionando con meco, et io con lui" ("but Love is always there speaking with me and I with him"). Petrarch's separation from nature reflects his *dissidio;* Laura's, her wholeness.

The landscape seems quieted and becalmed when she occupies its center. And even when there is movement it only serves to adorn her beauty. Witness this picture of Laura as Petrarch imagines her mourning over him when he is dead (such wish-indulgence is a good part of Petrarch's emotion in love):

> Da' be' rami scendea,
> dolce ne la memoria,
> una pioggia di fior sovra 'l suo grembo,
> ed ella si sedea
> umile in tanta gloria,
> coverta già de l'amoroso nembo;
> qual fior cadea sul lembo,

qual su le treccie bionde,
ch' oro forbito e perle
eran quel dì a vederle;
qual si posava in terra e qual su l'onde,
qual con un vago errore
girando parea dir: "Qui regna Amore."

From the beautiful branches there descended,
sweet to remember, a rain of flowers upon her lap,
and she sat modest in such glory, covered with
the nimbus of love; some flowers fell on her garment,
some on her blond locks, which that day
seemed furbished gold and pearls, some came
to rest on the ground and some on the waters,
and some with their lazy circling flight
seemed to proclaim: "Here Love is Queen."

(s. 126)

In her presence, even movement, softly falling, is not too far from stasis.

As on the day of her first appearance to Petrarch, it is natural that her beatitude should rival divinity:

Sì come eterna vita è veder Dio
né più si brama né bramar più lice,
così me, Donna, il voi veder, felice
fa in questo breve e fraile viver mio.

Just as it means eternal life to see God
and nothing more is desired or desirable,
so seeing you makes me content in this
brief and frail life of mine.

(s. 191)

This sonnet continues to praise the "ora beatrice" in which he has seen Laura more beautiful than ever, when every great hope and every desire are subdued ("che vince ogni alta speme, ogni desio"). This capacity of Laura to fill his every craving operates even in death, when she returns to his imaginative reveries, as in sonnet 284: "pur mentr'io veggio lei, nulla mi noce" ("while I see her nothing troubles me"). And in the subsequent poem, like lover or mother, she speaks to him of the chances of life and the need to raise his sights to better things, "e sol quant' ella parla ò pace o tregua" ("and only for as long as she speaks do I have peace or truce").

It is part of Petrarch's speculative distance from life that his vision of beauty in aesthetic stasis is not violated by any grasping hand or forward movement on his part. This is very different from Shakespeare's lovers (or Spenser's), where physical consummation is valid: "quick, and in mine arms." Petrarch, however, complements his lady's repose by keeping his aesthetic distance and enjoying the miracle in regard only:

> Stiamo, Amor, a veder la gloria nostra,
> cose sopra natura altere e nove.
> Vedi ben quanta in lei dolcezza piove,
> vedi lume che 'l cielo in terra mostra!

> Stand, love, and observe our glory, a thing
> above nature lofty and new. See what showers
> of sweetness, see the light that shows heaven
> on earth!

> (s. 192)

The poem proceeds to build upon the pleasures of the eye. And in a preceding poem, the very important sonnet 188, Petrarch again urges the sun to stay with him in admiration: "Stiamo a mirarla."

Laura's stasis, her annihilation of the world of toil and time-ridden history, her satisfaction of all desires, inevitably summons up for Petrarch the vision of the earthly paradise, where heaven showered forth on earth. Such love-idealism represents for him the fullest flowering of nature, its highest reach. Out of the creatural world itself, whatever its associations with divinity, a means is available of abolishing the sweat and the labor, and returning man to the condition of the first people. Laura usurps the place of the Christian source of redemption just as certainly as she came into Petrarch's life on Good Friday. If, in sonnet 188, the sun should look at her, he would see a sight without equal since Adam first saw Eve. This unique and marvelous vision, evoking thoughts of the world before the Fall, is worthy of their admiration, Petrarch maintains: stop and wonder.

But in this sonnet, fairly early in the story-line of the *Rime,* the sun loses its mythological robes: it ceases to be Apollo struck by the beauty of Daphne (laurel) and reverts to its more terrifying physical being, the sun, the sign of the remorseless course of time in the cosmos. The sun does not stand still — the days for miracles are over — but proceeds inevitably on its way, overriding Petrarch's wishes, spreading ever deeper shadows until the "fronde" — the Laura-laurel object — is concealed in darkness.

> O sole, e tu pur fuggi, e fai dintorno
> ombrare i poggi e te ne porti il giorno,
> e fuggendo mi toi quel ch' i' più bramo.
>
> L'ombra che cade da quell'umil colle
> ove favilla il mio soave foco,
> ove 'l gran lauro fu picciola verga,
>
> crescendo mentr' io parlo, agli occhi tolle
> la dolce vista del beato loco
> ove 'l mio cor con la sua Donna alberga.
>
> O sun, you nevertheless fly on, and
> lengthen the shadows of the hills and bear
> away the day, and take from me what I most
> desire. The shade that falls from that
> small hill, where my full flame was once a
> spark, and where the great laurel was once
> a twig, spreading even as I speak, removes
> from my eyes the sweet sight of that blessed
> place where my heart resides with its Lady.

A fundamental hostility is played out here between the heart's desires and wishes and the irrevocable passage of time. This drama will be repeated throughout the Renaissance (we have only to think of *Romeo and Juliet*), when the pleasure principle of love awakes to the reality principle of time. And in Petrarch's other "love" poems the moments of fulfillment with Laura are rendered fugitive by the ever-pressing hours. Such consciousness is acute with Petrarch; in his prose he will frequently note the passage of time as he is in the act of writing. So here as he is speaking, time, premonitory of death, steals the wonder that Laura promises, and gives precocious instruction in her own unreliability as a source of being.

Great Hopes Defeated

Despite his victories and proclamations, inner and outer evidence impressed upon Petrarch the faultiness of his reliances and pushed him

toward a fundamental re-evaluation of his own commitments. Pestilence
had cast a pall over life's highest possibilities. In the preface to his familiar letters, Petrarch points to 1348 as "the year that made us alone
and miserable . . . irreparable are the losses and incurable the wound."
Life's hopes were interred with his great friends:

> Rotta è l'alta colonna, e 'l verde lauro
> che facean ombra al mio stanco pensero:
> perduto ò quel che ritrovar non spero
> dal borrea a l'austro o dal mar indo al mauro.

> The high column is broken and the green
> laurel which together sheltered my tired
> thought; I have lost that which I can not
> hope to find from north to south, or from
> east to west.

> (s. 269)

Not only is this a private loss, it is also a public lesson intended for
all mankind. The human condition is essentially defective if its grandest
forces, the Great Prince (Stefano Colonna, the supporting column of the
first line above, and Petrarch's patron) and the Lady are so vulnerable.
Laura's death, in particular, is used as a test case similar to the fall of
princes in medieval tragedy, "demonstrating" the superiority of death
over life's promises. Quite logically, death proves his point in the *Trionfi:*

> Così del mondo il più bel fiore scelse,
> non già per odio, ma per dimostrarsi
> più chiaramente ne le cose eccelse.

> Thus of the world he [Death] chose the
> loveliest flower, not out of absolute hatred
> but to demonstrate his powers most clearly
> among the highest things.
> (*Triumph of Death,* I.115–117)

The choice example covers all other cases; if the best burn, what will
happen to the lesser creatures?

> Che fia de l'altre se questa arse ed alse
> in poche notti e si cangiò piu volte?
> O umane speranze cieche e false!

What will happen to the others if she
[Laura] burns and chills in few nights
and is thus changed many times?
O human hopes blind and false!

(127–129)

Laura in death as in life is of paradigmatic relevancy. She had represented a potential of life, but a potential insufficient to deal with the ominous powers of death, just as fame will in the later *Trionfi* prove weaker than time. Petrarch's complaints about life's deceptions are as strong as had been his trust and expectations. Like Dante he realizes that those who yield themselves totally to life's promises are the more readily disappointed. "O che lieve è ingannar chi s'assecura!" ("How easy it is to deceive him who is unheeding!") Who would ever have thought that those lovely eyes would become earth? Such human hopes he now calls blind. "Misero mondo instabile e protervo / del tutto è cieco chi 'n te pon sua spene." ("Wretched unstable and changing world, one must be blind to place his hopes in you.")

True promise cannot be maintained in the world where time and death prevail. For the men of the fourteenth century, such is the drive toward permanence and stability that those earthly things which do not endure or whose tenure is brief are unworthy bases of hope: *Ingentibus animis* . . . . That same impulse that propelled them to the heights of worldly achievement now moves them to the rejection of love and fame as primary forces. There are, however, more subjective pressures that force Petrarch to reconsider his goals and even his temporary successes. Not only the more general evidence that death's triumph provides, but also the testimony of his own spiritual being persuaded Petrarch of his error and helped to precipitate the crisis which brought about a shift in his values.

We remember that for Petrarch the figure of Ulysses had become a representative Renaissance type. Petrarch may have been restoring to him the ideal of mobility and experience that he had embodied before Dante made him the negative instance of a world running amok. At least in the earlier Petrarch, Ulysses is the world traveler, learning of the different ways of people, and he is one who rightly separates himself from the benighted stay-at-homes and takes the primary Renaissance step of going beyond the regular routines that blight the human spirit. Ulysses thus becomes fit to imitate, a model for the necessary act of setting-out in the quest of experience and wisdom. Acquiring through his own travels and venturousness the highest attainments of the human intelligence, he becomes a higher type, serving the cosmopolitan Petrarch's defense of his own love of variety, mobility, and travel:

> If indeed experience teaches us, if she is the mother of the arts, what praiseworthy artistic achievement can he hope for who spends his life guarding the house of his fathers? It is a peasant virtue to stay in one's own fields, to know the qualities of one's own soil and cattle, the waters and the trees, and the sowing seasons and rakes and grub-hoes and plows. But it is a mark of a noble, an aspiring mind that one has seen many lands and the customs of many peoples and has reflected on his observations. What you have read in Apuleius is very true. He says: "The divine originator of ancient poetry among the Greeks, wishing to present a man of the utmost wisdom, very justly sang of one who had profited by the vicissitudes of many states and peoples." Our great poet, imitating him, led his Aeneas through numberless cities and shores. (Bishop, 87)

This passage from *Fam.* IX.13 is not the only occasion where, rather than separating Aeneas (or Virgil) and Ulysses, Petrarch values in them their authors' intentions, as he says in *Fam.* XV.4, to cast the perfect man "as a world wanderer, everywhere learning something new. They thought the kind of man they portrayed could not be formed if perpetually limited to a single spot." (Bishop, 134) And this voice will recur in the great literature of the Renaissance, as Rabelais, Montaigne, Shakespeare, and Milton value the adventurer setting out, the great spirit that takes its chances and is not content only to stay at home.

But in moments of self-doubt and frustration, this love of variety and flexibility can lead to bitter self-accusation, itself, perhaps, an abiding trait of Renaissance humanism. For instance, Petrarch admires Dante's singleness of purpose, while "so many superior and fastidious minds are swerved from their purpose by a mere breath." The tensions that he feels within his chosen lot are very similar to those that Dante exploited in the prototypic character of Ulysses: his flexibility can be mere purposelessness and lack of identity. In fact, in the later *Triumph of Fame* (II.18), Petrarch himself will characterize Ulysses negatively, as he "che desiò del mondo veder troppo" ("who desired to see too much of the world"). Thus it is that many of Petrarch's works reveal a hankering back to an earlier and simpler world he had abandoned, even an envy of those who are "perpetually limited to a single spot" or those who spend their lives guarding the houses of their fathers, or those who have a simpler, less ambitious religious faith. In times of crisis Petrarch's new freedom seems a terrible price to pay, and perilous indeed.

These tensions plainly exist in his relationship with his brother Gherardo, and the letter describing the ascent of Mont Ventoux is the expression of Petrarch's own pained awareness of the differences that show themselves even in the characters of brothers. Gherardo seems to have been one of those people blessed with a good personal economy, with little wasted movement. Forthrightly and with no side excursions he proceeds along the straight and arduous path toward the summit of the mountain. But in his own distractedness, Petrarch seems incapable of committing himself to a single line; rather he looks for short-cuts and byways, which turn out to be only roundabout ways of descent. The different procedures of the brothers that Petrarch records in their ways up the mountain obviously point to Gherardo's decision to enter a monastery, while Petrarch himself tarried, juggling several possibilities, before making a different kind of commitment. Within the letter to Dionigi, Petrarch meditates about this quality in himself, about his own inability to translate knowledge into willed action. What holds him back from resolving on the difficult climb to the top, a climb he knows must be made if he is to be saved? "Surely, nothing but the level road that seems at first sight easier, amid base earthly pleasures. But after much wandering you will have to climb upward eventually, with labors long shirked, to the height of the blessed life, or lie sluggishly in the valley of your sins. And if — I shudder at the thought! — the darkness and the shadows of death find you there, you will spend an eternal night in perpetual torture." (Bishop, 47)

One other aspect of Petrarch's dilemma, implied in his capacity for distraction and his apparent lack of purpose, is his neglect of himself. In the same letter concerning the ascent of Mont Ventoux, the climax rebounds terribly against the frivolity of Petrarch's interests when compared with the needs of his own self, "Men go to admire the high mountains, and the great flood of the seas and the wide-rolling rivers and the ring of Ocean and the movement of the stars, but themselves they consider not." (Bishop, 49) Early in the development of humanism, Petrarch, the father, utters a fear that will be repeated by many of his sons. The reviver and disseminator of classical culture, the avid student of a learned and highly-wrought poetry, was haunted by the doubt that because of these very pursuits, elevating though they were, he was forsaking his own most vital interests. As with the randomly-chosen passage from the *Confessions,* it is mainly in the voice of Augustine that such rebuke is leveled. In the *Secretum* this part of Petrarch's own spirit accuses him of devoting all his time and energies to the writing of the *De viris illustribus* and the *Africa,* while being "prodigal of the most precious and irreplaceable of things [almost certainly meaning time] . . . and writing about others, you are most forgetful of yourself." (*Prose,* 192) Further, Augustine feels that the host of literary allusions which Petrarch can bring to every situation, rather than strengthening his own will and resolution, seems to weaken it. The company — even the authority — he finds for his misery deprives him of the willingness to effect a cure. When Augustine points to his graying hair, indicating the need to take control of his life, Petrarch can cite Virgil, whose hair grayed at an early age. To which Augustine scornfully replies, "How filled your mind is with examples." (*Prose,* 178)

As I shall repeat throughout this study, it is a mistake to emphasize the universal applicability of the general patterns of Dante's and Petrarch's work to the extent that each becomes a kind of Everyman. Their fates are not common, but exceptional, as exceptional as the high dreams that moved their startings-out, exceptional in their earlier aspirations, their ascendant hopes which separated them from the more established and regular world. There is something of Ulysses in both of them, and much of the adventurousness of the Renaissance. But as they were men set apart in their lofty ambitions and avid questing, so in their misery and unfulfillment they sense their differences from the more accepting souls who remained within the accustomed order. The lives of the elect do not proceed simply and peacefully, but are beset by anguish, disturbance, and difficulty. They reach for the highest, only to have their aspirations result in waywardness and waste. In moments of terrible clear vision, they contrast themselves rebukingly with the souls of the world who seem to proceed unmolested and clear. This is the basis of Petrarch's contrast of himself with his brother Gherardo. In fact, in his *Rime,* some of his finest poems are built on this same divergence between his own dissatisfaction and the simpler effectiveness and faith of the common world.[20]

Such reflections on Petrarch's part differ, to be sure, from Dante's in that they do not denote the beginning of a determined effort; indeed, they show little sign of conscious effort toward relief. But still they are important, self-regarding and self-indulgent though they are, in that they indicate an appreciation of the more medieval sense of stability that had been left behind. These predilections, even if only nostalgic, are preparatory to a shift of values. And such a shift did quite consciously occur in Petrarch. It is explicitly signed in a letter (*Fam.* XIII.8), written in

the summer of 1352, Petrarch's last summer at Avignon, where he professes his newly won admiration for life's more solid virtue, and his
disaffection from the passing sights and sounds of beauty and art. He
has, he tells his correspondent, declared war on his body ("Corpori
meo bellum induxi"). Of all the senses, his eyes had caused him greatest
difficulty: now he has closed them to all the things he formerly valued,
including women, with the exception of his peasant maid. He then enlists some hyperbole to describe the ruggedness of her features. Despite
her epic homeliness, "no one could be more faithful, humble, or hard-
working." He praises highly her sturdiness and the simplicity of her
peasant strength, caring for people without a whimper of complaint and
tirelessly performing her duties so that she in truth appears to be a young
girl fresh from her bed. In contrast with this effective virtue, the pleasures of the eye seem pale, and so, too, the harmonies of the ear: "Where
is the sweetness of song, flute and lyre that so enrapture me? The wind
has blown away all that delight." (Bishop, 123) He has come to adopt
a more simple, rustic life, for what once pleased him no longer does:
"The chains that once bound me have been cast off; the eyes that once
I sought to please are closed in death; and if they were still open I think
they would not hold me under their accustomed spell." (Bishop, 124)

So, too, his prior devotion to fame has undergone some change. Like
Dante, Petrarch comes to find the self-perpetuation through one's work
to be a shadowy fulfillment:

> Ma se 'l latino e 'l greco
> parlan di me dopo la morte, è un vento:
> ond'io, perché pavento
> adunar sempre quel ch' un'ora sgombre,
> vorre' 'l ver abbracciar, lassando l'ombre.

> But if in Latin or Greek I am spoken of
> after death, it is only a breath: therefore,
> since I fear to be always accumulating what
> one hour will disperse, I want to embrace
> the truth, not shadows.
>
> (Can. 264)

This new emphasis on solid virtue changes Petrarch's stance toward
the object of value. Formerly he had been content with speculative
distance." Stiamo a mirarla" was his instruction to Apollo. But now
he wants more solid fare. The verb "abbracciar" is very significant, in-

dicating a personal need to take hold. Later verses, sestina 142 and sonnet 355, express this same quest and need. The former, early in placement but not in date of composition, tells of his prior dedication to the laurel. But arguing from the changeableness of all things, he justifies his own alteration of ideals:

> Tanto mi piacque prima il dolce lume
> ch' i' passai con diletto assai gran poggi
> per poter appressar gli amati rami;
> ora la vita breve, e 'l loco e'l tempo
> mostranmi altro sentier di gire al cielo
> e di far frutto, non pur fior e frondi.

> I was at first so taken with that alluring
> light that l climbed many hard hills without
> minding in order to approach the beloved branch;
> but now the brevity of life and the time and the
> place show me another way to mount to heaven and
> to bear fruit, not only flower and leaf.

While granting that his aesthetic appreciation of beauty had been uplifting, he can no longer be content with the activities and rewards of poetry ("fior e frondi") but desires the solid fruit of virtuous action. The time has come, he concludes, "che n'è ben tempo" to take his life in hand. The final line of sonnet 355 determines that "non a caso è vertute, anzi è bell'arte." The order he would like his life to represent is not achieved by aesthetic detachment or congenital drifting; it is a skill ("bell'arte"), requiring effort and conscious determination.

The pressure of time is an active determinant in Petrarch's new resolution. His remarkable historical importance—perhaps accounting for his present neglect — is demonstrated here. He most conspicuously shows the pattern that later Renaissance writers will follow.[21] In him we see the heroic setting-out, the high aspirations, the need for energetic response, the love of variety and experience. But in him we also see the sharp self-criticism and fear lest all his high ambitions result merely in personal fragmentation, lack of purpose, the absence of any vital self-concern. In Petrarch, as in his followers, time will be a critical agent in solidifying the individual consciousness, in calling out a new realistic determination and purposiveness. Time is the agent of limitation and reality that their high dreams encounter, and without extirpating their earlier hopes, it forces a profound personal reassessment and helps to effect a conversion from what could be called an "aesthetic" attitude toward life, with all its varying manifestations, to one of accepted, limited, historical and ethical reality. Under this new pressure, we can observe most of the writers with whom we deal taking a more aggressive or at least a more determining role in relation to their life. Of course, such gestures of taking hold, *carpe diem,* can occur under very different beliefs, decidedly religious or purely secular. Petrarch's decision to get control of his life results in a manifestly different program from that of Prince Hal, yet it is precisely because the figures of the fourteenth century, like Dante and Petrarch, differ so radically from the later men of the sixteenth century in the final goals toward which the temporal pressures compel them that the surprising number of constants in the argument of time becomes worthy of special attention.

The Argument of Time

Although time was always a real presence for Petrarch, it was only in his later years, he tells us, that he valued it properly. He concludes that time, like other things, becomes precious as it becomes scarce. This renewed and reaffirmed appreciation of time's force and power is an important part of Petrarch's spiritual evolution. Even if in his precocious responsiveness to the processes of time he felt himself different from his contemporaries, "Still I did not cherish it as I should have. I would, for instance, like to be able to say that I never wasted a day, but I wasted many, even, to my chagrin, years. But this I can say without fear of contradiction: as far as I can remember I did not waste a single day without being acutely aware of it. Time did not slip through my fingers, rather it was torn from me. Even when I was involved in some business or in the delights of pleasure it would still dawn on me 'Alas, this day is irretrievably gone.' I believe these contradictions existed because I had not yet given time its virtue value, the sort that Seneca intended when he wrote to Lucilius. I knew that time was precious, but I did not know it was priceless [inextimabile]." (*Fam.* XVI.11) Then in this letter on the preciousness of time (*quam cara res sit tempus*), he engages in a form of address which will recur in the argument of time: he turns to the young and the inexperienced and exhorts them to give credence to his new knowledge: "Young folk in the flower of your years, believe me, time is simply priceless."

Recurrently, time is an instrument of the ethical; it is the force invoked, the antagonist recognized when consciousness comes to grapple with its active life and attempts to exert some control over its direction and content. Despite his awareness of time's fleetingness and the brevity of life, Petrarch has not acted upon his knowledge; not being a lesson of experience, it has not passed into the practical realm where it might substantially affect behavior. Time must be more than an awareness, it must be experienced. In the 1350s, with his hair gray and his remaining years visibly short, Petrarch acutely senses how limited is his time and is equally determined not to waste or spare a moment. When he was younger, however uncertain he knew life to be, elemental hope was still more natural, and far from vanquished. Now, however, he and his hopes ("res et spes") are radically diminished. "Ego hec, que olim opinabar, scio et video." "Quod suspicabar experior." What he had believed on the testimony of others, he now experiences on his own account.

Once time is fully realized, new experience is sharply marked off from old illusion. Consequently, a sense of conversion becomes part of the argument of time. Conversion, we must recall, does not occur instantly; or at least, where there is changed behavior there must have been some prior disposition and preparation. The burning bush might only be the last straw. In Petrarch's life, conversion did occur over a period of years. Nevertheless, this does not dilute its force, certainly it does not in his own mind, so conscious of what he was and what he is, so sensitive to the "tunc" and the "nunc." He sends out his love *rime,* the products of "mio primo giovenile errore," with the clear addition that now, in part at least, he is a different man. They belong to a time "quand'era in parte altr'uom da quel ch'i'sono."

As it is normal that the difference between what we might call "aesthetic" and "ethical" realizations, between consciousness and experience, should be deeply involved with time, so, too, should the sense of conversion related to time, the sense of a sharply-marked difference (however lengthy and painful the process), between a period of delusion and one of experience. Given the energies and hopes of youth (at one point Petrarch writes that it is not in the nature of youth to appreciate time properly), it is also fairly inevitable that this contrast should be between the stages of youth and maturity (however belatedly the latter might arrive). These contrasts correspond to the more dramatic presentation of the pattern in the *Secretum,* where Augustine assumes the voice of the rational and concerned father while Petrarch himself is the personification of naive confidence. If we think back to the *Purgatorio* where Dante was under the strict tutelage of a time-conscious father figure, and if we think ahead to Shakespeare's sonnets and his history plays, we see that these two voices recur in the argument of time.

In Petrarch, as in Shakespeare (whatever their differences, and some of them are basic, as we shall see) this argument of time involves facts, attitudes, and requisite actions. The facts of time in Petrarch's poetry, major prose, and letters are two-fold, involving certainties and uncertainties. Time is swift and life is brief and all things move toward their ends. With some vehemence Augustine admonishes Petrarch in the *Secretum,* "In your blindness, you don't perceive the circling speed of the stars, whose flight devours and consumes the time of our most brief life, and so you are startled when old age is suddenly upon you." Death is certain for man, but the moment of its coming is uncertain. Time's massive regular procession can be awesome, and terrible, but for Petrarch even more horrible is the unexpected suddenness of death, that bitter finality of non-existence, where a few hours before there had been gay life.[22] Born in a time of optimism (however in exile), yet destined to survive through the dark decades of pestilence, Petrarch's hopefulness was clearly depressed by the terror of those times. As it did for Milton, the plague served to separate Petrarch from any long-range hopes in succession. In a letter of 1349 (*Fam.* VIII.8), Petrarch writes of Paganino da Milano, a man who survived the outbreak of the year before, and with whom Petrarch was enjoying a burgeoning friendship: "Now he too was suddenly snatched away by the pestilence that ravages the world. He dined in the evening with his friends, and afterward he spent some time with me in talk and in friendly discussion of our affairs. That night he was attacked. He bore his sufferings with a stout spirit; and in the morning death came swiftly. And that no evil should be spared him, within three days his children and his whole family followed him to the grave. Oh mortals, strain, strive, and sweat, range the earth and sea for riches you will not attain, for glory that will not last!" (Bishop, 75) More than once Petrarch quotes Cicero approvingly: "Death is certain, but uncertain in that it might occur this very day" ("Moriendum enim certum est, et id incertum ad hoc ipso die.") Time, in the Renaissance, as we see here in Petrarch's case, came increasingly to mean not only regular proceedings but quite the contrary — hard, unlooked-for confrontations.

In the face of the twin facts of certainty and uncertainty, insouciance or (still worse) procrastination is deplorable. Exasperation mounts as the experienced voice sets about to recall others from the attitude of heedlessness. Given the participants, this is not too unnatural, since the older voice is trying to instruct the younger man rationally in a truth whose full impact he himself was able to perceive only by experience. The lessons of time need to be acquired. Exhortation exists in rough

mixture with exasperation, and urgently tries to dispel the illusions
which prevent clear vision and essential action. Time is available for
freedom, yet that time is rapidly drawing to a close, and in no way can
any full "natural" length of time be relied upon. The young man is in
danger of squandering available means. While he still can, and his will
is free, he is urged to provide: "Proveggia ben, mentre è l'arbitrio in-
tero." (*Triumph of Time,* 44) While the kind of action can be largely
of a religious nature in Petrarch — placing one's hope in a locus of
greater permanence than earth — still the appeal, according to the argument of time, is to reason, free will, and effective action.

There are psychic and iconographic constants in Petrarch's argument
of time. The notion that the individual will have to give an account of
his use of time, the dread anticipation of the last day, the appeal to clear
vision, and the use of the true-seeing mirror all recur with consistency
and emphasis in his field of temporal interaction. Largely through his
use, they will become the common property of later writings on time.
In the Renaissance, the notion of being called to account is a blend of
Christian, mercantile, and classical thought. Examples are found in two
men mentioned in the introduction, Paolo da Certaldo and Domenico
Cavalca, in whose work the intermingling of various strands is clear.
For Cavalca the Biblical parable of the talents, and the fact that one
will be called to account for his stewardship ("sarà chiesta ragione")
are critical. But the need to balance one's books is also a commercial
bequest, and, in fact, the language of economics is used extensively
throughout the argument of time (as students of the earlier and latter
stages of its development have noticed).[23] This must be so once time
is regarded as a commodity to be used with diligent thrift. The early
Italian merger of Christian and mercantile ideas is sensed by Iris Origo
in her description of the merchant of Prato: "On the first page of Da-
tini's great ledgers stood the words, 'In the name of God and of profit,'
and these were the only goals to which these merchants aspired; profit
in this world or in the next, as if the whole of life were one vast count-
ing-house — and its end, the final Day of Accounting." [24]

Of classical writers, Seneca seems to have had greatest influence on
Petrarch's urgent sense of time. Along with the important reference to
time's preciousness (alluded to in *Fam.* XVI.11) and his attack on sub-
dividing time, in Seneca is also to found the notion of time as a personal
repsonsibility for which one eventually will have to render an explanation, if only to his own conscience. In the first of his *Epistles to Lucilius*

he develops his notions of time, almost, as it were, giving the basis for the following letters. As a mother hen over her brood, we must gather together and care for our time ("collige et serva"). The greatest crime is negligence of this precious commodity: "Nothing, Lucilius, is ours, except time. We are entrusted by nature with the ownership of this single thing, so fleeting and slippery that anyone who will can oust us from our possession. What fools these mortals be! They allow the cheapest and most useless things, which can easily be replaced, to be charged in the reckoning, after they have acquired them; but they never regard themselves as in debt when they have received time, and yet time is that one loan which even a grateful recipient cannot repay." As for himself, all things considered, Seneca feels that his accounts are in order: *ratio mihi constat inpensae*. He cannot claim that he has not wasted time, but he does know the reason and the manner of his losses. In conclusion he urges Lucilius (again, perhaps in prototype, constituting the personae of the argument of time): "I advise you, however, to keep what is really yours; and you cannot begin too early. For, as our ancestors believed, it is too late to spare when you reach the dregs of the cask [sera parsimonia in fundo est]. Of that which remains at the bottom, the amount is slight, and the quality is vile." [25]

As we shall see, much of Seneca's aroused militancy toward time will be appropriated by Petrarch. There is, however, a basic difference in their use of the call to account. Seneca looks backward at neglected opportunities, at an unlived life. Petrarch looks forward to the afterlife. For Seneca the moment of recognition may occur long before death, when one is already confronted with his wasted opportunities. For Petrarch the dread moment is the moment of death, that important last day, *dies extrema, supremus tempus,* when one must give an account of his living to God. In Petrarch's temporal anxieties it is the day of death toward which a man looks with such open-eyed fear. For him more moving than the regret of unfulfilled years is the terrifying prospect of damnation. The last day ("l'ultimo dì") thunders in his heart and waits threateningly in his imagination (s. 101). This is the moment for which one must prepare. All other pleasures and resources and regrets pale before this occasion when the soul must render a most strict account of its prior existence, as Augustine warns Petrarch in the *Secretum* ("totius vite preterite actuumque et verborum rationem exactissimam esse reddendam . . .").[26] This difference between Seneca and Petrarch — when and from what perspective the call to account occurs — is important, because on these matters the later Renaissance (and in particular Shakespeare) will be more similar to Seneca than to Petrarch.

Essential to the idea of accountability for Seneca as for Petrarch is the notion that time is a limited bequest (Petrarch in *Sen.* III.1 uses the image of a vase whose contents are slowly seeping out), for which the individual is personally responsible. This in itself represents a major revision of the medieval notion that time belonged to God (and hence usury — or charge for time-use — was unjust). Given the individual's stake in his time, he needs to be alert and vigilant, to have his eyes open. But there is some illusion in the mind that prevents the eyes from fully registering the testimony of their senses. For Petrarch, this illusion has two forms: the unexpressed confidence that the time of life is abundant, and the other deep-rooted optimism about life's possibilities. No one, he feels, seriously imagines that he will encounter that terrible wall of finality; everyone, enjoying what in military battle is the perhaps essential "exception syndrome," believes that he will still have time. "There are all kinds of men, and all sorts of things desired by them, but in this one hope they are all alike." (*Fam.* XXI.12) This hopefulness in its several forms is what prevents man from coping realistically with his mortality, and Petrarch's attitude toward hope is now decidedly different from what it was when he wrote *Fam.* III.19 ("On Indomitable Hope"). Over-confidence in time now proves to be a deception that leaves man unprepared not only for the full use of his life, but also for the more important Judgment. And yet it is natural that such delusion should plant itself in the way of a true vision of life. It is life's and time's function to deceive, to promise and then to take away. Not only Dante and Petrarch, but Shakespeare, too, consistently describes time in this way. It is only by experience, then, that one suddenly discovers, in a kind of revelation, his true condition. In order to spare the more deluded younger person from such bitter recognition, the older voice warns and admonishes. The advice to bestir oneself, to wake up, to open one's eyes is not merely a form of speech with Petrarch; these measures are necessary for the conversion required.

The dangers of blurred sight and the benefits of clear vision run throughout Petrarch's expostulations over time. In his youth he had been alerted through his reading to the brevity and uncertainty of life. But this acquired consciousness became obscured by his "youthful ardor and flings [iuvenilibus . . . amoribus et erroribus]." As he tells us, the smoke of things dulled his perception ("fumus rerum hebetavit visum") and clouded whatever natural light had been there. But now experience has repossessed him of what he had forgotten, or failed to act upon, and, he writes to a friend in XXIV.1, "now I know and I see, and you, if you do not blindfold your eyes, you too will see." So, too, in sonnet 355 experience restores sight:

> O tempo, o ciel volubil che fuggendo
> ingani i ciechi e miseri mortali,
> o dì veloci più che vento e strali,
> ora *ab experto* vostre frodi intendo.

> O time, O turning heavens which
> fleeing deceive blind and miserable mortals,
> O days faster than wind or arrow, now from
> experience I understand your fraud.

But such deception is not time's fault; like Dante's *fortuna,* it becomes a regular functionary of the cosmos, merely performing its appointed tasks. "Ma scuso voi," Petrarch commences the next stanza,

> e me stesso riprendo,
> che natura a volar v'aperse l'ali,
> a me diede occhi, ed io pur ne' miei mali
> li tenni, onde vergogna e dolor prendo.

> But I excuse you, and blame myself, since
> nature to fly gave you wings and to me gave
> eyes, but I in my own evil ways held
> them shut, whence I now derive sorrow and shame.

That he might not end up ruined by such false intelligence, "I am now beginning to open my eyes." (*Fam.* XXI.12) Indeed, given the Christian dispensation, it is better late than never. Where he was once prodigal of his time, he is now, as this letter relates, "sparing, even stingy."

Concomitant with this insistence on clear sight, and an important object in the iconography of time, is the faithful mirror, one that gives a true account of the passage of the years.[27] Besides plain experience, the source of this association is probably Horace (*Odes,* IV.10.2–6): "when rosy features have changed, you'll say 'alas,' seeing yourself in the looking-glass" ("dices 'heu' quotiens te speculo videris alterum"). This same passage is quoted in *Fam.* XXIV.1 and in the *De remediis* (I.2), where Ratio urges Gaudium to place his trust in "true and enduring goods, not false and passing." A day will come when he will not recognize himself in his mirror. "If you listen to me now," Ratio argues, "in the future you will be spared a shock at your transformation." (*Prose,* 614–616) In the *Secretum,* Augustine refers frequently to Petrarch's blindness.[28] "Nor," he adds, "was I fooling when I suggested that you look in a mirror. Remember what Seneca wrote in his *Natural Problems*: that mirrors were invented so that man should know himself."(*Prose,* 184) And in the *Rime* (as in the *Triumph of Death,* 55–57), although its uses are multiple, the mirror is an instrument of final, accurate insight:

> Dicemi spesso il mio fidato speglio,
> l'animo stanco e la cangiata scorza
> e la scemata mia destrezza e forza:
> "Non ti nasconder più, tu se' pur veglio."

> Frequently I am told by my faithful mirror,
> my tired soul, my wrinkled skin and my
> diminished uprightness and strength: "Don't
> hide it any more, you are now an old man."

Although time is a critical enemy in the "Coronation Oration," and Petrarch stoutly maintains the triumph of art over time, it is in the *Secretum* and later works that the argument of time is specifically used — and mainly to religious purposes. From its reliances on future rewards in the realm of succession, the wayward understanding is admonished, by the brevity of life and the uncertainty of death, to abandon its habits of deferral and to take hold of its life in the present.[29] Petrarch's hopes in the realm of succession are ill founded, Augustine argues. And should he chance to realize his dreams of great accomplishment, a fulfillment that is granted only to few, fame itself has limitations that the severe bishop is only too willing to present in detail.[30] But even this curtailed success cannot be taken for granted in a world as precarious as the one Petrarch has come to know. Gaping after the future, Petrarch neglects what is present and important ("Venturis inhiantes presentia non curatis"). Why does he spend so much effort on work of such uncertain outcome ("exitum inceriti")? Augustine constantly warns Petrarch of the uncertainties in his natural faith, and thereby represents a fear of sudden death, with his work unaccomplished, that particularly haunted Petrarch. Would it not be terrible if, before he had completed his *Africa* and *De viris,* death should strip from his hand his laboring pen ("utroque inexpleto opere, mors calamum fatigatum e manibus rapiat"), "and thus, because of your immoderate searching for glory, you hurry down two roads, and in neither do you achieve your destination." (*Prose,* 192)

Distractedness and ambition are the charges that Petrarch levels at himself in the famous letter concerning the ascent of Mont Ventoux. They are parts of a larger confidence and optimism which, if we recall Millard Meiss, was the essential faith of early Renaissance Florence: Petrarch hopes for glory in this life and salvation in the next, presuming that the demands of this life and the needs of salvation are one. With a sense of terror that the plague was to confirm, Augustine pounces on this illusion: "O man, little in yourself, and of little wisdom! Do you, then, dream that you shall enjoy every pleasure in heaven and earth, and everything will turn out to be prosperous and fortunate for you always and everywhere? But that delusion has betrayed thousands of men thousands of times, and has sunk into hell countless hosts of souls. Thinking to have one foot on earth and one in heaven they could neither stand here below nor mount on high. Therefore, they fell miserably, and the moving breeze swept them suddenly away, some in the flower of their age, and some when they were in the midst of their years and all their business." He then applies this hard law to Petrarch's own case, warning him of the bitter recognition such an unlooked-for confrontation would cause: "And do you suppose what has befallen so many others may not befall you? Alas! if (which may God forbid) in the midst of all your plans and projects you should be cut off — what grief, what shame, what remorse (then too late!) that you should have grasped at all and lost all." (*Prose,* 200) The general association of Augustine and time becomes reinforced in the early Renaissance literary mind, when his severe sense of life becomes the interlocutor expressing life's vicissitudes and uncertainties.[31]

This "naive" trust in life has two very specific forms in Petrarch, both of which, interrelated, presume on an order in the realm of natural succession. One expression of this natural faith is the notion that the order of death follows the order of birth, that the oldest will die first. Consequently, Petrarch affirms dramatically in the *Secretum* that he will never see Laura dead; that since he is older he will predecease her. *Prius entravi, prius egrediar.* But this presumption of regular functioning is folly, Augustine warns: "O what folly to deduce the order of death from the order of birth! What does bereaved old age lament if not the precocious death of its sons? . . . This small number of years by which you have preceded her is a weak basis on which to build your hopes that you will die before her, the source of all your folly. You think that this order of nature is immutable." (*Prose*, 138–140) The plague of 1348 defeated that hope (perhaps an indication that the writing of the *Secretum* continued well beyond the 1343 period normally given, and that Augustine here is voicing as warning a fear that had already materialized); and similarly, under the renewed outbreak of the plague in the 1360s, Petrarch's letters again lament how ill founded is the hope in nature's order. The *Seniles*, begun in 1361, bear as one of their major burdens the cluster of deaths which removed from Petrarch's life several friends and his young son Giovanni. This last death was particularly bitter not only because of his youth (he was not yet 24), but because Giovanni had shown signs of reforming a life that had been painful to his father. But Petrarch, like Job, will not accuse divine providence; he is compelled to recognize "That he who gave has taken away. We must not cry out against death, which has merely exercised its rights, or against fate, or against nature. We must not seek an order in the world that has never existed." (Bishop, 224) In a later letter (III.1), lamenting the death of Simonides, to whom the *Seniles* were dedicated, Petrarch relapses into the old questioning: "Why was he the first to leave this bitter road of life who of all our group was the last to enter it?" Then Petrarch mildly rebukes himself for needing new lessons in the facts that have in the past so forcefully been taught him: "already through thousands and thousands of cases I have learned that in this respect there is no order in human life."

Even in later letters, the same desolate discovery is mentioned. He consoles Donato Albanzani in *Sen.* X.4 on the death of his son (lamenting also over the death of his own grandson, Francesco). In these deaths there should be no surprise, nor should it be said that they died before their time, since nowhere is the length of life appointed ("cui nullus est ascriptus dies"). And in *Sen.* XIII.1, written to Niccolo, the Marquis of Este, on the death of his brother Ugo, he states more fully his realization of life's lack of order: "I did not think it possible that he would have died before me, nor could it have occurred if there were any order in human life. It did happen, however, because here there is no order, no constancy, no stable and certain joy."

One other faith by which Petrarch clings to the realm of succession, and which underlies his habit of postponement and his confidence in time, is his acceptance of stages of life. Such segmentation is artificial, Augustine warns, and has the added danger of inducing a kind of temporal laziness, the belief that there are periods of safety in which some practices are permitted which can be corrected at another period. After sowing one's wild oats, there will be time to make the proper recompense with one's soul. This is another assumption that Augustine denounces: "This most restricted extent of human life you divide some in four parts, some in six, and others in still smaller particles, as if not being able to enlarge life in its length you increase the number of its sections. But of what use is this segmentation. Imagine as many parts as you want, the whole will still be gone in the wink of an eye. . . . In vain you try to extend that which the law of nature, our common parent, constricts." (*Prose,* 180) And in another place he urges Petrarch not to be deceived by the large number of days or the elaborate stages of life ("etatis operosa distinctio"): "all of human life, no matter how it is extended, has the length of a day, and sometimes not even that." (*Prose,* 210)

The same thought is repeated in XXIV. 1, under the shadow of the ninetieth psalm: "Let us divide life into as many parts as we like, let us multiply the number of years, and invent names for the various stages, nevertheless the life of man is only a day, and a wintry one at that." The tone is Hebraic, Augustinian, but the specific argument against the stages of life derives from Seneca's forty-ninth epistle: "An event which in its entirety is of brief compass cannot contain long intervals. The time which we spend in living is but a point, nay, even less than a point. But this point of time, infinitesimal as it is, nature has mocked by making it seem outwardly of longer duration; she has taken one portion thereof and made it infancy, another childhood, another youth, another the gradual slope, so to speak, from youth to old age, and old age is still another. How many steps for how short a climb!" [32]

Besides having an important place in Petrarch's argument of time, these reflections have for us the added advantage of showing the significance of a commonplace which, as modern scholars, we are too content at times merely to recount. The stages of life invest natural succession with a greater regularity than it has, whereas the direction of Petrarch's thought tended toward less faith in life's possibilities and in mere succession. Life is as uncertain for the young as for the old. In fact, "sepe tutior est qui minus sperat." There are no periods of safety, and since youth is more inclined to believe there are, it is frequently a more perilous stage than old age. We can see how one part — perhaps the most powerful part — of Petrarch's personality differs from the confidence a Wife of Bath or a Montaigne has in time. Both feel that *chaque chose a sa saison,* that some things are allowable in youth and other things more appropriate for age. But for Augustine in the *Secretum* it is shameful for man to waste the best years of his life in frivolities, and reserve the dregs for serious devotion to God. Even if Petrarch were certain of the future, is not this postponement of better things ("meliora postponere") an inversion of their right order? Behind Petrarch's rejection of a reliance on the stages of life there are definite questions of value and significance which set him in clear contrast to others with greater confidence in nature.

However unwilling Petrarch was to give himself over totally to the Augustinian view, he was indebted to that spokesman for a profound and enduring part of his mental habits. In the decades that followed, though he did not choose the monastic life for himself, he was, like many literary men with strong religious instincts, not too far from the yew tree. In fact, this clarification of religious priorities seems to have had a salutary effect on his personal economy. He finally seemed satisfied that he was converting his energy to more effective use. Once careless of time, he now proved avaricious of it. Although never perhaps fulfilling his ideals, in the fifties Petrarch made distinct strides toward the proper recognition of time and the fuller application of his energies to goals that he thought more and more worth while.

From Milan in August 1353, he writes the letter on the preciousness of time, "quam cara res sit tempus" (*Fam.* XVI.11), to which we have referred several times. Now that it is beginning to leave him, he begins to take account of time ("tempus agnoscere"). He recognizes its incredible flight and its precipitous fall. But these recognitions, instead of depressing his capacities, seem to call forth heroic energy. Time of such force cannot be braked except by means of ardent and tireless virtue ("nullis nisi ardentis atque impigre virtutis arcendum frenis"). He then goes on to enumerate the practical steps he is taking to save time: his letters will be briefer, with a more subdued style and simpler sentences.

His Augustine had attacked the more artificial means of enlarging the space of life, but Petrarch in a letter of 1359 (*Fam.* XXI.12), "de laxandis temporum angustiis sistendaque vite fuge," sets out to show precisely, not only how it can be done, but how he is doing it. The language is from Seneca's epistle XLIX, on the shortness of life: "angustias temporis mei laxa," but the remarkable energy of the piece is Petrarchan and Renaissance. Paradoxically, such economic and dedicated utilization of time occurs only when Petrarch himself rejects the notion of life as stretching into some unlimited future and instead regards it as definitely coming to a close. A new liberation is achieved when the soul is disposed to love the end of its life. This recognition of limitation preserves desire from the insatiable craving which is *concupiscentia.* The ideal for Petrarch would be Seneca's rounded life, and he quotes from epistle XXXII, "vivere vita peracta," to live a life completed. But, as usual, Petrarch is on neither one side nor the other, but somewhere in between. While he inclines by preference toward the vision of being that Seneca describes, he has not attained it. Nevertheless, he has come to live more in the present and to set limits on his prospects: "I am one of that flock whose life holds the middle way, whose life has no sense of completion, but neither is it dragged at length or driven by *concupiscentia.* Other things, many other things I desire, but these are limited; the goals that remain do not require centuries for completion, but they do require time and they fear life's brevity. Which is why I said that the art of expanding that narrowness is necessary." (XXI.12)

Confronted with the fallacy of his earlier hopefulness and feeling the pressures of time's passage in the stark brevity of his remaining years, Petrarch issues a typical Renaissance call to action. The hour is late, and the necessity is clear. And with the mounting urgency increase also his determination and resolution (and the staccato rhythm of his sentences): "This is not time for joking, believe me. We shall be surprised and defeated in the middle of our enterprises unless we wake up and make defense, and unless we resist with all the strength of our soul we shall be beaten down."

The cry of alarm is natural to the argument of time. It is the language of military attack, especially on a drowsy and unaware citadel. And for the men of the Renaissance it is the call for an awakening and response that shakes off the sloth and numbness of a long sleep. In the *De remediis* (I.1) Ratio cries out, "Expergiscimini, consopiti: tempus est, caligantesque oculos aperite!" ("Wake up you sleepyheads, it is time; open your glazed eyes!") In the *Secretum* and the *Africa* the passage of time is likened to a sneak attack on a slumbering camp, a Trojan horse ready to burst upon the sleepy populace. As in Seneca, time arouses to militancy, and inspires an aggressive seizure and taking in hand. Seneca urges Lucilius, "comes horas complectere," and Petrarch, with a literal vengeance, vows to make up for lost time, to be avaricious where time is concerned: "This I grasp, this I hold, that I might restore the ruins of lost time."

In a fairly typical way in *Fam.* XXI.12, he proceeds to draw up a schedule to make sure that no amount of this precious commodity is wasted. His *emploi du temps* is not as full as Rabelais', nor is it as smug as that of Benjamin Franklin, but it is a time schedule nevertheless.[33] Although Augustus allotted seven hours to sleep, Petrarch tries to get by on six. Two hours he gives to other necessaries, and the remainder are for study. He maintains that such a regimen is possible, and shows the fervor that can co-exist with such system, quoting the Horatian "Nil mortalibus arduum." In tone we are back again with the "Coronation Oration" and with the related letter to King Robert; we are in the midst of the heroic Renaissance, where nothing is impossible to human energy and will. It is only sloth and torpor, those unadventurous conditions of human sluggishness, that prevent us from pushing our strengths to superhuman levels. Humanism, as it would do later, invokes the heroic, the gigantesque. Such performance is rare, Petrarch acknowledges, but its rarity ought to make it more desirable. Toward this heroic end, Petrarch is determined to utilize every moment. Like Augustus, while shaving or having his hair cut, he is accustomed to reading or writing, or being read to, or dictating to some scribe. And — a practice he feels is unique (he does not remember having come across it in his reading) — he does the same even while riding horseback or eating. "What?" Montaigne would later complain, "next they'll have us shitting on the run." But Petrarch is delighted with the almost inhuman dedication of resources that he always found desirable yet wanting in himself, and the concentrated drive that he always envied in others. He describes with some pride a testimony of his own involvement, and an experience that every writer who is working well knows: such total absorption in a work, such full-powered involvement that ideas occur to him in his sleep, and he must force himself up out of bed to scratch on a shred of paper some urgent notion he will have difficulty deciphering in the morning light.

Rabelais' educational regimen for the young Gargantua almost naturally comes to mind when we observe in Petrarch that strange alliance of energy and tight scheduling. In fact, this conjunction of unlikely bedfellows is the basic problem of time in the Renaissance: on the one hand, time is a cosmic force and a fervid discovery, but it is a cosmic force that leads to, and even extols, practical prudence and mundane virtues; it is a passionate discovery that translates itself into system and schedule. In the course of the Renaissance, these differing approaches, united in the greatest writers, will come to assume positions of separation and antagonism. Rival energies though they might become, in Petrarch and Rabelais and Shakespeare they seem to abet each other. In Petrarch we see the purpose of imposing a system: it effectively reduces the demands of the body, and hence transcends its needs. Such maximum exploitation of time in writers like Rabelais and Petrarch is introduced so as to forget time. Petrarch has discovered a psychological fact which Piaget would render in a quasi-physical formula:

> Psychological time is the time of work accomplished in relation to the speed of the activity in progress, or motor activity. . . . We are all well aware that an interesting task seems to cover a shorter period of time than a boring one. What is interesting . . . is the mobilization of the strength of the individual when he whole-heartedly attacks a task important to him. On the other hand, boredom, disinterest, disassociation, can cause visible diminution of strength, or in other words, a shutting off of available energy.
>
> Consequently, remembering the relationship according to which time = work ÷ power, if one increases the power, the time seems to diminish. By contrast, during a period of expectation, the inverse occurs.[34]

We see here the close association between two fundamental Renaissance characteristics: its sense of human energy and its sense of time. One can become oblivious to time, not only when he is indifferent, but also when he is totally aroused by its consequences; then the energy that is released can be all-consuming and one forgets the clock. We can see how intrinsic to the Renaissance is the language of revivification and arousal by which Petrarch warns of the insidious attack of time. What is a man, Hamlet would cry out, if his chief good and market of his time be but to sleep and feed? Time, in between sleeping and feeding, is tedious for Rabelais' slumbering giant; indifferent to the message of time, he is nevertheless distracted from his weighty studies, his eyes on his books, but his heart in the kitchen. But with his new humanistic mentors and their rigorous sense of time in the direction of his studies, time is lost sight of as energy is awakened. For the men of the Renaissance their activism, as well as the products of their labor, is time-transcendent.

When we think back to the "Coronation Oration," we realize that in isolating Petrarch's tremendous energy and heroic busyness we are dealing not with an incidental part of his character but rather with an enduring stratum of his personality. Even in pieces more exclusively concerned with the salvation of his soul, the same kind of aroused exploitation of time is apparent. In September of 1348 or 1349 Petrarch wrote a long letter (*Fam.* X.3) to his brother Gherardo, urging him to "banish sloth and languor; when you are waken in the morning, think that you are summoned to a conversation with God." (Bishop, 98)

In a letter (*Fam.* XXII.10) that marks a very specific stage of religious conversion, Petrarch shows the same eagerness and wholeheartedness: "Nor am I to be criticized, if I, who so often used to rouse by night to work for empty fame and celebrate the futile lauds of men, should now arise at midnight to recite the lauds of my creator, and devote the hours proper to quiet and repose to him who shall neither slumber nor sleep while he keepeth Israel." (Bishop, 190–191) Even when we look to the end of Petrarch's life, that period of most pronounced religious dedication, we find him resisting any diminution in his life-giving habits of study and writing. In a letter to Boccaccio in 1373 (*Sen.* XVII.2), he counters most vociferously the younger man's suggestion that he retire. Boccaccio praises Petrarch, as he had done in the letter to Jacopo Pizzingha, as the leader in the revival of learning we have come to call the Renaissance. But Petrarch refuses to accept the conclusion that his work is, as a consequence, completed. Rather than retire he will continue to serve as a model for the young, through his own prolonged activity. To Boccaccio's suggestion that men of his day, unlike the ancients, come to old age earlier, Petrarch takes up the argument of his letter to King Robert. Resisting the implications of historical decline, he declares that such ideas are used to belittle the industry of the ancients and to excuse the laziness of the moderns ("ad deprimendam veterum industriam et excusandam ignaviam modernarum"). Petrarch goes on to affirm that "constant work and application are the food of my soul (labor iugis et intentio pabulum animi mei sunt); when I begin to relax and look for repose you can be sure then that I shall soon cease to exist." (Bishop, 301–302)

In the same year as this letter to Boccaccio, Petrarch addresses to a young Augustinian monk, Luigi Marsili, a letter (*Sen.* XV.6) urging him to make fullest use of his time. It is a duty of the young to marshal their forces so that not one day is wasted. The young especially must avoid laziness and not be deceived by an unconscious reliance on the length of life. When young one must hurry, if he wants to enjoy the fruits of his labor when he is old, if he wants to live through fame beyond the tomb, live, as Ennius says, "on the tongues of the wise." Another practical suggestion Petrarch advances is frequent stock-taking — a suggestion Alberti would later act upon. As a provident master of the house will do with his steward, so the individual ought to call himself to account. Not one day ought to have passed without his having done something of value. And if in his daily examinations he finds that he has done nothing, that day is wasted: on that day he did not live. Petrarch concludes the letter by urging Luigi Marsili to compose a refutation of Averroes, something Petrarch had long intended, but never fully achieved. Adding to the chain of continuity, it is to this same Luigi Marsili that Petrarch passes on the copy of Augustine's *Confessions* that he had received much earlier from another Augustinian monk, Dionigi da Borgo San Sepolcro (*Sen.* XV.7).

Despite our emphasis on the unattached, cosmopolitan, and solitary Petrarch, we must not imagine him isolated to the extent that he ignored the larger issues of his day, especially when Rome was the matter. The great concerns of Petrarch's later years were the receding twin ideals of medieval universalism: an Emperor and a Pontiff both established in Rome. In each concern, undeniably the humanistic picture of Rome's past greatness played a large part. And in Petrarch's exhortations to the religious and secular leaders, a substantial part of his argument utilizes various facets of the argument of time. So deeply part of Petrarch's consciousness is the impression of time's uncertainties, the dangers of postponement, and the calling to account, that the issues of his most personal crisis are given public force and persuasiveness. As in Shakespeare, the argument of time links the private and the public, showing the personal experience behind the public decision. So, too, Rome and the argument of time go hand-in-hand. The pressures of time are spurs to great actions for which the preeminent model is Rome. In fact, in one of his most vibrant letters to Charles IV (*Fam.* XXIII.2), he gives ten quotations from Latin authors describing time's transience, death's finality, and the need for virtuous actions if one is to live through fame.

In a letter assigned to 1350–1351 Petrarch exhorts the soon-to-be-crowned Charles to assume his rightful position in Rome. Why does he delay, wasting his time in counsels, "quasi venturis certus"? The affairs of men do not suffer dilatoriness: "Life is uncertain and fleeting, and although you are in the flower of your youth, it is still unstable and continually flies and consumes itself; without your being aware every day carries you toward old age. While you are looking around, while you delay, suddenly grey hair is upon you." (*Fam.* X.1) Petrarch's plea is urgent: life's uncertainties brook no delay. And what is most useful for a man intent on great actions," singulos dies magni extima": time is the only thing of which people should be avaricious; one must weigh out each day. If he is a friend to virtue, if he is desirous of glory, Charles will busy himself now with the great task that Petrarch envisions. In *Fam.* XXIII.2, written, as Petrarch tells us, eleven years after the earlier one, this insistence on present action forms the impassioned heart of his appeal. The present is all we have; the past is only a memory and the future is unknown: "Why do we always reach after what is absent? Let us seize hold [complectamur] of the present lest it slip away from us, let us endeavor [enitamur]." In fact, throughout this letter the language of revival and arousal is very common: "Excute torporem," "Expergiscere . . . hora est."

The temporal urgency behind these letters derives from the fear of the final call to account. If the individual is accountable for the use he has made of his time, think how much more will be the demands made on an emperor (in the letter to Pope Urban V [*Sen.* VII.1] the same will be said). To himself, to his age, to the ensuing centuries, and finally to the Eternal Emperor he will have to give an account. He was not given his temporal rule so that he should possess the signs of government in name only, but so that he might reign and rule and make the downtrodden his concern. Urban will be reminded that his position is not a gift outright, but one for which he will have to render a personal account. Such personal responsibility is a crucial aspect of the Renaissance argument of time. "Why do you hold yourself back" Petrarch asks the emperor, "why, looking towards tomorrow, do you neglect the things of today?" Whatever tomorrow requires, you or someone else can take care of; the time will not be lacking in their leaders, and if they are, it is not your fault. You take care, he urges the emperor, that you are not wanting unto your own time ("Tu ne tempori tuo non desis, cura . . .").

Temporal Ease and "Readiness"

Petrarch's letters are artfully controlled and manipulated in arrangement for proper effect. They do not have that searching, immediate quality suggested by Montaigne's *essais*. Nevertheless, in the familiar and unsystematic nature of Petrarch's studied reflections, he is as hard to pin down and at times as complex in his many ways of regarding his subjects as Montaigne. He has that quality of double vision so important for the fourteenth century (and, I suppose, for any great writer): at one time active and fervently heroic, and at another time, or perhaps even coincidentally, rising above the furor, distancing himself, to regard with "magnificent contempt" the vanities of our endeavor. At not too great a separation in time, Petrarch can write *Fam.* XXI.12, exhorting the necessity and demonstrating the art of managing one's time, and XXIV.1, "de inextimabili fuga temporis," where such art is farthest from his mind, and where the vision rises to the withering prospect of the ninetieth psalm, which he quotes. Curiously enough, this letter serves to introduce the last book of familiar letters, which is devoted to the re-establishment of communication with the masters of the ancient world. "De inextimabili fuga temporis" he seems to regard as the suspension under which historical discourse takes place.

But the important attitude to which Petrarch came most clearly and abundantly in the 1360s is somewhere in between activism and nothingness. In his letters of this period a new sense of patient trust is expressed, introducing a higher tone of spirit into what had threatened to be the pure monotony of bustling exhortation. God's lordship over time becomes one of his favorite themes. He is the "etatum temporumque omnium Conditor," the "omnium temporum Auctor" and the "Rex seculorum." Petrarch promises, as he turns away from secular to sacred literature, to devote his hours, as we quoted earlier, "to him who shall neither slumber nor sleep while he keepeth Israel; nor is he content with universal custodianship, but he watches over me personally, and is solicitous for my welfare. I am clearly conscious of this, and all men capable of gratitude must feel the same. He cares for each individual as if he were forgetful of mankind *en masse;* and so he rules the mass as if he were careless of each individual. Thus I have it firmly fixed in my mind that if it be heaven's will I shall spend the rest of my life in these studies and occupations." (Bishop, 191) Now his orators will be Ambrose, Augustine, Jerome, and Gregory; his philosopher Paul and his poet David. The same elevation of the Psalms we shall encounter in Milton when that poet also moves forward, with patient trust, into a world of uncertainty.

In times of trouble people seem especially prone to look for certainty in the future and to try, by whatever means, to decipher the cryptic time to come, even if the message relayed portends disaster. This will always be, T. S. Eliot tells us in "The Dry Salvages,"

> especially
> When there is distress of nations and perplexity
> Whether on the shores of Asia, or in the Edgware Road.
> Men's curiosity searches past and future
> And clings to that dimension.

And there was indeed much perplexity in the second half of the fourteenth century, especially for Petrarch in the 1360s, when pestilence broke out with renewed ferocity, and there seemed to be no reprieve from its devastating blows. And, as in Milton's time in the 1660s under similar circumstances, prognostication abounded. Boccaccio in particular, through some guilty ascetic susceptibility, seemed especially sensitive to such predictions. In *Seniles* I.5, III.1, VIII.1, and VIII.8, Petrarch is forced to calm him, to restore his faith in the rightness of literature and give evidence of his own faith against the incursions of fanatic monks, astrologers, and superstitions about the sixty-fourth year. Petrarch, like Milton in *Paradise Regained*, and for essentially the same reasons, will vehemently attack the illusions and presumptions of such predatory quackery. Such intrusions into the unknown future violate the prerogatives of divinity; they are products of a prideful misconception of man's true position in the world and attest to a lack of Christian faith. Importantly enough, then, the portents and devices of augury in Milton's masterpiece are diabolical suggestions, tempting Christ from his true way of proving his divinity. Dante, too, in placing the divinators in Hell, can ask, "Chi è piu scellerato che colui / che al giudicio divin passion porta?" ("Who is more guilty than he who makes the divine counsel subject to his will?" *Inf.* XX.29–30). And for most of these writers divination, as the word itself suggests, represents a false understanding of the world. In fact, with some consistency in this study augury will be defied whenever true being is approached.

In a world of universal shipwreck such information is trivial. What surprise is there in being told that disasters are imminent? As Montaigne, writing in another period of turmoil, would say, one does not need to go to the heavens for such a report. Indeed, the monk of Siena is privileged if he can assure Boccaccio and Petrarch of a year of life. Life is a continual dying. "We are all hurrying along . . . Nature herself carries us toward a reunion with the extinct. There is no rest; there is no stopping." (*Sen.* I.3) We are not in the world of assured continuities but rather in the inscrutable world of divine comedy. "We came crying hither" is inauspicious enough for King Lear and shows the tragic dimensions of his awareness. "From the day that we are born," writes Petrarch in *Sen.* I.7, "we are surrounded with dangers, trouble, hardship, and sorrow, and even though they do not descend on us immediately, still at every hour we mortals must expect them." It is foolish to fear or lament what must be. Yet it is just such recognition and acceptance of man's mortal condition that augury opposes. "They [augurers] disturb the present life and trouble it with lying fears of the future." (*Sen* I.7) Rather than peace their false knowledge seems to provoke fear and temporal anxiety, propelling the agitated souls madly and destroying any quiet and dignified faith.

Augury and medicine, unfortunately, are sometimes scarcely separate in Petrarch's mind. For him they both cling to the dimension of the future, and both try to eke out our years. Neither, however different their means, seems to prepare the individual to meet the closing rhythms of his own life. Life is not open-ended, Petrarch believes, and essential peace comes when man admits this fact, when he makes himself familiar with the notion of his own death. A greater human dignity seems to be achieved when, impatient with the need to be perpetually adding on years, one can say, "I have lived long enough." This is the basic argument of Petrarch's letter (*Sen.* XII.1) to one of the few doctors whom he respects, rejecting three of the doctor's six suggestions for better health. (Petrarch was sixty-six and trying to recover from a serious illness.) Whatever his superficial arguments might be, the fundamental source of Petrarch's disinclination to place himself in the tow of medical knowledge is his willingness to say "satis vixi." One must eventually be freed from the need to cling to life and to fear death, "otherwise our desires will never have an end . . . we will feed ourselves on illusions, and we will always need to appear and act youthful until death elicits the truth." It is in the attitudes they inspire — the need to hold onto life and the unwillingness to admit the fact of death — that the bogus peepers into the future and the doctors who are committed to keeping the patient alive, no matter at what level of capacity, disturb the quest for being, that final dignified attitude of readiness for death whenever it might come.

Most significantly, here and in other places, it is to the attitude of Job, and his very phrasing, that Petrarch turns, as other writers will do, in his attempt to express this readiness: "I shall live as long as it pleases Him of whom it is written, 'You have set the limits beyond which it is impossible to pass.' Gratefully always yielding myself to God, I shall hold myself ready to live or to die as he wills [paratus ad utrumlibet, seu ille vivere iubeat seu mori]." [35] Again and again, in I.7, III.1, VII.2, and here in XII.1 he explicitly confronts the larger world's hopelessness with the language of Job. "Keep in mind," he urges Francesco Bruni in *Sen.* I.7, "that old man, much tried in hardship but unsubdued, who was the voice of patience itself. When speaking with God he said, 'Then call thou and I will answer.' So, too, let us be ready for our call [observemus et nos revocatorem nostrum]." Similarly, in *Sen.* III.1 he will justify this translation of "readiness," when he writes, again echoing Job, "we must live in such a way that we are always ready to be called, not allowing any new or unforeseen thing to frighten us [ut parati simus dum vocabimur, ne quasi res nova ac improvisa nos terreat]." In a letter to Boccaccio praising old age (*Sen.* VIII.2) Petrarch writes of his willingness to leave his death to the "judgment of Him, of whom it is written, that he directs the steps of men and has prefixed the end of each man, even the number of his months and days, in comparison with whom a thousand years are as yesterday that has passed. 'Ipse vocabit me, et ego respondebo sibi.' "

More incumbent than the simple repetition of instances (however admirable they are) is a closer inspection that isolates the moral and psychological components that give such special majesty and lyric appeal to this condition of readiness. Of first importance to this attitude is trust in a providential cosmic power, in particular reference to the moment of death. Death is the fact that occupies the center of the argument of time and being, the obstacle over which the aspiring, questing Renaissance energy breaks down. The fundamental division between the continuities of civilization and the race and the mortal, limited condition of the single life is shown by death. The normal temporal rewards then seem distant and vicarious to the man who requires a more personal possession of fulfillment. This is the particular relevancy of "readiness" for time: it marks the point at which man is prepared to gather together his individual life. Unless man is willing to do this, to confront his life as close-ended, not as infinitely stretching into some desired future, he will be the constant prey of what Petrarch has called *concupiscentia,* and rather than countering time, his aroused energies will merely comply with time's own insatiability. But the danger here is fear, some blind and irrational panic in the soul that refuses to accept and transcend the inevitable. Martin Heidegger acutely analyzes this fear that results in such bewildered and vague thrashing: "This bewilderment is based upon a forgetting. When one forgets and backs away in the face of the factical potentiality-for-Being which is resolute, one clings to those possibilities of self-preservation and evasion which one has already discovered circumspectively beforehand. When concern is afraid, it leaps from next to next, because it forgets itself and does not take hold of any definite possibility. Every "possible" possibility offers itself, and this means that impossible ones do so too." [36] It was such unwillingness to face the fact of death that caused the distractedness and lack of definition that Augustine had charged in the *Secretum.* But in the condition of readiness we are outside the narrow bounds and the purgatorial astringency of that argument. Readiness involves an end to questing, an absence of fear, but also, more positively, an air of happiness, a kind of blessed release from burden, when one gives up the anxious attempt to control that one area of human life that cannot be controlled. A kind of resoluteness is implied, as man, with clear sight and free will, embraces an action that he cannot escape. Petrarch even shows a heroic abandon in a letter to the Paduan ruler Francesco da Carrara (*Sen.* XIV.1): "Why worry about the future, if even our next hour is not sure? Leave aside these worries. Is it not written, 'Abandon yourself into the arms of the Lord: he shall think to feed thee; nor will he leave the just man eternally in his troubles.'" This is not absolutely sound advice to give to a political leader, but even such leaders must at times take their chances, and give up the policy-ridden attempts to anticipate what will happen. Petrarch is here writing in refutation of the proverbial expression, "I am here today, but where will I be tomorrow?" and the grim need for calculation and provision that such a fear inspires. As an example of the opposite point of view, an interesting comparison can be made with Paolo da Certaldo's maxim 305. It too has as its premise the terrible uncertainties of the future, and it also attempts to contradict a proverb very similar to the one just quoted. Yet Paolo da Certaldo proceeds obliquely from the carefreeness and abandon that Petrarch had recommended. This representative of the merchant mentality, whose book is a model of prudence and reserve, urges renewed diligence. Since man does not know what the future holds, one should always work and labor for gain ("Sempre t'affatica e ti procaccia di guadagnare"). Petrarch, to be sure, does not urge prodigality, but he specifically counters the kind of desire and tight-fisted fear that unrelenting industry promotes. Despite their loose similarities and common premises, we can mark here a clear divergence between the literary-religious interests and the commercial.

But the same niggardliness of spirit that dominates the need to be constantly "getting" can also prevail in humanism. One can hold back spiritually as well as monetarily. The need for intellectual order and aesthetic prearrangement can shy away from risking the unknown. For this reason readiness means not stasis but forward movement. Petrarch trusts in God and awaits his call, but he also proceeds courageously: "procedo interea indies laetior." (*Sen.* VIII.2) He goes more happily about his daily business. The unforeseen and the new, those things that gave the Renaissance mind such pause, and that it labored to limit and control, no longer hold terror for him ("ne quasi res nova ac improvisa nos terreat"). In this forward movement without fear of the irrational, we can think of *Hamlet* and the end of "Lycidas."

A lightening (although not into what could be called gaiety) and a sense of release must accompany this new-found freedom. That larger and final shipwreck that casts its shadow over all the smaller accidents and fears of life has been confronted, and this seems to open the way for fuller participation. For this reason being will always be considered a profounder apprehension of life than that which is committed to the triumph over time through succession. A final, more crucial enemy is firmly faced, and man finds means to survive his sense of dislocation and orphanhood. In the more heroically aroused humanists, failure to arrive at such rock-bottom conclusions can breed inner tensions and unresolved anxieties, feelings of insufficiency. Even at the height of his temporal triumphs, Petrarch, for one, experienced great inner dissatisfaction, as if troublesome loose ends negated his victory.

There is something particularly characteristic of the Renaissance in the fullness that these writers experience in being. Their attitudes of divine trust and patient waiting seems courageous and affirmative. Perhaps what we respond to is the sense of release and discovery at the end of a long, scrupulous, and agonizing search. Involved, too, is a sense of return after the difficult years of separation to the condition of nonchalance that had been abandoned. Readiness returns the searching soul to a kind of temporal easiness that had been vacated for the sake of higher goals. It shows the way home for an individual heroism that is not self-destructive, and that is able to reconcile its goals with the world of time, history, and the limitations of man's state. The final return seems to incorporate the richness of the early setting-out, and to retain the accumulated pressures of the way traveled. In this sense, the approach to being breathes a new passion, even a religious passion, that is so dominant in the Renaissance.

As mentioned, the primary voice through which Petrarch expresses his own condition of readiness for God's "recall" is that of Job. His is the firm faith that Petrarch imitates when deeply valued things are torn from him. Yet it must be said that the figure of Job does not fit Petrarch well. Perhaps it is because Petrarch avoided most of the commitments to place and position, to family and children, that made Job's losses so heart-wracking and profound. Petrarch's voice seems more an isolated and individual one, perhaps even disembodied, when it is compared with the full substance and experience that Dante and Shakespeare, with all of their public and private involvements, were able to give to the "readiness" of Job. We might even say that while Petrarch's achievement seems akin to the ending of *Lycidas,* it falls short of the ending of *Paradise Lost.*

In practical terms, Petrarch's new faith meant no diminution of energy; quite the contrary, it seemed to inspire a reasonableness and ease in his relation to those things that had earlier competed with his sense of total dedication to God. Despite the scare Boccaccio receives from the monk of Siena, Petrarch (*Sen.* I.5) does not intend to give up his study of literature. In defense of his life's work he restates his preference for energy over sloth and the high road of glory over the lower — however saintly — road of ignorance. The detractors of literature are more often motivated by incapacity and sloth: they deprecate what they cannot attain. With a new sense of a bountiful Creator, whose custodianship is over each individual, Petrarch sees with largeness and generosity the many ways of reaching the Lord: "All good men have the same goal, but there are numerous ways thither, and much variety for the pilgrims. One goes slow, another goes fast; one in darkness, one in the bright light; one takes a low seat, one a higher. Every such journey is a blessed one, but the way of knowledge is certainly more glorious, illumined, and lofty. Hence there is no comparison between the simple piety of a rustic and the intellectual faith of a scholar. Give me an example of a saint who arose from the mass of the unlettered, and I will match him with a greater saint of the other sort." (Bishop, 227) There are gradations in Paradise, and for Petrarch they confirm the energy and the heroism that we had sensed in his earlier writings. In outline, our synopsis of Petrarch's career, followed through the theme of time and its corollaries, fits the scheme established by Hans Baron when, following other threads, he concluded, "In all three lines of change in Petrarch's historical outlook, therefore, we encounter the situation that a trend characteristic of his younger years was over-shadowed by contrary tendencies and at times almost obliterated by the early 50's, but subsequently revived, so that the earlier attainments were not lost and finally a kind of equilibrium emerged." [37]

This statement is accurate in the main, but one qualification is necessary. If by "equilibrium" we mean "a state of balance or equity between opposing forces," then that is not the right word to describe the settlement that Petrarch was able to make between those things useful for life and those things needful for salvation. His writings after the resolution of crisis make this clear. Where vital matters are the concern, "supreme truth and true happiness . . . eternal salvation," Petrarch professes that he is no Ciceronian or Platonist, but a Christian. Such is the critical argument in *Of His Own Ignorance (and That of Many Others)* — an invective of Petrarch's embattled later years that seems to revert to the dire alternatives of the *Secretum.* Once, however, this priority has been established, little conflict exists between Petrarch's literary vocation and his Christian belief, and he can go on to ask, "In what way is Ciceronian eloquence opposed to the Christian dogma?" And through a curious turnabout, the *Ignorance,* a major treatise of

Renaissance fideism, is converted into a specific defense of a certain kind of classical writing. Petrarch appears to be attacking the Averroistic Aristotelianism of Paris ("contentious Paris with its noisy Straw Lane" — we remember Dante's aversion to the Rue de Fouarre and the Averroistic "double truth"), but in reality the battle lines are divided between those who adhere to the misconceived philosophic tradition of Greece and those who espouse the humanistic literature of Rome. Without belittling Plato, who, bolstered by the testimony of men like Cicero, ranked very high with Petrarch, and whose works Petrarch had indeed begun to collect (without being able to read), and while sure that Aristotle had been subverted by his adulators, still it is with the Roman moral philosophers that Petrarch expresses a deeper personal kinship. Partially ethnic and geographic, this preference primarily derives from the struggles and resolutions of Petrarch's own moral evolution.

His own experience had taught him the difference between knowledge and virtue, and the anomalies of the human personality. In the famous canzone 264, he confesses, "Veggio 'l meglio et al peggior m'appiglio." One can indeed know the good and yet will the bad. More than knowledge is required to transform consciousness into character. It is the Latin authors, not the Greeks, who through their eloquence appeal to the will as well as to the mind. It is they who "stamp and drive deep into the heart the sharpest and most ardent stings of speech, by which the lazy are startled, the ailing are kindled, and the sleepy aroused, the sick healed, and the prostrate raised, and those who stick to the ground lifted up to the highest thoughts and to honest desire. Then earthly things become vile." [38] It is just this preference, before the onset of the Platonic revived, that allied the Latin authors with the Christian message.

It is obvious that Petrarch's humanistic regard for eloquence as opposed to scholastic method is part and parcel of his larger vision of life and his personal sense of human needs. Knowledge, incomplete by itself, must lead to a better life, to the ethical. The act of changing one's life, of actually doing what one knows he ought to do, of effecting the dictates of consciousness — these were the all-important areas of human life in which the Roman writers were most effective. It was they who had the sense of temporal urgency, an emphasis that one rarely finds amidst Hellenic serenity, however conscious of time the Greeks were. It is for this reason that Rome, the ethical, conversion, and time are intimately connected in Petrarch's understanding and response to the world. In proclaiming the triumphs of art over time, Petrarch quotes

Roman vaunts. In attempting to describe the unaccountable flight of time, he enlists Horace, Seneca, Cicero, Ovid, and Virgil. More specifically, his witnesses to life's uncertainties and brevity are Cicero (the same quotation more than once) and Horace. That the time of death is fixed he knows from Virgil. And perhaps most importantly, from Seneca he utilizes the argument against any reliance on "stages of life," the notion of the call to account, and the consuming sense of time's preciousness. In fact, in Petrarch's hostility to the dialecticians and the logicians we sense the same kind of temporal urgency that compelled Seneca to ridicule the quibbles of logic and grammar. The time of life is too short for such parlor games: "Even if there were many years left to you, you would have to spend them frugally in order to have enough for the necessary things; but as it is, when your time is so scant, what madness is it to learn superfluous things!" [39]

Hebraism and Hellenism were the two broad terms by which Matthew Arnold, writing in the nineteenth century with a facility that we now can envy, chose to understand the critical period in his country's development, the end of the Renaissance. The terrible division that he sensed in his contemporary society between the sweetness and light of culture and the unrelieved doggedness of those forces that were coming to control the destinies of England, Arnold traced to the seventeenth century, when the Hebraic impulse checked and changed the current of Hellenism more natural to the Renaissance: "This turn manifested itself in Puritanism and thus has had a great part in shaping our history for the last two hundred years. Undoubtedly it checked and changed amongst us the movement of the Renascence which we see producing in the reign of Elizabeth such wonderful fruits." [40]

If Arnold's terminology is to retain its validity for us, we should not seek too literal manifestations of the Hellenic or the Hebraic influence. Literally understood, the qualities of scholastic education that were indebted to Aristotle would seem to have little room for that "spontaniety of consciousness" which Arnold valued in Hellenism. And also reminding us of the limits of his theory — literally understood — is the fact that the experience and language of the Psalms, the Book of Job, and the Gospels, with their sense of patient waiting and divine trust, will do much to relax the ardent questing and time-consciousness of the new Renaissance energy. We have seen this happen in Petrarch and we shall have occasion to witness the same in Milton. Arnold's terms are simply focusing rubrics under which abiding aspects of personality are understood. Hebraism is the governing word for "this energy driving at practice, this paramount sense of the obligation of duty, self-control, and work, this earnestness in going manfully with the best light we have." (p. 129) Hellenism is a *humour,* a gift of "imaginatively acknowledging the multiform aspects of the problem of life, and of thus getting itself unfixed from its own over-certainty, of smiling at its own over-tenacity." (p. 142) While Arnold primarily limited his remarks to the English Renaissance, we can clearly observe their applicability, understood in the broadest way, to Petrarch and other men we shall study. A primal thrust that seems more speculative, individual, and free, which we could call the "aesthetic," is beaten down by forces that insist on "practical life and moral conduct," by the need to convert observation to practical action and to integrate the various facets of personality and understanding into a single entity, historical and ethical. Cato in the *Purgatorio,* Augustine in the *Secretum,* and the father (or his surrogate the Chief Justice) in *1* and *2 Henry IV* are the figures that embody this harder view of the world. Arnold's terms usefully describe a Renaissance process that is extensive, and of special importance in the argument of time.

But it is here that more serious and far-reaching objections can be laid to Arnold's theory. Only one of these figures, Augustine, is part of what we might call the Hebraizing-Christian tradition. Cato is Roman and Henry IV seems more like Aeneas than Augustine. This indicates, as our frequent references to Seneca and Virgil and Horace and Cicero also do, that when we speak of Hebraism in the Renaissance we are also speaking of the ethical and practical seriousness of Rome. From this we can determine that the diligent work- and time-consciousness which for Arnold destroys the true purpose of the Renaissance is not accidental, but a fundamental part of its development. Far from being a foreign graft that diverts true growth, this development is rather an important conquest of the Renaissance itself, an elementary and necessary response that serves to distinguish it from the Middle Ages. In fact, there is a connection of growth and development between Petrarch's sense of time, his schedule of hours, and the diligence of a Puritan like Baxter, or even the founder of Methodism, Wesley. The difference is, of course, that Petrarch can combine energy with learning and ease, patience in God's call with remarkably long hours at his desk; Rabelais can endorse the vigorous educational system for Gargantua as well as describe the Abbeye de Thélème, where there is no clock and everyone is free to do as he likes; and Shakespeare can understand the demands of the hard world of history as well as the release of the green world. But it must also be said that all of the writers we study came to detect the hazards and pains and dissatisfactions of the world view that triumphed in the industrial revolution, utilitarian philosophy, and the Methodism of Arnold's century. Precociously, in the Renaissance itself, some men, at least the greatest talents, were alarmed by the forces that they themselves had helped to unleash. Their discovery of being was an individual leave-taking — with universal implication — of a society to which Arnold would later try to minister with sweetness and light.

Last Things

In another invective of his later years, the *Contra eum qui maledixit Italie,* Petrarch continues to argue the superiority of the Roman writers over the Greeks, and for essentially the same reasons: Aristotle teaches, but Cicero moves the soul. In Aristotle there is more acumen, but in Cicero there is more power ("efficacie"). And in a terse sentence summing up the differences between the speculative intellect and the ethical life, Petrarch concludes, "Ille [Aristotle] docet attentius quid est virtus; urget iste [Cicero] potentius ut colatur virtus." (*Prose,* 800) The separation is clear between the writer who distinguishes and defines and the one who "more powerfully urges us to cultivate virtue." However, removed from the restricted alternatives of the *Ignorance,* Petrarch's defense of Rome in the *Contra eum* goes beyond qualified acceptance and rises to inspired panegyric. What is all history but the praise of Rome? Mundi caput, urbium regina, sedes imperii, arx fidei catholica, fons omnium memorabilium exemplorum." Not only is Rome all of this, but historical continuity and the possibilities of human achievement themselves are synonymous with praise of Rome. Validated with Rome and through Rome is some hope in the ways of succession, and consequently human effort. In praising Rome's continuing inspiration to those eager for fame and glory, Petrarch, as Hans Baron has shown, connects his latter end with his earlier beginnings. Here, as elsewhere, Petrarch opens the way and provides the form for later Renaissance response to Rome.

Like his literary descendants Spenser and Du Bellay, he turns the ruins of time into the triumph of Rome. Rome will have the permanence of time itself. This is the argument to which Petrarch returns — the argument of his younger days, of which the coronation was the crown and the oration the faith. In the *Contra eum* he ridicules the argument that the mere fact of change could diminish Rome's stature, "as if Rome only were continuously being transformed, and not all of the cities and all of the kingdoms, and especially individual men; and as if we were not always exposed to the vicissitudes of time until we reach eternity." Although such temporal triumph is obviously limited in contrast with eternity — and this is a qualification that the period of crisis introduced — still Rome is worth much, and, unlike other earthly cities, resists inclusion in the dolorous *ubi sunt* intonation. Babylon, Troy, Carthage, Athens, Sparta and Corinth — these are now merely names, "But Rome has not fallen to such ruin, and however seriously decayed, she is still something more than a name. Her walls and palaces are crumbling, but the glory of her immortal name remains. . . . The fame of the city [urbis] will not be lessened until the end of the world [orbis]; Rome will always be the world's high water mark [semper altissimus mundi vertex Roma erit]." (Prose, 774) In the life of the Renaissance, the worth of Rome will be kept alive in the spirit of those who continue her work.

Nevertheless, however affirmative is Petrarch's stand on the values of civilization, he cannot, whether early or late, disperse from his mind the shadows of a vast, terrifying and all-too-imaginable extent of time that simply dwarfs and reduces to nothingness all human efforts. In the letters to the classical authors that comprise Book XXIV of the *Familiares,* where Petrarch most stoutly proclaims the possibility of historical continuity, he reprimands the sloth of the preceding age and of his own, which has allowed so many excellent things of the past to be lost or mangled. To Homer he can complain, "How many things are lost!" But then he corrects the implication that only carelessness or accidents are responsible. Disappearance is a more universal phenomenon: "Nay, all things perish — all that our blind activity accomplishes beneath the course of the ever-returning sun. Vain are the labors and the cares of men! Time flies and short as it is, we waste it. Oh, the vanity and the pride of men over the nothingness that we are and do and hope for." (Cosenza, 153–154) And to Varro he urges a kind of resignation and desistance from grief, since all things perish: "Even while writing thou must have known that thy work was destined to perish; for nothing immortal can be written by mortal men. Forsooth, what matters it whether our work perish immediately or after the lapse of a hundred thousand years seeing that at some time it must necessarily die?" (Cosenza, 73) Distinction and extension — the great deeds that separate the uncommon man from the masses and earn the gratifying rewards of fame — are shrunk by the triumph of time. This is the vision which humbled Dante's pride in *Purg.* XI, which is utilized by

Augustine in the *Secretum,* and which Petrarch himself invokes in *Fam.*
XXIV.1.

The *Triumph of Time* is Petrarch's anatomy of the world, and as in
Spenser's *Mutabilitie Cantos,* or John Donne's *Anniversaries* it has
joined with it a companion piece that describes the heart's final desires,
the *Triumph of Eternity.* As the world of time is dominated by change,
this second world, totally other, is remarkable for its stability:

> Qual meraviglia ebb'io quando ristare
> vidi in un punto quel che mai non stette,
> ma discorrendo suol tutto cangiare!

> What was my surprise when I saw stand in one
> point that [time] which never has stood still,
> but running away changes all things!
>
> (25–27)

Time is movement and change, and these are repugnant for Petrarch,
who is still writing within the philosophical tradition of an Augustine
or a Boethius, with their distinctions between eternity and time. So
Benedict can urge Dante to look toward the ultimate sphere, "in quella
sola / è ogni parte la dove semp'era," and Bernard can pray for the
Virgin's care to overcome "i movimenti umani." In God's eternity there
is no such movement, but rather stability; there is not even succession
— no past, present, or future, those processes that make human life
for Petrarch "varia e inferma." (33) Whatever had been their earlier
zestful need for change and novelty, for these men of the fourteenth
century variety is at last only an indication of life's infirmity. By the
time we come to the end of this cycle of Renaissance literature, a great
alteration will have taken place. Milton's "change delectable" and
"grateful vicissitude" even in paradise are alien to Petrarch's highest
desires. Although both poets have a hunger for permanence, Petrarch's
paradise is more insistently unchanging. In what can man place his
trust? "In che ti fidi?" is the question he asks his heart. And the
progress of the *Triumphs* is from one trust to a higher one, until all
earthly fidelities seem unworthy of his commitment. The swiftness of
time, the brevity of life, these have been Petrarch's constant concerns,
and they lead to a conclusion that must share summary focus in Petrarch's writings:

> e parvemi terribil vanitate
> fermare in cose il cor che 'l Tempo preme,
> che, mentre più le stringi, son passate.

> It seems terrible vanity to fix our heart on those things that
> time gathers, and which, while
> we strive to hold them, slip by and are past.

(40–42)

At war with time, Petrarch is like a disappointed lover who has waked from a dream to face an empty reality.

Part mythological figure, part awe-inspiring cosmic force, Time here follows the triumph of Fame and indignantly protests: if a man's life through fame continues after his death, this contradicts the eternal law that all things mortal must die. Like Cato in the *Purgatorio,* Time has a strict legalistic mind, and above all resents man's encroachments on his own powers. Time is envious of man and determined to root out this challenger — "io porto invidia agli uomini e nol celo." (24) After speaking, Time continues on his way, "more swiftly than a falcon heading for its prey." Petrarch summons up images of terror to summarize the "inextimabilem fugam temporis"; but Time's most daunting quality is his ever-sameness: his motion is and has always been singularly undeviating. As in the prologue to Act Four of the *Winter's Tale,* Time is the great "I am":

> tal son qual era anzi che stabilita
> fosse la terra, dì e notte rotando
> per la strada ritonda ch'è infinita.

> I am that which I was before the very
> earth was established, day and night
> circling the heavenly cycle that is
> infinite.

(28–30)

The suggestion of unending momentum is more fully carried out by the Italian words — I believe untranslatable in their impact — "rotando" and "ritonda." Such a picture of uniform infinite motion Petrarch had to set aside before, in *Fam.* XXI.12, he was able to consider seriously the possibilities of using his own time more fully. Prospero in *The Tempest* will be aghast and stunned by the prospect that outlasts the great globe itself, and Newton will make such time a law.

And for those who seem to escape from the "commune gabbia" — those illustrious souls of special force and power — Time enlarges its flight:

> Volgerà il sol non pure anni ma lustri
> e secoli, vittor d'ogni cerebro,
> e vedrà il vaneggiar di questi illustri.

> The sun will turn not only years
> but lustra and centuries, victor over
> man's genius, and it will witness the
> disappearance of all these bright ones.
>
> (103–105)

Long time, as Petrarch concludes, is poison to those great names: "e'l gran tempo a' gran nomi è gran veneno." Time more than death is the great equalizer: even those who manage, through fame, to surmount death, come to the same end as those who have achieved nothing. Man would be able to see this if his own life were not so brief; fame is held in high repute only because man is short-lived. Such a vista of long time denies the vital Renaissance goals of distinction and extension after death. All are reduced to the undistinguished sameness typical of time itself. Life has no value, and the motto now indicates praise not of those who risk and struggle, but of those who are unborn: "Beato chi non nasce." (138)

In Dante the more significant contraction occurs in paradise at the joyous collocation of his birthtime and his ascent into the starry sphere. Even in Shakespeare, the contraction that brings together womb and tomb, deathdays and birthdays, the mortiferous and the creative, still suggests some awesome and terrifying power. Petrarch himself creates the same tragic ethos in the coincidence of his *innamoramento* with the crucifixion and the death of Laura. But here in the *Triumph of Time* contraction is reductive: it has neither joy nor tragic potential. Rather it is part of that terrible backward perspective where all the individual things that make up a life are shrunk to mere beginnings and mere ends: "stamani era un fanciullo ed or son vecchio" ("only this morning I was a babe and now I am aged") is Petrarch's desolate conclusion. Nothing emerges in between, no line of development, no significant events. In their prose works, both Petrarch and Seneca refer to this depressed possibility. With such a thought Petrarch opens that valuable letter to Phillip of Cavaillon, *Fam.* XXIV.1: "Thirty years! How time stealthily slips away! If I cast a glance backward, those thirty years seem so many days, so many hours." (Bishop, 200) He then adds, however, that if he singles them out one by one they seem to be thirty centuries. In his *Triumph of Time,* Petrarch was little disposed to parcel out the events of his life. Rather they bunched together to create a despair similar to that caused by time's own undifferentiated flow — the enemy against which Petrarch was warring in his heroic, even desperate attempt to tell the time, to single out and locate significantly an event in time. Time does have a wallet at his back, wherein he puts alms for oblivion. Such thoughts are also Seneca's in his forty-ninth epistle to Lucilius: "All past time is in the same place; it all presents the same aspect to us, it lies together. Everything slips into the same abyss." [41]

God's eternity is a "redoing" of all that on earth has been "undone" by time. The words *rifar* and *disfar* recur in the *Triumph of Eternity,* where Petrarch imagines the new world that will be remade "più bello e più giocondo" from the dissolved old one — a thought Milton would well have understood. There the destructive forces that so wracked Petrach's world and that figure so prominently in his works will themselves be undone.

> E 'l Tempo, a disfar tutto così presto,
> e Morte in sua ragion cotanto avara,
> morti insiem saranno e quella e questo.
>
> And Time, so ready to undo everything, and
> Death so greedy about its business, will
> themselves both be dead.
> (124–126)

Like Dante, Petrarch saw life as a process of undoing, but we can gauge the difference between their various styles, and the energies of their conceptions, when we note the vivid sense of process and imagery implied in Dante's words "spolparsi" or "sfogliarsi," and the more generalized "disfar" of Petrarch. Nevertheless, like Dante, Petrarch deplores the organic change that time, as represented in the animal procession of the zodiac, was felt to mean. At the desired future transformation,

Petrarch will be freed from the growth and sloughing-off, the coming hither and going hence:

> Non avrà albergo il sol Tauro ne Pesce,
> per lo cui variar nosto lavoro
> or nasce or more, ed or scema or cresce

> The sun will not rest with the Bull or the
> Fish [Taurus and Pisces], through whose
> variations our works now are born and
> now die, now diminish and now increase.
>
> (40–42)

As we have seen, Petrarch suffered from temporal anxiety more than most men do, from worry over his past mistreadings and fear over his future; and more than most he accused himself of the normal sins of distraction, lack of purpose, diffusion of personality. In his conception of eternity, man's temporal fragmentation will be healed, his scattered identities collected and made one. Here man will achieve that unchanging wholeness, the being which, to the credit of Petrarch's honesty, he never felt fully possible on earth. The points of past and future, the language of the tenses, will no longer be used:

> ma "è" solo in presente, ed "ora" ed "oggi"
> e sola eternità raccolta e 'ntera;
>   quasi spianati dietro e 'nnanzi i poggi
> ch' occupavan la vista, non fia in cui
> vostro sperare e rimembrar s'appoggi;
>   la qual varietà fa spesso altrui
> vaneggiar sì che 'l viver pare un gioco,
> pensando pur: "che sarò io? che fui?"
>   Non sarà più diviso a poco a poco
> ma tutto insieme.

> but "is" only in the present, and "now"
> and "today" and only eternity collected
> and entire; it will be as if the hills
> in front and behind that occupied the sight
> were levelled, and there will be nothing
> on which your hopes or memories can work;
> the alternation of which, one removing the

other, makes our life appear a game, as we
think, "What shall I be, what have I been?"
We shall not there be taken apart little by little
but all stand together.

Fame and ideal beauty are restored in the experience of eternity —
meritorious fame, which time extinguished, and the joyous faces which
were destroyed by change and bitter death. Returning more beautiful
than ever, they will leave the oblivion they are abandoning to "morte
impetuosa, a' giorni ladri" ("impetuous death and the thieving days"):

> ne l'eta più fiorita e verde avranno
> con immortal bellezza eterna fama.

> as in their most flourishing springtime
> they will have eternal fame with
> immortal beauty.
>
> (133–134)

A kind of fortunate fall is implicit in Petrarch's earlier ascendant aspirations: his higher vision, although insecurely based, eventually led him
to the highest. As Laura is singled out as the first of those who go to be
"remade," so Petrarch, through his attachment to her (and his lack of
physical fulfillment), is saved:

> Ecco che pianse sempre, e nel suo pianto
> sovra 'l riso d'ogni altro fu beato!

> Here is he who always wept, but who
> in his tears was more blessed above
> the laughter of the others!
>
> (95–96)

Important in Petrarch, and in the other writers of the Renaissance, is
this final sense of vindication — a joyous justification of their earlier acts
of separation, and their initial individual quest. In many of the writers,
despite, or mainly because of, a middle period of pain and alienation,
of crisis and doubt, of limitations experienced and reality faced, a final
stage is reached where their earlier strivings are reconsidered and found
not to be wayward, but to lead to, to be part of, the highest possibilities
of life. Their rejection of premature being, of serving as unventuresome

guardians of the family hearth, their striving and seeking that led to a kind of imbalance, their lostness and suffering, they finally see, allowed them to reach higher and go farther than those around them. They had, in a modern sense, gone out to the edge, but they had also returned home. And, as a consequence, home was a far richer place. In their final senses of being — paradisal or otherwise — their earlier Renaissance energies and ideals persist.

Part Two

Chapter 4
The Backgrounds
of History and Tragedy
in Sixteenth-Century Thought

However divided they were by the inevitable tensions of dual loyalties, the men of the fourteenth century made key contributions to the gradual unfolding of many elements of the Renaissance. While they themselves deeply needed and would eventually return to a larger religious unity of experience, their earlier spirited commitments to the validity of earthly rewards would persist, and even grow, in their *quattrocento* followers. Dante and Petrarch importantly announced a "new time" and boldly maintained the right of their "present" talent to march with the ancients, and thus restore the interrupted classical tradition "ch'era dipartita." Their avant-gardism and self-confidence would be emulated in the other national renascences. And in matters of poetry, their achievement would help provide the Renaissance with its own evolving tradition of the most serious subject matter treated in a highly imaginative and graceful style. Thematically, within the terms of this study, their great attention to time, children, and fame would also endure. The temporal milieu in which they wrote, with its modern forms of reckoning time, the development of the mechanical clock, and the increased consciousness of time in the commercial sector, would hardly be diminished in subsequent centuries, and their own meditations over time and the ways of man's response would become the property of literature. Petrarch, in particular, left a vivid legacy urging the fullest utilization of time. Progeny and fame, the forces of succession that so alternately attracted and disappointed them, would in fact grow in legitimacy, and be presented more frequently in the forefront of values. These ideas would come to have greater freedom from religious challenge in the subsequent centuries. Vittore Branca considers the family as the center of all aspects of life in Morelli's *Ricordi*. And to gauge their growth in validity one has only to refer to Palmieri's *Vita civile* and Leone Battista Alberti's *Famiglia*. The harvest of fifteenth-century educational tracts also shows a greater attention to children, to the ways of continuity, and ultimately to the well-being of the earthly city. These attitudes, which I have taken out of their larger circumference and development in the works of Dante and Petrarch, all have in common a greater willingness to accept the values and satisfactions of the city or — if we are to include the author of the *Vita solitaria* — the ways of time and succession. Within these terms and values and rewards, man would seek to define himself and his goals.

One of the clearest and most controversial spokesmen for these new developments was Machiavelli. His work caps a remarkable period of intellectual growth and social change — Florence from Dante to Machiavelli stands out as one of the most critical centers for historical development in the West. Decisive changes, according to Hans Baron's classic study, took place around 1400, when the Florentine Republic struggled to repulse the aggrandizing powers of the Visconti of Milan.[1] If formerly the Florentine intellectuals had recourse to the arguments of empire and looked at history theologically, as the manifestation of God's providential plan, now when these were the very arguments utilized by their attackers, the beleaguered Florentine citizenry worked out a new intellectual order. They had to believe that not providence, or some blessed *fortuna,* but rather man's virtue and will and dedication control the outcome of events. As these intellectuals rejected the claims of universal church and empire, they turned for their ammunition to the Roman Republic — not the Rome of the Empire. Unlike Dante, they looked with favor upon Brutus as the defender of the values of free Romans. The picture that emerges is that of an aroused and militant people who reject, under the pressure of contemporary political events, the traditional eschatology and frame of beliefs to which the preceding generations were able to turn.[2]

Such were the civic republican antecedents to Machiavelli's own thoughts about man and fortune. Yet it is clear that whatever his indebtedness to these predecessors, Machiavelli invests his prince with startlingly new qualities. Felix Gilbert concludes that Machiavelli differs from the earlier Florentines by virtue of his greater "realism," by his insistence that the conduct of the prince cannot always be determined by the ethics of the private man.[3] The requirements of public order and the realities of human nature inspire in Machiavelli a greater tolerance for ambiguity of means. In very specific instances, Machiavelli represents a radical departure from the thought of Augustine or of Dante. These Christian thinkers turned to the heavenly city because of the inherent defectiveness of the earthly city, a defectiveness that was revealed in legend when Romulus killed Remus, and archetypally when Cain slew Abel. But Machiavelli, in chapter nine of the first book of his *Discorsi,* defends Romulus. The killing of his brother was excusable since Romulus performed that act not out of personal ambition but for the common good ("il bene commune"). The virtue of Romulus' intentions was proved subsequently when he convened a senate, with which he consulted. He created as well as obeyed laws and ordinances that acted as a limitation on any absolute prerogative. His original act, rather than leading to a concatenation of actions and reprisals, served to establish a continuing public order. In a dramatic reversal of Augustine's or even the later Dante's notions, the true prince can thus surmount the inevitable taint necessitated by historical change. Rather than linking Romulus with Cain, Machiavelli associated him with Moses (and other founders of state), who similarly was compelled to kill many men so that his laws and ordinances could succeed. (*Discorsi,* 1.9 and 3.30)[4]

Machiavelli's conception of his prince is eminently dramatic. Taking upon his shoulders all the ambiguities of political conduct in a time of elemental change, the prince must be willing to enter into evil, while still not losing sight of the public good and public order. Literally on his own, cut off from any traditional past, he must respond instinctively to the realities of the situation, with its new and different requirements. Felix Gilbert admirably senses the dramatic implications of Machiavelli's new world, when he writes that "Machiavelli's ideal political order was one in which man lives in time and is subject to his ravages," and "Man was placed in a constantly changing world in which new forces and new situations were thrown up at any moment."[5] The Christian view of history has little relevancy for the challenges with which the new prince is faced.[6] Professor Gilbert concludes, "In placing politics in the stream of history, in demonstrating that every situation is unique and requires man to use all his forces to probe the potentialities of the moment, Machiavelli has revealed — more than anyone before him — that, at any time, politics is choice and decision."[7] And yet the problem of Machiavelli's prince is even greater, since the only true and successful resolution of these charismatic qualities is for them to become institutionalized, to translate themselves into regularly functioning laws and orders.

It was this dual aspect of Machiavelli's thought that captured the imagination of Elizabethan dramatists like Marlowe and Shakespeare.

In their work, too, man is placed in the reign of time, where the values and social alignments that served in the past are no longer valid in the present, and man must proceed darkly, moved by his energies and ambitions, and trusting in his own resources. The problem is more grandiloquently stated by Marlowe, whose Tamburlaine finds his triumph within the dimensions of the earthly city, "That perfect bliss and sole felicity, / The sweet fruition of an earthly crown." His more than human powers are no longer subject to any arbitrary fortune: "I hold the fates bound fast in iron chains / And with my hand turn fortune's wheel about." At the heart of his universe is struggle, and rather than condemning such restlessness he extols it as a universal principle. The defeated Cosroe calls him "bloody and insatiate Tamburlaine." Not so, replies the aggressive hero, and he proceeds to defend himself by the examples of the gods and of Nature:

> The thirst of reign and sweetness of a crown,
> That caused the eldest son of heavenly Ops
> To thrust his doting father from his chair,
> And place himself in the imperial heaven,
> Moved me to manage arms against thy state.
> What better precedent that mighty Jove?
> Nature, that framed us of four elements
> Warring within our breasts for regiment,
> Doth teach us all to have aspiring minds.
> (1 *Tamburlaine*, II.vii.12–20)[8]

Awesome and charismatic, Tamburlaine still looks to continuity, and, at his death, leaves the reins of government to his surviving sons, establishing himself as the model for their political conduct.

Shakespeare is much more serious and realistic; he has more of a sense of conflict and dilemma in his presentation of these political problems. Nevertheless, the legacy of Machiavelli is strongly present in the fundamental data of Shakespeare's historical world. I am thinking not only of the palpable Machiavellians of the Elizabethan stage, for which Richard III can stand as the type, but of a more basic picture of a great world on the move, the felt presence of historical change that destroys unfit kings like Henry VI and Richard II, and elevates a Bolingbroke to the throne, clouded in all the ambiguities of political action. If there is one clear fact in the world of the history plays, it is that the unarmed prophet perishes (we could also think of the gentle and naive Duncan)

— the other fact is that the armed butcher does not fare much better. Shakespeare's hope and ideal, the hope and ideal of any grand establishment, lie in the fusion of justice and power, the harmonization of energy and order, of *virtù* and value. In this regard, he had as precedent and model the Tudor establishment, its members themselves adept at bringing political and religious innovation within the frame of continuity. Shakespeare, benefitting from the Tudor solution, was in a much better position than Machiavelli himself, whose basic prescriptions, hopeless in an uprooted Italy, only elsewhere were applied to form the foundation of the modern nation states.[9]

Whatever else might be said of Machiavelli's thought — and it is complex — it shows faith in man's powers to exert some control over his social world, and as such it bulks large in one major trend of sixteenth-century thought, that represented by the dimension of history. But we must not forget that there evolved a counter-thrust to the image of man steering the wheel of fortune, that the sixteenth century was also the great age of skepticism and that it produced some of the supreme creations of Western tragedy.

Here again the Italian experience was prototypic. Written when the full consequences of the French invasion of 1494 had not yet been realized, Machiavelli's *Prince* could still urge political response. A few years later, however, that invasion was seen not as a passing burden or a local situation, but rather as something more fundamental and long-lasting, a larger situation against which man could do little. Felix Gilbert, like Hans Baron highly interested in the interactions of events and ideas, shows the impact of these realizations on the Italian conception of the world: "The continuance of the invasions of Italy heightened the significance of the campaign of Charles VIII in 1494, and when, in the 1520s, Italy was the chief theatre for struggle between Hapsburg and Valois for European hegemony, it became apparent that the beginning had been the French campaign of 1494, which increasingly was seen as the event of lasting impact and significance for the entire course of European history." This new realization brought about a change in the interpretation of the causes of the war. It was not the fault of the Italian princes, who lacked the capacities of the ancients, but of forces "beyond human power: it had been decreed in the stars and the heavens." These speculations led to very different notions about Fortune and man's capacity for control:

The *Fortuna* which emerged as the ruler of world history in the sixteenth century was the power behind everything that happened: it was an embodiment of the uncontrollable forces determining the course of events. This view of *Fortuna* was the outcome of the experience that no single event has a clear beginning, and the investigation of causal connections only exposes the vista of an infinite number of further relationships and interdependencies. Such a view of *Fortuna* destroyed the fifteenth-century belief in man's power to control, or at least to influence events. Yet this notion of *Fortuna* did not lead to a return to the medieval concept of a world directed according to God's plan. Italians of the sixteenth century saw no straight course or rational purpose in history; man was driven by forces which he could not fathom.[10]

Students of Renaissance literature may find here a remarkable exposition of the development of the sense of tragedy. First of all what was needed was a growth in the sense of man's powers and the greatness of his achievement, a faith in his capacity to determine events. But this then is followed by the bitter realization that periods of brilliance are short-lived, that man's triumphs do not extend into some limitless future, but are likewise circumscribed and have their falls, that the organic metaphor of nature applies to human civilizations as it does to the individual life. Man cannot escape the darker powers that close in on him, and he too is swept along by events over which he has little control. But as Gilbert and others have shown, in the sixteenth century man does not revert to the medieval scheme, however similar some of its conceptions might be. The resources of divine comedy are hardly available.

Tragedy occurs when faith in man's controlling powers is denied. But of course one other factor is needed — an unappeasable will and desire that refuse to accept the consolations of change. Such aspiration takes its growth in a world of optimism and hope, when human ideals have acquired great validity and promise. At that time, fidelity, remembrance, generational order and continuity, the powers of man's mind and his achievements — those values that distinguish man and set him apart from the beasts — become highly-prized objects of attachment. And when they are destroyed by the normal human tendency to forget, by the powers of time, by human faithlessness, or by ambition, then a world itself and a collection of values are destroyed, and with them all those who refused to relinquish their hold. Humanistic ideals are wrecked by the natural insufficiencies of man, but in the greatest works of Renaissance literature they are also challenged by an aggressive doctrine of change and social emulation, which can be most generally understood under the rubric of Machiavellism. Chaucer's Troilus, too, was destroyed by a combination of human passivity, Diomede's aggressiveness, and his own misplaced aspirations. But eventually his aspiring idealism was housed in a philosophy of eternity. For the writers we cover, such triumph over change and death was not possible (again allowing for exceptions among certain of the later English writers). From their conflict of aspiration and ideal with a hard and unyielding reality, the anguished hero can either learn to live among the pieces or perish.

For this background material we have relied to some extent on works of political history, which showed the interactions of political events and changes of attitude and conception. In the breakdown of faith in man's powers to master his destiny, and in the defeat of his aspirations, a sense of tragedy was one of the consequences, as the literature of the later Renaissance richly illustrates. But there is a condition of mind that survives after tragedy, which is not simply comic, but shows a more profound reintegration of man's desires with his experience. This attitude follows tragedy and probably has its greatest literary representation in the third book of Montaigne's *Essais* and in Shakespeare's last plays. One large philosophical frame which allows us to follow developments to this third stage is provided by Ernst Cassirer's *The Individual and the Cosmos in Renaissance Philosophy*.[11] Whether or not he succeeds in showing the "philosophic unity" of the Renaissance, Cassirer provides us with highly useful concepts, whose relevancy for the various forms of literary expression in the Renaissance has not yet been fully exploited. His notions of "graduated mediation," *"chorismos,"* and *"methexis"* have great importance for an understanding of the complex development of men like Rabelais, Montaigne, Shakespeare, and, to some degree, Spenser.

Graduated mediation might be called the inherited, orthodox medieval world-view built upon neo-Platonic and Aristotelian bases. Cassirer sees one part of this system as deriving from the Aristotelian notion of "development": "The world is a self-enclosed sphere, within which there are only differences of degree. Force flows from the divine unmoved mover of the universe to the remotest celestial circles, there to be distributed, in a steady and regulated sequence, to the whole of being; to be communicated, by means of the concentric celestial spheres, to the sublunar world. No matter how great the distance between the beginning and the end, there is no break." This notion of development joins with the neo-Platonic notion of "transcendence" to produce what Cassirer calls "emanation":

> The absolute remains as the super-finite, the super-one, the super-being, pure in itself. Nevertheless, because of the superabundance of it, the absolute overflows, and from this superabundance it produces the multiformity of the universe, down to formless matter as the extreme limit of non-being. A look at the Pseudo-Dionysian writings has shown us that the Christian Middle Ages adopted this premise and re-shaped it to suit its own ends. It gained thereby the fundamental category of graduated mediation, which on the one hand allowed the integral existence of divine transcendence, and on the other mastered it, both theoretically and practically, with a hierarchy of concepts and spiritual forces. (p. 18)

This is a highly philosophical statement of a spiritual sense of the world, where man has his means of communication with the higher forces and principles. It is anticipated in the Biblical image of Jacob's ladder, with angels ascending and descending, and it receives its finest embodiment from that chief imagination of Christendom, Dante, in his *Commedia*. In more human terms, at the heart of the Christian experience is the Incarnation, where man exists in relation to the universe as a son to a father, a creature to a creator, so that Dante at the conclusion of his poem can look into the divine effulgence and see there "nostra effige," our image. From a sense of exile man can reachieve a sense of belonging, of returning to a true home. All of this results from superabundance and produces a sense of *commedia:* as man had first conceived the world in all of his childlike innocence, so it has turned out finally to be. The world corresponds to man's conception of it.

But when we come to the later Renaissance, this notion of a true home for man is lost and the very possibilities of Jacob's ladder destroyed: man has no communication with being; time is not the image of eternity. This dark and skeptical thought in the later Renaissance can be called *chorismos,* and it follows upon an early stage of humanistic optimism, which if lacking the theocentric tensions of the fourteenth century, still entertained the same relative possibilities of graduated mediation. Confident neo-Platonism and humanism embraced figures like Rabelais and even the more religious Spenser, who deeply sensed that man's heroic possibilities were at one with the spiritual forces of the cosmos, that "here" and "there" were harmonious. But even these writers underwent their dark periods of doubt and skepticism. In writing of Nicholas of Cusa, Cassirer explains the general and far-reaching roots of *chorismos:* "All knowledge presupposes comparison, which, in turn, more precisely understood, is nothing but measurement . . . [which assumes] a condition of homogeneity. By its essence and by definition, the absolute object lies beyond every possibility of comparison and measurement and therefore beyond the possibility of knowledge . . . 'Finiti et infiniti nulla proportio.' " (pp. 10–11) In graduated mediation there was no break between beginning and end, but in *chorismos* there is no way of closing the gap: "The only relationship that exists between the conditioned, endlessly conditionable world and the world of the unconditioned is that of complete mutual exclusion. The only valid predications of the unconditioned arise out of the negation of all empirical predicates." (p. 21)

This separation brings about a profound reduction in man's condition, in relation not only to the eternal, but also to any sense of stability he had cherished. God has hidden his face, and as man's possibilities of transcending time are voided, so are his possibilities of any historical continuity. The world which had stood before him having a past and a future, an order and correspondence to his conception of it, is now void. Man lives only in the isolated moment, and a dark world of no past and no future, such as presented itself to Hamlet or Montaigne, emerges. Of course, this experience of chorismos is no real resting place or terminus; it is rather a way station where, if man survives, his baggage is rearranged so as to make a more bearable load, where his expectations and ideas of life are brought into closer line with life's realities. It is for his third concept, *methexis* (or participation), and for his important insight into the connection between it and *chorismos,* that Cassirer's account of Cusanus thought is important: "This conclusion [of *chorismos*] brings with it a peculiar reversal. The division that separates the sensible from the intelligible, sense experience and logic from metaphysics, does not cut through the vital nerve of experience itself; indeed, precisely this division guarantees the validity of experience. . . . Far from excluding each other, separation and participation, chorismos and methexis, can only be thought of *through* and *in relation* to each other." (p. 22)

Cusanus himself had considered the " 'apex of [his] theory' to be the insight that the truth which he had sought earlier in the darkness of mysticism and which he had determined to be the antithesis of all multiplicity and change, reveals itself, in fact, in the very realm of empirical multiplicity; indeed, it is a common, everyday matter." (p. 36) When we think of the last phrase, "truth is a common everyday matter," we suspect that for Montaigne at least Cassirer would have succeeded through his study of Nicholas of Cusa in showing the "philosophic unity of the Renaissance." And when we think of the words "experience," "participation," "truth in multiplicity," we see that the concept of *methexis,* added to his other notions of graduated mediation and *chorismos,* can be an extraordinary schema for talking in a new way about much that is superior in sixteenth-century literature.

This section began with a discussion of the changed conception of *fortuna* which occurred when divided Italy became a pawn of the European national powers. This changed attitude toward man's power to influence his world has definite implications for tragedy, and could be easily placed under the rubric of *chorismos.* This is especially true when we ponder Guicciardini's *Ricordi.*[12] These speculative maxims carry over into a broader field the principle of separation. If God's ways are an *abyssus multa* (92), history is almost as obscure. No one can proceed with assurance into the future: "58. How wisely the philosopher spoke when he said: 'Of future contingencies there can be no determined truth.' Go where you will: the farther you go, the more you will find this saying to be absolutely true." And the past has almost as little illumination: "110. How wrong it is to cite the Romans at every turn. For any comparison to be valid, it would be necessary to have a city with conditions like theirs, and then to govern it according to their example." (See also 117: "To judge by example is very misleading.") Curiously enough, such divorce from the more optimistic stays of life does not provoke Guicciardini to withdrawal. By that "peculiar reversal" of which Cassirer spoke and which we shall see operating again and again in sixteenth-century thought and literature, this stage of *chorismos* is transitional and leads to a renewed participation in life, a greater faith in the durability of nature and trust in experience. In Guicciardini's mind, future uncertainties can be the cause of present hope and a source of encouragement:

54. Anyone charged with defending a land must make it his principal object to hold out as long as possible. For, as the proverb says, he who has time has life. Delay brings infinite opportunities that at first could not be known or hoped for.

116. A man who governs a state must not be frightened by the appearance of dangers, though they seem great, close, and imminent. For, as the proverb says, the devil is not as ugly as he is made out to be. Often dangers will evaporate by chance. And even if some-

thing bad should happen, you will always find some remedy or alleviation within the situation itself.

And then, as he does following a similar *ricordo,* 162, he emphasizes
the importance of this message: "Ponder this *ricordo* well, for it is a
matter of daily life." With his proverbial lore, with his emphasis on daily
life and the cohesiveness of nature itself, Guicciardini presents what we
have called the comedy of existence, and it can be seen no accident that
he was Montaigne's favorite modern historian.

In his awareness of the fearful imaginings of the inexperienced intellect, Guicciardini is one of the early sixteenth-century praisers of folly,
a genre of developing importance.[13] By his frank and innocent forward
movement, the fool sometimes has better results than the man who holds
back. Trusting in nature and experience, *methexis* sees in life greater
forces working for survival than the intellect has conceived:

136. It sometimes happens that fools do greater things than wise
men. The reason is that the wise men, unless forced to do otherwise, will rely a great deal on reason and little on fortune; whereas
the fool does just the opposite. And things brought about by fortune
sometimes have incredible success. . . . This is just what the proverb says: *Audaces fortuna iuvat.*

60. A superior intellect is bestowed upon men only to make them
unhappy and tormented. For it does nothing but produce in them
greater turmoil and anxiety than there is in more limited men.

Thinking of these two maxims, and others in Guicciardini, it almost
seems inevitable that the century that began with Erasmus' *Praise of
Folly* should terminate with *Hamlet.* Yet, from Petrarch we could see
that while humanism was aspirant and heroic it was also profoundly
self-critical. This almost native doubt of humanism was complicated in
the sixteenth century by skepticism, or philosophical nominalism, and
bourgeois realism. It was then even more fitting for men to reflect on
the follies of wisdom and the wisdom of down-to-earth practicality. Don
Quixote and Sancho are the constant figures of the mind. And in England, where the onset of a "profit-seeking age" was most feared, one
lesser-known spokesman for this bourgeois realism was Philocosmus in
Samuel Daniel's *Musophilus.* On the eve of *Hamlet,* and in the presence
of the advent of Montaigne's *Essais* into England, he asserts the hazards
of learning and the advantages of ignorance:

Whilst timorous Knowledge stands considering,
Audacious ignorance hath done the deed.
For who knowes most, the more he knows to doubt,
The least discourse is commonly most stout.

(490–493)[14]

In the fourteenth century, the pilgrim is the image of the man who has separated himself from historical reliances, and who goes out separated from home, family, and friends to meet whatever God sends his way. In the sixteenth century this type is replaced by the fool, who can be representative of man's universal condition, but who also comments upon folly-fallen wisdom from the lore of proverbial experience. But here it must be remembered that while the pilgrim was the type with which the author could identify, the fool was the creation of the wise man, who was capable of appreciating the irony that the best-endowed are frequently the worst-prepared. By the very act of his creation the author transcends the figure of the fool. And, of course, the best writers were capable of surmounting the painful truth of their own folly, and reintegrating their knowledge and their experience into a rich unity.

These new attitudes and patterns of development have very obvious temporal implications. They will serve as the frame when we pick up the threads laid down through the first three chapters of this study and draw them through the works of Rabelais, Montaigne, Spenser, Shakespeare, and Milton.

Chapter 5
Rabelais

Children, Education, and Time

It is clear that a sturdy defense of progeny and the ways of succession had been part of Renaissance developments before the sixteenth century. Nevertheless, this process received further impetus and important philosophical endorsement from Florentine neo-Platonism. Notably in the famous letter from Gargantua to his son (*Pantagruel,* viii), a clear infusion of Platonic language is apparent: "Amongst the gifts, graces and prerogatives with which the sovereign plasmator God Almighty hath endowed and adorned human nature at the beginning, that seems to me most singular and excellent by which we may in mortal state attain to a kind of immortality, and in the course of this transitory life perpetuate our name and seed, which is done by a progeny issued from us in the lawful bonds of matrimony." [1] In Rabelais' creative world the regenerating powers of the universe are so great that they will not allow themselves to be countermanded by the original fall and so frustrated that "by death should be brought to nought that so stately frame and plasmature, wherein man at first had been created." In this life, through succession, man can achieve a kind of perpetuity. Gargantua is particularly grateful that he has lived to see and benefit from this process of regeneration: "Not without just and reasonable cause do I give thanks to God my Saviour and Preserver, for that he hath enabled me to see my bald old age reflourish in thy youth; for when, at his good pleasure, who rules and governs all things, my soul shall leave this mortal habitation, I shall not account myself wholly to die, but to pass from one place to another, considering that, in and by thee, I continue in my visible image living in the world, visiting and conversing with people of honour and other my good friends, as I was wont to do."

The essential background to these thoughts is Socrates' speech in the *Symposium,* but especially the refraction of that discourse in Marsilio Ficino's commentary *In convivium Platonis sive de amore* (VI.xi). Following Plato, Ficino gives his sense of the never-ending processes of emulation and change in the world. The individual is involved in replacement, not only of his organic being but also of his mind and emotions. It is in opposition to this process of change that procreation, moved by love, promotes a continuity whereby the mortal nature approaches the immortal: "We all desire to have goods, and not only to have them but to have them eternally. The single goods of mortals change and fade and they would all quickly disappear if new ones were not continuously made in place of those which leave. Therefore, so that goods may somehow endure for us forever, we desire to re-create those which pass away. That recreation is effected by generation. Hence has been born in everyone the instinct for generation. But since generation, by continuation, renders mortal things like divine, it is certainly a divine gift." [2]

In the specific argument of this study, a fundamental difference exists between Ficino and Rabelais, on the one hand, and Plato on the other. Ficino, representing, as Vittore Branca has made clear, the line of Italian civic interest, crucially differs from Plato in his valuations of children and fame. For Plato, while each is a product of man's aspirations for continuation, fame has superior merit: "Who, when he thinks of Homer and Hesiod and other great poets, would not rather have their children than ordinary human ones? Who would not emulate them in the creation of children such as theirs, which have preserved their memory and given them everlasting glory?" [3] Petrarch, with similar language and examples, took the same side of the argument, and so, too, will Montaigne (if we keep in mind his deep distrust of all future issues, fame included). But, perhaps following Ficino, Rabelais does not elevate fame over children. He calls physical procreation "the most singular and excellent way," and Shakespeare (to extend the thematic lines that we have been drawing) will regard it as the "mightier way."

To say that Ficino and Rabelais, and Shakespeare for that matter, thought children a superior way of response to time, is not to say that they were unconcerned with honor and achievement. On the contrary, for Ficino, knowledge and love of truth are the cognitive corollaries of the physical possibilities of renewal, preserving through memory what would otherwise be lost. And it is precisely in Gargantua's famous letter that the link is fastened between children and time and education. His son will be a better monument if, in addition to continuing "the perfect image of [his father's] body" he also shows his father's moral qualities ("les meurs de l'ame"). Only then will the son be the "perfect guardian and treasure of the immortality of our name." As the son is the reward and product, the father is the source and guiding hand, a new paideutic function in the Renaissance, where the father, time, and education unite in the formation of an adult ready for mature involvement in society.

Rabelais summarizes with great vividness and startling contrasts the educational ideal of fifteenth-century Italian humanism. If we consider the practices of such educators as Guarino da Verona and Vittorino da Feltre, and such treatises as Vergerius' *De ingenuis moribus,* Alberti's *I libri della famiglia,* Palmieri's *Vita civile,* Aeneus Sylvius' *De liberorum educatione,* and Battista Guarino's *De ordine docendi et studendi,* we cannot but be struck by similarities not only in general design and inspiration but also in specific details. For us, the new sense of time that these works exhibit, and the importance of time for their new educational programs, can serve as a bridge joining Petrarch and Rabelais.

Through men who had fallen under his tutelage, like the prominent university lecturer Giovanni da Ravenna, who had as students the future leading school masters Vittorino da Feltre and Guarino da Verona, Petrarch's connection with Padua and the north is clear and specific. In more general terms, W. H. Woodward can conclude, "The spirit of Petrarch — in the study of the Renaissance we find ourselves inevitably harking back to Petrarch — was still a living force in Padua." [4] In fact, throughout Italy, in Florence as well as in the north, the spirit of Petrarch was a living force, particularly his superhuman devotion to study and his conviction of the preciousness of time. We have already referred to Manetti, who nearly became consumptive through his determination not to waste time and who in a career as a distinguished civic leader was most conscious of time. A student of Vittorino da Feltre describes the extent to which he denied his body's needs for food and sleep in order to have more time for study and work. This same student remembers "that Vittorino, now well advanced in years, would of a winter's morning come early, candle in one hand and book in the other, and rouse a pupil in whose progress he was specially interested; he would leave him time to dress, waiting patiently till he was ready: then he would hand him the book, and encourage him with grave and earnest words to high endeavor." [5]

Later, in a period of intensive study before his journey to Italy, Erasmus too showed the same disregard for health and normal comfort, so fired up he was by his zeal for study and his determination to master Greek.[6] As in Petrarch, this zeal translates itself into a vigorous exploitation of every available moment. Vergerius' *De ingenuis*, using among others Petrarch's model of Augustus, urges the more intensive use of spare hours: "To give a fixed time each day to reading . . . is a well tried practice which may be strongly recommended. Alexander read much even on campaign; Caesar wrote his Commentaries, and Augustus recited poetry, whilst commanding armies in the field. With such examples what distractions of peaceful city life can be pleaded as excuse for neglect of daily study?"[7] While his argument is less militant than Petrarch's, still his sense of the need to utilize all time available for study is the same: "Many leisure hours now wasted may be saved by devoting them to the recreation of lighter reading. Some wisely arrange a course of Readings during dinner; others court sleep, or banish it, amidst books, although physicians are, no doubt, right in condemning the abuse of this latter practice." Then he makes a suggestion that is memorable for bringing together the technological advances of the fourteenth century and the aroused concerns of humanism for time (although it is more often cursed by today's students who labor under its psychic burdens): "Of no little use would also be the placement in our libraries of clocks, well in view, which could inform us of the measured lapse of time."[8]

In defense of this labor of love, Battista Guarino in his *De ordine docendi et studendi* can cite the examples of Pliny ("No one was more careful in rescuing every minute for his beloved studies") and Theophrastus, who "was in the habit of reproaching nature for granting long years of life to the stag and the crow, who could not use them, whilst denying them to man who has before him the illimitable task of knowledge." (Woodward, p. 177) Guarino then issues an exhortation that has already become familiar to his contemporaries: "Let us, then, heeding these great names, see to it that we allow not our short working years to pass idly away."

The clear enemy of this impassioned commitment to the new learning is time, which becomes all the more crucial when life is seen to be brief and the new worlds to conquer so great. This Petrarchan legacy receives its clearest expression in Leon Battista Alberti's *I libri della famiglia*. In the dialogue of Book Three, time, along with body and soul, is considered among the three most precious of man's belongings. Significantly, when we consider the frequent Renaissance relations between time and thrift, this third book is entitled "Economicus," and has to deal with the evils of prodigality and the virtues of "masserizia" (husbandry). Like money, the value of which is greatly stressed in the opening pages of this dialogue, time must be used; in fact, it perishes through non-use: "Perdesi adunque il tempo nollo adoperando, e di colui sarà il tempo che saprà adoperarlo." [9] *Never waste time* is the constantly stressed rule of this Florentine civic humanist. "Fuggio il sonno, e l'ozio, sempre faccendo qualche cosa" ("I flee from sleep and idleness, and I am always busy about something," p. 176). For such men, busyness is essential to business, even extending to their walk; the very accomplished Niccolaio Alberto used to say that he never knew a diligent man who did not walk quickly. Diligence is able to manage affairs with dispatch and order, but negligence — and here we witness the argument of time taking a secular turn — "once the proper time has been lost is obliged to perform in haste and with waste that which first would have been done easily" ("Allora quasi perduta la stagione gli sta necessità fare in furia e con fatica quello che in sua stagione, prima, era facile a fare," p. 177). Not in relation to the afterlife, but in the successes and accomplishments of earthly affairs, time involves a calling to account, where past negligence will come back to haunt present endeavor. The most dramatic presentation of this theme will be Shakespeare's *Richard II*.

Alberti is very concerned to regulate his busyness, so that his many activities do not confound one another, so that he has not begun many enterprises and finished none, or completed evil ones while neglecting the better (p. 176) — fears that were, of course, Petrarch's constant companions. Consequently, when he awakes in the morning, he makes a list, charting out what is to be done that day, and assigning to each event a set time. And in the evening he takes stock of what he was able to do and not do. Through this means all of his affairs are accomplished "with order and with almost no trouble" ("E a quello modo mi vienne fatto con ordine ogni faccenda quasi con niuna fatica," p. 176).

Love of variety is intimately connected with the Renaissance approach to time. In education, the writers we have been examining conceived of richer and more varied possibilities for knowledge. This was largely the product of the fuller acquisition of classical texts, presenting not only more knowledge but also greater diversity of matters for study. Consequently, in Renaissance treatises on education, scheduling is more important than it had been under the medieval system, where the number of materials with which education dealt was more limited. This is an important difference between the two. In the Renaissance, then, the titles of educational tracts imply such rational distribution of time, methods, and material: *De ordine . . . , De ratione. . . .* Describing his own miseducation, Erasmus, as Rabelais following him will also do, regrets the time spent in sophistries and vain mazes of logic, but also the lack of method: "Further, as to the manner of teaching, what confused methods, what needless toil, characterized instruction!" [10] Since the men of the Renaissance want so much, and there is so much to be wanted, and the time of life is so short, scheduling is a natural product of these pressures — of their love of variety and their fear of time. Thus it is that Vives justifies the teacher's selection of texts, "so that the course of life, so short and fleeting, may not be consumed in what is superfluous and (as is not infrequently the case) in the positively harmful." [11] As Alberti has already done, Battista Guarino, in his *De ordine docendi et studendi,* gives the connection between variety and scheduling in the Renaissance:

> In ordering our reading it is of great help to allot specific hours to each subject, and to observe this rule, once made, with strictness. In this way we may check our progress day by day. Hesiod long ago pointed the lesson — that the heap after all is only an accumulation of tiny grains. So to rescue even a few minutes each day for definite study of a particular author is always a gain. In the pursuit of learning as in other activities order and method are the secret of progress. [He gives examples of a chorus and an army.] Hence we see the crucial importance of system, which applies not less to study than to the captaincy of an army. For unless we map out clearly our course of reading and arrange our working hours in accordance with it, so many subjects claim our attention that concentration and thoroughness are impossible; our mind is divided between books of equal attractiveness, with the result that no solid work is done at all.[12]

This connection between variety and scheduling is essential to the nature of the Renaissance and can be observed in other areas as well. We recall that the mechanical clock found great receptivity in craft and merchant circles of the big cities, where the great variety of interest and duties could be better regulated by the single measurement of hours than by the various bells. We saw too that the great variety of interests of Dante and Petrarch — aesthetic and contemplative — were brought to some working and ethical order by their increased consciousness of time. In fact, time in the Renaissance is the agent of an external reality that serves to limit the freer flow of the human mind or human activities.

But here, as the examples above indicate, the clear conception and use of time serve to channel human energies for the purposes of greater effectiveness. This is another illustration of the paradox of time which we have discussed in connection with Petrarch and shall have further occasion to discuss in connection with subsequent writers — the unique combination of fervor and system that we find in the Renaissance approach to time, where discovery translates itself into schedule.[13]

While some of these educational tracts can indeed be methodical, we must not lose sight of their basic inspiration. In Erasmus, in Rabelais, in Milton, we sense the fervent discovery that things can be better done than in the past. Not many years ago, Matteo Palmieri can observe regretfully in his *Vita civile* (1435–1440), a large part of the student's life was consumed in the art and construction of grammar, with "tristi maestri con tristi auctori. . . ." But today, he emphasizes, "Oggi in brevissimo tempo si vede molti con tale eleganzia scrivere e dire in latino che in tutta la vita sì tolerabilmente non si dicea per maestri de' nostri padri" ("Today in the shortest amount of time many are able to write and speak Latin with such elegance as even in a lifetime our fathers' masters could not have attained.").[14] In a shorter period of time the student can be better learned in material that is more relevant for his life among men. The new sense of time and the new order of teaching come together in Palmieri's summary prediction that in not too many years "filosofia ed altre scienze potersi in sui principali autori più brievemente e perfecte imparare" ("philosophy and the other disciplines will be taught in their primary authors more briefly and more perfectly"). "Più brievemente e perfecte," will be the cry of educational reform heard again and again in the Renaissance.

In the *Gargantua* (XIV–XXIV), Rabelais describes in greater detail the process of separation from the infelicitous methods of the Goths. His account of the exhaustive and weighty regimen under which Gargantua suffered, "corrompant toute fleur de jeunesse" is, as could be expected in comedy, neither kind nor just, but outrageously funny. While using Rabelais as witness might smack somewhat of giving the prosecuting attorney the powers of judge, still beneath his gross hyperbole there is the fabled "moelle substantifique." Three basic impressions can be gathered from his portrait of the older methods of education: a disregard for time, a tremendous sense of physical weight, and untapped human resources.

Disregard for time is one conspicuous means Rabelais uses to indicate the unworthiness of the former method of education. Under the tutelage of Thubal Holofernes, the young giant spent five years and three months learning his ABC's with such skill that he was able to recite them by heart backwards (chapter XIV). Thirteen years, six months, and two weeks were spent in hearing lectures on the standard medieval grammarian, Donatus, and three authors from another standard text. For eighteen years and eleven months he read another grammar then in fashion, *De modis significandi,* with all of its commentaries. This too he could recite by heart backwards. He was sixteen years and two months about the *Compost.* In the midst of the work his tutor died of syphilis — the irruption of reality into an insulated system which Montaigne also would have occasion to exploit. With Thubal's replacement the mode of study did not alter, except that Grangousier brings about a necessary change of method and tutor when he notices that education is working no improvement in his son, but rather making him worse so that he "grew thereby foolish, simple, doted and blockish." (XV) A vivid lesson of contrast is presented in the manners, appearance, and grace of learning of the young page, Eudemon, who had studied only two years. This faith had found expression before, indirectly in "Cornificius," and more prominently in the line of fifteenth-century humanistic educators who held, as Palmieri put it, that the great authors could be learned "più brievemente e perfecte." Eudemon is a living example of the cry of the reformers: a better education could be acquired in a shorter period of time.

The expenditure of time is aggravated by the childish unworthiness of the materials, of which little games such as proving "de modis significandi non erat scientia" on one's fingers are all too often, unfortunately, in evidence — the silly byproduct of the cloistered imagination. The materials lack variety and anything like rich personal, public, or natural reference. It is no wonder then, that one main impression of this educational regimen must be its sheer sense of physical weight and boredom as a vital spirit is limited to time-consuming pettiness. Since Gargantua's school days passed before the invention of printing, he had to write all of his books in the Gothic script (printing and the use of Roman, or Italian, letters, are two indications of time-saving in Pantagruel's education). To do this he had to carry a great pen and inkhorn, weighing seven hundred thousand pounds, "the pencase whereof was as big and long as the great pillar of Enay, and the horn was hanging to it in great iron chains, it being of the wideness of a tun of merchant ware. (XIV)

His breviary, which had to be carried for him to mass, weighed "in grease, clasps, parchment, and cover, little more or less than eleven hundred and six pounds." (XXI) Rabelais deals as freely with poundage as he does with years, for in this closed system numbers are strangely without significance. At church Gargantua heard "six and twenty or thirty masses." The careless statement of number indicates the lack of attention paid to any one mass. While numbers proliferate, the thing itself is unimportant. So it is with the "confused heap of paternosters . . . of Saint Claude" brought to Gargantua on an ox-drawn cart. Since each was the size of a hat-block, "he said more in turning them over, than sixteen hermits would have done."

More oppressive than the weight of the objects is the heaviness of that spirit which without thought or interest merely follows prescribed routines. After all the masses and the paternosters, "then did he study some paltry half hour with his eyes fixed upon his book; but as the comic saith his mind was in the kitchen." Time passes slowly for such distracted energy. The spirit is oppressed by the organic necessities of eating, sleeping, and discharging wastes — stultifying natural rounds that it was the very meaning of humanism to surmount. This atmosphere is far from the reaction of Pantagruel when he received his father's letter: he seemed so fired with a new avidity for learning that "you would have said that the vivacity of his spirit amidst the books was like a great fire amongst dry wood, so active it was, vigorous and indefatigable."

Such liberated energy must be kept in mind when we make our way through the rigorous *emploi du temps* that Gargantua's new mentors designed for him, "qu'il ne perdoit heures quelconques du jour, ains tout son temps consommoit en lettres e honeste scavoir" ("that he lost not any one hour in the day, but employed all his time in learning, and honest knowledge," XXIII). Despite the tight scheduling, time is paradoxically overcome through the zest and pleasure with which the human appetite moves toward goals that arouse its limitless resources. We have shown in the case of Petrarch how little the spirit seems to drag and the time to weigh in such total commitment of endeavor. Control of time involves a more confident view of human resources.

Along with the injection of vitality, important techniques are practiced to utilize time more exhaustively. One could be called "doubling-up" — a practice that Petrarch cites Augustus as using, and one to which he added embellishments.[15] Upon awaking (his day started at 4 A.M. under the new system, not at 8 or 9 A.M. as under Thubal) Gargantua was rubbed down — and as this was being done he was read some pages from the Bible. Next, at elimination, the same lessons were read, with his tutor dwelling on the points that were difficult and obscure. The lessons from the day before were repeated while Gargantua was dressing. Repetition — not of courses, but, on a day-to-day basis, of materials recently covered — helps the student to secure the great variety of materials. It is important to realize that Rabelais is respecting historical probability in his description of Gargantua's education. Humanistic it was, but it still took place before the invention of the printing press; consequently it was based on "leçons orales" — lectures and memorization. But to the recitation and memorization the student was enjoined to adduce practical examples from daily life — "y fondoit quelques cas practicques et concernens l'estat humain." (XXIII)

Another variation of "doubling-up" is the perennial searching for causes. To aid digestion, they brought out cards, "not to play, but to learn a thousand pretty tricks, and new inventions, which were all grounded upon arithmetic." Learning is made pleasant, but recreation, too, is not exempt from that investigation of causes and reasons which was part of the need to exploit all time and all resources. Over dinner, they "discourse merrily together, speaking first of the virtue, propriety, efficacy and nature of all that was served in at that table; of bread, of wine, of water, of salt, of fleshes, fishes, fruits, herbs, roots, and of their dressing," to which they mustered a phalanx of classical commentary. Music, sport, conversation, games — all add variety to the main endeavor, but are not too distant from it — given the drive to search out the causes and qualities of things. In gigantesque form, the Ulyssean impulse is reincarnate in Rabelais.

A fairly direct relationship can be established between Petrarch and Rabelais; at least they are on the same line of development. But Rabelais, too, in his intense Renaissance concern with scheduling, looks forward to the same need in Robinson Crusoe or Benjamin Franklin. Perhaps this would be clearer if we recomposed Gargantua's schedule in the following manner:

4 A.M.	Rise, rub-down, lecture from Holy scriptures. Adoration and prayer to the good Lord. Excretion, lecture. Dress, repeat lessons of day before.
5 6 7	Lecture of day.
8	Exercise.
9	Dinner, thrifty and frugal.

10   Digestion, cards and music.

11 ⎫
12 ⎬   Second lecture of day.
1   ⎪
2 ⎭

       Lengthy period of outdoor activity.
       Supper, copious and large. Games and merriment.

     At full night, praise God the Creator. Sleep.

It is obvious that some of my arrangement depends upon time-esti-
mates, since in Rabelais the only specific references are to the 4 A.M.
rising, the two three-hour lecture periods, and the one-hour period of
digestion after the morning "diner." Indeed, there is some flexibility:
when the student repeats the preceding day's lessons, this can last several
hours, but ordinarily terminates when he has completely dressed. Exercise after the first lecture of the day may be terminated at their pleasure.
But despite the latitude and the imprecise intervals, this rough *emploi
du temps* is still fairly systematic, much more so than Petrarch's attempts
to marshal his time, and is well on the way to the thorough domination
of schedule, with hours well defined, that we have in Benjamin Franklin's list. What is absent in the latter, and what is uniquely combined
with the schedule of Gargantua's studies, is the sense of enthusiasm and
dedication, the presence of a liberating fervor that annihilates the very
time-consciousness which guides it. As in other areas of Renaissance
development, we are in the presence of a discovery.

One of the forerunners of Rabelais' humanistic educational system,
Vergerius, in his *De ingenuis moribus,* suggests that in every library a
clock ought to be in full view. Indeed, beginning with the sixteenth century, the clock was frequently present in portrait paintings.[16] Relatively
rare, it was an item *de luxe,* a matter of conspicuous display — but one
that indicated a kind of public or intellectual seriousness. The man
whose portrait contained this time-indication would be like Botticelli's
Augustine or Pencz's Jerome (with hour-glass), wrestling with problems
of utmost importance, or he would be a public man of some substance
and responsibility, like Holbein's Charles Solier, the French ambassador
to London. A necessary adjunct of churchmen, scholars, and diplomats,
when they presented themselves to the world in their essential nature,
was this sure indication of a personal seriousness. But there was another

reaction to the domination of the clock, one that would much later be expressed by Mme. De Sévigné, who refused to wear a watch with a second hand: "it would chop one's life too fine," or Mme. Louvigny who left her residence in Rue Vieille-du-Temple in Paris — because the clock of the Hôtel d'Epernon struck the quarter hours. This too "cut her life into too many pieces." [17] To be sure, most of the world then still lived according to "temps vécu" — a natural world of vague and general temporal reckoning linked to events of nature or daily life.[18] As Rabelais in the education of Gargantua is far in advance of this easier world, anticipating the more vigorous lists of a more sober era, so too in his Abbey of Thélème he anticipates the desire to escape the felt pressures of time's movement, the elitist desire for freedom and spontaneity, the kind of freedom the new monk John of the Funnels represents when he declares, in regard to canonical hours, "I never tie myself to hours . . . for they are made for the man, and not the man for them." (*Garg.* XLI) Consequently, in Rabelais' golden world of the Abbey, as in Shakespeare's green world, there must be no clock. In this kingdom of possibilities, Gargantua founds for John of the Funnels a Utopian religious community "contrary to all others": "And because in all other monasteries and nunneries all is compassed, limited, and regulated by hours, it was decreed that in this new structure there should be neither clock nor dial, but that according to the opportunities and incident occasions, all their hours should be disposed of; for, said Gargantua, the greatest loss of time that I know, is to count the hours — . What good comes of it? Nor can there be any greater dotage in the world than for one to guide and direct his course by the sound of a bell, and not by his own judgment and discretion." (LII)

At first glance, this Utopian abbey seems to contrast starkly with the method by which Gargantua was educated: in the one fairly rigid scheduling, and in the other, an openness and spontaneity that proceeds by the inspiration of the moment. Gargantua was wakened at 4 A.M., but the members of the Abbey "rose out of their beds when they thought good." (LVII) There are, in fact, substantial differences between the two, and these are important to the problem of time. Yet both are prompted by the same Renaissance spirit, by the image of human possibility. In each, this spirit is triumphant: in the one, it is voracious and energized, packing as much activity as possible into the passing moments; in the other, it is the spirit of gaiety and delight in spontaneity. In both, what stifles is abhorred. The two regimens are further alike in that each is explicitly anti-medieval. Rabelais' new program of humanistic studies shows a vivid sense of time and a sharp notion of personal and social relevancy. As in the academy, the walls of the cloister are removed, and greater freedom of movement and involvement in society is allowed. The three vows of monastic life are to be replaced by three freedoms: for chastity, that the Thelemites might be honorably married; for poverty, that they might be rich; for obedience, that they might live at liberty. In all three, although certainly there is an aristocratic admixture, the new bourgeois values of goods and succession are clearly represented. Yet despite this fundamental similarity, we are right to sort out elements that will in history be sorted out for us, when the bourgeois sense of time will be separated from the aristocratic sense of leisure. That they should be united in the Renaissance, and pre-eminently in Rabelais, by some truly kindred and undifferentiated bond of common impulse, is an integral part of the nature and problem of time in that period.

The *Tiers Livre:* The Skeptical Reaction

Gargantua (1534) and *Pantagruel* (1532) are united in their optimistic, progressive resources, which, despite the shadows of the diabolic artillery, can be traced in the opportunities that opened before father and son. With all the comic style, their worlds are heroic worlds, instinct with great possibilities and energies, where man is capable of acting upon the world and ordering his affairs with some rational and vitalistic faith. The *Tiers Liver,* separated from the first two by some twelve years (1546), is radically different. Lacking the strong forward impulse so typical of the first two books, the *Third Book* is somewhat depressurized and frankly unheroic, as Panurge recoils from the most painful of ignominies, cuckoldry. Instead of a world luminously open to knowledge and human endeavor, this skeptical work shows the diversity and perplexity of human subjectivity that puzzles Panurge's will. The assembled authorities of the rational sciences, each reflecting the assumptions of his own discipline, can give him no certitude; so contradictory is the evidence that Gargantua, remembering the halcyon days of promise, can only reflect, "En sommes-nous là?" [19] ("Are we come to this?")

In this world that seems to have ground to a standstill, to have lost even its desire for forward movement, it is the fool who becomes the wise man, and one important fool, Bridoie (or Bridlegoose), utters the temporal wisdom of the piece. Rather than managing time, Bridoie temporizes. And yet his nonchalance is very distant from the resources of the abbey. Neither utopian nor avant-garde, his manner seems a return to a more muted natural world, instinct with distrust of man's rational capacities. His long-standing habit of deciding law cases by the throw of the dice, while not ordinarily recommended, still strangely enjoys some justification by the very intellectual atmosphere of the *Third Book*, where the uncertainty of judgment and the diversity of opinion suggest the essays of Montaigne. In fact, in *Of Presumption* (II.17) Montaigne, too, will submit to hazard: "The uncertainty of my judgment is so evenly balanced in most occurrences that I would willingly submit to the decision of chance and of the dice. And I note, with much reflection on our human weakness, the examples that even sacred history has left us of the custom of entrusting to fortune and chance the determination of choice in doubtful cases. . . . Human reason is a two-edged and dangerous sword." (Fr. 496/Th. 739)[20]

In chapters XXXIX–XLIII, the story of Bridoie unfolds. He must defend one of his unfavorable decisions before the parliamentary court of Paris. Bridoie pleads old age and failing sight — he cannot see the dice as well as he used to. But why, the question must be answered, if he decided by chance, does he go through all the routine of court procedure? He lists his reasons, and his third brings us to the new temporal perspective of the *Third Book*:

> Thirdly, I consider, as your own worships used to do, that time ripeneth and bringeth all things to maturity, — that by time everything cometh to be made manifest and patent — and that time is the father of truth. . . . Therefore is it, that after the manner and fashion of your other worships I defer, protract, delay, prolong, intermit, surcease, pause, linger, suspend, . . . and shift off the time of giving a definitive sentence to the end that the suit or process, being well fanned and winnowed . . . may, by succession of time, come at last to its full ripeness and maturity.
>
> (XL)

By this time all the passions and convictions of right are allayed, and people are much more willing to accept a settlement. In his further defense, Bridoie tells the story of Perrin Dendin, who was famous as a reconciler of parties in court cases. But his son, more "actif et vigilant" and operating under a more aggressive banner, somehow was never able to duplicate his father's success in settling differences. Wherever throughout his part of the country he heard of a trial or division under way, he immediately intervened to settle the issue ("il se ingeroit d'appoincter les parties"). But his over-eagerness led rather to anger and exasperation than to reconciliation, and the tavern keepers of the area used to say "that under him they had not in the space of a whole year so much reconciliation-wine . . . as under his father they had done in one half hour's time." The son complained bitterly to old Perrin Dendin, and was answered that his lack of success was due to his failure to wait: "Thou hast not the skill and dexterity of settling and composing differences. Why? Because thou takest them at the beginning, in the very infancy and bud as it were, when they are green, raw, and indigestible. Yet I know, handsomely and featly, how to compose and settle them. Why? Because I take them at their decadence, in their weaning, and when they are pretty well digested." (XLI) The word is right time, *oportet,* but the ethic is very different from the Renaissance injunction to seize the day, *carpe diem.* The method of Bridoie and the story of Perrin Dendin revert, within a Renaissance context, to an older, more enduring and patient level of nature, which is alien to fiery humanistic endeavor. The idea of ripeness here, rather than encouraging militant seizure, leads to patient waiting and a contentment within the regular rounds of things, which have their own logic and rhythm, and to which the human mind must adjust. It was the purpose of humanism, with its energetic ardor, to rise out of these regular rounds — which seemed more suited to dull and torpid natures. For the arduous struggle Bridoie, and perhaps the entire *Third Book,* substitutes a natural ease. Rather than aggressive attack, a kind of holding-action is required. This world-view, as we shall see later in Montaigne, has much in common with the gray world of the administrator, not so much interested in adjudicating right or wrong, but more concerned with keeping the ship afloat, with reaching amicable agreements. Such an impulse runs counter to the humanistic need to gain distinctions, and in fact undermines man's claim to being a rational creature. In the subsequent chapter (XLII), Bridoie relates how court suits grow, and offers his solution for passionate conviction: sleep it off. He uses the story of the angry Gascon who had lost his money at cards and then went around challenging everybody to a fight. When he found no takers, he fell asleep, only to be awaked, uncomprehendingly, by another belligerent. But after his rest he saw no reason to fight, and Bridoie concludes: "Avecques l'oubliance de sa perte il avoit perdu l'envie de combattre" ("Thus, in forgetting his loss, he forgot the eagerness which he had to fight"). This vision is of course essentially comic and reductive, making light, as in his way Montaigne will also, of both the stability and the rationality of man's strongest convictions: "Thus by a little sleep was pacified the ardent fury of two warlike champions."

The extent to which the posture of Bridoie deviates from the basic

Renaissance response can be shown when we contrast his attitudes with several episodes in the *Gargantua*. John of the Funnels refuses to resign himself to God's will when his monastery's vineyards are being uprooted by the armies of King Pichrochole. (XXVI–XXVII) His fellow monks, amazed at the attack, can only sing, "Impetum inimicorum non timueritis": "Whom when he hears sing, im, im, pe, ne, ne, ne, ne, nene, tum, ne num, num, ini, i mi, co, o, no, o, o, neno, ne, no, no, no, rum, nenum, num: It is well shit, well sung, said he. By the virtue of God, why do you not sing, Panniers farewell, vintage is done?" Representing the active energy of the aroused and engaged Church militant, he takes up the cross and uses it as a weapon to lambaste and scatter the attackers. A similar antipathy toward do-nothing monks, who represent no social utility, is expressed in chapter XL, which explains "Why Monks are the Outcasts of the World." Gargantua believes that the monk, like the ape, is good-for-nothing; the monk —

> I mean those lither, idle, lazy monks [ces ocieux moines], — doth not labour and work, as do the peasant and the artificer; doth not ward and defend the country, as doth the man-of-war; cureth not the sick and diseased, as the physician doth; doth neither preach nor teach, as do the Evangelical doctors and school-masters; doth not import commodities and things necessary for the commonwealth, as the merchant doth. Therefore is it, that by and of all men they are hooted at, hated and abhorred.

As in the education of Gargantua, the emphasis is on social service, practical utility, with preaching included; here we should recall that the much earlier opponent of the do-nothing monks, Domenico Cavalca, with his sense of time, was a member of the order of preachers. So, too, when Grangousier later gives his counsel to the pilgrims (XLV), he urges them to stay away from "ces otieux et inutiles voyages" ("idle and unprofitable journeys"): "Look to your families, labour every man in his vocation, instruct your children, and live as the good apostle St. Paul directeth you."

While certainly Rabelais does not repudiate the good sense of these passages, still in the *Third Book* their aroused and active energy is more disquieting. It is Dendin's son Thenot who is the spokesman for vigorous enterprise, and even for the motto of social utility, "Qui non laborat non manige ducat." This Pauline phrasing (here mangled) was also prominent in Domenico Cavalca's treatise: "Chi non vuole operare non mangi." But as this notion of busyness is satirized in the son, so is it repudiated in the patient waiting of the father. They also serve, Milton will write, and like Rabelais and Montaigne, although from a far different base, he will be more willing to defend the value of "standosi" and "ozio" — those indolent qualities of man which were so offensive to Cavalca, and even to the earliest notions of Rabelais and Milton themselves. These are specific instances of endorsement and then recoil from a rigorous implementation of an intrinsic Renaissance message.

Chapter 6
Montaigne

Introduction

Montaigne stood in determined opposition to many of the larger developments in Renaissance temporal response, and in so doing, he became startlingly modern. His thought betrays none of that aroused militancy in organization and scheduling of time, none of that need to cast into the future, to transcend the debased present. His nonchalance ("toward which I clearly lean by temperament"), so disquieting to Pascal, was alien to Renaissance fervor and heroism and energy. Yet, on a smaller, more personal and intimate scale, the *carpe diem* motive, prominent in the Renaissance, was finally his. In his willingness to engage the thing itself, without any metaphysical structuring, without any historical extension, Montaigne was modern, indeed, and as free from the great motivations and needs of a Dante as he was from the humanistic pursuit of continuity.[1] "Presenti cose," Dante confesses before Beatrice, "Present things with their false pleasure turned my steps as soon as your face was hid." For Dante, the vision of permanence needs prayerful protection from "human movements"; motions and energies of life must be comprehended within an enduring idea, texture contained in a text, before what is present can be redeemed. This was true for medieval Christianity and it was equally true for Renaissance humanism deriving from Petrarch. But for Montaigne, present things in their passingness and materiality are not debased; they are, in fact, all that man possesses. "I easily console myself," he writes in "Of Vanity," "for what will happen here when I am here no longer; present things keep me busy enough."[2] Such radical transformations must extend to imagery, and Michaël Baraz, in a valuable article, "Les Images dans les *Essais* de Montaigne," has shown what totally new valuations of experience are introduced in Montaigne's writing. In both the Middle Ages and the Renaissance, loftiness, light, spirituality, transparency, seriousness, permanence, stability, nobility were images indicating superior value; but for Montaigne, low places, darkness, materiality, density, humor, variety — areas that had previously been reserved for comedy or worse, become choice and desirable.[3] Similarly, and more closely related to temporality, over words connoting length or extension Montaigne prefers words that suggest "filling-out" ("remplir le maintenant"), penetration in depth, thickness of immediate experience. Whether hierarchical or lateral, Montaigne upsets the terms valued by Christian philosophy and Renaissance humanism.

Cassirer's *The Individual and the Cosmos in Renaissance Philosophy* provides some larger frame for Montaigne's transformation of values. Formerly, in the inherited Aristotelian-Platonic system of "graduated mediation," "the higher an element stands in the cosmic stepladder, the closer it is to the unmoved mover of the world, and the purer and more complete is its nature. But Cusanus no longer recognizes any such relationship of proximity and distance between the sensible and the supersensible. If the distance as such is infinite, all relative, finite differences are annihilated. When compared to the divine origin of being, every element, every natural being is equally far and equally near to that origin. There is no longer any 'above' and 'below,' but a single universe, homogeneous within itself." (pp. 25–26) Thus it is that in Rabelais the objects in the world are food for the intellectual appetite; all things, great and small, reveal and lead to fundamental causes, and all are worthy of study — or mention (and hence his delight in listing). Thus it is that Shakespeare can weave his play with plot lines from various social strata, and feel no neo-classical compunction about joining kings and clowns. Erich Auerbach, in "The Weary Prince," shows the rich scale of stylistic levels that go into Shakespeare's works — "the ever varied nuances of the profoundly human mixture of high and low, sublime and trivial, tragic and comic." [4]

For the Christian Middle Ages, "Everything in the world was an effect of something beyond the world; everything in life was a step to something beyond life." [5] The same deferred fulfillment and ulterior references were part of humanism, which explains why fears of early and sudden death haunted the imaginations of Petrarch and Milton. But Montaigne would have us focus on the thing at hand, in itself, and find our fulfillment in its own basic worth. His modernity lies here.

Harry Levin, writing of aesthetic realism, contrasts it with medieval allegory: "The world-view of the Renaissance and its aftermath can be differentiated from that of the Middle Ages by its vivid interest in . . . objects for their own sake." [6] In fact, Montaigne anticipates what Ortega y Gasset has called "the modern theme." For this most influential Spanish philosopher, nineteenth-century culture and science were themselves "progressivistic":

> The meaning and value of life, which is essentially present actuality, are forever awaking to a more enlightened dawn, and so it goes on. Real existence remains perpetually on the subordinate level of a mere transition towards an utopian future. The doctrines of culture, progress, futurism and utopianism are a single, unique "ism." Under one denomination or the other we find invariably the attitude of mind in which life for its own sake is a matter of indifference, and only acquires value if it is considered as an instrument or as a basis for the use of a culture operating in the "Beyond."

The theme of Ortega's generation, the modern theme, challenges the "cultural tradition," and instead of saying "life for the sake of culture," replies (with Montaigne, we might add), "culture for the sake of life." [7]

In his intellectual origins, Montaigne does not derive from the line of civic humanists with their endorsement of public involvement and children. Rather he seems more akin to those Stoical humanists, in the manner of Petrarch, who declined to submit themselves to Fortune. Essays such as "Of Solitude," "That to Philosophize Is to Learn to Die," "That the Taste of Good and Evil Depends in Large Part on the Opinion We Have of Them," "That Our Happiness Must not Be Judged until after Our Death," "Of the Inequality That Is between Us," "Of Democritus and Heraclitus," all largely of the early 1572–1574 period, show an attempted separation and retreat from life's troubles. In this stage of Montaigne's thinking, death dominates life and casts its shadow over all else. It is the final moment where our philosophy will be tested. It is the *but* and the *bout,* not only the end but also the goal and aim of life. And along the way, we must keep a backroom of life to ourself where we cannot be touched by what happens. Scornful indifference rather than hate is the proper attitude; rather than Timon's rage indicating care, Diogenes' disdain is proper to the Stoic. Montaigne's faith in man's rational tools and his goal of a severe and highly perfected character are summarized in the story of Pyrrho, the fearful man in the storm and the calm pig. The philosopher reprimands his companion, reminding him that he was endowed with reason so as to be superior to a pig. Montaigne goes on to ask,

> Shall we then dare to say that this advantage, reason, that we make such a fuss about, and on account of which we think ourselves masters and emperors of the rest of creation, has been put in us for our torment? What good is the knowledge of things if by it we lose the repose and tranquillity we should enjoy without it, and if it puts us into a worse condition than Pyrrho's pig? The intelligence that has been given us for our greatest good, shall we use it for our ruin, combating the plan of nature and the universal order of things, which says that each man shall use his tools and means for his advantage?
>
> (Fr. 36–37/Th. 75)

The rhetorical questions imply their own answers. Later on, however, although the *dramatis personae* will remain the same, the questions will draw different answers. The personal Stoic ideal will seem remote and impossible, and man's rational powers given him only as a curse, in contrast to which the instinctive repose of the pig seems a blessing.

Montaigne's experience of man's larger incapacities shatters his notions that man through rational powers can rise above his nature. This experience also intrudes upon his disdainful retreat and, paradoxically, pushes him more intensively into life. Death is the end of life, the *bout*, but not the goal of life, he will later conclude. "Philosopher c'est apprendre à vivre." Death is not at the end of life, it is all the way through life. In the "Apology" he tells us that "we stupidly fear one kind of death, when we have already passed and are passing through so many others." Experience of *chorismos*, or a more or less universal failing, seems to propel Montaigne, in a manner contrary to his intellectual heritage, all the more deeply into the things that perish.

Usually such conversion is not outrightly new, but rather a reconversion. And in Montaigne's case, to follow the argument of his recent biographer, Donald M. Frame, this seems to be the case.[8] Montaigne's Stoical humanism was a not quite congenial reaction to the death of his friend, Etienne de la Boétie. Although the relationship was a good deal more complex than that, it appears that before his friend's death in 1563, Montaigne was the more pleasure-seeking of the two, with a gay love of life, while La Boétie was the mentor of "high moral strenuousness" for whom the "good life" was an "unending struggle for perfection." (p. 76)

It was after his death that Montaigne resolved to follow the high road of his friend. For ten years after La Boétie's death, according to Professor Frame, "Montaigne tried hard to follow in La Boétie's footsteps. As long as his friend lived — to judge by our few glimpses of the two — Montaigne preached and practiced a code and ideal more natural for himself and less rigorous than La Boétie's. After 1573 he was to renew his quest for a way of his own. For the ten years in between he was under the sway — almost the shadow — of his friend's ideals." (p. 83) The Stoical humanism of Montaigne's early essays shows Montaigne's attempts, somewhat unnaturally, to imitate his friend, and while there were other influences in and out of books, it was mainly La Boétie's impact that helped convert "Montaigne in his thirties from a reflective but gay young hedonist into an apprehensive stoical humanist." (p. 84)

Chorismos, for Montaigne, would imply the rejection of all human claims to constancy and permanence, the abnegation of man's pretensions to a purposeful, rational control of events and experience. While at first devastating and even tragic, such realization, as Cassirer has indicated, can eventually lead to better things, to a more modest yet positive evaluation of human life. For Montaigne, this radical skepticism did help to resolve the contradictions that arose between his Stoic assumptions and his more hedonistic nature, and helped him return to a more congenial pattern of thought. The massive "Apology for Raymond Sebond," speaking for universal mankind, together with several other essays containing more personal and individual revelation, explains why Montaigne himself was compelled to relax his hard Stoic line.

The final pages of the "Apology" (Fr. 455 ff./Th. 679 ff.) form a magnificent discourse of sustained philosophical lyricism, worthy — although devoid of their sonority — to be placed among the great French *hymnes* of the Renaissance. Although a cento from Plutarch with trimmings from Lucretius, this conclusion will serve to summarize Montaigne's consciousness of the pervasiveness of change, and of man's helplessness against the great forces of mutability. Prior to this section, after having developed at length the argument for perpetual change in the world of objects and in the cognitive and emotional world of the subject, Montaigne even more profoundly showed the fundamental unreliability of our senses as accurate indicators and conveyers of external phenomena. Where our instruments are faulty, how can the lines of our judgment be true? "Finally, there is no existence that is constant, either of our being or that of objects. And we, and our judgment, and all mortal things go on flowing and rolling unceasingly. Thus nothing certain can be established about one thing by another, both the judging and the judged being in continual change and motion." Montaigne cannot attribute the possibility of being to man: he is only involved in the passage from one state to another, neither of which *is*. "Thus, all things being subject to pass from one change to another, reason, seeking a real stability in them, is baffled, being unable to apprehend anything stable and permanent; because everything is either coming into being and not yet fully existent, or beginning to die before it is born." This section summarizes the great role of flux in Greek classical philosophy. Homer, according to Plato, made Ocean the father of the gods and Thetis his mother, in order "to show us that all things are in perpetual flux, change and variation." Pythagoras thought that all matter is flowing and sliding ("coulante et labile"); the Stoics, that there is no present time; Heraclitus, that no man steps twice into the same rivers; and Epimarchus, that no man owes money to him from whom he borrowed it, since both have changed. This "course" shows the tremendous place of change in the thought of the Greek philosophers, and one aspect of their influence on the later Renaissance.

Contemplating the processes of man's growth, Montaigne admits a philosophy of temporal replacement. "So that what is beginning to be born never arrives at the perfection of being; forasmuch as this birth is never completed, and never stops as being at an end, but from the seed onward goes on ever changing and shifting from one thing to another." "This being born commeth never to an end," John Florio will render it in his Elizabethan translation. The ages of man indicate the same development, "So that the subsequent age and generation is always undoing and destroying the preceding one." Coming to be born and coming to death are coincidental in the vast elemental processes. Life is not an achievement of a perfect state, since all is in mixture, or as Louis LeRoy had almost contemporaneously declared, in vicissitude.[9] Later Montaigne himself would declare the world's rule to be in "compensation et vicissitude." The notion is Heraclitean and is made clearly so when the Ephesian philosopher is quoted again, "the death of fire is the generation of air, and the death of air the generation of water." But this fragment is transcended when the same lesson is applied to ourselves: "Our prime dies and passes when old age comes along, and youth ends in the prime of the grown man, childhood in youth, and infancy in childhood. And yesterday dies in today, and today will die in tomorrow; and there is nothing that abides and is always the same."[10] This passage then goes on to declare that only God *is,* and that it is only to an eternal being that the language of time does not apply. The separation is vast and unbridgeable in the "Apology" between the eternal and the human, between the timeless and time, and between being and becoming. Only grace can elevate man is Montaigne's fideistic conclusion to the essay. We must remember, however, that the experience of *chorismos* is not terminal but transitional. Here Montaigne maintains the insubstantiality of the present, but later this will lead to the qualified dominance of the "present" in his thought. The "Apology" could be subtitled the "Triumph of Time," but it leads to no Petrarchan rejection of all those perishable goods, to no "Triumph of Eternity," but rather to a deeper immersion in things and life in all their present substantiality.

Montaigne's cosmic picture of the world is highly emulative, where the elements themselves die and give birth, and where the same process is observable in the stages of man's individual life. Such meditations are common in the Renaissance: they form the powerful substance of Dante's sense of life, of Machiavelli's, of Marlowe's, and of Shakespeare's. And yet, obviously, the ways of response differ. Although Dante had once entertained the vision of a political solution to his highly energized sense of man's questing, finally after the *Monarchia* he accepted only religious directions as being fully satisfactory. Not by running to keep up, but by participating in the higher spiritual directions of the universe does man save himself. Machiavelli essentially disregarded these higher possibilities and involved political man willy-nilly in the tragic-historical world where he had to maintain himself through power or else be swept aside. One of the great lines of intellectual descent in the sixteenth century derives from Machiavelli, and has its literary flourishing in Marlowe, and to a more limited degree in Shakespeare's history plays. Man is involved in a changing world, and can only save himself by aggressively controlling his fate. But as we have seen in Guicciardini, and shall observe in Montaigne, the experience of *chorismos* essentially debilitates any faith in man's controlling powers. Guicciardini is speaking of politics, but Montaigne even extends it to man's personal life. Even the sagest of men are buffeted by the instabilities of human nature, by being creatures of change in a changing world. "Of Drunkenness" gives a more mundane version of the "Apology's" assault on man's reason and capacities: "To how much vanity are we driven by the high opinion we have of ourselves! The best-regulated soul in the world has only too much to do to stay on its feet and keep itself from collapsing to the ground through its own weakness. . . . For all his wisdom, the sage is still a man: what is there more vulnerable, more wretched, and more null? Wisdom does not overcome our natural limitations. . . . The sage must blink his eyes at the blow that threatens him; if you set him on the edge of a precipice, he must shudder like a child. Nature has willed to reserve to herself these slight marks of her authority, invincible to our reason and Stoic virtue, in order to teach man his mortality and frailty." (Fr. 249–250/Th. 382)

And there are qualities more peculiar to Montaigne's own personality which made his earlier adoption of La Boétie's Stoic position more uncomfortable and alien. If, in the Machiavellian sense, one desires to control his experience, it requires great powers of self-control, calculation and containment. But Montaigne, as he tells us in "Of Presumption" (Fr. 488–489/Th. 727–728), is congenitally unsuited for the rigors of disciplined endeavor. Unable to control fortune, he abandons himself to her (a pose most unlike that prescribed by Machiavelli), and is at his calmest when he expects the worst. Deliberation disturbs him. Like several of Shakespeare's imaginative creations, Brutus, Hamlet, and Macbeth, Montaigne is highly apprehensive before the event. "Calamitosus est animus futuri anxius," he quotes Seneca. The only way that he found himself able to be careless of what was to come was by discovering his own inability — and a more generalized and universal inability — to control his fate. Cassirer's argument about the relationship between *chorismos* and *methexis* is hence borne out by Montaigne's spiritual evolution. Montaigne needed to face the personal and philosophical experience of man's nullity before he could move to redeem whatever was of real value.

Montaigne's experience of *chorismos* is important for what it leads to. By closing the door on a limitless future, it brings man face-to-face with his finite existence. Only in God's will, in the perception of that beatitude, did Dante see any resolution and satisfaction to man's passionate energies; yet Montaigne found some contentment in the experience of limitation itself by settling into what was his own. He feels that man's own energies and values are dissipated by the restless need to be looking "ailleurs." Such half-heartedness in the present taints existence, and adds to dissatisfaction and anxiety. Montaigne, "the wisest Frenchman who ever lived," administers to his own ills and those of his emotional and heroic time by recommending salvation, not in any transcendence or heroism, but in the present itself, and in the normal rounds of existence: "Others always go elsewhere, if they stop to think about it: they always go forward . . . as for me, I roll about in myself." (Fr. 499/Th. 743) Curious ramifications in his thought stem from Montaigne's conviction that men must find their contentment in what is at hand. On the one hand it leads to a social conservatism, horrified at any innovation, but, on the other hand, it leads in his personal life to a sense of freedom and liberation.

"The Vanity of the Human Position"

When at the conclusion of his essay "Of Three Kinds of Association" Montaigne speaks of *obligations civiles* and *occupations particulières,* he provides us with labels for the important directions his thought took after his experience of *chorismos.* Each of the attitudes connected with these phrases begins with profound skepticism and returns from Utopianism to the present, and each takes a comic view of man's separation from being, of his involvement in change. The first French phrase implies a passive acceptance of public duty, and an accommodation of the self to existing social standards. This vision belongs to the old and the experienced (perhaps they could be called the tired and the defeated). They are practical skeptics for whom nothing is new; they have seen it all. Their vision is essentially reductive, and in Montaigne's case they are painfully aware of the fortuitousness of our emotions and opinions, the simple changeableness of the human mechanism. If the activities of the human consciousness are not taken seriously one can see how this vision is closely indebted to *chorismos.* Behind it we hear the laughter of the gods, deriding our claims to deliberateness or permanence, mocking our passionate attachment to ideas that grew in time and will alter in time. In fact, this vision uses time to expose our violent passions and great schemes, to reduce their seriousness by revealing their genesis. Spokesmen for this attitude could be Pandarus in *Troilus and Criseyde,* Bridoie in Rabelais' *Third Book,* or, after Montaigne, a presence in the background of Shakespeare's tragedies that seems to reflect on the high ambitions of the agonists. The great motto of this vision would be, after Montaigne, "tant l'humaine posture est vaine." The vanity of the human position deflates any high pretensions; in fact, it deflates tragedy itself, and man is closed in the comedy of existence, where the main interest is in survival.

If a useful phrase for this vision is closed comedy, its counterpart involving *occupations particulières* could be called open comedy. This is the realm of the young (and those old men who would be explorers). Typically it approaches the present pleasure with vigorous attachment and without any doubts as to its validity. Such comedy is not one of derision but rather of vigorous participation in the pleasures of multiplicity. In closed comedy, the individual sacrifices his own doubts and desires to the general will and continuing order of society; he sets himself against the menacing encroachments of change. But in the personal realm of private thought and conduct, rather than seeking to halt change, he positively delights in diversity and novelty for their own sakes. While seriously taking hold of pleasure, these people differ from tragic characters in that they are more at home and more resilient in a world of variety and change. If, using Shakespeare's comedies as a basis of judgment, the reasonable and loving young woman is a touchstone of reality and representative of this vision, the outcast is the tedious pedant who would use his bookish learning to reduce the real worlds of nature, love, and experience. The vision of open comedy does not look to the vanity of our dreams, but rather to their sufficiency and reality. Yet it does not cling to any notions of permanence. Those who belong in the world of open comedy accept things as naturally passing, but that does not detract from their pleasures, which they pursue and possess with gaiety and strength.

In closed comedy man is a creature of change. Montaigne emphasizes process, whereby human pretensions towards permanence and deliberation are undermined. Man has no *réelle subsistence;* in the "Apology," the same is true for his institutions and his thought: "If nature enfolds within the bounds of her ordinary progress, like all other things, also the beliefs, judgments, and opinions of men; if they have their rotation, their season, their birth, their death, like cabbages; if heaven moves and rolls them at its will, what magisterial and permanent authority are we attributing to them?" If the "form of our being" — not only our complexion, stature, health, and physical attributes but the very "faculties of our soul" — depends on the habits and climate of the place where we have lived, if we see that some areas incline toward certain characteristics, "if we see flourishing now one art, one opinion, now another, by some celestial influence; such-and-such a century produce such-and-such natures, and incline the human race to such-and-such a bent; the minds of man now lusty, now lean, like our fields; what becomes of all those fine prerogatives on which we flatter ourselves?" (Fr. 433–434/Th. 647–648)

Rather than men of prerogative we are bondsmen to custom, habit, and natural change. Yet this inconstancy has its benefits. Custom, a monster, is angel yet in this, as Hamlet would say. And Montaigne recounts that after the death of his intimate friend, La Boétie, he threw himself into violent distractions in order to forget. "Variation always solaces, dissolves, and dissipates. If I cannot combat it, I escape it." In fact, this is nature's way. "Nature proceeds thus by the benefits of inconstancy. For time, which she has given us as the sovereign physician of our passions, gains its effect principally in this way: furnishing our imagination with other and ever other business, it dissolves and breaks up that first sensation, however strong it may be." (Fr. 634–635/Th. 934)

Rather than tragic in his intransigency, man is eminently adjustable. Custom can be a "violent and treacherous schoolmistress"; still there is some advantage to be had from the way she "dulls our senses" and the way, in time, we grow accustomed to what at first seemed insupportable. So with the big bell which in its ringing shook Montaigne's tower and seemed intolerable — in time he grew used to it ("en peu de temps m'apprivoise"), to such an extent that he was able to sleep through its "tintemarre." (Fr. 78/Th. 137) So, too, in married life, the absence of a fixed being in man, his prevailing susceptibility to change and custom, help him to make his peace with its incommodities. It is too late to complain about marriage, once one has taken on its obligations. Individual liberty is subjected to general and universal laws and duties, as man becomes part of nature's large continuing actions: "We do not marry for ourselves, whatever we say; we marry just as much or more for our posterity, for our family. The practice and benefit of marriage concerns our race far beyond us." (Fr. 645–646/Th. 956)

Montaigne compartmentalizes the worlds of married love and sexual passion. He does not see any cruel and tragic choice between them — in fact, he finds that their divided ends are quite compatible, serving separately man's needs for ordered peace and his desire for sudden, violent passion. By maintaining each in its own sphere, Montaigne's attitude toward each is essentially comic. Love, he believes, is harmful only to fools. And he would have agreed with Plutarch that Antony was mad to destroy himself for a woman. Unlike Shakespeare, he would not have shared Antony's quest for permanence, or any time-transcending union of married love and romantic passion.

And if he had little sympathy with an Antony, he would have had even less with Othello. One of the byproducts of sixteenth-century *chorismos* and closed comedy — where the will of men is compliant with the world's changeful necessities — is the quest for equanimity in cuckoldry. From Ariosto to Rabelais' *Third Book* to Montaigne's essays, man must endure his bad fortune with good grace. It is his destiny, not his dessert, to be so used. For such comedy of existence, Othello is ill-suited, both by his commitment to a world of sustained lyrical love and his inner psychic needs. But, Montaigne would ask, why should any man stir in this world of reduced expectations, where man is a creature of change, not constancy? "Lucullus, Caesar, Pompey, Antony, Cato, and other brave men were cuckolds and knew it without stirring up a tumult about it. In those days there was only one fool of a Lepidus who died in anguish over it." (Fr. 657/Th. 966) The large number of the good and great companions so dishonored detracts from the stain: "I know a hundred honorable men who are cuckolded, honorably and not very discreditably. A gallant man is pitied for it, not disesteemed." And besides, he brusquely reminds the injured: each of you has cuckolded somebody else: "now nature is all in similarities, in compensation and tit for tat [vicissitude]. The frequency of this accident should by this time have moderated its bitterness; it will soon have become a custom." (Fr. 662/Th. 973)

In the private world of the heart's desire, as well as in that social world of public expectation, Montaigne adjusts to the shrunken vistas of closed comedy: a not too desirable necessity must be accepted. But man is a fragile creature who more easily than he imagines can learn to live in changed circumstances.

Montaigne does not complain that people behave according to their own "manners and customs." That is a common vice, shared by fine intellects as well as by ordinary people, and he finds this a universal and excusable limitation. But he does complain when people are so lacking in discernment and self-awareness that accidental matters of "present usage" and personal preference are treated as standards of universal validity. Such temporal provincialism — ignorant of, or choosing to disregard, the inveterate vicissitudes of human activity — is presumption. Speaking of his fashion-minded contemporaries, Montaigne continues this argument in "Of Ancient Customs": "When they wore the busk of their doublet between their breasts, they maintained with heated arguments that it was in its proper place; some years later, it has slipped down between the thighs, and they laugh at their former custom and find it absurd and intolerable. The present fashion in dress makes them promptly condemn the old, with such great positiveness and such universal agreement that you would think it was a kind of mania that thus turns their understanding upside down." (Fr. 216/Th. 333–334) This essay, as others have done, stresses the importance of Montaigne's focus on the present. But from this passage, as from others quoted in the following section, it is clear that even his attitude toward the present is, as usual, complex. He scorns the lack of judgment shown by those who so heatedly will defend a present fad — with the usual positiveness and ignorance of their own status as creatures of change. If our concern is wisdom, a former custom is not to be scoffed at without the awareness that the present observance is also caught up in the same processes of replacement.

Sharply observant of the changes that time brings in our beliefs, Montaigne can ridicule our furious present attachments, the vanity of our contentions. In his collocation of the large and the small, the vehement and the trivial, he has the makings of a satiric vision. He can marvel at the "fameuses impressions" that derive from such "vains commencements et frivoles causes." He delights in showing the simple causes — overlooked for their very *petitesse* — behind prodigious happenings. His aim is to effect a relaxation in the intensity of commitment by showing how insignificant are some of the reasons for conflict and passion. *De mesnager sa volonté,* to husband one's will, is imperative. "Most of our occupations are low comedy [farcesques]." "Mundus universus exercet histrioniam," he quotes Petronius, "And the whole world plays a part." And in the same essay, "Our greatest agitations have ridiculous springs and causes. What a disaster our last duke of Burgundy incurred because of a quarrel about a cartload of sheepskins!" (Fr. 779/Th. 1142) We can also recall how Rabelais debunked the great wars in their starting points: "How there was a great strife and debate raised betwixt the Cake-bakers of Lerné, and those of Garguntua's country, whereupon were waged great wars." Do we see the same principles operating behind the opening scene of *Romeo and Juliet,* where tragic consequences derive from a family feud revived by a foolish clash between servants?

But Montaigne does not take our present practices (at least those upon which society has depended for some time) back to their sources in order to dethrone them, or even to invalidate a custom. His aim, he tells us, is to inform our judgment, to take the wind out of presumption: "I want to pile up here some ancient fashions that I have in my memory, some like ours, others different, to the end that we may strengthen and enlighten our judgment by reflection on this continual variation of human things." Dante's observation of the processes of replacement in human affairs and in universal nature drove him to search for a firm anchor against all change. He found it in the transcendent presence of the Eternal Idea. With Montaigne this same perception of the tides of change is quite simply accepted, and not transcended, but only slightly mollified by awareness. The evil is presumption, or ignorance of this "continual variation of human things," while wisdom, or judgment, is crucially aware of our changeableness.

As a consequence of this awareness, Montaigne tended toward neither of the two large social and temporal directions of the Renaissance, Utopia and the Golden Age, which, though basically opposed one to the other, enjoyed a common rebirth. In this he somewhat resembled Machiavelli, who, bowing before the realities of time and history, was determined to speak only of the way things were. And Spenser and Shakespeare, presented with Utopian arguments, converted them into dystopias. For Spenser, whose Artegall can argue that "All change is perilous, and all chaunce unsound," the levelling instincts of the Giant in V.ii of the *Faerie Queene* are foolish; and Shakespeare's own sense of paradox and complex reality undercuts the pretensions of Cade in *2 Henry VI*.[11]

Utopian thought can be summarized by three concepts: impulse, reflection, and design. It rests first upon the faith that things can be better, and it dreams of a perfect society. But it has every intention of actually implementing these dreams not in the present, but most certainly at some future time. The wonder — the horror — of Utopias is their tendency toward eventuation. However delayed, they burn with the possibilities of realization. Secondly, while it looks to the far future, Utopian thought has its origins in contemporary abuses and injustices. Not simply reformist, it still holds up a satiric mirror that reflects the social inequities of its own time. And finally, "design" is involved because there is something in Utopian strategy that appeals to every tinkerer's delight, that is based upon the elaboration of gadgetry and the abstract working out of hypothetical systems. Although strongly motivated by the impulse to actuate itself, there is much in Utopian thought of the geometrician's games. Of these three concepts, only toward the second, the reflective, satiric mode, does Montaigne have any attachment. With the other two, the impulses toward radical betterment and toward rational design, Montaigne admits to having little sympathy. He sees little practical possibility in these endeavors, which are more properly meant to be intellectual exercises and drawing-room games (for which he expressed both his inaptitude and impatience) than serious attempts to cope with man and society as they are: "And indeed all those imaginary, artificial descriptions of a government prove ridiculous and unfit to put into practice. These great, lengthy altercations about the best form of society and the rules most suitable to bind us, are altercations fit only for the exercise of our minds; as in the liberal arts there are several subjects whose essence is controversy and dispute, and which have no life apart from that. Such a description of a government would be applicable in a new world, but we take men already bound and formed to certain customs; we do not create them, like Pyrrha or Cadmus." (Fr. 730/Th. 1070–1071) Both Utopia and the Golden Age derive psychologically from man's inability to accept his present condition: "Not in theory, but in truth, the best and most excellent government for each nation is the one under which it has preserved its existence. Its form and essential fitness depend on habit. We are prone to be discontented with the present state of things." (Fr. 731/Th. 1071)

Literature extolling a Golden Age looks backward to a past of greater simplicity and innocence; it yearns to negate the complications of life and society toward which human existence naturally seems to tend in time. Civilization, it contends, has largely been a mistake. Before the eighteenth century and Rousseau, Golden Age literature was primarily nostalgic in ethos; it had no intention of translating emotional yearning into social action. And where it did, Montaigne found the results ridiculous. People who urge a return to the "originelle source" generally fare far worse, he argues, than those who are compliant with the present mores. They are prey to what Montaigne calls "sauvages opinions," like Chrysippus, "who in so many places strewed his writings with remarks displaying the little account he took of incestuous unions." (Fr. 84/Th. 146)

Montaigne's "Of Cannibals," although dealing with the "new world" — where men might be formed anew — and rather primitivistic, shows his distance from either the Utopian or Golden Age motivations. Montaigne is a relativist, not a revolutionary: he would alter not our actions but our judgments. He despises the presumption of sheltered arrogance, for whom everything is barbaric that is not of its own usage. His aim in this immensely influential essay is to scandalize settled persuasions, and to promote uncertainties. The natives might be cannibals, but he wonders upon what grounds the cruelty of the civilized Portuguese would be preferable. While Montaigne is a relativist who knows no certainties, both Golden Age and Utopia deal in terms of absolute conviction. Possessing the "first and universal reasons," which Montaigne finds beyond his comprehension, they have brought the certainty of being into the realm of history. Whether far in the past or in the distant future, they have replaced the hierarchical development of religious thought with a linear one, a religious process toward stasis with a secular one. But Montaigne, who has passed through *chorismos,* considers all that is human as subject to time and change.

Montaigne shares no hankering to return to a simpler form of existence. The appeal of the new world is mainly in its physical reality, its actual primitivism, not something poetically yearned for, nor some phil-

osophical projection. Indeed, the newly discovered natives are not exotic or strange, but simple, clear, and pure — they show the common
way of nature. They have about them the solid crunch of reality, a
substantiality that Montaigne, when he looked to the past, admired in
the Romans. The natural virtues that they possessed Montaigne tried
to recapture in his private life — and we approach here the freedom of
open comedy. But, when it comes to considerations of society as a
whole, Montaigne feels the weight of history and he closes the open
door with some regret: "We may regret better times, but not escape the
present; we may wish for different magistrates, but we must nevertheless
obey those that are here." (Fr. 760/Th. 1114) "Mes-huy c'est fait,"
he says resignedly in "Of Repentance," and he resists both reformation
and repentance.

"Of Repentance" tells us of two forces that mold man's conduct: one
is the "condition universelle" and the other is the pressures of the
"times" — that particular configuration of forces and issues within the
limits of his contemporary experience. Thus far, in showing how Montaigne's concern with the present has led to the social conservatism of
closed comedy, we have emphasized man's universal condition and
Montaigne's acceptance of man's imperfection: "Life is a material and
corporeal movement, an action which by its very essence is imperfect
and irregular; I apply myself to serving it in its own way." (Fr. 756/
Th. 1108) Still we must ask why, in the public sphere, this vision of
man's involvement in movement and change should lead to a conservatism that was quite hostile to progressive reform, while in Montaigne's
private world it should lead to a liberating, if not exhilarating, pursuit
of diversity. The answer lies, I believe, in the "times," and the turmoil
that disturbed France during the entire span of Montaigne's adult life.

Religious fanaticism was only one manifestation of a passionate and
volatile age. Georg Weise writes of France: "In no other part of Europe did the heroic ideal exercise an influence as profound and lasting
as it did in France." And to that passion for glory that seems to have
consumed much of French interest, he correctly places Montaigne in
determined opposition.[12] Montaigne is convinced that the itch to perform great deeds, or worse yet, to have the renown of greatness, is the
infectious disease disturbing the inner rest and equilibrium of his country: "Men of our time are so formed for agitation and ostentation that
goodness, moderation, equability, constancy, and such quiet and obscure
qualities are no longer felt." (Fr. 782/Th. 1147) He scorns the com-

pulsion to erect monuments to insignificant deeds. Like Dante, also writing in a time of tumult, he could exclaim, everyman wants to be a Marcellus. "Renown does not prostitute itself at so cheap a rate. . . . We have the pleasures suitable to our lot; let us not usurp those of greatness. Ours are more natural and all the more solid and sure for being humbler. Since we will not do so out of conscience, at least out of ambition let us reject ambition. Let us disdain this base and beggarly hunger for renown and honor which makes us grovel for it before all sorts of people." (Fr. 783/Th. 1148) We see here one of the major causes and targets of Montaigne's essentially reductive vision, of his attacks on pretension, and of his insistence on pointing out the process and mechanism involved in our great contentions.

"Of Husbanding Your Will" is Montaigne's superb defense of his own tenure as mayor of Bordeaux. It shows his intelligent responsiveness to the demands of the age. His government was not spectacular for its achievements; he had to fight a holding action. Gestures which attract attention and praise were impossible then; the purpose of his government — which he accepted — was to keep the lid from blowing off: "I had nothing to do but conserve and endure, which are noiseless and imperceptible acts. Innovation has great luster, but it is forbidden in these times, when we are hard pressed and have to defend ourselves against innovation [nouvelletes]. Abstention from doing is often as noble as doing, but it is less open to the light; and the little that I am worth is almost all on that side." (Fr. 783/Th. 1149) He is not unaware, given his own personal urge toward freedom and creativity, of how valuable for society is the impulse toward change and innovation, and how appealing it is in the eyes of the world. But those are precisely the virtues that are being abused in his time, and contributing greatly to the general destruction.

I cannot but think what words of encouragement Montaigne would have afforded the young men and women of the fifties in America. They were the silent generation, for whom *abstinence de faire* was preferable to the alternatives offered by their times. Unlike the epigone-liberals they did not desire a return to the action of the thirties, a most suspicious nostalgia, where the appropriateness of outspokenness and action would have been dependent upon the hardships and miseries of the time. So too the tranquillity over which his government presided was "gentle and mute": "I have not had that iniquitous and rather common disposition of wanting the trouble and sickness of the affairs of this city to exalt and honor my government." (Fr. 783/Th. 1149) The generation of the fifties was unfortunately like Montaigne in that, if it did not hanker after worse times, neither did it militate for better. For better or worse, it was only the less deceived. It could not answer — if it had heard — the stifled cry of the bored suburban housewife, "Is it just enough not to be bad?"

"Conserver et durer" . . . it is to this rhythm of existence that Montaigne inclined by temperament, by philosophy, and by his career as an administrator in those troublesome times. While it does not lead to radical transformations, Montaigne's sense of life as durable and enduring does not incline toward doom. In fact, it is in the nature of Montaigne's present concern, his interest in the day-to-day and the regular functioning of society, that he shies away from such tremendous conclusions. The experience of *chorismos* leads to a sense of solid reality, of strata of existence that persist. Underneath the changing façade of social custom there is an abiding nature. His "Of Cripples" begins, "It is two or three years since they shortened the year by ten days in France. How many changes were supposed to follow this reform! It was literally moving heaven and earth at the same time. Nevertheless there is nothing budging from its place: my neighbors find the hour for sowing and reaping, the opportune moment for their business, the harmful and the propitious days, exactly at the same point to which they had always assigned them."

If this sense of the enduring rhythms of existence might approach a peasant's consciousness — an association, incidentally, that Montaigne found at times attractive — a similar sense in public affairs of the true cohesiveness and durability of the state might be called an administrator's view. Montaigne's awareness of long temporal processes, his faith in a continuity, rhythm, and life of the state which is frequently independent of man's actions, means also that there is little that we can do to destroy a long-established government. A great walrus with far-flung and hidden recesses, it still manages to pull through in its awkward, sluggish, flip-flop mode of existence.[13] In this sense of durability Montaigne is somewhat like Bridoie in Rabelais' *Third Book*. They both insist that man must learn to control his impatience, and somehow adapt himself to the rhythms that nature and institutions have in themselves. By that "peculiar reversal" which Cassirer has noticed, Montaigne's sense of separation leads him to a qualified optimism. In "Of Vanity," he concludes: "Perhaps we are not on our last legs, for all that. The preservation of states is a thing that probably surpasses our understanding. As Plato says, a civil government is a powerful thing and hard to dissolve. It often holds out against mortal internal diseases, against the mischief of unjust laws, against tyranny, against the excesses and ignorance of the magistrates and the license and sedition of the people."

Despite the misery of his country, it will survive. And, as usual, to support his conclusion he returns to Rome, because in Rome's history, as in epitome, one sees all the "forms and vicissitudes" that could befall a state. Despite the horrors of the first emperors, and the over-extension of its dominion, containing so many disaffected people, poorly administered and unjustly conquered, nevertheless Rome "endured it and continued in it": "All that totters does not fall. The fabric of so great a body holds together by more than a single nail. It holds together even by its antiquity, like old buildings whose foundations have been worn away by age, without cement or mortar, which yet live and support themselves by their own weight." (Fr. 732–733/Th. 1074–1075) Montaigne suspects the theoretician's grand conclusions, be they millennial or ruinous. Through *chorismos* he has passed to the comedy of existence, which deals not with significance but with survival and endurance.

All around him Christendom is in turmoil; the old order seems finally to be giving out. Wherever one looks he can see clear testimony of alteration and ruin. The astrologers are silly to search the stars for premonitions of approaching disaster; you don't need to go to heaven for that — the signs are all around us, Montaigne insists, present and palpable. But from this vision of a fallen and falling world, Montaigne derives more than consolation, he derives some hopefulness "for the duration of our state, inasmuch as naturally nothing falls where everything falls." And in one of his stirring aphoristic phrases, easily detachable from the text, he concludes, "La maladie universelle est la santé particulière" ("Universal sickness is individual health"). Reconciliation to the tragic world of *chorismos* by that peculiar reversal leads to *methexis,* participation, or the vision of qualified hope. Things have got so bad, they now are safe.

"A nous la liberté"

In open comedy the background of *chorismos* is just as strong, but it is far from leading the individual to subject his personal pleasures to the larger demands of the race for continuity and social order. Primarily in this private world, Montaigne shakes off *obligations civiles* and applies himself with a joy and curiosity truly remarkable to an active pursuit of diversity. The here and the now, instead of being subordinate and reduced, become the primary objects of his experience. In the *Apol-

ogy, Montaigne denied man's possession of being, and philosophically confuted the possibility of his having any present existence. But in his later development, he threw himself all the more eagerly into the present. If man has no communication with being, if he is a creature of change and inconstancy, if he cannot rationally control his experience, if all life is involved in the processes of replacement, then each moment and each thing as they are in their present existence become precious and irreplaceable. A future which is uncertain and unavailable and a past from which he would prefer to turn his glance, if he could, cast man all the more earnestly into the present. "Life on earth is the only one he has. He wants to savour it to the last drop: car enfin c'est nostre estre, c'est nostre tout." [14]

Old men should be explorers, a later poet would say, who himself struggled to escape the metaled tracks of appetency leading from past to future. And Montaigne is engaging and zestful as a traveler. In fact, in no way do we see his freedom of movement, his commitment to the present, his loathing for organized planning and scheduled events more than in his attitude to travel. It is a symbol of life as he would have it: cut off from all connections, man encounters with open intelligence the diversity of ways and people. Imbrie Buffum has indeed gone so far as to make Montaigne's travel experience a critical influence on his later thought and style.[15] It would be more accurate, however, to say that the conditions of travel allowed Montaigne to manifest his ideals of living. The sense of life which Montaigne exhibits *en voyage* he had already advocated in "Of the Education of Children." Perhaps in no other area do older men who have lost their way and are struggling to regain it more reveal the vision of possibility that moves them than in their ideas for educating the young.

In his public life Montaigne bowed to his *devoir,* but in his private life he resented it. His hostility was primarily based on a personal distaste for any enforced routine or compulsion. In "Of Presumption" he attributed this fact of character to the pleasures and easiness of his earlier training at home. He despised the drudgery of learning by rote and memorization. Like all good humanists he was fearful of our attachment to the past, fearful that we lose thereby our own natural vigor and independence of judgment. And he of course despised those "furieux maistres d'escole." "Our mind," he will complain, "moves only on faith, being bound and constrained to the whim of others' fancies, a slave and a captive under the authority of their teaching. We have been so well accustomed to leading strings that we have no free motion left; our vigor and liberty are extinct." (Fr. 111/Th. 183) And while this thought is an addition of 1588 to the essay that first appeared in 1580, still it is in accord with the earlier material. To foster the young person's judgment Montaigne especially recommends travel. But as usual he dismisses scornfully the tidbits of knowledge which tourists love to return with, showing how little they engaged themselves when living in another land. It is shameful that the young French nobility (Florio calls them "galants") should only be interested in the length or breadth of the Santa Rotonda, or the cost of Signora Livia's drawers, or the discrepancy between the size of Nero's face found in the Roman ruins and that on the medallions found elsewhere, rather than bringing back knowledge of the "characters and ways of those nations." And further on, although more broadly involved with what Montaigne calls "le commerce des hommes," and not only travel, Montaigne urges silence and modesty: "instead of gaining knowledge of others we strive only to give knowledge of ourselves, and take more pains to peddle our wares than to get new ones." (Fr. 113/Th. 187) Far from the provincial defensiveness of big-city people, Montaigne in a new land is driven not to impress the natives, but rather to learn. And he wants to learn something new, not repeat stalely what he has already acquired. The great purpose of travel is to "rub and file [limer] our brains by contact with those of others." (Fr. 112/Th. 185) The vigor of the verbs is indicative. He is not looking for what he has known, the dull, solipsistic game of rehearsing one's pronouncements, but something new: the felt contact of original response.

These same attitudes are found in the 1588 edition of the essays, where travel has become, in Thibaudet's words, the image of life: "My plan is everywhere divisible; it is not based on great hopes; each day's journey forms an end. And the journey of my life is conducted in the same way." (Fr. 747/Th. 1095) The backdrop of *chorismos* has fallen over any great expectations. Montaigne's openness to the present comes through a disregard for any future contingency. He lives "from day to day, and, without wishing to be disrespectful, I live only for myself; my purposes go no further." In his travels he has no overriding schedule: "If it looks ugly on the right, I take the left; if I find myself unfit to ride my horse, I stop. . . . Have I left something unseen behind me? I go back; it is still on my road. I trace no fixed line, either straight or crooked." That strange tension produced by the need to keep a prearranged plan can harm life. A kind of double attention is created, whereby one does not deal fully with the present object, but seems to push it aside in order to get to the next stop, where contentment is similarly disturbed. Most of his countrymen, Montaigne fears, "take the trip only for the return. They travel covered and wrapped in a taciturn and incommunicative prudence, defending themselves from the contagion of an unknown atmosphere." (Fr. 753–754/Th. 1104–1105) One delights to imagine Montaigne's reaction to modern freeway traffic. Most certainly the irony of the phrase "freeway" would not have escaped him. The mechanization of the human response would have troubled him as much as it does us, who are obliged to scurry pent-up with nervous stomachs along these congested modern highways.

Man's imagination has always taken pleasure in summarizing the human condition by the image of movement. Ulysses is the prototypic traveler, even when he is rejected by Dante for the sake of a higher figure of mobility, the pilgrim. Indeed, the figure of the pilgrim differs radically from Montaigne's notion of travel. Assured of his goal, on which all his attention rests, the pilgrim has only passing interest in the objects along the route. But Montaigne, practically careless of his final goal since it is unknown, has less concern about wandering. In fact his delight in travel lies in the freedom to approach the various and sundry objects along the way without any ulterior concerns. The difference between the fourteenth and the sixteenth centuries can perhaps be exemplified with Petrarch as a contrasting figure. Petrarch too took Ulysses as the model of travel and the highest representative of man's condition. But Petrarch could not endure simple wandering, as Montaigne did. His own love of mobility and variety eventually informed against him, and he accused himself of flightiness, lack of purpose, and irresolution — qualities which for Montaigne came to summarize man's true nature.

One of the values of Montaigne's *Travel Journal* is the corroboration it gives to his lyrical notions of travel; he actually did put them into practice. Montaigne's amanuensis writes:

> I truly believe that if Monsieur de Montaigne had been alone with his own attendants he would rather have gone to Cracow or toward Greece by land than make the turn toward Italy; but the pleasure he took in visiting unknown countries, which he found so sweet as to make him forget the weakness of his age and of his health, he could not impress on any of his party, and everyone asked only to return home. Whereas he was accustomed to say that after spending a restless night, he would get up with desire and alacrity in the morning when he remembered that he had a new town or region to see. I never saw him less tired or complaining less of his pains;

for his mind was so intent on what he encountered, both on the road and at his lodgings, and he was so eager on all occasions to talk to strangers, that I think this took his mind off his ailment.

And in that amazingly persistent and universal image, Montaigne *en route* seemed to be "like people who are reading some very pleasing story and therefore begin to be afraid that it will soon come to an end, or any fine book; so he took such pleasure in traveling that he hated to be nearing each place where he was to rest." (Fr. 915) Totally unselfconscious, forgetful of sickness and age, Montaigne experiences completeness by fixing his mind intently on the objects he encounters. He does not approach things for any extrinsic purpose, nor does he feel the pressure of time weighing down on him and forcing him to participate with distracted impatience, one eye on the object and the other on what is still to be done. It is quite possible to say that, in this total absorption, Montaigne arrives at the condition of childlike simplicity, and seems to have reversed the fall into time that the pressures and consciousness of adulthood produce. For this reason, the image of reading is apt: it suggests the "lostness" that children have, which is really total concentration in the book or play, so that they actually regret when the last page is turned, or the curtain dropped.

But if Montaigne recovers the lost capacity of childlike concentration, still the mind that is working and judging is that of an adult. The sign of the adult is the loss of provincialism that comes from having experienced the larger world. Similar to Alcofrybas Nasier, who discovers in Pantagruel's mouth that one half of the world does not know how the other half lives, Montaigne discovers that the common assumptions about the Alpine passages are mistaken. His own experience contradicts the received information that the passes were full of difficulties, the people uncouth, the lodgings primitive, and the air bad. (*Travel Journal*, Fr. 910) Freedom and lively perceptiveness show the true dimensions of Montaigne's mind. Rather than insisting on his accustomed ways and settled practices he is consumed by the sheer pleasure of multiplicity. Travel is an earthly paradise of sorts, free from history, and Leah might be Montaigne's attendant genius: "Each custom has its reason. Let there be plates of tin, wood, or earthenware, boiled meat or roast, butter or nut oil or olive oil, hot or cold food, it is all the same to me." (Fr. 753/ Th. 1104)

If ever there were lyricism in man's social experience it is here with Montaigne *en voyage*. And certainly the most engaging and — in more than word choice — the most revealing self-description of Montaigne the traveler is his refusal to be served *à la française:* "I have laughed at the idea and made straight for the tables thickest with foreigners." In its depiction of a man eager to learn by being an involved participant, this passage reveals Montaigne's almost passionate concern with the density and thickness of experience, rather than its extension.

As Montaigne in travel is the emblem of his life, so the language of travel filters into his style and helps to form it. He avoids the clear pre-announcement of subject matter, as Bacon would do with his well-organized tripartite topic sentences; he refrains from enumerating his points as he makes them. Schedule is as distant from his style as it is from his voyaging: "It is the inattentive reader who loses my subject, not I. Some word about it will always be found off in a corner, which will not fail to be sufficient, though it takes little room. I seek out change indiscriminately and tumultuously. My style and my mind alike go roaming [vagabondant]." (Fr. 761/Th. 1116) There is much of the vagabond's comic gaiety in Montaigne, hitting the open road and singing "à nous la liberté." Similarly, he is comic in his refusal to limit experience to a single level of life. High and low, dark and bright mingle in his quest for fullness. "Life is an uneven, irregular, and multiform movement." His image of man becomes Socrates, who seemed adept at moving on all these multiple levels of existence. "The fairest souls are those that have the most variety and adaptability [souplesse]." (Fr. 621/Th. 914) Shakespeare, in his multiple plot levels, in his admiration for the man who can, like Hal or Hamlet, be at home in all of them, joins Montaigne in his Renaissance love of variety. The traditional wise man is on his way to becoming the melancholy Jaques of Shakespeare's comedies, and even a Malvolio, when Montaigne concludes, with some anticipation of Sir Toby Belch, that one must be "a little mad if he does not want to be even more stupid" ("Il faut avoir un peu de folie qui ne veut avoir plus de sottise," Fr. 761/Th. 1116).

Far from harboring the accustomed humanistic scorn for the lower classes, Montaigne admires their openness and their freedom from mental stress. He contrasts the life of a learned man, with his anxious sweating over the future, to that of a plowman, "letting himself follow his natural appetites, measuring things only by the present sensation, without knowledge and without prognostication, who has pain only when he has it; whereas the other often has the stone in his soul before he has it in his loins. As if he were not in time to suffer the pain when he is in it, he anticipates it in imagination and runs to meet it." (Fr. 362/Th. 544)

It is well known that Montaigne's own anxiety over the stone and death led him to admire the more passive stolidity of the common people in the face of pain and suffering.

But more than mere endurance, there is a positive gaiety in his exhortation to self-reliance. Do not dwell on future misfortunes, they will come soon enough, is his admonition as he proceeds to quote Seneca: "Meanwhile favor yourself; believe what you like best. What good does it do you to welcome and anticipate your bad fortune, to lose the present through fear of the future, and to be miserable now because you are to be so in time?" (Fr. 804/Th. 1178–1179) The necessity of future sickness and death, and inescapable limitation, serves to redeem the present. Do not lose the present by the fear of a future, which must be. Let be, is Montaigne's anxiety-free resolution.

Traditionally, Montaigne complains, "our distaste for present things" ("le desgoust des choses presentes") has been regarded as wisdom. Montaigne's repudiation of this conventional stance, his redemption of the present, is connected with his deep disinterest in two large ways of personal extension, progeny and fame. The men of the Renaissance may have leaned toward the future, with its rewards, but Montaigne was not one of them. He took no pleasure in the "au-delà"; "beyonding" was not for him: "We are never at home, we are always beyond. Fear, desire, hope, project us toward the future and steal from us the feeling and consideration of what is, to busy us with what will be, when we shall no longer be." (Fr. 8/Th. 35) Ever concerned with the present time in all its "thickness" and density rather than in some deferred and perhaps even non-existent future, Montaigne finds ridiculous the rather common "humor" of Tiberius, "who was more concerned about extending his renown into the future than about making himself estimable and agreeable to the men of his own time." And in a passage pregnant with summary and typical sentiment, he concludes (this is a post-1588 addition): "If I were one of those to whom the world may owe praise, I would ask for payment in advance and hold it quits. Let the praise make haste and pile up all around me, concentrated and massive rather than extended and durable [plus espesse qu'alongée, plus pleine que durable] and let it vanish abruptly together with my consciousness of it, when its sweet sound will reach my ears no longer." (Fr. 595–596/Th. 878–879) Post mortem pleasures leave Montaigne cold, as does post facto regret. Although in an earlier essay he advises the reader not to judge of his happiness until after his death, the later Montaigne gravely questions this assumption. It was Solon who said that no man before his death could be called fortunate, but it was Aristotle who wondered if this meant that he who lived virtuously ("selon ordre") was less so if his fame went badly, or if his posterity were miserable. Montaigne goes on to add, and even consciously to improve upon Aristotle: "While we move about, we transport ourselves by anticipation wherever we please; but once out of being we have no communication with what is; and it would be better to say to Solon that man is never happy, then, since he is so only after he is no more." (Fr. 10/Th. 36–37)

The present is all that man has, and present things offer Montaigne preoccupation enough. But man's thoughts are always "ailleurs": "Our thoughts are always elsewhere; the hope of a better life stays and supports us, or the hope of our children's worth, or the future glory of our name. . . . Even Epicurus consoles himself at the end with the eternity and utility of his writings." (Fr. 633/Th. 932) While Montaigne's tone is far from hostile, while he recognizes how all too human is this need to divert attention from the thing itself, still the different procedure of Socrates is more to his liking (however high and difficult might be its lesson): "It is only for first-class men to dwell purely on the thing itself, consider it, and judge it. It belongs to Socrates alone to become acquainted with death with an ordinary countenance, to become familiar with it and play with it. He seeks no consolation outside the thing itself." (Fr. 632/Th. 930)

Progeny and fame are powerful enough instincts to subdue, but even more important for Montaigne is his reluctance to engage himself to any emotion, no matter how powerful, that is unchecked by his judgment. Montaigne, for whom nature can be a powerful mother, *douce,* yet reasonable and ordered, to whom on occasion he advises us to commit ourselves simply, still reserves the right to separate his own judgment from the commands of nature. The final goals of the individual and nature might be different; the great mother is more interested in the continuation of the race than the judgment of the single man: "Those who accuse men of always gaping after future things, and teach us to lay hold of present goods and settle ourselves in them, since we have no grip on what is to come (indeed a good deal less than we have on what is past), put their finger on the commonest of human errors — if they dare to call an error something to which nature herself leads us in serving the continuation of her work, and which, more zealous for our action than for our knowledge, she imprints in us like many other false notions." (Fr. 8/Th. 34–35) Our discourse of reason was given us in order that we might separate ourselves from the instincts of the herd — especially the instinct of generation. In "Of the Affection of Fathers for Their Children," Montaigne confesses, "I, for my part, have a taste strangely blunted to these propensities that are produced in us without the command and mediation of our judgment." (Fr. 279–280/Th. 424) And as an example he cites his inability to understand how people can fuss over a newborn child who has not yet taken on any individual characteristics. "And I have not willingly suffered them to be brought up near me." Montaigne does not share "that strong bond that they say attaches men to the future by the children who bear their name and their honor." (Fr. 764/Th. 1120) Those that do, he accuses of taking too seriously "male entails." "And we look forward to a ridiculous eternity for our names." (Fr. 289/Th. 437)

Thibaudet has called Montaigne "un célibataire manqué." [16] The solitary life has its advantages, Montaigne finds, and to be without children has never seemed to him "a want that should make life less complete and less contented. The sterile profession [la vocation sterile] has its advantages, too." (Fr. 764/Th. 1120) Children are for Montaigne an unneeded subjection to fortune — a thought that discloses a basic consistency stretching from his early Stoic period to the last addition to the *Essays,* and further places him as a vital link between Petrarch's Stoic humanism and Bacon's *Essays*. "Of Solitude" professes the need for that "arrière-boutique" of the mind, that place reserved apart, so that should the time come when we must lose wife, or children, or goods, we can do so with equanimity, being already prepared for such losses. We should have these attachments, "but we must not bind ourselves to them so strongly that our happiness depends on them." (Fr. 177/Th. 278) In "Of Husbanding Your Will" he can write in the same vein, "He who does not brood over his children or his honors with a slavish fondness manages to live comfortably after their loss." (Fr. 778/Th. 1140) As a further argument against such dependencies he points to the degeneracy of the France of his day, where, given the personal disorders and public chaos that civil war can create, children might be more cause for dismay than consolation. (Fr. 764/Th. 1120) This is the leitmotif of Montaigne's *Essays,* the historical pressure that complements his philosophy. In the same "Of Vanity," he expresses the wish to have a son-in-law whom he could trust, but then counters his own wish by reminding himself that "we live in a world where loyalty in our own children is unknown." (Fr. 727/Th. 1022) In "Of the Affection" he advocates easy amicability with his children, except if they should be "raging beasts, such as our time produces in profusion." (Fr. 284/Th. 431) Not unaccountably, for Montaigne as for Dante (although the latter did not have that prior sense of apathy), hope in one's children is definitely one of the casualties of historical dislocation.

Indifferent to children as sources of continuity, and hence of consolation, Montaigne is deeply interested in their personal development, the type of adults they become. While his need to preserve reason and individual judgment little disposes him to ecstasy over their childish games and gestures, his indulgence toward change permits him to be gracious in granting the rising young people their places in adult society. Emulation, perhaps because Montaigne had no sons, is not for him a source of personal tension. Consequently he rejects the niggardliness and severity of some fathers, and considers criminal the refusal to allow children "a share and association in our goods, and as companions in the understanding of our domestic affairs." If they fear to be replaced, then they should not have meddled with being fathers, "since in the nature of things [the younger generation] cannot in truth either be or live except at the expense of our being and our life." (Fr. 280/Th. 425) This freedom and liberality, so typical of the later stages of Montaigne's thinking, result in his willingness to make room for those who come after — and not only to make room, but to positively encourage them in their development.

His two basic statements on the subject, "Of the Education of Children," and "Of the Affection of Fathers for Their Children," are, interestingly enough, addressed to women, titled women, whose concern, Montaigne feels, should be the greater that their children receive the proper education. Not unexpectedly, the rigors of scheduling, the need to "double-up," and any long-houred lucubrations such as we have seen as one part of Renaissance temporal response from Petrarch to the Italian educators of the fifteenth century, and on to Erasmus and Rabelais, are absent from Montaigne's "Institution des enfants": "For all this education I do not want the boy to be made a prisoner. I do not want him to be given up to the surly humors of a choleric schoolmaster. I do not want to spoil his mind by keeping him in torture and at hard labor, as others do, fourteen or fifteen hours a day, like a porter." (Fr. 121/Th.198) Always he has in mind that the product of the educational system is to be a man in society, with larger responsibilities, and that this is especially true for the aristocracy. Montaigne's program is for the education of a prince, and the Aristotle he invokes is the tutor of Alexander, the author of the *Ethics,* rather than the master of the schools. Montaigne's stride here is thoroughly of the

Renaissance; it moves away from the quibbles of grammar, the vapidity of logic, and the vain disputations of dialectic, and toward matters of practical import: moral philosophy and history. Here if anywhere temporal pressure is felt by Montaigne, and his thrust and purpose are typical of the line whose sire might be Cornificius, and which was to gather force in the course of the Renaissance — a line from which, on so many other vital interests, Montaigne differed profoundly: "They teach us to live, when life is past. A hundred students have caught the syphilis before they came to Aristotle's lesson on temperance. Cicero used to say that even if he lived the lives of two men, he would not take the time to study the lyric poets. And I find these quibblers still more pathetically useless. Our child is in much more of a hurry: he owes to education only the first fifteen or sixteen years of his life; the rest he owes to action. Let us use so short a time for the necessary teachings." (Fr. 120–121/Th. 197) As in Gargantua's letter to Pantagruel we are reminded of the larger social and civic demands to which the time of schooling is prelude and preparation.

In the same "Of the Affection of Fathers for Their Children," Montaigne shows his indebtedness to the preferences of Petrarch when he finds accomplishments and works a more noble and personal means of braving time. He resents our helplessness in loving our children for the simple fact of having engendered them, when there is another possibility of production: "For what we engender by the soul, the children of our mind, of our heart and our ability, are produced by a nobler part than the body and are more our own. We are father and mother both in this generation. These cost us a lot more, and bring us more honor, if they have any good in them." (Fr. 291/Th. 440) The value of our children is their own; the value of our work is our own. And in a post-1588 addition he quotes Plato, observing that these works of the mind are "des enfans immortels," who immortalize their parents.

But Montaigne is as searching in his criticism of fame as he has been of children. His attitudes toward fame represent a fundamental break with the strong Renaissance tradition, in which are listed men like Petrarch, Boccaccio, Ariosto, Ronsard, and Spenser, to mention only the most prominent. But in rejecting the pursuit of fame, he does not necessarily revert to the belittling arguments of Macrobius or Boethius, as Dante had done in *Purgatorio* XI and as Petrarch had done especially in his *Triumph of Time*. It is rather in defense of present things that Montaigne rejects fame, not, as was the case with the earlier writers, because fame suffers the fate of present things when contrasted with the vast centuries of time or with eternity. Montaigne's two essential arguments against this reliance on fame are the same as his objections to children (the third, historical argument will also be active): it serves to divert our attention from the thing itself, and defer our own vigorous satisfaction in the present to some sentimental and perhaps unfounded future consolation. Moreover, putting oneself in the hands of fame is tantamount to putting oneself at the mercy of others — a concession Montaigne, who is only at ease *chez soy,* is never willing to grant.

Montaigne's future vistas are radically circumscribed. His remarks *au lecteur* advise us that his ends in writing are "domestique et privée." He has given no thought either to the reader's service or to his own glory — accomplishments he pretends (bowing and scraping) to be far above his capacities. In 1588 he still writes that he has no illusions about the worth of his book: "I write my book for few men and for few years." If he were concerned with durability, he would have written in Latin ("un langage plus ferme"), rather than in the vernacular French. When Montaigne does look to the future, he envisages communications that are intimate and real. He writes for friends who will be able to discern his character in his works, and refresh their memories of the man they once knew. To Madame de Duras, at whose visit he broke off writing "Of the Resemblance," he expresses this hope: "These same traits and faculties that you have been familiar with and have favored, Madam, with much more honor and courtesy than they deserve, I want to lodge (but without alteration or change), in a solid body that may last a few years, or a few days, after me, in which you will find them when you are pleased to refresh your memory of them." (Fr. 595/Th. 878) The fear of a contradiction existing between his life and his work compels him to write in a manner that is recognizably his. "I do not at all seek to be better loved and esteemed dead than alive." If fame is to be his, it will have to be on Montaigne's own terms — as it was eventually to be.

Again we return, as a basis of his thought, to Montaigne's impressions of his century: the men of his time are only given to ostentation. Things are done for show, in the sight of others and for their approval, rather than for their own intrinsic merit and pleasure. In opposition to this pervasive "other-direction," Montaigne's defense of his writing involves the interests of private development and self-knowledge. First, to pass so many idle hours with useful and pleasant thoughts — does that need to be defended? Yet, utility is there: his writing has brought him toward a surer knowledge of himself. As much as he has made his book, his book has made him. It is a book consubstantial with its author: "Have I wasted my time by taking stock of myself so continually, so carefully? For those who go over themselves only in their minds and occasionally in speech do not penetrate to essentials in their examination as does a man who makes that his study, his works, and his trade, who binds himself to keep an enduring account, with all his faith, with all his strength." (Fr. 504/Th. 750) His ultimate defense of writing is not what it does for others, not its lastingness, but what it does for him in helping him to perfect his thought: to write is to think better.

Earlier Montaigne had adopted the country gentleman's tic of deprecating those activities that consumed a good part of his time and interest. Here he admits, for the first time, to be a professional man of letters — it is his study, his work, his trade ("son mestier"). And also, as in the earlier writers, once the fundamental priority of primary and secondary goals has been rectified, a just hope in the duration of his writings can be recorded: they can be an "enduring account."

Montaigne's attitude toward the past is more complex than his nonchalance toward the future: the future, after all, is nonexistent. One's hopes in it, even if they are primary causes of action, are pure fantasy and vicarious consolation, diversion from the responsibility of meeting the present squarely. The past too has its dangers; one's reliance on it could be stifling of the present — a relationship the classically formed sixteenth century struggled to transform. Montaigne deplored such dependency on authority and memory rather than on judgment and personal experience. But the important difference is that our relationship to our past is not vicarious, but a real part of our formation and personality. "We have no grip on what is to come (indeed a good deal less than we have on what is past)," is the introductory phrase we have already quoted from "Our Feelings Reach Out Beyond Us." The presence of the past is a vivid reality for Montaigne, the root, in George Eliot's phrase, of one's piety.[17] Despite his concern with the thing itself, Montaigne had, with Hamlet, "le culte de la mémoire des morts." [18] Care for the dead must be our concern, he writes, and after La Boétie's death it was Montaigne who saw to the publication of his works. And, Professor Frame continues, "He took pride in protecting La Boétie's memory against misinterpretation. In all these acts, and in his chapter on friendship, centrally placed in Book One of the *Essays* and worked over with loving care, he seems to consider himself as mainly the guardian of La Boétie's shrine." [19] It was not for Montaigne, the most civilized of men, to turn barbarian by any single-minded and cruel rejection of those things and people that had been swept away by time.

He presumes in his family and friends, for whom the *Essays* were intended, the same interest that he expresses in "Of Giving the Lie": "What a satisfaction it would have been to me to hear someone tell me, in this way, of the habits, the face, the expression, the favorite remarks, and the fortunes of my ancestors! How attentive I would be! Truly it would spring from a bad nature to be scornful of even the portraits of our friends and predecessors, the form of their clothes and their armor. I keep their handwriting, their seal, the breviary and a peculiar sword that they used, and I have not banished from my study some long sticks that my father ordinarily carried in his hand." (Fr. 503/Th. 749–750)

The dead deserve this gratitude because they are dead and because they are great.

> They are dead. So indeed is my father, as completely as they; and he has moved as far from me and from life in eighteen years as they have in sixteen hundred. Nevertheless I do not cease to embrace and cherish his memory, his friendship, and his society, in a union that is perfect and very much alive.
>
> Indeed, by inclination I pay greater service to the dead. They can no longer help themselves; therefore they need my help all the more, it seems to me. It is here that gratitude shows in its proper luster. . . . It would be ingratitude to despise the remains and images of so many worthy and most valiant men, whom I have seen live and die, and who give us so many good instructions by their example, if we only knew how to follow them.
>
> (Fr. 762–763/Th. 1117–1119)

A personal sense of honor engages Montaigne to preserve some relic from his own past. He is not interested in constructing theoretical exhortations to memory; rather such action derives from an honorable nature: to be indifferent toward one's past bespeaks "une mauvaise nature." And as this concern prevails in relation to Montaigne's familial past, so it does in relation to his cultural past. Rome, the metropolitan city of Christendom, receives his veneration. He has seen other ruined cities, but they are only matters of fact, as they were for Petrarch. Rome is a different experience. "I could not revisit the tomb of that great and mighty city so often that I would not marvel at and revere it." And this is the way it should be. Rome is not external, but an integral part of himself. In comparison, the things of the present are "fantasies." He cut his teeth on Rome. He knew the events of Roman history long before the affairs of his own household; he had, as a schoolboy, participated in a hundred "querelles" in defense of Pompey and Brutus; he knew the Capitol and its plan before he knew the Louvre, and he knew the Tiber before the Seine. The fortunes and conditions of Lucullus, Metellus, and Scipio were more with him than any of the men of his own time. These are not casual acquaintances, but ones that have become part of himself. Useless in his own time, Montaigne throws himself back into the past of Rome, "libre juste et florissante," where he amuses, interests, and even involves himself passionately. He recognizes it as a sort of folly, knows that he is to a degree being bamboozled, but still the pleasure is too great.

Vanity? Yes. But where is there not vanity, asks Montaigne, whose purpose was to "faire valoir la vanité meme et l'asnerie" if it brings him pleasure. And by that "peculiar reversal" he transforms his great impression of passingness into the positive human action of preservation. He does not mind being made an honorary citizen of Rome: "Being a citizen of no city, I am very pleased to be one of the noblest city that ever was or ever will be. If others examined themselves attentively, as I do, they would find themselves, as I do, full of inanity and nonsense. Get rid of it I cannot without getting rid of myself." (Fr. 766/ Th. 1123) And we could repeat, "La maladie universelle est la santé particulière." A new freedom and natural indulgence in ordinary pleasures and everyday things emerges from his experience of the vanity of all things. The universal vulnerability to time makes it all the more incumbent to keep alive one's own vital links with the past.

This contribution of Montaigne to the development of modern Western thought is radical indeed, altering the very substance of attachment. That mere passingness does not mean defect is the great revolutionary message of this social conservative. Or, if it does indicate imperfection, it is a taint so common, so universal and all-encompassing, that it loses any real significance. Wisdom for Montaigne does not necessarily imply disgust with present things, with the ephemeral, nor does it involve the placement of a superior goal or level of perfection toward which the individual ought to aspire. In fact it is the very seriousness with which Montaigne regards the radical imperfection of life that compels him, in a manner contrary to Dante or Petrarch, who yearned "sine tempore vivere," to immerse himself so fully in the passing present things. And it is Montaigne's redemption of the present, even in its passingness, that moves him to redeem other present moments, now past, from the movements of time. Universal transience, or *chorismos,* brings back the past as well as the present. Any arrant notion of progress that presumptuously looks down its nose at what went before, ignoring how vulnerable it is to the same fallibility and transience, is alien to his thought. If Montaigne does not censure the past, neither, in his writings, does he censor it: "I do not correct my first imaginings by my second — well, yes, perhaps a word or so, but only to vary, not to delete. I want to represent the course of my humors and I want people to see each part at its birth. It would give me pleasure to have begun earlier, and to be able to trace the course of my mutations." (Fr. 574/Th. 848) Although Montaigne would have had important differences with post-Romantic literature, still on the more basic levels of approach and style, Montaigne is very similar to the post-Romantic mode of apprehension and presentation (a fact that partially accounts for his great vogue in ninteenth- and twentieth-century literature and thought). His aims are more genetic than teleological. He is more interested in the development of a thought than in its final, stationary product. Renaissance appeals to continuity fail to move him; religious or heroic models of perfection are not for him; nor even, in his thought, is there any single line of development. Everything is in mutation and change. Montaigne travels with the foxes, with their appreciation of life's many individual moments.[20] His writing is a record of those moments, and he does not try to change an earlier perception by a later. That it is later is no sure proof that it is better, merely that it has followed in time. *Chaque chose en sa saison,* is almost desperately true in Montaigne. Nor does he mean by seasons general and large stages of life, but rather individual moments, "de jour en jour, de minute en minute."

"Others form man; I tell of him" ("Je le recite"). In its first paragraph, worthy to be committed to memory, as it frequently is, "Of Repentance" summarizes the role of Montaigne's overwhelming sense of change in his literary method and his ideal of life. The world is only a "branloire perenne," staggering with a kind of "natural drunkenness," carrying in its wake our intentions as well as our fortunes (or, as Hamlet would say, our wills and our fates). "My history needs to be adapted to the moment." One idea at one time can contradict another idea at another time. But the truth, Montaigne affirms, is not contradicted. The lines of his painting do not go astray, although they vary and change. It is the world that changes, and in his book of good faith, he is honest to that register: "This is a record of various and changeable occurrences, and of irresolute and, when it so befalls, contradictory ideas: whether I am different myself, or whether I take hold of my subjects in different circumstances and aspects. So, all in all, I may indeed contradict myself now and then; but truth, as Demades said, I do not contradict. If my mind could gain a firm foothold, I would not make essays, I would make decisions; but it is always in apprenticeship and on trial."

This line of thought reaches its highest and most moving expression when Montaigne disdains the "dolorous reformations of old age" that tend to look with sanctimonious horror at the follies of greener years. Montaigne erects no palinode, as his predecessors of the fourteenth century had done — notably Dante, Petrarch, Boccaccio, and Chaucer — recanting their "giovenile errore." If anything, now that old age is upon him he tries to balance its necessary weight and seriousness with the gaiety of his youth, and with voluptuousness. "Let childhood look ahead, old age backward: was not this the meaning of the double face of Janus? Let the years drag me along if they will, but backward. As long as my eyes can discern that lovely season, now expired, I turn them in that direction at intervals. If youth is escaping from my blood and my veins, at least I want not to uproot the picture of it from my memory." (Fr. 639/Th. 940) And in the equally memorable conclusion to "Of Repentance," he hopes that now when old age and death are creeping up on him, as he loses more and more the vigor of life and is less and less in possession of himself, his book will serve as a reminder (in Florio's inspired translation) "from what height I tumbled."

Being

There are rhythms that continue and rhythms that come to a close. Newness is always in the world, with each succeeding generation: nature is solicitous of the continuance of her work. But within these larger continuing processes, obligations which Montaigne dutifully accepted, many individual rhythms are dying out. The self, then, at least as Montaigne describes his personal feelings, is not much interested in the processes of continuity, in novelty or in renewal. It experiences a deep limitation of possibilities, a hardening of the form of response. Life is no longer made up of separable, even contradictory, present moments, but acquires a formation of its own; the events it has experienced become part of an identifiable, organized whole. "Habit is a second nature," Montaigne wrote in "Of Husbanding Your Will," "and no less powerful." Whereas formerly he had rejected being and substance (we have no communication with being, nor any real substance) he now admits a greater coherence to the individual's experience: "In short, here I am in the act of finishing up this man, not of making another out of him. By long usage this form of mine has turned into substance, and fortune into nature." (Fr. 773/Th. 1133)[21]

Montaigne has come to experience a necessity in his life, one which, typical for the general easiness of his response and development, is non-tragic. Neither is it reductive, as was the case in closed comedy. It is a valuable contraction in which the ends of life are brought together to form a qualitative whole: "The range of our desires should be circumscribed and restrained to a narrow limit of the nearest and most contiguous good things; and moreover their course should be directed not in a straight line that ends up elsewhere, but in a circle whose two extremities by a short sweep meet and terminate in ourselves." (Fr. 773/Th. 1134) The actions of those "who run in a straight line, whose course carries them ever forward" he would consider astray.

One of the major stages of Renaissance paideia, a study suggested by Werner Jaeger but still to be written, is marked by the change from the imitation of Christ to the imitation of Socrates.[22] As Socrates had been Montaigne's model in readiness, in suppleness, in his ability to be at ease on many levels of existence, so Socrates is still his model when the lines of the individual life are about to be drawn in. What he offered Montaigne was an image of a life that is self-contained, without exaggeration or external reference. Socrates did not rise up or look forward; rather he returned to his original starting place and from that center he managed all vigor, bitterness, and difficulties. "It was he who brought human wisdom back down from heaven, where she was wasting her time." In his ways of life there is nothing borrowed from art or science: "Even the simplest can recognize in him their means and their strength; it is impossible to go back further and lower. He did a great favor to human nature by showing how much it can do by itself." (Fr. 793–794/Th. 1163–1164) Not upward or forward, neither transcendent nor heroic, but down and backward were the directions of Socrates' movements to bring the person into a more fundamental contact with himself, perhaps best summarized by the homely phrase, "He was always himself" ("Il fut aussi tousjours un et pareil"). Life is thus of a piece, rounded out and completed, and of its nature sufficient. Out of human life itself, out of the everyday, one can achieve an absolute simplicity, a relief from anxiety, which is akin to being. In his refusal to make use of Lysias' prepared supplication, Socrates becomes Montaigne's unmodeled model in the art of dying: "He did very wisely, and like himself, not to corrupt an incorruptible tenor of life and such a saintly model of human nature [une si saincte image de l'humaine forme] in order to prolong his decrepitude by a year and betray the immortal memory of that glorious end." (Fr. 807/Th. 1183) The human form, overwhelmed in the universal experience of *chorismos*, is once again of some importance, even holiness, when man is concerned to exercise that one power indubitably his: his right to hold to the quality of his life at the expense of mere extension, his right, as Robert Lowell has put it, to choose life and die. Certainly we are in the midst of a sense of being, when man can refuse the mere prolongation of life — the kind of extension that Montaigne always rejected — at the expense of its lived quality. Readiness, Petrarch's "satis vixi," recurs in this choice of Socrates. But it is important to note that this is not merely a sudden act *in extremis*: his manner in death is of a piece with his habits of life.

Formerly, in his Stoical days, death was the end and the aim of life for Montaigne: *le bout et le but*. It was the final step of a long dying, toward which all our efforts of preparation ought to be directed. The change in this idea that Montaigne's thought underwent as he himself grew older and experienced the crises of sickness has been covered by other writers.[23] Death had dominated life; what was needed was the capacity to see death as merely a natural part of life. "But you do not die of being sick, you die of being alive. Death kills you well enough without the help of illness." (Fr. 837/Th. 1127) Montaigne's final thoughts, especially in "Of Experience," show this ability to see life as a total, self-contained entity, not something of indefinite extension; to see it rather as a work of art, self-enclosed, with a beginning, middle, and end. The fearful need to add to life is useless and debasing — in Heidegger's phrase it frantically envisages impossible possibilities. With that natural easiness so typical of Montaigne's thought, he makes allowance for death as part of the natural process. From Cicero he adapts the thought, "Whatever happens contrary to the course of Nature may be disagreeable, but what happens according to her should always be pleasant." A tooth falls out "without pain, without effort." The limits of nature must be observed: for the tooth it was "the natural term of its duration." (Fr. 845/Th. 1239) So, in "Of Repentance," Montaigne, who has seen the bud, the flower, and the fruit, now sees the bare winter of his existence, "happily, since it is naturally": "I bear the ills I have much more easily because they are properly timed, and also because they make me remember more pleasantly the long felicity of my past life." (Fr. 620/Th. 913)

But as we have seen in the personal sphere of open comedy, Montaigne is also aggressive and vigorous, resisting mere passivity. It is a fault to consider death too closely, so as to lose or damage the sense of one's own life. The goal of life is still to seek strongly those pleasures that have served to constitute the self. Montaigne insists on the art of application, of vigorous seizure, as well as the art of acceptance: "I have a vocabulary all my own. I 'pass the time,' when it is rainy and disagreeable; when it is good, I do not want to pass it; I savor it, I cling to it. . . . This ordinary expression 'pastime' or 'pass the time' represents the habit of those wise folk who think they can make no better use of their life than to let it slip by and escape it, pass it by, sidestep it, and, as far as in them lies, ignore it and run away from it, as something irksome and contemptible." (Fr. 853/Th. 1251) While reconciled to losing life, he regards it as "something that by its nature must be lost; not as something annoying and troublesome." In the meanwhile, death is a future concern, not one that should daunt the present and agitate his experience.

In fact, this recognition impels him, in Renaissance fashion, to gain from his life all the good that he can. By this he does not mean provision for the future, but rather a much more determined and even passionate concentration on the present: "It takes management to enjoy life. I enjoy it twice as much as others, for the measure of enjoyment depends on the greater or lesser attention that we lend it. Especially at this moment, when I perceive that mine is so brief in time, I try to increase it in weight; I try to arrest the speed of its flight by the speed with which I grasp it, and to compensate for the haste of its ebb by my vigor in using it. The shorter my possession of life, the deeper and fuller I must make it [plus profonde et plus pleine]." Through the art of application, of management, of consciousness applied to sense, he "amplifies" the moments of genuine pleasure.

Montaigne transcends time not by prudentially looking to the future, but by disregarding the future and sinking into the present. Like God, he would "remplir son maintenant." The verb "to fill out" is crucial to Montaigne's qualitative sense of life. His favorite words suggest in-depthness, fullness, amplification, thickness, and density. Life possesses a reality in which he can immerse himself — not in order to lose himself, he reminds us, but to find himself. It is from filling up his present that man arrives at the sense of completion that he had previously sought — like time itself — by running anxiously after the future. Man redeems the solidity of the subject and the reality of the object by looking to the thing itself. "When I dance, I dance; when I fuck, I fuck." This is the ungentle Montaigne's sense of life with bite and reality.[24] Only by immersing himself in things themselves did Montaigne achieve wholeness. As Professor Baraz succinctly summarizes Montaigne's development: "Montaigne starts from the experience of continuous flux in order to reach the experience of timeless being [être atemporel]." [25] By applying himself, without anxious other thoughts, to things as they present themselves to him in the processes of time, Montaigne recovers his sense of being.

Chapter 7
Spenser

Monuments of Time

Spenser's great concern is to transcend time. It is the end and justification of his heroic conception of life, and it is the basis of many of his larger preoccupations. Poetry, history, the continuity of civilization, the ideals of excellence and distinction in an aristocratic society — all of these turn on success or failure in rising above the present moment. Love and progeny too are exalted in their capacities to surmount time. Indeed, in the struggle against time all of these human resources assume cosmic importance, for it is in truth a religious battle that is being fought, which at its farthest touches the creation of man. To submit to the normal dissolution of the organism in time is to impugn the divine part in man's origin. There is then a religious factor — and this is important to remember for our discussion — in Spenser's impassioned and heroic striving for fame, and in his great tributes to love — those things regarded by Petrarch's Augustine as creatural possibilities that lured man away from the true permanence and security to be found in the creator. But the complex relation of fame and love to time in Spenser renders their attainment religiously sanctioned. In fact, the excellence of man's creation shines through his achievements that brave time, so that we can say with justice that time is the element of man, and the heroic impulse to resist time — to find temporal extension in the future and to retain the models of the past — is a distinguishing human feature.

It is a relatively late work, *An Hymne of Heavenly Love,* that details the origins and provides the cosmic scaffolding for Spenser's ideas. Before time itself, God, the Son, and the "almightie Spright" reigned in "endlesse glorie and immortall might." (22–42)[1] Out of a desire to share his pleasure and "to enlarge his race," this fruitful love next created the angels. This second brood was, however, not as powerful as God, "yet full of beautie." But it is to their temporal existence that we must look. God is literally before time, but the angels are involved in time, and yet it is not a time that man knows. They are privileged to look on and share in God's light, in whose presence they "caroll Hymnes of love both day and night." While they sing and experience succession, still it is a pleasurable experience:

> Both day and night is unto them all one,
> For he his beames doth still to them extend,
> That darknesse there appeareth never none;
> Ne hath their day, ne hath their blisse an end,
> But there their termeless time in pleasure spend.
>
> (71–75)

The angels are below God's eternity, since they were created; they experience succession and they move through the skies. But their changes are not distasteful — they know no night, and they share in the creator's peace and bliss.

But the Child of Light fell, and God created man to replace the emptiness left by the now eternally damned angels. (99 ff.) Man differs from the angels in that his "root from earths base groundworke" was taken. And his time is "prescribed," or as the other poems will say, "short," not the termless time of the angels. Not pure spirit, his vision of God's glory is less direct, and unlike the angels, man is mortal. But still he was formed in the image of God and consequently has the taste for endless bliss.

> Therefore of clay, base, vile, and next to nought,
> Yet form'd by wondrous skill, and by his might:
> According to an heavenly patterne wrought,
> Which he had fashioned in his wise foresight,
> He man did make, and breathd a living spright
> Into his face most beautifull and fayre,
> Endewd with wisdomes riches, heavenly, rare.
> Such he him made, that he resemble might
> Himselfe, as mortall thing immortall could.
>
> (106–114)

Man is a compound creature, in his mortality committed to clay and dust, but in his divine resemblance suited to heavenly things. From this we see incidentally the destructive and sinful connotations that earth has in Spenser, as well as the reason for his frequent commands to rise up and look to higher things.

Although man is not an angel, still he is not a beast. And it is in terms of temporal extension that Spenser makes this distinction. The animals (and we look now to the earlier *Hymne in Honour of Love*), following the divine creative act, seek to enlarge themselves in kind. But they are only seeking

> To quench the flame, which they in burning fynd:
> But man, that breathes a more immortall mynd,
> Not for lusts sake, but for eternitie,
> Seekes to enlarge his lasting progenie.
>
> (102–105)

Man's mind, resembling the immortal mind, has greater constructive aims than the momentary impulse; he seeks endless monuments, whether in the eternity in heaven, or in the continuity of line here ("lasting progenie"). Akin to, and deriving from, God's own creative thrust to beget creatures like himself, this desire for self-projection and self-perpetuation in time is a radical impulse in man. It serves that basic distinction, which Spenser is so intent on making, between man and the beasts, and has its corollary in an equally vital discrimination he draws between lust and love. Its social implications emerge when in the important *Ruines of Time* Spenser accuses the aristocracy, careless of their past, of being

> Like beast, whose breath but in his nostrels is,
> And hath no hope of happinesse or blis.
>
> (356–357)

But in Spenser's world view, man's spirit was inbreathed by God, so he has a hope of a "heavenly place" in addition to the earthly compensations of continuity and achievement. And even these latter two, progeny and poetry, love and fame, are incorporated into a grand system. They are ways by which mortal man shows his divine resemblance.

Spenser's endorsement of the heroic possibilities of human experience is all the more impressive for its occurrence in that section of the *Faerie Queene* where one would least expect it: Book One. There the lesson of man's religious experience is summarized by Spenser himself:

If any strength we have, it is to ill,
But all the good is Gods, both power and eke will.

(I.x.i)

Nevertheless, in the same tenth canto that this specimen of dire Cal-
vinism helps to introduce, the Red Cross Knight is warned against forsaking the Earthly City. In contrast with the appeal of the New Jerusalem that God has built for his chosen, the Great Cleopolis, which he
had thought the fairest of cities, shrinks in importance. Yet, while granting the rightness of the Red Cross Knight's preference for celestial matters, St. John still shows the validity, within a Christian context, of heroic
effort and affirmation:

"Yet is Cleopolis for earthly frame,
The fairest peece, that eie beholden can;
And well beseemes all knights of noble name,
That covet in th'immortall booke of fame
To be eternized, that same to haunt,
And doen their service to that soveraigne Dame,
That glory does to them for guerdon graunt:
For she is heavenly borne, and heaven may justly vaunt."

(I.x.59)

The religious origins of proper time-transcendence are here affirmed.
Unlike Faustus, who was damned for seeking to be eternized, Spenser
endorses its human possibilities within a religious system.

The heroic strivings of humanism which Georg Weise has so fully
described are extremely strong in Spenser or, at least, strong enough to
support a contrast with Chaucer, in so many other respects his precedent
and model.[2] With all of their similarities, still a root difference inheres.
Spenser has a fundamental high Renaissance, Elizabethan commitment
to the ways of succession, and in his greatest works (one has only to
think of the Garden of Adonis and the *Epithalamion*) he expresses this
faith in the possibilities of continuity. Children and fame — the two
ways that man through succession simulates eternity and resists time —
are not debased values, but rather incorporated into a system of higher
possibilities. The man of earth becomes England's patron saint, George,
and simulates Christ, not in his sacrifice, but in his triumphant entry.
Nation and religion, the earthly and the heavenly, merge in splendor.
In Spenser's humanistic lexicon, the contents of Christianity are raised

to the level of heroism. But when Chaucer refers to the Parson's "noble ensample," heroism is humbled to the sturdier, simpler stuff of Christianity.

When we turn from Spenser's cosmology to his ideals of civilization, prime consideration must be given the *Complaints* of 1591, where, as the title indicates, tears and lamentation abound. Indeed, in the balance of Spenser's world the vision of vanity counts for much. Like Petrarch, he was early impressed with the instability and distress of things. In fact, his first poetic appearance was in Van der Noodt's *Theatre for Worldings* (1569), which, accordingly, represents the miseries and calamities that follow the voluptuous. There eleven of the fifteen *Visions of Bellay* and six of the seven *Visions of Petrarch* first appeared unrhymed. For the *Complaints* Spenser tagged his blank verse, but did not alter the content very much. The Petrarch sonnets derive from the famous canzone 323, written after the death of Laura, where a series of visions all repeat the same theme: the sudden destruction of what was glorious and flourishing. As a young man's work, Spenser's productions in the *Theatre* betray a precocious fascination with desolation and loss. And, when in the seventh sonnet of *The Visions of Petrarch* Spenser expresses the wish, "this wearie life [to] foregoe, / And shortly turne unto my happie rest," we see that his early poetic predilection fatally anticipates the final wish of the *Mutabilitie Cantos*. Like Petrarch's, Spenser's earlier poetic courting of the great themes of mutability will be fulfilled in his final works. But also, as in Petrarch, this melancholy duplication of beginnings and ends will be separated by periods when his sense of human vigor and constructiveness offers some hope for redress.

The Shepheardes Calender, far from being a rosy pastoral piece, continues some of the young man's melancholy. Surely an insistence on defeat and decline is one major emphasis of this epoch-making Renaissance poem: the churchmen have fallen off from the Christian simplicity of earlier times, and a cankerworm has crept into the bud of love and spoiled all fruitful expectations. The flowers are spilled with which the young man would have decked his lady's garland. In simple terms, this work could be called a Renaissance *Waste Land* (complete, like its twentieth-century variant, with erudite notes for the unlearned, exotic language, and regret for a simpler world). Yet there seems to be an equally powerful counterthrust to this vision of depletion. In the epilogue, the poet's voice can jubilantly proclaim his verse-achievement:

> Loe I have made a Calender for every yeare,
> That steele in strength, and time in durance shall outweare:
> And if I marked well the starres revolution,
>   It shall continewe till the worlds dissolution.
> To teach the ruder shepheard how to feede his sheepe,
> And from the falsers fraud his folded flocke to keepe.

The tone is one of triumph: while following his destined calling — it is marked out by the stars — he imitates Horace and Ovid in the claims on permanence they made for their work, "aere perennius."[3] This faith in the potentiality of human accomplishments, particularly in the arts, to surmount time will persist in Spenser's work up through the *Epithalamion*. But the power that he sensed in his calling will be transformed from the admirable and unabashed vaunt into a consciousness — no less impassioned — of its valuable service as an integral part of civilization. Under the necessity of persuading, through flattery and admonition, the aristocratic elite of his time to show more concern for the arts, and the eventual and perhaps inevitable disappointment in these ambitions, he explored with passionate devotion the ramifications of poetry until he saw its importance extend into many practical — and unsuspected — relationships with society. Significantly for our purposes, the means of persuasion is the argument of time. In works like *The Ruines of Time* and *The Teares of the Muses* the issues of vanity and vigor, which were present but separate in the *Calender,* are joined. In typical Renaissance fashion, it is the very reality of nothingness and the keen possibility of degeneration that call forth vigorous response here.

The ideal of cultural continuity was for Spenser, as for Petrarch or DuBellay, best represented by the example of Rome. Spenser's translations of the latter's *Les Antiquitez de Rome* — the *Ruines of Rome: by Bellay* — pit Rome's fallen grandeur against the universal forces of time and change. They introduce into the English sonnet sequence the great meditative themes which Daniel and Shakespeare would exploit.[4] In the fall of Rome, Spenser, following DuBellay, sees the epitome of the world's inconstancy. And well might Rome serve as such a model, since Rome was the world. (s. 26) But from these reflections upon change, other thoughts suggest themselves that work counter to the conclusion of vanity. The young poets are obviously thrilled by the grandeur of their subject. Rome and time are resounding words that they love to repeat and roll. This tonal impression is not belied by their thoughts about Rome. There is a flicker of the old glory in the ghost, and from the ruins we can imagine the former greatness. The historical and poetic imagination of DuBellay, to which Spenser so readily responds, sets out to give a sense of the living reality through the prospect of ruin. It does not allow what was great in life to perish, unknown and unrecalled. There is a revivifying and vital perspective in their backward look. Rome is a model of cultural continuity as well as an instance of ruin. As her "antique furie" continued to inspire poets of the Renaissance, so her architecture and sculpture served the renascent arts with materials and models, served it to such an extent that there was some point in believing, as DuBellay did, that the spirit of Rome, itself, was raising up the rebuilt city. Implicit in the efforts of these young Renaissance poets was the idea (not yet given conscious formulation by Spenser) of an intimate connection between art and society: in reviving the past, in keeping its memory alive, the backward-looking historical and poetic arts transcend time and, by preserving for the enrichment of the present the forms and ideals of the past, perform an essential service for the continuity of civilization.

The Ruines of Time are closely connected with the *Ruines of Rome*.[5] In each, the fall of an earthly city is the symbol for the larger reign of time in human events. There is the further evidence that although the English poet chose as his model an ancient English city, Verulam, still the city was from Roman Britain and was drawn into the powerful orbit of its falling mother city. Rome is still the great model:

> O Rome thy ruine I lament and rue,
> And in thy fall my fatall overthrowe,
> That whilom was, whilst heavens with equall vewe
> Deignd to behold me, and their gifts bestowe,
> The picture of thy pride in pompous shew:
> And of the whole world as thou wast the Empresse,
> So I of this small Northerne world was Princesse.
>
> (78–84)

On however reduced a scale, Verulam, as a fallen earthly city, repeats the function of Rome. Yet it is not their similarity in fates but their dissimilarity in achievements that dictates Verulam's presence in the poem. Unlike Rome she has produced no works to perpetuate her fame: she is not celebrated nor recalled. She is a city

> Of which there now remaines no memorie,
> Nor anie little moniment to see,

> By which the travailer, that fares that way,
> This once was she, may warned be to say.
>
> (4–7)

It is in thus falling short of Rome that Verulam is significant, and as such she serves as a warning instance to Spenser's contemporaries:

> O vile worlds trust, that with such vaine illusion
> Hath so wise men bewitcht, and overkest,
> That they see not the way of their confusion;
> O vainesse to be added to the rest,
> That do my soule with inward griefe infest:
> Let them behold the piteous fall of mee,
> And in my case their owne ensample see.
>
> And who so els that sits in highest seate
> Of this worlds glorie, worshipped of all,
> Ne feareth change of time, nor fortunes threate,
> Let him behold the horror of my fall,
> And his owne end unto remembrance call;
> That of like ruine he may warned bee.
>
> (456–468)

And although Verulam requests pity for her fate, still the warning indicates the possibility of positive action. In fact, the sense of the poem repeats the argument of time. Time is a threatening force, but if alerted, man still has the freedom to withstand its hostility in some measure.

In fact, as Rome is a positive model of proper response, so in the poem, in the midst of the wailing, there emerge two instances of man's ability to overcome time. In a series of *ubi sunt* stanzas, Verulam laments her passed glory, which is wasted "as if it never were." She is unlamented and unsung, except for the work of one man, who

> maugre fortunes injurie,
> And times decay, and envies cruell tort,
> Hath writ my record in true-seeming sort.
>
> (166–168)

One man has been concerned with restoring Britain to her antiquity and her antiquity to Britain.[6] Spenser's panegyric of William Camden, whose *Britannia* was used by Daniel, Drayton, and himself, far from being "irrelevant" to the poem, is central as a portrait in miniature of the ideal

functioning of art and the great alliance between poet and historian in
their attempts to transcend the ruins of time:

> Cambden the nourice of antiquitie,
> And lanterne unto late succeeding age,
> To see the light of simple veritie,
> Buried in ruines, through the great outrage
> of her own people, led with warlike rage;
> Cambden, though time all moniments obscure,
> Yet thy just labours ever shall endure.
>
> $(169–175)$

The function of the historian fitted well with the great urge to transcend
time that possessed writers like Spenser. Harrington in his translation of
the *Orlando Furioso* shows the two crafts were considered together at
that time, when he translates Ariosto's "poeti" — the saving swans who
rescue the imperiled names from oblivion — as "historians learned and
poets rare." (35.22)[7]

The lamenting Verulam then turns (176 ff.) to survey the contemporary English scene as continued evidence of man's neglect. But here,
as elsewhere, the vision of death and passingness is tied up with models
of response and possibility. Her perspective of the *stemmata dudleiana*,
and its losses as proof of the world's ruin, is actually, as Spenser relates
in his preface to the Countess of Pembroke, "speciallie intended to the
renowning of that nobel race, from which both you and he [Philip Sid-
ney] sprong, and to the eternizing of some of the chiefe of them late
deceased." On the world's ruins and in the face of death, the poet repays his portion of a transaction. Not only do we witness the powers of
the poet to confer immortality, but, further, the patronage of the arts
that this house afforded serves as a model to the nobility. In this praise
of a line, so representative of the alliance between literature and an
aristocratic society, Spenser quite naturally singles out Sir Philip Sidney,
that soldier-poet of his race, who in his person summarized both ideals.
While Sidney himself was quite nonchalant about the Renaissance fever
for fame — it is negligible in his *Apologie* and in his *Astrophel and
Stella* — his achievement came to represent an unsurpassable ideal for
the writers of his circle. Not only the jeopardized ideals of art and society but also the other polarity of fame and religious reward seem to
be reconciled in his life. In Spenser's memorable salute, Sidney is in the
blessed fields, talking shop with all the great poets, while he is also
praised by his survivors here on earth:

> So there thou livest, singing evermore,
> And here thou livest, being ever song
> Of us, which living loved thee afore,
> And now thee worship, mongst the blessed throng
> Of heavenlie Poets and Heroes strong.
> So thou both here and there immortall art,
> And everiewhere through excellent desart.
>
> (337–343)

Rather than "here" and "there" being antinomous, they reward similar merit. Spenser is about his destined task, the task of any grand establishment poet, of reconciling opposites, of amalgamating contraries, and Sidney is his great example. But outside of the Dudley line and after the death of Sidney this ideal relationship between art and civilization is being threatened. Spenser complains that the hyphenated ideal of Sidney has been ruptured. Verulam is not Rome, and Burghley is not Sidney. The barbarians, with only the vision of the present, are in the saddle. The Sidneys, he warns, were responsive patrons when they did not have to be, possessing their own literary talent. Those who are not so ideally endowed should be more provident:

> But such as neither of themselves can sing,
> Nor yet are sung of others for reward,
> Die in obscure oblivion, as the thing
> Which never was, ne ever with regard
> Their names shall of the later age be heard,
> But shall in rustie darknes ever lie,
> Unles they mentioned be with infamie.
>
> (344–350)

The language here is not uncharged, as Spenser's imagination shudders at the prospects of nothingness. The direction of this stanza indicates that namelessness is not a simple phenomenon in Spenser's moral system; its implications extend beyond the merely physical to the moral and the spiritual. The final line suggests that the society which is neglectful of its past will probably be a notorious society in other matters. When oblivion is bestial, fame has these more serious and far-reaching consequences.

> What booteth it to have been rich alive?
> What to be great? What to be gracious?
> When after death no token doth survive,

> Of former being in this mortall hous,
> But sleepes in dust dead and inglorious,
> Like beast, whose breath but in his nostrels is,
> And hath no hope of happinesse or blis.
>
> (351–357)

Montaigne, of course, ridiculed such humors, and considered it foolish to rely on fame to justify one's life. But Montaigne was ministering to a society in which, he believed, the senseless craze of heroism was responsible for the violence of civil war. Spenser, on the other hand, was addressing a society that Daniel called "profit-seeking," that was represented by the hard-headed Philocosmus, and where a thoroughgoing practicality would be only too triumphant. Moreover, from the first, whenever Renaissance man sought to make more vigorous and energetic use of his time, he contrasted the purpose of such vital potential with the sloth of the beasts. From Ulysses to Hamlet the cry will be heard, "What is a man, / If his chief good and market of his time / Be but to sleep and feed? A beast, no more." The word "humanism" in this sense takes on added meaning, having at its base a consciousness of time that serves as a distinguishing human trait. In addition to making a more spirited use of time, humanism also came to invoke the reward of human activity, fame. Basic to humanism is Petrarch's assertion, "Ingentibus animis nichil breve optabile est." A similar need to deny the common fate of man and beast is behind the heroic humanism of Spenser. Assuming in the nobility the same grand propensities that move him, Spenser then launches into the classic exhortation of the argument of time, "Provide, provide":

> Provide therefore (ye Princes) whilst ye live,
> That of the Muses ye may friended bee,
> Which unto men eternitie do give;
> For they be daughters of Dame memorie
> And Jove, the father of eternitie.
>
> (365–369)

While, from the swing of the trope, we could well expect the poet to urge a *carpe florem* or a *carpe diem,* Spenser's temporal concern looks beyond the present pleasure to the larger dimensions of history and civilization, even eternity.

Spenser shares with Shakespeare the recognizable dimensions of the argument of time. In each writer, time is used as a warning principle in order to shatter illusion. While time is thus an agent of a limiting reality, it also, for each, heightens reality so that relatively mundane virtues like prudence and patronage become factors in a battle of cosmic importance. Each writer experiences a horror at the nothingness that results when no adequate response is made against time. Together they differ from their fourteenth-century predecessors in that their response is more directly historical, involving government, or children, or fame, and less directly religious. It is here, of course, that their means of response practically diverge. Spenser's drama takes place on the high plane of civilization and through the large dimension of history; he is more often dealing with cultural ideals. Shakespeare, while deeply involved in history, is much more individually concerned (although we shall be forced to qualify this generalization). Both Spenser and Shakespeare venerate the memory of the dead, but Shakespeare is more personal (consider Hamlet's remembrance of his father, for instance) while Spenser is given more to historical extension, the monumental. The bestial oblivion he deplores is barbarism; the ideals and values of civilization are what he would not allow to be forgotten.

While certainly deriving great present inspiration from the past, Spenser's art is much more backward-looking, more memorial. Memory, extended beyond the personal dimension that it has in Shakespeare, becomes part of this grand avenue of culture and, as the allegory of Alma's tower tells us (*F.Q.* II.ix), it plays an important part in the life of man and the life of a country.

The message of time for the aristocracy is even more detailed in the *The Teares of the Muses,* where the neglect of poetry leads to profound social and cosmic ramifications. The expressiveness of Spenser's language in regard to as mundane an item as patronage must be understood in this system of interconnecting spheres, where disorder in one area involves the whole. A kind of "domino theory" is operative here. Disregard for the artist indicates a disregard for the muses and a concern with the present that is nonchalant about antiquity and posterity. The heroic impulse, the desire for excellence that should be proper to any aristocracy, is thereby frustrated, and virtue lies dormant. Dominated by the present pleasure, such a society rather than merely being unknown runs the risk of infamy. Distinctions are lost, and with distinctions knowledge is neglected. At its farthest reaches this dislocation touches the creation. If God's plan is affirmed by man's heroic transcendence of time, so it is subverted by ignoble oblivion. The world reverts to the uncreated mud and slime, before the hand of God brought forth sig-

nificant forms. Such are the dismal effects that the interruption of the
circuit of history suggests for Clio, one of the tearful muses:

> So shall succeeding ages have no light
> Of things forepast, nor moniments of time,
> And all that in this world is worthie hight
> Shall die in darknesse, and lie hid in slime!
>   (103–106)

When the muse of epic and heroic poetry, Calliope, bemoans the lack
of contemporary subject matter, we see that for Spenser neglect of the
past has important sociological consequences. A lack of interest in raising from the dust what was once noble bespeaks an ignobility, a narrowness of heart and vision, that will result in the eventual namelessness
of the present generation. Historical isolation will be their fate, since
they themselves will be lacking in motivation to transcend the present
and perpetuate their own names. Deeds and learning are therefore connected. By failing in their function as patrons, the members of the aristocracy undermine the heroic ideals of distinction and extension; it is
themselves that they are undoing, and the aristocratic bases of their society. The levelling processes of death and time are triumphant, as Calliope complains: "What oddes twixt Irus and old Inachus, / Twixt best
and worst, when both alike are dedd . . . ?" (447–448) Fame is the
spur for Spenser as it had been for other Renaissance writers, and the
basis of their heroic vision. The heroic poem has this social purpose:
it retains the names of the past and provides models for conduct, but in
its act of recognizing merit and preserving for posterity the superior
names and deeds of its own time, it provides the motive spark for heroic
effort. For this reason Calliope calls herself the "nourice of virtue," just
as the muses are termed "nourses of nobility," and Camden's historical
efforts serve as lantern and nurse.

The Bower of Bliss and the Garden of Adonis

An indication of the large place the foregoing considerations have in
Spenser's moral universe is their helpfulness in glossing the episodes of
the Bower of Bliss and the Garden of Adonis. Spenser's dedication to
the transcendence of time, the bestial consequences of total concentration on the present, his appreciation of aristocratic family line and historical continuity, and finally the connection of all of this with man's

divine origins — these arguments and concerns are useful in throwing into relief important details that might otherwise be neglected in the two great sections of *The Faerie Queene*. While true means are offered man to preserve his excellence from decay, so, too, are false means. The contrast — and a contrast is clearly intended — between the Bower and the Garden is partially effected through two differing responses to Time.[8]

The ethic of the Bower is simple naturalism. Look at the lily, Cymochles is urged in Book Two, Canto VI: she "neither spinnes nor cardes, ne cares nor frets, / But to her mother Nature all her care she lets." Concomitant with this naturalism is the exhortation to take the present pleasure:

> Why then doest thou, O man, that of them all
> Art Lord, and eke of nature Soveraine,
> Wilfully make thy selfe a wretched thrall,
> And wast thy joyous houres in needlesse paine,
> Seeking for daunger and adventures vaine?
> What bootes it all to have, and nothing use?
> Who shall him rew, that swimming in the maine,
> Will die for thirst, and water doth refuse?
> Refuse such fruitlesse toile, and present pleasure chuse!
>
> (II.vi.17)

When we come upon the young man lulled in Acrasia's bower, the message is the same. The sheer labor required of the heroic ambition is unnatural madness when old age is waiting. *Carpe florem* is the short-term advice, for which nature serves as example:

> Gather therefore the Rose, whilest yet is prime,
> For soone comes age, that will her pride deflowre:
> Gather the rose of love, whilest yet is time,
> Whilest loving thou mayst loved be with equall crime.
>
> (II.xii.75)

Spenser's refrain is the English addition to a literary motif that has had a long and flourishing career. From Ausonius' "Collige, virgo, rosas" to the "Cogli la rosa" of Lorenzo de'Medici and his more talented poet, Poliziano, to Ariosto and the Pléiade, "Cueillez, cueillez," and finally from Tasso to the English writers, Spenser and Daniel and their followers, this theme has produced exquisite poems that have been gathered and studied.[9] My notes will contain some of these references; here let me expand on two more general problems involved. While the *carpe florem* motif had a vigorous poetic life in the circle of Lorenzo and later, both it and *carpe diem* exhortations were present much earlier in European literature. They are the implied injunctions of the *Roman de la Rose,* the active ethic in Boccaccio's *Decamerone,* and are clearly stated in Pandarus' advice to Criseyde (in Chaucer's version, as well as in Boccaccio's). They were also both present in the classical quotations that Petrarch incorporated into his essentially religious goals.[10] They differ only by virtue of the greater inclusiveness of the *carpe diem* idea, which extends beyond simple amatory persuasion. The second point to be stressed here is that in English writers like Spenser and Shakespeare, whenever *carpe diem* or *carpe florem* suggestions seem to isolate man in the present, that is, whenever they suggest a separation from the larger associations open to him within society and history or the order of the cosmos, then such arguments are almost certainly coming from unreliable spokesmen (or women).[11] In Sidney's *Arcadia* (III.10) Cecropia's arguments, a veritable summary of Renaissance themes, are rejected by Pamela. Marlowe's invitation to love is countered with the realism of Raleigh's response. The invitation to love in Shakespeare's *Venus and Adonis* is disordered. Andrew Marvell, who wrote "To His Coy Mistress," also wrote "Clorinda and Damon." Giles Fletcher wrote "Christ's Victory and Triumph." Perhaps we must look to Milton's poetry, most grandly in *Paradise Lost* and *Paradise Regained,* to see the fullest gathering and rejection of these Renaissance themes. It is in relation to these works and others like them, where the *carpe diem/carpe florem* motives are used dramatically, that Spenser's Bower of Bliss must be understood. The discriminations here are slightly complicated in that, far from totally rejecting succession, the Elizabethan writers were thoroughly committed to its rewards. The same argument, rejected in the *Venus and Adonis,* is espoused in Shakespeare's sonnets, when the course of action suggested, marriage and children, means connection with past and future. It is with Shakespeare's sonnets and histories, whatever their different scope and sensibility, that Spenser's Garden of Adonis must be grouped.

Time is the great enemy in the Bower, but the means proposed to counter time are damaging, unnatural, and constrictive. To make nature man's emblem in response as well as in fate is to deny civilization and the human means afforded for continuity within time. Such naturalism is unnatural, Spenser would say, thwarting man's greater possibilities. There is the suggestion that even the sex of the Bower is not thoroughly satisfying; it has much of the peep-show about it, and the young man seems more the victim of an experience *manqué* than the enjoyer of any virile sexuality. Perhaps the strongest condemnation of the Bower is the contrast between the youthful, growing nature of Verdant, the young nobleman, and the coy, artificial, and entangling atmosphere. But for Spenser, so conscious of time and civilization, an equally important condemnation is found in the young man's apparent disregard for his past and his future:

> His warlike armes, the idle instruments
> Of sleeping praise, were hong upon a tree,
> And his brave shield, full of old moniments,
> Was fowly ras't, that none the signes might see;
> Ne for them, ne for honour cared hee,
> Ne ought, that did to his advauncement tend,
> But in lewd loves, and wastfull luxuree,
> His dayes, his goods, his bodie he did spend:
> O horrible enchantment, that him so did blend.
>
> (II.xii.80)

His total devotion to the present pleasure has reduced the young man to the same barbarism against which Spenser warned the aristocracy, a barbarism of total presentness, which is careless of past and future. With our previous argument in mind, meaningful poignancy can be read into the details where the "old moniments" of his shield were so erased that "none the signs might see." The past of his own house is forgotten and consigned to nothingness, and with the old monuments also perish the examples and incentives for heroic and even moral effort in the present. The young gentleman lost in the Bower is a practical instance of the dangers Spenser warned would befall the aristocracy from their neglect of those who keep the past alive.

Acrasia's discarded lovers are unmanned and beastly, and, as we have shown, this has special relevancy in Spenser's own detailed thought, where one definition of man lies in his capacity to transcend time. To be so oblivious of anything but the present pleasure is to debase man's stature as a creature of God. See, says Guyon, at the unreconstructed Grylle,

> See the mind of beastly man,
> That hath so soone forgot the excellence
> Of his creation, when he life began,
> That now he chooseth, with vile difference,
> To be a beast, and lacke intelligence! [12]

(87)

These final thoughts return the distinctions Spenser is intent on making to their first origins.

With Shakespeare's sonnets and his second tetralogy, Spenser's Garden of Adonis is Elizabethan England's grandest endorsement of the ways of generation. Where Shakespeare's procedure begins with passions and people in conflict and then approaches myth, Spenser begins with myth containing strong suggestion for personal apprehension. In the Garden Spenser sees not a person, but a process, a process so awesome as to inspire the imagination to describe it only in universal terms. The Porter

> letteth in, he letteth out to wend,
> All that to come into the world desire:
> A thousand thousand naked babes attend
> About him day and night . . .
>
> (III.vi.32)

> Daily they grow, and daily forth are sent
> Into the world, it to replenish more.
>
> (36)

Mind sits back and contemplates the formation of all the creatures that come to be born. It is a key to Spenser's imagination and sensibilities that he responds so passionately to these larger ongoing processes. As he figured forth the continuities of history and civilization, so he projects the race itself: change is subsumed under a more thrilling dimension, universal in its scope, and man feels enlarged by identification with such process. The individual is not alone, he suffers no orphanhood, no nakedness, but rather feels comforted, even exalted, by this means of perpetuation. Abiding lifelines dominate change and become the image of eternity. Adonis, the mythic personage embodying the spirit of the Garden, is "eterne in mutabilitie / And by succession made perpetuall."

The Garden of Adonis is Spenser's earthly paradise. It is his contribution to that long line of "pleasant places" that man's desires and imagination and mind have created to summarize what they conceive to be the best operations of the natural order. Residual materials from the earthly paradise *topos* help to identify its lineage. Labor is absent:

> Ne needs there Gardiner to set, or sow,
> To plant or prune: for of their owne accord
> All things, as they created were, doe grow.
>
> (34)

In this place "There is continuall spring, and harvest there / Continuall." And yet it has its differences from the tradition. Unlike Dante's earthly paradise, where a chaste intellectual love that spiritually enjoys the many objects of the world is celebrated, the Garden is involved in the processes of generation, and physical love is extolled:

> Franckly each paramour his leman knowes,
> Each bird his mate, ne any does envie
> Their goodly meriment, and gay felicitie.
>
> (41)

Whereas Dante would be removed totally from the dung and death, Spenser accepts death and change for the sake of the regenerative potential and cosmic participation. Moreover, Dante's allegory represents an essential stage in the journey of the mind toward God. It is only, however, a temporary one, where the citizen of the City of God is "poco tempo silvano." Spenser's garden is a recreation and exposition of fundamental forces working for continuity in the world. While clearly subordinate in hierarchy to the more religiously conceived virginity of Belphoebe, and the Virgin Queen, still it is a highly respected level of existence with its own integrity and justification, supported by God's command: "Increase and multiply." For Spenser, then, as for Rabelais and, as we shall see, for Shakespeare, there is no essential conflict between the ways of succession and of salvation.

Spenser's Garden is not dominated by an ethos of nostalgia. It might simulate the desire for a Golden Age, but one of its gates is iron. Time is not dissolved but is a distinct presence in the Garden; beauty of form is not immune:

> Great enimy to it, and to all the rest,
> That in the Gardin of Adonis springs,
> Is wicked Time, who with his scyth addrest,
> Does mow the flowering herbes and goodly things,
> And all their glory to the ground downe flings,
> Where they do wither, and are fowly mard:
> He flyes about, and with his flaggy wings
> Beates downe both leaves and buds without regard,
> Ne ever pitty may relent his malice hard.
>
> (39)

And although the gods pity this cruel truth and Venus laments, still it is part of the nature of things about which nothing can be done:

> For all that lives, is subject to that law:
> All things decay in time, and to their end do draw.
>
> (40)

In the Garden the pleasure principle dominates, but time, a principle of reality, and one could almost say fate, against which even the gods are helpless to save beauty, is not denied. The Garden embodies Marlowe's invitation to love, but it also includes Raleigh's grim reminder. In fact, it is possible to say that the poetic impact of the Garden of Adonis is effected through the precarious sense of loveliness obtained and lost in time. Yet strong forces of continuity do exist.

In this way the Garden differs from its obvious competitor, the Bower of Bliss. Time is the great enemy there, but as a reality its force is missing. Everything in that Palace of Art is done to obscure the nature of man's involvement in organic process, in growth and decay, in individual termination and racial continuity. In a modern poet's phrase, the Bower is "reprehensibly perfect." [13] Just as it seeks to conceal man's true temporal condition, it also neglects the means of response that nature affords. Its commitment to present pleasure seems sterile and dead-end. Brought together thus, indicating erroneous and viable responses to time, the Bower and the Garden of Adonis are part of Spenser's argument of time and show that the Garden, while a mythic treatment of a cosmic process, is not automatically open to all, but is an acquisition dependent upon right understanding. It is a product of that important Spenserian world, "trial." Spenser leaves no doubt that the vision and promise of this joyous paradise must be achieved. While its true location is obscure (an indication that while literally somewhere, it is of course everywhere), wherever it be,

> Whether in Paphos, or Cytheron hill,
> Or it in Gnidas be, I wote not well;
> But well I wote by tryall, that this same
> All other pleasant places doth excell.
>
> (29)

While active exhortation to proper attitude, as in Shakespeare's address to the young man of the sonnets, is missing, this great interlude represents a tried and conscious investment in the processes of succession.

"Trial"

Glorious spoile
Gotten at last with labour and long toyle

By "tryall" Spenser knows that the Garden of Adonis is the most realistically fulfilling of the pleasant places, and particularly superior to the Bower of Bliss, whose present-centered naturalism scorns the "fruitlesse toil" that goes into heroic endeavor. Finally, in the Garden, Cupid and Psyche, those forces of love and mind that are so tragically dissevered, come together "after long troubles and unmeet upbrayes." Although the course of true love does not run smooth in Spenser (we remember Colin's December song in *The Shepheardes Calender*), the defeats of early love are eventually resolved. Man can obtain a guilt-free attitude toward sexual love, represented by mature womanhood. But it is not done easily, as the trials of Britomart indicate. This same process of long struggle with eventual success glorified in Britomart will be particularized with happy results in Spenser's sonnet sequence and the crowning *Epithalamion*.

The notion of trial is a highly significant and consistent portrayal in Spenser's works of man's involvement in succession, and calls for special treatment. On the one hand it is clear that the concept of trial is part of Spenser's heroic heritage. Difficulties must be overcome before the aspirant earns the right to the prize. Since the way is hard and the companions few, Petrarch, in his noteworthy sonnet 7, urges the young man not to grow tired, "non lassar la magnanima tua impresa." High merit is proved by constancy and persistence in the face of never-ending obstacles. But at the same time that trial calls out man's heroic potential, it also deeply signifies life's imperfections. To be in time is for Spenser to be involved quite seriously in succession. While this means that after error and straying man can eventually right himself, it also means that such moments of triumph and perfection are short-lived. Toil recommences: how deeply alluring then for Spenser is the notion of rest. While man can live through defeat, he also survives after victory, survives to see his triumph qualified and tested again. In Shakespeare, more dramatic in his art and conception, life will be seen as highly emulative, with tense confrontations and tragic endings. His historical and tragical works move more resoundingly toward a denouement, but in Spenser such a solution is more attenuated. He is given more by form and vision to the longer work. Lacking the higher tensions of emulation, he strings things out: stories overlap, and supposed victors in one book continue their quest in the following. The Red Cross Knight presumably has completed his mission, but at the moment of his wedding celebration an anticlimax occurs: Archimago intrudes with his insidious accusation. After unmasking the deception, the Red Cross Knight cannot remain with his wife, but must return to Gloriana's court, and further journeying in Book Two. In the manner of Ulysses, he arrives at home, but he cannot stay. The world is not a place of abiding arrivals, but only of contingencies. At the end of Book Two, Acrasia's bower is destroyed and the victims restored, but there is still Grylle, who resists reconversion. If an integral part of Christian vision is the "saving remnant," an equally persistent part is the "damaging remnant." Victories, while clear, are only temporary, and the battle lines quickly regroup to meet on another front. While time is a reality for Spenser, and events do have their own right and merit, still it is clear that time is only a staging ground for a higher resolution. Spenser seems viscerally committed to a sense of continuity that deprives individual actions of their self-containment. This is perhaps a basic difference between his vision and that of Shakespeare's more emulative world, where finalities are keenly realized. It also means that Spenser, unlike Dante or Shakespeare, never approaches the contracted present, whether as divine comedy or tragedy, and it suggests that, wed to the ways of succession and historical extension — and they can be heroic — he never seems to penetrate the enclosure of being.[14]

Psychologically, Spenser knew what he was about when he affirmed his kinship to Chaucer. In this sense of trial, he approximates Chaucer's own sense of process — the missing ingredient in Chaucer is of course the heroic dimensions of trial. They both seem given to visions of variety, to processions of figures and seasons and calendars. For both, change does not bode as ominously as it does for Shakespeare with his sense of emulation and replacement. For both, the process of change seems bound within a larger order, and both seem to have an inner stability and even confidence that permits them to live through the change. In the February *Shepheardes Calender,* the aged character Thenot gives a clear presentation of this Spenserian preoccupation. As in Dante's *Paradiso* X, the play of the weather is again the instant that suggests the need for human endurance:

> Lewdly complainest thou laesie ladde,
> Of Winters wracke, for making thee sadde,
> Must not the world wend in his commun course,
> From good to badd, and from badde to worse,

From worse unto that is worst of all,
And then returne to his former fall?
Who will not suffer the stormy time,
Where will he live tyll the lusty prime [spring]?
Selfe have I worne out thrise threttie yeares,
Some in much joy, many in many teares:
Yet never complained of cold nor heate,
Of Sommers flame, nor of Winters threat:
Ne ever was to Fortune foeman,
But gently tooke, that ungently came.
And ever my flocke was my chiefe care,
Winter or Sommer they mought well fare.

(9–24)

From this elderly piece of fortitude in the face of life's root mutability, we can see how far the Boethian-Chaucerian ideal stretches into English literature. Good times and hard times are intermixed in the cycle of the seasons. Life's doubleness, if it brings pain, also wheels back to spring and growth. In the face of these vicissitudes what is required is staying power and small expectations. An almost inalienable inner sphere of temporal confidence permits the aged man to go about his business until the weather clears. If things are beyond his powers, still their course is common and fairly regular. We have a representation here of an older sense of being, perhaps even pre-existing the medieval, attached to the soil and the processes of nature, where man exhibits inner stability and forbearance. Dante and Petrarch in their higher and more individualized pursuits are forced to abandon this level of existence, and then must try to incorporate it into their more heroic visions. For Spenser, despite his deep attraction to the heroic sense of life, this older habituation to change persists as an essential element of his artistic vision.

This vision promises little durable joy — in fact, little durability of anything. The shifting conditions of human life call for inner reserves of patience and fortitude. In Book One, the Red Cross Knight can easily detect the plain English of the House of Pride, but when he encounters its spiritual variant, the super-subtle Italian, Orgoglio, he has no preparation for such an enemy. On the day of his success over Pride, he falls victim to that enervating nonchalance which is another form of pride, and which leaves him exposed, unarmed, and defenseless. Such lassitude is harmful in Spenser's active Renaissance world, where one must always be moving and doing. After rescuing him from Orgoglio, Arthur summarizes the lesson of man's condition: "blisse may not abide in the state of mortall men." (I.viii.44) But even here there is no resting place. The Red Cross Knight loses courage at this grim message and succumbs to Despair, the vision that all of his life will be subject to strenuous and painful risings, only to be offset by sudden falls, an interminable prospect of new defeats following old triumphs. Only God's grace can rescue him from man's condition of essential imperfection and unfulfillment. For his part, he has only the sad lessons of a chastened experience:

> th'onely good, that growes of passed feare,
> Is to be wise, and ware of like agein.
>
> .   .   .   .   .
>
> Henceforth sir knight, take to you wonted strength,
> And maister these mishaps with patient might.
>
> (44, 45)

But patience is not an exhilarating virtue: it follows the debacle and tries to restore peace and order. Its usefulness is after the event, or with experiences that are old and hence open to mastery. The sad thought presents itself that where experience is new man will fail. Paradise, where man's instinctive response is the right one, has been lost. And indeed, there is much resembling Spenser's religious and historical thought in Books XI and XII of *Paradise Lost,* where patience before man's inherent incapacities in a changing world is only occasionally lightened by the sought-for thrusts of grace.

In Spenser, love is the source and testing ground of heroic merit. It seems most beset by hazards that try the mind's devotion and vision. Britomart is one of the most significant questers in a book whose pages are marked by people who are running and people who are seeking. Love's power is moving her,

> Making her seeke an unknowne Paramoure,
> From the worlds end, through many a bitter stowre.
>
> (III.iii.3)

Yet in Spenser love is a less tragic emotion than in Shakespeare. There is hope that through perserverance the bitter trial will yield fruit, and love enjoy extension through progeny and fame. If love seems to scatter and divide, love also joins, bringing together the predestined pair,

From whose two loynes thou afterwards did rayse
Most famous fruites of matrimoniall bowre,
Which through the earth have spread their living prayse,
That fame in trompe of gold eternally displayes.

(*ibid.*)

Love combines with social forces, with history, and with progeny to become an heroic force for the transcendence of time. Ever the great amalgamator, Spenser sees no opposition between society at its highest and true love:

For it of honor and all vertue is
The roote, and brings forth glorious flowres of fame,
That crowne true lovers with immortall bliss,
The meed of them that love, and do not love amisse.

(IV.Prologue.2)

Spenser invokes the muse of history, Clio, for his account of tried and glorious love, but in Shakespeare there is less of a fusion between forces of love and history. Love's play is in the comedies, where the spokesmen for history are unmasked as pedants and self-servers, and where the values of spontaneity, rejected in the histories, have some validity. In the histories, the love element is well-nigh absent. In *Henry V,* Henry's wooing provides comic relief after the great victories have been achieved; it represents Shakespeare's correctly-felt need to humanize his hero. The Lancasters' flame is dimmed by the heavy seriousness required of a ruler, and the high emotions of love and heroism are considerably tempered. The discards from this society are those who seem to show too much fire, whether of wit or heroic aspiration. The Shakespearean historical world is a manly world, and the generational link is mainly between father and son. In the sonnets addressed to the young man, there is little concern for the vessel he would enrich with his seed. In the histories and tragedies, wherever women are active, those who put on the breastplate of manliness are forces of disorder and disruption. But for Spenser the Faerie Queene is more of an active ideal, and in the trials of Britomart the poet represents the successful integration of love with history and children.

The beginnings of love in Britomart are troubled because she is not captivated by a real object but rather by the image of a man in the mysterious mirror (which, by the way, has a political relevancy in being designed by Merlin to warn King Ryence of any invasion to his king-

dom). The image of her future husband is a remarkable projection of
the young girl's ideal emotions and desires. Despite these strange incep-
tions and its troubled course this love story will be gloriously successful,
resulting in the foundation of the line of English royalty.

What is moving Britomart is a sacred fire, extolled in the invocation
of Canto III, which leads to "noble deeds and never-dying fame." But
in this case there is another force at work. The mystery of her love is
part of God's providence directing human history:

> Well did Antiquity a God thee deeme,
> That over mortall mindes hast so great might,
> To order them, as best to thee doth seeme,
> And all their actions to direct aright;
> The fatall purpose of divine foresight,
> Thou doest effect in destined descents,
> Through deepe impression of thy secret might,
> And stirredst up th'heroes high intents,
> Which the late world admyres for wondrous moniments.
>
> (III.iii.2)

Love is then an instrument of divine providence ("the fatall purpose of
divine foresight"); it is, in fact, its means of directing human conduct
through the efforts of its heroes. The providential program is the basis
of the Tudor myth, which Spenser here celebrates. The mystery of the
mirror is partially explained by the historical election of Britomart:
she is the first mother of the line that will culminate in the last virgin.
Aspiring love, historical extension, and progeny converge in this unfolding line whose flower will be "the perfect love . . . of chastity."
It is indicative that the thought of Spenser was not struck by the paradox
that the Queene's virginity would also mean an end to the Tudor myth.
Even Shakespeare's Cranmer, at the conclusion of *Henry VIII,* must
lament that the "most unspotted lily" would pass, a virgin, into the
ground.

The *Amoretti* and the *Epithalamion* are much more personal and
more pleasing expressions of the issues that had been elevated on the
historical stage and the Platonic ladder — England and formal Platonism
being Spenser's great interests in the 1580s. The sonnet sequence and
its accompanying and culminating marriage song join with the later
two *Hymnes* in replacing the Word of the earlier "greener" pieces with

Flesh. Christ and married love are much more palpable and pressing realities than the impossible confusion and the unreal subtleties of transformation in Platonic ascent. The picture of the nineties will be complete when the grand design of providential history — whose particular concern seems to be England — is shaken by the insurrection of radical historical change.

In these companion pieces recording his courtship and celebrating his wedding day Spenser fuses the two related strands of thought that we have been following: after long trial the determined and dedicated lover brings a successful resolution to the potentially divergent forces of love and progeny. Spenser shows himself to be the true lover and constant quester who gains his "glorious spoile / Gotten at last with labour and long toyle." In this context it may be appropriate that Spenser should have named the first fruit of that marriage Peregrine.

Many of the traditional and overworked themes of the sonnet sequence exist in the *Amoretti*: the warnings against hard-heartedness and the transience of youthful beauty, the unapproachability and ineffability of the beloved, the oxymoronic agonies of the lover, and the traditional vaunt of the immortalizing powers of the poet's verse. But this particular sequence differs from the conventional repetition of Petrarch's long-deceased woes by the successful and real consummation that it brings to an actual courtship. No bromide this! The *Amoretti* show Spenser's great genius in transforming the moral and thematic ends of a particular genre. This is a gathering not only of the usual postures of the sixteenth-century sonnet sequence, but also of the material that we have seen play so persistent a part in Spenser's other works.

It is the lover who must undergo the trial of constancy. The obstacles that Spenser encounters differ from the expected tests of the courtly love game or the normal suffering of the hopeless lovers in the sonnet sequences: his pain is the product of his lofty aim, but it will be offset by the obtained success. And the traditional *hauteur* of the object-lady within the concept of trial is transformed into a loftier virtue betokening sounder and more durable pleasure:

> Doe I not see that fayrest ymages
>   of hardest Marble are of purpose made?
>   for that they should endure through many ages,
>   ne let theyr famous moniments to fade.
> Why then doe I, untrainde in lovers trade,
>   her hardnes blame which I should more commend?
>   sith never ought was excellent assayde,

which was not hard t'atchive and bring to end.
Ne ought so hard, but he that would attend,
   mote soften it and to his will allure:
   so doe I hope her stubborne harte to bend,
   and that it then more stedfast will endure.

(s. 51)

Fascinating in this extract is Spenser's mingling of his experiences in art and his experiences in love. Unfading temporal extension through fame is the reward for ambitious accomplishments in marble, just as in Spenser's age — and for the young man not yet thirty who tried to overgo the Italian Ariosto — the heroic poem was the highest goal. But allied with this hard task is a native confidence in the powers of constant dedication, and the fire of love. We naturally recall Petrarch's interweaving of the laurel-Laura motives, and the "Coronation Oration." Spenser's experiences in art have provided him the model for hope of attainment in his approaches to love: for preliminary difficulty and pain they both promise long-lasting rewards.

Spenser, like Petrarch, labored under the fascination of what was difficult. As his devotion to love and fame derive from the Italian poet-humanist's tradition, so his abhorrence of the merely present pleasure coincides with Petrarch's self-dedication to high and heroic tasks. Spenser, too, tried to rise out of his age. At the same time he was deeply committed to succession, and unlike Petrarch, to children. The temporal confidence of Spenser was not shared by the fourteenth-century father of humanism and of heroic poetic strivings. Petrarch felt guilt and anxiety, while Spenser sensed a legitimate area of human conquest. To stretch out one's hand and take, under the cosmic conditions envisioned by Spenser, was justified. But Petrarch, perhaps because of his children born out of wedlock, frequently felt guilt at such penetration into human experience. At the same time, Spenser's courage and confidence in succession could be limiting. Petrarch's temporal anxiety pushed him to achieve the highest vision of divine comedy, a presentness in which he stands ready for God's every call. "The readiness is all" is a tone rarely, if ever, achieved by Spenser.

Unlike Petrarch, when the lights that were his guides are obscured and his traditional galley is lost, Spenser, with his more masculine confidence, is not dismayed:

   Yet hope I well, that when this storme is past
   my Helice, the loadstar of my lyfe

> will shine again, and looke on me at last,
> with lovely light to cleare my cloudy grief.
>
> (s. 34)

The image, as with Guyon in Book Two of the *Faerie Queene* going toward the Bower of Bliss, is one of voyage, where, despite the darkness and the turmoil, safe harbor is sure to be reached:

> Most happy he that can at last atchyve
>   the joyous safety of so sweet a rest;
>   whose least delight sufficeth to deprive
>   remembrance of all paines which him opprest.
> All paines are nothing in respect to this,
>   all sorrowes short that gaine eternall blisse.
>
> (s. 63)

Joy is the emotion of these final sonnets and of the *Epithalamion,* joy in the resiliency of the human condition, joy in the rewards of an enduring constancy — an almost miraculous joy that cancels out all past sorrows and torments.[15] Time indeed becomes short in qualitative contrast with such possession and in quantitative contrast with enduring fame. Time is an element of reality against which man must struggle, but it is also here clearly subordinate. Man's victories are measured not in time — its expenditure is unimportant — but in the endless monuments heroically achieved.

The sense of joy and wonder is increased when the final victory comes not only as a product of resolution, art and "long attent" but when one had least expected it (similar to the victories that Arthur or the Red Cross Knight achieve when they are fallen). As in Shakespeare's last plays, the sense of miracle only adds to the joy. So, the remarkable sonnet 67 records the softening of his lady's pride, in pity for her discouraged lover, who had finally wearied of the chase:

> Lyke as a huntsman after weary chace,
>   seeing the game from him escapt away,
>   sits downe to rest him in some shady place,
>   with panting hounds beguiled of their pray;
> So after long pursuit and vaine assay,
>   when I all weary had the chace forsooke,
>   the gentle deare returned the selfe-same way,
>   thinking to quench her thirst at the next brooke.
> There she beholding me with mylder looke,

> sought not to fly, but fearelesse still did bide,
> till I in hand her yet halfe trembling tooke,
> and with her own goodwill hir fyrmely tyde.

The image of the coupling of male and female is not that of plucking the rose or seizing the day, but a gentle fitting together. Maleness, however, still asserts its mastery, reaching out a hand and firmly tying her, and she, consenting at last to have her freedom ended, is before the strangeness of this new experience of life fearless but still "halfe trembling."

The subsequent sonnet is Spenser at his boldest and most imaginative. Just as when the Red Cross Knight enters the redeemed city, where he is likened to Christ entering Jerusalem,

> And all the way the joyous people singes,
> And with their garments strowes the paved street
> (I.xii.13)

and as in the *Epithalamion,* when Spenser's love is about to enter the church and the poet cries out

> Open the temple gates unto my Love,
> Open them wide that she may enter in,
> (204–205)

so here the lovers' realization of themselves as a couple (if not the actual physical consummation) is given broad imaginative amplification when it shares the joy of Christ's resurrection:

> This joyous day, deare Lord, with joy begin,
>   and grant that we for whom thou diddest dye
> being with thy deare blood clene washt from sin,
>   may live for ever in felicity.

Their love receives religious endorsement in the love of Christ (thereby linking these two poems not with the earlier *Hymnes* and their formal Platonism but with the later two). With this support Spenser exhorts his Elizabeth:

> So let us love, deare love, lyke as we ought,
>   love is the lesson which the Lord us taught.
> (s. 68)

This sonnet provides religious coverage for sonnets 67 and 70, where the *carpe florem* and *carpe diem* themes are strong. In the last, Elizabeth seems careless that winter has passed and spring is upon them; she should be warned:

> Tell her the joyous time wil not be staid
> unlesse she doe him by the forelock take:
>
> .   .   .   .   .
>
> Make haste therefore, sweet love, whilest it is prime,
> for none can call againe the passed time.
>
> (s. 70)

These pagan motives, and the resounding promises of eternal fame (sonnet 69), do not jostle Spenser's religious conscience. They are absorbed in the service of higher ends and purposes, from which they derive legitimacy. They are part of the deeper emotion of a just and indisputable joy. Here again Spenser shows an instinct which is perhaps typical of Elizabethan England. As in the Garden of Adonis, earthly responses to time, which are menacing when they stand alone, are placed in a broader context where they actually serve continuity and religious values. This connection of "here" and "there" is most richly drawn in the *Epithalamion*.

"The wished day is come at last" and the poet who had consistently praised others now turns to his own deserved pleasure. As all the various parts of the day and the members of the wedding pageant ceremoniously fulfill their functions, the poem slowly flowers into rising exultation. Although apparently derived from Catullus' epithalamia, Spenser's "progressive montage" differs considerably from the Latin example. The point in Spenser is that in contrast with the sheer happiness of the marriage and the hope of progeny, the time of trial is short. In fact, time as an urgent pressure on human activity is disallowed in the sheer concentration on the moment of contentment and its possibilities for "eternal bliss." But in Catullus' marriage song, the quality of which is hard to describe but mainly shares in the practical, common shrewdness of the city street, the passage of time becomes a frequent refrain. The progression is a hurried, not a stately movement. "Sed abit dies: / prodeas, nova nupta," and to the young groom, he urges, "perge, no remorare," Step on it, for time is passing.[16]

In Spenser's poem the hours are in attendance in their reparative functions, for the end of this marriage is the natural continuity that is the image of eternity and even extends to heaven's bounds:

> But first come ye fayre houres which were begot
> In Joves sweet paradice, of Day and Night,
> Which doe the seasons of the year allot,
> And al that ever in this world is fayre
> Do make and still repayre.
>
> (98–102)

As the world is renewed in time, so the human line through marriage is continued and repaired. But in Catullus no such cosmic concerns exist. Spenser, part of that line of Renaissance poets who, since Dante, wanted to be more classical by joining together eloquence and philosophy, who wanted to be no superficial humanist but a "curious universal scholar" for whom poetry was, in DuBartas' phrase, "docte artifice," turns out to be more classical than Catullus. For the Latin poet, children do not possess that universal time-transcending significance that they do for Spenser. In Catullus it is nice to have children, since it is not right that an old name should be without heirs. And whereas in Spenser the resemblance of child to parent reinforces the aims of self-perpetuation and self-projection, in Catullus (as in Boccaccio's version of the Griselda story) the concern is again more practical and social: the honesty of the mother is proved when the child looks like the father.[17]

It is against the background of the concept of "trial" that Spenser's prayerful requests in the *Epithalamion* take on greater poignancy. Finally, the man who had been bound by duty to the hardness of the world's imperfect ways asks that a pure day of pleasure be legitimately his. His claim on pleasure is not in defiance of the powers of the universe, but rather a plea that in their more beneficent functioning they honor for a day the world order's loyal upholder:

> O fayrest Phoebus, Father of the Muse,
> If ever I did honor thee aright,
> Or sing the thing, that mote thy mind delight,
> Doe not thy servants simple boone refuse,
> But let this day, let this one day be mine,
> Let all the rest be thine.
>
> (121–126)

It is now legitimate, in the hard Spenserian world, to relax one's guard and defenses. High, even unruly emotions of popular celebration are now allowed:

> Make feast therefore now all this livelong day,
> This day for ever to me holy is,
> Poure out the wine without restraint or stay,
> Poure not by cups, but by the belly full,
> Poure out to all that wull,
> And sprinkle all the posts and wals with wine,
> That they may sweat, and drunken be withall.
>
> (248–254)

Festival spirit, if anywhere, reigns here. And, to borrow C. L. Barber's thought, Saturnalian release, rather than defying the forces of order, actually, in its clear status of exception, confirms their power.[18] For once, rejoice. Normally threatful forces are invoked in their more benign aspects. Night becomes protective:

> Now welcome night, thou night so long expected,
> That long daies labour doest at last defray,
> And all my cares, which cruell love collected,
> Hast sumd in one, and cancelled for aye:
> Spread thy broad wing over my Love and me,
> That no man may us see.
>
> (315–320)

And although it seems to have been his luck to have chosen for his wedding the time of summer solstice when the day is longest and the night shortest, this does not daunt him: he has lived through much and knows that it will pass ("Yet never day so long, but late would passe"). Through long time and trial their patient love is rewarded, and they share in that peculiar power of man to forget past suffering: love makes up in height for what it lacks in length. But here, especially in this stanza where night is invoked in its dark protective intimacy, we are inevitably drawn to reflect upon the fates of two doomed young lovers, who enjoyed their love without any hope for future extension. Love and extension through progeny coincide in Spenser, and unlike Romeo and Juliet, he does not try to extend or alter the natural processes of day and night; he abides within them and they become holy:

> let the night be calme and quietsome,
> Without tempestuous storms or sad afray:
> Lyke as when Jove with fayre Alcmena lay,
> When he begot the great Tirynthian groome;

> Or lyke as when he with thy selfe did lie,
> And begot Maiesty.
>
> (326–331)

The product of this durable love is progeny. The moon, at other times the symbol of woman's fickleness, becomes, as Lucina, the patroness of woman's more productive involvement with the organic world:

> And sith of wemens labours thou hast charge,
> And generation goodly dost enlarge,
> Encline thy will t'effect our wishful vow,
> And the chaste wombe informe with timely seed,
> That may our comfort breed.
>
> (383–387)

To Juno and Genius — here the porter to the gate of life — he also prays for "fruitful progeny," life-continuing results of the wedding band.

Through the larger divine and cosmic associations we "earthly clods" arrive at extension in time, and time-bound mortality can become the image of eternity. Succession is graced, for the individual soul in this line can hopefully arrive at endless rest. This is the prayer and thought of the poem's penultimate stanza:

> And ye high heavens, the temple of the gods,
> In which a thousand torches flaming bright
> Doe burne, that to us wretched earthly clods,
> In dreadfull darknesse lend desired light;
> And all ye powers which in the same remayne,
> More than we men can fayne.
> Poure out your blessing on us plentiously,
> And happy influence upon us raine,
> That we may raise, a large posterity,
> Which from the earth, which they may long possesse,
> With lasting happinesse,
> Up to your haughty pallaces may mount,
> And for the guerdon of theyr glorious merit,
> May heavenly tabernacles there inherit,
> Of blessed Saints for to increase the count.

Again extension in time and vertical ascent are reconciled, and not only reconciled, but combined, so that the one leads to the other. Prayed for and envisaged is not only physical augmentation but also spiritual increase. The historical realm of succession includes the personal grant of salvation: "the guerdon of glorious merit." Heroic continuity and blessedness are jointly possible.[19]

Mutability

Despite all its tribulations and delay, the concept of trial indicates a fundamental temporal trust in Spenser. The universe is ordered toward spiritual ends and the protagonists themselves have an inalienable inner confidence. Like Thenot, they weather hard times with the faith that spring will follow winter. Succession thus deprives history of all sense of tragic termination. Spenser reveals no anxiety that the long labor of heroic dedication to humanistic ideals will be frustrated. He does not seem to share the fears of Petrarch or Milton that early death can cut short the long-postponed rewards of learning and poetry. Consequently he does not seek that rounding out of present fulfillment. Unlike Montaigne's, his faiths are extended.

Even time, as we have seen in contrast with the sure acquisition of enduring goals, is reduced to its proper insubstantiality. In fact, rarely in Spenser does time receive any real embodiment. The great exception is of course the Garden of Adonis, but even there devouring time is mastered in a more significant life process. Rarely does time stand forth in irrational and pugnacious opposition to man's properly achieved attitudes. At the basis of Spenser's allegorical method is the internalization of conflict: it is with himself and his false attitudes that man must war, not with an external world. In Shakespeare's more dramatic and social world, Lear and Hamlet eventually come to proper understandings of themselves and the universe, but this does not preserve them from bitter ends. It is in this sense that we can call Spenser's world "ideal" rather than "historical." One does not hear in Spenser the tragic cry of replacement, nor feel the agony of being pushed aside. No Bolingbroke now rides roan Barbary, no Hotspur or Fortinbras threaten to usurp one's position, no Shallow has land and beeves. In the material that we have studied thus far, time simply is not emulative in this personal and social sense in Spenser.

The *Two Cantos of Mutabilitie* cancel these generalizations. While it is true that the rejoicing of the *Epithalamion* is the reward for years of trial and labor, and that mankind are "wretched earthly clods" dwelling in "dreadefull darknesse," still the heavens "lend desired light." Despite the trial of existence, inner and outer sources of guidance and encouragement exist to hearten the true quester. But when we come to *Mutabilitie* those few remaining stabilities are threatened. The moon whose course "joy to weary wandring travailers did lend" is challenged by a different principle of cosmic direction, and its effect is a blackout, reminiscent of the pre-creation chaos:

> Mean-while the lower World, which nothing knew
>   Of all that chaunced here, was darkned quite;
>   And eke the heavens, and all the heavenly crew
>   Of happy wights, now unpurvaide of light,
>   Were much afraid, and wondred at that sight;
>   Fearing least Chaos broken had his chaine,
>   And brought againe on them eternall night.
>   (VII.vi.14)

In his large associative method, Spenser clearly draws into the significance of Mutabilitie's actions effects which are analogous to the Fall (stanzas 4, 5, 6). At that time it was Mutabilitie, who, in her ambitious attempt to extend her domain, brought an end to man's earthly paradise:

> For, she the face of earthly things so changed,
>   That all which Nature had establisht first
>   In good estate, and in meet order ranged,
>   She did pervert, and all their statutes burst:
>   And all the worlds faire frame (which none yet durst
>   Of Gods or men to alter or misguide)
>   She alter'd quite, and made them all accurst
>   That God had blest; and did at first provide
> In that still happy state for ever to abide.
>   (5)

Mutabilitie altered the provisions God had made for man "at first." In the beginning the promise was for pleasant abidance in a happy state. Instead man must endure change and alteration. This policy of alteration has more than physical attributes; it involves moral confusion:

> Ne shee the lawes of Nature onely brake,
>   But eke of Justice, and of Policie;
>   And wrong of right, and bad of good did make,
>   And death for life exchanged foolishlie:
>   Since which, all living wights have learn'd to die,

And all this world is woxen daily worse.
O pittious worke of Mutabilitie,
By which, we all are subject to that curse,
And death instead of life have sucked from our nurse.[20]

(6)

Yet, however far-reaching her associations and however mythological her dress, the point of the poem is not the distant first Fall, with its curse, its conversion of life processes into death processes, and its attendant sense of historical decline, but the later assault upon the heavens, a threatened second fall, which is taking place in Spenser's own life time.[21] An older order, to which Spenser committed his faith and from which he derived his hope, is threatened by a newer order, which he regards as morally dangerous. Emulation, replacement — those processes which were heretofore largely absent — now force themselves upon his consciousness. *The Two Cantos of Mutabilite* represent the eruption of deeply experienced history on what had been Spenser's ideal landscape. Former faiths and aspirations, promising a degree of security and continuity, are radically challenged. Whatever might be said of the poem's connection with the Tyrone rebellion in Ireland, and with Spenser's forced evacuation and bitter end, it is clearly not the work of an administrator who sees some future open to him.[22] There is certainly more than usual significance in the report (unverified) that a newborn child of the writer of the Garden of Adonis and the *Epithalamion* perished in the Irish uprising.[23]

Mutabilitie's associations with the first Fall are extremely important, both in larger intellectual import and in their revelation of Spenser's preoccupations. In Spenser's concept of trial we noted the persistence of sin and evil. Archimago returns to deprive Guyon's victory of its total satisfaction; Grylle remains unredeemed. While legacies from the past are sources of inspiration for Spenser, as we have seen, and while he once planned to write a poem in praise of the *stemmata dudleiana* (which was partially achieved in the *Complaints*), he was nevertheless aware of other unregenerate continuities. Mutabilitie is the recurrent and damaging remnant from the first assault on the heaven. Although Jove seemed to defeat the Titans, "Yet many of their stemme long after did survive." The earth in conjunction with chaos has produced these rebellious powers which never seem to be completely mastered and periodically return to overextend their power. Though defeated for a

time, they too have their perseverance, so that the battle is never entirely
ended. The earth, we remember, is fruitful, and chaos lent substance to
the great creative processes of the Garden of Adonis. Jove explains that
while he destroyed his assailants,

> Yet not so quite, but that there did succeed
> An off-spring of their bloud, which did alite
> Upon the fruitful earth, which doth us yet despite.
>
> (VII.vi.20)

Beyond this Spenserian proclivity for genealogies, Mutabilitie's connection with the first Fall helps to place this new phase of Spenser's work
in Renaissance developments.

If there is any meaning to the progressive enlightenment of the neo-
Platonism that helped to promote the greater optimism of the high Renaissance, it was in its faith that somehow the lapse of the first parents
had not been as all-destructive as was traditionally supposed. As Cassirer has shown in his *Platonic Renaissance in England,* Plato's melior-
ism replaced Augustine's rigor.[24] Similar to the introduction of Thomistic
Aristotelianism in the thirteenth century, this later touch of Hellenism
reinvigorated the human spirit. Upon the ashes of the first ruin, a more
optimistic Christian philosophical and social edifice was constructed
which gave man some possibility of communicating with divinity, of
having an integrated view of the cosmos and an important position in
the scheme of things. Spenser's world view, his vision of history and
love and children, is an important endorsement of these possibilities.
Although in the sublunary world all was change and confusion, in the
spheres above the moon there was constancy and rest, and true directing
order and spiritual light. The physical heavens in their imputed immu-
tability and unchanging perfection were the symbols of more permanent
values which continued to serve as guides and standards for men. But
now in Spenser's time these apparently enduring values and man's capacity to know them are challenged. Into this world of graduated mediation intrudes another principle, regarded as a second historical fall
(Dante's "twice-robbed tree"), that calls into question the order and
direction of the universe, and plunges man into the darker world of
chorismos.

Mutabilitie is more than change. Her attempt to become a cosmic
principle — that is, a principle by which men should direct their actions
and in which they should place their faiths — symbolizes Renaissance
developments in science and in moral and political philosophy which,

Spenser feared, tended to kill man's prior sense of rapport with the spiritual forces of the universe and his own hopes for continuity. Her endorsement of change and her own aggressive behavior plunges man into brute conflict and emulative struggle. A root irrationality inheres in the working out of things; the order of history is not continuity, but change based on power. Although Spenser's style and method of presentation might still be part of what Danby has called Great House literature, his present vision of the world shows the unmistakable influence of the stage, and particularly that genre which first began to deal with vital Renaissance energies, the history play. Behind Mutabilitie's ascensionism is the emulative spirit of Tamburlaine:

> The thirst of reign and sweetness of a crown,
> That caused the eldest son of heavenly Ops
> To thrust his doting father from his chair,
> And place himself in the imperial heaven,
> Moved me to manage arms against thy state.
> What better precedent than mighty Jove?
>
> (II.vii.12–17)

The cosmic and natural precedent that Tamburlaine claims for his thrusting out of the older order is dramatically duplicated in Mutabilities's attempt to wrest control of the heavens. In each, broader Renaissance developments are more specifically embodied in this new sense of struggle and emulation within the processes of succession.

She is a descendant of the Titans "that did whylome strive"; like Bellona, so did she "aspire." But unsatisfied with control of the earth,

> She gan to cast in her ambitious thought,
> T'attempt the empire of the heavens hight,
> And Jove himselfe to shoulder from his right.
>
> (VII.vi.7)

She boldly ascends to the circle of the moon, whose splendor she admires and envies:

> Shee gan to burne in her ambitious spright,
> And t'envie her that in such glorie raigned.
> Eftsoones she cast by force and tortious might,
> Her to displace; and to her selfe to have gained
> The kingdome of the Night, and waters by her wained.
>
> (10)

Like Tamburlaine in front of Mycetes or Richard of York with Henry VI, she feels herself "more worthy" of the ivory throne. Undaunted by any threats, Mutabilitie presses forward to expel Cynthia from her throne: "boldly preacing-on raught forth her hand / To pluck her downe perforce from off her chaire." (13) Spenser, as we have seen, like Shakespeare, participates in the general Renaissance *carpe florem* and *carpe diem* themes. It is legitimate for man to reach out his hand, provided, these English writers insist, such action is within a broader frame of religious or social sanction. Mutabilitie represents single, isolated seizure without any larger concerns. Her endorsement of change, similar to that of the Richards in Shakespeare's first tetralogy, leads to no larger good. Milton, too, in highly dramatic comment, would qualify this act of reaching out the hand to take. We see Eve: "forth reaching to the fruit, she plucked, she eat." But her hand is "rash," and the hour "evil."

Mutabilitie's intellectual parentage and relations are further clarified when she decides, in the manner of many of the opportunists of the history play, to take occasion by the forelock and force her way into Jove's court, rather than wait for his leave. Before the gods can rally themselves she resolves to set upon them, "And take what fortune, time, and place would lend." Up she marches, armed with the proverb of political expediency that echoes throughout Shakespeare, particularly among his villains, "good on-set boads good end." (23)

Mutabilitie's boldness is electric. Jove's functionaries are more than unsettled by her brashness: they are somewhat astounded and abashed by her vitality. She crashes through the older conceptions. The conventional image of time, "hory / Old aged Sire, with hower glasse in hand," seems decrepit and clearly passé in contrast with her energy: "she entred, were he liefe or sory." (8) The stars, witnessing the struggle between Cynthia and Mutabilitie,

<blockquote>
still did stand,
All beeng with so bold attempt amazed,
And on her uncouth habit and sterne look still gazed.
</blockquote>

(13)

Mercury, too, is at first taken back by the sight of Mutabilitie:

<blockquote>
At whose strange sight, and haughty hardinesse,
He wondred much, and feared her no lesse.
</blockquote>

(17)

Into the counsel of the gods she barges, uninvited, and finds them

> All quite unarm'd, as then their manner was.
> At sight of her they sudaine all arose,
> In great amaze, ne wist what way to chose.
>
> (24)

And after she speaks and literally challenges Jove's birthright, the gods

> Stood all astonied, like a sort of steeres;
> Mongst whom, some beast of strange and forraine race,
> Unwares is chauns't . . .
>
> (28)

It must be said that the members of Jove's court suffer from a malady most incident to long-continuing civilizations. The whetstone of ambition has been worn smooth; they have been domesticated, and their air of defenselessness reveals their shock at Mutabilitie's bold challenge. The woods have been cleared for them and they no longer remember the primitive struggle. They themselves have been victimized by the very order and continuity of their regime. The emotions they feel are not unlike those of a son who, abiding within the overarching parental control, suddenly witnesses those figures on whom he depended challenged by another son on equal ground. No little envy and self-blame enters into their combined fear and admiration of the challenger.

Jove's courtiers, however, like their lord, are sturdy and recover. And in a way, there had been cosmic justification for their admiration. The gods are moved by Mutabilitie's beauty, as Jove will later be in allowing her to speak:

> (Being of stature tall as any there
> Of all the Gods, and beautifull of face
> As any of the Goddesses in place . . .)
>
> (28)

And this is as it should be, when we consider how much Spenser admires and participates in the role of change within the universe. Time is ideally the image of eternity, and Spenser will always detect the presence of divinity and spiritual order behind the moving pageants of seasons and months and hours. Mutabilitie's attractiveness also has its prototype in Christian myth. Lucifer was, after all, the brightest angel, the Child of

Light. In *Paradise Lost* he is ignorant of how much he is diminished, but in Spenser's poem Mutabilitie still enjoys the beauty she has as God's means of bringing his creation to fulfillment. We can measure then the difference between her attractiveness and that of Shakespeare's villains, a Richard III or an Edmund. Theirs lies in the sexual appeal of arrogant will itself, of brutal cunning and enforcement. Shakespeare has a much more human sense of evil and of passion. But in Spenser, Mutabilitie is more a principle of cosmic proportions — however far-reaching and painful her practical ramifications might be — and as such she still enjoys divine favor, shown in her beauty.

Mutabilitie's person does not challenge the gods as much as the content of her speech. Not only is she a goddess in appearance and spirit (*de facto,* we might say) but *de jure,* too, she has some rightful claim to sovereignty. And it is here that Spenser's Tudor myth encounters Tudor reality. The established order has not always been so. At its beginning violent change and guile helped to usher in the new order. By what right is peaceful succession urged on Mutabilitie when the establishment itself was born in violence and revolution? What Mutabilitie is practicing she has merely learned from her betters. In dramatizing this fundamental problem of history — the problem of original sin — Spenser's mythic treatment covers the contemporary American scene as well, where the explosive demands of the unjustly deprived challenge the order of a beleaguered establishment.

As the Mortimers will haunt the Lancasters, and eventually topple the weak Henry VI in Shakespeare's first tetralogy, so Mutabilitie is up on her genealogy when she shows that Jove's father, Saturn, obtained power by displacing an elder brother. For Mutabilitie, as it was for Tamburlaine, emulation is indeed a cosmic process, with divine precedent:

> For, Titan (as ye all acknowledge must)
>   Was Saturnes elder brother by birth-right;
>   Both, sonnes of Uranus: but by unjust
>   And guilefull meanes, through Corybantes slight,
>   The younger thrust the elder from his right:
>   Since which, thou Jove, injuriously hast held
>   The Heavens rule from Titans sonnes by might.
>   (27)

Mutabilitie's challenge carries with it the implication that at the heart of the historical process are emulation and blood beginnings. Consequently, a vision of history akin to the Augustinian view would be confirmed, if not by the Cain-Abel motif, then by Jacob-Esau. Man can not redeem himself in time, and rather than enjoying continuity he is exposed to a series of replacements. In the historical vision of man's struggle with time, the concept of original sin is a recurring obstacle, a force that must be overcome. Wherever original sin predominates, the earthly city is an invalid locus of redemption. So Augustine looks to the heavenly city — precisely because of this process; so Dante abandons the city of his youth, beset by the contentious waves of struggle and exile and the fratricidal desolations of civil war. So, in Shakespeare's first and second tetralogies, the fundamental issue will be to redeem the original curse, which is almost synonymous with redeeming time. In Dante's temporal realm, the *Purgatorio,* the pattern also exists: redemption proceeds against the stain of original sin. But rather than being an antagonist, original sin is the essential memory — a kind of viaticum — that Dante must carry with him on his ascent before he reaches his deliverance. But in a later age, in the presence of the Platonic optimism of the high Renaissance and the Elizabethan faith in succession and the ideals of continuity, the original fault radically challenges these hopes with the inescapable facts of replacement and emulation.

Jove does not answer this deep argument with Tudor myth, but rather with Tudor reality. Unlike Henry VI he does not consider his title weak, but rather as secured by conquest. But it is a conquest that is destined, and part of the order of things. *A View of the Present State of Ireland* shows that Spenser is not being ironic in giving Jove the tyrant's plea.[25] The Elizabethans, as E. W. Talbert has argued, considered necessity to be a highly valid argument.[26] This is Spenser's defense:

> For, we by Conquest or of our soveraine might,
> And by eternall doome of Fates decree,
> Have wonne the Empire of the Heavens bright . . .
>
> (33)

An awesomeness in great rule links it with the powers that be in the universe. Spenser, ever the poetic idealist, or one might say Hellenist, confers upon the nature of things the dread power of fate and necessity. Whatever his origins in time, Jove is better deserving to be a higher principle than Mutabilitie. In fact, as with the other devotees of emulation, say, a Richard III or an Edmund, there is something self-destructive in Mutabilitie's plea. In embracing her program men foolishly exchange death for life. And nature warns her in her final judgment, "thy decay thou seekest by thy desire." For Shakespeare, as for Spenser, to advocate change and to resist the possibilities of continuity is to go against basic life forces. This is sufficient proof of unworthiness for rule.

If thus far Mutabilitie's arguments, touching the complexities and ambiguities of politics and history, derive from Machiavelli, her further and terrible insights into change could derive from Montaigne. When she informs the assemblage (vii.18) that all earthly things are involved in the processes of birth and decay, this is not new. Even the next stanza, which traces the progress of man's pilgrimage, is still conventional up to a point:

> And men themselves do change continually,
> From youth to eld, from wealth to poverty,
> From good to bad, from bad to worst of all.

The language even echoes Thenot's earlier piece of consolation. But what follows gives it an essentially different flavor. Thenot encountered the world of change with an essential inner equilibrium and stability, which was typical of the simpler type of being that the men of the Renaissance, with their great strivings to overcome time, abandoned. They did not recommend acquiescence, but rather effort. Spenser in his notion of heroic trial combined both of these approaches. But Mutabilitie undoes both possibilities when she describes not only external change but a new awareness of inner change:

> Ne doe their bodies only flit and fly:
> But eeke their minds (which they immortall call)
> Still change and vary thoughts, as new occasions fall.
>
> (vii.19)

As the Player King in *Hamlet* will see it: " 'tis a question left us yet to prove / Whether love lead fortune, or else fortune love." For the newer Renaissance idealism, this skepticism had disastrous consequences. Mutabilitie's claims, or Hamlet's own increased awareness of her powers, imply an end to any sense of man as a creature of rational choice and heroic determinations. Discourse, looking before and after, enjoying historical connection and extension, is ruled out by the present pressures.

Any conception of heroism or fidelity is impossible, and achievement is robbed of heroic distinction when it becomes merely a product of adrenalin. Ideal considerations are lost under the force of matter.

As with man's mind, so with his institutions and his beliefs: "Nothing doth firme and permanent appeare." Tudor myth must finally encounter cosmic reality. The reign of Mutabilitie suggests the end of that era of Elizabethan glory and accomplishment to which Spenser had dedicated himself and which he had celebrated. Mutabilitie's lesson of time is clear:

> who sees not, that Time on all doth pray?
> But Times do change and move continually.
> So nothing here long standeth in one stay.
>
> (47)

History itself is negated as a source of repair for Spenser; those thrilling consolations experience their own twilight, and man is forced more and more to seek an individual recovery for his existence in time.

Mutabilitie's assault further robs man of any immortal pretensions, any communication with divinity. The lights are hid that shone with such fragile reassurance in a dark world. Jove might claim that spiritual direction exists and controls the processes of change, but in a brash, young, rationalistic way (anticipatory of Edmund's iconoclastic scoffs, partially justified, at Gloucester's notion of heavenly influence) Mutabilitie wonders who has seen these powers:

> The things,
> Which we see not how they are mov'd and swayd,
> Ye may attribute to your selves as Kings,
> And say they by your secret powre are made:
> But what we see not, who shall us perswade?
>
> (49)

In a scientific manner, is she not insisting that things, in order to have existence, must have location in space and time? Such are the implications for the development of the modern world that Mutabilitie represents. The Gods themselves are subject to change. Far from being a universal principle, Jove himself was born in time, although some might say his birthplace was Crete, some Thebes, and others elsewhere. (53) Cultural anthropology and comparative religion combine to shatter any absolute basis for existing belief. In a world of mutability, Spenserian man is cut adrift, facing only the isolation of the historical moment and the horizons of birth and death in time.

To be sure, nature corrects the picture. Mutabilitie's presentation of the progress of the months and the seasons works against her own argument. Change occurs, but there is greater continuity. Nature's presiding sergeant is Order, and the rich pageants of the seasonal calender scenically reveal the beauty of multiplicity, where life's continuities predominate over its terminations. Old senile February, drawn by fishes because he cannot walk, still looks ahead to ploughing and pruning. The dead and the dying look to the duties of the season. And while it is Death that concludes the parade, it is Life that is finally described. Spenser's own inner faith in an outward directing order shines through the actual natural processes of Mutabilitie. Time, rather than the enemy of the organism, is actually the arena of his development. Inherent formal principles are brought out through time; consequently, time is not a determining principle, but rather a subordinate one: it works a higher purpose. Nature's summary judgment is that, while all things hate steadfastness,

> yet being rightly wayd
> They are not changed from their first estate;
> But by their change their being doe dilate:
> And turning to themselves at length againe,
> Do worke their owne perfection so by fate:
> Then over them Change doth not rule and raigne;
> But they raigne over change, and do their states maintaine.
>
> (58)

A Swiss theologian, Theodor Bovet, provides a useful modern gloss on this thought. In his short essay, *Have Time and Be Free,* he senses the larger possibilities of fulfillment triumphing over the pressures of time: "Time also is not an inexorable, austere pacemaker governed by the swing of a clock pendulum, hurrying us through our life, demolishing our previous work, and finally conducting us to our death. It is much more our framework, according to which we unfold, and realize ourselves, and which finally guides us to another aspect and another time." [27] But despite Spenser's reliance on the presiding order of continuity and his participation in the large cosmic processes, the cry of individual loss and replacement is not muted. In the first stanza, in the last, and even in the interlude, the suffering of men is too plainly felt to be ignored:

What man that sees the ever-whirling wheele
   Of Change, the which all mortall things doth sway,
   But that thereby doth find, and plainly feele,
   How Mutability in them doth play
   Her cruell sports to many mens decay?

                                         (vi.1)

Even the delightful interlude of mythologized geography is used to explain why wolves and thieves flourish in what was once a pleasant place. Diana abandoned it and afflicted it with a curse:

   Since which, those Woods, and all that goodly Chase,
   Doth to this day with Wolves and Thieves abound:
Which too-too true the lands in-dwellers since have found.

                                         (vi.55)

In keeping with the thrust of these cantos, events are seen through the image of an original offense that continues to have consequences. But it is in the two stanzas from the eighth canto of the unfinished book of Constancy that Spenser's individual voice most painfully cries out. The heroic consonance between "here" and "there" is shattered, as Spenser returns to the vanity literature of his youthful translations. Here, it is not unfair to remark, Spenser for once speaks what he feels, not what he ought to say. The power of Mutabilitie persuades him to

        loath this state of life so tickle,
   And love of things so vaine to cast away;
   Whose flowring pride, so fading and so fickle,
Short Time shall soon cut down with his consuming sickle.

Short Time does not yield endless monuments. The consolations of perpetuation through process or achievement no longer hold true, and Spenser yearns for an individual redemption. In the second stanza he requires an eternity that is "contrayr to Mutabilitie," not a continuity that is "eterne in mutabilitie." If the *Two Cantos of Mutabilitie* represent the triumph of time, the added two stanzas pray for the triumph of eternity. The restless condition of mankind, which he so manfully and dutifully shouldered in his heroic conception of trial, is now unbearable, and his final plea is for rest and steadfastness.

    With all of his individual variation and undeniably strong medieval qualities, Spenser still repeats a general Renaissance pattern. His heroic strivings sought a victory over time through the avenue of succession, only to lose faith in the reliability and endurance of those rewards. He then must turn (or return) to a religious source for a more individual possession of being. In this he is like his predecessor Chaucer and his contemporary Donne, and unlike Shakespeare. The final vision of the *Mutabilitie Cantos* is much like the epilogue to Chaucer's *Troilus and Criseyde,* with the important difference that, unlike Chaucer, Spenser had great expectations. This is why Mutabilitie is not calmly accepted, but rather her triumph provokes urgent desire for rest outside of time. As in Donne's *Anniversarie Poems,* the two cantos anatomize the world, while the final two stanzas, like the second of the *Anniversaries,* urge the soul's progress to a better life. Loss of trust in man's powers and life's promise does not lead to tragedy, as it does in the Shakespearean experience of *chorismos,* nor does it lead to that strangely wonderful third stage of *methexis,* or participation. While Spenser's death can in no way be called premature, given his splendid accomplishments, still it is to be regretted as cutting short a life before its fullest development. Given Spenser's great investment in succession, his love of change and nature, and his virile imagination and talent, one can well imagine that he would have been capable of breaking through into that final blessed harmony represented by Shakespeare's last plays and Montaigne's *Third Book*.

Chapter 8
Shakespeare's Histories

An Overview of Basic Issues

Early and late, the values of continuity express for Shakespeare the fertile richness and order of life itself. In its growth, ideally, the temporal process regenerates. In one of Shakespeare's last plays, *Henry VIII,* while blessing the newborn princess Archbishop Cranmer rises to prophetic rapture to speak of the promise that Elizabeth holds for England, "which time will bring to ripeness":

> Good grows with her.
> In her days every man shall eat in safety
> Under his own vine what he plants, and sing
> The merry songs of peace to all his neighbors.
> (V.v.33–36)[1]

And it is in similar terms of stablity, continuity, and fertility that the *pater patriae,* the still uncrowned Henry of Richmond, urges his followers against Richard III,

> The wretched, bloody, and usurping boar,
> That spoil'd your summer fields and fruitful vines . . .
> (V.ii.7–8)

Forces anticipatory of *Macbeth* frighten Richard and encourage Henry. The ghosts of the two young princes whom he had murdered weigh on Richard, but urge Henry to "Live, and beget a happy race of kings."

And among the many advantages Henry foresees in the end of Richard's tyranny is the possibility that one might just live long enough to see his children's children:

> If you do free your children from the sword,
> Your children's children quits it in your age.
>   (V.iii.262–263)

Richard III, the most hellish of Shakespearean plays, terminates with a marriage that opens the future. Literally, as in an inferno, the time, or future, was closed to Richard III; but to Henry it opens with the promise of peace and generation:

> And let their heirs (God, if thy will be so)
> Enrich the time to come with smooth-faced peace,
> With smiling plenty, and fair prosperous days!
>   (V.v.32–34)

Of course Shakespeare is here exercising his dramatist's right to express as a wish and a prayer what was in fact a reality. But that is precisely the point: the fact of Tudor continuity became more than historical record; it helped shape a code of values. Historical fact assumes value, and becomes illustrative of a way of viewing the world. King Henry's reaction to Archbishop Cranmer's prediction is indicative:

>   O Lord Archbishop,
> Thou hast made me now a man! Never before
> This happy child did I get anything.
> This oracle of comfort has so pleas'd me,
> That when I am in heaven I shall desire
> To see what this child does, and praise my Maker.
>   (V.v.64–69)

In the second tetralogy, we shall witness another king vindicated by the proved promise of his heir, another man's somewhat harried life efforts redeemed by his lineal successor. In the face of death, continuity lends more than reassurance; it has something of triumph, a triumph, importantly enough, not at odds with the true designs of the Creator for man. And while it is certainly clear that throughout Shakespeare the source of such triumph is also the cause of greatest anguish (and our purpose is to indicate these wild swings), still it is obvious that Shakespeare's plays of English kings are more than historical in subject; they are historical in value.

Nevertheless, while benefitting those who honor her, history can also be a jealous mistress and destroy those who would deny her. And despite its potential fruitfulness, to enter into history is to enter into limitations which can be cruel in their exactions. To those who accept these limitations, history offers great rewards of order and stability, the settings for continuity and development. But Shakespearean drama is rich with characters who seek to escape from history, from the processes of time and change, and from the necessities of choice and decision. They are lovers and kings who begrudge the limitations that time imposes on their desires. Love is brief, and kings who had enjoyed an absolute prerogative of command are given lessons in subjection and mortality.

Although his stature in history and tragedy is different, Richard II, like King Lear, could proclaim, "They told me I was everything," when he refuses, or is unable, to temporize. In the hard world of the histories he resists subjection and is consequently punished by that supreme article of limitation, time. Another "weak king" yearns for subjection, but Henry VI's flight is the same as Richard II's — away from time and his present responsibilities. Shakespeare's historical vision allows no privileged sanctuary, no retreat to a simpler mode of existence. All precocious presumptions on a state of being, on any inviolable prerogatives of will, or on a nonchalant garden existence are rudely confronted with the harsh antagonism of a stern and unavoidable reality.

Henry VI in *Part Three* of that play has been chased from the battle between his forces and those of York. Typically enough he has forfeited his own resources, sits on a molehill, and leaves victory "to whom God will." He yearns for a simpler life, and in one of Shakespeare's first time speeches, arranges it by the dial.

> O God! Methinks it were a happy life
> To be no better than a homely swain;
> To sit upon a hill, as I do now,
> To carve out dials quaintly, point by point,
> Thereby to see the minutes how they run —
> How many makes the hour full complete,
> How many hours brings about the day,
> How many days will finish up the year,
> How many years a mortal man may live.
>
> (II.v.21–29)[2]

By this prospect, the life of man is contained and known, orderly and peaceful. Time implies a benign order with no discontinuities, no sudden disruptions or cruel choices, and man lives in a natural, unmolested harmony with the processes of the world. Petrarch, too, looked with yearning to such stability, and Dante, moving towards his terrible solitary journey, observes with regret that the simpler creatures of the earth were given a reprieve from such hardships. The urge is great to have the stages of life settled and assumed, but such a possession of being would be premature (and even perhaps unworthy), as Shakespeare's characters, like Dante and Petrarch, are pushed to fuller visions of life.

Henry yearns for the trouble-free pastoral life, leading to a natural fulfillment: "minutes, hours, days, weeks, months, and years, / Pass'd over to the end they were created." But brutal specimens of civil war crash in upon his hankering for ordered and peaceful existence. A son discovers he has killed his father and a father his son. Frequently in Shakespeare the hopes for free and easy continuity are broken by a disruption in the family, reflecting a larger disorder. Society's development is doomed when ignorant armies clash in the very heart of the family. One senses that the guilt-ridden cry of the ignorant son could be taken out of its immediate context and made to summarize a more fundamental dilemma of fathers and sons:

> Pardon me, O God! I knew not what I did.
> And pardon, father, for I knew not thee!
> (69–70)

Although Henry is a sympathetic witness to this scene, it is clear that he does not escape responsibility for the disorder of his kingdom. Too inclined to be a spectator, he was congenitally incapable of taking the actions necessary to preserve the order of the state. In *Part Two*, beset by the Cade rebellion, Henry despairs at the difficulties of rule:

> Was ever king that joy'd an earthly throne
> And could command no more content than I?
> No sooner was I crept out of my cradle
> But I was made a king, at nine months old.
> Was never subject long'd to be a king
> As I do long and wish to be a subject.
> (IV.ix.1–6)

Richard II invested too much belief in his own grandeur and authority; Henry VI too little; but nevertheless in their resultant inaction and fates they are similar. This brief scene that Henry's speech introduces is followed — in a revealing dramatic juxtaposition — by one that takes place, significantly enough, in Iden's garden, the property of a Kentish squire. When we first hear Alexander Iden he sounds very much as if he were realizing Henry's dream:

> Lord, who would live turmoiled in the court
> And may enjoy such quiet walks as these?
> This small inheritance my father left me
> Contenteth me, and worth a monarchy.
> I seek not to wax great by others' waning,
> Or gather wealth, I care not with what envy.
> Sufficeth that I have maintains my state
> And sends the poor well pleased from my gate.
>
> (18–25)

This Montaignesque solitude and the pleasures of the retired life are destroyed by the intrusion of the desperate rebel Cade. Certainly an emblematic scene, even Iden's garden, it would appear, cannot escape the confrontations and choices of history. The garden world has suffered a fall into time, and Iden must either master Cade, or else be killed by him. Involved in a highly competitive society, the very processes of the court that he sought to escape are thrust upon him inescapably: he must wax by another's waning. This element of either/or choice is essential to Shakespeare's vision of history, and also to his dramatic procedure. It will continue throughout his work. We recall that King Lear, anticipating carefree final years, is bitterly disappointed. And when, even in defeat, he would from prison observe the life of the court, he still would see it in terms of change and replacement: "Who loses and who wins; who's in, who's out — "

Time involves man in a process of change and replacement. This is the fundamental emulative fact of the Shakespearean historical world. Not only his natural world but his social world is filled with pushing, aggressive energies eager to replace what went before them and now stands in their ways. The realities of Shakespeare's vision into nature and society are hardly static, but dynamic and passionately striving. The first tetralogy abundantly represents this power. Passionate, hot-blooded energies enter from opposite sides of the stage and contend in the center. Such head-on meetings form the dramatic situation and emphasize inevitable struggle and contention. In Temple Garden, the lines of Red and White are formed as one by one the parties of York and Somerset choose their colors. Their allies Vernon and Basset repeat the dissension on the way to France, thus provoking the king's incrudulity:

> Good Lord, what madness rules in brainsick men
> When for so slight and frivolous a cause
> Such factious emulations shall arise!
> (IV.i.111–113)

Emulation is the word by which Shakespeare characterizes the struggles within the courtly society. It is given some descriptive substance when Exeter, in soliloquy, expresses his own fears for England's order:

> no simple man that sees
> This jarring discord of nobility,
> This shouldering of each other in the court,
> This factious bandying of their favourites,
> But that it doth presage some ill event.
> (187–191)

This vision is not only contained in the first tetralogy but extends throughout the sonnets, the histories, and the tragedies. As sonnet 60 makes clear, emulation is the method of time:

> Like as the waves make toward the pebbled shore,
> So do our minutes hasten to their end;
> Each changing place with that which goes before,
> In sequent toil all forwards do contend.
> Nativity, once in the main of light,
> Crawls to maturity, wherewith being crown'd,
> Crooked eclipses 'gainst his glory fight,
> And Time that gave doth now his gift confound.[3]

Echoing the language of this sonnet, Ulysses in *Troilus and Cressida* warns the sulking Achilles of this law of nature and human existence, thus suggesting a connection between the temporal vision of the sonnets and the social world of the histories and the tragedies:

> Keep then the path,
> For emulation hath a thousand sons

> That one by one pursue. If you give way,
> Or hedge aside from the direct forthright,
> Like to an ent'red tide they all rush by
> And leave you hindmost
>
> (III.iii.155–160)

Emulation involving radical competition and bitter struggle persists throughout Shakespeare's historical and tragic worlds. In the dramatic opening scene of *3 Henry VI,* the king enters to find the Yorkist forces already in possession of the throne. Henry's question is basic: "And shall I stand, and thou sit in my throne?" He is presented with the choice of securing his crown or relinquishing it. Indeed, to be or not to be is a choice more real and practical in the histories than in the tragedies. But true to his general defection from the order of time, Henry seeks a compromise that violates the important principle of generational continuity. He disinherits his own son, naming York his heir. As so often happens where temporal continuity is disrupted, this action soon leads to total dispossession.

Unlike Henry, Prince Hal enters into the temporal order and re-establishes continuity. This penetration involves him in a crucial either/or conflict:

> The land is burning; Percy stands on high;
> And either they or we must lower lie.
> (*1 Henry IV*, III.iii.226–227)

Hal and Henry Percy are pitted in combat, and both recognize it as a destined, inevitable confrontation. "Two stars," Hal instructs his rival,

> keep not their motion in one sphere,
> Nor can one England brook a double reign
> Of Harry Percy and the Prince of Wales.
> (V.iv.65–67)

Hotspur concurs, "Nor shall it, Harry; for the hour is come / To end the one of us." Hal is ready to accept the limitations of history, and, whereas Henry VI breaks the line of his fathers, he returns to a grand tradition of generational continuity.

Emulation is a real and dramatic substance of Shakespeare's world. But just as real are the resources available to man for providing continuity and regeneration. The dynamic struggle between the two alternatives forms the argument of time that will be important in Shakespeare's early sonnets and his second tetralogy. As we shall see, there are many quite detailed connections between the sonnets and the histories, but mainly they cohere in affirming the power of life's lines to repair life's decay.

The Dramatic Exploitation of Time

In the early 1590s a spate of English works appeared with time as a vital concern. These included poems, where time was conceptually quite important, and stage plays, where time in its acutal passage was a vivid presence and an instrument of dramatic intensification. At the headwaters of this interest was probably Spenser's *Complaints,* with its strong indebtedness to Du Bellay. It was entered in 1590; there followed Daniel's *Delia* (1591–92), Shakespeare's longer poems (with Lucrece's lengthy address to Time, and the *carpe diem* argument in *Venus and Adonis*), and presumably also his sonnets. Some of the material is conventional, but in the others, as we have seen, time is a highly realized force that enters into an important dynamic relationship with man.

It is perhaps natural in drama, where events lead up to a critical hour of decision, that time should be physically present. In Greene's *The Honourable History of Friar Bacon and Friar Bungay,* in Marlowes's *Dr. Faustus,* and in Shakespeare's *Richard III* we are involved with the actual unrolling of time in its crucial aspect of decisiveness. For seven years Friar Bacon has been preparing to hear the message of the Brazen Head. This time is further divided into the last sixty days and nights, which he and Friar Bungay have shared in their watches. Now the moment is come when the labor of this jingoistic necromancer will be rewarded. The Brazen Head will enable him to "girt fair England with a wall of brass." Oddly enough, this seer leaves the critical watch to the inept Miles, who does not understand the utterances of the Head. "Time is." "Time was." "Time is past." These words are all that it intones, and we are involved in a suspenseful moment of decision where possibility presents itself, only to be dramatically and irretrievably retracted when the moment is missed and the Head is destroyed by lightning.[4]

The very nature of drama is dependent upon such an intensification of action. A new discovery for the young dramatists, it reaches its early height in *Dr. Faustus.* Conceptually, as in Greene's play, time is here a definite article of limitation used to rebuke illicit magical pretensions. Faustus has none of Friar Bacon's laudable nationalistic aims; consequently time seems all the more pressing when his soul rests in the balance, and we are dramatically involved in his possibilities of choice and then his strange and anguished paralysis. The twenty-four years of the bargain narrow down to the final hour that he never thought to encounter. Throughout the performance the audience should, however, be reminded of the passage of time through the visible effects of Faustus' aging. Time is the reality that is slowly but certainly closing in on him. Suspensefully, the final hour is actually represented on the stage. "The Time is come," Lucifer announces as the final scene begins. (V.ii.6) We are told that Faustus is laboring to overreach this reality that is tracking him down, "but all in vain." Faustus bids farewell to fellow scholars, who are horrified to learn of the infernal agreement that accounted for his powers. Payment is now due, Faustus tells them: "The date is expired. This is the time, and he will fetch me." Good and Bad Angel plead and persuade; the jaws of hell open and are closed. And then "The clock strikes eleven." Faustus, self-pitying and observant, records the time:

> Ah Faustus,
> Now hast thou but one bare hour to live,
> And then thou must be damned perpetually.
> (130–132)

The half-hour is struck, and the greatest soliloquy in English drama up to that point continues. The audience in the meantime must be driven wild by the inevitable movement of time, the constriction of possibility, and yet Faustus' pained refusal to say the simple words of repentance. "The clock strikes twelve," and Faustus encounters the fierce God he had always feared. One single problem gets more and more urgent until it is resolved in the most terrible way. Terror and pity are rarely more effectively combined.[5]

Although time in *Richard III* might not be as significant conceptually as in later Shakespearean drama, still it is a highly exploited dramatic presence, as it was in the two other plays. Their difference is that while *The Honourable History* and *Dr. Faustus* placed a single man before a moment of possibility and then slammed the door shut forever, in *Richard III* the climax is a result of the developing confrontation between two rival claimants. Towards this battle all English history of the preceding half century seems to have been leading. Finally the moment of denouement arrives, when one man will be king. But like Greene and Marlowe, Shakespeare utilizes "psychological time," in which the final short period before the climactic event is drawn out, and whereby the smaller actions before the momentous period receive a focus which in the preceding longer run of time would have been inordinate. A modern psychologist, using the phrase "le temps psychologique" discusses two of the phenomena that the young Elizabethans discovered to their dramatic advantage: "The twenty-four hours that immediately precede the present moment seem in memory relatively long, in comparison with the preceding week or months. At the rate that the time of an awaited event approaches we tend to double our attention. The interest that we feel in this event increases." [6] This explains why, of course, in an automobile ride, when we are approaching a destination for the first time, the ride seems longer, but when we return it seems to go much faster. So here, the twenty-four hours preceding the battle of Bosworth field receive a detailed temporal attention such as no other event receives in the first tetralogy. In V.ii we learn from Richmond that Tamworth, where his forces wait, is one day's march from Leicester and Bosworth field. In the next scene we see Richard pitch his tent at Bosworth. (The cutting from one force to another, the montage effect, as in *High Noon,* increases the dramatic suspense.) Then in a matter of several hundred lines we follow the progress of time from sunset to after four the next morning. "The weary sun hath made a golden set," says Richmond announcing his arrival at Bosworth. At the end of the speech he calls good night to Captain Blunt, and invites his men into his tent for consultation; "the dew is raw and cold." We switch to Richard, where he asks the time of Catesby: "It's supper time, my lord; / It's nine o'clock." (47–48) He asks Ratcliffe to come to his tent "about the mid of night" to help him arm. There follows the swift-cutting visitations of the ghosts, suggesting that at this decisive battle the past will be told, and Richard's sins will catch up with him. Richard awakes frightened: "It is now dead midnight," by which he means that it is completely dark—for his soul and for his chances. When Ratcliffe enters at the end of Richard's soliloquy he announces that the village cock has crowed twice. (210) Richmond, awaking, is told that the morning is "upon the stroke of four." Shifting to Richard, the clock strikes (we are not told how often), and Richard consults an almanac, where he learns that on this date the sun should have arisen an hour before. Despite his resurgence of bravery, his thoughts are ominous, "A black day will it be to somebody." (281) Concept and powerful dramatic device merge in this remarkably accurate psychological use of time references on the stage. When we recall that Jacqueline de Romilly has concluded, writing of the developing anxiety in the *Medea,* "This continuous and regular procession, where one single problem gets more and more urgent, till it bursts into crime, is the very core of tragedy," [7] we can see what a vital conquest for Elizabethan drama was not only the concept of time as a force of limitation but also the deliberate exploitation of its psychological resources on the stage.

The Early Sonnets and the Argument of Time

Shakespeare's first tetralogy has the dimensions of an inferno: the future is closed, man has nothing to leave behind or look forward to, fruitfulness is blighted, children are violated, and fame is considered an empty dream. A severe system of ironic retribution imposes itself. The protagonists are pawns believing themselves to be acting freely, but they are really abetting a higher process that converts them into agonists. The figures who present themselves to us are negative instances, models of destruction to be avoided. In the first tetralogy, after more than half a century things eventually sort themselves out. England is regenerated, but only partially through human effort. Henry VII, while fully embodying the values of continuity and political skill, is actually a *rex ex machina,* a source of blessed innocence and light, come from afar — who was absent when the terrible deeds were being done. Out of the entrails of the play itself there is no active force which we follow that leads to rejuvenation. Consequently, throughout the first tetralogy, time as a conceptual force is rarely addressed, and when it is, it presents not a choice but an echo: it shares in the ways of fortune and is an instrument of rebuke. In fact, this characteristic of time will not be lost throughout Shakespeare (however much it becomes less formalized). Instead, it will become part of a battery of time-centered materials, where the possibilities of choice and positive, constructive action are not foreclosed. In short, it will become the threatening portion of the larger argument of time, where man does have some chance of redeeming himself in history.

It is in the second tetralogy that active models in their effort and growth occupy our attention. The political ideals of continuity implicit and violated in the first tetralogy are positively reconstructed through the second series. The house of Lancaster overcomes the menace of the curse, seems to improve with time, and eventually vindicates itself in its children. Despite the fears of the father that his "dissolute as desperate" son is a curse on his own misreadings ("If any plague hang over us, 'tis he"), still he is able to spy a glimmer of hope in his son's true characteristics: "I see some sparks of better hope, which elder years / May happily bring forth." (*Richard II,* V.iii.21–22) and in 2 *Henry IV,* when in a totally different atmosphere the weary king again despairs over his son — an "unweeded garden" — Warwich speaks confidently of the prince's redemption in the "perfectness of time." (IV.iv.74) This root confidence is vindicated when in the pivotal confrontations of both parts of *Henry IV* the prince reveals himself his father's true son. Henry's revolution succeeds and is justified because of his son, while Richard of York's revolution fails when his Richard turns into a nemesis, a hellhound who, embodying his father's very principles, directs them against his own house. The son executes the curse in the first tetralogy, while in the second Hal breaks the chain of repeated crime.

This is enough to indicate that at the heart of the Shakespearean argument of time is the father-son link of generation. That this link forms an important value for Shakespeare and is intrinsically involved with his war against time the earlier sonnets abundantly illustrate. There we have prototypic expression of the argument of time with emphasis on continuity as augmentation. In the sonnets and the histories this argument involves the persuasion of a younger spirit by an older, more experienced voice; the voice is admonitory and urgent under the felt pressures of time; the young man is still free to act, but the need to act is great and time is passing; his freedom is precarious, especially since there will be a strict calling to account, and the clarity of the young man's vision seems to be blocked by some ignorance, illusion, or infatuation. But when we come to the argument of time in its specific application, we see immediately that there are two fundamental differences between Shakespeare's use of the argument and the uses of Dante and Petrarch. One of these is most relevant now, and justifies our retention of the specific cognomen "augmentative" when referring to the dominant code of values in the sonnets and the second tetralogy. The other we will come to shortly. The argument of time is used religiously in Dante and Petrarch (although in the latter it has more practical application and historical influence) and consequently involves their souls in a bitter struggle and choice between reliance on God and reliance on the ways of succession, whether children or fame. The argument of time, calling attention to the uncertain moment of death and yet its inevitability, the unreliability of children and the arbitrariness of fame, precipitates a crisis, a purgatorial state, that forces them to make a cruel rejection of the ways of succession, which because of their purely human means of transcending time constituted a threat to man's absolute reliance on God. In Shakespeare's sonnets and histories no such division between faith in the Creator and faith in the ways of succession occurs. Succession itself is fruitful, and the temporal garden, properly husbanded, leads to fulfillment. Henry VIII's final speech, we recall, in gratitude for the promise of his daughter, leads to praise of his

Maker. As in Spenser, at least the Spenser before the *Mutabilitie Cantos,* succession and fruitfulness do not contradict divinity: here and there are in consonance, as the magnificent Garden of Adonis illustrates.

To account for this renewed Elizabethan faith in the processes of generation and succession is difficult. I suggest two very large causes, one a European phenomenon, and the other more strictly Tudor. As we have seen, the period of the later thirteenth and early fourteenth centuries in Florence witnessed the development of an optimistic, bourgeois humanism associated with the names of Aristotle, Aquinas, and Latini, and even including, in his earlier commitments, Dante. In Millard Meiss's view, which I quote in the introduction to this study, these well-rounded burghers were assured "that they could enjoy themselves in this world without jeopardizing their chances in the next." Later, Ficino would be a link between the Florentine civic humanism and the new surge of northern European optimism that neo-Platonism helped to create.[8] From Ficino's commentary on Plato's *Symposium,* clear connections can be observed with the letter of Gargantua to Pantagruel. However, in my studies a hiatus was present between the work of the Florentines and the great expression of this faith that we witness in Spenser and Shakespeare. This gap in information was filled by Erasmus, particularly the letter of advice to a young nobleman, urging him to marry, that was translated and printed by Thomas Wilson in his *Arte of Rhetorique* (1553).[9] This filiation from Ficino via Erasmus to the Elizabethans is very clear, and is the more impressive since it roughly parallels the growing interests in time and education, natural corollaries of the concern with children and all attesting a renewed faith in the possibilities of succession and a vital civic concern.[10]

Secondly, faith in continuity and the celebrative vision of dynastic sucession within English history that we find in Spenser and Shakespeare are also Tudor in emphasis. Compared with our notions of stability, the Tudor age might well appear raucous and hectic. But compared with the world that Dante knew, or even the turmoil in other contemporary nation-states, the Tudor dynasty typified order, for it had succeeded for more than three generations in imposing order on the wild vicissitudes of history and human fortune. This balance, as R. B. Wernham has recently maintained, was precarious and not unthreatened, but nevertheless it was there, and perhaps all the more valued because of its precariousness.[11] It is a fact that the ruling national life that Spenser and Shakespeare knew suggested the virtues of human control and the possibilities of succession. It is also true that this vision of success upon which they were bred would come to an end; that the near misses, so triumphantly averted, would not be near misses after all, but the ever-pressing line of disaster. But this involves us in the argument of tragedy and the eruption in the *Mutabilitie Cantos,* not the possibilities implied in the argument of time.

The comings and goings of emulative process are the lessons provided by nature in Shakespeare's first sixteen sonnets — but with more distinct peril for man since he does not personally enjoy the cyclical recurrence that nature does. The deceptiveness of early promise followed by later decay, so disillusioning for men like Dante and Petrarch, forms the brunt of Shakespeare's admonitions to the young aristocrat. Time's inconstancy is described in terms that would be even more fearful for the subject of a monarch; it becomes tyrannical, promising great promotions and then reneging — the way of Richard III with Buckingham:

> Those hours that with gentle work did frame
> The lovely gaze where every eye doth dwell
> Will play the tyrants to the very same
> And that unfair which fairly doth excel;
> For never-resting time leads summer on
> To hideous winter and confounds him there,
> Sap checked with frost and lusty leaves quite gone,
> Beauty o'ersnowed and bareness everywhere.
>
> (sonnet 5)

This "ingratitude" attends the universal law of replacement and impermanence, where man can attain no unchanging position, but shares in growth, maturation, and decay:

> When I consider everything that grows
> Holds in perfection but a little moment
>
> .   .   .   .   .
>
> When I perceive that men as plants increase,
> Cheered and check'd even by the selfsame sky,
> Vaunt in their youthful sap, at height decrease,
> And wear their brave state out of memory . . .
>
> (sonnet 15)

How naturally powerful and vital is Shakespeare's conception of growing youth and manhood, and how painful is the contrast between "brave" life and its final end.

Sonnet 7 provides more dramatic dimensions to the natural processes: human ingratitude complements nature's own inconstancy. The arch of the sun from horizon to horizon sums up the stages in man's life, his youth, his middle and then his feeble age. But the poem is more sensitive to the attitudes of the onlookers of this "golden pilgrimage." In the upward climb, each underling

> Doth homage to his new-appearing sight,
> Serving with looks his sacred majesty.

And so it is in manhood — "mortal looks adore his beauty still." The change comes at the decline, and the sonnet with its natural shift at the sestet emphasizes the painful alteration:

> But when from highmost pitch, with weary car,
> Like feeble age he reeleth from the day,
> The eyes (fore duteous), now converted are
> From his low tract and look another way.

The agony of such "ingratitude" will be more painfully presented in the dramas of "sacred majesty." It is at the center of action and reflection in *Hamlet,* where the prince cannot tolerate the poor example of his uncle now having the prerogatives of his father, and in *King Lear,* where the Fool can explain to Kent in the stocks why the king comes with so small a retinue of men: "there's not a nose among twenty but can smell him that's stinking. Let go thy hold when a great wheel runs down a hill, lest it break thy neck with following; but the great one that goes upward, let him draw thee after. (II.iv.70–74)

Given these "natural" tendencies, we can see why issues of children extend so far in Shakespeare. As posterity, they are valid channels of continuity, prolonging man's life, but more personally, they are cherished shelters of care and continuity that serve to counter natural and social ingratitude. Erasmus' epistle, tracing the benefits of marriage and family, employs this argument: "You have them that shall comfort you in your latter days, that shall close up your eyes when God shall call you, that shall bury you, and fulfill all things belonging to your Funeral, by whom you shall seem to be new born. For so long as they shall live, you will never be thought dead yourself." (Wilson, p. 56) Other eyes will turn to the new sun, sonnet 7 concludes, but the man with children will still be an object of dignity, despite his declined powers:

> So thou, thyself outgoing in thy noon,
> Unlook'd on diest unless thou get a son.

Here is the germ of a preoccupation that will grow to King Lear's desire
to find a nursery in his daughter's home. Early and late in Shakespearean
thought children are intended to be great means of protection against
emulation and sheer replacement. In the sonnets and the histories we
have perhaps the greatest Renaissance expression of the newly won faith
in progeny, and in tragedies like *Hamlet* and *King Lear* the nature of the
investment in this ideal is measured by the chaos and outrage that its
violation occasions.

Children console not merely through the fact of continuity, but through
the added pleasure of physical resemblance to the parent. They are a
reminder, a portrait, as it were, of his own youth. This delight is not
neglected in Erasmus' epistle: "Now again, what a joy shall this be unto
you, when your most fair wife shall make you a father, in bringing forth
a fair Child unto you, where you shall have a pretty little boy, running
up and down your house, such a one as shall express your look, and your
wife's look." (p. 56) In Shakespeare such duplication is a fundamental,
irreducible natural pleasure which emphasizes the fact of continuity and
seems to reverse the sting of age and replacement:

> Thou art thy mother's glass, and she in thee
> Calls back the lovely April of her prime.
> So thou through windows of thine age shalt see,
> Despite of wrinkles, this thy golden time.
>   But if thou live remem'bred not to be,
>   Die single, and thine image dies with thee.
>   (sonnet 3)

But, as Gargantua reminds Pantagruel, formal resemblance without
moral virtue merely intensifies the pain. So Richard II will be charged,
and so the mistaken Henry IV complains about his own apparently rowdy
son:

> Most subject is the fattest soil to weeds,
> And he, the noble image of my youth,
> Is overspread with them.
>   (*2 Henry* IV, IV.iv.54–56)

Not only has Hal's uncertain development threatened all of his father's
efforts, but in a related sense it robs him of the consolation that we see

from the sonnets is important to Shakespearean man. Hal is an unweeded garden, and the processes of generation, rather than serving to restore Bolingbroke's golden time, merely aids the emulative work of nature.

In their attention to beauty and the need to continue the "image" or "model" of beauty, the sonnets show Platonic influence. "From fairest creatures we desire increase." (sonnet 1) Procreation is much more incumbent upon the young man because of his beauty. "Make thee another self for love of me," Shakespeare pleads in sonnet 10, "That beauty may still live in thine or thee." The young man's "image" must be kept alive:

> Let those whom Nature hath not made for store,
> Harsh, featureless, and rude, barrenly perish.
> Look, whom she best endow'd she gave the more,
> Which bounteous gift thou shouldst in bounty cherish.
> She carv'd thee for her seal, and meant thereby
> That thou shouldst print more, not let that copy die.
>
> (sonnet 11)

But as in Homer, Dante, Petrarch, and Yeats, so in Shakespeare the most gifted seem to have the greatest opportunities for mistreading: "Most subject is the fattest soil to weeds." Like the young man in the sonnets, Richard II, Falstaff, and Hamlet all seem to have something too much which incapacitates them, while lesser people thrive. The added burden increases the responsibility, the difficulty, and the pain.

Despite the appeals to wrinkled middle age, some infatuation prevents the young gentleman from seeing the overwhelming evidence provided by the concerned older voice of the sonnets. Some illusion of invulnerability, born of youthful vigor and confidence, blocks his true perception of reality. Participating in the rising movement of his life he has no mind for the declining portion of time's progress. This presumption of being, while involved in the processes of change, allies the young man of the sonnets with the dramatic kings of the histories and tragedies, the nature of whose positions similarly blinds them to their mortal existence. But there is in the young gentleman further complications of character. He combines prodigality and niggardliness. On the one hand, like Hal, he is an "unthrift," wasting his beauty's treasure and heedless of his own vulnerable position. But on the other hand, this seeming lack of care does not stem from an overabundant, risk-taking nature, but, Shakespeare suggests, from some chariness, perhaps based on self-liking. Erasmus makes similar accusations (where, since the reference is not as pointed, the langauge can be more severe): "Now I think he is most worthie to be despised above all other, that is born as a man would say for himself, that liveth to himself, that seeketh for himself, that spareth for himself, maketh cost only upon himself, that loveth no man, and no man loveth him." (p. 55)

In sonnet 4, the young man represents "unthrifty loveliness," who spends his legacy of beauty only on himself; he is a "beauteous niggard," who abuses "the bounteous largess given thee to give," and he is a "profitless usurer" who only traffics with himself. Beauty, and beyond beauty, one's entire life, was given one for use and increase, for addition to oneself and others. The law, against which the young gentleman's ungenerous nature offends, is summarized in this sonnet:

> Nature's bequest gives nothing but doth lend,
> And, being frank, she lends to those are free.

To hold back, to fail to use profitably, and with increase what was loaned to one, is to abuse natural requirements of frankness. This principle from the parable of the talents brings with it the sterner call to account. If the young man refuses to add to himself,

> Then how, when nature calls thee to be gone,
> What acceptable audit canst thou leave?

These two elements, the parable of the talents and the call to account, and associated with them the language of economics, are intrinsic to the Renaissance argument of time. Shakespeare uses them again in sonnet 2:

> When forty winters shall besiege thy brow
> And dig deep trenches in thy beauty's field,
> Thy youth's proud livery, so gaz'd on now,
> Will be a tatter'd weed of small worth held:
> Then being ask'd where all thy beauty lies,
> Where all the treasure of thy lusty days,
> To say, within thine own deep-sunken eyes
> Were an all-eating shame and thriftless praise.

An heir would help him "sum [his] count," that is, adequately repay the loan of life and talents. However, should he fail to do this the laws of nature and the recognitions they bring are bitter indeed, as Richard II, or any of the dramatic characters who waste their time, are forced to acknowledge. It is to spare such unacceptable accounts that Shakespeare holds up a mirror to reality. The final sonnet addressed to the young man, 126, shows this basic concern. Nature only deludes him into thinking that his beauty and powers will last. She is only preparing him for a final betrayal:

> Yet fear her, O thou minion of her pleasure!
> She may detain, but not still keep, her treasure;
> Her audit, though delay'd, answer'd must be,
> And her quietus is to render thee.

The call to account was of major importance in Petrarch and, behind him, in the letters from Seneca to Lucilius. Its background is also Biblical: Matthew's rendering of the parable of the talents and the foolish and wise virgins continued to appeal to the provident personality. And in the secular writings of Paolo da Certaldo and the religious writings of Domenico Cavalca we have seen how this concern could merge in the lay commercial and urban evangelical currents of the fourteenth century. But if we are considering possible sources, the popular morality play *Everyman* is far closer to Shakespeare in both nationality and artistic form. Quite surprisingly, in some 920 lines the notion of being called to account and the need to face up to that "dredefull rekenynge" are referred to in at least 33 specific instances. In fact, an actual Book of Account is part of the physical properties of the play. Concomitant with the idea of reckoning is the notion that man is merely borrowing, taking on loan, his earthly existence and that he is bound to give an account of himself. God complains that men take no heed of him, nor are they grateful "for theyr beynge, that I them have lent." Life is not an outright gift, but rather a temporary loan. Further there are some six references to the urgency of time: time passes, "wete thou full well the tyde abydeth no man." [12]

As Shakespeare exploits that fatal moment of finality, where life and character are revealed, we see that the dramatist in him carried over much of the medieval heritage. Yet with all these similarities we see that there are profound differences. And this brings us to Shakespeare's second major divergence from Petrarch's argument of time. In Petrarch (as in Dante and *Everyman*), the call to account is at the moment of death — *l'ultimo dì, supremus tempus, dies suprema*. There man shall have his soul measured, and the stewardship of his spiritual life judged. Shakespeare is closer to Seneca: not one's soul, but rather one's use of his given expectations and hopes will be clarified. Earthly royalties — capacity, adulthood, manliness, what one has done and what one has to show for it — are then counted up. In *Everyman* the calling to account brings one to a singleness — the state of one's soul before God. The other accidents of life — fellowship, kinship, and goods — pale. But for Shakespeare it is mainly in relation to these things that man defines his success. When he loses his goods — like Richard's roan Barbary now in the possession of Bolingbroke, or Falstaff heinously unprovided for, while foolish Shallow has land and beeves — he feels his loss keenly. Not singly, but with kin and comrade, Shakespearean man settles his account in time. In Petrarch, too, the summons can arrive at any time, and quite arbitrarily; not being part of historical process, its terror comes from its suddenness. But at the moment of reckoning for Shakespeare we are dealing with the accumulated operations of a lifetime which finally, in a moment of need, reveal themselves perniciously. In short, in both event and loss, in Shakespeare's call to account we are still in history. This can have some very uncompromising effects, which still differ from the religious argument of time. Despite its pressure in Dante's *Purgatorio,* in Petrarch, and in *Everyman,* time is not an irreversible force. Even in that tragedy of damnation, *Dr. Faustus,* had the doom-ridden scholar made his peace, he could have found salvation. Buonconte da Montefeltro and Manfred in the *Purgatorio* are saved through last-minute appeals to the spiritual order of the universe. And, quite frankly in *Everyman,* Time is only superficially essential, because the needed "layser" (leisure) is granted for Everyman to get his things in order. "God gyve you tyme and space!" is Knowledge's hopeful prayer. We are not dealing with the irreversible world of hard, historical realities, but rather with spiritual possibilities that intersect that order. But in Shakespeare, once the time to come is closed and man loses his freedom, his loss is irreversible. Richard II, Falstaff, and Henry VI stand helpless before an end they did not foresee. There is no reprieve. This is the hard law of being called to account in Shakespeare's historical world, and it is just such a bitter recognition that Shakespeare would spare the young man of the sonnets by showing him, from his own experience, the argument of time.

To persist in refusing to read the evidence is suicidal; in fact, images of self-consumption occur frequently in Shakespeare's appeals to the young aristocrat. To be so "self-will'd," as sonnet 6 warns, is to run the risk of being "self-kill'd." His unmarried state will make the young man "the tomb of his self-love." Betrothed only to himself, he burns himself out: "feed'st thy light's flame with self-substantial fuel. . . . Thyself thy foe, to thy sweet self too cruel." To be so tight and self-involved is to hoard one's talent, and eventually to destroy it:

> Look, what an unthrift in the world doth spend
> Shifts but his place, for still the world enjoys it;
> But beauty's waste hath in the world an end,
> And kept unus'd, the user so destroys it.
>> No love toward others in that bosom sits
>> That on himself such mur'drous shame commits.
>>> (sonnet 9)

And in the subsequent sonnet 10 the same thought is elaborately developed: such "unprovidence" indicates a lack of love toward others and a conspiracy against oneself ("'gainst thyself thou stick'st not to conspire").

Fundamental to Shakespeare's code of augmentative time is the revulsion and horror the soul must experience when it is face-to-face with nothingness. To be nothing draws out fervent protests from Richard II and King Lear, and the word has an important play in both their dramas. In the sonnets, as in the histories, children are a means, in their varying ways, of warding off that dread reckoning. Shakespeare warns the young man,

> But if thou live remem'bred not to be,
> Die single, and thine image dies with thee.
>> (sonnet 3)

In sonnet 5 the young man is urged to distill the essence of his being, otherwise

> Beauty's effect with beauty were bereft—
> Nor it nor no remembrance what it was.

In the eighth sonnet, the concord of various strings sounds discordant to the young man because they ring home the unpleasant truth, "Thou single wilt prove none."

We come even closer to the very issues of the history plays in sonnets 10 and 13, where the waste of individual beauty is metaphorically associated wiith the ruin of a house. The poet in sonnet 10 cannot believe that the young man bears love to anyone, since to himself he is so improvident,

> Seeking that beauteous roof to ruinate
> Which to repair should be thy chief desire.

And in sonnet 13, the young man is asked

> Who lets so fair a house fall to decay,
> Which husbandry in honour might uphold
> Against the stormy gusts of winter's day
> And barren rage of death's eternal cold?

The same thought inspires Erasmus' address to his young gentleman, since the only other surviving heir of that family lines, his sister, had entered a nunnery: "Now, be it that others deserve great praise for their maidenhead, you notwithstanding cannot want great rebuke, seeing it lieth in your hands to keep that house from decay, whereof you are lineally descended, and to continue still the name of your ancestors, who deserve most worthily to be known for ever." And clearly noting the public and civic confines of his argument, Erasmus regards a general adherence to the ideal of virginity as "perilous to a commonweal." (p. 51)

Husbandry, in its several meanings, is a valuable term in Shakespeare's argument of time, and provides an easy passage from the fundamental ideas of the early sonnets to the second tetralogy. Agriculturally and domestically, to practice husbandry is to provide for continuity through natural means. One season dies, but through care and management one is prepared for the next. Nature itself offers means of overcoming natural terminations. "As fast as thou shalt wane, so fast thou grow'st / In one of thine." (s.11) In the context of the sonnets, one is a good husband by providing for continuity through children. And in a more social order, this means also the protection of the family estate against the wintry season of death and oblivion. Since the processes of change and emulation in the histories are not merely natural, but also social, husbandry there means more than begetting of children. One must provide against the enemies that would usurp one's position, that threaten one's house. Those who fail to respond to the needs of husbandry — who are uninformed or willfully vain — who fail to heed the lessons of time and recognize the threatening nature of their universe, are condemned to loss and nothingness. Especially to these faulty kings (Henry VI or Richard II) the language of husbandry applies, since their failure as husbands is related to the inadequate husbandry of their kingdom.[13]

Richard II

In *Shakespeare's Imagery,* Caroline Spurgeon notes the advance of clarity in conceptualization that *Richard II* makes over the first tetralogy. Writing on the importance of the garden imagery, she concludes: "And so what has been but an undertone — at first faint, later clear and definite — in the earlier historical plays, here in *Richard II* gathers strength and volume, until it becomes the leading theme, which is, as it were, gathered up, focussed and pictorially presented near the middle of the play in the curious garden scene (3.4).[14] The garden is not the single leading theme, but coalesces with time and family to form Shakespeare's historical horizon, the metaphysic of his political ethic. As in the sonnets, they shape the world of external force and limitation and reward in which Shakespearean man must operate. The importance of these three themes — at times inextricably united — is underlined by the frequency of their appearance and by the essential fact that none of them is stressed by Shakespeare's sources in the chronicles: they are all Shakespeare's interpolations, reflecting his basic preoccupations.[15]

In *Richard II,* time is an article of limitation as well as accusation. In the early scenes of the play the king appears to preside with confidence and authority over the aroused energies of the combatants. We are given an important picture of kingly control, restraining dangerous passions. "Wrath-kindled gentlemen, be ruled by me." "Lions make leopards tame." "We were not born to sue, but to command." With some flair he removes four of the ten years of exile that he had imposed on young Hereford. The challenger, passionately fascinated by the prerogatives of royal power, reflects on Richard's capacity to abridge time:

> How long a time lies in one little word!
> Four lagging winters and four wanton springs
> End in a word, such is the breath of kings.
>
> (I.iii.213–215)

But other reflections are advanced that severely qualify that power. They are consistently offered in terms of time. In one of the first, John of Gaunt anticipates death because of his son's absence — a typical enough concern, given the play's theme and its proximity to the earlier sonnets. When Richard jocularly tries to persuade him that he has many years to live, the father speaks to the point:

> But not a minute, King, that thou canst give.
> Shorten my days thou canst with sullen sorrow
> And pluck nights from me, but not lend a morrow.
> Thou canst help time to furrow me with age,
> But stop no wrinkle in his pilgrimage.

> Thy word is current with him for my death,
> But dead, thy kingdom cannot buy my breath.
>
> (226–232)

Richard's apparent security and aplomb crack as the play proceeds. The effects of his offenses and poor rule come to a head. With typical misdirection he pursues his Irish Wars, while trouble brews at home. As York laments, Richard is "gone to save far off, / Whilst others come to make him lose at home." (II.ii.79–80) His delayed return from Ireland discourages his Welsh soldiers, who disband at the lack of news. When Salisbury reports this defection to Richard, it is again in terms of implied temporal limitation:

> One day too late, I fear me, noble lord,
> Hath clouded all thy happy days on earth.
> O, call back yesterday, bid time return,
> And thou shalt have twelve thousand fighting men!
> To-day, to-day, unhappy day too late.
>
> (III.ii.66–71)

But time is more than just an item of physical limitation; it has moral implications, assuming the values of history and continuity. It expands to its full conceptual use in Shakespeare when York, outraged by Richard's confiscation of Bolingbroke's patrimony, plainly allies it to the peaceful progression of generations. Through this act Richard has violated a fundamental code, almost too basic to reason over, and York is at first reduced to self-evident questioning. He proceeds to defend his outburst rationally, and in so doing justifies our discussion of Shakespearean time in its larger significance:

> Take Hereford's rights away, and take from Time
> His charters and his customary rights;
> Let not tomorrow then ensue to-day;
> Be not thyself — for how art thou a king
> But by fair sequence and succession?
>
> (II.i.195–199)

Overriding the fact of change is a continuing order with expectations and rewards: sequence and succession can be fair. Richard has tripped upon a moral bar to the absoluteness of his will. This father-son code, moreover, is not only an ideal: it has quite specific practical reality and effect. In traducing that benefit of law and civilization, Richard threatens his own right to the throne. He seems determined to "be not himself." As we have seen, in the sonnets self-consumption was the consequence to those foolhardy enough to neglect the essential realities of Shakespeare's historical world.

So it is with the two other major themes, the family and the garden; their violations inevitably lead to self-destruction, as though a powerful force had been trod upon. Since the possibilities of generation, growth and ripeness within the historical process are clear Shakespearean values, the interruption or desecration of this process is an almost sure indication of faulty values. Richard III wars on his father's house — "I am myself alone." The young man in the sonnets threatens to bring a halt to his family line — "Thou single wilt prove none." And Richard II is neither father nor son. In the tragedies, as we shall see, such an orphanhood is man's true condition, but in the histories such a position is unnatural and condemned, especially when the protagonist actually pursues hostility against his family.

In several scenes that are Shakespeare's additions, family is a lifeline whose neglect means disaster. While Richard culpably disturbs this order, John of Gaunt innocently harms himself. In not the only such scene in Shakespeare's plays, a firm-willed woman, with a clear sight of reality, warns a more scrupulous man of the dangers of his patience. The widow of Thomas, the duke of Gloucester, whose murder Bolingbroke importantly enough was determined to revenge at the play's outset, warns John of Gaunt of his folly. In 2 *Henry VI* in a similar scene, the Duchess of Gloucester warns her husband that their enemies are using her to get at him. Here in this scene of *Richard II,* with an increased conceptual importance, action is advocated in terms of family:

> Finds brotherhood in thee no sharper spur?
> Hath love in thy old blood no living fire?
> Edward's seven sons, whereof thyself art one,
> Were as seven vials of his sacred blood,
> Or seven fair branches springing from one root.
>
> (I.ii.9–13)

Some died natural deaths, but her husband Thomas of Woodstock was brutally hacked down, "his summer leaves all faded." She proceeds to stir Gaunt to action by invoking the doctrine of the sonnets — in the death of the son the image of the father also dies:

> though thou livest and breathest,
> Yet art thou slain in him. Thou dost consent
> In some large measure to thy father's death
> In that thou seest thy wretched brother die,
> Who was the model of thy father's life.
>
> (24–28)

Such willingness to tolerate harm to his family's line is suicidal in Gaunt:

> In suff'ring thus thy brother to be slaught'red
> Thou showst the naked pathway to thy life,
> Teaching stern murder to butcher thee.
>
> (30–32)

The Duchess is proved right in the next scene and subsequently when, though not overtly violent, Richard's practices do extend to Gaunt. The exile of his son is a death blow, as Gaunt himself admits. This covert hostility of the king toward his father's line is capped in the confiscation of Gaunt's property and goods. Instrumental in Gaunt's death, Richard thoroughly undoes him by disinheriting his son. This act provokes the most tolerant of the uncles, York, to a condemnation of Richard, again in terms reminiscent of the sonnets. Richard's resemblance to his father, the Black Prince, only points up the divergence of their conduct. York's tirade echoes that of the more impassioned Gaunt, who had earlier linked Richard's hostility towards his father's brothers with consequences of self-destruction:

> O, had thy grandsire, with a prophet's eye,
> Seen how his son's son should destroy his sons,
> From forth thy reach he would have laid thy shame,
> Deposing thee before thou wert possess'd,
> Which art possess'd now to depose thyself.
>
> (II.i.104–108)

The echoes in the phrasing themselves suggest the network of relationships, the bonds of mutual involvement, that family imposes in the historical world. (The same phenomenon is observed when Gaunt's lecturing exasperates Richard, and the king warns him that it is only the fact that he is his father's brother that saves him. With the impunity of the dying, Gaunt cries out, "O, spare me not, my brother Edward's son, / For that I was his father Edward's son!")

Richard, in warring against his father's house, violates the augmentative code of the sonnets. He is self-willed and (the sonnets provide the consequence) self-killed. That strong, steadying influence of father, or father-figures, is absent or disregarded, and he must face up to the dire consequences of his own faulty attitudes. He rushes toward the fate against which Shakespeare warned the young aristocrat of the sonnets: he consumes his means, loses his name, and soon will be no thing. In language that further reveals the qualities which make for the historical success of the house of Lancaster (in fact, they will be repeated in Henry IV's advice to his erring son), Gaunt predicts Richard's imminent doom:

> His rash fierce blaze of riot cannot last,
> For violent fires soon burn out themselves;
> Small show'rs last long, but sudden storms are short;
> He tires betimes that spurs too fast betimes;
> With eager feeding food doth choke the feeder;
> Light vanity, insatiate cormorant,
> Consuming means, soons preys upon itself.
>
> (33–39)

The steadiness that leads to extension in time is lacking from Richard's personality, just as the possibilities of continuity are missing in his life. Some immaturity of ego, some lack of settledness, seems to jeopardize any possibilities of long tenure. Yet maturity and settledness are precisely the values that are required in history, and the values that the Lancasters abundantly represent. In the histories, intense aspiration seems doomed by a world that respects the more enduring skills and values. It is no accident that time should play so great a thematic and dramatic role in the second tetralogy, where the value of long-lastingness is so prominent.

Temporal richness is most symbolically expressed in terms of the garden and natural growth.[16] Edward's sons were seven branches springing from one root. Richard of Gloucester's designs on the "golden time" of the kingship rest upon his rooting out the "hopeful branch" of his brother's loins. In both tetralogies garden scenes quite artfully assume large emblematic significance. In the first series of plays, the garden provides a natural setting of innocence and repose which human antagonism violates as fiercely as the plucking of the white and red roses. Basically, in those plays, it is the locus for man's Edenic urge that is overcome by his involvement in history: Iden cannot escape Cade, who forces upon him the either/or choice he sought to avoid. But in *Richard*

II (III.iv) the garden, still emblematic, assumes a slightly different function. True to the order of nature represented in the sonnets, it no longer serves as peaceful background, but itself contains, in its natural growth and vigor, the possibilities for good or evil that are in human life. It has become not a sanctuary from labor but symbolic of the laborious requirements of life itself. The garden is the kingdom, as Gaunt earlier regrets, when he accuses Richard for leasing out "This other Eden, demi-Paradise. . . . This blessed plot, this earth, this realm, this England." (II.i.42, 50) Husbandry must be exercised in the realm as in the garden. Possibilities exist for true benefit, but they must be nurtured and cared for. Richard's tenure is no good example for their work, the gardener's man complains:

> Why should we, in the compass of a pale,
> Keep law and form and due proportion,
> Showing, as in a model, our firm estate,
> When our sea-walled garden, the whole land,
> Is full of weeds, her fairest flowers chok'd up,
> Her fruit trees all unprun'd, her hedges ruin'd,
> Her knots disorder'd, and her wholesome herbs
> Swarming with caterpillars?
>
> (III.iv.40–47)

Richard himself will later regret this loss of "form and due proportion"—this keeping time; his kingdom is an "unweeded garden" not through any necessity, but rather through his own failures. The gardener silences his outspoken man with the information that Richard's neglect has drawn on his inevitable defeat:

> He that hath suffer'd this disordered spring
> Hath now himself met with the fall of leaf.
>
> (49–50)

Richard II, although in not quite the formalized way of *Richard III,* is a hard universe of powers that catch up with the delinquent. The gardeners exercise strict control over their domain. At the proper time they wound the bark,

> Lest, being over-proud in sap and blood,
> With too much riches it confound itself.
> Had he done so to great and growing men,

> They might have liv'd to bear, and he to taste,
> Their fruits of duty.
>
> (59–63)

The gardeners cut away the superfluous, "that bearing boughs may live":

> Had he done so, himself had borne the crown,
> Which waste of idle hours hath quite thrown down.
>
> (65–66)

The entire emphasis of the lesson in government is on the potential for fruitfulness that has been needlessly wasted.

The queen interrupts this painful parable. When she calls the gardener "Thou old Adam's likeness" and regards his news of the king's downfall as coming from Eve or a serpent, she reminds us of the larger extensions of this garden scene. The garden is not the world of bliss and easiness, but the real world of history, history that can be converted to fruitfulness, but which destroys any negligent presumption on being. She scorns the gardener, "thou little better thing than earth" for daring to "divine his downfall." But this is merely part of the general movement of the play, where mortal limitations impinge upon kingly prerogative. The queen, typical of Richard's party, is reduced to a helpless curse: "pray God the plants thou graft'st may never grow." Saddened, but unperturbed, the gardener places his confidence in his managed skill:

> Poor Queen, so that thy state might be no worse,
> I would my skill were subject to thy curse!
>
> (102–103)

In all three areas — and they do indeed come together — of time, family, and the garden, Richard has run afoul the nature of Shakespeare's historical world. And that world is such that he is held to a stiff reckoning. "Now comes the sick hour that his surfeit made." The evidence suggests that Richard's loss is self-inflicted and that his deposition turns out to be, in fact, abdication. It is not in Richard's manner personally to control events; like Henry VI, although for different reasons, his reliances and supports rest outside of himself. Arriving in

England to meet the rebellion (III.ii), he invokes a special relationship between his native soil and his kingship. The very stones will prove "armed soldiers" on his behalf, and the earth will send up offensive creatures to molest his enemies. His faith — febrile, to be sure — that God's angels will fight on his behalf is another indication of Richard's presumption on being, on a felt immunity to change. But this superstructure of confidence collapses very quickly into despair when confronted with the defections from his camp and Bolingbroke's solid reality. "Of comfort no man speak."

> For God's sake let us sit upon the ground
> And tell sad stories of the death of kings!
> (144–156)

There is some psychological need in Richard that resists settling for anything less than the totality he had been accustomed to. He cannot separate himself from the order of being to which he was committed. Aumerle suggests that he temporize by granting Bolingbroke's demands, "Till time lend friends, and friends their helpful swords." (III.iii.132) Such a concession would plunge the king into the rough and tumble world of calculation, skill, management — in short, the world of time. But Richard, like King Lear, is victimized by the expectations of one of the King's Two Bodies. Accustomed to the privileges of the office, the dimensions of permanence, and the absoluteness of the will (again his early accession to the throne and the absence of a father are relevant), Richard cannot tolerate the subjection and limitation on his will that time imposes, which he is, nevertheless, powerless to resist, "O that I were as great / As is my grief, or lesser than my name!" And he is compelled to realize the painful difference existing between what he once was and now is: "Or that I could forget what I have been! / Or not remember what I must be now." (136–139) Like Shakespeare's tragic heroes, Richard falls prey to time in its most dramatically exploitable aspect, that of change. Thus, Margaret in *Richard III* welcomes the latest reject from fortune's wheel:

> Thus hath the course of justice whirled about
> And left thee but a very prey to time,
> Having no more but thought of what thou wast,
> To torture thee the more, being what thou art.
> (IV.iv.105–108)

Richard II is also a soul caught in the agony of change, and yet the missing element could be called necessity. Unlike the other tragic heroes he seems to have some proclivity, some excess of willingness to identify himself with the line of fallen princes. There at least he will still retain something of his former royal nature. "A king, woe's slave, shall kingly woe obey." (III.ii.210) He yields to this wound of hysteria, in which the old order of being is still intact:

> Swell'st thou, proud heart? I'll give thee scope to beat,
> Since foes have scope to beat both thee and me.
>
> (140–141)

Both Marlowe and Shakespeare in their earlier works were beset by two fundamental myths: one of the controling father and the other of the destroyed, tragic son. These two come together in Tamburlaine's final advice to his remaining sons (he had already killed the one defector, the effeminate Calyphas). At the end of a successful reign, the father is able to meet death nobly because he has passed on his achievements to his sons. The play would seem to indicate that man can exercise a firm control over the events of life, and that the father is the model for such possibilities. The situation is summarized in the metaphor of horsemanship, which like the garden, suggests energies (more vital in this case) which must be firmly managed. The opposite of the successful Tamburlaine, or father figure, are the tragic young men, the mythic Phaeton, Icarus, Hippolytus, caught up in their mismanaged powers and destroyed. This is Tamburlaine's charge:

> So, reign, my son; scourge and control these slaves,
> Guiding thy chariot with thy father's hand.
>
> .   .   .   .   .
>
> Be warned by [Phaeton]; then learn with awful eye
> To sway a throne as dangerous as his;
> For if thy body thrive not full of thoughts
> As pure and fiery as Phyteus' beams,
> The nature of those proud rebelling jades
> Will take occasion by the slenderest hair
> And draw thee piecemeal, like Hippolytus,
> Through rock more steep and sharp than Caspian cliffs.
> The nature of thy chariot will not bear
> A guide of baser temper than myself,

More than heaven's coach the pride of Phaëton.
(2 Tamburlaine V.iii.228–244)

Richard will himself repeat the image and the thought and some of the language when he descends into the base court:

> Down, down I come, like glist'ring Phaëton,
> Wanting the manage of unruly jades.
> (III.iii.178–179)

The metaphor of ineffectual horsemanship is relevant, since time and the halter have been traditionally associated in art. They both imply control and, in these plays, a control associated with a fatherly adult world.[17]

Fatherless tragic sons, Richard II, Edward II, and we can include Faustus here, who turned his back on his "base parentage," have much in common in their fates. They are all joined by the fact that the reality of time is hostile to their expectations and to their aspirations, and that eventually it is the article of limitation that impinges upon the infinitude of their will. Confronted with change and loss, they all have recourse to imaginary beings. The imprisoned Edward II unfurls the multiple possibilities of his heart's desire. He cannot be reconciled to the bitterness of his lot: "The griefs of private men are soon allayed, / But not of kings." (V.i.8–9) His mind is dauntless, and like the lion he would rage. At times his soul is so outraged that he soars to the gods to complain against Mortimer and Isabel. But then he remembers that he is king and should revenge himself for the wrongs he has suffered, whereupon he recalls that he is powerless, and what are kings without power, "But perfect shadows in a sunshine day?" Edward's address to the sun shows fully the hostility that exists between man's kingly expectations and his changeful existence:

> Continue ever thou celestial sun;
> Let never silent night possess this clime.
> Stand still you watches of the element;
> All times and seasons, rest you at a stay,
> That Edward may be still fair England's king.
> (64–68)

Like Richard, Edward suffers the agony of a man caught in the inevitable process of replacement. Time's unrelenting movement is clear indication both of the implacable process to which he has engaged himself and of his failure to temper his will to an objective reality. Time's unstoppable passage shows him the truth of what he is:

> But day's bright beams doth vanish fast away,
> And needs I must resign my wishèd crown.
>
> (69–70)

In *Dr. Faustus,* time is again a terrible instrument of inevitability — here much more dramatically present throughout the play. Faustus himself tries all manner of illusory beings in order to escape the final reckoning, and like Edward II he would summon superhuman powers to limit time:

> Stand still, you ever-moving spheres of heaven,
> That time may cease and midnight never come.
> Fair nature's eye, rise, rise again, and make
> Perpetual day; or let this hour be but
> A year, a month, a week, a natural day,
> That Faustus may repent and save his soul.
> *O lente, lente currite noctis equi!*
>
> (133–139)

But, of course, additional time would not alter Faustus' fate, merely postpone it. His damnation does not lie in time, but in his will, where he had been unable to translate conception and desire into willed action. We are reminded of Augustine's warnings to Petrarch. Indeed, for Faustus at this point to resort to a literary tag from Ovid is indicative of how far he has forgotten himself, how far his learning has robbed him of moral consciousness, and contributed to a paralysis of his will. Time proceeds, indifferent to his desires

> The stars move still; time runs; the clock will strike;
> The devil will come, and Faustus must be damned.
>
> (140–141)

The horror of this tragedy of damnation is that Faustus knows what his fate will be; and although he still has time, refuses or is incapable of altering it. Time's inevitable movement, rather than provoking conversion, mesmerizes a man already captivated by his own damnation.

Time is so dramatic a presence in *Dr. Faustus* because it still implies freedom and the possibility of choice. Until the final moment, in the play's Christian medieval context, Faustus could repent. This is precisely the terror and the suspense that engages the audience so deeply in the drama. In *Richard II*, however, that possibility of choice does not exist: the accumulations of a lifetime will be told and Richard has only to recognize his own folly. "Learn, good soul," he instructs his wife at their leave-taking,

> To think our former state a happy dream;
> From which awak'd, the truth of what we are
> Shows us but this. I am sworn brother, sweet,
> To grim Necessity, and he and I
> Will keep a league till death.
>
> (V.i.17–22)

His stature grows when it is most diminished, not through our sympathy, but because of the dignity, honesty, and intelligence with which he sees into his own heart and condition. But, like Edward II and Faustus, he does not yield to his loss without flashes of anger and will. Alone in Pomfret Castle, he seeks to people his miniature world:

> My brain I'll prove the female to my soul,
> My soul the father; and these two beget
> A generation of still-breeding thoughts.
>
> (V.v.6–8)[18]

His solitary imprisonment summarizes his solipsistic position in life. Curiously enough, although they started from different assumptions, both Richard II and Richard III meet their ends in isolation, and both are consequently voided in history. There is an absence of reality to Richard II's projections, and like Faustus he at last cancels the word with the word. In the mind all things are possible and equally impossible. As in Lear, ambitious thoughts plot unlikely wonders:

> how these vain weak nails
> May tear a passage through the flinty ribs
> Of this hard world, my ragged prison walls;
> And, for they cannot, die in their own pride.
>
> (19–22)

There are thoughts that seek consolation in the fact that Richard is not the first of fortune's slaves. In one person Richard plays many people, "And none contented." From king he becomes beggar, from beggar, king, until he is brought back to his present loss "And straight am nothing." Richard is faced with the stark prison walls, grim reminders of a reality that he cannot shuffle; his fancy cannot cheat him as she used to do. In his profoundest conclusion he proceeds to explain why man nevertheless continues to raise up imaginary beings:

> But whate'er I be,
> Nor I, nor any man that but man is,
> With nothing shall be pleas'd till he be eas'd
> With being nothing.
>
> (38–41)

Only when dead will man finally become reconciled to being nothing, but as long as he lives, he will resist the end toward which life and time move him. Caught between time and being, Richard could not shift. His premature and unreliable possession of being was shattered by the intervention of a more powerful reality, one that pitilessly exposed the insufficiency of his attitude. But he could not relinquish the taste of being, because the alternative was nothingness. This accounts for all those imaginary flashes of role-playing: they were means of disguising an unpalatable reality and change. Richard II is an incipient King Lear, and one can easily see in this younger play issues which, given more thrust and sturdiness, cast into a more universal context, can provide the key to the motives and drives of Lear. But it must be said that Lear's nothingness is more inevitable, it is death at the end of life. It is also something that he resists more passionately. Before he can create a Lear, Shakespeare must progress from studies of the decadent, weak king to plays involving those who achieve some mastery over experience and are capable of management in time. Richard has none of this; and so, after his fundamental insight into the needs of the human psyche, he comes to realize his own culpability, providing another summary instance of the role of time in the second tetralogy. (V.v.41 ff.)

Time is not kept in the serenade to Richard, and he is instantly aware of it. But in his acute self-awareness he is also alert enough to draw the moral: that he has the delicacy of ear to notice a musical discord, but did not have the requisite sensitivity to detect the disorder in his own personal time. "I wasted time, and now doth time waste me" is the deposed monarch's summary phrase. The time that he had failed to use properly now turns against him and presents him with a bitter reckoning. Time as a potentiality was neglected, and he is now called to account. Richard's sighs and groans and tears now tell the time that rings him out and Bolingbroke in. He sees himself converted to a timepiece, that is, the helpless record of another man's triumphs. The world which was Richard's is now Henry's, and the nothingness of the erstwhile king is maddening.

Although time is not redeemed in *Richard II,* it is easy to see that the argument of time is indeed active throughout the play. Richard fully suffers the hazards and the risks against which Shakespeare warned the young man of the sonents. In his ruin it is neglected time that brings its accusation against the willful king. That proper use of time is not developed in this play is no reason to assume that it is not a vital force.[19]

The Growth of Hal

The shadow of Richard II hangs over the waywardness of Hal in *1 Henry IV.* The young prince is threatened with the same historical isolation and discontinuity. In their critical confrontation, his father the king accuses him of straying "quite from the flight of all thy ancestors." His place on the council has been "rudely lost" to his younger brother. "The hope and expectation of thy time / Is ruined." He then startles his son's self-possession by declaring that Percy is more like his true heir, and that he (Hal) is more like Richard.

> [Percy] hath more wordly interest to the state
> Than thou, the shadow of succession.
> (III.ii.29–99)

To be sure, the scope of Hal's conversion can be exaggerated. As we insisted with Petrarch and Montaigne, before one can be reformed there must be some prior inclination to reformation: something convertible must inhere before conversion. And Hal's first soliloquy where he shows some of his father's calculation and vows to redeem his time, can be taken to show that the ground was ready. Yet there is a difference between vowing to do something, knowing that one will, and actually doing it. There is something headstrong and, in a way, deceived in that young man who knows his capacities and yet feels no need to demonstrate them to other people. This is no mean alteration; it can be summarized in the change from adolescence to adulthood. The father is crucial in this transformation as is the sion's personal pride, his felt need to redeem his time and to fulfill his "hopes and expectations." As we have seen in Dante and Petrarch, both of these elements, the father-figure (in Hal's case, his actual father) and a sense of time, are crucial in this phase of commitment. The argument of time, in its ramifications, is the instrument of conversion from the aesthetic to the ethical stage of existence.

Kierkegaard's terminology is highly useful in describing Shakespeare's character delineation. In Dante and Petrarch the aesthetic stage importantly includes a reliance on the substitute satisfactions of art and beauty. But in each it extends somewhat beyond that to the aesthetic personality. In the *Purgatorio* Dante had to change his interest as he ceased to be a passive witness and began to take more positive action. Petrarch's aesthetic stage had even more to do with a preference for contemplative distance and consciousness rather than commitment and moral effort. Although Shakespeare's characters have something of the "literary" in them (Richard II and the "bookish" Henry VI), they fulfill the aesthetic function more in terms of personality. What strictly joins Hal with Richard II (and through him with other representatives of the aesthetic — although at the time we did not so designate them — Marlowe's Calyphas in *2 Tamburlaine,* Edward II, and Dr. Faustus) is (1) the inclination to be a spectator rather than an actor, (2) a divorce between consciousness and willed action, and (3) a kind of identity-diffusion. Not all of these figures fully enjoy all three characteristics, but all have a sufficient share of them to invalidate their effectiveness in the temporal realm. It is to spare his son their fates (particularly that of Richard II) that the concerned father puts before Hal an objective picture of his actions — the way his behavior is read by both the public and his father.

The structure of *1 and 2 Henry IV* — the multiple plot levels — is essential to the character of Hal. This technical device (also employed in *A Midsummer Night's Dream*) was of major usefulness to Shakespeare from the mid-nineties on.[20] If in *Henry IV* he has found his character and his theme, in the multiple plot he has found the mechanism for revealing them. Richard II, too, has multiple personalities, but they are all imaginary, and he only gives flight to them when the hard world of history presents him with the truth of his nothingness. But Hal still has time, and with time, choice. Hal is a fluid participant in multiple levels of existence. In many ways that is his glory and, as we shall see, his redemption. But it can also be his destruction if he refuses to commit himself to a single identity, and if he refuses to accept the responsibilities and historical limitations into which he was born. We come here again to a basic characteristic and function of time in the Renaissance and its relationship with the possibilities of variety. Petrarch, too, accused himself of distraction, of having too many options, and thus neglecting the most important condition of his soul. Time was a crucial element in his conversion. Later in the Renaissance, in Alberti's *regola,* we saw the rationale for scheduling. Each morning he charted the things to be done that day, and assigned a time to them. In this way the variety of his interests did not prove his undoing, and all things were accomplished "con ordine." In Guarino, too, we observed an explicit connection between scheduling and variety. "So many subjects claim our attention that concentration and thoroughness are impossible" unless we regulate our existence. And the education of Gargantua is a greater dramatic example of the arrangement of time required to order many interests. Although there is no odor of schedule in Hal, still time is about its same purpose as in these other Renaissance writers: it channels and makes more effective, it marshalls into a functioning unity, the variety of interests and talents that otherwise might be merely dissipated, and to their possessor's harm.

This quality in his prince attests also to Shakespeare's talent for comprehensiveness, his ability to recreate imaginatively various levels of existence. It further shows his concern with the many ways of regarding reality, with consciousness trying to feel out and determine the nature of the world. Yet while this multifaceted world reveals a rich Renaissance sense of variety and possibility, and is related to the artist's own protean capacities, Shakespeare fully recognized the dangers involved. Not only are potentially ideal characters threatened or destroyed by a dissipation of energy, but Shakespeare's evil characters also seem unsettled and chameleon-like:

> Why, I can smile, and murther whiles I smile,
> And cry "Content!" to that which grieves my heart.
> And wet my cheeks with artificial tears,
> And frame my face to all occasions:
>
> .   .   .   .   .
>
> I can add colours to the chameleon,
> Change shapes with Proteus for advantages,
> And set the murderous Machiavel to school.
> (*3 Henry VI,* III.ii.182–185, 191–193)

We must remember that Iago, too, was "motiveless" in his malignity. The mind is a dangerous and shifting place, "no-man fathomed." And while Romantic critics like Bradley and Yeats groaned at the heavy ethic of Lancaster, there is every indication that their "strong fixed" house, "like a mountain" lent some stability to a world that for Shakespeare was becoming increasingly complex. Their world of time and consequence might bear too great a yoke (although we must remember that Hal's own modified comprehensiveness represented a more graceful advance on that "silent king" his father), yet it was preferable to the uncontrolled actor Richard III and to the vainly deluded and destroyed Henry VI and Richard II.

In discussing the argument of time it is relevant to mention a very consistent factor in the "weak king" type that Hal must transcend. *Edward II* opens with Gaveston reading a letter telling him of the death of the king's father. *Henry VI* begins with the inauspicious funeral procession of his father. Richard II, too, was a child king, who warred on his father's house. Dr. Faustus, with infinite possibilities before him, came from parents "base of stock" and consequently in no position to give him guidance. And what must assume some significance, given these other details, the young man of the sonnets is without a father. Sonnet 3 refers to his mother in the present tense, as still living, while sonnet 13 distinctly refers to his father in the past tense — "You had a father — let your son say so." The absence of Northumberland in Hotspur's defeat is thus crucial. The office of the father is to educate the will, to deflate the "swoll'n cunning of self-conceit" — to strip the young man of vain illusions of permanence and omnipotence. He stands for an external objective world that is threatening to any deluded vanity. As such the father embodies the sense of time, and we are justified, I believe, in recalling the role of Cato in Dante's temporal *cantica,* the *Purgatorio,* and that of Augustine in Petrarch's *Secretum.*

That Hal required the important interview with his father in the very center of *1 Henry IV,* even after his seemingly self-assured soliloquy, is proved by the fact that the intervening scenes all show him as an uninvolved participant in actions where the play element is strong and where he believes that his real self is essentially untouched by his involvements. To justify the Gadshill episode, he declares, "Once in my days I'll be a madcap." (I.ii.160) He is in rollicking humor as he tells of the drinking buddies he has just encountered, and will play with Francis, the rather limited waiter, "to drive away the time till Falstaff come." (II.iv.31) He is "now of all humours that have showed themselves humours since the old days of goodman Adam to the pupil age of this present twelve o'clock at midnight." (104–107) He is not of Percy's mind, "I prithee call in Falstaff. I'll play Percy." (122)

And after the jest of catching Falstaff in his "incomprehensible lies," he yields to the gaiety of the moment and Falstaff's urging, "Shall we have a play extempore?" (308) But the outside world intrudes on this play world. Sir John Bracy brings news of the Percy uprising, yet Hal takes it all lightly. And at the prospect of a chiding from his father the next day, he agrees with Falstaff's suggestion to play out the scene: "If thou love me, practice an answer." (411) This action, while ostensibly comic, reveals some serious motives: Falstaff's insistent defense of himself, and the prince's suddenly serious vow of banishment "I do, I will." (628) But this scene also is interrupted — this time by the knocking of the sheriff's men. Falstaff urges, "Play out the play. I have much to say in the behalf of that Falstaff." (531) The prince covers for him, one of several crucial scenes in the play where he pays the bill and spares Falstaff a reckoning. Despite all the wonderful fun and humor of the prince, it is obvious that here he is a different individual from the one who emerges following the interview with his father.

Several other elements in the father's lecture to his son remain important. We get some notion of what it means to redeem the time, when the king declares what he would have been if, at their relative stages, he had been like Hal, "so stale and cheap to vulgar company." The opinion of the people would have still remained loyal to Richard,

> And left me in reputeless banishment,
> A fellow of no mark nor likelihood.
>
> (III.ii.44–45)

To be a "somebody," to have a name, is crucial in Shakespeare's historical argument of time. (How much young Bolingbroke's sense of identity, "Harry of Hereford, Lancaster, and Derby / Am I" contrasts with Richard's subsequent namelessness and nothingness.) And to achieve this status one must learn the importance of "appearances" and the necessity of manipulating the human mechanism. That is how Bolingbroke came to be king, while

> The skipping King, he ambled up and down
> With shallow jesters and rash bavin wits,
> Soon kindled and soon burnt.
>
> (60–62)

An interesting element in the house of Lancaster is the way the son will repeat the attitudes and even words of the father. "Soon kindled and soon burnt" recalls the fate old John of Gaunt predicted for Richard's "light vanity," which "consuming means, soon preys upon itself." There is a fundamental seriousness in the house of Lancaster that has only scorn for the ineffective bursts of wit and fancy that play themselves out and produce nothing of solid and enduring reality. Hal, too, will be in a position to reject "light vanity."

But at the moment, his antagonist Hotspur is the occasion that informs against him. How irritating it is for the son to hear invidious comparisons with a more successful coeval. It is of course to emphasize this rivalrous competition and their destined confrontation and to increase the sting of the comparison that Shakespeare tranforms the ages of Hal and Hotspur, making them contemporaries, when, in historical fact, Hotspur was older than Henry IV. But Hotspur is now Hal's Fortinbras. And to his father's lavish praise of "this Hotspur, Mars in swathling clothes" and to the suggestion that Hal would more likely fight in Percy's hire through fear and his patent inclination toward lowness, Hal's native pride stiffens.

> Do not think so. You shall not find it so.
> And God forgive them that so much have sway'd
> Your Majesty's good thoughts away from me.
> I will redeem all this on Percy's head
> And, in the closing of some glorious day,
> Be bold to tell you that I am your son.
> (129–134)

Despite the sunny avowal, the language of economics persists. Percy is but his factor,

> And I will call him to so strict account
> That he shall render every glory up,
> Yea, even the slightest worship of his time,
> Or I will tear the reckoning from his heart.
> (147–152)

In tracing the fortunes of Hal in *Parts One* and *Two,* one is indeed surprised to learn that after his splendid reformation he must again prove himself to his father. Yet the tone of *Part Two* has become so sombre, so intensified, and so dark, with such new problems raised, that one does not object to the replay. Howevermuch it may have been an afterthought, *Part Two* is radically different in atmosphere. The gaiety and the sun-drenched possibilities of *Part One* are weighted down by sickness, guilt, and the apparently unending troubles of Henry IV's reign. Falstaff's age and melancholy are more apparent; when we first meet him he is desperately in need of money. Hal himself is wearied with his former friends. At a crucial point of father-son feeling, Hal's cronies cross his true sentiments and make it appear that Hal would only be a hypocrite were he to show sadness at his father's illness: "By this hand, thou thinkest me as far in the devil's book as thou and Falstaff for obduracy and persistency. Let the end try the man. But I tell thee, my heart bleeds inwardly that my father is so sick; and keeping such vile company as thou art hath in reason taken from me all ostentation of sorrow." (II.ii.48–54) His father had warned him of "vile participation," and Hal comes now to experience it in his own way.

Time is no longer altogether in front of Hal. He begins to feel the weight of his own waste. Here, by focusing on some elements of the argument of time, we can perceive a dramatic justification of *Part Two*. As in all father-son encounters, the older voice tries to persuade the younger person of a truth that he did not learn abstractly himself, but rather gained from experience. The absence of the same experience in the son and the importance of the lesson account for the mounting exasperation and impatience in the father. It is not until the son himself knows by experience the lessons of time — and this lesson all too often is only learned, unfortunately, in the shadow of the father's death — that he comes to appreciate in his own marrow the truths that previously were mere abstractions. We have seen this already in the dynamic of Petrarch's development. It was only by experience that the lessons of time could be really learned, and a true conversion take place. The advance of *Part Two* over its predecessor is precisely here. In *Part One* Hal was still glorious; in *Part Two,* he begins to feel the waste of his own energies and talents. Falstaff's overweening letter tells the prince that Poins has been speaking of a marriage between his sister and Hal. When Hal asks if this is true, Poins in effect declares that he could do worse. These involvements depress the prince: "Well, thus we play the fools with the time, and the spirits of the wise sit in the clouds and mock us." (II.ii.154–157) Yet he undertakes one more jest to catch Falstaff. Hiding behind the arras he has the opportunity to observe "desire outlive performance." And although Falstaff, as in *Part One,* wriggles out of the trap, the scene ends disappointingly. News of war again intrudes, but this time only serves to burden the prince with guilt:

> By heaven, Poins, I feel me much to blame
> So idly to profane the precious time,
> When tempest of commotion, like the South,
> Borne with black vapour, doth begin to melt
> And drop upon our bare unarmed heads.
>
> (II.iv.390–394)

So, too, the king's burden is heavier in *Part Two*. The end of his life is approaching and the crucial action of his life is still unjustified. The source of concern is his as yet unredeemed son. Through Hal's dereliction the king sees his own guilt reflected. Rather than an event leading to a better future, his accession to the throne seems only to be a curse. Should Henry IV provide an orderly succession, the ambiguities surrounding his rise to power would be resolved. The doubtful resolution of the prince turns back on Bolingbroke. In *Richard II* he is already aware that "if any plague hang over us, 'tis he." And in *Part One,* his first words to his son emphasize this fear that Henry is Henry's punishment:

> I know not whether God will have it so,
> For some displeasing service I have done,
> That, in his secret doom, out of my blood
> He'll breed revengement and a scourge for me;
> But thou dost in thy passages of life
> Make me believe that thou are only mark'd
> For the hot vengeance and the rod of heaven
> To punish my mistreadings.
>
> (III.ii.4–11)

In *Part Two* (III.i), the worn and sleepless king has time to reflect on the ironies of history. Ten years ago Richard and Northumberland were friends; eight years ago he and Percy were friends. Rather than simple "revolution of the times," a formal line, reminiscent of the curses of the first tetralogy, is given these events by Richard's prediction of them. To a certain point, then, the issues of the first and second tetralogy follow similar courses. Action in the first merely brings on further action; a curse seems to operate over the whole. In the second, as far as Henry IV is aware, the same is true. His act of revolution seems to have involved him in a series of necessary actions that hold no promise for resolution. His hope in the time to come is also blighted by his son. Not only has Hal, as we have seen, turned the garden of his youth into a weedy patch, and thus reversed one benevolent process in generation, he threatens the more public hopes of the king:

> The blood weeps from my heart when I do shape,
> In forms imaginary, th' unguided days
> And rotten times that you shall look upon
> When I am sleeping with my ancestors.
>
> (IV.iv, 54–61)

This same double curse that produces bitter emulation within the family and disorder in society is the object of the king's attack on his son in their moving interview in *Part Two*. "See, sons, what things you are . . ." (IV.v.65 ff.) Believing that Hal seized the crown before his death, Henry IV assails this ingratitude:

> For this the foolish over-careful fathers
> Have broke their sleep with thoughts, their brains with care,
> Their bones with industry;
>
> .   .   .   .   .
>
> When like the bee tolling from every flower
> The virtuous sweets,
> Our thighs pack'd with wax, our mouths with honey,
> We bring it to the hive, and, like the bees,
> Are murd'red for our pains. This bitter taste
> Yields his engrossments to the ending father.

That his son will dance on his grave, is the fear — perhaps ages old — that the anguished father expresses. His sense of injury at the apparent ingratitude is strong, "Canst thou not forbear me half an hour?" As in *Tamburlaine,* but without that play's zesty endorsement, the universe becomes an arena of naturalistic place-taking from which no service or relationship is immune. Henry IV, so the curse would run, who usurped the position of Richard II, is driven from office by his son. This is the way of the universe, where no channels exist that offer protection against the currents of emulation. The dilemma of Henry IV is precisely here: although he came to the crown through ambiguous means, he hopes to establish an orderly and a clear succession. His war is preeminently with an original sin, which his son's behavior seems to confirm. Yet his concern extends beyond his personal situation to the national consequences that his distraught fears imagine:

O my poor kingdom, sick with civil blows!
When that my care could not withhold thy riots,
What wilt thou do when riot is thy care?
O, thou wilt be a wilderness again,
Peopled with wolves, thy old inhabitants!

(134–138)

It is part of Shakespeare's eminent reasonableness, of course, that the accusing father is wrong in his opinion of his son. But the concern is genuine, and it is this concern which turns out to be an expiating factor, in the second tetralogy, in the validation of the house of Lancaster.[21] The two tetralogies assume a fundamental relationship with the *Oresteia*, where similarly two basic acts are performed, one vindicated, the other not. The House of York in the first tetralogy was unable to muster valid principles to justify its revolution. Yorkist vision, consumed by the golden crown, rarely rose to larger perspectives of time and place; its motives proved to result in a root individualism that in turn devours York's own house, "I am myself alone." It is precisely this vision of life that Henry IV, however tainted he might be, criticizes in his own son. The Yorkists are like Clytemnestra, who brazenly exults over the fallen husband. Her own impure motives reveal themselves in the way her kingdom grinds to a dead stop, in the horror of fear and nightmare. On Orestes, however, a necessity operates that compels him toward the horrendous deed, and his own righteousness is revealed in the guilt that he feels, and by the pilgrimage of expiation he must undergo. His conscience has not been brazened by the act. Like Henry IV, his very guilt is part of the breaking of the curse.

This is especially so, to return to Shakespeare's second tetralogy, when the father's guilt is centered on Hal and his tenure, on the kind of king he will be. In one of his denunciations of his son, Henry IV charges that his attitude toward government is frivolous: "O foolish youth! / Thou seek'st the greatness that will overwhelm thee." (*2 Henry IV*, IV.v.96–97) Yet it is precisely in his sense of the burdens of rule and the other difficulties and either/or necessities of the world of time that Henry most duplicates his father. Unlike the Yorkists' frequent apostrophes to the Elysium of the crown (in the Marlovian vein), the Lancasters are impressed with the hardships and burdens of kingship. "O polished perturbation! Golden care" is Hal's address to the crown he finds beside his sleeping father. And after his father's denunciation, in his own defense he proceeds to recount what he actually had said. The golden crown is carnivorous: it eats the bearer up, as it has fed upon the body of his father:

> if it did infect my blood with joy
> Or swell my thoughts to any strain of pride,
> If any rebel or vain spirit of mine
> Did with the least affection of a welcome
> Give entertainment to the might of it . . .
> (170–174)

This oath, sworn with gravity and determination, pleases the father in two ways; it shows that his own labors have been appreciated, and that like himself Hal will be a serious ruler. Through their very sense of guilt and responsibility, added to determination, the Lancasters show a capacity for effective rule. The original sin, so dominant in the first tetralogy and looming in the second, has been purged through the very father-son ideal that is at the heart of Shakespeare's political ethic. The crown sat uneasily upon the head of the father. Bolingbroke, as the original man in the middle, had to assume the guilt of historical action. But that guilt has been broken. To his son the crown will descend with better quiet,

> Better opinion, better confirmation;
> For all the soil of the achievement goes
> With me into the earth.
> (189–191)

Henry is the scapegoat who carries the sins away. But his burden has been eased by his son's proving his right to succession. Henry IV does not die as a tragic figure, nor as a Christ-figure who simply absorbs the blow. At the end, as with Henry VIII, Henry IV's victory is historical. His action at a crucial moment of historical change, rather than being doomed by a sense of life that fears all doing, is justified in his son. As Henry VIII exclaims with pride and praises his Maker, so Henry IV finds his life's work vindicated, and cries out "Laud be to God." Where he does this is important. Waning fast, he asks in what room he fainted. Told it is called the Jerusalem room, he rejoices and then explains that he was once told he would die in Jerusalem, which he had thought to mean the Holy Land. Some critics have considered this to be a "juggling prophecy" which robs Henry IV of any contentment and shows him in the end to be a defeated man. Correct reading of this scene and Henry's attitude would seem to dispose of that interpretation. Far from being a juggling prophecy, it places the seal of approval on his actions. If he could not go to Jerusalem, Jerusalem came to him. And as in *Henry VIII,* there is some religious confirmation of this man who faced with resolution and courage the bitter choices that the new times presented to him.

This tetralogy is at the core of the larger developments of the study of time in the Renaissance. It shows, as in Spenser, the basic Elizabethan reinvestment in the ways of succession. In Dante, we recall, all rightness comes from God, and not through the lines of succession. We do not have to go back as far as Dante for that. Samuel Daniel, whom some have thought Shakespeare followed in his historical vision, also sees a controlling providence at work in the lines of English kings. After the superb attainment of Edward III and the promise of his sons, disaster strikes when the Black Prince predeceases his father and the throne is left to a child.

> But now the Scepter, in this glorious state,
> Supported with strong power and victories,
> Was left unto a Child, ordain'd by fate
> To stay the course of what might grow too hie:
> Here was a stop, that Greatnesse did abate,
> When powre upon so weake a base did lie.
> For, least good fortune should presume too farre,
> Such oppositions interposed are.[22]

The world is still governed by the inscrutable powers that allow man his glory but are jealous when it seems to continue too long, and for the same reason as in Dante: then he will believe that he, and not these mastering powers, is the measure of things. But Shakespeare's vision differs even from that of Daniel. There is a kind of human effectiveness that does not act in opposition to the great powers of the world, but, as in the *Oresteia,* seems willing to give them their place of honor and their due of guilt, and the sweat of scrupulous preoccupation with law and government. This effectiveness is not of the Yorkist-Clytemnestra type, whose brag and insolence merely add to the processes of retribution they thought they were breaking, but neither does it share the vision that utterly despairs of any redemption in time. That man can act safely in time — however harrowing and difficult it might be — is the credo of Shakespeare's development in the second tetralogy. Importantly, then, where the argument of time is seriously used, it works to dissolve the hold of original sin.

Also related to the development of time in the Renaissance is the fact that a secular paideia replaces the Christian. In the Dante of the *Commedia,* man is a truer man the less he has of manliness, and the more he regains of the purity, innocence, and sense of life's coherence that a child has. As in other Renaissance works fundamentally concerned with education, so in Shakespeare's second tetralogy, the ideal formation takes place strictly between father and son. The older figure leads the son to maturity, responsibility, and order. Time is redeemed when this secular paideia functions, just as time is forfeited in the *Inferno* and in *Richard III* when that process is destroyed. In two speeches, one of which is memorable, Hal vows to maintain the processes of succession that his father feared were broken. Taking to himself the crown that (as he believed) killed his father, Hal affirms his right to it and his willingness to defend it:

> and put the world's whole strength
> Into one giant arm, it shall not force
> This lineal honour from me. This from thee
> Will I to mine leave, as 'tis left to me.
>
> (44–47)

We have already observed the "lineal honour" operating in the several reformations of the son, especially in *Part Two,* and also indirectly in the many echoes and resemblances passed on from father to son. Falstaff, especially, courts disappointment when he seeks to insert himself between the father-son relation.

The same order of stability that Hal comes to represent is absent from the worlds of Hotspur and Falstaff, but, significantly, they can be validly discussed in the temporal terms we have established. Hotspur is Hal's foil not only in reaped honors, but also in awareness. Hal's broadgauged participation in many levels of existence is a kind of fortunate fall. While it seems to present him with greater difficulties ("most subject is the fattest soil to weeds") it also indicates greater possibilities — the "sparks of better hope" — which his father quite early detects. Separate and diffuse, his multiple identities can be damaging, but unified they show greater tolerance, broader perspectives, and a disposition to embrace life. Hotspur, of course, has none of these qualities. He is caught in that older way of reducing life to ultimate alternatives: honor or death, "or sink, or swim!" This tendency derives from his basic devaluation of life's normal activities and his fierce devotion to those moments of combat when all will be determined. Before battle he has no time for the letters brought by a messenger — "I cannot read them now":

> O gentlemen, the time of life is short!
> To spend that shortness basely were too long
> If life did ride upon a dial's point,
> Still ending at the arrival of an hour.
> An if we live, we live to tread on kings;
> If die, brave death, when princes die with us!
> (V.ii.80–87)

His code of honor actually compels him to seek out dangerous situations:

> Send danger from the east unto the west,
> So honour cross it from the north to south,
> And let them grapple. O, the blood more stirs
> To rouse a lion than to start a hare!
> (I.iii.195–198)

Hotspur is a man possessed, and when he speaks it is rarely to others, but rather out of some demonic trance within himself. These words, for instance, spoken at a council of war, are not really addressed to the group. Some inner jockey is spurring him on, and the crowd stands back in amazement at his frenzy. Northumberland, his father, provides the actor's cue:

> Imagination of some great exploit
> Drives him beyond the bounds of patience.
> (199–200)

But Percy proceeds:

> By heaven, methinks it were an easy leap
> To pluck bright honour from the pale-fac'd moon,
> Or dive into the bottom of the deep,

> Where fadom line could never touch the ground,
> And pluck up drowned honour by the locks,
> So he that doth redeem her thence might wear
> Without corrival all her dignities.

Worcester, his uncle, grows somewhat impatient at all of this fantasy:

> He apprehends a world of figures here,
> But not the form of what he should attend.
>
> (201–210)

With Hal, however, despite his own kind of isolation, we have none of this blind imagination. He seems to see better into people and situations: "I know you all . . ." And while he is deluded in thinking that he is in control of the situation (other forces must help effect his regeneration), still his presence in the easy world of jokes and stories, of small beer, provides a larger perspective from which to view the ludicrous warrior-myths and pride of the Glendowers and Hotspurs. In *1 Henry IV,* when Falstaff tells of the spreading rebellion, his very telling satirizes the spectacular pretensions of the soldier clan:

> That same mad fellow of the North, Percy, and he of Wales that gave Amamon the bastinado, and made Lucifer cuckold, and swore the devil his true liegeman upon the cross of a Welsh hook — what a plague call you him?
>
> (II.iv.369–373)

Hal picks up the marvelous puncturing, completing Falstaff's similar description of Douglas, "that runs a-horseback up a hill perpendicular —"

> *Prince.* He that rides at high speed and with his pistol kills a sparrow flying.
> *Fal.* You have hit it.
> *Prince.* So did he never the sparrow.
>
> (378–382)

His sense of fun and humor is sparkling when he puts Francis' inarticulateness on parade or when he makes sport of Percy:

That ever this fellow should have fewer words than a parrot, and yet the son of a woman! His industry is upstairs and downstairs, his eloquence the parcel of a reckoning. I am not yet of Percy's mind, the Hotspur of the North; he that kills me some six or seven dozen of Scots at a breakfast, washes his hands, and says to his wife, "Fie upon this quiet life! I want work!" "O my sweet Harry," says she, "how many hast thou kill'd to-day?" "Give my roan horse a drench," says he, and answers "Some fourteen," an hour after, "a trifle, a trifle." I prithee call in Falstaff.

(110–122)

The prince too knows that Hotspur apprehends a world of figures, and not what he should attend. His parody of Hotspur emphasizes his lack of responsiveness, his lack of consecutiveness. All consumed in his own world, time is unimportant. Rather than answering his wife's question (still in Hal's parody) he gives an order instead, and one hour later registers his response. There is strong evidence in the play that Hal's comic version of Hotspur is not inaccurate.

With the exception of the material in the section on "The Dramatic Exploitation of Time," I have generally ignored the interesting problems of the sequences of actual plot time. But because of the conceptual value of the presentation of dramatic time in *1 Henry IV*, I make an exception here. Mable Buland has studied the problems and development of double time in Elizabethan drama, with particular attention to Shakespeare. In brief, she states that double time in the plays results from "an attempt to give the effect of close continuity of action, and to use at the same time a plot requiring the lapse of months or years." I find that the use of double time in *Henry IV* serves the added purpose of reflecting the two young heroes' varying attitudes toward life. Miss Buland summarizes the plot-times of the play:

In *1 and 2 Henry IV* . . . Shakespeare reverted to the epic type of the chronicle, but not to the kind of construction used in the *Henry VI* plays; for into the episodic scenes of Hotspur's rebellion he has woven a comic story possessing such close continuity that a semblance of coherence is imparted to the whole play. In *1 Henry IV*, we hear Falstaff and Prince Harry plan to take a purse "to-morrow night in Eastcheap" (I.ii); we see the early morning robbery, we enjoy the supper scene after the night's adventures; we hear the Prince resolve, "I'll to the court in the morning" (II.iv.595); and presently we find the son and father together (III.ii). It is then ar-

ranged that "on Wednesday next" the prince shall set forward with
his troops, and a few days later, at the battle of Shrewsbury, the
play is concluded. Nevertheless, the affairs of Hotspur, which should
be concurrent with those of the Prince of Wales, cover a period of
three months, and their long-time extension is clearly indicated.[23]

Although Hotspur's activities cover a longer period of time, they do not
suggest continuity. They represent a disrupted sequence of heightened
moments: they are crisis episodes. Human interest is kept up by the
sheer eccentricity and "humor" of the wild-eyed devotee of soldier's
honor. Yet there is no suggestion of the fuller life, or any interest other
than honor (which has a strong echo of cracking heads). Time between
the crucial episodes is of little value:

> Uncle, adieu. O, let the hours be short
> Till fields and blows and groans applaud our sport!
> (I.ii.301–302)

The prince, on the other hand, is involved in the more quotidian world
of community and consecutive experience. His plot time, if briefer, is
more continuous, and therefore more open to extension. Hotspur's time,
while covering a longer period, is actually contracted into short moments: it is more suggestive of the tragic world of passion to which his
end is the consummation.

Beneath Hotspur's devotion to crisis-time is a certain devaluation of
the small things in extended time. Underlying his stance is a desperate
skepticism that comes out in his last speech:

> But thoughts the slaves of life, and life time's fool,
> And time, that takes survey of all the world,
> Must have a stop.
> (V.iv.81–83)

As his approach to time has indicated and as this final turning away
shows, Hotspur's attitudes do not promote the kind of temporal stability and controlling powers that Shakespeare valued in his more life-seeking monarchs.

In the histories, Falstaff is Shakespeare's prime creation of a negligent
greatness. Hal is determined to redeem the time and move against the

tempest of commotion that drops on his "unarmed head." But there is strong evidence that Falstaff misdeems the time and is by his own admission heinously unprovided. He is the latter spring, and the all-hallown summer. His desire outlives performance. The man of incongruities and incomprehensible lies, whose predilection was for the latter end of a fray and the beginning of a feast, brought laughter in *Part One.* His sheer extravagances were rewarded, and his inconsecutiveness was much to the point. But a move persists to expose Falstaff, whether after Gadshill, or when Poins and Hal oversee him in *Part Two.* And like the Wife of Bath, Falstaff is an aging, melancholy comic hero, beset by occasional religious anxiety, but also driven by hard economic motivation. Underneath his inconsequence there is a hard line of practical shrewdness: " 'When thou art king' runs like a refrain through what he has to say, and reveals the anxieties beneath the jesting. . . . What is to happen when the old king dies? That, as we are reminded time and time again in this scene, is the leading problem of Falstaff's existence." [24] The hope is that the prince will spare him the reckoning of his more extravagant ways, that the prince will provide and set Falstaff's accounts in order.

The call to account is crucial to the argument of time. It is the fatal moment for which one must prepare, the sick hour that Richard's surfeit brought, the bitter realization against which Shakespeare warns the young man in the sonnets, and the crucial hour of combat for which the interview with his father prepares Hal. The call to account is the inevitable summons that breaks through illusion and presents a hard world of reality. But Falstaff, we are told at once in *I Henry IV,* is superfluous in demanding the time of day. "What a devil has thou to do with the time of day," unless the signs and acts of pleasure were fitting marks for the world of time. Attached to the prince, Falstaff is the allowed jester: he never is called to pay. The prince may have called the hostess to a reckoning many a time, but he never called Falstaff to pay his part. "No, I'll give thee thy due, thou hast paid all there." (I.ii.59) The prince's credit redeems Falstaff's activities. As Gadshill, the spotter explains: his team of robbers includes some who are involved in the robbery for sport's sake, "that would (if matters should be look'd into) for their own credit sake make all whole." (II.i.79) Falstaff's world is a merry play world. Watch tonight, pray to-morrow. . . . "A play extempore" is the proper happening for those who live by their wits. After the robbery, when the play world has been interrupted by the knocking of the sheriff's men, Hal engages his word that Falstaff (hidden fast asleep behind the arras) will answer the complaints. The prince promises that the money will be paid back "with advantage," and persists in being good "angel" to Falstaff.

Falstaff is ill-prepared for the emulative struggle to which the prince is called. The either/or challenge of Hotspur which Hal must answer is for Falstaff merely

> Rare words! brave world! Hostess, my breakfast, come.
> O, I could wish this tavern were my drum!
> (III.iii.228–229)

He is somewhat reluctant to settle accounts, especially in a world of struggle and real threats; in London's taverns his wit and verbal skills could get him by, but not in combat: "Though I could scape shot-free at London, I fear the shot here. Here's no scoring but upon the pate." (V.iii.30–32) As the moment of battle approaches, Falstaff asks Hal's assistance. But Hal is not colossal enough to bestride him in battle: "Say thy prayers, and farewell."

> *Fal.* I would 'twere bedtime, Hal, and all well.
> *Prince.* Why, thou owest God a death.
> *Fal.* 'Tis not due yet I would be loath to pay him before his day.
> Why need I be so forward with him that calls not on me?
> (V.i.126–130)

While it would be foolhardy to rush toward that reckoning, still the postponement he seeks here is only part of the larger practice of deferral that is typical of Falstaff throughout both parts of *Henry IV*.

In the battle Hal significantly does not bestride Falstaff, but rather his father. And when Falstaff pulls the bottle of sack from where his pistol should be, the prince rebukes his poor timing: "What, is it a time to jest and dally now?" (V.iii.57) The preparation for rejection proceeds — even if premature and bound to be deferred. When Hal sees the fallen Falstaff, whom he mistakenly believes to be dead, the prince hardly expresses any regret:

> O, I should have a heavy miss of thee
> If I were much in love with vanity!
> (V.iv.105–106)

Again the Lancastrian seriousness returns to judge the frivolity of those whom they reject or oppose. But Falstaff is not dead, only counterfeiting, and he springs to life to pull off his most incredible stunt: claiming he killed Hotspur. The claim has all the more chance of success in the world of *Part One,* the more preposterous and patently incredible it is. Falstaff lands on his feet, and the prince again uses his credit to spare him a reckoning:

> For my part, if a lie may do thee grace,
> I'll gild it with the happiest terms I have.
>
> (161–162)

In *Part Two,* the law is not so easily fobbed off. The Lord Chief Justice holds the keys to this terrain, as the law-bound Cato did in the *Purgatorio.* He is just as severe in his retention of the past, and the object of his implacability is Falstaff: "It is not a confident brow, nor the throng of words that come with such more than impudent sauciness from you, can thrust me from a level consideration." (II.i.121–124) He is determined that Falstaff pay his debt to Hostess Quickly "both in purse and person." Earlier the Chief Justice showed that he at least had not forgotten the events of Gadshill: "Your day's service at Shrewsbury hath a little gilded over your night's exploit on Gadshill. You may thank th' unquiet time for your quiet o'erposting that action." (I.ii.168–171) Falstaff's pretensions of youthfulness, and his brawling are unseemly to the serious man of order, "Doth this become your place, your time and business?" (II.i.73) Such a complaint will be echoed by the newly-crowned Henry V: "How ill white hairs become a fool and jester!" (V.v.52)

Falstaff is ill attended in *Part Two.* Like the Chief Justice, the prince's brother John is not an ideal audience for his antics. He warns Falstaff of the danger he is running by his eccentric ways:

> Now, Falstaff, where have you been all the while?
> When everything is ended, then you come.
> These tardy tricks of yours will, on my life,
> One time or other break some gallows' back.
>
> (IV.iii.29–32)

For one scene only, prior to rejection time, Falstaff and Hal appear together in *Part Two.* (II.iv) And as in *Part One,* Poins and the prince have designed a trap to expose Falstaff. The directions of both plays seem toward Falstaff's exposure. But in *Part Two,* much of the former gaiety has passed out of the scene, and it ends unsatisfactorily and unresolved. The final impression is one of time profaned. Indeed, it is "Falstaff, good night."

Although Falstaff has not altogether lost his charm in *Part Two,* he is no longer so outlandishly inconsequential. He has acquired authority, and he uses his new employment to deliver himself from the officers of the Chief Justice. But as he becomes more consequential in speech and behavior, he becomes more of a real problem and hence more open to rejection: "You speak as having power to do wrong." (II.i.141)

Debts past due, of which the Chief Justice is the unrelenting collector, are closing in on Falstaff. There are signs that his good angel of the past will no longer pay the reckoning. One indication of Hal's future behavior is in his father's accusation that under his reign any kind of hoodlum and criminal would find refuge: "England shall double gild his treble guilt." The same term of covering was used by Hal in *Part One,* and by the Chief Justice in *Part Two* to describe the royal credit that was redeeming Falstaff's carelessness and illegality. The father's charge is pointed. But rather than to Falstaff, it is to the Chief Justice that Hal gives his hand, "you shall be as father to my youth." In *Parts One* and *Two* Falstaff loses out to time and the Law. As in Dante's *Purgatorio,* these two principles, part of the argument of time, necessitate a rejection that continues to be debated.

It is quite natural that we should recoil at Falstaff's rejection, just as we did at Virgil's — even though the latter seemed to represent more positive ideals. After Romanticism, as Professor Langbaum has shown, the quandary of moral categories and sympathetic character seems only to have become thicker.[25] Naive readers have continued to protest, and overly severe teachers have continued to pursue rigorously the textual logic that requires dismissal. However much we might wish to see Falstaff's presumption deflated and delight in the dramatic effects that build up to his final exposure, however much we might be aware that Falstaff's egotism personally intrudes on the proper and serious business of governing a country, and however much we are brought to realize that lurking on the verge of Falstaff's domain is disorder, crime, and even murder, still it is not without regret that we see the world deprived of his good force. It is this to which Edmund Wilson responds when he joins in association Falstaff and the later tragic figures, Lear and Antony.[26] In their loss a great force has gone out of the world.

Falstaff's merits become apparent, not in contrast with the virtues required of the monarch, but when set next to the lesser characters who seem to thrive. Shallow, a simple fool, except where money is concerned, is everything that Falstaff is not. Ever in the rearward of the fashion, this country squire still has more than Bardolph for security. His beeves and Falstaff's lack of provisions presents another of those occasions that inform against one, those bitter lessons that reveal a clear reality. Shallow sounds the depths of his name. He is nostalgic and backward-looking to a past he never had. In his great soliloquy (III.iv), Falstaff has nothing but scorn (and some designs) for this lying old man, who in his youth was no way like himself. He only sang outmoded songs, and never had the courage, enterprise, or wit to be the blade he later imagined himself to be. He was a hanger-on, one who circled around the outskirts of the tumult. He was never at the center of things; he never took the risks of the thrust. Yet, now he is wealthy and Falstaff desperately in need of provisions. This speech shows Falstaff's virtues in proper dialectic; Shallow's triumphant narrowness is degraded in contrast with the risk-taking Falstaff. It was Falstaff who ventured, who drew the laughs, who was wit itself and the cause of wit in other men.

Falstaff had always misdeemed the time and ignored the need to provide prudently. And while there was always a latent cynicism in his profane detraction from heroics, still it is only in his advanced age, when he sees fools provided for, that he grimly sets about to hunt for himself: "If the young dace be a bait for the old pike, I see no reason in the law of the nature but I may snap at him [Shallow]. Let time shape, and there an end." (III.ii.356–359) Falstaff can hardly inspire his wonted affection in us when he speaks of the "law of nature." This latter-day lapse into an opportunistic ethic, similar to that of the Yorkists, is a startling reversal from the earlier gaiety (for all its undertone of future gain). His freedom has become victimized by its own excess and desperately converts from happy inconsequence into hard calculation; perennially out of season, Falstaff too late in life adopts a grim code of provision. And ironically, it is this final resolve to take advantage of the time, that element which he had so grandiosely scanted, which helps to make Falstaff dramatically ripe for rejecting.

The Significance of Time in Shakespeare's Histories

True to its form, Shakespeare's argument of time exhorts response. And the response, as proclaimed in the sonnets, involves a faith in the augmentative potential of the ways of succession. Wherever these ways are open, and man places his confidence in them, children and fame are valuable counters in the war against nothingness and oblivion. And this perhaps is one of the values of the argument of time: it provides a bridge between the private voice of the sonnets and the more public world of the drama. It concentrates on the problems that help to make the histories intense personal as well as political drama. But it also gives larger scope to the virtues of good government: prudence and responsibility and even decorum are more than that when they are stabilizing guards against a chaotic and destructive world of willful vanity, negligence, and nothingness. The argument of time provides such enlargements for Shakespeare's political ethic.

We have already had occasion to observe this double dimension of time in the Renaissance: it is a cosmic discovery that translates itself into schedule; with fervor it combines practicality. These aspects of time in the Renaissance help to explain the division in modern criticism over Shakespeare's successful House of Lancaster. Whether defending Richard II or Falstaff, men like Yeats or Bradley are repulsed by the calculation, priggishness, and prudence of the Lancasters. "To suppose that Shakespeare preferred the men who deposed his king is to suppose that Shakespeare judged men with the eyes of a Municipal Councillor weighing the merits of a Town Clerk; and that had he been by when Verlaine cried out from his bed, "Sir, you have been made by the stroke of a pen, but I have been made by the breath of God," he would have thought the Hospital Superintendent the better man." [27] Indeed, there is part of us that wishes Yeats to be right, that feels uncomfortable whenever we insist too pompously on the correctness of deposition or dismissal. But, at the same time, we also feel that Yeats, bristling under the divisions of his own time, has stripped the growth and significance of Hal of half the interest it holds for us. He belittles the prudence, but he forgets the cosmic issues of time and nothingness against which prudence is a defense. He mocks the decisions of the public man, but he forgets the private setting for those decisions. In short, Yeats is prevented from seeing the crucial nature of time in the Renaissance. Time is a principle of reality that limits human freedom, but it also heightens reality. It is these deeper issues in Hal's development that the argument of time brings out. Yet Yeats is historically percipient. Just that severe division which would eventually come about between Verlaine's spirited vanity and the dull Municipal Councillor has its roots in the Renaissance triumph of time. And Shakespeare's own tragedies will show the split that Yeats detected in the histories. But for a while, with Shakespeare, as with other Renaissance writers, when time was still an important and fervent discovery, the union of energy and control was still possible. Rabelais could have his education of Gargantua and the freer air of the Abbey. The practical results of the discovery of time

could still be exciting, especially when man was trying to liberate himself from an unworthy torpor, or in Shakespeare's case, from older ways
that no longer served the modern prince. The modern world, especially
in literature, would like to return to the world before time became a
pressure and a commodity. Yet it was just this discovery of time that is
intrinsic to the nature and accomplishments of the Renaissance.

The first tetralogy shows the transition from the high point of England's medieval achievement to the first Renaissance English monarch.
So, too, the second tetralogy deals with the "change of times," as it
moves from a king whose values are medieval to one whose values are
more like those of the Tudors (whether represented by Henry VII or
the Cranmer oration in *Henry VIII*). In the first tetralogy Henry V is
the last of the medieval kings; in the second, he is the glorious representative, shown in his growth and development, of the modern notions of
realism, effectiveness, comprehensiveness of appeal. His contrast with
Hotspur transcends mere competition between coevals; it is rather between two different ways of life. There is more in Hal that seeks and
deserves survival; there is more in Hal that is in tune with the nature
of the world and the demands of the time. With all of his tremendous
vitality and spirited vision, Percy is still food for worms.

> Ill-weav'd ambition, how much art thou shrunk!
> When that this body did contain a spirit,
> A kingdom for it was too small a bound;
> But now two paces of the vilest earth
> Is room enough.
>
>   (*1 Henry IV*, V.iv.88–92)

Hal's vision includes human limitations and vulnerabilities. His spirit is
not as doom-eager and death-insistent as the tragically motivated chivalric and aristocratic Hotspur. J. Dover Wilson's comments on these
lines, especially "ill-weaved ambition," are suggestive: "Such is the
quality of Hotspur's ambition . . . and such the language of Shakespeare, the wool-dealer's son, who well knew that cloth loosely woven
was especially apt to shrink." [28] Shakespeare, the wool-dealer's son,
finds the values and personality of a Hotspur inappropriate for true
management, stability, and safety in the world. There is not enough in
Hotspur that seeks life over death. He shows too much willfulness, too
great a reluctance to adjust one's spirit to the realities of existence. And
one of the great realities is time.

Continuing to follow larger historical suggestions, it has been clear from our study that the sense of time as an urgent pressure was coincidental with the rise of bourgeois society and the middle class. More to the point, time figures prominently in the formation of middle-class values. It suggests an external world of real limitations, against which one must make provisions if he is to be spared an unsatisfactory reckoning. If, then, Shakespeare's England witnessed the great alliance under the Tudors between the throne and the middle class, it is clear why time is so important a force in Shakespeare's second tetralogy. Historical in value, the history plays reflect historical reality: Hal is the embodiment of the Tudor revolution in values that Shakespeare sought to dramatize. Against the bedeviled turmoil of a Hotspur, he sets Falstaffian life. But against Falstaff's nihilism, he sets a modified code of honor and historical continuity that is a consolidation of the traditions of the old in harmony with present realities. In his most stirring affirmation in *2 Henry IV*, Hal draws a particularly English bridge over the gap of historical change, uniting in a single unit the old and the new. "The tide of blood in me," he confesses,

> Hath proudly flow'd in vanity till now.
> Now doth it turn and ebb back to the sea,
> Where it shall mingle with the state of floods
> And flow henceforth in formal majesty.
> (V.ii.129–133)

Despite the disruption of Bolingbroke's revolution, despite the new realism of his house, continuity has been maintained — and more than maintained, gloriously advanced. Aristocratic and bourgeois, Hal represents the great tendency toward amalgamation of virtues that we had already observed in Spenser, and had further seen to be crucial to the problem of time in the Renaissance.

For Harry Levin, in his important essay "English Literature of the Renaissance," Bacon's "Merchants of Light" symbolize "the belated yet determining role that Englishmen played in the Renaissance, the mediating practicality that reshaped its ideas into those of the Enlightenment." [29] While we could see in "Merchants of Light" the several facets of time, it is the phrase "mediating practicality" that is justified by many points in this study, and which the history plays dramatize. We could say that the fundamental contrast between the house of York and the house of Lancaster was the absence of this mediating practicality in the former. They too unreservedly in Shakespeare's plays took over the Machiavellian line, without submitting to the larger needs of time and place. In the Marlovian vein, they were too unmitigated in their adoptions, without transforming their desires to the larger needs of life and order. If Richard II, Henry VI, and Falstaff were too negligent or improvident, the Richards of the first tetralogy were too aggressive and belligerent. And yet Shakespeare, and the directions of English thought in the Renaissance, sensed the importance of time and the need for man to manage it effectively, to husband it. Somewhere between the premature reliance on being and the unscrupulous seizure of time must, unfortunately, lie the difficult shadow area of proper action. Man can act safely in time, but it involves heavy responsibilities and burdens, with the quieter rewards and consolations of the ways of peace and succession. Indeed, given the Baconian context of Professor Levin's remarks, the second tetralogy — with its faith in a virtuous control of experience stabilized by the successful father-son relationship, with its recognition of a hard objective reality and the need for man to be modest in the face of his vulnerable exposure, yet through this submission to the laws of nature to be able, in turn, to control experience — the later group of history plays seems to have found its proper setting.

Civilization can indeed be said to progress in the sense that tendencies which were streams and springs continue to develop until they are rivers. So it has been with the growing capitalist, middle-class society of roughly the past millennium. At various stages in the course of the Renaissance we have seen a general compatibility of views between the writers examined in this study and the developing rhythms of their society. But in most cases this presumed coincidence of energies was based upon mistaken identification of interests. On the one hand, while civilization continues to develop and perfect its instruments, the life of the individual man comes to an end. This is one rub that compels us to pause before the issues of time and being. The other dilemma is caused by the casualties attending the particular development of the West, and its concern with time. In their responses to time most of the writers we have discussed experienced something redemptive and illuminating, stirring and heroic. But the development of society was to leave behind the more generous and fulfilling aspects of time, to disunite the earlier combinations of elements, and lay bare its narrow, utilitarian, and money-saving implications. These two discoveries — that social identification and continuity hardly provide the kind of fortification required against the larger enemies of life, and that the triumph of time itself seemed to invalidate the more heroic qualities of individual life — brought most of our writers to the realization that man needed to be defined not in relation to on-going society, but in relation to the cosmos and his own abiding nature. When Shakespeare moves from the world of history to that of tragedy, these two discoveries will play an important part. The ways of civilization will develop along the realistic, prudential lines for which not Henry V but Benjamin Franklin would be a typical voice, but Shakespeare will call back Falstaff, at least in his new incarnations as Hamlet, Lear, and Antony, and rivet our attention to the tragic cry of change.

Between History and Tragedy: *Macbeth*

E. M. W. Tillyard has called *Macbeth* "the culminating version . . . the epilogue to the Histories," and thus justifies its present position in this study.[30] Quite rightly he links *Macbeth* with *Richard III,* "where likewise the body politic asserts itself against the monstrous individual." (p. 357) The many points where the two plays touch are not to our purpose here, but it must be pointed out that Macbeth's hellish character, like Richard's, is finally determined by the massacre of the innocent children. Like Richard, Macbeth is a "hellhound," and the same infernal infrastructure prevails in both plays. If anything, it is more apparent in the later play: the porter to Macbeth's castle makes plain the dismal area that Macduff and Lennox are entering; Macbeth himself dramatically visits some underworld, and finally, in his disintegration, his remaining confidant is "Seyton." But, as in the history plays, countervailing potentials for growth exist. Duncan vows to increase Macbeth's honors: "I have begun to plant thee and will labour / To make thee full of growing." (I.iv.28–29) But Macbeth, so committed to the future, despoils the possibilities of such growth, and this is most sharply evident in the determined war he wages against lineage. The Prince of Cumberland is the added step over which he is obliged to leap, and to the stunned children of Duncan he profanes the commonplaces of the father-son link when he informs them of the death of their father. "What is amiss?" Donalbain asks, and Macbeth replies,

> You are, and do not know't.
> The spring, the head, the fountain of your blood
> Is stopp'd, the very source of it is stopp'd.
> (II.iii.102–105)

The Weird Sisters' prophecy that Banquo will father a line of kings sticks in Macbeth's throat. In his rivalry with Banquo's promising future, the typical dead-end fate of the tyrant is the direct object of Macbeth's concern:

> Upon my head they plac'd a fruitless crown
> And put a barren sceptre in my gripe,
> Thence to wrench'd with an unlineal hand,
> No son of mine succeeding. If't be so,
> For Banquo's issue have I fil'd my mind.
>
> (III.i.61–65)

Macbeth has given his "eternal jewel" to the devil — "the common enemy of man" — and his very actions will help to make Banquo's heirs kings. But even beyond these future rewards — where Macbeth feels his own ambition to be repudiated — the anxious conspirator senses a deeper-lying character division, a more fundamental rebuke, in the personal integrity of Banquo, as much the object of his fixation as is Banquo's line:

> Our fears in Banquo
> Stick deep; and in his royalty of nature
> Reigns that which would be fear'd. 'Tis much he dares,
> And to that dauntless temper of his mind
> He hath a wisdom that doth guide his valour
> To act in safety. There is none but he
> Whose being I do fear; and under him
> My Genius is rebuk'd, as it is said
> Mark Antony's was by Caesar.
>
> (III.i.49–57)

Banquo's capacity to act in safety would have its most natural habitat in the world of the histories, where he would be a prototypal figure. That he does not live to see his efforts — in this instance his restraint — justified, his line established, is one of the painful facts that separates *Macbeth* from the histories.

The scene in which Banquo falls victim to Macbeth's plot while his son Fleance is able to escape is richly significant, emblematic of the large place that the father-son, augmentative code occupies in Shakespeare's vision. As prelude to this scene, Macbeth, showing how far he has advanced in the arts of black magic, summons up the murderous forces of the world:

> Come, seeling night,
> Scarf up the tender eye of pitiful day,
> And with thy bloody and invisible hand
> Cancel and tear to pieces that great bond
> Which keeps me pale. Light thickens, and the crow
> Makes wing to th' rooky wood.
> Good things of day begin to droop and drowse,
> Whiles night's black agents to their preys do rouse.
> (III.ii.46–53)

Lady Macbeth can only stand aside, a passive marveling spectator, as her husband shows his proficiency in the arts of which she was his teacher (see I.v.39–53, where she similarly calls on the spirits of dark night). The audience, too, must gasp when in the next scene of ambush it witnesses the dark powers apparently responding to Macbeth's conjurings. Night spreads slowly throughout the universe (and presumably the stage world) as Banquo and Fleance approach the waiting assassins. One of the murderers paints the scene in words:

> The west yet glimmers with some streaks of day.
> Now spurs the lated traveller apace
> To gain the timely inn, and near approaches
> The subject of our watch.
> (III.iii.5–8)

This picture might suggest some flickering moral qualm, some instinctive recollection of a time before the speaker was made reckless by the world's buffets. The complement of this remnant of light is the suggestion of man's creations, which provide protection against elemental and human darkness. The inn is timely, a pocket of light in a world given over to blackness. It represents the order that man attempts to impose, and it corresponds to the lighted torch that Fleance carries, and which Banquo calls for as they approach the treacherous castle. This is a wonderful metaphoric scene, showing the value Shakespeare placed on the great bond of father and son. Banquo and Fleance carry their own light. They symbolize peaceful succession in which man tries to make his way and bestow the legacy of his person and achievements on his children. Observing the sky, Banquo notes its darkness. Earlier, at the beginning of Act Two, Banquo had remarked to Fleance that the stars are extinguished, but attributes it to "husbandry," or economy, thrift, in heaven (the word of course suggests procreation, also), and at the approach of an unknown (Macbeth) he warily calls for his sword. The treachery felt then in Act Two is fully realized in Act Three: Banquo's observation that it will rain is the murderers' cue to strike, "Let it come down!" The scene is rich with symbolic significance: emphasizing the irony that Macbeth's own actions pave the way for Banquo's descendants (an irony that operated when Richard III made possible the accession of the Tudors), so in this scene it is under the very cover of blackness that Fleance manages his escape.

In *Macbeth* tensions exist between the grasp for the extraordinary, the attempt at grandeur, and the enduring strengths of the commonplace world that has been left behind — and in this the play invites comparison with other tragedies of damnation, Dante's *Inferno* and the first several books of *Paradise Lost*. It is further part of the dialectic of the histories, and part of the problem of time in the Renaissance, that the mundane should be invested with prestige. Macbeth violates the father-son bond and it becomes richly representative. Similarly, in contrast to the horrid tyranny of Macbeth, Edward the Confessor, the English king who receives Malcolm, is more valued as the healing king, *le roi thaumaturge*. (IV.iii.141–159) It is with his help that the Scottish lords hope to give again

> to our tables meat, sleep to our nights,
> Free from our feasts and banquets bloody knives,
> Do faithful homage and receive free honors —
> All which we pine for now.
>
> (III.vi.33–37)

These overlooked dignities and necessities of normal civilization acquire richness in their disruption — then they are pined for. So it is in the witches' own words that Banquo, who despite some temptations remained within the bounds of order, is "lesser than Macbeth, and greater," "not so happy, yet much happier." Oddly enough, Macbeth himself seems more heroic when he is operating as Duncan's subordinate than when he moves to violate the regular orders of vassalage. In the treacherous waters of conspiracy, Macbeth is torn by doubts and irresolution, panic and even cowardice, but he is Bellona's bridgegroom, valour's minion when he himself beats down rebellion, and curbs the "lavish spirit" of proud Norway (assisted by the Thane of Cawdor). He then knows no division between mind and action, but enjoys a wholeness and instantaneousness of response, "point against point, rebellious arm against arm." (I.ii.50–57) As a subordinate he enjoyed a security which he will always be seeking outside that order — then he was "lapp'd in proof." Later Macbeth, with his kingdom in dissolution and all the chickens coming home to roost, with his end of life before him, will make a desperate gesture to recapture that old heroism. But there has been too much abuse along the way, and we look beyond his remnants of martial skill to the story of his life, to his earliest beginnings, and reflect more upon human life itself. A gash has been made (in *King Lear* we think of the state as being gored, but in *Macbeth* it is a gash) and now the wound is closing. We do not envy Macbeth, nor do we regret his passing, but still we sit in awe and terrible reflection before the passage of his life. This is why the Weird Sisters preside throughout the play. They do not determine actions but rather dance in attendance whenever fatal choices are made. Two men, flush with success, encounter their destinies in an as yet undetermined terrain: the day is still ambiguous, "foul and fair." Directions are in suspension which will thereafter clarify and harden:

> If you can look into the seeds of time
> And say which grain will grow and which will not.
> (I.iii.58–59)

We should like to say that it was at the crossroads, even where three roads meet, that two lives acquire their character and definition. But we do not need to make that addition from *Oedipus Rex* to see how similar Shakespearean fate is to that of Greek tragedy.

Answering Macbeth's own call, the objectification of his deepest desires, the Weird Sisters precipitate the crisis of his life. All thoughts and actions will lead up to that single, decisive event, the killing of Duncan, from which all future consequences will derive. The nature of that act will require further actions, as the usurper is himself aware, but it is primarily his own personality that places Macbeth in bondage. A terrible anxiety, a tragic vulnerability reveals Macbeth's lack of aptitude for the role toward which he aspires. He is one of those souls — apprehensive before the event — of whom Montaigne was thinking when he quoted Seneca, "Calamitosus est animus futuri anxius." Removed from common discourse Macbeth is lost in his own soliloquy:

> Present fears
> Are less than horrible imaginings.

> My thought, whose murther yet is but fantastical,
> Shakes so my single state of man that function
> Is smother'd in surmise and nothing is
> But what is not.
>
> (I.iii.137–142)

As Bellona's bridegroom, Macbeth could "disdain Fortune," that is, be careless of consequences as he cuts his way through his opponents' lines; but as a secret conspirator his cloth is ill fitting. His own imagination invokes comparisons with Banquo's more stable and successful qualities. A regal kind of Peter principle is here revealed, as Macbeth rises to the level of his incompetence.

In his role as a conspirator, Macbeth is an unlikely man of action, lacking the necessary decisiveness and determination. Early in the plot, we see in him a tendency to place the outcome of an event in other hands than his own; he is shown to incline toward drift: "If chance will have me King, why, chance may crown me, / Without my stir," and "Come what come may, / Time and the hour runs through the roughest day." (I.iii.143–147) Not that he abandons his ambitions, but their realization must be brought about by agencies external to himself:

> Stars, hide your fires!
> Let not light see my black and deep desires.
> The eye wink at the hand; yet let that be,
> Which the eye fears, when it is done, to see.
>
> (I.iv.50–53)

Lady Macbeth understands this characteristic in her husband; he would not play false, and yet he would wrongly win. In a play of many external agencies, from the Sisters to the knife that "marshalls Macbeth the way that he was going," Lady Macbeth — challenging her husband's manhood — is strongest in propelling him toward destruction.

There is another division between the partners in greatness and evil. His wife at first is utterly without Macbeth's anxiety over the future. In fact, although her husband is not yet king, she seems to savor by foretaste the greatness of the office: "I feel now / The future in the instant." The assassination of Duncan is "this night's great business,"

> Which shall to all our nights and days to come
> Give solely sovereign sway and masterdom.
>
> (I.v.58–59, 69–71)

Her ambitions are fairly clear, and once they are attained she is willing to rest with the attainment: she has none of her husband's mad projections into the future.

> Naught's had, all's spent,
> Where our desire is got without content.
> 'Tis safer to be that which we destroy
> Than by destruction dwell in doubtful joy.
>
> . . . . .
>
> Things without all remedy
> Should be without regard. What's done is done.
>
> (III.ii. 4–12)

Yet in her own disintegration, her mind shows itself to have been seared by the terror of their actions. As she relives in her sleep the actions of the past she is dramatic testimony to the play's theme that what is done is not done, but continues to spread: "who would have thought the old man to have had so much blood in him?" and "Here's the smell of the blood still." (V.i.44–45, 56) The morality function of the play is reinforced when the great queen's madness is witnessed by the gentlewoman, who keeps to the order of pieties ("I would not have such a heart in my bosom for the dignity of the whole body," 61–62), and the doctor, the representative of bodily order.

Macbeth does not have his wife's determination or her willingness to be content in the present (although in each trait her capacity falls somewhat short of her speech). He betrays a need for an absolute security that plunges him wildly into the future, and that consequently precludes any possibility of final safety. "To be thus is nothing, / But to be safely thus" — and he determines the plot against Banquo and Fleance. (III.i.48–49) Macbeth's own need to find the "be-all and end-all" converts him into the living example of his homiletic soliloquy: his own actions will return to plague their inventor. Macbeth's persistent need is this requirement of total certainty. The Weird Sisters "have more than mortal knowledge in them." In fact, all the external agencies upon which Macbeth is so reliant provide for him a sense of sufficiency that he could never find in himself. This play of "political ambition" is moved by strangely non-political motives. When told that Fleance is escaped, Macbeth's security is again dashed:

> Then comes my fit again. I had else been perfect;
> Whole as the marble, founded as the rock,

> As broad and general as the casing air.
> But now I am cabin'd, cribb'd, confin'd, bound in
> To saucy doubts and fears.
>
> (III.iv.21–25)

Macbeth's own pathetic and eager helplessness comes out in his desire to know the future. He "burn'd in desire" to question the witches further, he writes to his wife; before his real journey to the underworld, he is "bent to know / By the worst means the worst. For mine own good / All causes shall give way"; and in his audience with the apparitions, his "heart throbs to know one thing." The strongest non-political motivation is his rivalry with Banquo. What Macbeth throbs to know is if Banquo's line will ever reign in Scotland, and it is these future projections that cause Macbeth to expend his energy on personal issues out of proportion to their present realities. The division between the worlds of Banquo and Macbeth runs deep in this play. Banquo chose to remain within the order of history, with its consolations of order and succession, while Macbeth rose out of that order through violence. He will always be haunted therefore by images of growth that escape the slash of his knife. Fleance and through him Banquo's line are that part of future regeneration and growth that elude the clutches of the tyrant. To Lady Macbeth's plea for contentment in the present, Macbeth can only argue,

> We have scotch'd the snake, not kill'd it.
> She'll close, and be herself, whilst our poor malice
> Remains in danger of her former tooth.
>
> (III.ii.13–15)

Banquo, the grown serpent, lies dead, but Fleance, the offspring, has fled. While he cannot harm them in the present, still Macbeth reflects that the fled worm "hath nature that in time will venom breed." The world of the future, of growth, always eludes Macbeth's absolutist grasp. Since Macbeth the tyrant is punished in his "unlineal hand," he shares the fates of the other rulers who ran afoul of the ethic of Shakespeare's history plays, whether the over-aggressive Richard III, or the ineffectual Henry VI and Richard II. We can see here how critical is the notion of progeny that extends with profound ramifications throughout Shakespeare's political and historical world.

Oddly enough, rather than Richard III, whose superficial fate Macbeth reproduces, in his fundamental character he more resembles

Richard II. He too requires external forms of support; in his case they are infernal rather than providential reliances, but they condemn him to the same political ineffectiveness. The witches' doggerel, another instance of common wisdom under a specious façade, is almost explicit in its prophecy of Macbeth's pending defeat:

> He shall spurn fate, scorn death, and bear
> His hopes 'bove wisdom, grace, and fear;
> And you all know security
> Is mortals' chiefest enemy.
>
> (III.v.30–33)

Macbeth believes his life "charmed" but is immediately cowed when Macduff discloses the nature of his birth; and the formidable castle, which would scorn an attack, he abandons when told of the movements of Birnam Wood. The banal outcomes of the high-sounding witches' prophecies is part of the plot of the play, which shows such commonality asserting itself against lofty assurances and insecurities.

Like *Richard III,* Macbeth is aetiological: it makes use of past history to provide a dramatic explanation of current values. The Tudors emerge at the end of the earlier play, and the later one looks forward to the Stuarts. But the plays are more valuable in filling in the spiritual background, rather than the political background. Like Aeschylus in his *Oresteia,* Shakespeare shows the dramatic personal reasons behind current practice. The commonplaces of order must be measured against the public and private chaos represented by Richard III and Macbeth. When Macduff proclaims "The time is free," the meaning of that phrase is reinforced by our awareness of the full terror of a system of fear and of spies, of sleepless nights and of haunted feasts.

Despite all of these important relationships with the histories — and they operate on fundamental levels of imagery and consistent pattern — still *Macbeth* as a play eludes that category. It simply leads us to a level of reflection that the histories do not. And this is primarily due to that speech, so appropriate for Macbeth's anxious, projecting mind: "To-morrow, and to-morrow, and to-morrow . . ." At the end of his tether, Macbeth is told that Lady Macbeth is dead, and he catches himself in the commonplace reflection — toward which he was so prone near the end — that "there would have been a time for such a word"; that is, in Samuel Johnson's reading, "Her death should have been deferred to a more peaceful hour; had she lived longer, there would have been a more conventional time for such a word." [31] The following famous speech shows his awareness that he too has fallen into the common fallacy of always looking to a tomorrow. The moral pattern of the play is expressed in this amoral speech — the ironic, retributory action of the play, where a rebellious thane of Cawdor has replaced a rebellious thane of Cawdor, and has come to something of the same end: "all our yesterdays have lighted fools / The way to dusty death." Basically, however the speech is nihilistic; it does not take account of the restorative and healing powers in life, of the possibilities for growth, of all the satisfactions, successes, and even wisdom available to historical man. Macbeth errs in his description of life, as the play itself and its re-establishment of order attest. Yet, while he is talking about life, we are thinking about him, his essay at greatness, his agony — all the sound and fury — and then as the wound in the state closes, his nothingness. The advancement in internalization of experience that this play makes on *Richard III* aids our distinctive concentration on the fate of this hero, whose beginning and end we have witnessed, and whose own speech makes the final nothingness resound. Perhaps even some of his own nihilism rubs off on us. When man has grown fat and satisfied, and loses any authentic connection with his own welfare, when the commonplaces of existence become again banal, will not another thane of Cawdor make his push for grandeur, gash the body politic and perish in his own chaos? While existence is not meaningless, nevertheless the almost periodic basis of such revolutions suggests man's terrible need to pass beyond peaceful historical succession.

Chapter 9
Shakespeare's Tragedies

Introduction

Man in the histories ideally looks to past and future. Continuity, whether in the form of allegiance to past models or provision for the future through children, is practically a touchstone, and those characters who run afoul the nature of the world and proper government are doomed to isolation and discontinuity. The sonnets stress the relation between singleness and nothingness. Richard III assassinates the children, Henry VI disinherits his, Richard II has none: and all are destroyed. Shakespeare's dramatic scope, the tetralogy itself, seems to provide physical endorsement of this historical value. Given sufficient length, he seems to intimate, the temporal process will eventually yield fulfillment. The first tetralogy culminates in the founder of the reigning house of Shakespeare's day, and the second in the ideal representative of the values of the modern English ruler. In the perfection of time, through growth and development, order will be achieved. In his histories Shakespeare is very much like Aeschylus, who also required a series of plays in order to show his own reconciliation of opposites, his own sense of order eventually coming out of chaos.

In his tragedies, on the other hand, Shakespeare is closer to Sophocles, particularly the *Oedipus Rex*. The values of continuity are no longer effective (although they might still operate as values). Lines of extension cannot be maintained. Historical connections vanish as the thread of the present is cut off from past and future. Hamlet says there will be no more marriages, and Antony and Cleopatra and Romeo and Juliet are reminders of that tragic truth. The children revolt in *King*

Lear, and Hamlet is deprived of his succession (while his mother marries the interloper). Hal was only temporarily the shadow of succession; the hopes and expectations of his time were eventually realized. But the expectations that serve as attainable values in the histories are blighted at their very source in the tragedies. The flowers with which Gertrude had thought to deck Ophelia's marriage bed she strews on her grave. The garden is no longer potentially fruitful; it is from the very beginning "unweeded." The on-going rhythms of the race and civilization do not provide the needed consolation or triumph. Quite literally Hamlet must endure an "orphanhood in time," and find his redemption in the height and depth of the present. In the ripeness of time Hal will come to fulfillment, but Hamlet must learn, with Edgar, that the ripeness is all.

The narrowing focus of tragic contraction seems to reduce life to the enigmatic present. The future is unforeseeable. The situation is quite different in the two historical tetralogies. In the first a curse is operating, and the action is rounded out by means of dire predictions and their fulfillments. But in *Hamlet,* "We defy augury." In plays so dominated by error, by "accidental judgments, casual slaughters," what is to come is by its nature unknowable. Man must stand ready, with Petrarch, to answer any call. "Since no man knows aught of what he leaves, what is't to leave betimes? Let be." (V.ii.233–234) The skepticism of the tragedies is even more distant from the second tetralogy, where curse was replaced by plausibility and the master-process by human control. We remember Henry IV's fears that Richard possessed some special knowledge when he predicted the events of the subsequent years; but another interpretation is offered — Warwick's — that past events lend reasonable grounds for future possibilities: "Such things become the hatch and brood of time." Time partakes of its essential nature in the histories: showing promise and connection, or continuity. This means that the properly attuned mind can act in safety, and Warwick's explanation is answered by Henry IV's firm resolve of action: "Are these things then necessities? / Then let us meet them like necessities!" (*2 Henry IV,* III.i.92–93) But in the tragedies neither knowledge nor action is reliable. Ophelia's deranged cries show essential knowledge: "Lord, we know what we are, but know not what we may be." Here man does not act upon but rather suffers his necessities: "I hope all will be well. We must be patient . . ."

In the second tetralogy, at least, time is ample and still free. Irremediable actions have not yet been taken. Its very length suggests hope and possibility. But in the tragedies, length of time is abridged to briefer periods, and attempts are even made to conceal the actual extent of those durations. Things happen in the "thrice of time." There is no time for deliberation, that rational distancing which allows for long-range conclusions. As the future appears constricted, so are the horizontal possibilities of succession. The very pulse of the plays seems aroused, like that of the tragic heroes, wanting to gain by intensity what it cannot have by duration. Illumination breaks out of the middle level of history and civilization and seems to unfold the vertical stretches of heaven and hell. Cosmic extension is given to the issues which were held within social forms in the histories. This intensity, this brief but all-revealing light, is part of the contracted measures of the tragedies.

In formal and thematic ways tragedy serves the impression of contraction. One of Aristotle's definitions of tragedy calls it "an imitation of an action that is serious, complete and of a certain magnitude." [1] Completeness, the comprehended beginning, middle, and end of any action, is pleasurable in itself. If we think back to the events of Dallas and their aftermath, we see that, mixed with the world's reaction to the wretched end of Jack Ruby, was a feeling of satisfaction that it had seen the beginning and now was witnessing the end of a very significant action. Completeness satisfies a fundamental human instinct, where we seem to apprehend causality. This perception of coherence can be fulfilling, since it represents an important victory over time.[2] From the turmoil of experience, the flux of continuity, a pattern is perceived, and the lines of a life stand revealed.

These purely formal attributes obviously shade off into thematic corollaries. And indeed, a close relation exists between the completeness of the tragic story and the metaphysical content of tragedy. Process of time is not just arbitrary: there is an inevitable connection between events. The agonists are in the grips of the necessary relation between the past and the present. For Alfred North Whitehead, the essence of tragedy "resides in the solemnity of the remorseless working of things." [3] And in a book whose title, *Moira,* ought to be used more frequently in the discussion of Shakespearean tragedy, W. C. Greene writes, "The development of tragedy . . . no less than the propensity of serious poets, drew attention from the mere sequence of events to some conception of their relationship." [4] Such interrelations of experiences reside partly in the objective flow of events themselves and partly in the perceptions of the participating characters, but whatever their origins they give to the plays their tragic ethos.

As an example, one could look at *Julius Caesar,* that "gateway to the tragedies," where a fatal canopy of beginnings and ends hangs over its resolution.[5] As his presence and his plans dominated the action in the first three acts, the ghost of Caesar returns to continue that dominance in the last two. There is no escaping his track. Events do not seem to be moving toward an open future, but rather toward some fatal, pre-determined end. And yet remorselessness can have its solemnity, and the hours of farewell and final things can breathe a cleansed air. Brutus will not go bound to Rome, "But this same day / Must end that work the ides of March begun." (V.i.112–113) When Caesar's ghost visits Brutus the second time, he knows his "hour is come." (V.v.20) As death approaches, Brutus' "bones would rest, / That have but labour'd to attain this hour." (41–42) All of his efforts, his apparent free actions, were merely laborious ways — "rough-hewn"? — of achieving this destined conclusion. Caesar's restless ghost can now "be still." In fact, there is a retributive completion, seen by both Cassius and Brutus, in their deaths. As Pindarus stabs him, Cassius addresses the absent but ever-present giant,

> Caesar, thou art reveng'd
> Even with the sword that kill'd thee.
> (V.iii.45–46)

And coming upon the catastrophe of the dead Cassius and Titinius, Brutus echoes his comrade's words,

> O Julius Caesar, thou art mighty yet!
> Thy spirit walks abroad and turns our swords
> In our own proper entrails.
>
> (94–96)

There is another kind of contraction, which is less related to action, and more to perception. Before the battle at Phillipi, Cassius informs Messala, "This is my birthday; as this very day / Was Cassius born." (V.i.71–72) And when he sends Pindarus to spy out the fortunes of war, he again reflects ominously:

> This day I breathed first. Time is come round,
> And where I did begin, there shall I end.
> My life is run his compass.
> (V.iii.23–25)

The tragic pattern contains no linear projection; rather, the future is closed, and our attention is fixed on the significant closing of a life. Two elements are important here. They are both summarized in a phrase from Tolstoy, whose short stories richly attest to this strange power of final things. In *Hadji Murad,* Tolstoy himself intervenes to comment on the business-as-usual attitude with which the men met the death of another: "None of them saw in this death that most important moment of a life, its termination and return to the source whence it sprang." This final hour itself is powerful in any man's life, but its significance is increased when it is conjunctive with the first hour. In a way not possible when the future still remained hopeful, the individual (and also the audience) achieves a sense of being in the tragic rounding-out and completion of the individual life. In a way, the premonition of Cassius, and such fatal coincidence, is a common human reaction, lending the mind alleviation in disaster. The search for coincidence, or pattern, seems to rob death of some of its mad sting, and, as in the completeness of the story, seems to extract meaning from pointless event. On the death of Queen Elizabeth, the historian William Camden fixed on the fact that "on the 24. of March, being the Eve of the Annunication of the Blessed Virgin, she (who was born on the Eve of the Nativity of the same Blessed Virgin) was called out of the Prison of her earthly Body." [6] And it is perhaps to honor Shakespeare's own preoccupations with such significant contractions that tradition continues to observe his birthday on April 23, which was also the date of his death.

In all of the tragedies significant contractions occur. Faced with the fact of their own termination, the tragic heroes, like tragedy itself, pack with intensity their shorter periods of existence. Although they might be different from the type represented by Cassius in *Julius Caesar,* nevertheless their perceptions serve the same purpose: in the approach of death, life is energized by significant collocations, as if, in ending, it is also enjoying completion.

Despite the sublimity of the last act of *Julius Caesar,* where characters rise out of the historical world to perceive a destiny and the rhythm of tragedy, this play reveals a close relation to the histories: it has none of those lyrical resources of human love or remembrance or fidelity that the tragedies raise and advocate, nor the contest between these ideal forces and the human vulnerability to time and change. The great issues of Shakespeare's tragedies have not been joined. In this regard, *Romeo and Juliet* might serve as a better gateway.

Tragedies of Love

Santayana's formula treats Shakespeare's tragic vision with the comprehensiveness it requires: "For everything in nature is lyrical in its ideal essence, tragic in its fate, and comic in its existence." [7] Unlike the histories, where ambition and glory are the only activators of human energy, in the tragedies love is a powerful force. In plays like *Romeo and Juliet, Troilus and Cressida, Antony and Cleopatra*, fidelity in love is a means of continuity. In its renewing and creative energies it represents a triumph over time. If the earlier sonnets (as I discussed them in the last chapter) provide the frame of augmentative time by which we can understand the histories, the profession of faith in sonnets 116 and 124 helps us to understand the aspirations in these tragedies of love.

Juliet is the model for all of Shakespeare's frank heroines when she pledges her willingness to yield herself to her lover. Like the sea, she withdraws herself only in order to give herself again:

> My bounty is as boundless as the sea,
> My love as deep; the more I give to thee,
> The more I have, for both are infinite.
> (II.ii.133–135)

Romeo too speaks of the awakening powers of love.

> Love goes toward love as schoolboys from their books;
> But love from love, toward school with heavy looks.
> (157–158)

The same contrast between the heaviness of schoolboys and the energies aroused by love is the basis of Berowne's lectures to his fellow academicians in *Love's Labour's Lost*.

> Why, universal plodding prisons up
> The nimble spirits in the arteries,
> As motion and long-during action tires
> The sinewy vigour of the traveller.
> (IV.iii.305–308)

Love, learned in the woman's eyes, rather than fatiguing and wearing down the primal energy seems to add to the total resources of the individual, giving to "every power a double power / Above their functions and their offices." (331–332) While normal "slow arts" appeal to the brain, the desires of love arouse the total being with heightened powers.

Indeed, it is "the true Promethean fire," one stolen from the gods, and which raises man above his mortal heaviness.

In *Romeo and Juliet,* the time and the fates of those who respond to the Promethean fire contrast radically with those who are more at home in the easy world of the comedy of existence, the plodding imperfect world of change. We must qualify these remarks with the understanding that ideally love is not by itself an antisocial force. In the comedies, for instance, love comes to terms with the surrounding realities and eventually serves as a renewing force in society. In *Romeo and Juliet* the same possibilities are suggested; after his marriage with Juliet, Romeo loses all of his doom-eagerness and serves as a willing peacemaker. Requited love in Shakespeare is an introduction to a sane reality, lending support to the banner, "Make love not war." But when, in the tragedies, this experience of love is denied continued existence, the high idealism of love becomes its terrible opposite. Isolated from society and the guiding hand of older wisdom, the young lovers are thrown back on the dangerous tendencies within their own natures and are exposed to tragic fate.

There is something in the very nature of the love to which they open themselves that exposes them more readily to disaster. On the one hand, passion clouds reason (witness the mistaken suicides of Romeo and Antony) and limits their field of maneuver. But on the other hand, their experience in love is so overwhelming that other considerations appear banal, and the ordinary world moribund and constrictive. Love is at the cutting edge of experience. Intensity is not relaxed with disappointment, but rather diverted to an equal passion for death. Denied normal extension to their desires, the lovers no longer entertain hopes of continuity, but instead contract experience, bringing together in a terrible way, the womb and the tomb, the penis and the asp. In their march toward death there is something as dark and as powerful as sex itself that draws them on. Love is a killer and death a lover. "The stroke of death is as a lover's pinch / Which hurts and is desired." "Unsubstantial death is amorous and keeps Juliet as his paramour." The same resoluteness is seen in Romeo's toast to the poison. Far from being resigned to a providential system, Romeo is an angry young man who has been fed the bitter end and will bite it to the very stalk:

> Come bitter conduct; come, unsavoury guide!
> Thou desperate pilot, now at once run on
> The dashing rocks thy seasick weary bark!
>
> (V. iii. 116–118)

And after Cressida's betrayal, Troilus seems to call for death, shouting down its very throat. While this response differs from the kind of contraction we will meet in *Hamlet,* or even *King Lear,* nevertheless the principle of tragic contraction persists, where lovers hope to seize in depth the experience that is being denied them in length.

Around the young lovers, committed to life as lyrical essence, are older people who have adjusted to the world of change. They tend to look to the past and suggest a time older than the moment of passionate love. Their vision of the world has much in common with Montaigne's closed comedy. Containing little lyricism, making do with small insistencies, they manage to survive and, in an uninspired way, convert passionate intensity into social choice. Unlike the lovers, the representatives of what could be called extended time are in no hurry to come to the point. The garrulous Nurse will tell and tell over again the events of the past. She estimates the present age by the deaths, births, and earthquakes in her memory. It is hard for her to take seriously the passions of the girl whose bumps and knocks she ministered to. This vision is essentially reductive, living in small expectations. It is not an unattractive world, and it has its own ease, humor, and stability. Rich in the comedies, where it shows an overseeing wisdom and flexibility, its most fertile ground is Shakespeare's last plays. Those who entertain these longer vistas have the primary virtue of flexibility in the face of man's changing conditions. But in the tragedies when this flexibility hardens into pure insensitive stubbornness, or when its exponents become mere opportunists, or worse, then those who contract time and those who extend it cross swords.

In an ordinary world of festivities, of parodic speeches on Queen Mab, of old men thinking back some thirty years and a wet nurse back some fourteen, in short, in a simply human world of change with some stability, in the pandaric world of the comedy of existence, a different order of perception and desire is introduced:

> my mind misgives
> Some consequence, yet hanging in the stars,
> Shall bitterly begin his fearful date
> With this night's revels and expire the term
> Of a despised life, clos'd in my breast,
> By some vile forfeit of untimely death.
>
> (I.iv.106–111)

Earlier Romeo's love melancholy had given his father cause for worry. His perversion of the activities proper to day and night appears noxious:

> all so soon as the all-cheering sun
> Should in the farthest East begin to draw
> The shady curtain from Aurora's bed,
> Away from light steals home my heavy son
> And private in his chamber pens himself,
> Shuts up his windows, locks fair daylight out,
> And makes himself an artificial night.
>
> (I.i.141–147)

To the father who cannot understand this strange and unaccustomed behavior cutting across his normal expectations, this "humor" is "black and portentous." The voice of the father, as we saw in the histories, is the voice of good counsel, urging appropriate actions in time, those which would further the development of the experienced adult. But Romeo closes himself to scrutiny and counsel. It is as hard to find out his malaise as it is to discover the canker in the closed bud. And this introduces another note of inauspiciousness and fear that Romeo's life might be cut short by this premature sickness,

> As is the bud bit with an envious worm
> Ere he can spread his sweet leaves to the air
> Or dedicate his beauty to the sun.
>
> (158–160)

Against this higher pressure of ominousness, Romeo's friend Benvolio introduces a common, easier world of change. To Romeo's love sickness he administers the potion (as a sestet) which Ariosto had espoused and Montaigne advocated: change.

> one fire burns out another's burning;
> One pain is less'ned by another's anguish;
> Turn giddy, and be holp by backward turning;
> One desperate grief cures with another's languish.
> Take thou some new infection to thy eye,
> And the rank poison of the old will die.
>
> (I.ii.46–51)

One nail will drive out another; one screw spin out another. In this world there are few things that are permanent and that cannot be reversed. It is an uninsistent, non-tragic, everyday world, represented by the convivial comfort and good humor of Capulet, the loquaciousness of the Nurse — with their bumbling sense of easy natural time — and even the profanity of Mercutio. The fact is that after he meets Juliet, Romeo would gladly be part of this familiar world. His love-sickness over the inaccessible Rosaline disappears in the reciprocated love of Juliet; her living responsiveness counters his adolescent fondness for death. When Friar Laurence chides him for thus forgetting Rosaline over whom he shed such tears, and accuses him of fickleness, Romeo vindicates himself;

> She whom I love now
> Doth grace for grace and love for love allow.
> The other did not so.
>
> (II.iii.85–87)

But the presence of the long-standing feud — which few people take seriously but none repudiates — converts the secret marriage of the young lovers from a means of reconciliation (as Friar Laurence had hoped) into an agent of death. This perversion of a life force into the means of destruction was Shakespeare's early sense of tragedy in the mid-nineties. While the feud was hardly taken seriously, it still was part of the atmosphere that allowed killers like Tybalt to operate. Fresh from his marriage, Romeo comes upon the embroiled Tybalt and Mercutio. At Tybalt's hurled insult Romeo can only respond with the benevolence he now wishes toward the house of Capulet:

> Tybalt, the reason that I have to love thee
> Doth much excuse the appertaining rage
> To such a greeting.
>
> .   .   .   .   .
>
> I do protest I never injur'd thee,
> But love thee better than thou canst devise
> Till thou shalt know the reason of my love.
>
> (III.i.65–73)

Mercutio (also ignorant of the marriage) explodes at this presumed cowardice, challenges Tybalt, and destruction follows. In this southern tragedy, Romeo, who was on his way toward entering a world of stability and bounteous love, relapses into his old fatalism:

> This day's black fate on moe days doth depend;
> This but begins the woe others must end.
>
> (124–125)

Like the other tragic heroes who are swept away by quick and incomprehensible events, he is "fortune's fool."

As the feud's recrudescence allows Tybalt his right of maneuver and gives events a bad turn, so the humdrum world of existence loses its comic resilience and hardens into unreasoning and unyielding social convention. It is now her father's will that Juliet marry Paris — a person, we are told, she loathes. As the feud squeezes into its fatal noose the freedom that Romeo had gained, the stubborn hand of another past constricts the spirit of the lovers. Society dooms the creative powers of its own renewal.

Caught between banishment and an unwelcome choice, the young, isolated lovers feel at enmity with the passage of time. Although they would have earlier been most willing to merge with the processes of succession and society, now these processes are alien, part of a world of heaviness and exile. Like the fallen monarchs in the histories, their desires are at odds with normal sequence, and they desperately seek to maintain their precarious happiness. But time moves steadily on. Juliet refuses to believe that they must face separation, insisting that the lark's song is really that of the nightingale. But Romeo is realistic — "night's candles are burnt out." He knows he must be leaving or face death. In a remarkable dramatic scene the doomed lovers watch the inevitable spreading of day throughout their lives. Again the normal world is reversed, and the light of comfort which should be a modulated part of their love's night is only its dark reversal:

> *Juliet.* O, now be gone! More light and light it grows.
> *Romeo.* More light and light — more dark and dark our woes!
>
> (III.v.35–36)

Society — by means of the feud and the forced marriage to Paris — removes from the lovers any chance of bringing together ideal essence and the comedy of existence. Tragic ethos and character converge in their ill-divining souls:

> *Juliet.* Methinks I see thee, now thou art below,
> As one dead in the bottom of a tomb.
> Either my eyesight fails, or thou look'st pale.
> *Romeo.* And trust me, love, in my eye so do you.
>
> (55–58)

Romeo is wed to calamity, the lovers are star-crossed and death-marked. The past maintains its fatal grip; the choric prologue dictates the end of the play: everything is predetermined from the loins of these feuding households. Yet, this experimental tragedy does not reach a catharsis.[8] Rather we experience indignation. And as a matter of fact, whatever may have been lacking in the young lovers, their loss is regarded as an accusation and penalty against the feuding families. In language that suggests both the inversion and the contraction of the play, the prince charges Capulet and Montague:

> See what a scourge is laid upon your hate,
> That heaven finds means to kill your joys with love!
> (V.iii.292–293)

While Romeo and Juliet do not reflect on it, still their tragedy dramatically represents the truth of which the comic lovers of *A Midsummer Night's Dream* were fortunately aware: there is some hostility to love in the universe,

> Making it momentany as a sound,
> Swift as a shadow, short as any dream,
> Brief as the lightning in the collied night,
> That, in a spleen, unfolds both heaven and earth,
> And ere a man hath power to say "behold!"
> The jaws of darkness do devour it up:
> So quick bright things come to confusion.
> (I.i.143–148)

This passage summarizes the impressions of tragic love gathered from *Romeo and Juliet*: its brevity, its power (which, denied extension in time, seems to break loose in vertical destructive potency, unfolding heaven and hell), and the almost inevitable descent of those quick bright things into the tomb. Yet, despite these impressions *Romeo and Juliet* is domestic and local tragedy. Cosmic extension, necessary for tragedy, is not given their condition. But when we come to *Troilus and Cressida* and *Antony and Cleopatra* the desires and problems of the lovers have undergone a metaphysical heightening. The issues of love and time have become much more immediate in these plays: in fact, they form the patterns of reflection. In this context, love can supply the substance of tragedy, representing man's hopes and ideals, which are sadly and rudely negated by the facts of his existence. Love is a force of revival and transcendence that seems to redeem the heavy plodding world of mortality — it is Promethean, and as such, a challenge to the gods. As happiness flees from their grasp, the lovers are only left to reflect upon the cosmic enmity that tragically reminds man he is not a god.

Romeo has no cosmic quarrel. But in *Troilus and Cressida* and *Antony and Cleopatra*, clearer formulation and reflective extension are given to the issues of the earlier play. On the one hand, fidelity in love as a source of triumph over time becomes a dominant ideal, centrally placed and powerfully advocated, while on the other, the forces of change and human mutability correspondingly assume greater significance. In *Troilus* the intransigence of the young hero ("Never did young man fancy / With so eternal and so fix'd a soul") is placed in obvious combat with man's acknowledged changeableness. Even in love itself conflict exists between spiritual aspiration and physical fact: "This is the monstruosity in love, lady, that the will is infinite and the execution confin'd, that the desire is boundless and the act a slave to limit." (III.ii.87–90) "Infinite will" and "boundless desire" are the forces released in love, and yet throughout the play these forces are confronted with obstacles to their fulfillment. The division is sharp between man's spirit and his physical existence, and, while Troilus is firmly committed to unendingness, the play unmistakably presents the fact of change. And looming above all the rest and summarizing the essential conditions that limit fervent desire is time. Even before news arrives of the lovers' forced separation, the passing of night frustrates their need to preserve their moment of happiness. Cressida complains "Night hath been too brief." And Troilus curses,

> Beshrew the witch! With venomous wights she stays
> As tediously as hell, but flies the grasp of love
> With wings more momentary-swift than thought.
>
> (IV.ii.11–14)

"Momentary-swift" — (language reminiscent of the passage from *A Midsummer Night's Dream*) — these are the words with which the lovers are forced to reflect on their love. Some enmity does exist between man's desires and his realities in love, making the moments of happiness as ephemeral as a dream. The hostility is increased when the fortunes of war and larger reasons of state join with this spiritual dilemma. "Have the gods envy?" (IV.iv.30) asks Cressida when she must leave Troy for the Greek camp. And to Troilus the answer is too plain: their separation is an act of vengeance on the part of the gods

for the purity of his love to Cressida. (26–29) Not only are they forced
to leave, but suddenly.

> We two that with so many thousand sighs
> Did buy each other, must poorly sell ourselves
> With the rude brevity and discharge of one.
> Injurious Time now with a robber's haste
> Crams his rich thiev'ry up, he knows not how.
> As many farewells as be stars in heaven,
> With distinct breath and consign'd kisses to them,
> He fumbles up into a loose adieu,
> And scants us with a single famish'd kiss,
> Distasted with the salt of broken tears.
>
> (41–50)

Earlier Cressida also senses the enmity existing between man-in-love
and the gods. Anticipating regrets for her unpreventable frankness in
love and her clear willingness to yield herself to Troilus, she excuses
her lapse of more prudential reason as being the handicap man bears in
love. Her words join Shakespearean perception to the tragic worlds of
Homer and William Butler Yeats. They did not give us their wisdom
with their power: "for to be wise and love / Exceeds man's might: that
dwells with gods above." (III.ii.163–164) Cassandra wails at the
broken wall and tower: "Our firebrand brother Paris burns us all."
(II.ii.110) The spark of life can yield the conflagration. How similar
are Dante and Shakespeare in their sense of the power of love. Ezzelino
was the firebrand of the north. His flame was destructive, while his sister
converted the same passion to better use. Francesca can also contract
love and death, "Amor condusse noi ad una morte." And the irony of
the canto informs against her. But when Helen speaks indulgently of
love — "This love will undo us all. O Cupid, Cupid, Cupid!" (III.i.119–
120) — despite Thersites' scabrous hostility to the song of love, there
is no certain irony that bears the conviction of the author against it.
Love is a terrible irresistible passion that with all its destructive power
still contracts experience in a very basic way. That men are not gods
is Shakespeare's tragic conviction, and nowhere is this more apparent
than in the spectacle of love's fleetingness and the alliance with death
that it can foster.

There is something melancholy in Troilus' personality, as in Romeo's,
that makes death active in his imagination. Before the encounter with

Cressida he is giddy with expectation and imaginary relish. What will the reality be like?

> Death, I fear me;
> Sounding destruction; or some joy too fine,
> Too subtile-potent, tun'd too sharp in sweetness
> For the capacity of my ruder powers.
> I fear it much.
>
> (III.ii.23–27)

And after her loss, he reverts to the same death thoughts. Aeneas' call for Cressida reminds Troilus of the summons that man's attendant genius makes when he is about to die: "Some say the genius so / Cries 'Come!' to him that instantly must die." (IV.iv.52–53)

But along with his characteristic penchant for death, Troilus introduces resources that convert tragic love into a living and enduring reality, one that resists time not by means of contraction, but by continuity:

> O that I thought it could be in a woman —
> (As, if it can, I will presume in you)
> To feed for aye her lamp and flames of love;
> To keep her constancy in plight and youth,
> Outliving beauties outward, wtih a mind
> That doth renew swifter than blood decays!
>
> (III.ii.165–170)

Shakespeare's noblest heroes conceive of a human quality that does not yield to the inevitable decay of nature, but rather seeks its own furtherance. While, like Dante, Shakespeare has a remarkable sense of the propensity of physical matter to run down, to lose its early fire, so, too, in Troilus and Hamlet, in the sonnets, and in any number of heroines, he introduces qualities which, if allowed, would give horizontal enlargement to the vertically aspiring will. These possibilities for something like richness within continuity are denied in the tragedies, but find their proper expression in the vision of the last plays.

The position most contrary to this ideal of fidelity receives its summary formulation in *Troilus and Cressida*. Paradoxically enough, it is Ulysses, the frequently invoked spokesman for a very static Renaissance conception of "degree" and "order," who, in his great speech on time (III.iii.145–190), gives expression to a world view that is most hostile to the ideals and desires of the renewing mind. As it was for Tamburlaine, the natural world of time and change becomes in his oration the exhortative model and example for aggressive human conduct. Ulysses' vision represents acceptance of and immersion in the world of struggle, where time is distinctly emulative. What follows overwhelms what went before, and nature herself justifies man's own ingratitude and forgetfulness:

> Time hath, my lord, a wallet at his back,
> Wherein he puts alms for oblivion,
> A great-siz'd monster of ingratitudes.
> Those scraps are good deeds past, which are devour'd
> As fast as they are made, forgot as soon
> As done.

In order to survive, man must acknowledge that his natural condition is one of struggle; he must be prepared to seize the ready opportunities that present themselves and keep ahead of the competition.

> Take the instant way;
> For honour travels in a strait so narrow
> Where one but goes abreast. Keep then the path,
> For emulation hath a thousand sons
> That one by one pursue. If you give way,
> Or hedge aside from the direct forthright,
> Like to an ent'red tide they all rush by
> And leave you hindmost.

This passage provides the social corollary to the emulative world of nature expressed in sonnet 60 ("Like as the waves make towards the pebbled shore") and indicates some of the fundamental data of man's political condition. Its summary position is further increased when it places emulation in the heart of the family: "emulation hath a thousand sons," a fact Henry IV feared and Gloucester learned to regret. Willynilly, Ulysses reminds Achilles, man is a temporal creature, and consequently he is involved in an either/or situation, where the penalty for negligence or retreat can be severe and pitiless. Things do not enjoy permanence, but are rather part of the cosmic flow. This somewhat Machiavellian world view, partially appropriate for the histories, is especially threatening to lovers who want to preserve their happiness, or to kings who are wedded to their absolute prerogatives — those creatures of the Shakespearean dramatic world who seek a permanence and a continuation of what was. For them time's casualties are painful:

> Let not virtue seek
> Remuneration for the thing it was!
> For beauty, wit,
> High birth, vigour of bone, desert in service,
> Love, friendship, charity, are subjects all
> To envious and calumniating Time.

The predominance of what is present unites both man and nature: "The present eye praises the present object." As Dante warred against the "presenti cose" and Spenser opposed the "present pleasure," so Shakespeare dramatically protests against the human failure to withstand change. It is such concern with the present that leads to forgetfulness and ingratitude, the horrors that so bedeviled Hamlet and Lear. And interestingly enoungh, Cressida herself echoes Ulysses' view when she laments the weakness of her sex:

> Ah, poor our sex! this fault in us I find,
> The error of our eye directs our mind.
> What error leads must err. O, then conclude
> Minds sway'd by eyes are full of turpitude.
>
> (V.ii.109–112)

We recall that the purity of Juliet's intention was shocked by the Nurse's suggestion that she marry Paris and forget the banished, and hence harmless, Romeo (III.v). Some six years later in Shakespearean drama the woman does not come off so well when fidelity is at the stake. Gertrude and Cressida both show that at once unnerving and yet fascinating capacity of woman to make herself at home in changed circumstances, to accommodate herself so readily to the limits of her immediate environment. It is woman by her acquiescence to change that most challenges with suspicions of boyishness the aspiring mind of man.

Much of Ulysses' account is at the basis of Shakespeare's own vision into the realities of history. They do not differ in their assessment of the raw natural and social data; rather they differ in the responses each would consider suitable. If we return to the histories we see that even there the ethic of the Yorkists (Ulysses' "Take the instant way" is akin to their opportunism) was successfully improved upon by the larger historical and social concerns of the Lancasters. Especially when we consider the tragedies, where a new ideal of fidelity and another temporal perspective are introduced, we are aware of how alien Ulysses' exhortation has indeed come to be. The new values and vision are related to the love-idealism of the later sonnets, especially 116 and 124, where the renewing and faithful mind is Shakespeare's great hope:

> Love's not Time's fool, though rosy lips and cheeks
> Within his bending sickle's compass come.
> Love alters not with his brief hours and weeks,
> But bears it out even to the edge of doom.

Not only does this sonnet express the sturdy ideals of a constant love, but it also calls into question the shortsighted policies of the "instant way." These practices, dominated by the demands of the changing present, possess no larger directions and values; they are "subject to Time's love or to Time's hate / Weeds among weeds, or flowers with flowers gather'd." The love that Shakespeare professes seems to have more solid substance to it (again in contrast to shifting political currents):

> It fears not Policy, that heretic
> Which works on leases of short-numb'red hours,
> But all alone stands hugely politic,
> That it nor grows with heat nor drowns with showers.

These are the greater ideals of Shakespeare's tragedies, and their great theme, where man's desires for fidelity, for spiritual continuity, encounter the harsh facts of change.

Inner and outer forces — human change and the fortunes of war — combine to destroy Troilus' hopes in love and to expose him once again to the thoughts of self-destruction. Ulysses takes him in hand, serving as mentor and guide, to reveal the truth of Cressida's infidelity. Her defection exposes Troilus to the supremacy of a view he had most combatted; rather than accept such regiment he desperately seeks his own death. His mind, eternal and fixed, can find no other outlet for its intensity. In Chaucer's world there was greater philosophical accommodation for change, and there was less hope in any human sort of continuity. Consequently there was less rage and storm at the dissolution of the love pledge. Such "troth" is only to be placed in Christ, and oblivion is not bestial, but merely human. On the other side, the philosophy of eternity behind the works of the great fourteenth-century writers is not present in Shakespeare's dramatic world. Therefore, a greater stake is had in purely human means of continuity, and greater resistance is offered when these ideals succumb to the pressures of time. With nowhere to go, Shakespeare's crushed idealists can only rage at a world they are being forced to acknowledge. Only Hamlet and Lear seem to arrive at anything like a just understanding.

For Antony and Cleopatra, the present is the object of their passion. They scorn more prudential considerations. Antony is a child of the time, but Caesar possesses the time (to make a quotation apt by removing it from context). To him Antony's neglect of time is childish:

> But to confound such time
> That drums him from his sport and speaks as loud
> As his own state and ours — 'tis to be chid
> As we rate boys who, being mature in knowledge,
> Pawn their experience to their present pleasure
> And so rebel to judgment.
>
> (I.iv.28–33)

Plutarch had similar judgments about Antony's indulgence of the present pleasure. He writes (in North's translation): ". . . yet, as though all this [Fulvia's wars, Caesar and the Parthians] had nothing touched him, Antony yielded himself to go with Cleopatra into Alexandria, where he spent and lost in childish sports (as man might say) and idle pastimes, the most precious thing a man can spend, as Antiphon sayth: and this is, time." [9] But this judgment is not necessarily Shakespeare's. In the histories, true to its Renaissance function, time was a precious commodity, and historical values of continuity were crucial. Man must encounter his life with a deliberative seriousness and choice. But Antony is not merely an aesthetic personality. His downfall does not occur in the pre-historical world of Richard II, but rather in the post-historical world of tragedy. Despite the apparent contradiction, he is one with the other Shakespearean tragic heroes, since his mad devotion to the present derives from a disenchantment with the policy of short-numbered hours. Theodore Spencer, in his *Shakespeare and the Nature of Man,* recognizes this when he writes that "Antony and Cleopatra, unlike the chief characters of the other great tragedies, are never disillusioned, for they had no illusions to start with. Antony knows what he is doing when he chooses Egypt instead of Rome." [10] Early in the play Antony takes his stand in Egypt (even though somewhat jocularly, and even though he is destined to vacillate):

> Let Rome in Tiber melt and the wide arch
> Of the rang'd empire fall! Here is my space.
> Kingdoms are clay; our dungy earth alike
> Feeds beast as man.
>
> (I.i.33–36)

In this play Antony begins with the conclusions at which Hamlet arrives in the graveyard. Yet, while Hamlet would more readily enter into the human activities that are contained within dust and death, Antony would rise out of them. Empire smacks of the mortality of earth and clay; it does not permit enough freedom for the aspiring spirit. The requirements of empire — small war on the heels of small war — are too burdensome without the illumination of the spirit, without love, daring, and generosity. In both Antony and Cleopatra are seen vital revivifying fires. Age cannot wither her, nor custom stale . . . Life is enjoyed as alacrity of spirit, as vital response and fulfillment rather than ponderous calculation which does not appear to make a real answer to decay.

> For his bounty,
> There was no winter in't; an autumn 'twas
> That grew the more by reaping.
> (V.ii.86–88)

This is Cleopatra's great version of Antony. But even the play's *raisonneur,* Enobarbus, calls him a "mine of bounty." Caesar, operating ever on the principles of political expediency, repays those who defected to him with death or front-line service, while Antony rewards betrayal. Overwhelmed with guilt, Enobarbus (who is practically a pure creation of Shakespeare in the play) seeks out some foul ditch in which to die. His practical wisdom, necessary in the histories, in the tragedies is revealed as being more knavish than his fidelity was foolish.

The fire of love only makes more acute such contrasts between its vitality and powers of renewal and the moribund operations of normal life. Placed against what the lovers experience with one another, Caesar's reasoned world of empire seems banal. Cleopatra asks for a soporific when she learns of Antony's departure, "That I might sleep out this great gap of time / My Antony is away." (I.v.5–6) When Antony learns the false news of Cleopatra's death, he vows his own death. Long time without her would be tedious, and all effort would be mere plod and self-defeating labor:

> So it must be, for now
> All length is torture. Since the torch is out,
> Lie down, and stray no farther. Now all labour
> Mars what it does; yea, very force entangles
> Itself with strength. Seal then, and all is done.
>
> (IV.xiv.45–49)

Riper lovers, to be sure, but nevertheless the experience they relate is one that Berowne, as well as Romeo and Juliet, would have understood. The double power of the Promethean fire (Falstaff converted it to sack) enhances life above its normal sub-average operations. Without it, in the tragedies at least, why live the death that is life and why not reach into the life that is in death? When Antony dies, whatever was remarkable has been removed from life. And like Hecuba, Cleopatra should pronounce treason on the gods:

> It were for me
> To throw my sceptre at the injurious gods,
> To tell them that this world did equal theirs
> Till they had stol'n our jewel.
>
> (IV.xv.75–78)

That men are not gods is the tragic realization in this play, where reason and passion, wisdom and power are so sorely divided.

As in *Troilus* a backdrop of ironic reflection on the human mechanism of change does much to qualify the heroic projections of the central lovers. Saddened by the news of Fulvia's death, Antony has reason to notice his own changed feelings:

> The present pleasure,
> By revolution low'ring, does become
> The opposite of itself. She's good, being gone;
> The hand could pluck her back that shov'd her on.
>
> (I.ii.128–131)

Man stands helpless before the alteration of events, and deep antagonisms are transformed into deeper regrets. As with the great, so with the people:

> Our slippery people,
> Whose love is never link'd to the deserver
> Till his deserts are past, begin to throw
> Pompey the Great and all his dignities
> Upon his son.
>
> (192–196)

Caesar, too, similarly reflects on the upsurge of popular sentiment for Pompey:

> It hath been taught us from the primal state
> That he which is was wish'd until he were;
> And the ebb'd man, ne'er lov'd till ne'er worth love,
> Comes dear'd by being lack'd. This common body,
> Like to a vagabond flag upon the stream,
> Goes to and back, lackeying the varying tide,
> To rot itself with motion.
>
> (I.iv.41–47)

This trait of the people is part of the comings and goings of the world of time. And Antony, in his decline, is deeply sensitive to change. When attention turns another way (or seems to), Antony is indignant at the prospect of such betrayal:

> Authority melts from me. Of late, when I cried "Ho!"
> Like boys unto a muss, kings would start forth
> And cry "Your will?" Have you no ears? I am
> Antony yet.
>
> (III.xiii.90–93)

Antony, too, is a great prey to time, caught between was and is, and obliged to endure the cruel agony of replacement. Octavius seems to him

> Proud and disdainful, harping on what I am,
> Not what he knew I was.
>
> (142–143)

His involvement in a world of political ambitions, the either/or world of emulative time, and his neglect of the proprieties of rule in that world, mean his end. As he declines, his temporal orientation shifts from the present to the past, to the time when, as he encourages Cleopatra to recall, he had been the "greatest prince o' th' world." As the end approaches, the split between effective control in this world and the lovers' visions widens. Antony finally looks outside of time entirely, to a place "where souls do couch on flowers." (IV.xiv.51)

If Antony loses in the game of politics, his great aspirations, unlike those of Troilus, are affirmed in Cleopatra's ultimate fidelity. Cleopatra joins him in this projection of the spirit beyond the end of life. Her speeches (V.ii) reach philosophic heights. Her losses (and Antony's) in the mortal world of empire induce her to take greater benefit from the life of the spirit:

> My desolation does begin to make
> A better life. 'Tis paltry to be Caesar.
> Not being Fortune, he's but Fortune's knave,
> A minister of her will. And it is great
> To do that thing that ends all other deeds,
> Which shackles accidents and bolts up change,
> Which sleeps, and never palates more the dung,
> The beggar's nurse and Caesar's.
>
> (V.ii.1–8)

Change which so typified the people, and which Antony experienced both in his own emotions and in his fate, is not atypical, or merely part of the ups and downs of political life: it is intrinsic to man's universal life. As Antony's early lines did, so these lines of Cleopatra's remind us of the graveyard scene in *Hamlet*. Her insight into the base origins and physical limitations placed on high and low alike is akin to Hamlet's discovery that the dust of Alexander might be found stopping a bunghole. This common vulnerability levels whatever distinctions their spirits required.

> The odds is gone
> And there is nothing left remarkable
> Beneath the visiting moon.
> (IV.xv. 66–68)

While Hamlet consents to enter into that new world, Cleopatra would be free forever from accident and change. Caesar's triumph is actually his loss. He triumphs through practical control in the world of time, but his practical reason is still subject to life's necessities and physical limitation: rather than mastering fortune he is merely her servant. In contrast, the lovers' defeat in the world of time calls them to the better life of the spirit. Cleopatra has immortal longings. Indeed, Douglas Bush's query whether Christian premises do not underlie the exaltation and ruin of Antony and Cleopatra is sensitive and to the point.[11] She looks for a perpetuation of her love outside of time: "Husband, I come." The title suggests the anticipation of extended love, missed in life. She even has a sympathetic enjoyment of the place Antony envisioned, where souls couch on flowers, "As sweet as balm, as soft as air, as gentle." Cleopatra is fire and air — all Promethean; her mortal elements she leaves to baser life. (V.ii.283–293) The division is complete between the spiritual and the physical. Why should she stay in this wild world?

In the face of the facts of the changeful human mechanism and the lessons of mortality, which ironically comment upon the grand figures of the central characters, I believe we separate ourselves from the high insistencies that Antony and Cleopatra throw up in their destined downfall. However much we are moved by their premises, we are reluctant to accept their conclusions. The dull dog within refuses to march to their music. Nevertheless, *Antony and Cleopatra* is a major Shakespearean play not because it simply exposes the pretensions of that old ruffian Antony and his whore, but because it shows how much is lost when their virtues and aspirations are no longer valid in a world of organized empire. It would be an easy error to underestimate the character and triumph of Octavius, the era of "universal peace" that he most ideally suited and served, but the basic impression of the play leads us not to rejoice at his victory, but rather to regret the loss of Antony. Enobarbus can only destroy himself when he deserts Antony, when he loses the forces of fidelity and generosity, when the head triumphs over the heart. Other characters who survive into a new world find their victory deprived and themselves diminished:

> The death of Antony
> Is not a single doom; in the name lay
> A moiety of the world.
>
> (V.i.17–19)

In the world governed by fortune, the gods, according to Cleopatra, gave Octavius victory only "to excuse their after wrath." Like us, Dolabella is a sympathetic but nevertheless independent audience for Cleopatra's description of an Antony who dominated the world and the universe. Was there ever such a man? "Gentle madam, no." But in his response

Dolabella knows that his own stature has been reduced: her loss will always detract from whatever success he might achieve. (V.ii.94–105)

While the play anticipates a new epoch, still it is valedictory in mood. And herein lies its precise suitability to Shakespeare's own age. The play's setting is pre-Christian, but its message is post-Christian and post-Renaissance. A new age is being ushered in that is without the greatness, either personal or cosmic, of the preceding. The post-Renaissance world will be schematized, methodized, and organized, and there will be little room for the dream of an Antony. He and Octavius could not stall together, and this is the tragedy of the Enlightenment, the Augustan Age, whose foremost writers were so divided between what they respected and what took their breath.

The play is ideal for the argument of this book. Renaissance vigor, which first revealed itself in its victory over time, now comes to find its success too costly. The triumph over time, which Shakespeare found an urgent and compelling need in the second tetralogy, has been too triumphant. The thrill of discovery has gone out of it, and temporal consciousness and control have revealed their own nemesis. The new age that is being ushered in has little use for the old vanities and excesses. But in their loss, much more is extinguished. The death of Antony is not a single doom. Man's desires, his hope that things will not come to an end, his quest for permanence — these bases of Antony's greatness and loss — are also doomed. The metaphors of personal experience — which were once important ways of understanding the world and placing oneself in it — are no longer valid in an Age of Reason. But if Antony and Cleopatra reject the race of time — which for them was no longer that, but lengthy tedium — it is questionable if the play supports their flights out of time. It is mainly to *Hamlet* and *King Lear* that we must look for a sense of being that is supported by the evidence of the play.

Hamlet and *King Lear*

Hamlet is the thematic companion piece to *Troilus and Cressida,* and yet in universality of appeal it vastly surpasses that play, just as it and *King Lear* surpass the other tragedies of love. The reason for this is, I believe, that Hamlet and Lear embrace the two great orders of continuity, the public realm of succession and the more private order of fidelity — the two areas that were so separate in the tragedies we have just discussed. We see Romeo, Troilus, and Antony mainly as lovers, with their ideals scarcely penetrating to other human functions and roles.

Troilus and Antony are involved in the world of empire, but contrary to their wills, which would gladly shelter their happiness in love from the encroachments of the historical world. The circles of Hamlet and Lear expand to include man's ideals in all of his large human activities. Lear is father and king, Hamlet is son and prince, and their ideals and expectations are related to each of these functions. Similarly, they must face the challenge of change in each of their functions. What Ulysses characterized as the great ravages of time — forgetfulness and ingratitude — assaults them in all their relationships. Their exposure seems more fully human. And it is this many-faceted fullness of their involvement, meeting in a central consciousness, which makes them Shakespeare's most satisfying tragic heroes.

There is one other important similarity between the two. All of their roles and relationships come to crisis at a particular stage of life. Interestingly enough, their universality derives from the problems they encounter at a determined age. *Hamlet* is Shakespeare's tragedy of a young man, *King Lear* his tragedy of an old man. *Nel mezzo del cammin,* the prince, who was too much in the sun, came across a dark way. Not only in the middle way, but all the way, Lear discovered there are no areas of safety. In the confrontation of their expectations with the different realities of a new stage in the human life cycle, they stand for the pilgrimage of all men into the dark and unexpected. Behind each of the different ages, death is the reality that must be faced. In order to meet his life, Hamlet must resign himself to death. His perspective is that of consciousness trying to contain, of experience being felt out, and finally the inscrutable penetrated. His young, inexperienced mind must query existence before it becomes ready for its mission; indeed, the question of Hamlet seems all-important. Hamlet must circle round and round before he is ready to take on (or off) his life. Lear's destiny emerges after the trying-out, after experience. His tragic cry surmounts Hamlet's interrogations, as his death, for some reason, is more painful (perhaps because pain is more present in his play). "We came crying hither" and "the fierce dispute" are proper titles with which the 1960s came to comprehend *King Lear*. Before the final ingratitude and oblivion, Lear's instincts rage and passionately revolt.

Yet, with all his rage, Lear at the beginning of the play would gladly accept the code of succession, just as Hamlet seems adjusted to the expectations of the historical world. Both deal essentially with historical expectations — hopes of continuity and succession, orderly, even unmolested, progress through the stages of life — joined with the higher claims of fidelity and remembrance. It is because, in each figure, man's

enduring hopes and solid achievements — love and history — confront
bitter disappointment and final limitation, that they surpass the other,
more limited tragic figures. Perhaps we can look backward and recall
that even in the histories, presumptions on reality, as in *Richard II,* or
on an automatic progression through the stages of life, as in *Henry VI*
(or Petrarch), are rudely answered by a harsh external reality. But
Hamlet is different from these kings: they refuse to accept the historical
and the ethical, while Hamlet is beyond history. Unlike Hal, he would
gladly accept the responsibilities of power, the limitations and goals of
succession and continuity. He has already subordinated himself to the
ethical, in Kierkegaard's language. It is to a new order of apprehension
that he is called to lead the way, and he enters on that way with fear
and trembling. Like Lear's, Hamlet's tragic possibilities are more fully
realized because he so staunchly upholds or would so willingly embrace
the order of continuity and succession. He is neither decadent nor a su-
perman, neither a Richard II nor a Richard III. He is committed to
the highest values of civilization. But it is these very values that tragedy
limits. Tragedy only occurs, in Niebuhr's phrase, when solid achievement
is shown to be insufficient. Hamlet must pass from the comforts and
consolations of history and continuity to an orphanhood in time; he must
pass from the communal to the particular and individual, but in so doing he rises to a greater universality. The dreadful summons he receives
brings him out of the world of time into the world of being, and somehow the world he achieves fulfills us better than the world he had expected to enter.

History occupies the mythic over-plot of Hamlet. In their mistaken
explanation of the ghost's presence, Horatio and Marcellus nevertheless
provide a valuable dimension to the play. Horatio conjectures that the
ghost of Hamlet is restless because young Fortinbras is making moves
to recover his dead father's lands and honors. The first order of explanation in the play, despite the extraordinary eruption of the ghost and
the atmosphere of foreboding, is historical. In fact, in his narration of
the single heroic fight between old Hamlet and old Fortinbras, Horatio
brings to mind the duel between Hal and that other young man who was
pricked on by most emulate pride. It was an old-time challenge of individual combat, *mano-à-mano,* almost heroic in its simplicity. Even the
names of the antagonists (Fortinbras, Hotspur) abundantly make plain
their simplified qualities. And in the world of personal expectations, the
values of the histories are at the threshold of response. When Hamlet

is informed of the murder, he promises to "sweep to his revenge." And throughout the play he contrasts himself, as Henry IV contrasted Hal, with his more "timely-happy" coevals. Will Fortinbras prove his right to succession, while Hamlet remains merely the shadow? The retention of this basis of judgment brings flashes of hot anger and self-criticism.

Another world of expectations preoccupies Hamlet. His insistence on remembrance and fidelity in love gives to the play a lyrical force that was absent in the histories. Polonius reads Hamlet's version of "Dover Beach" (as Harry Levin has so aptly termed it) sent with a love-letter to Ophelia:

> Doubt thou the stars are fire;
>   Doubt that the sun doth move;
> Doubt truth to be a liar;
>   But never doubt I love.
>   (II.ii.116–119)

He opens himself with friendly confidence to Rosencrantz and Guildenstern, "in the beaten way of friendship, what make you at Elsinore?" "Come, come, deal justly with me." But they would rather attempt to manipulate him in the transparent manner of the political climber, and Ophelia, under Polonius' prodding, returns what she should never have — "his remembrances."

While the context is already one of violation, Hamlet shows himself sensitive to Troilus' ideal of the renewing mind (another indication that for Shakespeare love and time are not necessarily at odds):

> Why, she would hang on him
> As if increase of appetite had grown
> By what it fed on.
>   (I.ii.143–145)

This same ideal of a continuing love is expressed by Hamlet's father (although again with regret and sorrow):

> O Hamlet, what a falling-off was there,
> From me, whose love was of that dignity
> That it went hand in hand even with the vow
> I made to her in marriage.
>   (I.v.47–50)

In the confusion and chaos of reality, the disruption of this ideal — given the specific malefactress — is unbearable. Hamlet cannot leave his mother to heaven, and thus he taints his mind. He squares the general sex by Gertrude's rule, "Frailty thy name is woman!" The prologue to the play is brief "As woman's love." It is one of Ophelia's misfortunes to come between Hamlet and his line of sight on his mother. Before the dumb show she corrects Hamlet's bitter gaiety to remind him it is four months, and not two hours, that his father has been dead. He interprets this as a defense of his mother's merriment: "O heavens! die two months ago, and not forgotten yet? Then there's hope a great man's memory may outlive his life half a year. But, by'r Lady, he must build churches then, or else shall he suffer not thinking on." (III.ii.138–143) Although all around him he finds instances and arguments of change and acquiescence, Hamlet, a fidelist in love and memory, holds out, the lone intransigent. A world order is at stake, a vision of life and man that he is reluctant to give up. *Hamlet,* perhaps better than any other of Shakespeare's plays, supports Reyher's idea that Shakespeare cultivated the memory of the dead.[13] Remembrance is a distinguishing human feature, which throws up resistance to the downward sweep of time, fortune, and nature. It is part of man's godlike reason that helps to provide the continuities of civilization. The ideal is Spenserian, and as with Spenser, oblivion is bestial.

> What is a man,
> If his chief good and market of his time
> Be but to sleep and feed? A beast, no more.
> Sure he that made us with such large discourse,
> Looking before and after, gave us not
> That capability and godlike reason
> To fust in us unus'd.
>
> (IV.iv.33–39)

In Hamlet's detestation of sloth and torpor, in his sense of man's separation from the animals, in his veneration of that large discourse which, divinely given, allows man to consider past and future, he fully characterizes one large thrust of the Renaissance response to time. Like Spenser, he would say that when man provides for the achievements of temporal continuity and the glories of civilization, he is fulfilling a divine function. In the optimistic fervor of the Renaissance, energetic response to time is not necessarily alien to eternity. In fact it comprises the world of graduated mediation which Tudor success and continuity helped to foster. But *Hamlet* is more fully a Renaissance piece in that it oversees the confrontation of this ideal with the stubborn facts of change and mortality: "what a falling off was there!" The whole inspiration of greatness and continuity is undone by man's vulnerability to change. "O woe is me / t'have seen what I have seen, see what I see" (III.i.168–169) — is Ophelia's tragic cry. And like Shakespeare's other tragic heroines, so utterly defenseless, she cannot manage the change. But Hamlet seems more comprehending, more realistic. The play summarizes the Renaissance not only in its ideals of history and of love, but in its sober register of the larger forces of time and change that necessarily qualify that idealism.

Quite early in the play Hamlet's intransigence and sense of particularity come into conflict with his mother's passivity in relation to man's fate: "All that lives must die, / Passing through nature to eternity." And while the mourning prince is obstinate in his condolement, to Claudius it is clear that nature's common theme is death of fathers: "you must know your father lost a father; / That father lost, lost his. (I.ii.72–90) How different at its very source is *Hamlet* from the histories and the earlier sonnets, where the common theme was provision for children, the father passing his legacy on to the son. *Hamlet* deals not in such continuity, but rather in termination. Later, in the graveyard where all the lines converge, Hamlet will come to similar conclusions — but in his case they will be earned realizations, and will carry the same charged energy that his bereavement did. He knows not "seems."

Hamlet's scholarly mind always looks for lessons in events: "this should learn us." And his instructions come mainly in the force of mutability over man. He is astounded to hear that the players have been replaced by children (thus corroborating the general impression of emulation that is so powerful in Shakespeare's world). Upon reflection it is not strange but rather a universal phenomenon, "for my uncle is King of Denmark, and those that would make mows at him while my father lived give twenty, forty, fifty, a hundred ducats apiece for his picture in little." (II.ii.380–384) The present eye praises the present object. Always looking for cause and principle, Hamlet sees in it something "more than natural, if philosophy could find it out." The principle of change and replacement, thus isolated and reflected on, acquires a consistency of presence in the play: it is its more than natural metaphysic.

In the Player's speech, the matter of Troy lends universal and fatal proportions to the individual tragedies. With the fall of Pyrrhus' sword,

> "Then senseless Ilium,
> Seeming to feel this blow, with flaming top
> Stoops to his base, and with a hideous crash
> Takes prisoner Pyrrhus' ear."
>
> (II.ii.496–499)

Hamlet asks to have the speech recited not only for the world of change and death of fathers that it relates, but for the stubborness that it shows against fortune's changes. Pyrrhus' sword — momentarily suspended — completes its inevitable fall on the hapless Priam, and for that event Hamlet's heart too cries out against fortune's dominion:

> "Out, out, thou strumpet Fortune! All you gods,
> In general synod take away her power;
> Break all the spokes and fellies from her wheel,
> And bowl the round nave down the hill of heaven,
> As low as to the fiends!"
>
> (515–519)

As Hamlet stands out intransigently against the world of emulation, so he sees in Hecuba an ideal ally that was not to be found in his mother. Her appearance and clamor justify his own idealism. Anyone seeing her, "with tongue in venom steep'd / 'Gainst Fortune's state would treason have pronounc'd." (533–534) It is, of course, with such treasonous behavior that Claudius charges Hamlet in the second scene of the play. Hamlet shows a natural and understandable proclivity for the play world, where things proceed heroically and clearly. But the play world, like the historical world that occupies his consciousness, must come to terms with the present reality. Hamlet must leave the world as it was or as he would have it be and come to understand and participate in the world as it is. The play world only momentarily assuages. At its termination, Hamlet in a bitter soliloquy breaks out in curses against his own delay, when this actor, over Hecuba, "Could force his soul so to his own conceit" and simulate tears. "What's Hecuba to him, or he to Hecuba?" (579, 585) The play world of Hamlet has a way of returning and focusing on reality.

Hecuba, or Gertrude, is much to Hamlet. In the play world his spokeswoman is Hecuba, but in the real world, which he translates into a play, he comes to an understanding of mutability and change that places him in closer relationship with the real Gertrude. In "The Murther of

Gonzago," the players recite some lines which, if they are not the "some dozen or sixteen" that Hamlet promised to provide for them, still go far in summarizing Hamlet's own growing realization of the inconstancy of human behavior — his own as well as his mother's. The lines could be Shakespeare's version of Montaigne's *Apology*; and they are not random reflections. Like the player's speech, these lines of the play-within-the-play mirror the real plot of *Hamlet* and reflect its wisdom. The dying king answers his wife's protestations of faithful memory with a saddened and yet calm exposition of human changeability:

> I do believe you think what now you speak;
> But what we do determine oft we break.
> Purpose is but the slave to memory,
> Of violent birth, but poor validity;
> Which now, like fruit unripe, sticks on the tree,
> But fall unshaken when they mellow be.
>
> .   .   .   .   .
>
> This world is not for aye, nor 'tis not strange
> That even our loves should with our fortunes change;
> For 'tis a question left us yet to prove,
> Whether love lead fortune, or else fortune love.
> The great man down, you mark his favourite flies,
> The poor advanc'd makes friends of enemies.
>
> (III.ii.195–214)

Time has become more than an article of reality inviting response. In the histories it represented some freedom in man's social relations, but in the tragedies time is a more universal and cosmic force that defeats the best of resolutions. Firm resolutions, therefore, though essential for the growth of Hal, are no longer enough. Time becomes an instance not of man's freedom but of man's fate. The sonnets, too, register this change of purpose:

> But reckoning time, whose million'd accidents
> Creep in 'twixt vows and change decrees of kings.
> Tan sacred beauty, blunt the sharp'st intents,
> Divert strong minds to th' course of alt'ring things . . .
>
> (sonnet 115)

Unforeseeable accidents and changed purposes limit the firmest resolutions: all mankind is seen under the aspect of changefulness. And to return to the player-king, his concluding lines bid fair to summarize the play as well as provide the new attitude of skepticism informing Shake-spearean tragedy:

> But, orderly to end where I begun,
> Our wills and fates do so contrary run
> That our devices still are overthrown;
> Our thoughts are ours, their ends none of our own.
>
> (220–223)

Chorismos, or the separation of man's mind from his world, contributes to the tragedies an atmosphere of error, which is the Shakespearen equivalent of *hamartia.* Wills and fates are contrary and devices are overthrown; when we commit our thoughts to action, we seem to enter them into an order quite different from our conceptions. In the histories, plots do not fail — they might succeed only too well, as in the first tetralogy. But in the tragedies, especially *Julius Caesar* and *Hamlet,* calculation does miscue to a remarkably consistent extent. Brutus' words and his deeds are at odds, and every decision he makes for the best of reasons is mistaken. In this mood that expresses the growing philosophical skepticism of the Renaissance, "men may construe things after their fashion, / Clean from the purpose of the things themselves." So Cassius, in his wasteful suicide, "misconstrued" things. Hateful Error, apostrophized in *Julius Ceasar* (V.iii.67), is abundantly present in *Hamlet,* where every plot fails, sometimes rebounding with vengence upon the conceiver.

In his savage determination to get to his mother, Hamlet, with the most curious of reasons, relinquishes the hold he has over the praying Claudius. Had he killed him then, the object of the play-within-the-play would have been achieved, and his plot would have succeeded. But Hamlet's belief that the praying king is truly repentant is mistaken, and the error is really unavoidable, although one might say that Claudius has been replaced by Gertrude as the object of Hamlet's attention. His onslaught on her sexuality is highly extra-curricular; his own adolescent fears of motherly betrayal do, indeed, "taint his mind" quite contrary to the instructions of the ghost. He is not willing to "leave her to heaven" but stamps and rages in a rather uncontrolled way about her bed. Another visitation by the ghost, this time wearing less intimidating dress, is required. In the process of Hamlet's own penetration into a real world, the ghost too has become less of a figure from imposing legendary history; he has become more humanized and closer to the everyday world. Hamlet, as he himself is only too aware, is "laps'd in time and passion." (III.iv.107) And yet he is at his most passionate. His fixation on his mother was a means of avoiding man's true condition under time as it is a quite literal detour from his true mission. "This visitation / Is but to whet thy almost blunted purpose." (110–111) And indeed after the ghost's admonition, Hamlet does speak in calmer language; he is less victimized by his sense of betrayal. "Assume a virtue, if you have it not," he tells his mother. (160) Custom, the product of long time, is a monster in dulling purpose and habituating rational awareness to evil practice, but Hamlet sensibly recognizes that custom can also strengthen one's hold on good actions. Man's changeful condition has its benefits:

> Refrain tonight,
> And that shall lend a kind of easiness
> To the next abstinence; the next more easy;
> For use almost can change the stamp of nature,
> And either [curb] the devil, or throw him out
> With wondrous potency.
>
> (165–170)

Such calm realism Hamlet had earlier heard from the player-king; now after a more human picture of his father has presented itself, Hamlet is able to adopt the same knowledge and tone. In independence from his mother, and in moral superiority, Hamlet has become the king-father he had earlier imagined. His growth in understanding and control is evidenced by the realistic use he would make of the powers of time. With his motives purified, it remains for him to penetrate the inscrutable, and to learn his own capacities.

In his prescriptions for the world of the play and players, Hamlet showed himself to be a man of refined sensibilities, whose judgments were set apart from the groundlings and the multitude. (So, too, *Hamlet* was praised by Gabriel Harvey for pleasing the "wiser sort.") But in the situation to which he has been called he finds this same quality an impediment, for he is prone to think too precisely on the event. He feels himself discredited by contrast with Fortinbras, who scorns

> the invisible event,
> Exposing what is mortal and unsure
> To all that fortune, death, and danger dare.
>
> (IV.iv.50–52)

Accustomed to clarity, certainty, and intellectual order, Hamlet is thrust into a world that shows few of these attributes. It is thus significant that at the beginning of the play he should want to return to the university, and that even after the mission imparted by the ghost, Hamlet should see it as a "cursed spite" that selects him to rectify the country's disorder. Something in Hamlet is holding back from the "invisible event," the unknown future, where "fortune, death and danger" threaten. We learn more about what had been restraining Hamlet when he recounts to Horatio his adventures at sea. While the ranting Laertes, operating on the stock level of history, was being immobilized and then converted to Claudius' own purposes by the wily usurper, Hamlet was behaving like a swashbuckling prince:

> Rashly —
> And prais'd be rashness for it; let us know,
> Our indiscretion sometime serves us well
> When our deep plots do pall; and that should learn us
> There's a divinity that shapes our ends,
> Rough-hew them how we will —
>
> (V.ii.6–11)

A man who had lived in the theatre world of arrangement and order now praises rashness and indiscretion — happenings. He comes to recognize that the perfection he desired with such scrupulosity is beyond life's imperfections and uncertainties. The finishing process is not ours to give; we merely initiate directions: *ébaucher* is Montaigne's word, which Florio translated "rough-hew." [14] This is a lesson Hamlet feels the generality of men must learn, but obviously it is a truth he previously felt he himself needed to acquire.

Montaigne is again in mind when Hamlet approaches his final action. His resolution in answering the challenge of the duel helps to give ultimate clarity to the fear that was holding him back: "If it be now, 'tis not to come; if it be not to come, it will be now; if it be not now, yet it will come: the readiness is all." (231–233) Death is the ultimate invisible event that gave such humanists as Petrarch and Montaigne pause. And from Hamlet's earlier soliloquy we should recall that it was this "undiscovered country" that puzzled the will. But here his confrontation with death carries with it some of the liberation of *methexis,* or participation. Cassirer has argued, and Hamlet magnificently attests, that the background of error and ignorance and mortality leads to commitment: "Since no man knows aught of what he leaves, what is't to leave betimes? Let be." Fear of death was holding Hamlet back from the land of the living; acceptance takes him from an anxious time-ridden existence into being. But the tragic fate of Hamlet is different from the allowances that Montaigne found in his own life. At the beginning of the play Laertes could be assured that "Time be thine," and Hamlet upon his return could vow "The interim is mine." Both projections never, of course, materialize. Events continue in their unpredictable way, and time is an instance of an external reality that in the tragedies, at least, disappoints human desire.

In his sense of a divinity that shapes our ends and the providence that cares for a sparrow, even in his Job-like readiness, Hamlet's resolutions are clearly within a Christian framework. Yet there are quite serious differences that separate the play from what could be called Christian tragedy. If we consider *Samson Agonistes* the perfection of that genre, we find it very difficult to repeat some of the benedictions of that play over Hamlet.[15] At Samson's end it was fitting for us to hear:

> Nothing is here for tears, nothing to wail
> Or knock the breast, no weakness, no contempt,
> Dispraise, or blame; nothing but well and fair,
> And what may quiet us in a death so noble.
> (1721–1724)[16]

Yet, despite Horatio's valediction, we could not repeat these lines at the end of *Hamlet* without a sense of jarring inappropriateness, no more than we could say them at the end of *Oedipus Rex*.

> Samson hath quit himself
> Like Samson, and heroicly hath finished
> A life heroic.
> (1709–1711)

Samon Agonistes is really a divine comedy, where ends confirm beginnings, and existence eventually supports essence. But in *Hamlet* there is a strong feeling of dissatisfaction, of lack of fulfillment. Hamlet has not quit himself like Hamlet. "Had he been put on" he would have proved most royal. But this is a condition contrary to fact. And so, too, Hamlet has much to tell, to explain about the bloody appearances:

> Had I but time (as this fell sergeant, Death,
> Is strict in his arrest) O, I could tell you —
> But let it be.
>
> (V.ii.347–349)

Hamlet does not have time, and the scholar whose genius was language is stilled: "The rest is silence." There is no triumphant look to the humanist's glory, fame. But Samson will continue to live in glory. A monument will be erected by the succession-conscious father, where his acts will be enrolled

> In copious legend, or sweet lyric song.
> Thither shall all the valiant youth resort,
> And from his memory inflame their breasts
> To matchless valor and adventures high.
>
> (1737–1740)

As in divine comedy, fame and the rewards of succession are here re-introduced, but in *Hamlet* despite Fortinbras' succession, the play ends on the dead drum beat of final termination.

If this is the case, what is the nature of our tragic pleasure in reading or seeing *Hamlet*? One cause must be in the energy of realization, and this is intimately connected with contraction and tragic ethos. "La maladie universelle est la santé particulière" was Montaigne's grand conclusion. In *Hamlet,* where some of the same psychic development occurs, it is no accident that the most significant scene occurs in the graveyard. This is not the first or the last life-study which began in the house of death. In the histories, the emblematic scenes took place in the garden, where the world was growing or open; but in Hamlet the grave represents the *maladie universelle* that the young prince must face.

The conclusions Hamlet comes to in this scene resemble those offered as consolation by the king and the queen. But the contexts are all-decisive. His elders' conventional wisdom is really a covering for moral passivity in the queen and for murder in the king. But in Hamlet we sense more of the conviction of discovery. Man is seen in a more universal horizon, stretching from Adam to doomsday. Yet there is a basic sameness of pattern within this duration. The essential stages of life between the termini of birth and death are reduced to the termini themselves. Hence, the paradox that time of such vast extent is actually single in its pattern: earth returns to earth. The gravedigger's refrain is apt, summarizing the basic return: "O, a pit of clay for to be made / For such a guest is meet." (V.i.129–130) The transparent cunning of the politician, the foppery of the courtier, and the superficial glossing of the lady — all are vanities when measured against this background of beginnings and ends. In the graveyard the differences between the mythic historical-legendary overplot and the unheroic present are abridged. In their creatural connection, kings and clowns come together: a king may go a progress through the guts of a beggar. "To what base uses we may return." And not only common men, but Julius Caesar and Alexander:

> O, that that earth which kept the world in awe
> Should patch a wall t' expel the winter's flaw!
>
> (238–239)

Hamlet comes to see man under a more universal, if mortal, aspect.

There is another profound contraction of beginnings and ends in this scene. The sexton took up his employment thirty years ago, the day old Hamlet defeated old Fortinbras, and the day young Hamlet was born. The cycle of events is swinging round to completion. Before the day is over, Hamlet will be dead, and the succession will fall on young Fortinbras. Within the suggestion of extended time, a pattern is imposed which inevitably joins beginning and end. The serpent takes his tail in his mouth; the wheel is come full circle. The sense of inevitability, of necessity, which pervades the tragedy is built on such significant contractions of extended time to essential termini, coupling in a necessary way birth and death. Yet, with all this dust and death, the pattern is not wholly reductive. We are thrilled at the significant contraction and the basic discovery that prepare Hamlet for his final steps. We are moved deeply by the calm realism of this young hero who passes so nobly through the graveyard of life and tries to restore a world destroyed.

King Lear deepens and universalizes the great concerns of the histories. In *Hamlet,* although the focus was familial, the family itself does not come under any bitter scrutiny; it is an outsider, an interloper, who poisons the waters. But in *King Lear* the family, rather than being the one anchor and channel of stability, is more like the unfathomable deep. Rather than a protective enclave, the family is the bed of deepest acrimony and the source of fiercest competition. Feelings of fear and hatred are there compounded by the intensest rivalry. Rather than one's hope, children are one's despair, as they persist in mirroring one's most repressed defects. The closeness of the family grants no reprieve, no cooling-off period, and deliberation is blasted by explosive feelings so near to the surface. It all takes place, suddenly, "upon the gad" that a festive ceremony becomes a dread quarrel. However desirable its quality, the force that *King Lear* embodies, and that Shakespeare knew, was not rationality, at least in the affairs of the family.

Although conclusions are different, the family in *King Lear* continues to epitomize the nation and the world, as it did in the second tetralogy. Eventually in that earlier series of plays the wild vicissitudes of history and human fortune are stabilized in the harmonious succession of the son. The Tudor values of continuity within change, and their own generational triumphs, are here given their greatest mythic representation. The fears of the father, that he himself is caught in a master process of crime and punishment, of curse and fulfillment, are relieved by his son's serious intent to be a responsible ruler. The son's imitation of the father, that important Renaissance version of paideia, brings human order and control to history. This is, from our perspective, one of the significant contributions of the Renaissance: a restored faith in the order of succession. But before his son proves his merit, the father unburdens his chest of essential fears. "See, sons, what things you are," is Henry IV's complaint. "Emulation hath a thousand sons," is Ulysses' more objective statement. For their pains, the worn-out fathers are murdered and pushed aside, like the industrious bee. This is the "bitter taste" that the "ending father" must suffer. Henry IV is astonished at his son's apparent haste to remove him, "Canst thou not forbear me half an hour?" Henry was mistaken, but Lear is not. When he feebly protests, "I gave you all —" it is Regan who responds, "and in good time you gave it." In contrast to his vision in the second tetralogy, in *King Lear* Shakespeare no longer saw the family as protection from the grasping and seeking acquisitiveness that destroys a human society. The bond which seemed to promote the larger historical order is no longer effective, and the tragedies revert to a world order in some ways similar to that of the first tetralogy, or to the world which preceded the stabilities of ordered succession. A rational paideia whereby the son (or daughter) could be nurtured until ready to assume adult values has been undone. Rather a mysterious and irrational process seems to put our children beyond our reach:

> It is the stars,
> The stars above us, govern our conditions;

> Else one self mate and make could not beget
> Such different issues.
>
> (IV.iii.34–37)

Such were the conclusions of the writers of the fourteenth century, Dante, Petrarch, and Chaucer; they persisted even in some of Shakespeare's contemporaries, like Samuel Daniel. Tragedy is a reintroduction of medieval values into the Renaissance ethic — yet with a great difference. Those earlier authors moved from the unreliability of children, representing the order of succession, toward hope in God, from whom true virtue derives. Beyond earthly mystery is a spanning and controlling divine comedy that is different from Kent's fatalism. With similar bafflement, King Lear can ask, "Is there any cause in nature that makes these hard hearts?" (III.vi.81) No longer a promise and a hope, children are "a disease that's in my flesh." (II.iv.225) In seeing the mortified flesh of Tom o' Bedlam (Edgar), Lear can only conclude that he has had daughters:

> nothing could have subdu'd nature
> To such a lowness but his unkind daughters.

He asks,

> Is it the fashion that discarded fathers
> Should have thus little mercy on their flesh?
>
> (III.iv.70–75)

And in answer to his own question, sees the justice of the punishment, since " 'twas this flesh begot / Those pelican daughters." In his fears of "filial ingratitude," Henry IV foresaw the end of civilization, so far does its importance extend in his mind. England will be "a wilderness again, / Peopled with wolves, thy old inhabitants." Such reversion materializes in *King Lear* and extends to the cosmos. Albany protests that unless the heavens take an active part against this newly-erupted evil,

> Humanity must perforce prey on itself,
> Like monsters of the deep.
>
> (IV.ii.49–50)

Barbarism, cannibalism, "he that makes his generation messes" —this is the reversion that the turbulent atmosphere of *King Lear* evokes. An older world returns:

"The hedge-sparrow fed the cuckoo so long,
That it had it head bit off by it young."
So out went the candle, and we were left darkling.

(I.iv.235–237)

The disordered family in *King Lear* extinguishes the small light that the histories, with proper family functions, had made.

With the break-up at the center, the lateral stability of history is destroyed and we are plunged into a world of risings and fallings, of sharp tumbles and sudden shifts of fortune's world. Life is filled with "strange mutations" — fierce outbursts and unexpected change. Kent, Cordelia, Edgar, and the Fool are all suddenly cast into new lives. And, of course, over-arching all of these changed beings, is the great figure of the king.

Does any here know me? This is not Lear.

.   .   .   .   .

Who is it that can tell me who I am?

(I.iv.246, 250)

The processes of change that we had seen delineated in sonnet 7 are realized in Lear: he is the aged man and the declined majesty, but, belying the assurances of that earlier order, he is also the discarded father. And in the language of *Edward II,* his griefs, being kingly, are not soon allayed. He swears and curses and promises:

Thou shalt find
That I'll resume the shape which thou dost think
I have cast off for ever.

(330–332)

He would be the omnipotent creature he once was, but the more he rages the more we are impressed with the pathos of his helplessness:

No, you unnatural hags!
I will have such revenges on you both
That all the world shall — I will do such things —
What they are yet, I know not; but they shall be
The terrors of the earth!

(II.iv.281–285)

The coming of tears presages the coming of storm and madness. Rather than Isabella's lion who lashes out, if only to paw the earth, Lear is more like Edward II's imperial lion, who rends and aggravates his own gored body, while all around him are his allies — the rejects of the fathers, Cordelia, Edgar, Kent — who, like the humbler deer, seek to heal their wounds.

Kent had always honored Lear as king, father, master, and patron. Change does not affect his fidelity: "He'll shape his old course in a country new." (I.i.190) One of the faithful whom Lear dismisses from his side, Kent adjusts easily to banishment. Despite his "raz'd likeness" and new identity, he persists in his service to the king:

> Now, banished Kent,
> If thou canst serve where thou dost stand condemn'd,
> So may it come, thy master, who thou lov'st,
> Shall find thee full of labours.
>
> (I.iv.4–7)

Like the other exiles who adopt new identities, Kent does not rage against fortune. He seems to carry a settledness and equanimity within him. Ignoring his "shameful lodging" in the stocks, he looks to better times, "Fortune, good night; smile once more, turn thy wheel." (II.ii.180) "Turn Fortune her wheel then as she list — and the clown his mattock" is Dante's own expression of readiness for the shaft of exile.

Cordelia, too, resists alteration. Unlike the sisters and Edmund, who return evil for good, she turns evil into good. She has "no cause" to hate her aged father. Like Kent she accepts fortune's shifts with equanimity:

> We are not the first
> Who with best meaning have incurr'd the worst.
> For thee, oppressed king, am I cast down;
> Myself could else outfrown false Fortune's frown.
>
> (V.iii.3–6)

Edgar, too, is forced to flee and assume "the basest and most poorest shape." His name is lost: "Edgar I nothing am." (II.iii.21) And yet like Cordelia he accepts his changed condition and lives to return care and service to his mistaken father.

The lines in *King Lear* are sharply drawn, and people like France are forced to choose. His choice, too, echoes the more idealistic voice of the sonnets.

> Love's not love
> When it is mingled with regards that stands
> Aloof from th' entire point.
>
> (I.i.241–243)

So, too, the Fool, although laboring to "out-jest" Lear with the lessons of practical wisdom, adheres to his fallen king:

> But I will tarry; the fool will stay,
> And let the wise man fly.
> The knave turns fool that runs away;
> The fool no knave, perdy.
>
> (II.iv.83–86)

In their abidance, their relative indifference to change in their own fortunes, and their fidelity, these figures are the great dramatic embodiments of the ideals of the sonnets. They are all of Lear's party, although he does not know it. Instead he commits himself to those whose worldview and practice are quite opposite to his own sense of grandeur and generosity.

Edmund is not only the prime disturber of the play, he comes equipped with a rationale of behavior that justifies his actions and those of Lear's daughters. There is a natural union between the three, announced in II.i.99, sexually proposed in the later action, and finally consummated in death. When Edmund proclaims, "Thou, Nature, art my goddess," his provenance goes back beyond Richard III to Marlowe's Tamburlaine, and beyond him to Machiavelli, who provided a nationalistic rationale for the aggressive tendencies that Dante deplored in his "gente nova." Ulysses' occidental journey has found other energetic spokesmen and activists. Edmund looks forward to Hobbes, to Milton's Satan, whose "Evil, be thou my good" sounds familiar, and beyond them to social Darwinism, another rationale for the "gente nova" industrialists of the nineteenth and twentieth centuries. Marlowe's Tamburlaine might be idiosyncratic, but certainly he is not atypical. Edmund repeats him not only in his imitation of nature, but also in his sense of emulative struggle within the family. As the coming to power of Jupiter justifies

Tamburlaine, so Edmund invokes the cruel laws of natural replacement to justify his betrayal of his own father to the Duke of Cornwall:

> This seems a fair deserving, and must draw me
> That which my father loses — no less than all.
> The younger rises when the old doth fall.
> (III.iii.24–26)

This is the emulative world, aggressively endorsed and put into practice by the party of hostility in *King Lear,* which was more rationally espoused by Ulysses, and which draws the protestations of those who look to continuity, whether lyrical or generational. The protests are raised high in *King Lear,* in the main because Edmund's code is omnipresent. It is behind the daughter's cruel behavior: "I pray you, father, being weak, seem so." (II.iv.204) Edmund is wily enough to twice attribute his very thoughts to Edgar, thereby setting his father into a rage. We see how important is the notion of family and continuity, when the universal discord in *King Lear* is caused by the argument of emulation that attacks both. Gloucester is a deluded man, whose gullibility compounds the break-up he regrets. But nevertheless his words, however foolish and superstitious they sound to Edmund, accurately reflect the scene of *King Lear,* and serve, with their echoes in John Donne's *Anniversarie Poem,* to form the *loci classici* of the Jacobean sense of decline:

> These late eclipses in the sun and moon portend no good to us. Though the wisdom of nature can reason it thus and thus, yet nature finds itself scourg'd by the sequent effects. Love cools, friendship falls off, brothers divide. In cities, mutinies; in countries, discord; in palaces, treason; and the bond crack'd 'twixt son and father. This villain of mine comes under the prediction; there's son against father: the King falls from the bias of nature; there's father against child. We have seen the best of our time.
> (I.ii.112–123)

Edmund can mock this attempt to see a pattern of relationship in events. Yet he is callous to the "sequent effects" of his behavior — effects his father would do everything he could to avoid.

In tracing Edmund's genealogy and descent we ignored the greatest figure of filiation, Spenser's Mutabilitie. Like that Titaness, Edmund is shoving, aggressive, individualistic, rationalistic, and a dangerous threat to order. At the same time, the beauty and vigor of such figures contrasts with the more innocent establishment. Edmund's "lusty stealth of nature" contrasts with a tired legitimacy; and indeed, like Richard III, there is something sexually attractive in his position outside the law. Both Mutabilitie and Edmund are the victims of some taint within the established order, and consequently present together an essential myth of Spenser and Shakespeare: the confrontation of a beleaguered establishment with the destructive demands of the unjustly deprived.

As *King Lear* looks more deeply into family feeling, so events force the upholders of civilization to look beneath the veneer into its insubstantiality. As Gloucester bred a bastard, so society in time breeds its own nemesis. Society is not unimpeded progress, good heaped upon good; rather its very development seems to bring with it the defects of civilization: a loss of contact with the roots of existence, a moral carelessness. Society stands in need of periodic purgatives, and this itself dooms an absolute confidence and faith in succession. Rather than linear, the development of society, by its own processes of decay and renewal, is more organic or even cyclical. It partakes of the very rises and falls of time and nature. However disastrous, this shared process is not always an evil, but serves the need of taking man from a falser to a truer picture of reality. It replaces negative success with positive failure, takes man from time and places him in being. Gloucester summarizes this transition when he admits that he has no way: "I stumbled when I saw." In his physical blindness he recovers a spiritual sight which the ways of civilization seem rather to have hindered:

> Full oft 'tis seen
> Our means secure us, and our mere defects
> Prove our commodities.
>
> (IV.i.18–21)

Desolation makes a better life, when the accretions of civilization had muffled a true sense of man's condition and made callow his moral feelings. The process of the play is to strip bare this insulation, to penetrate the dark, and to recover the true bases of society. Lear can cry out,

> Take physic, pomp;
> Expose thyself to feel what wretches feel,
> That thou mayst shake the superflux to them
> And show the heavens more just.
>
> (III.iv.33–36)

Gloucester too urges the heavens to enter into human affairs:

> Let the superfluous and lust-dieted man,
> That slaves your ordinance, that will not see
> Because he does not feel, feel your pow'r quickly.
>
> (IV.i.68–70)

Lear and Gloucester and their society are broken on the contradictions between their own ideals and their reality. "Plate sin with gold." "Robes and furr'd gowns hide all." (IV.iv.169) The ideal of society to which they adhered was only a veneer — or worse, a legitimization of the same process of exploitation that existed in the natural state. The fallen state of man is not redeemed in history or civilization, it is merely covered. If this is the case, by what standards can those who challenge society be answered? "None does offend, none — I say none!" (172)

As Edgar progresses through the play he shows greater complication of character than his simple naive innocence led us to suspect. When Lear asks, "What hast thou been?" His response indicates a participation in the society that Lear and Gloucester also knew. "A servingman, proud in heart and mind; that curl'd my hair, wore gloves in my cap; serv'd the lust of my mistress' heart and did the act of darkness with her." (III.iv.87–90) He, too, finds the journey to the bottom somehow healthful.

> To be worst,
> The lowest and most dejected thing of fortune,
> Stands still in esperance.
>
> (IV.i.2–4)

But in the world of *King Lear* there are false bottoms to the consolations one is allowed. When his father enters blinded, Edgar realizes that even defeat is not a final resting-place: worse may proceed upon worse. "The worst is not / So long as we can say 'This is the worst.'" And when Lear's forces are defeated in battle, Edgar dispels his father's ideas of suicide with the only kind of being that is allowed in the mutable world of *King Lear*:

> Men must endure
> Their going hence, even as their coming hither;
> Ripeness is all. Come on.
>
> (V.ii.9–11)

The world of emulation, of coming and going, of ripening and then rotting, occupies the vision of Shakespeare's tragic world. And it is this creatural perspective that historical man is obliged to entertain. Its very instability, even inscrutability, rules out the controlling intellect that prevailed in history. Rather the proper attitude betokens a kind of patience that moves forward into darkness. Edgar's "ripeness" recalls Hamlet's "readiness"; yet even the phrases themselves suggest something of the difference between the two plays — the one involving mental attitude and the other so deeply involved in physical processes.

While Edgar's important realization is akin to Hamlet's, in *King Lear* it does not absorb our consciousness in the way that Hamlet's central resolution does. Partly this is because Hamlet's development is the most momentous in the play's action. But more important is the fact that Hamlet occupies the height of his world, while in *King Lear* there is a passion that rises above Edgar's "ripeness." King Lear stands out in obvious contrast to his environment. His impulse is to expand things, make them greater than they are, while all around him are people, good and bad, who, in their different ways, would reduce things. Lear would push into the background his obvious and justified preference for Albany over Cornwall, and not belittle a splendid ceremony and occasion with such petty differences. Scorning more prudential considerations, his passion is magnificence. Kent, Cordelia, and Edgar could, without too much fanfare, accept their changed necessities. They move in a world of smaller expectations. But as king, Lear is keystone and stands atop a grand order of continuity that persists through the rhythms of succession. It is quite natural then that his agony should be more intense, his change more convulsive as he undergoes the prototypal tragic progress from man as everything to man as nothing.

"They told me I was everything," is Lear's great cry; "they flatter'd me like a dog." (IV.vi.98–107) We come here to the ideal suitability of king as tragic hero. Possessing "two bodies" — one of absolute will, of enduring tradition, and the other of creatural mortality — the king summarizes the human condition, both in its rising towers of the spirit and in its inevitable limitation. And while Richard II was a decadent, who yearned to lose, who possessed no real thrust, who had not yet entered the ethical and historical world, it is clear that King Lear is a fuller, more tragic realization of the issues of that history. King Lear is "every inch a king," and the break-up of the world he had mastered and required is cataclysmic. The grander the possibilities, the more terrible is the fall. In this way, it is clear that the king as tragic figure in Shakespeare fulfills a similar function to that of the semi-divine heroes in Homeric tragedy; they more fully pose the dilemma of man's lot. The presence of the divine in the human spirit only makes it more difficult to accept mortal limitations. The heroic potential (even achievement), the divine discourse, the established greatness and absolute will only serve to conceal true tragic fate. While abetting his pretensions, they must yield to the essential truth that men are not gods, and their solid achievements must come to an end.

Lear's quarrel is greater and less apparent than that of those around him. Whether benignly or aggressively, they seem to embrace a world of change that leads to essential nothingness. Behind Cordelia's "nothing" is the unkind truth that she will marry, Lear will die, and all will come to that dread nothing. "Death of fathers" is also the theme of this play. Lear passionately resists the realistic appraisal of man's creatural existence toward which events and the force of reality move him. "Reason not the need" he finally exclaims against the humiliating numbers game that Goneril and Regan have forced on him. "Allow not nature more than nature needs, / Man's life is cheap as beast's." (II.iv.267–270) For Lear as for Hamlet, the discrimination between man and beast is a forceful thought. In Regan and Goneril, Lear senses the reductive social Darwinism for which Edmund is spokesman. Nature is aggressive and emulative, rising and falling. Lear's position, similar to that of Alfred North Whitehead in the *Function of Reason,* is that man has desires and needs which differ from those of simple survival. For Whitehead, the fault of the evolutionary formulae is that they do not allow for the contrary tendencies of human nature. "The struggle for existence gives no hint why there should be cities. Again the crowding of houses is no explanation why houses should be beautiful. But there is in nature some tendency upwards, in a contrary direction to the aspect of physical decay. In our experience we find appetition, effecting a final causation towards ideal ends which lie outside the mere physical tendency." [17] Lear, too, proceeds to explain the aesthetic impulse,

> If only to go warm were gorgeous,
> Why, nature needs not what thou gorgeous wear'st.
> (271–272)

But these are not his true needs. He more strongly feels the need for kindness, respect, and reverence, for generosity reciprocated and acknowledged, for attention being paid, for still being somebody, although he has lost the power to command. Nature rises and falls, but human nature seeks to resist physical decay. The difference here is as acute as that between Ulysses' view in *Troilus and Cressida* and the vision of the later sonnets, between Hamlet and the world of acquiescence and change around him. In *King Lear,* Edmund translates into a philosophy of action what is an observation of the ways of nature, while Lear, like Frost's west-running brook, would throw up resistance against the stream of everything that runs away.

The king who assumes Regan knows "the offices of nature, bond of childhood, / Effects of courtesy, dues of gratitude" (II.iv.181–182) resists the unconnected singleness toward which the forces of the play seem to compel him. "Orphanhood" in temporal or communal terms is abhorrent. The thing itself, from which Montaigne could derive such fulfillment, leads to the impoverished condition of which the matted and mortified nakedness of Tom is the object lesson. "Is man no more than this?" is the summary cry of Lear, who clings to the achievements and functions of civilization:

> Thou ow'st the worm no silk, the beast no hide, the sheep no wool, the cat no perfume. Ha! Here's three on's are sophisticated! Thou art the thing itself; unaccommodated man is no more but such a poor, bare, forked animal as thou art.
>
> (III.iv.105–114)

But despite his reluctance, Lear slowly moves toward an immersion in another reality, one that he had perhaps too much ignored. As we saw in the lot of the Gloucester family, society can breed its own nemesis in the braz'd consciousness of the father, and in the bastard son. Lear, too, betrays an anxiety in his reliance on society and his unwillingness to acknowledge man's true condition. It is of this that Maynard Mack writes, "Can it be that here, as on that map, is a realm where everything is presumed to have been charted, where all boundaries are believed known, including those of nature and human nature; but where no account has been taken of the heath which lies in all countries and in all men and women just *beyond* the boundaries they think they know?" [18] Tragedy takes man out of assured certainties and forces him to encounter another reality, to find another security in uncertainty. Arthur Sewell knows this when he writes, "In general, the tragic hero is conceived as pursuing a settlement not only with secular society but also with his universe. Settlement with society is not enough; for he must also find himself an identity which, while giving him mastery over his temporal problems, justifies that mastery with a more than temporal sanction." [19] From history man moves to tragedy, from time to being. And Lear is, after the storm, finally willing to admit his creatural mortality — although he does it with the usual flair. Gloucester would kiss his royal hand, but Lear protests that he must first wipe it, "it smells of mortality." (IV.vi. 135–136)

> We came crying hither;
> Thou know'st, the first time that we smell the air
> We wawl and cry.
>
> (182–184)

Man is seen in a more fundamental aspect than as a social being. After the storm the scorched brain of Lear mends, his rage is abated, and he comes to accept the age that he defied. "I am a very foolish fond old man." "Pray you now, forget and forgive. I am old and foolish." (IV. vii.60, 85)

With the storm assuaged in King Lear's mind, the lines of the play converge in the contracting atmosphere of tragedy. As before the momentous battle at Philippi, a protagonist senses the approach of life's end — not only as termination, but also as completion, with destiny fulfilled. Before the apparently decisive battle, Kent introduces the tone of finality:

> My point and period will be throughly wrought,
> Or well or ill, as this day's battle's fought.
>
> (IV.vii.96–97)

Another life comes full circle, mainly with retributive justice but not without some tragic dimension, when Edmund realizes he has been mortally wounded by his wronged brother, Edgar. Edmund was the lax Gloucester's nemesis, and Edgar points the moral of a fitting *contrapasso:*

> The gods are just, and of our pleasant vices
> Make instruments to plague us.
> The dark and vicious place where thee he got
> Cost him his eyes.
>
> (V.iii.170–173)

Edmund acknowledges the truth: "The wheel is come full circle; I am here." His beginning and his end meet in a fallen condition: he started in the depths of fortune's status as a bastard, and now, fallen and defeated, he senses a return. And while other parties seem to come together (Gloucester's heart burst smilingly in the arms of Edgar, knowing his true son at last, and Kent continues his dogged perseverance in the steps of his master), Edmund sheds some tragic lustre on the joined fates of the antagonized sisters and himself. When information is brought of their deaths, he adds their epitaph: "I was contracted to them both. All three / Now marry in an instant." (228–229) The ethos of tragedy is enhanced by these series of contractions (despite the retributive nature of some of them).

Lear's earlier hopes of settling his rest on Cordelia's kind nursery seem, after the agony and the defeat, finally to be realized. His beginnings and ends are brought together, as the reprieve he had first desired is now apparently granted. In her presence all change is converted to inconsequence. Lear seems finally to have come upon that freedom from the rising and falling emulative struggles of life and natural process that had first been behind all his desire and rage:

> . . . we'll wear out,
> In a wall'd prison, packs and sects of great ones
> That ebb and flow by th' moon.
>
> (V.iii.8–19)

The struggle from which Henry VI averted his ken, which Iden tried to flee in his garden, and which Richard II thought he had transcended, Lear finds absorbed in the stabilizing presence of his daughter. Their condition in its simple felicity is more enduring than all the scrambling of the great, and yet, unlike Henry VI and his rather flat pastoral idyll, the vision of Lear is substantially fixed on the rough and tumble processes of life, "Who loses and who wins; who's in, who's out." The play — should this vision be allowed — would anticipate the last plays, where father and daughter enjoy the Happy Island together. In fact, the aptest description of the vision of the last plays is certainly that of God's spies, looking on the mystery of things.

And if Lear had been allowed this resolution and conclusion, he would, of course, have participated in the converging lines of the play. But as he had, in his rage, transcended the assuagement and readiness to which the others more willingly came, so in his conclusion his passion rises out of his surroundings. External reality in Shakespearean tragedy, as in history, continues to defeat the heart's desire. The cut of time is still sharp, and Edmund does not send for help in time. The pattern of disappointed expectations persist: as his earlier hopes were defeated for a privileged sanctuary, free from responsibility and struggle, so his final vision of reprieve is doomed. The conditions of Shakespeare's temporal world do not allow for many carefree clearings. Yet there is something fitting in Lear's rage. Disappointed and unappeased, he seems, in his powerful passion, a truer representative of tragic man. From the beginning Lear's quarrel was with "nothing." And now at the final nothingness which waits for all men, he raises his howl, "that heaven's vault should crack." Death is the final ingratitude which is part of life's process of coming and going. It stood behind all of his complaints and raging. Lear's passion cannot be mollified. "Thou'lt come no more" and five "nevers" enforce that terrible finality, and in a way feebly attempt to understand it, to arrive at a verbal equation for it. Tragic statement can go no farther.

Chapter 10
Shakespeare's Comedies
and Last Plays

Paradoxically, yet understandably enough, the growth of the myth of the golden age was coincidental with the Renaissance discovery of time. Neither of these themes was a critical force in the Middle Ages, yet in the Renaissance they seem to coexist, the one almost necessarily provoking the other. The pressures of the temporal world of history produce the need to escape from time. But on the other hand, the removal to an idyllic kind of existence, in the manner of Alexander Iden or Henry VI of Shakespeare's first tetralogy, can be rudely countered by interventions of the real world. In writers like Rabelais and Montaigne we saw what forms these two ways of organizing experience took: Rabelais allowed for the energetic education of Gargantua and the more spontaneous Abbey of Thélème, and Montaigne was equally sensitive to the different requirements of the public and private worlds. Shakespeare observes similar divisions in his world of the histories and that of the comedies. In the histories, which deal with national interest and public responsibility, the sway of time is severe and the sense of external reality almost unmitigated, so that the individual, if he is to redeem himself from the chaos and nothingness that attended willful vanity, must submit to historical limitations. But in the comedies another dispensation prevails, with different horizons. There is no clock in the forest of Arden, and the banished Duke Senior has a certain appeal for the young: "They say he is already in the Forest of Arden, and a many merry men with him; and there they live like the old Robin Hood of England. They say many young gentlemen flock to him every day, and fleet the time carelessly as they did in the golden world." (I.i.120–125) Behavior that was repudiated in the histories receives justification in the comedies. Falstaff, rejected under a more serious code, enjoys a return to favor as Sir Toby Belch within the festive dimensions of *Twelfth Night*. Conversely, Hal chooses the Chief Justice, but the time-serving censor Malvolio is exposed.

Obviously we are dealing with a different order of relationships, with different allowances and sanctions. The motive of the comedies is love, its aura is gaiety, and its ethic devoted to the present pleasure. In the histories the love element is practically nonexistent; gaiety is suppressed under the burdened seriousness of the house of Lancaster, and man must look beyond the present to the long-range good and stability. But in *Twelfth Night*, the Medicean carnival song springs forth in all its youthful exuberance:

> What is love? 'Tis not hereafter;
> Present mirth hath present laughter;
>   What's to come is still unsure:
> In delay there lies no plenty;
> Then come kiss me, sweet and twenty!
>   Youth's a stuff will not endure.
> (II.iii.48–54)

"Take the present time" is the advice from *As You Like It*. While dominated by youth, the wisdom of the comedies is also ages old. As Sly, in the Induction to *The Taming of the Shrew*, prepares to drift off into the world of the theatre, he urges his stage wife, "Come, madam wife, sit by my side, and let the world slip. We shall ne'er be younger."

Shakespeare's comedy is open. Rather than submission it seeks out freedom, and rather than reflecting on the vanity of the dream, it works to possess the reality.[1] The restrictions of old father law, so dominant in the histories, are the points of departure in the situations of comedy. From its rigors characters in *The Comedy of Errors, A Midsummer Night's Dream,* and *As You Like It* seek a reprieve and another world of a more natural order. Unlike closed comedy, where society uses laughter to correct excess, Shakespeare's comedies use the spirit of youth and love—even in excess—to correct society. Love is also a key to reality, and is used to show up the excesses of the overly ambitious scholars in *Love's Labour's Lost,* the affectations of lovers, the melancholia of a Jaques, the moroseness of a Malvolio. Love is connected with genuine experience and with a pleasurable and fresh approach to nature. Consequently it avoids rational constructs and elaborate formulae, and has its prime representative in the woman. Relatively absent in the

histories, in the comedies the woman at times holds the upper hand—
the highest perspective, as Bertrand Evans has shown—and as she is
the resident genius of the true seriousness and freshness of Shakespeare's
comic world, so too she seems best endowed to sort out matters and
bring them to a fortunate conclusion.[2]

The hard line of history is the oppressive frame from which comedy
departs and to which it returns as a force of rejuvenation. At the outset
of *The Comedy of Errors* and *A Midsummer Night's Dream*, private
feelings suffer under the severity of public demands. Old Egeon is
caught in the power politics of Syracuse and Ephesus, "the mortal and
intestine jars / 'Twixt thy seditious countrymen and us." (I.i.11–12)
And while the Duke, were he free, might pity the poor victim, still he
can only delay, not change, the exacting laws. Moreover, the authority
of his position forbids him to alter a sentence once it has been passed.
In *A Midsummer Night's Dream*, the old hand of the past, Egeus, arrives to block the freedom of love. He begs the "ancient privilege":
"As she is mine, I may dispose of her." (I.i.41–42) His adamancy
presents his daughter with unpalatable alternatives: if she refuses to
marry her father's choice, the consequences are either death or a cloistered existence. The intervention of the father frustrates that fruitfulness
which is the end of comedy. While calling the religious life thrice-bles-
sed, still Theseus reflects the fundamental Elizabethan preference for
generation when he presents the choices to Hermia:

> But earthlier happy is the rose distill'd
> Than that which, withering on the virgin thorn,
> Grows, lives, and dies in single blessedness.
>
> (76–78)

Whatever Theseus' personal feelings, what with his own wedding but
four days off, still he is helpless to extenuate the severity of the law.

In these two plays the initial plot shows private emotion suffering
under the inflexible law of history. But in *As You Like It*, twisted personal feelings lend an edge to power and make it unjust. The historical
theme of this later comedy is the falling-out of brothers. As much as in
the histories, or *Hamlet* or *The Tempest*, the Cain-Abel, Esau-Jacob
syndromes are here relived. Orlando is kept under boot by his older
brother Oliver, while at the court the same "old news" of in and out is
true: "the old Duke is banished by his younger brother the new Duke."
Oliver obviously lives in fear of his stronger, more attractive brother,
and the duke's "humorous" and "envious disposition" is well known.

It is these "unnatural" turns that force Orlando and Rosalind to take refuge in the forest of Arden, away from the emulation of society, and where the duke senior holds his more attractive court. While the golden world is not free from the penalty of Adam, still the seasons' difference is preferable to the perils of emulative society. Escape here is not toward a world of fanciful unreality, but from the emotional turbulence that corrupts nature and society. As this play and others will show, the forest is the place where saner attitudes may be acquired, the better self more fully possessed.

The world of Shakespearean comedy is not innocuous, nor does the source of difficulty and complication come only from the older establishment. The attractive younger world has its share of immaturity, affectation, changeableness, and ignorance. The discrepancy of awarenesses, which, as Bertrand Evans has shown, is a key device in the comedies, is not based on a lofty view of mankind. Ignorance at times invincible seems to prevail; hearts are fickle and protean, imagination is easily deceived by mystifying appearances and dream-like realities; and deeply submerged within the social personality are fear and hysteria, irrational elements that reveal themselves in moments of impotent bafflement—at which incidentally we laugh. Hermia and Helena can regress to the world of schoolgirl tyrannizing and name-calling. Although not as cosmic as Montaigne's depiction of *chorismos,* at the core of Shakespearean comedy is the same sense of human instability. In the entanglements of love and disordered imagination, Viola can profess her helplessness:

> O Time, thou must untangle this, not I;
> It is too hard a knot for me t'untie!
>
> (II.ii.41–42)

Yet there are sources of assurance. When the upper world of what-you-will, as-you-like-it, and much-ado-about-nothing becomes too complicated, the subplot provides more than comic relief. Bottom and his crew represent a simple and solid reality, undaunted by its own ignorance and confusion. We breathe more easily in *Much Ado* when Dogberry's men overhear the plot of Borachio—although their leader's dilatoriness is tantalizing. Borachio's admission might be summary for much of the spirit of these comedies: "What your wisdoms could not discover, these shallow fools have brought to light." (V.ii.239) We are reminded that at the headwater of Shakespearean comedy stands perhaps the most influential book of the sixteenth century, Erasmus' *Praise of Folly.*

Viola reinforces this impression when she defends the wise fool. There is an art in being a clown: "For folly that he wisely shows, is fit . . ." but the wise man who turns fool is the subject of abuse: "But wise men, folly-fall'n, quite taint their wit." (III.i.74–75)

In *Love's Labour's Lost,* the intentions of King Ferdinand to redeem his time through study are, in themselves laudable:

> Let fame, that all hunt after in their lives,
> Live regist'red upon our brazen tombs
> And then grace us, in the disgrace of death,
> When, spite of cormorant devouring Time,
> Th'endeavour of this present breath may buy
> That honour which shall bate his scythe's keen edge
> And make us heirs of all eternity.
>
> (I.i.1–7)

This defiance of cormorant, devouring time is heard in Shakespeare's own voice in the sonnets. But here the conditions of the enterprise qualify its value. The regulations concerning women, sleep, and food are extreme and exclusive. Berowne protests against these stipulations, claiming all they will serve is a barren pedantry unrelated to any human experience and productive of no independent judgment:

> Small have continual plodders ever won
> Save base authority from others' books.
>
> (86–87)

It is love which shows up affectation in the comedies. Love introduces the deluded to a natural and appropriate reality. This is Berowne's argument after the betrayal of the academic pledge was discovered:

> Let us once lose our oaths to find ourselves,
> Or else we lose ourselves to keep our oaths.
>
> (IV.iii.361–362)

The experience of love restores them to a right participation in their time. Their early vows represented a deviation from what was normal for their period of life: "Flat treason 'gainst the kingly state of youth." (293) Abounding in rhyme (in fact, the speech is the sestet of a sonnet),

Berowne excuses himself and his friends for bowing to the force of their affections:

> Sweet lords, sweet lovers, O, let us embrace!
>   As true we are as flesh and blood can be.
> The sea will ebb and flow, heaven show his face,
>   Young blood doth not obey an old decree.
> We cannot cross the cause why we were born;
> Therefore of all hands must we be forsworn.
>
>   (214–219)

Most memorable is Berowne's paean to the quickening powers of love:

> Other slow arts entirely keep the brain,
> And therefore finding barren practisers,
> Scarce show a harvest of their heavy toil;
> But love, first learned in a lady's eyes,
> Lives not alone immured in the brain,
> But with the motion of all elements
> Courses as swift as thought in every power,
> And gives to every power a double power
> Above their functions and their offices.
> It adds a precious seeing to the eye.
>
>   (324–333)

Yet however much this idea of inspiration draws our assent, there is still in Berowne's banquet of wit something which smacks of unreality. Although by their ability to laugh at the Armado-Jacquenetta mix-up and the foolish brag of the Knight, the would-be academicians show they are not entirely lost, yet, in many ways Armado's love affair informs against them just as much as Holofernes' use of learned language does. It is the caricature of their own folly in love. Their situation might be seen as analogous to Jaques' laughing at the contemplative fool who moralized the time, while being blind to the humor of his own situation. Armado's case is of course more blatant, but we cannot but think of Berowne and the lovers (and their later model of the type-cast love sonneteer, Orlando), when the melancholy Armado prays for the inspiration of love's muse: "Adieu, valour! rust, rapier! be still, drum! for your manager is in love; yea, he loveth. Assist me some extemporal god of rhyme, for I am sure I shall turn sonnet. Devise, wit! write, pen! for I am for whole volumes in folio." (I.ii.187–192)

As the untimely vows of study were overthrown by the reality of love, so the exclusive predominance of love's claims is qualified by the fact of death. The literary theme of *carpe diem* and the supremacy of youthful affections that reigned in the gay royal park of rhyme, plays, and songs are subdued by the news of death. J. Dover Wilson gives a lively description of his response to the dramatic performance of *Love's Labour's Lost,* where the bright and flashing colors of wit are toned down by the stark, black messenger of death.[3] There is no greater harbinger of manhood and seriousness than the death of fathers. It casts a shadow over the lovers' youthful unconcern with a time larger than their own. A larger view, which takes into account some other necessities of life, tells against the lovers' exclusive preoccupation with their present. The entertainment is cancelled ("Worthies, away! The scene begins to cloud").

The intervention of this news from the outside world forces the king to bring the issue of marriage to a head, although in his pompous speech he still shows a trick of the old rage:

> The extreme parts of time extremely forms
> All causes to the purpose of his speed;
> And often at his very loose decides
> That which long process could not arbitrate.
>
> (749–752)

The mourning princess does not understand the prolix marriage suggestion, so Berowne tries to pierce the ears of grief with "honest plain words." He confesses that "for your fair sakes have we neglected time, / Play'd foul with our oaths." Time is again a principle of reality and seriousness; the gay young people were neglecting their time. The reaffirmation of their earlier vow is emphasized by the return to the blank verse of seriousness.

When Ferdinand invokes the urgency of the immediate hour in his marriage proposal, the princess qualifies that concern by referring to a longer vista — "a world-without-end bargain." Yet she does not outrightly refuse him, but instead imposes a period of trial, in which she is followed by all of her ladies in regard to their suitors. The king must seclude himself for twelve months in a "forlorn and naked hermitage";

> If this austere insociable life
> Change not your offer made in heat of blood —

> If frosts and fasts, hard lodging and thin weeds
> Nip not the gaudy blossoms of your love,
> But that it bear this trial, and last love —
> Then, at the expiration of the year . . .
>
> (808–813)

she will be his in marriage. The gaudy blossoms of love must be tried in the course of the seasons. It is significant that at the outset of her sentence, the princess describes the probationary period as involving "twelve celestial signs," rather than simply a "year," thereby implying the change of the seasons, and the fuller varieties of human experience. Berowne's argument of the overpowering force of youthful affection, and even his argument of fit time, is modified by a larger regard for the human cycle. Especially here, we find the immediate *carpe diem* invitation to love qualified by something like Raleigh's reminder of grimmer experience. Despite its removal from the hard consequences of history, Shakespearean comedy does not totally forsake such reality. Neither, however, does it accede to such mournfulness. The final songs of Spring and Winter repeat the seasonal bias of the play, and suggest its larger awareness.

In the world of the histories, the metaphor of music was occasionally used to express the concord of properly managed time, and the discord of disordered time. In sonnet eight, the young man's ear is offended by the "true concord of well-tuned sounds" because such "unions married" rebuke his own singleness. And in the great time speech of Richard II the dejected king regrets his failure to hear his "true time broke." His attention had been politically misguided, and hence his lack of concord. But in the comedies, discord is produced by the overly serious person. His dislike of music is indicative of his alien intentions, "treasons, stratagems, and spoils." And typically enough, Shylock, the bitter outsider of Venice, closes his doors on the carnival times of masque and music — "the vile squeaking of the wry-neck'd fife." Thus it is that in *Twelfth Night* the sombre Malvolio is exposed in terms of music. His untimeliness has its musical correlation. On any Twelfth Night, the overseer of responsibility must be out of time. But it is also a mistake to have Malvolio merely stand for order and sobriety. His views of society are not discredited, but rather his motivation, or, as Adonis would say, his device in propriety. Maria sees that he is a time-pleaser and an "affection'd ass." He is fantastically ambitious and vain, and his undoing is the comic revelation of his true self-seeking nature.

Sir Toby and Sir Andrew are in high spirits, and when the Clown enters they ask him to sing a song. Would they prefer a love song, or a song with a moral ("a song of good life")? "A love song, a love song," shouts Toby, and Andrew adds, "Ay, ay! I care not for good life." The sentiments of love admirably express their own festive spirits. The time of life is short; what's to come is still unsure; enjoy the present while you can. Sir Toby is in excellent strutting form, as he waves aside Maria's pleas to stop the caterwauling. Then Malvolio enters: "My masters, are you mad? or what are you? Have you no wit, manners, nor honesty, but to gabble like tinkers at this time of night? Do ye make an alehouse of my lady's house, that ye squeak out your coziers' catches without any mitigation or remorse of voice? Is there no respect of place, person, nor time in you." (II.iii.93–99) There then follows a "triple-play" on the idea of timing. Malvolio reproaches their breach in de-corum, although his sense of their music (with which Maria might agree) sounds very much like Shylock's harangue of the masquers. And in the phrase "mitigation or remorse of voice," does not the stuffed-shirt show a kinship with Holofernes? Toby does not reply directly to Malvolio's main criticism. Although there is no rhyme in his response, it has its own reason. They are not out of time, because their fun and singing has its own time. "We did keep time, sir, in our catches." He then taunts Malvolio with snatches of songs. But the thought that he was out of tune returns to his mind, and he denies it again, providing the unanswerable and perpetually quotable justification of harmless pleasure against the intrusive morality of the busybody: "Out o'tune, sir? Ye lie. Art any more than a steward? Dost thou think, because thou art virtuous, there shall be no more cakes and ale?" (122–125) The Clown adds the spice, and Malvolio gets heaped on him the abuse that all wet-blankets re-ceive: Go hang yourself! Go shake your ears! Go polish your chin! Sir Toby returns the reproach back to the original speaker. Sir Toby is in time, both in his song and in his season. Malvolio is discordant in resting selfishly outside the human community. His egoistic separation from society is represented in his fanciful interpretation of the planted letter, and is justly recompensed in the trick of madness. The Clown reminds us that Malvolio got what was coming to him: "But do you remember — 'Madam, why laugh you at such a barren rascal? An you smile not, he's gagg'd'? And thus the whirligig of time brings in his revenges." (V.i.381–385) Malvolio shows wisdom folly-fallen. The Clown becomes the wise man, and Malvolio the fool. Olivia sighs, "Alas poor fool, how have they baffled thee!"

Open Shakespearean comedy posits a faith in the reality and significance of the present experience. As in Montaigne, the firmness of Shakespeare's attachment to life discredits the posture of traditional wisdom, that "disgust with present things." For Jaques in *As You Like It* that vigorous commitment to things, essential in love, is absent. This comes out most clearly in his famous soliloquy on the "Seven Ages of Man." [5] (II.vii) Orlando, desperate from hunger, breaks upon the duke's party with his sword drawn, demanding food. The kindness and gentleness of the deposed courtiers soften his determination, and he is persuaded to sit and eat with them. Before he will eat, however, he must go "like a doe . . . to find my fawn / And give it food." (128–129) He tells them about faithful Adam. The duke uses the straitened fortunes of Orlando and Adam to arouse Jaques, in hope of getting some matter, and Jaques responds:

> All the world's a stage,
> And all the men and women merely players.
> They have their exits and their entrances,
> And one man in his time plays many parts,
> His acts being seven ages.
>
> (139–143)

The Duke's cue, "This wide and universal theatre" with its "woeful pageants," has a very different tone from Jaques' summary of human activity, where we are "merely" players. His overview reduces to mockery the passions and actions of men. His patterns incline toward ignobility for several reasons. The first is the essential baseness of the activities he isolates, e.g. the puking infant, the whining schoolboy. But the more reductive factor is the sheer repetition. The impression is that we all go through foreordained parts; it's all been done before, and will continue so. Yet despite this unchanging cast, we rant and rave in our roles, puffed up with self-importance. Everybody plays a part as if it were original with him: the lover, sighing like a furnace, writing blazons to his mistress' eyebrow; the soldier, full of strange oaths. And each individual goes through all the stages in time. Past follies are repeated. One man comes to play the part of the justice, "with eyes severe and beard of formal cut," straining hard to fill the role he saw others in. The impression that emerges from this portrait of the human life cycle is one of vanity and evanescence. To Jaques, humanity is typecast. There is a total lack of any variety that would imply a real power of choice. Instead we have the illusion of choice and significance, when we are making gestures in parts that have been acted before we were born, and will continue when we are gone.

> Last scene of all,
> That ends this strange eventful history,
> Is second childishness and mere oblivion,
> Sans teeth, sans eyes, sans taste, sans everything.
>
> (163–166)

In its cynicism this speech is almost the equal of Macbeth's reduction of human activity to meaninglessness in "Tomorrow, and tomorrow . . ."

Quite naturally then, there should be essential opposition between Rosalind and Jaques, between the girl most seriously in love (whatever her disguise — and there is a reason for it) and the commentator upon the human scene, who is himself only a spectator: "It is a melancholy of mine own, compounded of many simples, extracted from many objects, and indeed the sundry contemplation of my travels, in which my often rumination wraps me in a most humorous sadness." (IV.i. 16–20) But Rosalind replies with a native strength that pierces Jaques folly: "A traveller! By my faith, you have great reason to be sad. I fear you have sold your own lands to see other men's." (21–23) Jaques' overview is at the expense of concrete and practical involvement, which give experience and personal sturdiness. Hence his melancholy. He has neglected his own lands even in language. "Come, more! another stanzo! Call you 'em stanzos?" Rosalind takes a parting swipe at this tendency to put more value on other men's lands and language: "Farewell, Monsieur Traveller. Look you lisp and wear strange suits, disable all the benefits of your own country, be out of love with your nativity and almost chide God for making you the countenance you are; or I will scarce think you have swam in a gundello." (32–37) Love's concern with the unaffected present, its confidence in its own experience, its natural vitality, all show up the attenuated Jaques.

The neglect of true nature is also part of the love-plot. The passage of the play is toward the discovery of a nature free from posturing. We must not forget that when duke senior abandoned the painted pomp of the court, he came into relationship with his true nature. Even when bitten with cold:

> I smile, and say
> "This is no flattery; these are counsellors
> That feelingly persuade me what I am."
>
> (II.i.9–11)

But Rosalind is in disguise and Orlando is fairly well fulfilling the ludicrous mold in which Jaques cast the lover. When Orlando answers Jaques that Rosalind is "just as high as my heart," he seems to confirm his antagonist's impression that the actors in life's farce have conned their parts: "You are full of pretty answers. Have you not been acquainted with goldsmiths' wives, and conn'd them out of rings?" (III.ii. 287–289) Signor Love and Monsieur Melancholy take leave of one another. Orlando is obviously indulging in a preposterous attitude which excludes the real world. As in *Love's Labour's Lost*, the real world must enter to qualify the single-mindedness, though not the seriousness, of love. But here love is not lost when it comes into contact with reality; rather it loses its false tone, and is strengthened.

Rosalind's disguise as Ganymede suits Orlando's covering of his true nature in love. In boy's costume she acts the love-struck Orlando's mentor, and tries to impress him with the impossibility of excluding all of life from love. She does this by showing how he does not live up to his claims in love:

Ros. I pray you, what is't o'clock?
Orl. You should ask me, what time o'day. There's no clock in the forest.
Ros. Then there is no true lover in the forest; else sighing every minute and groaning every hour would detect the lazy foot of Time as well as a clock.

> (III.ii.317–323)

Consistently in Rosalind's playful banter, time is the element which represents the fuller considerations of the real world. Orlando is an hour late for a meeting: "Break an hour's promise in love? He that will divide a minute into a thousand parts and break but a part of the thousand part of a minute in the affairs of love, it may be said of him that Cupid hath clapp'd him o'th'shoulder, but I'll warrant him heart-whole." (IV.i. 44–49) And when other obligations call Orlando away, he vows to return by two o'clock. Rosalind feigns that this is an instance of a false lover who will not give all his time to love: "Ay, go your ways, go your ways! I knew that you would prove. My friends told me as much, and I thought no less. That flattering tongue of yours won me. 'Tis but one cast away, and so, come death! Two o'clock is your hour?" (186– 190) Orlando vows that he will keep the rendezvous religiously, and Rosalind, with a sigh of resignation, concludes, "Well, Time is the old justice that examines all such offenders, and let Time try. Adieu." Rosalind stresses the folly of Orlando's role in love by reprimanding him according to his own preposterous code when he perforce fails to live up to it. She expresses surprise that other interests could so occupy his time, and mocks the exclusiveness of love, "Men have died from time to time, and worms have eaten them, but not for love." When Orlando affirms that he will have Rosalind "for ever and a day," she corrects him: "Say 'a day,' without the 'ever.' No, no, Orlando! Men are April when they woo, December when they wed. Maids are May when they are maids, but the sky changes when they are wives." (146– 150) Rosalind tries to bring Orlando's love into firmer touch with reality, not to weaken it, but to purify it.

The betrothal of Oliver and Celia seems to wake Orlando from his dream of love. This is another of those Shakespearean situations that powerfully inform against the illusions one has been content to remain in. However much one disguises real feelings, there comes a time when illusion is dispelled by the palpable realization or disappointment of true desires. The happiness of his brother makes Orlando feel

> . . . how bitter a thing it is to look into happiness through an-
> other man's eyes! By so much the more shall I to-morrow be at
> the height of heart-heaviness, by how much I shall think my brother
> happy in having what he wishes for.
>
> *Ros.* Why then, to-morrow I cannot serve your turn for Rosalind?
> *Orl.* I can live no longer by thinking.
> *Ros.* I will weary you then no longer with idle talking.
>
> (V.ii.47–57)

Unlike Jaques, Orlando is not content to look on the world through other men's lives. Love is a force which compels men to become men. As in the tragedies, it involves them in a deeper reality. They come face-to-face with their own world, and their own pleasures and emotions. It teaches them to respect the just claims of their own present time. It is when Orlando decides the play has gone far enough and he cannot be satisfied with the surrogate Rosalind, that the real Rosalind decides it is time to end the charade. The woman was waiting for the man to become a man, before she could become a woman. She stops the idle banter and proceeds to resolve, in a grand finale, all the complications of love.

In effect, the new regime for Gargantua and the abbey of Thélème, and Montaigne's open and closed comedies, represented different solutions to man's existence in time. Yet, more fundamentally these responses were joined together by root similarities. Rabelais' essential Renaissance hope and fervor united the two apparently dissimilar temporal responses, and Montaigne's attitudes in the divided world of public and private life originated in his experience of *chorismos*. So, too, Shakespeare's histories and comedies, the works that predominated in his early manhood and that seem devoted to such different horizons and patterns of behavior, are united at the more substantial level of needs and perceptions. In a world that was becoming increasingly complex, both the histories and the comedies reveal a search to find reality. It is no accident that the technical device Shakespeare should have resorted to in the nineties, one which suited his needs so brilliantly, was the multiple-plot structure, where the full range of his comprehensive consciousness could have play. Here courts and taverns, kings and clowns, love and war, show how varied is the world and how many are the ways — proper in all — of regarding it. Not only does a "middle period" comedy like *A Midsummer Night's Dream* have the same multiple levels, but the comedies by their nature have the same Renaissance love of variety, of that "souplesse" Montaigne so admired in Socrates. It would seem that any "totalitarian" claims are fair game for laughter. Any exclusiveness that is either single-minded or unseasonal becomes ludicrous in the comedies. This we recall is for Bergson the essential matter of comedy (however much Shakespeare's romantic comedy differs from Bergson's more satiric models). The single-minded Hotspur is as objectionable in the histories as the restricted scholars in *Love's Labour's Lost*. The jaded philosopher, the affected lover, the severe Puritan, when they become types through the narrowness of their preoccupations, destroy the personal variety required in the life of comedy. On another plane, the background of the seasons that loom in song or metaphor suggest the sort of ease and flexibility that the art of life in the comedies requires.

But variety can also be a danger. Hal's virtues, his ability to participate on all levels of existence, can also be a menace, representing the danger that he will never tie his different strands of personality into a unit, that he will suffer identity diffusion and aestheticism and will be, with disastrous consequences, a spectator of his own times. The probing of reality in the histories and comedies, reflected in the multiple plot, is balanced in each by the need to possess reality, finally to grasp a life. Affectation in the comedies, role-playing, any attitudinizing that severs a vital relationship with life or love, need similarly to be confronted. In Orlando's case, reality does intervene to cut short the play world. As in the histories, an informing occasion breaks through the periphery of his game to reveal his true needs. In the histories, the educative force is his father; in the comedies, it is a woman. In each, a lesson strikes home, a basic hurt is experienced that tells the deluded individual what he wants.

The comedies and histories are united by these fortunate conclusions that rest on proper understanding of reality. A mature and capable adulthood is the end of these processes of growth. In the comedies, reason and love, normally at odds, ultimately merge. People can get control of themselves, and lovers can arrive at a genial maturity. The end of love is not merely the present pleasure, but marriage and generation. For this reason, any purely love ethic, such as Berowne's extravagances, must be qualified by experience. The same Shakespearean social sensitivity that in the histories qualifies the Machiavellian and Marlovian *carpe diem* ethic of the House of York, in the comedies serves to restrain and purify any outright *carpe florem* ardor. The flame must be subdued to a longer existence for the sake of fruitful and peaceful life. In the resolutions of the comedies, as in the second tetralogy, the hostile wars of generation must be pacified, and more than a truce, positive guidance must be available for the true entrance of the younger generation into the adult world. It is indicative that the spanning arch of *A Midsummer Night's Dream* is the soon-to-be-secured marriage of Theseus and Hippolyta. In a world that is contained and comprehended by such graceful intelligence, natural fruitfulness will not for long be prevented — despite all the efforts of the hard-headed remnants of the past. To Theseus' premarital impatience, Hippolyta's temporal confidence more truly indicates the reasonableness and possibilities of success that belong to comedy:

> Four days will quickly steep themselves in night;
> Four nights will quickly dream away the time;
> And then the moon, like to a silver bow

New-bent in heaven, shall behold the night
Of our solemnities.

(I.i.7–11)

This is slightly over-sanguine; sailing will not be so smooth. Yet, she and Theseus are the presiding patrons of Shakespearean comedy, with no inclination to rush, no desire to lose. These are the models toward which the young lovers aspire, after the chaos in the woods.

Length of Time in the Last Plays

Time is change, and Shakespeare's tragic heroes do not take easily to that fact. The fall from position, the loss of stature and identity, the change from the way things were to the way things are — such experience is the unbearable burden of tragedy, the source of pain and anger for Richard II, Lear, and Antony. Caught in time's duplicity, these men, accustomed to the rising rhythms of their greatness, believing that they were everything, do not accept with easy good grace the discovery of their nothingness. They rage and storm, providing an inner equivalent for the more elemental unrest sweeping through their worlds. Increasingly in Shakespeare, the storm, the tempest on the uncontrollable high seas becomes a figure of life. But in the world that Shakespeare envisioned after the tragedies, the tempest breaks early, at the beginning, and the discoveries that a Hamlet or a Lear come to are made with considerably less trauma. Cast ashore, Pericles learns his larger helplessness. The surges of resistance and rage, typical of the tragic hero, subside sooner:

Yet cease your ire, you angry stars of heaven!
Wind, rain, and thunder, remember earthly man
Is but a substance that must yield to you;
And I, as fits my nature, do obey you.

(II.i.1–4)

Although a prince and unused to hardships, Pericles bows to natural necessity and begs assistance from the fishermen:

A man whom both the waters and the wind,
In that vast tennis court, hath made the ball
For them to play upon, entreats you pity him.
He asks of you that never us'd to beg.

(63–66)

His change in fortune provokes no rage:

> What I have been I have forgot to know;
> But what I am, want teaches me to think on:
> A man throng'd up with cold.
>
> (75–77)

More basic creatural needs demand his attention; what he was is forgotten. In the storm he has been stripped of his rich royal dress: "What
cares these roarers for the name of king?" the Boatswain shouts in
The Tempest. In the last plays great claims on permanence seem less
insistent. The ghost of Hamlet's father can cry "Remember me!" But
in *The Tempest,* Alonso is urged: "Let us not burden our remembrance
with / A heaviness that's gone." And when Paulina conjures up the
ghost of Hermione which would follow the remarrying Leontes, her
hauting cry of "Remember mine," is dramatically less compelling and
spiritually at odds with the needs and wisdom of *The Winter's Tale.*
Although there are great instances of fidelity and even memorable
professions of faith in the last plays, man's expectations are more
modest in the face of the changeful and vast universe.

The last plays, like the tragedies, deal in elemental things, and time
is one of the great elements. Cutting through social conventions and
familial connections it reduces man to a basic orphanhood. Marina's
ancestors were once like mighty kings,

> But time hath rooted out my parentage,
> And to the world and awkward casualties
> Bound me in servitude.
>
> (V.i.93–95)

Pericles can give a similar account, as he contrasts his present poor
condition with the luminousness of the king his father:

> Whereby I see that Time's the king of men;
> He's both their parent, and he is their grave,
> And gives them what he will, not what they crave.
>
> (II.iii.45–47)

The choric speech at the outset of Act Four of *The Winter's Tale* is
thus representative, in the power it communicates, of the dramatic role
of time in the last plays. In his speech Time is an absolute master. No
one escapes from his reign — he tries all and is "both joy and terror

/ Of good and bad." More even than death, Time is the leveller. At the same moment he is busy planting new customs and overwhelming the old. His hour is "self-born" without any external needs. As in Augustine (*The City of God,* XIII.10) or Petrarch (*Fam.* I.3, XXI. 12), the true terror of Time's nature is its unchangeability. Always in the present, he is self-avowedly "the same I am." Evidencing a genetic relativism of the sort that Montaigne demonstrated, Time is present at the origin and at the end of all social order and custom.

> Let me pass
> The same I am, ere ancient'st order was
> Or what is now receiv'd. I witness to
> The times that brought them in.
>
> (9–12)

And more pathetically for Shakespeare, his sway includes "the freshest things now reigning," "the glistering of this present" — all of which Time will make stale. Consequently, and this is the dramaturgical corollary to such relativism, even the convention of the classical unity of time must bow before the precedence of this great force.

In its presentation of human patterns within long periods of time, the last plays differ from each of the preceding stages of Shakespearean development, while, at the same time, taking something from each. The contracted intensity of the tragedies has been dissolved. The storm breaks early, and man yields to his creatural nature and then survives to taste the benefits of nature's doubleness. In the tragedies the comings and goings ended painfully. In the last plays, the final turn is for the better. Attitude is replenished, and the shocked mind is restored. The sea that takes can also give in return. The storm that wrecked Pericles also tossed up his father's armor, thus allowing his good success at Pentapolis: "the rough seas, that spare not any man, / Took it in rage — though calm'd, have given't again." (II.i.137–138) The duality of nature and time in the last plays emphasizes the fortunate conclusion. Ferdinand echoes Pericles when, in the final restoration of *The Tempest,* he tells the assembled on-lookers, "Though the seas threaten, they are merciful." (V.i.178)

The comedies, too, have happy endings, but they differ on several counts. Sheer length of time is a striking contrast between the comedies and the final romances. The time-span in the comedies usually covers only several days, or, at most, several months. But significantly, even when the length of time is relatively great, this duration is concealed by the activities that cover the foreground of interest. In the final romances no effort is made to foreshorten time; in fact, every effort is made to emphasize the wide gap of time separating the important events. Twelve, fourteen, sixteen, twenty years — these are the durations that enable men to look at their passions and wrongs, suffered or committed, with new understanding and feeling. And it is of course here, in vision, that the last plays differ from their predecessors. Confusion in the comedies, even when protracted, hardly seems gravely threatening, and while resolutions do depend on some character development, they scarcely occur as the result of any deeply experienced change or chaos. But the last plays survive through tragedy. Hard weather and estrangement in them are real and of long-lasting effect. In the comedies, separation exists, but without any real break. Assurances abound that things will work out well. The needed one thousand marks float in and out of the mad world of Ephesus. Love complications rest on quadrangular bases, rather than triangular, indicating that pairing off is at least possible. But in the last plays there are no such assurances. As Bertrand Evans has demonstrated, the world of the storm appears as senseless to the audience as it does to the participants: "From the point of view of the management of awarenesses, what most distinguishes the first three romances from the comedies is that here, while action continues, we are denied that to which we have grown accustomed — the comforting assurance that, in spite of seeming danger, all is well." (p. 221)

In the histories man is involved with time, but that time is historical and more or less proportionate to man's dimensions. Man is part of society; his identity is social and national, and he has a horrid fear of isolation and of being found short in the ultimate calling to account. But coming after the tragedies, the last plays deal with much larger, almost cosmic, time — by its very nature unmanageable. Far from the comforts of society, man discovers his creatural nature, and when such nakedness has been known there can be little fear of any narrow inventory. From habituation to loss, man acquires an attitude of endurance. Marina was

> Born in a tempest when my mother died!
> This world to me is like a lasting storm,
> Whirring me from my friends.
>
> (IV.i.19–21)

"The Emperor of Russia was my father," is Hermione's magically poignant recollection amidst her present humiliation. (III.ii.120) And yet, for those who clung to the dimensions of civilization this orphanhood is not as terrible as they had feared. In the powers of endurance shown by the older woman, in the natural grace, innocence, and courage of the young girls, a human stability persists which is at the basis of civilization.

The linear stability that formed so much of the value and promise of Shakespeare's House of Lancaster — in the modern world the control of social fluctuations would only grow — is replaced by a deeper experience of change. "Temporal royalties" have been lost, but, as with Prospero, a "kindlier" vision is restored. This vision — it could simply be called that of *methexis* — involves, as it does for Montaigne, the collocation of new things coming into being and the old that are dying out. But it differs from Montaigne's in that the new and the old are intimately connected with generation, with fathers and children. This was a concern of Shakespeare's since the sonnets and the history plays, but here, in the last plays, the facts of generation do not look to continuity or dynasty. Where the histories were properly linear, the last plays are mythic and Hellenic. The *Aeneid* might be the pattern of the histories, but the myth of the last plays is closer to the *Alcestis*. In the generational connection of the histories the vital link is that of father and son. The fear is lest the son fail to master the adult world. But in the last plays the vital link is father and daughter. It is not the child but the old man who requires assistance. There the return of health of mind, or simply of the proper attitude, is coincidental with the recovery of the nature and innocence of the daughter. As Dante in the *Commedia* turns from the historical code involving father and son, and the secular paideia of the city of Florence, so, too, Shakespeare shows his passage out of the dimension of history by looking to the values of innocence, where mother and daughter seem to merge. Yet this is no virginal process; it is deeply involved with wifehood and childbirth and generation.

Despite the valued presence of the young woman in the last plays, her vision does not predominate as it does in the comedies. Any exhortation to the "present pleasure" would seem out of place in the world of such mingled sadness and joy. The vision here — and this is natural considering the large extent of time the romances cover — is that of the middle-aged. We follow their misfortunes and reunions, and it is through their eyes (and experiences) that we look at the young.

This helps explain why Prospero, whose overview is so unrepresentative of the trials of the afflicted in the last plays, is still their titular monarch. The family resemblances of children suggest a pattern within generation. The emphasis is on kind, rather than lineal continuity. Time is not cyclical in this world, but we do see the human life cycle where essential lines of human nature stand revealed. Not outside of time, nor in the lines of history, but within the very developments of life itself a rich and satisfying pattern can be discerned. The last plays, born in *chorismos,* reach *methexis,* where the condition of being is a property of existence itself.

The Winter's Tale

The Winter's Tale is Shakespeare's paradise regained. Leontes is an Othello who threw away his happiness, and yet was allowed to repossess it. After long time — sixteen years — and real estrangement and grief, joy is once again miraculously granted. It is mixed with wonder, and all the more intense because of the sadness, because it is beyond comprehension and even beyond deserving. Oracularly, the return of what was lost is the major movement of the play.

The natural hope in children and continuity that was so important in the histories, as we have seen, forms the level of expectation in *The Winter's Tale* (with the exception that the mother is an important and loved participant, rather than the mere vehicle). Where dynastic royalty is at stake, succession is very important. Florizel, in his aroused youthful passion, can erase himself from his succession. He will be heir to his affections. Leontes' determined refusal to remarry creates problems for his state, where the "fail of issue" might lead to more general destruction. But, in more personal terms, children are consolation and support. Mamillius indeed "physics the subject," we are told in the exchange between Camillo and Archidamus that occurs in the play's very first scene. Old men will hold onto life merely for the benefit of seeing him a man. In the next scene we learn of the joys that young Florizel gives his father. Polixenes is indeed as fond of his prince as Leontes seems to be of Mamillius:

> If at home, sir,
> He's all my exercise, my mirth, my matter;
> Now my sworn friend, and then mine enemy;
> My parasite, my soldier, statesman — all.
> He makes a July's day short as December,

> And with his varying childness cures in me
> Thoughts that would thick the blood.
> (I.ii.165–171)

In the progress of this work, I have illustrated with examples from many sources the great importance in the Renaissance of the notion of progeny. Such possibility of continuity helps man to bear up under the melancholy thoughts of age and death. Here in Polixenes' speech it is not simply the idea of continuity, but rather the gaiety and humor of the boy that takes from his father's mind all brooding. He reminds his father of his own youth, and, in a way that the sonnets suggest, returns the older man to the freer days of natural innocence. In the same scene, Leontes, looking on Mamillius, seems to recall his own past by virtue of his son's resemblance:

> Looking on the lines
> Of my boy's face, methoughts I did recoil
> Twenty-three years, and saw myself unbreech'd,
> In my green velvet coat.
> (153–156)

As Camillo and Archidamus had affirmed of the king's subjects, so Hermione actually clings to life sixteen years for the sake of seeing her own child alive and an adult. It was this hope that gave her the necessary courage (anticipating Prospero's own "undergoing stomach"):

> Tell me, mine own,
> Where hast thou been preserv'd? where liv'd? how found
> Thy father's court? For thou shalt hear that I,
> Knowing by Paulina that the oracle
> Gave hope thou wast in being, have preserv'd
> Myself to see the issue.
> (V.iii.123–128)

The connection which in the early sonnets is vicarious is here personalized in the mother's deep sense of involvement — "mine own."

The fact of family continuity is emphasized by the resemblance of parents and children. The carry-over of visible facial and physical similarities into the succeeding generation has great relevancy for the themes of *The Winter's Tale*. Obviously, where jealousy and imputed adultery are sore points, the visible proofs of paternity are a consolation. Except for the horns, Leontes and Mamillius "are / Almost as like as eggs." When Paulina lays the newborn baby at Leontes' feet, she disproves its bastardy by pointing out the infant's resemblance to Leontes. (II.iii.95–107) There is no greater indication of Leontes' madness and, as in the histories, his self-victimization, than the fact that the victims of his delusion are "copies" of himself. Even after the disaster, when reconciliation is pending, this enduring assumption re-emerges in Leontes' greeting to Florizel:

> Your mother was most true to wedlock, Prince,
> For she did print your royal father off,
> Conceiving you.
>
> (V.i.124–126)

In the sonnets and the history plays, children represented some possibility of temporal response and renewal. The individual might die, but some portion of him would continue to live. In the last plays, although with far deeper personal meaning, children again show Shakespeare's natural faith. "The King shall live without an heir, if that which is lost be not found." Perdita becomes part of the returning current of great creating nature but here, in the final romances, rather than representing some future consolation or historical possibility, she brings present fulfilment and wonderful joy for those who had long been separated. Pericles calls Marina "Thou that beget'st him that did thee beget." (V.i.197) In this play of recognitions and returns, resemblances add to the joyous reunions, suggesting that portions of the principals themselves have returned. Children show Shakespeare's sense of an innate natural link that becomes part of a code of value — a moral DNA — leading to physical and spiritual regeneration.[6]

In the last plays, ordered continuity and lateral stability are broken. We are cast into a tragic world, one perhaps of comings and goings, rather than of rises and falls. Submerged under the apparently calm, complimentary, and gracious manners of adult courtly life exist the wildest possibilities of irrationality and infatuation. Tragedy seems predisposed to assume great instability under the superfices of cultural security; its resolution serves to discover creatural securities within cosmic insecurity. The readiness that Shakespeare's heroes achieve seems to belong more naturally in the last plays to the women, like Hermione:

"There's some ill planet reigns. / I must be patient." Woman herself
— perhaps from her own organic and periodic basis — seems to embody the contained yet rich and patterned world of the last plays. Such
periodicity, associated with the changing seasons, was hostile in the
tragedies of love and was repudiated by the aspiring Cleopatra. But
here, showing the degree to which natural change has been acclimated
into Shakespeare's final vision, it becomes the point of highest wisdom.
Hermione seems devoid of any aggressive pushing into the future,
either in relation to objects or in search of the fleeting goal of happiness. Even the youthful Perdita shows some of the same qualities. It
was as if against her will that she played the role of queen in Act Four
of *The Winter's Tale*. When Polixenes reveals himself and rebukes his
son, she blames her momentary lapse in trying to rise above her station:

> This dream of mine —
> Being now awake, I'll queen it no inch farther,
> But milk my ewes and weep.
>
> (459–461)

Yet, in her profession of fidelity (as her mother's own actions testify),
she espouses the values of fidelity and permanence that are always noble
and heroic in Shakespeare: "I think affliction may subdue the cheek
/ But not take in the mind." Like her mother, she is capable of the
combined qualities of strength and acceptance.

In the return of what was lost, the story of *The Winter's Tale* comes
into contact with the myths that hover around human actions and give
mysterious enlargement and suggestiveness to them. Through mythic
resonances, the basic life lines of man and woman emerge. The myth
of the Christian Fall helps explain the loss of boyhood innocence shared
by Polixenes and Leontes. Polixenes tells Hermione that the two boys

> were as twinn'd lambs that did frisk i' th' sun
> And bleat the one at th' other. What we chang'd
> Was innocence for innocence; we knew not
> The doctrine of ill-doing, no, nor dream'd
> That any did. Had we pursu'd that life,
> And our weak spirits ne'er been higher rear'd
> With stronger blood, we should have answer'd heaven
> Boldly, "Not guilty," the imposition clear'd
> Hereditary ours.
>
> (I.ii.67–75)

Hermione jokingly takes this to imply that they have fallen since, and Polixenes agrees, graciously complimenting her and his own queen as the respective sources of temptation. Although this explanation of the fall is offered with grace and humor, it does correspond to the real changes that have come upon the former friends in their male maturity. The loss of innocence is coincidental with the age of sexual maturity and the ego-possessiveness in man's relations with woman. Also jeopardized by this fall is the paradise of male friendship. In this period of jealous turmoil, the former friend removes himself and the woman suffers patiently: like Alcestis, Hermione must go underground, as it were, and endure death until, with the growth of her daughter and her husband's middle age, she can be seen by Leontes with the understanding and unselfish affection that suffering in long time has produced. In his daughter Leontes can see his wife when young; and in his wife he sees what his daughter must endure. This vision is the product of sheer length of time: the perception of patterns of resemblance produces a growth of the understanding that works toward reunion.

If the essential stages of male growth are suggested, so are those of womanhood, from Perdita's innocent natural grace to her mother's return as a middle-aged woman. Here, too, the reader is moved by an irresistible urge to respond to the mythic suggestivity of the piece. Proserpina is there in Perdita's lovely apostrophe,

> O Proserpina,
> For the flowers now that, frighted, thou let'st fall
> From Dis's wagon!
>
> (IV.iii.116–118)

And like the mythical prototype, her absence is coincidental with the blight of estrangement. But, although Perdita is absent, she is never underground. In Florizel's description of her she is natural grace in all its completeness and self-sufficiency:

> What you do
> Still betters what is done. When you speak, sweet,
> I'ld have you do it ever. When you sing,
> I'ld have you buy and sell so; so give alms;
> Pray so; and for the ord'ring your affairs,
> To sing them too. When you do dance, I wish you
> A wave o' th' sea, that you might ever do
> Nothing but that; move still, still so,

And own no other function. Each your doing,
So singular in each particular,
Crowns what you are doing in the present deed,
That all your acts are queens.

(IV.iv.135–146)

What Laura represented for Petrarch, this portrait of natural beauty represents for Florizel, with two essential differences. Although this description is qualified by the over-arching experience of the play, still there is no sense of conflict between this fulfilling role of woman and a religious sense of life. Secondly, the English sense of the legitimacy of sexuality and generation (witness Spenser's "Garden of Adonis") is alien to Petrarch's aesthetic distance from his ideal woman. Perdita would strew the flowers of springtime on Florizel, but not to deck a corpse — "or if — not to be buried, / But quick, and in mine arms."

While Perdita suggests a world before the Fall, she lives and is surrounded by a world in the latter part of the seasons. While she helps the autumnal atmosphere to reflourish, the wisdom of the play is not that of simple spring. Perdita does not possess the chastened wisdom of destroyed happiness; this is the experience of the older members, who, like the play itself, see two times: what they once were and what they have become. It is they who repossess the innocent virtue of spring in the winter of ruined expectations.

It is Hermione who goes underground, lost to the spectator as well as to her family. Like Alcestis, she endures death. Hers is the maternal sacrifice that the woman must undergo when she enters into marriage. There is a special bond between mother and daughter in the last scene of the play. Perdita kneels before her mother in reverence for the sacrifice Hermione made when Perdita came into life. And here her simple utterance seems to have greater reverberations, just as the actions of the play have airy extension:

Lady,
Dear queen, that ended when I but began,
Give me that hand of yours to kiss.

(V.iii.44–46)

The bringing together of beginnings and ends is important in *The Winter's Tale*. But here, unlike the contraction of the tragic lovers, the collocation is not of essential facts of experience, as love and death, but rather of essential stages in the life process; the emphasis is not on termination, but the discovery of continuity and pattern. The stage of Hermione's innocence ended symbolically with the birth of Perdita. Perdita now takes Hermione's place in the human chain of repeated birth. It is this discovery and this acceptance of the essential stages of human life that gives profundity to the joys of the final reconciliation.

The Tempest

In *The Tempest* Prospero is the bearer of an ancient grudge. This conflict between his name and his past is resolved in the very acceptable conclusion of Bertrand Evans: "Plainly, in *The Tempest* Shakespeare did not seek to represent struggle itself, but to proffer its fruits." (p. 336) We come upon Prospero when he is in his full powers, with a daughter grown, and having had the years to assimilate and understand his earlier loss and replacement. Although he is a beneficent power, raising and then allaying the storm, and ensuring that no one has been harmed, still Prospero's first appearance is as the upholder of past memories. The story he tells is of the primal eldest curse, the Cain-Abel motif, which was so present in the material of the histories and tragedies, and which was one frame from which youth escapes in the comedies. It is the more painful social equivalent of the original sin. The liberal arts were all Prospero's study; for these he grew a stranger to his state, neglected worldly ends: "Me (poor man) my library / Was dukedom large enough." This was the extent of Prospero's complicity with his "perfidious brother"; nevertheless through his absence the lesser Antonio did manage the mundane arts,

> how to grant suits,
> How to deny them, who t' advance, and who
> To trash for over-topping.
>
> (I.ii.79–81)

His craft calls to mind the essential lesson learned in the garden scene of *Richard II*. The reappearance of this political message in a highly unfavorable context suggests something of the change Shakespeare's own views underwent from the time of the histories to that of the last plays. The higher arts, imperfectly possessed by Richard II, are vindicated in the character of Prospero. Unlike Richard II, he was not a decadent: his signory was first in the land, and Prospero himself was well loved. His true, and more ideal, interest in government is revealed by the particular pain he felt that his free state of Milan should have to enter into a tributary relation with Naples, in order for his brother to obtain assistance from Alonso.

Although Prospero is educating Miranda in order to have her properly appreciate his dramatic virtuosity, still her reaction (perhaps the one he hopes for and anticipates) is in contrast to his hectoring insistence on reopening past wounds. All pity and love, she is not by nature inclined to want to know more about the past; she is content with the present: "More to know / Did never meddle with my thoughts." (21–22) It was the presence of the infant Miranda that gave Prospero "an undergoing stomach, to bear up / Against what should ensue" (157–158) in the tempest of personal crisis. Although in different circumstances, and to different effect, the child in the last plays fulfills the same beneficent, life-saving functions as in the earlier histories. And as in the histories, so here, the child is helpful in attitude. It is her response to the plight of his enemies — caught in the storm that Prospero's art has created — that serves to educate his response.

While such a conclusion would also seem foregone, still Prospero's virtual power must be made actual, and he must forgive his enemies — not only in his dramas, but also in his life. The lack of dramatic struggle here does not contradict the need for such action. After years of remembering earlier injury and plotting revenge — what prodigies, what terrors they will be — Prospero must finally react not according to the wrongs suffered but according to his better reason. Long years have brought changes in his enemies, too. Facing imminent shipwreck, Alonso, who was returning from marrying his own daughter, is more sympathetically presented by the pious enthusiast Gonzalo, "The King and Prince at prayers! Let's assist them, / For our case is as theirs." (I.i.57–58) In fact, as the play proceeds, Alonso becomes exposed to the same kind of plot that deposed Prospero. That wide-ranging, empathic dramatic virtuosity so typical of Shakespeare's art becomes the special moral vision of his chief characters. Hamlet is sorry that he became furious at the mourning Laertes, "For by the image of my cause I see / The portraiture of his." (V.ii.75–78) So, Miranda's appeal is to human empathy, "O, I have suffered / With those that I saw suffer!" These virtues now have become redemptive, as Prospero, combining both functions of dramatist and moralist, uniting the aesthetic and the ethical which were so severely disjoined in the histories, lives to see the larger disorder and helplessness of his enemies. Ariel relates their pain:

> Your charm so strongly works 'em,
> That if you now beheld them, your affections
> Would become tender.

Pros.   Dost thou think so, spirit?

Ariel. Mine would, sir, were I human.
Pros.   And mine shall.
 Hast thou, which are but air, a touch, a feeling
 Of their affections, and shall not myself,
 One of their kind, that relish all as sharply
 Passion as they, be kindlier mov'd than thou art?
 Though with their high wrongs I am struck to th' quick,
 Yet with my nobler reason 'gainst my fury
 Do I take part. The rarer action is
 In virtue than in vengeance.

           (V.i.17–28)

Miranda's pity, like Perdita's regenerative potential, seems to have become part of nature itself. The very air is inclined toward compassion, and so is Prospero's nobler reason. Although practical reason recognizes that he has been wronged (the wound is still present — "with their high wrongs *I am* struck to the quick" —) and that revenge is justified, his "nobler" reason, his sense of kind, must subdue his fury. When put to the test, Prospero must reveal his finer self — the real end of the Shakespearean journey in time.

Prospero's supremacy is more seriously challenged in another episode that can serve to summarize not only Shakespeare's but perhaps all the Elizabethans' war with time. In the masque that he created for the newly pledged lovers, Prospero shows the very aspirations of his mind, seeking to lend permanence and continuance to the passing things of this world. Generational continuity and married love are granted extension in his remarkable vision of bounty and grace — Shakespeare's "Prayer for a Daughter." The songs of Juno and Ceres bring an abiding spirit into the earth:

Juno. Honour, riches, marriage blessing,
  Long continuance, and increasing,
  Hourly joys be still upon you!
  Juno sings her blessings on you.
Ceres. Earth's increase, foison plenty,
  Barns and garners never empty,
  Vines with clust'ring bunches growing,
  Plants with goodly burthen bowing;
  Spring come to you at the farthest
  In the very end of harvest!

          (IV.i.106–115)

This bountiful sense of life, of fruitfulness and growth, naturally involves Prospero in intimations of immortality. But just as Henry VI and Iden were deprived of such satisfactions to their yearning, so Prospero's art is interrupted by the rude entrance of history. He had momentarily over-looked Caliban and his plot. The emulative motif of the histories here reveals the strong hold it had on Shakespeare's consciousness. Caliban's return plunges Prospero into a cosmic despair; like Dante, or the Spenser of the *Mutabilitie Cantos,* he is confronted with a world of struggle, re-placement, and termination rather than the concord and continuity he had imagined. Almost literally he is cast into an absurdist universe: his dancers vanish to a "strange, hollow and confused noise." Caliban is that lingering original sin, that part of us that participates in decay — "as with age his body uglier grows / So his mind cankers" — and Prospero must admit to the relationship — "this thing of darkness I acknowledge mine." The presence of Caliban, the smell of mortality, counts for so much as to utterly discredit the aspirations of Prospero's mind and the reality of his art. The persistence of his unregenerate nature suggests a vast uni-verse, similar to that of Petrarch's *Triumph of Time,* which dwarfs all man's efforts and renders vain all his desires. Prospero's vision of bounty was a baseless fabric, his theatre an insubstantial pageant. Such con-structs of human ideality count for little in a universe that will dissolve not only man's more solid cultural achievements but the great globe itself. Nihilistic conclusions approaching those of Jaques and even of Macbeth are Prospero's:

> We are such stuff
> As dreams are made on, and our little life
> Is rounded with a sleep.
>
> (IV.i.156–158)

Yet, despite this temporary lapse, Prospero is soon restored to his more native optimism. What it is that calms his beating mind is not clear: he has several plots to complete and a daughter to marry. Whatever the cosmos might be, and despite Caliban and his higher relations in emula-tive rebellion, Sebastian and Antonio, Prospero regains his better nature. In fact, *The Tempest* shows an essential faith in human reasonableness. The disordered fits of ambition are seen to be precisely that: aberrations from the norm. Prospero is able to bring his enemies to their better senses; as with the coming of morning,

>   so their rising senses
> Begin to chase the ignorant fumes that mantle
> Their clearer reason.
>
>   (V.i.66–68)

With such restorations and with such reconciliations imminent, and given such basic faith in enlightenment, what need is there to threaten prodigies of revenge? In this most delicate treatment of art and of a condition that might possibly approach neurosis, Prospero can well abjure his craft. If the End of the Renaissance (a notion that could profitably be open to more systematic study) has any meaning, this is the gesture that best symbolizes it. For Shakespeare, man's soul will no longer be stretched those splendid and terrifying distances. And here he is certainly prophetic of the future, however much those grand strains will continue to be played by the metaphysical poets and by Milton.

In his most airy and imaginative work, Shakespeare bids farewell to Ariel and to his imaginative, cosmos-involving art. Reasonableness brings with it reduced dimensions. Unlike Spenser or Donne, Shakespeare does not turn his back on the new age of reason. Like Montaigne, although with greater dramatic struggle, he proceeded from the world where man was everything, through the necessary break-up of *chorismos*, toward a more integrated experience of aspiration and reality. After suffering and through sheer length of time, a new vision emerges in the last plays that represents a reconciliation of the demands of the histories and the desires of love, of the remarkable human capacity for continuity and the pressing realities of time and change. Shakespeare's last plays have, as does Montaigne's third book of *Essays,* a lofty sense of discovery and originality. Rich, mythic patterns closely linked with the human life cycle and man's more creatural nature persist and even predominate within a changing universe. Such achievements their more rational and enlightened successors could not hope to duplicate, and here lies the difference, as we have seen throughout the Renaissance, between a conquest and an inheritance.

Chapter 11
Milton

The Ways of Succession

For various reasons — personal predisposition and experiences, the accident of historical position — Milton suffered an earlier disillusionment in the ways of succession than did his Elizabethan predecessors. That grand Tudor establishment, which inspired and confirmed faith in generation and succession, came to an end; and like Augustine or Dante, Milton experienced the fall of a great order, the end of a line. Like Petrarch, Milton began feeling the fascination of death when still a youth, and as with the earlier Italian poet, whom he somewhat resembles, the experience and overhanging threat of pestilence tended to cancel an already shaky faith in succession. A plague that struck London in May 1625 grew to the extent that "as many as 35,000 persons were said to have died of [it]" in the autumn of that year. It revived soon after the start of Easter term, 1630, and made Cambridge a desolate place. "Whoever has read the records of those times knows that an almost constant subject of alarm to England, as well as to other nations, was the Plague. Every ten or fifteen years there was either a visit of it or a rumour of its coming." [1]

Infant mortality, always high in those times, was aggravated under the conditions of plague. In a time when, to unearth evidence of a marriage, an investigator from a later age would be obliged to search out the recorded burial entries of infant children; when a father could lose all his sons to the plague within three days, there was little reason to celebrate the ways of succession. Consequently, in one area of vital response to time — progeny — Milton was not hopeful. (As we shall see, his ideas on fame, that other form of temporal response, were more complicated.) When Milton came to undertake the poetic memorial for Edward King, it was not the first time that he addressed premature death, "yet once more, O ye laurels, and once more." Quite early in his poetic career he had devoted attention to the deaths of children. *On the Death of a Fair Infant* and *An Epitaph on the Marchioness of Winchester* deal with disruptions in the process of generation and normal expectations. Even in *On the Morning of Christ's Nativity* his realism obliges him to jump over the blessed event and to foresee the suffering the grown man must endure. However attractive it would be to anticipate a golden age on the morning of Christ's birth ("Time will run back and fetch the age of gold"), fate denies that untroubled consummation:

> The Babe lies yet in smiling infancy,
> That on the bitter cross
> Must redeem our loss,
> So both himself and us to glorify.[2]

The blood in *Upon the Circumcision* anticipates the scene of the crucifixion:

> Alas, how soon our sin
> Sore doth begin
> His infancy to seize!

Christian realism and the forms it gave to experience served to limit the possibilities of generation and made Milton less willing to extol it as a primary source of hope. For one thing to return to the earlier *Fair Infant,* it was only among the "wanton gods" that childlessness was held a reproach. And in the conclusion of the poem, religious consolation, echoing Isaiah (56.5), invokes a higher reward for patience under God's will, the offspring of immortality: "he will an offspring give / That till the world's last end shall make thy name to live."[3]

Later experience does nothing to change such early awareness and inclinations. Milton's unhappy first marriage, his tragic second, where fruit and tree were indeed spoiled, and his childless third all added to his earlier disinclination to place great hopes in succession. However, Milton stands apart from that line of humanism, represented by Petrarch and Boccaccio (and later by Francis Bacon), which preferred the products of the spirit to those of the loins. For Milton, as for Spenser in his Garden of Adonis, God's great command is to increase and multiply. This would have been an event of simple blessedness in the world before the Fall. After the Fall, however, Adam's pain at Michael's vision of the future is increased because he is the guilty father helplessly watching the destruction of his children. Far from being sources of regeneration, the children present the father with horrid mirror-images of his own malfeasance. Milton, like some other poets, did not have luck with his children. Edward Phillips gives some indication of the family turmoil, as the blind Milton tried to force his daughters to read to him by sounding out the syllables of languages they did not comprehend. Whether through "their failure or his stubbornness" he eventually had to farm them out to learn embroidery. And, with some resemblance to King Lear, Milton in effect disinherited his "unkind children." [4]

In his position as a son, Milton was distinctly aware of the tensions of fathers and children. From the earlier *Ad Patrem* to *Paradise Regained* and *Samson Agonistes,* the poems reveal essential cross-purposes deriving from the son's need to satisfy his heroic hunger in the face of his father's more practical concerns. The rival claims of the two fathers have their hold on Milton, and, in fact, become important parts of his work. The one looks to the securities of experience with its realization in the adult world of history, while the spiritual father requires greater risks, risks that might involve tragedy or divine comedy. It is no accident that the Renaissance, with its discovery of time and the tutelary figure of the father, and its simultaneous fostering of the great heroic desires of the son, should be painfully divided by the demands of these separate worlds. With Milton the fact remains that generation does not redeem itself so easily or so naturally: fate requires the crucifixion. Through blood and nails, in time, the tree of generation does reflower, but in a way far different from human expectations. When Christ in *Paradise Regained* returns home to his mother's house, it is because he has come to understand, by resisting Satan's false suggestions, the true way of accomplishing his father's business. And in *Samson Agonistes,* the consolations of the human father do not contain the higher and more heroic intentions of the spiritual father. The crucifixion, which the father would naturally prevent or soften, the son must face, for through it, as the *Nativity Ode* declares, lies his greater glory.

It is in his *Seventh Prolusion* (which, despite its occasional function, Milton clearly considered a serious pronouncement on vital matters) and his treatise *Of Education* that Milton shows himself to be a true son of the Renaissance. Like Petrarch and Spenser before him, he defends the value of letters for society, renounces that abuse of history, the doctrine of decay or decline, and extols the grand coincidence between "here" and "there," between man's glory and God's divine control. To be somewhat impressionistic, it is more in the spirit of these works, particularly the former, that Milton's Renaissance heritage reveals itself, as he sets out with energy and dedication to accomplish great things — things that can only be the products of lofty ideals and strenuous labor — and thus earn the rewards of glory and fame. As he values distinction and extension — the basic goals of Renaissance humanism — so he deplores the sluggishness and oblivion of beastly ignorance:

> Now in faith what truly is the blessedness of Ignorance? To possess its own for itself, to be defamed by nobody, to avoid every care and trouble, to spend life as easily and calmly as possible. But this is the life of a beast or of some bird which has its nest for safety as close to the sky as possible, on the height or in the depth of the forests, which trains its young, which flies to the feeding ground without fear of the fowler, which at dawn and at evening sings sweet strains. What does that ethereal vigor of the soul long for beyond these? Well, let it lay aside the human; let it be given the Circean cup; stooping let it migrate to the beasts.
>
> *(Works,* XII.281)

Despite the downright attractiveness of this life of the beast (his description foretells a future change), Milton's soul requires greater efforts and greater rewards. The *Areopagitica,* in its most famous passage, shows the heroic energy and activity that typified Milton's young faith: "I cannot praise a fugitive and cloistered virtue, unexercised and unbreathed, that never sallies out and sees her adversary, but slinks out of the race, where that immortal garland is to be run for, not without dust and heat." *(Works,* IV.311) Renaissance humanism involves the heroic act of separation, of risk-taking, of setting out from the easier, more common and natural patterns of life for the sake of the extraordinary. We can think of Dante, attempting at the outset of the *Inferno* to scale the mountain through his own efforts (it is noteworthy that in his *Commonplace Book (Works,* XVIII.141), Milton looks at sloth through Dante's presentation of it in *Inf.* III), or of Petrarch, in the ardor of the "Coronation Oration." In his announcement of his poetic vocation, Milton will also share their ideals and fervor. In the important poetic epistle *Ad Patrem,* he promises to take his place among that "learned band" of ancient poets (we recall *Inf.* IV) "and sit with a victor's ivy and laurel. Then I shall not mingle, unknown, with the dull crowd, and my footsteps shall shun the light of profane eyes." (101–104) Obscurity and sluggishness are loathsome to this Renaissance idealism.

Deeper satisfactions are required than the normal rounds of life can afford. At heart, religious assumptions and hopes infuse Milton's great striving. He takes it as a belief his audience shares, "That the great Framer of the universe, although He had founded all other things on change and decay, had intermingled in man, beyond what is mortal, a certain divine breath and as it were a part of Himself, immortal, imperishable, immune from death and destruction." (*Works*, XII.253–255) Man's true happiness, then, lies in satisfying this greater need. While this essential faith will be crucial in Milton's later works, especially in *Paradise Regained* and *Samson Agonistes*, here, years earlier, it is by knowledge that man fulfills this eternal part of his nature. It were a cruel joke for the great Framer of the universe to have given us this insatiable desire in vain, unless he meant for us to develop it fully. Moreover, by satisfying this hunger, by understanding his works, man gives greater glory to God. Milton, holds a belief that we have already witnessed in the early stages of Dante, Petrarch, and Spenser: that an amalgamation is possible whereby those things useful for life actually lead to those things needful for salvation. "Here" and "there" are more than reconcilable: they are necessarily, even heroically, conjoined.

We recall the famous phrase from *Of Education*, "The end then of learning is to repair the ruins of our first parents by regaining to know God aright." So, in the *Seventh Prolusion*, knowledge lends a weapon to contend with death. Looking before and after, into the past and the future, knowledge makes one "a contemporary of time itself." While granting all the obvious dissimilarities, we concede the justice with which this speech has been labeled "Baconian." When the full lamp of learning has been turned on, so that all the corners of the world are illuminated, "Then at length many accidents and consequences of things will become clear so suddenly that nothing in life can happen quite unexpectedly, nothing by chance to one who has gained possession of this stronghold of wisdom. He will seem to be one whose power and authority the stars will obey, the land and the sea will follow implicitly, the winds and the storms will strive to please; one to whom Mother Nature even will hand over herself in surrender, quite as if some god, having abdicated power on earth, had delegated to him his court, his laws, his executive power, as though to some prefect." (*Works*, XII.267) "Nothing unexpectedly, nothing by chance" — so goes this early testament. Yet, later, rather than such control, which he would come to think impossible, Milton will find more welcome a condition of readiness for what is unexpected and unforeseen.

In his ideas on education we find the same aroused and vigorous utilization of time that we had found in the other Renaissance tracts, where the need to order experience was pronounced. To teach the principal authors "più brievemente e perfecte," was Palmieri's slogan, and Milton too utters the cry of the educational reformer that superior material can be better taught in a shorter period of time. In *Of Education,* he outlines the ideas that he had slowly developed, "of a better education, in extent and comprehension far more large, and yet of time far shorter, and of attainment far more certain, than hath been yet in practice." In the *Seventh Prolusion* he complains of two obstacles to true education: "knowledge poorly taught" and "slothfulness." An earlier prolusion, "In the Morning Rise up Early," regrets that physical laborers make better use of their time than do scholars, "who aspire to the highest and best in human affairs": "We permit ourselves to be outstripped by laborers and farmers in nightly and early morning toil. . . . We guard our health against late hours and severe studies; shameful to say, we leave the mind uncultured." (XII.273–275) This is particularly shameful, since, given diligent application and a temperate life, the scope of what man can accomplish is practically limitless. Of course Milton was advocating what he himself had practiced. From his brother, Christopher Milton, John Aubrey learned that "when he was very young, he studied very hard, and sat up very late, commonly till twelve or one o'clock at night," and Aubrey also notes that Milton "was an early riser (*scil.* at 4 o'clock manè)." [5]

In the *Seventh Prolusion* Milton would save time by emphasizing useful material. He would discard the "trifles of the grammarians and the rhetoricians," save only what was worthy from logic, and avoid the perilous rocks of metaphysics. "With all of these things, which are of no value, despised and eliminated, it will be wonderful how many whole years we shall gain." In *Of Education* he holds that the amount of Latin or Greek that had been acquired in seven or eight years "might be learned otherwise easily and delightfully in one year." (*Works,* IV.277) The anonymous *Life of Milton* rightly observed that he had put his pedagogic ideas to work on his nephews John and Edward Phillips, and in Aubrey's notes Edward Phillips wrote that Milton "in a year's time made them capable of interpreting a Latin author at sight, etc., and within three years they went through the best of the Latin and Greek poets." [6] The glorious conquest of knowledge envisioned by Milton depended upon maximum utilization of time ("if from child-

hood we permit no day to pass without lessons and diligent study,"
Works, XII.279), and in *Of Education* he maintains that one reason for
his country's lack of proficiency in those classical languages "is our
time lost partly in too oft idle vacancies given both to schools and
Universities." (XII.278) Milton seems to be objecting not to vacations,
which he regarded as refreshing, but to the practice of suspending studies
on holidays.[7] Along with this concern for time goes, as we have seen
in other Renaissance educational tracts, a desire to introduce right
order in the system of studies. Milton opposes the composition of themes
and orations before the student has read sufficiently in "pure authors"
and his judgment and experience have been formed. Unlike the *Seventh
Prolusion, Of Education* does not throw out grammar or rhetoric, or
even logic and metaphysics; rather, in it Milton insists that these subjects be taught at a suitable age, after the student has learned and
mastered more convenient material, natural geography, physics, ethics,
politics.[8] By gradations ("The next step would be the authors of agriculture"), Milton would lead the student along, concerned equally with
the appropriateness of the material to the growth stage of the youngster
and with increasing his diligence and application to the limit (and
sometimes beyond).[9] Though hardly as programmed in daily detail,
still his systematic and inspired exploitation of time recalls Gargantua's
regimen, whereby "il ne perdoit heures quelconques du jour." In the
Seventh Prolusion, Milton declares that it is merely the excuse of Ignorance which holds that life is short and art is long. Given a true
vision of man's possibilities and a more profitable use of his time, Milton
believes that this easy formula can be reversed, so that life becomes
long and art short. Thus benefitted, the scholar will be like an Alexander
with no new worlds to conquer. (XII.279)

Milton's disenchantment with fame also occurred quite early, given
his commitment to the heroic possibilities of learning. Here the lines
of any chronological demarcation are complicated by an apparent division between his poetry and his prose. In his poetry, new values were
introduced as early as 1632 which would qualify his confidence in fame.
But in his prose, the ideas of the *Seventh Prolusion* are paralleled by
similar sentiments in *The Reason of Church Government Urged Against
Prelaty* (1642), *Of Education* and *Areopagitica* (1644), and even *The
History of Britain.* In the Second Book of the last, he writes that "great
Acts and great Eloquence have most commonly gone hand in hand"
and that true valour, "knowing that when he Conquers all things else,

he cannot Conquer Time or Detraction . . . honours and hath recourse to the aid of Eloquence . . . by whose immortal record his noble deeds, which else were transitory, becoming fixt and durable against the force of Yeares and Generations, he fails not to continue through all posterity, over Envy, Death, and Time, also victorious." [10] But in *Paradise Lost,* just this union between society and fame is seen to be broken by a general failure to discern true merit. "The better fortitude / Of patience and heroic martyrdom" is left unsung (IX.31–33) and "what most merits fame [is] in silence hid" (XI.699) while the destroyers are glorified. Although the lines are blurred, still the basic direction of Milton's thought is clear. The religious answer of patience to the call for fame is heard from the early sonnet "How soon hath Time." Its distinctions between inner ripeness and timely response extend through *Lycidas* and receive their fullest expression in the three great last poems, thus representing a repudiation of the active, energetic Renaissance spirit that values the ready response; the spirit that, by removing the unexpected and the uncertain, seeks to control events, and that culminates in Baconianism.

In this regard, *On Time* is worthy to be associated with sonnet VII, since the divisions between outer seeming and inner ripeness are there broadened into the more basic differences between the moving world of time, which, nevertheless, only consumes what is unworthy, and the more rewarding world of religious peace:

> Attired with stars, we shall for ever sit,
> Triumphing over Death, and Chance, and thee, o Time.

Milton's intention is not to capture time or to seize the day, but to let it run to its own dissolution. In fact one of the major themes of Milton's most serious poetry is quite simply resistance to the temptations posed by those arguments of time that had so clearly emerged in the earlier Renaissance.[11]

Sonnet VII ("How soon hath Time"), the contemporaneous letter to an unnamed friend, and the much later sonnet XIX ("When I consider how my light is spent") can be treated together, despite subtle shifts in emphasis, because in them Milton invokes patience to withstand the argument of time. For comparative purposes they are especially important because they, too, have behind them the parable of the talents and the idea of the call to account. In sonnet VII Milton feels that he has not much to show for his late spring, neither bud nor blossom. In the letter, although unasked, he feels obliged to give an account, and he recognizes the "solid good flowing from due and tymely obedience to that command in the gospell set out by the terrible seasing of him that hid the talent." And in sonnet XIX, although the "one talent which is death to hide" — his work of reading and writing so dependent upon his eyes — is of no use, he seems more pressed therefore to give his "true account." [12] Still, while recognizing the sway of these arguments, he is able here to suggest relief from anxiety through the sense of a higher calling. This struggle for psychological independence represents another stage in Renaissance temporal developments. In the fourteenth century, the argument of time was used by Dante and Petrarch for essentially religious purposes. But a bourgeois twist is given the Biblical instance when the clergyman Domenico Cavalca employs the parable of talents to discipline his brothers, largely in the matters of social relevancy. In Shakespeare the culmination of the secularizing process is seen when the parable of the talents, without any religious connotation whatsoever, is used as an argument to further generation. Indicating future directions, both for himself and for the argument of time where literature is concerned, Milton resists the incontinent need to show fruit. He is more aware of an inner process of ripening that enjoys religious favor.

"How soon hath Time" is one Miltonic poem that is sensitive to the emulative competition that brought the lessons of wasted time so sharply home to Hal, Richard, Falstaff, and Hamlet. Douglas Bush's headnote to the poem in his edition of Milton's poetry captures its spiritual context: "[Milton] had become a literary and intellectual figure in the Cambridge world, but now he has been for six months an obscure student under his father's roof, beginning the years of hard reading by which he hoped to prepare himself for the unknown future: meanwhile his contemporaries were forging ahead." Yet Milton is able to resist earlier and more strongly than Shakespeare the appearances of the "timely-happy." With all its complications, even in the histories, time for Shakespeare was competitive and social; its power demonstrated the reality of external phenomena. In his version of the argument of time, it was mainly in relation to things and achievements, position and power, that man defined himself. The tragedies would reverse this, of course, but still it was not until the last plays that Prospero's kindlier vision replaced his lost "temporal royalties." For Milton, however, it is the inner worth in tune with the will of heaven that matters.

It is at this point that the letter differs from the two sonnets. Presumably his correspondent had urged Milton to become a more useful member of society by joining the clergy, and had faulted him for having "too much love of Learning." Milton proceeds to give an account of his "tardie moving" — the man's arguments did not fall on deaf ears — and in so doing resumes the general Renaissance arguments for responding to time. "Natural proneness" or laziness must be discounted, because this would be insufficient to counteract the deep motives that man has to establish himself with "house and family of his owne to which nothing is esteemed more helpful than the early entring into credible employment." The second force operating in man ("Which is not of pure yet of refined nature . . . to dissuade prolonged obscurity") is the "desire of honour and repute and immortall fame seated in the brest of every true scholar which all make hast to by the readiest ways of publishing and divulging conceived merits as well those that shall as those that never shall obtaine it." The desire for fame, while not yet seen to be an impurity, is definitely a subordinate value (as it is in Augustine). Its lack of purity is indicated in Milton's description of the itch to publish and of its uncertain rewards. Higher aims move Milton above the instant way of response. In fact the very parable of the talents, instead of urging him to press forward, urges restraint; its consideration "keeps off with a sacred reverence, and religious advisement how best to undergoe not taking thought of being late so it give advantage to be more fit, for those that were latest lost nothing when the maister of the vinyard came to give each one his hire." (*Works,* XII.324) Too much haste, too much eagerness for fame propels his contemporaries to publish what they perhaps should not. Rather than neglecting his time, Milton, like Petrarch in his *On Solitude,* is making a tactical retreat, taking one step backward in order to take two forward. He uses the parable of the vineyard to balance that of the talents. It is a question not of time, but of the fitness of the work.

But in both sonnets, this element of superior calculation is absent. Perhaps this is because in the letter Milton is trying to reassure his friend, perhaps also because his prose is more assertive than his poetry, his "nightward thoughts." Whatever the cause, in the sonnets there is less certainty about the ultimate worth of his efforts, which nevertheless are covered by his act of religious dedication. In sonnet VII Milton is ready to accept God's will not only whether the results of his efforts come "soon or slow" but also whether they be "less or more" or "mean or high." In the prose letter, the fitter time for appearance is Milton's to consider, but in the sonnets the outcome is more in the hands of an external time, directed by the will of heaven. And in sonnet XIX, the day-labor, which the letter believes is now due, seems to have been cancelled literally by Milton's loss of sight. His fretfulness over an un-

just accounting implies a slight to God, and Patience silences his unnecessary murmuring. While there are those who are dispatched in
God's service, constantly posting "without rest," Milton still can find
peace in the knowledge that there are those close to God "who only
stand and wait." Though he does not uproot the notion of an active
use of time, Milton still provides other alternatives to Renaissance militancy. One can serve by enduring inaction. Over-eagerness, any Renaissance aggressiveness, will not cause him to withdraw from God's service,
or that portion of God's service that seems to be his.

The sonnet that opened the period of private study in his father's home
reflects Milton's realization that the standards of the world and its
vision might not be suited to recognize true merit. His disenchantment
with worldly fame and, more importantly, with the larger realm of succession, is developed in the poem that closes the Horton period, *Lycidas*.
Here early death and the real uncertainties of mortal existence stagger
the youthful confidence in a regularly functioning nature. Premature
death is even more painful in those areas of human life that depend
upon time and maturity for the realization of their high aims. Rewards
in the scholarly, humanistic world, unlike those of the more active life,
are deferred as the man of high dedication and lofty goals labors to
attain his proper skill. In *The Reason of Church Government* he declares that if he were seeking after glory, "I should not write thus out
of mine own season, when I have neither yet completed to my mind the
full circle of my private studies." (*Works*, III.i.234) In a letter to
Charles Diodati of 1637, he gives some indication of the order of his
studies: "I have by continuous reading brought down the affairs of the
Greeks as far as to the time when they ceased to be Greeks. I have
been long engaged in the obscure business of the state of Italians under
the Longobards, the Franks, and the Germans, down to the time when
liberty was granted them by Rodolph, King of Germany: from that
period it will be better to read separately what each City did by its
own wars." (*Works*, XII.29) Realization is postponed in Milton's
ambitious dedication to toil, long hours, and diligent and ordered study.
The experiences that intervened must have been fortunate, and the
ease that he felt must have been wonderful, when the author of *Paradise
Lost* could praise his

> celestial patroness, who deigns
> Her nightly visitation unimplored,

And dictates to me slumb'ring, or inspires
Easy my unpremeditated verse.

(IX.21–24)

"Unpremeditated verse" is far from the ambitious planning of the younger Milton. Such planning, of course, depends upon the hope that the time necessary for his plans to be realized will in fact be granted, but it is just such a hope that the early death of Edward King serves to extinguish. Fate can intervene cruelly to cut promise short; that long worked-for goal can be wiped out in an instant by the absurd and the irrational. Given such a reality, a larger containing principle beyond that of temporal achievement or confidence is required, with which one would be ready to face the dark and the unknown. In *Lycidas* the ideals of poetry and its rewards are discovered to be insufficient to the uncertain world and the possibilities of unfulfillment that Milton must face.

Lycidas contains a vignette of the enclosed and secure world of the undergraduate — a world that is quickly shattered in confrontation with adult life:

Together both, ere the high lawns appeared
Under the opening eyelids of the morn,
We drove afield, and both together heard
What time the gray-fly winds her sultry horn,
Batt'ning our flocks with the fresh dews of night,
Oft till the star that rose, at ev'ning, bright
Toward heav'n's descent had sloped his westering wheel.
Meanwhile the rural ditties were not mute,
Tempered to th' oaten flute;
Rough Satyrs danced, and Fauns with clov'n heel
From the glad sound would not be absent long,
And old Damoetas loved to hear our song.

(25–36)

This was the world — fittingly in a pastoral setting — before the fall, showing oblivious (yet creative) animal energies in tune with the apparently beneficent processes of nature. Morning, noon, and night proceed in regular pattern, and security is assured by the presence of the guiding evening star and the paternal old teacher, Damoetas. He lends stability, authority, and approval to their carefree days. As the idyll closes, his authoritative figure seems to ward off life's terrors and appropriately to confirm their youthful optimism.

They were together then, but at the end of college each must seek out his individual destiny and chosen lot. Old Damoetas is no longer there with his marks of approval, and life which had seemed so secure and enclosed is now open to all the fears that its hazards can bring. The early death of Lycidas introduces the note of tragic change.

> But O the heavy change, now thou art gone,
> Now thou art gone, and never must return!
>
> (37–38)

Rather than the returning cycle of the seasons, the developing man experiences a terrible finality. His experience and desires differ from continuing nature. Lycidas' death breaks the early unity with nature, and seems to rend the veil to expose processes that are far from benign and regular in their functioning:

> As killing as the canker to the rose,
> Or taint-worm to the weanling herds that graze,
> Or frost to flowers, that their gay wardrobe wear,
> When first the white-thorn blows;
> Such, Lycidas, thy loss to shepherd's ear.
>
> (45–49)

Far from being a source of security, nature has diseases that blight early promise. It shares in the vulnerability to early death that has precipitated Milton's fallen world. The basis of any natural faith — the regularity of the times and the seasons allowing for the full growth of the organism through the allotted stages of its life — is challenged by the plain facts of experience. As in Petrarch, nature is insufficient to triumph over that irrational phenomenon, and a faith more than natural is required to stand up to such bitter fate.

But even more important and more painful than the loss of faith in nature is the contrast experienced between the promises and rewards of poetry and the reality of a blighted young career. While nature herself is vulnerable to cankers, the ivy, myrtle, and laurel persist as rewards and as symbols, in their ever-greenness, of the time-transcending possibilities of human achievement, especially of immortal fame, which is the hope of poetry. But in the opening lines of the poem their perdurability only contrasts (like any Grecian urn or golden bough) with the bitter human experience, and the mortal human hand. Not only nature but poetry too cannot provide a suitable weapon for meeting with faith and courage the hard possibilities of life. This questioning of poetry and fame extends to the prototype of poets. In the *Ad Patrem,* Milton's ardent defense of poetry found a model in Orpheus, who "by his singing drew tears from the shades of the dead." And in *Il Penseroso* the contemplative mood finds its resources in the kind of song Orpheus sang:

> Such notes as, warbled to the string,
> Drew iron tears down Pluto's cheek
> And made hell grant what love did seek.
> (106–108)

Further, if in *L'Allegro* Orpheus' efforts only managed to "half-regain" Eurydice, still the type of song that Milton conceives "married to immortal verse" would have completed the reversal of death. But in *Lycidas* Orpheus and the tutelary muse of poetry are helpless against the irrational Bacchantes. How is poetry to provide a stay for Milton when the very prototype of the poet was helpless against the same fate that met Edward King:

> What could the Muse herself that Orpheus bore,
> The Muse herself, for her enchanting son
> Whom universal nature did lament,
> When by the rout that made the hideous roar
> His gory visage down the stream was sent,
> Down the swift Hebrus to the Lesbian shore?
> (58–63)

Earthly fame in *Lycidas* is a mixed and subordinate value. As in Dante and Petrarch and that line of Renaissance humanists who were determined to rise above present pleasure, fame is the motive spark and the reward that moves the heroic soul. Laborious days spent in pursuit of a slighted trade are all to find their recompense in the final achievement. Yet, it is the very precariousness of this hope that reveals fame's infirmity. In so far as fame promotes higher things, it is part of human nobility. But as a primary virtue it is insufficient. Life is too fragile, too "thin-spun," to give assurance of future rewards. Like the roaring Maenads the blind Furies intercept and cut off the high designs and future projections:

> But the fair guerdon when we hope to find,
> And think to burst out into sudden blaze,
> Comes the blind Fury with th' abhorrèd shears,
> And slits the thin-spun life.
>
> (73–76)

Not only is life too uncertain, but fame itself seems more a fanciful dream than a stable goal by which a man can guide his life. "Sudden blaze" suggests daydreaming wish-indulgence — imagined tumults of acclaim that seem, in fact, a desecration of the hard work and serious pleasures that are part of any genuine undertaking. But the fame that is being rejected is not merely an ignoble dream; it is precisely because it is so powerful an attraction for the heroic soul ("a desire of honour and repute and immortal fame seated in the breast of every true scholar") that it is here tested. In this purgatorial condition, dilemma exists because no base desires are being sifted, only time-transcendent possibilities. Milton's poem proceeds by "eager thought": by advancing antidotes to death and then testing them. Nature, poetry, fame, while appealing, are none of them quite able to provide a remedy for death and uncertainty. They all seem victimized themselves, or reliant on a temporal process that offers no real assurance.

Lycidas, then, is a continuation of the spiritual discoveries of "How soon hath Time." As it penetrates more deeply into the hazards of succession, it attests to the same separation between worldly appearance and true spiritual ripeness. Fame itself seems to share some of life's blindness: its symbol is the "glittering foil." As Milton in the early sonnet dedicated himself to labor under the true taskmaster's eye, so genuine fame in *Lycidas* does not find its just reward in "broad rumor,"

> But lives and spreads aloft by those pure eyes
> And perfect witness of all-judging Jove.
>
> (81–82)

This same division between worldly fame and a more perfect spiritual witness will persist, even be essential, in Milton's later poetry. In fact, important aggregations of values, intimately involved with time, will settle around blindness and true sight.

Milton's endings are justly praised, and the conclusion of *Lycidas,* with its quiet incorporation of the poem's preceding dramatic argument and thematic developments into its final attitude and action, is as fine as any:

> Thus sang the uncouth swain to th' oaks and rills,
> While the still morn went out with sandals gray:
> He touched the tender stops of various quills,
> With eager thought warbling his Doric lay.
> And now the sun had stretched out all the hills,
> And now was dropped into the western bay;
> At last he rose, and twitched his mantle blue:
> To-morrow to fresh woods, and pastures new.

The poem of *Lycidas* becomes the personal possession of the uncouth swain, and he inherits the wisdom that had been built through its "eager thought." While the faith seems chastened and mature, closer to the ordinary events of life and farther from the attenuated reliances that had been abandoned, still the facts of uncertainty and change persist. What differentiates the early oblivious participation in a nature whose veil had not been rent from the later one, fully aware of the thin-spun mortal life, is the intervention of Christ. Milton is perhaps the last English poet whose simple faith in the resurrection and the final vision of paradise could pass unchallenged even by a skeptical reader and, moreover, find no little empathic response.

In keeping with what has become the clear pattern of this study, Milton is led from the forced experience of the hazards of succession, hazards which dispossess him of natural and human reliances, to a secure sense of being. The motto of the final lines might be "The readiness is all. . . . Let be." Milton's religious faith, however, is firmer, and the presence of Christ and the resurrection is clearer, than in *Hamlet*. It is through Christ and the temporal ease and loss of anxiety which his faith has provided that Milton feels equipped to move forward into the unknown future, the "fresh woods and pastures new" of his larger time to come.

Paradise Lost

In moral courage and firmness of conscience and individual faith, Milton may have been part of the modern Protestant spirit of which Puritanism was one manifestation. Yet, in his sense of time, or the way he preferred to spend time, strong divergences exist between his attitude toward pleasure and any time-harried consciousness of work. The spirit of *L'Allegro* that admits "unreproved pleasures free" persists in two sonnets written around 1655. In the one (sonnet XX) written to Edward Lawrence, "of virtuous father virtuous son," he asks when they will be able to meet by the fireplace during the winter season and thereby "help waste a sullen day." The day will be made cheerful with food ("light and choice"), wine, and Tuscan song:

> He who of those delights can judge, and spare [afford time]
> To interpose them oft, is not unwise.

And in sonnet XXI, addressed to Cyriack Skinner, the grandson of the lawyer Sir Edward Coke, he tries to persuade the apparently over-serious younger man to leave off his ponderous considerations for the sake of "mirth that after no repenting draws." "Mild Heaven" provides for times of such relief,

> And disapproves that care, though wise in show,
> That with superfluous burden loads the day,
> And when God sends a cheerful hour, refrains.

While not exactly a refutation of Malvolio by immortal cakes and ale, a chaster version of Old England continues in this terrible Puritan, who introduces into the modern compulsion to control time the sense of a more benign controlling divinity on whom man ought to rely. In the process of Renaissance laicization, the parable of the talents had come to imply a regard for provisions, those things — material goods, children, fame — that one added to himself, and thereby served to lighten the bleak wintry season. But as Milton had already used the parable of the vineyard to resist that pressure (he calls it a "great commandment"), so he now uses another text from Matthew to urge reliance on God, not on what man is able to lay up. The natural ease that Milton urges on Lawrence will await the return of "the lily and the rose, that neither sowed nor spun," and bespeaks, like the flowers themselves, a divine trust. In fact — although these considerations do not strictly belong to the two sonnets under discussion — it is more in patient waiting, and perhaps even in a more leisured existence that man perceives his true relationship with divinity, while from the over-zealous race to defeat time, to lay up store for reckoning, can be induced a forgetfulness of man's dependence.

The Garden of Paradise is the epitome of this concern for a mode of existence free from time's pressures. When Adam and Eve fall, Milton draws the temporal implications very clearly. Before their lapse,

> God or angel guest
> With man, as with his friend, familiar used
> To sit indulgent, and with him partake
> Rural repast, permitting him the while
> Venial discourse unblamed.
>
> (IX.1–5)

But the introductory words rule out this possibility with a terrible finality: "No more" will this be done. Change, which had once been delectable on earth as in heaven, becomes the basis of tragedy, as Milton leads up to that decisive moment:

> O much deceived, much failing, hapless Eve,
> Of thy presumed return! event perverse!
> Thou never from that hour in Paradise
> Found'st either sweet repast or sound repose.
>
> (404–407)

Rightly Milton changes his notes to tragic, since tragedy depends on change. As in Greek tragedy, events converge toward the momentous action which will alter all future existence. The action here is all-decisive: not only do the protagonists experience the hard edge of time, but time itself and history begin with their sin. Prior to their fall, time was not felt; it held no urgent pressure, was no commodity for which the individual was responsible. Adam and Eve, typifying the condition of early being before the discovery of time, lived quiescent in the palm of unpressured amplitude. But their liberation draws them into a world of crucial events and bitter consequences that defy even God: "past who can recall, or done undo? / Not God omnipotent, nor fate" (926–927) is Adam's rhetorical question and deadly reply.

As readers we are of course suspensefully aware of the threatening developments — of which Adam and Eve are themselves oblivious. And it is their temporal apprehension which is typical of the innocence of the Garden. While time is of course present, it is not an enemy. This seems to comply with very basic characteristics of Milton's thought and work. Time and change are not in themselves debased factors of human experience. Milton differs profoundly from men like Dante and Petrarch, Spenser and Shakespeare, in whose quest for permanence one can detect the horror they experienced in their changeful existences. But Milton seems more open to change. Time in their works is a hostile force that brings low all the works of man. It rakes over their deepest commitments. But Milton did not have such an unyielding commitment to a social order: he could expect improvement only from political change. Petrarch looked to a time when man can live *sine tempore,* but for Milton even the difference between life on earth and in heaven is not as great as had been thought:

> what if earth
> Be but the shadow of heav'n, and things therein
> Each to other like, more than on earth is thought?
> (V.574–576)

There are days in heaven, and temporal measurement,

> (For time, though in eternity, applied
> To motion, measures all things durable
> By present, past, and future.)
> (580–583)

Change, succession, day and evening — all of these are experienced by the angels. Raphael parenthetically explains the coming of evening:

> (For we have also our ev'ning and our morn,
> We ours for change delectable, not need.)
> (628–629)

The crucial factor here is the absence of constraint. In a similar locution, at the outset of Book VI, the lodging and dislodging of day and night through the heavens make a "grateful vicissitude." Processes that might suggest emulative replacement are familiarized and made benign. Change itself is not offensive. A fine critic has recently seen change as the basis of Milton's style as well as of his metaphysics: "The Muse's method in *Paradise Lost* consists largely in the creation of movements in a world of space and time. It is an open question whether this should be considered primarily further accommodation to the limited perception of man, or whether it is a direct revelation of the divine reality. For Milton seems to have believed that motion, whether physical or mental or spiritual, was the chief manifestation of vitality, that quality which, in *The Christian Doctrine,* he placed first among the purely affirmative attributes of God.[13] Indeed, one of the contributions of Mr. Summers' book that has been followed by other scholars is the suggestion that *Paradise Lost* even requires a changing reader.[14]

In Milton's conception of *Paradise Lost,* while the Fall is literally *une chute dans le temps,* it is not time itself that precipitates it. In Book Nine, Milton describes the geography that existed before the expulsion: "There was a place, / Now not, though sin, not time, first wrought the change. . . ." (69–70) In the writers of the fourteenth century, time operates in a quasi-Manichean way, indicating a root imperfection in the world that is outside of God's eternity. And time itself destroys human achievement and shows the vanity of our efforts. But again in Milton it is not time, but sin, that is responsible. The Paradise of Fools in Book III is the storehouse

> Of all things transitory and vain, when sin
> With vanity had filled the works of men.
>
> (446–447)

Formerly, if anything, time was an agent of progressive evolution:

> Time may come when men
> With angels may participate, and find
> No inconvenient diet, nor too light fare;
> And from these corporal nutriments perhaps
> Your bodies may at last turn all to spirit,
> Improved by tract of time.
>
> (V.493–498)

The future is open until, in God's words, man by "degrees of merit raised" elevates himself, and earth and heaven become one. Such rapprochement is implicit in Milton's ideas on time and change. But such a destination is available to man conditionally — "if not depraved from good." Regretfully, the goodness with which God made all things did not find its correspondence in man's will, and time in reality did not come to mean progressive spiritualization. Truth is not the daughter of time — the temporal assumption very prevalent among the Elizabethans — but instead its primal inspiration seems to have been buried under the accretions of tradition and history. The reformist *ad fontem* is a major thrust of Milton's moral and imaginative directions.[15]

This is the way it must be when time and change have been perverted from their created efficacies. Change, once delectable, after the Fall becomes "mortal." Christ pities Adam and Eve, who stand "Before him naked to the air, that now / Must suffer change." (X.211–213) Like a bird of prey smelling carrion, Death fills his nostrils with "the smell / Of mortal change on earth." (272–273) The seasons' differences, with winter's cold and summer's heat, hardly become enjoyable in their changes. (651–714) Time itself acquires its scythe and becomes similar to the Renaissance picture of *tempus edax rerum,* time the great devourer. Sin gives this charge to death:

> Thou therefore on these herbs, and fruits, and flow'rs
> Feed first; on each beast next, and fish, and fowl,
> No homely morsels; and whatever thing
> The scythe of Time mows down, devour unspared.
>
> (X.603–606)

The alliance of time and death, mortality and change — qualities non-existent in the Garden — is effected through sin.

In their psychological senses of time, a similar change occurs for Adam and Eve. Hell's hours are "irksome" (indicating the absence of inner contentment, and the boredom that compels its legatees to rise up with unreal and doomed gestures); heaven's hours are expectedly "cheerful"; but when at the end of Book IX we are told that the fallen pair of lovers, Adam and Eve, spent the "fruitless hours" in mutual recrimination (neither of them "self-condemning") we are brought up short with this new temporal attitude. In the Garden before the Fall, hours could not be "fruitless" since there was no real conception of time as a commodity that could be profitably or unprofitably spent. Adam and Eve tilled the soil, but since their labor was not forced, it was delectable: it simply "made ease / More easy, wholesome thirst and appetite / More grateful." (IV.329–331)[16] Consequently, Eve's arguments before the Fall introduce an alien ethic into the true leisure of the earthly paradise. Invoking efficiency, she pleads for a division of labor. It appears that Adam with his small gestures of love or "casual discourse" slackens their productivity; these "intermit" their "day's work, brought to little, though begun / Early," and, as a result, "th' hour of supper comes unearned." (IX.224–225) Rather than trusting in God's bounty, Eve here betrays a more personal and aggressive attitude toward time and life. She senses herself measured by what she does, and feels guilty when she does not earn her supper. However laudable her home economics, her "husbandry," these arguments imply that need for personal mastery and independence which will later aspire to absolute independence, or Godhead.

As in *Richard II,* the garden is an important locus. Eve fears that their Garden will run wild:

> what we by day
> Lop overgrown, or prune, or prop, or bind,
> One night or two with wanton growth derides,
> Tending to wild.
>
> (209–212)

This passage provides another historical confrontation, since not only its argument but its language calls to mind the garden scene in *Richard II* with its "Superfluous branches / We lop away, that bearing boughs may live." But the point here is that the temporal management which that play endorsed is out of place in the true Garden. Richard's world was already the fallen world of history, but into the early sense of being enjoyed by Adam and Eve this extraneous notion of labor, diligent surveillance, and managed control helps to engineer the Fall. In mythic summary, and from one point of view, Milton confirms the changing attitude toward time that is the historical thesis of this study.

There is another passage that casts terrible and ironic reflection on Eve's utterances. Her code of labor and production is seen in a new light when we find it essentially contained in Sin's instructions to her son, Death. In fact, Milton's attitude toward the augmentative code that had reigned supreme in Shakespeare's histories can here be seen. Eyeing new worlds to conquer, Sin rouses her son to follow the model of their father:

> O son, why sit we here each other viewing
> Idly, while Satan our great author thrives
> In other worlds, and happier seat provides
> For us his offspring dear?
>
> (X.235–238)

Mr. Summers is correct in associating this passage with Eve: "Like Eve, Sin is an advocate of activity, of 'working within one's calling,' of imitating the efficiency of one's 'author.' " (p. 61) Milton here shows his inclination toward other values by placing the scorn for idleness in the mouth of Sin. Yet her words recollect those of Christ, "Why stand ye here all the day idle?" (Matthew 20.6), and point to the evangelical background of the modern work-discipline. But the Gospel according to Matthew can be complex. If it gives us the parable of the talents, it also points to the lilies of the field. And here Sin's recollection of Christ's words derives from the parable of the vineyard, where the ending, with its reliance on the munificence of the householder, subverts the earlier doctrine of work.

As Milton in sonnets XX and XXI reminded his younger friends, so Adam reminds Eve that her concerns, while praiseworthy in part, are too strict for man's garden existence: "not so strictly hath our Lord imposed / Labor . . ."

> For not to irksome toil, but to delight
> He made us, and delight to reason joined.
> (IX.242–243)

But this conception of delighted leisure was appropriate to the world before the Fall, before time and history. Labor, which was inoffensive before Adam sinned because not obligatory, but rather part of man's free condition, is now "enjoined." In the concluding lines of the epic, the simile of the evening mist gathering at the laborer's heels as he returns homeward fills in the details of the terrible judgment on Adam, and through him, mankind. And perhaps, in the larger frame of this study, some historical development is shown, when the laborious world that the first parents are required to enter exacts its due of punctuality. Adam, who had spent moments of timeless rapture listening to heavenly discourse, must abruptly descend from the mount of speculation: "For the hour precise / Exacts our parting hence." (XII.589–590) In all ways Adam and Eve are obliged to enter the world of pressured temporality.

It was David Masson who thought that "Shakespeare lived in a world of time, Milton in a universe of space." In an article that was originally entitled "Criticisms Criticized" the redoubtable E. E. Stoll challenged this all-too-summary thought and claimed time for Milton, too. "In fact, Milton takes very considerable account of time. . . . The mere map of it that he draws is as extensive [as that of space] — from eternity to eternity, from before the begetting of the Son to the ultimate Judgment and consequent purging conflagration (XI.900–901), with innumerable glimpses of world changes in between. And his feeling for time is perhaps as profound. . . . The sin of Eden overhangs *Paradise Lost* from the beginning, and the light of the atonement, of which there is a glimpse at the beginning, early rises to relieve the shadow deepening towards the end." [17]

This Miltonic sense of time and history has been since ably developed. With his usual synthesizing clarity Douglas Bush in his Claremont lectures, *Themes and Variations in English Poetry of the Renaissance,* reminds us that for thoughtful men of the Renaissance, "World history was pivoted on three supreme events: the Creation and the life and death of Christ, the first as well as the second within the measurable past, and, in the not immeasurably remote future, the end of the world and the day of judgment." [18] With great scholarly elaboration this same Christian schema has been studied by C. A. Patrides in his *The Phoenix and the Ladder: The Rise and the Decline of the Christian View of History* and, more recently, in several chapters of his *Milton and the Christian Tradition.*[19] As early as *On the Morning of Christ's Nativity,* the great events of the Christian historical drama formed the pillars of Milton's poetry. They are present imaginatively in Milton's first great poem: the music heard at the birth of the Christ child harks back to the Creation, "when of old the sons of morning sung," and forward to the last day, when Nature will have fulfilled her task. But the hard events of Christ's life, the crucifixion, introduce sterner notes, "the wakeful trump of doom," which is like the "horrid clang / As on Mount Sinai rang." Within the grander sustaining poles of creation, the incarnation, and the final fulfillment, Milton also registers the sad necessities of fate and law and history. Patrides rightly emphasizes the connection between this vision of history ("universalistic and Christocentric") and *Paradise Lost,* for which he calls the nativity ode a "dress rehearsal." [20] There, too, the great events of the Christian schema are given powerful repercussions, especially as they are perceived for the first time by the first father, who was their earthly originator and upon whose shoulders (and those of his children) their terrible consequences would weigh. In fact, Milton's great quality and imaginative virtue is the connection he senses, like Dante, between the large events of history and the individual life. Also writing of Milton's historical world (as realized in the formerly maligned last two books of *Paradise Lost*), Balachandra Rajan perceives these interlocking interests: "The massed resources of time and space are made to move inward on the moment of crisis, intensifying that crisis and to some degree measuring it by its endless involvement in a web of meaning and consequence." [21] While we have been emphasizing the deep personal cut of time as representing tragic and momentous change and as imposing laborious burdens on man, and while the historical stages (as well as the cosmogonic problems) have become something of a convention in Miltonic scholarship, it is well to be reminded thus of their dramatic prominence in Milton's poetry.

We remember that in Shakespeare's version of the "fall" of man, the greatest loss was suffered in political terms of deposition or usurpation — in short, in the more emulative world of aggressive and competitive energies. But in Milton, although the first parents are ejected from their happy place, the primal Fall is more painful (especially for Adam) in the lost relationship with divinity. Man had an earlier sense of harmony and of true connection with the spiritual forces of the universe. The Fall destroyed that sense of being part of a divinely ordered world:

> How shall I behold the face
> Henceforth of God or angel, erst with joy
> And rapture so oft beheld?
>
> (IX.1080–1082)

This contrast between loss of spiritual being in Milton and loss of position in Shakespeare holds true until we consider Satan. Satan is the founder of the earthly city, and it is no accident that the world he ushers in and presides over is one of emulation. At the crucial beginning of human history, fratricidal strife duplicates Satan's original offense. More than a consequence, emulation is a cause of man's fallen world.

From the great convocation of angels in Book V we learn that distinctions already exist in heaven. The banners they carry

> for distinction serve
> Of hierarchies, of orders, and degrees;
> Or in their glittering tissues bear emblazed
> Holy memorials, acts of zeal and love
> Recorded eminent.
>
> (590–594)

This is enough to indicate that for some, a sense of place and merit could already have been achieved. Amid this prior order, God expresses his preference for his Son, and elevates him to a new position of supereminence:

> Hear, all ye Angels, Progeny of Light,
> Thrones, Dominations, Princedoms, Virtues, Powers,

> Hear my decree, which unrevoked shall stand.
> This day I have begot whom I declare
> My only Son, and on this holy hill
> Him have anointed.
>
> (600–605)

It is in the marked political context of this designation of the Son for further advantages (one can think of Duncan establishing his estate on Malcolm) that alienation occurs in heaven. As Raphael continues to narrate to Adam, all heaven seemed to celebrate the new honors, and either slept peacefully or sang melodiously about the throne of heaven;

> But not so waked
> Satan — so call him now, his former name
> Is heard no more in heav'n; he of the first,
> If not the first Archangel, great in power,
> In favor, and pre-eminence, yet fraught
> With envy against the Son of God, that day
> Honored by his great Father, and proclaimed
> Messiah, King anointed, could not bear
> Through pride that sight, and thought himself impaired.
>
> (657–665)

This origin of discord is important, not only because of the dramatic tension it creates between Christ and Satan, but, thematically, for the role it will continue to play in Milton's vision of human history. In Michael's condensed pictorial history in Book XI, interesting connections exist between the first falling-out in the human family and the earlier one in the heavenly family. Despite the Fall and the exclusion from Eden, mankind continued to live in a familial unit and a tribal setting. The field pictured to Adam is pastoral, with still some strong remnant of religious identification: "I'th'midst an altar as the landmark stood / Rustic, of grassy sord. . . ." The center of the community was still Adam's and Eve's sense of service to God. To this altar a reaper and a shepherd brought their offerings, but the reaper, Cain, brought first fruits, some still green and "unculled, as came to hand." His offerings indicate haste, carelessness, and some disregard. His brother, the shepherd, "more meek came, with the firstlings of his flock, / Choicest and best. . . ." The shepherd's offerings found greater favor with heaven, at which Cain, in Satanic fashion, "inly raged" and then killed the sincere Abel. (XI. 429–460)

History begins when families divide. As it was for Augustine, so for Milton, too, the Cain-Abel motif is an archetype, since in the second installment of human history, after the flood, a corresponding crime occurs. The "second course of men, while yet but few," will live in peace and fear of God, and will prosper and multiply. The primitive tribal pattern, under parental rule, will give them peace and "joy unblamed,"

>   till one shall rise
> Of proud ambitious heart, who not content
> With fair equality, fraternal state,
> Will arrogate dominion undeserved
> Over his brethren and quite dispossess
> Concord and law of Nature from the earth.
>   (XII.24–29)

He, too, will build a city with towers to challenge the heavens, but Nimrod's Babel will be an earthly kind of Pandemonium, wherein the multiplicity of tongues reflects their "various spirit." As with Satan, their end ironically undoes their aspirations.

Obviously there is not a one-to-one relationship in all these events. Christ is not a brother to Satan, nor is he literally slain (yet essentially the sins of the world would be responsible for his martyrdom, and "meek" Abel's death is a figure of Christ's death). Nevertheless, Milton, within the possibilities of his story, seems to have intended significant areas of overlap between the incidents. The divisions within the two fraternal conditions of the human family derive from the original division propagated in heaven. Attention to this material also indicates Milton's awareness of the human truth that a fall occurred before the sexual fall; before man and woman were at odds, a spirit of rivalry or emulation existed within the human family, between brother and brother, that served to defeat concord. Satan felt himself "impaired" by Christ's new honors. He violated the spirit of charity and concord, and plunged his heirs of the earthly city into a pattern from which they could not escape. As in Dante, the hunger for things that cannot be shared produces the wild contest for things that do not last.

Deeply involved with Milton's attitudes toward time are his ways of presenting the actions and ideas of those who are driven by the spirit of personal glory or acquisition, and who separate themselves from any sense of a controlling divinity. They both typify and are victimized by the processes of time itself. Habitually in Milton, time is associated with mad forward movement ("the race of Time"), with ravenous appetite, and with a general loss of perspective and unregarding devotion to what is immediate and present. From the very early *Naturam non pati senium,* Milton speaks of the "eternal hunger of the years" and asks rhetorically, "Shall insatiable Time swallow up Heaven and take his father into his own entrails?" In its forward casting, time is insatiable; the Latin verbs suggest great hunger (*esurire*) and a strong action of seizure (*rapere*). Milton conflates Chronos (Time) and Cronos (Saturn), a combination Panofsky has described in his important article on Father Time.[22] But he further reverses the father-son role, and rather than have Saturn (or Time) devour his children, he casts Time in the emulative role of son threatening father. We can well witness behind this transmutation the experience of Marlowe and Shakespeare, and even Spenser in the *Mutabilitie Cantos,* for whom threatening change is contained within a larger frame.

On Time continues the same order of address. Time is "envious," and its actions resemble the aggressive competition of a race. In scornful contrast with the unending joys of the blessed, greedy Time's devouring action is self-destructive. It "gluts" itself on non-essentials, "dross," and finally will consume itself. Milton's personal temperance obviously led him to loathe such gorging. In the *Ad Patrem* he commends the songs that were heard at royal feasts, before luxury was known, or "the bottomless pit of the monstrous gullet." Such hunger is blind. In *Lycidas* Milton vituperates the "blind mouths" that have taken over the offices of the church. And Satan when he conceives Sin is struck dizzy, his eyes dimmed. So the quest for glory or fame can equally be a product of blind desire. To the Paradise of Fools in Book III are brought

> Both all things vain, and all who in vain things
> Built their fond hopes of glory or lasting fame,
> Or happiness in this or th' other life;
> All who have their reward on earth, the fruits
> Of painful superstition and blind zeal,
> Naught seeking but the praise of men.
>
> (448–453)

While Milton values mobility and vitality, a terrible loss can occur when man consigns himself so unreservedly to the movements of time.

All these areas of Miltonic preoccupation converge on the "evil hour" when Eve stretches forth her hand in an act of seizure that will be repeated throughout man's private and public history, to his own dismay. As her action summarizes the *carpe diem* motif ("Her rash hand in evil hour / Forth reaching to the fruit, she plucked, she eat"), so her motives are quintessentially Renaissance. In a fundamental act of separation, Eve discards the comfortable cloak of infantile dependence and ignorance and takes the risk of good and evil. Man was not meant to live like a beast, with his conscious powers undeveloped. This familiar Renaissance argument of time lies behind Eve's protest: Is this intellectual food denied to man yet allowed to beasts? Her felt powers and ambitions move her toward godhead. But rather than alert and seeing, as she should be in the normal argument of time, Eve is in Milton's ironic context blind and greedy:

> Back to the thicket slunk
> The guilty Serpent, and well might, for Eve
> Intent now wholly on her taste, naught else
> Regarded; such delight till then, as seemed,
> In fruit she never tasted, whether true
> Or fancied so, through expectation high
> Of knowledge, nor was Godhead from her thought.
> Greedily she engorged without restraint,
> And knew not eating death.
>
> (IX.784–792)

These hurried, rapacious, and unregarding actions, so characteristic of time itself, contrast strongly with the nature of God and the patient virtues of Christ. God is the great overseer, under whose purview all time is comprehended and contained. Literally in Milton, events unfold *sub specie aeternitatis* and "we take cognizance of the unique Jewish view that history unfolds under the vigilant eye of God." [23] In the early sonnet Milton has the patience to commit himself to service under the "great Task-master's eye." In *Comus,* the Attendant Spirit returns to the broad fields of the sky, "Where day never shuts his eye." Milton can accept his blindness with greater patience because he knows that God can read his true account. In *Paradise Lost,* Belial warns that God's "eye / Views all things at one view." Satan's uncertain voyage through Chaos is not unobserved:

> Him God beholding from his prospect high,
> Wherein past, present, future he beholds.
>
> (III.77–78)

In Book V the "unsleeping eyes of God" monitor the strategy sessions of the dissident angels. It is this higher vision and wisdom, contained and foreseeing, that converts Satan's tragic ambitions into derided grotesquerie.

The aesthetic operations of *Paradise Lost* conform to this spiritual vision. While the events of the epic run on a loose timetable, all the poet's effects seem designed to disrupt normal sequential relations. The contracted time of narrative fans its spokes into a cosmos of reference. But there is more than just this sort of "double time": "By deliberately dislocating time sequence, by his mastery of cumulative effects, by his genius for energy and movement in language, [Milton] secures the illusion that what is past is still present at the end when all is at last rounded out." [24] The very verse itself, with its transposition of tenses, its rising and falling rhythms, its winding sentences and irregular pauses, suggests a changing world, a world of surges and drops — in which the reader's own expectations are dislocated. A sense of co-temporality, challenging normal time sequence, emerges from the dynamics of Milton's artistry and suggests shared experience by those who have lived, are living, and will live. While Milton scholars have attended to this phenomenon with great interest and ability, the doyen of what are essentially "figural" studies, Erich Auerbach, ought to be heard, especially as he distinguishes between *figura* and more primitive or more modern historical understanding. In his classic essay, he emphasizes the historical reality of an event which, nevertheless, still looks to another event that completes it and gives it proper fulfillment.

> In this light the history of no epoch ever has the practical self-sufficiency which, from the standpoint both of primitive man and of modern science, resides in the accomplished fact; all history, rather, remains open and questionable, points to something still concealed, and the tentativeness of events in the figural interpretation is fundamentally different from the tentativeness of events in the modern view of historical development. In the modern view, the provisional event is treated as a step in an unbroken horizontal process; in the figural system the interpretation is always sought from above; events are considered not in their unbroken relation to one another, but torn apart, individually, each in relation to something other that is promised and not yet present. Whereas in the modern view the event is always self-sufficient and secure, while the interpretation is fundamentally incomplete, in the figural interpretation the fact is subordinated to an interpretation which is fully secured to begin

with: the event is enacted according to an ideal model which is a prototype situated in the future and thus far only promised. . . . Thus the figures are not only tentative; they are also the tentative form of something eternal and timeless; they point not only to the concrete future, but also to something that always has been and always will be; they point to something which is in need of interpretation, which will indeed be fulfilled in the concrete future, but which is at all times present, fulfilled in God's providence, which knows no difference of time.[25]

As God's eye contained the movements of Satan, so human actions are circumscribed by other patterns. Ths, with the experience of risings and fallings, serves to disrupt any straight linear approach to time. The temporal perspective of Satan, the appetitive ascendancy of Eve — in short, any temporal thrust that drives toward the future — is false to the nature of the world and to its highest wisdom. There is a fuller, better nature in which man can participate by standing and being.

And yet, despite the implications of recurrence, Christian eschatology is linear: the race of time must be run before time stands fixed. After the Fall there is no way of avoiding the reality of changed condition and keenly felt loss; and despite ecstasies of entrancement, time is still a reality to be felt and a weight to be borne. In fact, the basic problem of *Paradise Lost* is: How does man respond to the experience of time and change; and its argument shows two contrasting ways of recovering the spiritual identity that had been lost, Satan's way and that of Adam and Eve. That *Paradise Lost* is a poem of time and history is shown by the fact that Satan's refusal to bow to the new realities results in perennial defeat.

His mode is tragic: "O how fall'n! how changed." (I.84) He sees Beelzebub, yet defiantly resists the evidence of his senses; he does not intend to repent or change "that fixed mind / And high disdain. . . ." (97–98) To hell he brings "A mind not to be changed by place or time." (253) His instincts are barbaric, and his myth of himself becomes history. Without any sense of vulnerability he proclaims the power of the determined intellect:

> The mind is its own place, and in itself
> Can make a heav'n of hell, a hell of heav'n.
>
> (254–255)

A phrasing reminiscent of many of Shakespeare's tragic heroes returns as Satan is reminded of what he once was and now is. The beauty of the earth he is intent on subverting in Book IV reminds him of the place he had known:

> Now conscience wakes despair
> That slumbered, wakes the bitter memory
> Of what he was, what is, and what must be
> Worse.
>
> (23–26)

In order to retain his position Satan commits himself to a desperate heroism. His world is now fallen, but he would still hold on to the forms and prerogatives of his prior glory. But since the order he is repudiating is the true source of fulfillment, his government in exile can only be based on anti-values, and his dictatorship is a doomed one. His opposition to what is best in the nature of things commits him to negation and self-destruction.

Satan's rival kingdom seems in no way to recapture the condition that once belonged to unfallen man and angels. He is a defective model of recovery, which for Milton does not lie through any false assertiveness, but rather through humble and modest recognition of the reality of one's condition. The expiation of Adam and Eve commences with self-blame, and Book X is based upon the contrast between their initial steps toward reconciliation and the final ignominy of Satan and his band:

> so oft they fell
> Into the same illusion, not as man
> Whom they triumphed once lapsed.
>
> (570–572)

At the end of Book IX the man and woman for whom love had been spoiled, "in mutual accusation spent / The fruitless hours," and Milton adds with point, "but neither self-condemning." Importantly and typically, it is the woman, whose arrogance led to the fall, whose modesty and honesty of admission leads to renewal. Book X ends with the first parents, with sighs and tears — signs "Of sorrow unfeigned, and humiliation meek" — confessing their faults and praying for pardon. Christ is their final pattern in recovery: not in ostentatious yet brittle self-assertion, nor in a pained superiority-inferiority syndrome, but in humble recognition of man's new condition in time and history.

Time and place, disdained by Satan, become distinct realities for Adam and Eve when they come to suffer change and (Eve especially) lose the happy place. It is too often forgotten — the fortunate fall perhaps occupying too much attention — that paradise is really lost in this poem, that *Paradise Lost* is not a paradise regained. Time and change are formidable realities under whose burdens man must labor. Glory and spontaneous reciprocal love have passed out of this Virgilian epic. (E. E. Stoll is right to declare, "In his historical sense and compass, [Milton] is of course like Virgil, not Homer.")[26] With faith in providence and the eventual triumph of their seed, and given an indication of what true response to their changed condition must be, man and woman enter a world of history, where the defeats are many and the moments of grace rare and fleeting. They are supported by faith, but still the final prospect commits them to a future expectation that they themselves in their temporal lives can never experience. Their sadness is mixed with cheer, and their cheer with sadness. As prototypes of married man and woman, with their hopes in romantic innocence now replaced by a sad maturity, the first parents "hand in hand" together must live in the ruins of a world they helped to unmake.

Paradise Regained

The prologue to *Paradise Regained* makes clear that in the grander, earlier epic, paradise was really lost. While hoping for a future deliverance, Adam and Eve are still committed to the world of time and history; they have not recovered the lost world of being. It is in *Paradise Regained* that the Adam-Christ genealogy fructifies, "And Eden raised in the waste wilderness." Well could Milton be impatient with the cavilling critics who did not find in *Paradise Regained* the energy and issues of *Paradise Lost*: its issues are simply at the center of Milton's moral universe, and more directly than in *Paradise Lost* they are connected with the spiritual resolutions of "How soon hath Time" and *Lycidas* of the earlier period.[27] If *Paradise Lost* is his great poem of time and change, *Paradise Regained* is Milton's poem of being.

There is another sense in which *Paradise Regained* is the sequel to *Paradise Lost,* and that is in the advancement it represents in the order of the temptations. The lure to which Adam proved weak is lesser than the temptations that Satan spreads before Jesus. In repudiation of the sensualist Belial, who suggests that he use women to rob Jesus of his mission, Satan clearly establishes a hierarchy of values:

> Beauty stands
> In the admiration only of weak minds

Led captive; cease to admire, and all her plumes
Fall flat and shrink into a trivial toy,
At every sudden slighting quite abashed.

(II.220–224)

Loftier temptations must be used: those which in the noblest minds lead away from a prime reliance on God.

Therefore with manlier objects we must try
His constancy, with such as have more show
Of worth, of honor, glory, and popular praise,
Rocks whereon greatest men have oftest wrecked;
Or that which only seems to satisfy
Lawful desires of nature, not beyond.

(225–230)

This argument is, of course, not unfamiliar. As we have seen, it forms the basis of the purgatorial experience that Dante and Petrarch underwent, and which involved them, as it does Milton in *Paradise Regained*, in such painful exclusions. For the religiously minded, the highest ways of succession are quite simply the greatest sources of temptation because they transcend time while yet basically failing to provide the permanence and security that the soul requires. Consequently, A. S. P. Woodhouse is right in his statement that Milton's short epic runs "the gamut of worldly glory as conceived by Renaissance man." [28] Christ's temptations are largely those of the Renaissance. The spur of fame, *carpe diem* urgings, exhortations to take the instant way — these are the promptings by which Satan attempts to lure a Jesus approaching the critical choices of manhood away from his divine calling. It is the disproportion resulting from the measurement of Christ's promise and his goals against his "obscurity" that lends to Satan whatever efficacy his arguments possess. As Milton in the two sonnets "How soon hath Time" and "When I consider" felt acutely the passing time and his own apparent unproductiveness, his "belatedness," so Satan urges on the yet unproved Jesus, "Thy years are ripe, and over-ripe." The pressures of time in all their ramifications that this study has suggested converge on Christ and present him with the greatest danger, that of forcing God's will to his own.

But we should also recall that Biblical inspiration itself does much to promote a sense of responsibility for one's talents. That parable was for Milton a "great commandment," one to be transcended only in terms of a greater. Christ, moving into a solitary world, ponders "which way first / [to] Publish his Godlike office now mature." (I.187–188) It is incumbent upon man to make known, not to bury, his virtue. The very Jewish sense of history does much to commit Christ to future expectations, and hence make temptation possible. Past promise looks to future fulfillment, and disposes man to a linear conception of time. Jesus searched the book, and found "of whom they spake / I am." (262–263) He moves into the pathless desert alone "but with such thoughts / Accompanied of things past and to come / Lodged in his breast." (299–301) His mother, too, is a repository of ancient sayings and future promise:

> My heart hath been a storehouse long of things
> And sayings laid up, portending strange events.
>
> (II.103–104)

Very prominent in the poem (a Laury Zwicky has shown) is the New Testament notion of *kairos;* that is, a fore-ordained time for a significant God-appointed event.[29] The sense that such a time has now come increases the pressure on Christ for accomplishment. With his sense of mission, Christ "the time prefixed . . . awaited." (I.269) He is persuaded of his divine mission by his Father's voice, "by which I knew the time / Now full, that I no more should live obscure." (286–287) It is in terms of this very notion of *kairos,* indeed, echoing John's gospel, that Christ is able to answer Satan: "My time . . . is not yet come." (III.396–397)

The great achievement of *Paradise Regained* is the coincidence it creates between Christ's divine appointment and the expectations of Renaissance humanism. To put it another way, Christ for Milton is a literal model of the problems and resolutions of his own life. We sense the collocation, the exploitation of personal identification, when Christ muses over his own high seriousness:

> When I was yet a child, no childish play
> To me was pleasing; all my mind was set
> Serious to learn and know.
>
> (I.201–203)

Precociously ("above my years") he read the Law of God, and moreover, "found it sweet." Yet Christ speaks for the young Milton and even for the early Renaissance, when he records that his great impetus was heroism; beyond the Law his spirit aspired:

> Victorious deeds
> Flamed in my heart, heroic acts: one while
> To rescue Israel from the Roman yoke,
> Then to subdue and quell o'er all the earth
> Brute violence and proud tyrannic pow'r,
> Till truth were freed, and equity restored;
> Yet held it more humane, more heavenly, first
> By winning words to conquer willing hearts.
>
> (215–222)

In a very suggestive interpolation, Milton develops the character of the mother as the prime inciter of this heroic sense of calling and mission. Its autobiographical implications are intriguing when we reflect, with the *Ad Patrem* in mind, that a similar invention in *Samson Agonistes* casts the father as the exponent of practical wisdom and shrewdness, whose understanding is inferior to that of his heroic son. Contained in Jesus' soliloquy are the encouragements of his mother:

> High are thy thoughts,
> O Son, but nourish them and let them soar
> To what highth sacred virtue and true worth
> Can raise them, though above example high.
>
> (229–232)

She reminds him that, in the manner of the classical hero, one-half of his parentage was divine, and that his true father is a heavenly king. Not fully understanding yet the divine intent, as indeed neither Jesus nor his disciples do, she casts the divine promise in grand, yet still earthly political, terms. It was she to whom the Annunciation was made, and foretold concerning Christ:

> Thou shouldst be great and sit on David's throne,
> And of thy kingdom there should be no end.
>
> (240–241)

Imperium sine fine dedi. With these words Mary rises out of the Hebraic world, like some divine sibyl, to embrace the entire expectations of the classical world at the time of Virgil's epic and (importantly) his *Fourth Eclogue*. Grandly historical in imagination, Milton's vision rivals Dante's in its probings of the relations between the Christian and the classical worlds, of the hopes and predictions of the one and their fulfillment in a totally unforeseen and different way. One could also say that this transformation parallels the development of much of the Renaissance itself, with its own early rising concern with the kingdom on earth and its later more spiritual emphasis on the kingdom of the individual soul. Specifically, in the Biblical context, we see re-expressed Milton's transcendence of the Renaissance investment in posterity. From the notion that his seed will be a nation, and the idea that his earthly kingdom will be everlasting, it is clear that, while metaphorically retaining both of these concepts, Christ comes to comprehend the more spiritual nature of his line of descent. (IV.146–151)

A literal *contretemps* exists between the different levels of discourse and understanding on which Jesus and Satan operate. While Satan's intrusions focus on the present, Christ's answers seem to reach back to the beginnings and forward to the end; his vision is contained and comprehensive, while Satan's is momentary, groping, and hectic. To Satan's first inquiry, "What ill chance" brought Christ to the desert, the response is abrupt and yet extensive: "Who brought me hither / Will bring me hence; no other guide I seek." (I.335–336) And to the decorous scene that Satan stages, full of the delicacies of an elitist and sophisticated life, Jesus' response transcends the simple hunger that Satan has in mind: "With my hunger what hast thou to do?" (II.389) His hunger for deliverance and salvation cannot be satisfied by Satan's method or his domain. This higher need must be understood if Christ's rejections are to be properly understood. What Satan offers, even if "unreproved pleasures free," cannot satisfy Christ's hunger. To Satan's praise of glory, Christ's response indicates a higher power, "I seek not mine, but his / Who sent me, and thereby witness whence I am." (III.106–107) And when Satan prods him to take "occasion's forelock," Christ shows his final security in the will of his Father:

> All things are best fulfilled in their due time,
> And time there is for all things, Truth hath said.
> If of my reign prophetic Writ hath told
> That it shall never end, so when begin
> The Father in his purpose hath decreed,
> He in whose hands all times and seasons roll.
>
> (III.182–187)

When Satan refers to the "perfect season" he means the opportune time. Readiness here implies a capacity and will to act and force events to one's favor. But the fullness of time to which Christ refers is controlled by God. The readiness that he displays implies a greater capacity for endurance than for action, more of a reliance on God's plans; he is willing to leave his people "to his due time, and providence." (III.440)

In contrast to these larger considerations "of how the world began, and how man fell," there is a direct immediacy and command in Satan's phrasing: "Get riches first, get wealth." Belial, although his advice is rejected, anticipates his leader's style, "Set woman in his eye," in which words we recognize the tone of: "Put money in thy purse." Satan's vision does seem "bounded and limited," but despite his allusion to the "circling hours" it would be a mistake to say that his vision of time is cyclical.[30] Rather his temptations exhibit the new developments in Renaissance responses to time, those more aggressive attitudes that served, as far as Milton was concerned, to sever man from his larger associations.

Throughout the temptations, by utilizing Christ's obscurity, his age, the great predictions ringing in the past, and Christ's own hunger for great things, Satan tries to instill distrust, temporal anxiety, the need for immediate action by *carpe diem* urgings, and a primary emphasis on secondary forces, like "means" and glory, all of which would tend to diminish Christ's primary faith in the Father. The means he proposes seem to destroy the larger sense of man's spiritual being and importance. In his reply to Satan's argument that he should imitate his Father's own desire for glory, Christ reminds him that glory was not his "prime end" but rather a means to "show forth his goodness." Moreover, all glory belongs to God, not to man, who, by turning away from God, despoiled himself of true good. This retort, again coming from the mouth of righteous innocence, is pointed, and, as in *Paradise Lost,* makes the vulnerable tempter wince with pain:

> So spake the Son of God; and here again
> Satan had not to answer, but stood struck
> With guilt of his own sin, for he himself
> Insatiable of glory had lost all.
>
> (III.145–148)

Paradise Lost and *Paradise Regained* are profound Christian interpretations of the Renaissance itself, a story that our premier Renaissance historian, Jacob Burckhardt, sensed when he described the "diabolic" within the strong urge for fame.

Satan is ignorant not only of the larger perspective that Christ values and illustrates, but of the real means by which his kingdom is to be gained. What if Christ's end is not to be a "success story" — the only kind that Satan can envisage:

> What if he hath decreed that I shall first
> Be tried in humble state, and things adverse,
> By tribulations, injuries, insults,
> Contempts, and scorns, and snares, and violence,
> Suffering, abstaining, quietly expecting
> Without distrust or doubt, that he may know
> What I can suffer, how obey? Who best
> Can suffer best can do; best reign who first
> Well hath obeyed; just trial ere I merit
> My exaltation without change or end.
>
> (III.188–197)

Earlier Jesus had recounted the prediction "that my way must lie / Through many a hard assay even to the death." As the nature of his divinity becomes clear, so does the means of his triumph — both of which are beyond Satan's ken. And yet, ironically, it is Satan's own dogged instinct for self-destruction that serves to elucidate and bring out Christ's revelation of his divinity. It is not by going, but by standing that Christ re-establishes man's link with divinity. And as in *Hamlet* or *Lycidas,* or in the philosophy of Martin Heidegger, the sense of being comes not in the agony, but in the achieved condition of readiness for that event.

There is another pattern in Christ's demonstration of the patience and the trust that are for Milton the patent revelations of his gospel. Defiance of augury from Dante and Petrarch to Montaigne and *Hamlet,* from *Paradise Regained* to the *Four Quartets,* has been part of the approach to being. Particularly in times of trouble or pestilence, omens and augury proliferate, and a season of such portents occurred in England in 1665 and 1666 (although we have already referred to the plague's periodic returns). In Shakespeare's tragedies such foreknowledge was intrinsic to tragic effect, but in Milton premonitions of what fate intends (and this would be closer to Satan's terminology) represent a challenge to Christ's faith in a divine providence.

In Book I of *Paradise Regained* Satan unintentionally reveals in what way this recourse to prognostication offends the religious spirit. Co-partner with mankind, he says,

> [I] lend them oft my aid,
> Oft my advice by presages and signs,
> And answers, oracles, portents and dreams,
> Whereby they may direct their future life.
>
> (393–396)

Satan's oracular powers tend to the same end as his other temptations: they appropriate to man powers that are only God's. Even the Son of God does not know the future, and his contentment in that ignorance is the test of his faith and the revelation of his mission. With Christ's coming, "oracles are ceased."

> God hath now sent his living Oracle
> Into the world, to teach his final will,
> And sends his Spirit of Truth henceforth to dwell
> In pious hearts, an inward oracle
> To all truth requisite for men to know.
>
> (I.460–464)

Rather than the superstitious claptrap and the embarrassing observances of ritual (the kind of hocus-pocus dismissed as early as *On the Morning of Christ's Nativity*), the revelation toward which the will of God has been working in history is this living oracle of Christ. But Christ himself shuns the nervous probing into the future, and is content with God's will:

> And now by some strong motion I am led
> Into this wilderness, to what intent
> I learn not yet, perhaps I need not know;
> For what concerns my knowledge God reveals.
>
> (I.290–293)

As in *Paradise Lost,* Milton has come a long way from the Baconian prospectus of *The Seventh Prolusion.*

This first temptation emanates from an attitude of presumed power and authority, a knowledge that can control the future. In Book IV, however, augury is an agent of ill omen, of anxiety and distress, of "terrors dire." Following Christ's own suggestion in Book III, that the way to his kingdom might be hard, even to the death, Satan sees in the stars that

> Sorrows, and labors, opposition, hate,
> Attends [him], scorns, reproaches, injuries,
> Violence and strifes, and lastly cruel death.
> (IV.386–388)

Feigning then to leave the young hero, Satan troubles his sleep with "ugly dreams," which have their corollary in a fierce natural storm. This is the darkest moment in Christ's endeavor, when inner and outer weather join to urge fear and despair. But here the Milton of the famous proems and invocations of *Paradise Lost* uses the personal form of address to honor the model that Christ offers of inner calm and trust in the face of apparent defeat and contumely:

> Ill wast thou shrouded then,
> O patient Son of God, yet only stood'st
> Unshaken; nor yet stayed the terror there:
> Infernal ghosts, and hellish furies, round
> Environed thee; some howled, some yelled, some shrieked,
> Some bent at thee their fiery darts, while thou
> Sat'st unappalled in calm and sinless peace.
>
> (419–425)

Despite this outward disorder, to which even Christ appears subject, his own mind and spirit are really untainted. The experiences of Milton, like those of Dante, led him to locate the true divinity of Christ in the pattern he provided of such unshakable conviction and inner peace. Dante's corollary to this pattern is the story of Romeo in *Paradiso* VI. Both of these writers confirm Oscar Cullmann's conclusion, in *Christ and Time,* that when God's lordship over time becomes most obscure it is made visible again by Christ's patience.

Samson Agonistes and Divine Comedy

"He unobserved / Home to his mother's house private returned." This ending to *Paradise Regained,* blending so much of the poem's meaning in quiet understatement, indicates that even after the realization of his divinity Christ must still live in time. But, as Oscar Cullmann has shown in his Biblical studies, the time after Christ's fulfillment is different from the time at the end of *Paradise Lost,* when Adam and Eve make their way into a new world. While on the way to redemption, they, like the Old Testament itself, look forward to that great event. It still is to come, and their hopes rest in the future. In *Paradise Regained,* however, the event confirming the faith in providential history has already occurred. As in *Lycidas,* the attitude of spiritual readiness has been achieved through Christ and the pattern to follow is no longer in front of one, but behind.

Yet despite this attainment of being, *Paradise Regained* does not represent the highest possibilities of divine comedy. As it shows an advance on *Paradise Lost,* so on spiritual and aesthetic grounds *Samson Agonistes* advances beyond it. Indeed, it strikes one as rather fitting, in Milton's Christocentric world, that the mediating piece, as it were, between hell, time and history, and the fulfillment of paradise should deal with the revelation of Christ's divinity. In the trilogic chain of his great poems, it is properly located. Two obstacles to this interpretation are that (1) Christ's divinity, his overwhelming moral pre-eminence, make it difficult to consider dogmatically another hero as superior to him, especially when (2) the protagonist, Samson, existed historically prior to Christ's revelation. Yet Samson does not look forward, but rather has already benefitted, in the virtues he exercises, from the kind of patient trust in God's providence that Christ revealed in his brief epic. Moreover, there is a continued discrepancy, not bridged in the poem, between Christ's beginnings and his end that is part of the purgatorial attitude which Milton had developed from "How soon hath Time." Apparent heroism and real heroism are different; the glistering foil of fame is not as accurate as the true and perfect witness of all-judging Jove; the rugged-seeming heroic character might be miserable in his core, while the simple, patient man accomplishes much more, and in a sounder way. This separation between *virtù* and virtue, between energy and moral superiority, is sharply focused in *Paradise Lost,* testing the reliability of our own responses. It is at the basis of the educational process that Adam undergoes in Books XI and XII, and it is what Christ must himself come to understand in *Paradise Regained.* From physical triumph and temporal power to spiritual victory, from Mary's early "kingdom without end" to Christ's final "everlasting kingdom" — this is the progress that summarizes not only the differences between the classical and the Christian worlds, and between the Old and the New Testaments, but the spiritualization within the Renaissance itself. In this state of separation, fame and the ways of succession are not recovered, but still suffer under the general suspicion of the temporal.

Samson Agonistes represents a change from these purgatorial attitudes. As in Dante's *Paradiso,* a reintegration occurs between fame, the ways of succession, and the Christian experience. Endings essentially confirm beginnings:

> Samson hath quit himself
> Like Samson, and heroicly hath finished
> A life heroic.
>
> (1709–1711)

Not only does he win the vision of patience, "the exercise of the saints," but beyond that and his own merits, he is allowed through the majesty of God's grace to achieve his promised physical triumph. It is as when, in the middle of paradise, Dante encounters his real ancestor. There is some point in praising the spiritual father, but when one's guiding inspiration is also the real father of one's blood, then the intent of the creating universe must appear all the more miraculous.

In this sense of the final reintegration of Milton's vision we can speak of *Samson Agonistes* as advancing even spiritually beyond *Paradise Regained.* But to speak only in terms of aesthetic energies, Samson is also a fuller character than Christ. Primarily, Christ's defect as a character — as James Joyce observed — comes from his singleness, his lack of relation to the procreative aspects of life.[31] But in Samson we return to the basis of the Fall, man and woman. As a character he transcends Adam, since he has more of the hero in him to begin with. Samson, indeed, seems to be a blend of Adam, Satan, and Christ, experiencing the fall and chastisement of the first, but knowing the tragic sense of change of the second and the consolation and fulfillment of the last. In fact, speaking of energies, Samson is a virtuous Satan, one who transcends tragedy. This character, with whom Milton identified in his fall, is a fitting persona by whom the Renaissance poet of Christian faith could celebrate the victory (not only spiritual but also temporal) to which his rectitude, dedication, and talent brought him. Like Samson he fell, and like Samson he learned through blindness, and like Samson he eventually accomplished those great things that he had earlier learned to leave in God's hands. Far from being a work we should identify with Milton's despondency after blindness, whenever it may have been written, *Samson Agonistes* completes the pattern of development typical of the great poets of the Renaissance, bringing together their earlier hopes and final triumphs. If *Samson Agonistes* has a basis in biography, and it clearly does, it is in this sense of fulfillment that Milton knew in and through *Paradise Lost.*

In retrospect the drama informs us that, like other Miltonic heroes (Christ and even Satan), Samson was above the common run. Special events seemed to designate him as "separate to God," and his own physical prowess seemed to confirm that fact: "I was his nursling once and choice delight." (633) It is this very extraordinary course of Samson's career that is responsible, in his fallen condition, for his severe doubts and questionings:

> Why was my breeding ordered and prescribed
> As of a person separate to God,
> Designed for great exploits, if I must die
> Betrayed, captíved, with both my eyes put out,
> Made of my enemies the scorn and gaze;
> To grind in brazen fetters under task
> With this Heav'n-gifted strength?
>
> (23–36)

Change, as with Shakespeare's tragic heroes, or with Satan and the fallen angels, is the exploitable condition of Samson's present disarray. Softly approaching, the members of the chorus are astounded at the new Samson:

> O change beyond report, thought, or belief!
>
> .   .   .   .   .
>
> Can this be he,
> That heroic, that renowned,
> Irresistible Samson?
>
> (117–126)

A genuine prince (not by birth, but by merit, as lines 170–175 indicate) Samson serves in the manner of the *Mirror for Magistrates,* the *De casibus,* or the fall of princes as an example of the human condition:

> O mirror of our fickle state,
> Since man on earth unparalleled!
> The rarer thy example stands,

> By how much from the top of wondrous glory,
> Strongest of mortal men,
> To lowest pitch of abject fortune thou art fall'n.
>   (164–169)

Tragic provisions are ample. Samson himself echoes the line of Satan and of Shakespearean tragic heroes behind him. His thoughts, like hornets armed, present his greatest agony, "present / Times past, what once I was, and what am now." (21–22) And although these words are not used, it is clear that Samson's defeat casts some doubts, if only implicit on Samson's part, on the "special eye" and hand of providence. Were this line of doubting to be affirmed, we would be left not with a religious sense of the world but with a tragic one. It would be a story "Of fate, and chance, and change in human life." There would be no cosmic accommodation for the aspiring heroic soul, but Samson, like Achilles, would only be led to reflect on the differences between the gods and men. Hellenic and Hebraic, as in *Paradise Regained,* the issues are clearly joined. Samson, like Troilus in Chaucer's "little tragedye" (before the Christian dispensation is invoked) would be a hero in the classical manner, defeated, with no responsiveness in the universe to his higher ideals and dreams. However much this might be a mistaken vision of Greek culture (in Aeschylus the universe is decidedly moral, and in Sophocles savage destiny leads to Colonus a man scarred by the gods — Oedipus, who thereby becomes their charge and even their spokesman), nevertheless in the minds of the greatest Renaissance writers the highest achievement of the classical world was its sense of tragedy, and it was precisely this vision that the Christian subsumed and transcended. Achilles in Book XXIV of the *Iliad* is justification for Dante's vision of limbo in *Inferno* IV: a hemisphere of light in a world of darkness. Man has no communication with divinity:

> Rather accuse him under usual names,
> Fortune and fate, as one regardless quite
> Of mortal things.
>   (*Paradise Regained,* IV.316–318)

For Milton, while he incorporated many of its forms, the Incarnation rendered this tragic vision obsolete. And while we are emphasizing the heroic Samson, and in what ways dramatically *Samson Agonistes* is a fuller version of divine comedy than *Paradise Regained,* it must be stressed that the experience of Christ, anachronistically imitated in Samson, is the basis of that later fulfillment.

The chorus indicates two ways in which God shows himself through his just ones. One is the heroic way, reminiscent of the prelapsarian Samson:

> Oh how comely it is and how reviving
> To the spirits of just men long oppressed,
> When God into the hands of their deliverer
> Puts invincible might
> To quell the mighty of the earth . . .
> He all their ammunition
> And feats of war defeats
> With plain heroic magnitude of mind
> And celestial vigor armed.
>
> (1268–1280)

The other is the way exemplified by the Christ of *Paradise Regained*. Different from the heroic greatness that leads to physical victory is the suffering of the patient:

> But patience is more oft the exercise
> Of saints, the trial of their fortitude,
> Making them each his own deliverer,
> And victor over all
> That tyranny can inflict.
>
> (1287–1291)

Either of these, the chorus proceeds, is within Samson's lot, but his blindness

> May chance to number thee with those
> Whom patience finally must crown.
>
> (1295–1296)

The chorus is, of course, right and wrong. The exercise of saints, the renouncement of his own will, and the patient attendance on the will of God has been Samson's way. Like Christ in *Paradise Regained* he achieves a spiritual readiness for whatever divine providence sends his way. But the chorus is wrong in ruling out the heroic magnitude of mind armed with celestial vigor.

This is not unusual, since the energies of the piece habitually surmount the reach of the chorus (and Manoa). Samson is tried by tempters (Dalila and Harapha) and encircled by well-intentioned comforters. While not pernicious, the counsel of the latter is not satisfactory either. They are practical foils to Samson's special designation. Theirs are consolatory writs, while Samson is designed for heroic fulfillment. As usual in Milton, the protagonist is quietly superior to his surroundings. Although relatively inactive, he is at the center of concern. Through eager thought he rejects a series of temptations, and by these rejections manifests, beyond his knowing, his own capacity. While Shakespeare's agonists are more passionate, and have around them characters and incidents that rightly or wrongly cause them pain and self-doubt ("How all occasions do inform against me!"), Milton's characters have a remarkable and almost inalienable core of calm superiority. Even the tragic-heroic Samson, anguished though he is, shows his higher level of comprehension. This superiority comes from his responsiveness to divine impulses, and is part of the higher destiny planned for him. For example, Samson refuses to take part in the games of his oppressors, games with which the chorus, fearing the practical consequences, urges compliance. Like all choruses they retreat from the painful confrontation: "How thou wilt here come off surmounts my reach." At this moment the drama pivots. Under the influence of the old promptings, Samson decides to participate, a choice that leads to an ending more suitable to his heroic beginnings. "Be of good courage," he cheers the chorus:

> I begin to feel
> Some rousing motions in me which dispose
> To something extraordinary my thoughts.
> (1381–1383)

It is the practical father's plans and designs that are most ironically counterpointed by the higher purposes of divine intent. His sanguine beliefs are reminiscent of those of Adam and Eve before their real education in time and history. More like Gloucester in *King Lear* he is brought from one level of experience to another by his son; he has been forced to enter a world not of regular proceedings but of risings and fallings and sudden surprise:

> O ever-failing trust
> In mortal strength! and oh what not in man
> Deceivable and vain! Nay, what thing good
> Prayed for, but often proves our woe, our bane?
> I prayed for children, and thought barrenness
> In wedlock a reproach; I gained a son,
> And such a son as all men hailed me happy:
> Who would be now a father in my stead?
>
> (348–355)

Like every busy father, however, he tries to exploit his pull with City Hall to get his son relieved. He works to effect some accommodation for his ransom; he even hopes that Samson's sight will be restored. With typical poor taste the chorus reminds Manoa of how the normal expectations of fathers and children have been reversed in his case. While fathers normally save for their children, Manoa will be obliged to spend; whereas children are expected to care for their aged parents, Manoa will be obliged to care for his son — whose blindness has reduced him to helplessness. But the father would delight in such care, merely to have the comfort of the son's presence and safety. Yet Samson had earlier rejected such security, the ignominy of sitting like some static Ulysses:

> But to sit idle on the household hearth,
> A burdenous drone? To visitants a gaze,
> Or pitied object; these redundant locks,
> Robustious to no purpose, clust'ring down,
> Vain monument of strength; till length of years
> And sedentary numbness craze my limbs
> To a contemptible old age obscure.
>
> (566–572)

He would rather be a slave than entertain such retirement, where no little part of his pain, besides his own inoperancy, would be unwelcome obscurity. Essential cross-purposes divide the son and his dramatic world of heroism and grace from the father and his stable world of succession. Going beyond the pleasure principle, the son experiences greater needs that must be satisfied. Milton has created a tragic protagonist with all the fire and pure spirit of an Achilles or a Hamlet. "I set not my life upon a pin's fee," was Hamlet's response to those who would dissuade him from his fate; and Samson, too, rejects his father's reduced terms. He will not plead with God: "His pardon I implore; but as for life, / To what end should I seek it?" (521–522) Nevertheless, the differences between the relations to their fathers of these English tragic heroes are instructive. Hamlet must come to accept a more limited world, which Samson would rise out of. Hamlet's father stands for special heroic distinctions, while the action of the play is based upon mutability and serves to level the differences between Hyperion and a satyr. In Milton, reflecting his confidence in the heavenly father, the earthly father speaks practically, while it is the son whose higher aspirations are favored.

In *Samson Agonistes* the greater tension exists between the father's "timely care" — mainly seeking survival for his son — and the son's pursuit of his fate. Two fathers, with conflicting aims, make their demands upon Samson. As he did in his birth and his fall, so, by satisfying the promptings of his heavenly father, Samson brings his earthly father to a higher awareness:

> Nothing is here for tears, nothing to wail
> Or knock the breast, no weakness, contempt,
> Dispraise or blame; nothing but well and fair,
> And what may quiet us in a death so noble.
>
> (1721–1724)

It is the father who picks up the thread of Samson's heroism. Samson has quit himself like Samson, and brought "To himself and father's house eternal fame." We should not see this return of the notion of fame as an indication of Manoa's unregenerate limitations and mediocre perspective. There is other testimony in the play that supports such reintegration. Before his consent to enter the games, Samson's thoughts presage some great act that would make the day remarkable; he senses that something extraordinary is imminent. Earlier fame was presented in its doubleness as arbitrary and completely dependent upon the subjectivities of time and place: Dalila will be condemned in Judaea, but among the Philistines she will be lauded. But contrary to Milton's other attacks on fame, here the dispraise does not come from a reliable spokesman, but rather from a woman whose falsity is apparent. To return to the heroic conclusion, the chorus joins the medley and sees in Samson the fabled phoenix,

> And though her body die, her fame survives,
> A secular bird, ages of lives.
>
> (1706–1707)

Samson, as Manoa continues the final lengthy speech, will serve as a model. Like Edward King he will be the Genius of the Shore, not so much for protection or comfort, but rather for heroic encouragement and high inspiration. His father will build a monument,

> and plant it round with shade
> Of laurel ever green, and branching palm,
> With all his trophies hung, and acts enrolled
> In copious legend, or sweet lyric song.
> Thither shall all the valiant youth resort,
> And from his memory inflame their breasts
> To matchless valor and adventures high.
>
> (1734–1740)

Such confirmation had not been heard from Milton since the early days of the *Seventh Prolusion,* or the *Ad Patrem.* And here, importantly, the father is converted to the son's heroism. *Dividuumque deum genitorque puerque tenemus.* In divine comedy, at its highest stages, the divided world of early inspiration and middle defeat come together, and after its chastening, purgatorial process, fame returns. With fame also is restored the other broken link of the ways of succession, generation. Father and son are reconciled.

Chapter 12
Summary and Epilogue

At the core of this study, as its essential Renaissance theme, lies the argument of time. It brings together into patterned formations the many and variegated facets of Renaissance understanding and response. Its value might be the relationship it establishes among elements that have hitherto been considered separately. To be sure, Renaissance literature shows a keen sense of time's all-consuming power; *Tempus edax rerum* was no idle imagining, or, as Petrarch could say, no "somnium," but rather "present and real." A state of war was declared between man and time, requiring preparedness and militant concern. Yet time is no palpable villain: it can smile before it murders; it is a swift and subtle thief that creeps up on the unwary. Behind these fairly conventional expressions is the more interesting understanding of time's doubleness; its comings and goings convert early promise into bitter endings. Man's expectations, his ideas of himself or his community and nation, are created in the early, brighter, rising rhythms of existence. Built-in, then, almost from childhood, is an illusion of invulnerability. Time's doubleness lulls the unwary into a sense of false security, an attitude of untroubled drift; it is on the most unheeding, from Dante to Shakespeare, that changes fall most terribly, and cause the deepest anguish. For this reason, then, the argument of time involves that warning voice, urgent and exhortative, which presents to the deluded imagination the folly of its inactivity. The argument of time is a call to action, the marshaling of a more aggressive attitude toward experience. The *carpe diem* philosophy, broadly understood, inspires this summons to strenuous activity, urging man to get control of a portion of his life and not to rely on an ignorant sense of security. Even Petrarch for religious purposes wants, after his conversion, to grasp the truth, " 'l ver abbracciar." In the youthful familiar letter (I.3) Petrarch, as he does on other occasions, can use the decidedly pagan *carpe florem* motif within a clear religious context: "Collige, virgo, rosas dum flos novus et nova pubes." But in all of the writers, whether Augustinian or historical, religious or secular, lies the deep awareness that time can brutally break through all defenses. Time is the agent of a reality that contradicts any sense of carefree impunity. This reality must be encountered; if met properly, it can bring rich talents to a good end.

While considering the similarity of pattern that joins the different writers in this study, we must also bear in mind historical development and change. One of the most important transformations is the religious use to which the argument of time was put in the fourteenth century and its more purely secular purposes in the sixteenth. In both, time is an agent of conversion from what we have called aesthetic awareness to ethical action. This latter phrase implies an active taking in hand, a refusal to leave the outcome to events themselves, and is essential to the enduring pattern. Augustine in Petrarch's *Secretum* uses the argument of time to stress the uncertainty of succession and the need for the properly alerted soul to look outside its realm for his rewards. Spenser, on the other hand, in his frequent and unavailing addresses to the English nobility, urges just such a concern with succession — in despite of the ruins of time. Under the hard law of the argument of time, which seems to require such infamous rejections, Dante in his *Purgatorio* must leave behind Virgil, who represents succession and continuity, seriousness and temporal diligence. Yet in Shakespeare's history plays, under the impress of another father law and time, Henry V rejects Falstaff's license on the basis of values that Dante found insufficient in Virgil. Other areas of the argument reveal similar transformations. Very early among the fourteenth-century writers (long before any strict Protestant ethic), the use of the call to account and the parable of the talents revealed the accommodations made between religious concern and economic success.[1] The metamorphoses of these two notions, the first from Seneca to Petrarch to Shakespeare and then to Milton, and the second from its use in Domenico Cavalca and then in Shakespeare and Milton, help us to see, through very specific themes, the broad lines of change in the Renaissance attitude toward time. They show the interpenetration of the religious and the secular in the fourteenth century, the secular exhortations of the sixteenth, and then a return to a more spiritual understanding in the age of the "metaphysicals."

Advancing along a wide front of preoccupations, the argument of time enters into the largest meanings of the Renaissance when it reflects that age's double face. It is no accident that time should be the concern of a period whose works are marked by energy and a love of variety. The very sense of time that calls for an awakening, for militancy, is intrinsic to the nature of a renascence. So, too, the challenge of time in the Renaissance calls out heroism: "ingentibus animis nichil breve optabile est." Time can thus elicit fervent heroic aspiration, but it also can present a practical aspect, especially in moments of doubt and despondency, when the heroic impulse is confronted with wasted possibilities, unfinished projects, the sins of overreaching, and the ruins of paradise. Energy needs to be channeled and variety brought into some working order. Thus Petrarch concludes (and in so doing gives expression to this need as he had done to the heroic): "Totum in ipsius temporis dispensatione consistit" ("Everything consists in the ordered disposition of time"). Whether for Petrarch, for the younger Guarino, or for Shakespeare, time is the agent and the reality invoked to marshal energy and variety.

This dual nature of time — and its historical development in the West — has created modern critical problems. While Matthew Arnold's terms, Hellenism and Hebraism, are useful if properly qualified, the fact is that Hebraism, in the time-related sense in which he employs it, was not an incidental usurper of the Renaissance's true Hellenic function: that age's new sense of time was a fundamental conquest, joining together cosmic argument and practical ends, fervent discovery and scheduling. Modern critics who have reacted only to the implied business ethic and calculation of this new sense of time have failed to see what an important and necessary cultural advance it was, and how many of the values and possibilities they themselves enjoy derive from that primary Renaissance act of endeavor and separation from the more quietistic medieval world. Nor do they sufficiently respond to the dynamics of individual development, to the personal issues raised in the public choice, and to the need for the questing spirit to liberate itself from idleness or from the destructive possibilities of willful aestheticism. In much Renaissance literature where time was a passionate discovery, practicality and enthusiasm could be successfully combined. That this did not hold true in later developments served to prejudice post-Romantic criticism against the Renaissance argument of time.

Time was a theme that Jacob Burckhardt did not include in his study of the Renaissance, yet it is in relation to time that his special claims for the distinctiveness of fame in that period hold true. He has been seriously challenged, however, by Johan Huizinga in his *Waning of the Middle Ages*. The Dutch historian thought that Burckhardt "here, as elsewhere, exaggerated the distance separating Italy from the Western countries and the Renaissance from the Middle Ages. The thirst for honour and glory proper to the men of the Renaissance is essentially the same as the chivalrous ambition of earlier times, and of French origin." [2] The argument of time enables us to affirm the essential validity of Burckhardt's point. In the Renaissance, fame was at war with time. One responded to time because one hoped to shore up an extremely vulnerable and exposed condition of being with heroic achievements. Whether this response was or was not known in chivalry, still Burckhardt is right, and Dante and Petrarch our witnesses, that the motive was primarily Roman in origin. Chivalric honor did not derive from any sense of man's exposure to time, but from the sense that within man was an inviolable essence that ought under no condition to submit to lower contingencies. Far from being at war with time, as Petrarch is in the "Coronation Oration" and Shakespeare in his sonnets, chivalry, like feudal society, was relatively indifferent to time. Its desired goal did not come from temporal management, from diligence, constant application, and long effort, but rather from a repudiation of such paltry considerations. It lacked the practical Renaissance awareness of time, and its moments of splendor seemed alien to the continuous effort that Renaissance fame and time required.

The development of notions about fame and children shows that the modern world has been much less inclined to make such fervent claims for the realm of succession. Oliver Elton was right when he saw a new somberness and lack of optimism about fame in seventeenth-century literature. "The *Urn-Burial* (1658) is almost the burial, in England, of the old hope." [3] Professor Benjamin is also right when he considers the eighteenth-century expressions of the idea of fame as "tending to become more and more of an elegant, meaningless abstraction. In the nineteenth century the word ceases to be associated with poetry and history as new poetic and historical standards are evolved." [4] There are exceptions, but in the main these conclusions support the basic trend of declining investment on the part of high literature in the long-range possibilities of succession, and even the reduced claims for poetry itself, until Robert Frost with all the strength of modesty could call poetry "a momentary stay against confusion."

Beneath the apparent relation of progeny and fame in the Renaissance — both indicating a renewed faith in the order that man could impose upon succession — there existed profound differences, as contemporary controversy and future directions revealed. Lines were drawn during the Renaissance between, on the one hand, the humanists who valued their freedom and their spiritual offspring, and, on the other, those with more civic or national allegiance who thought that it was in relation to the encumbrances of fortune, politics, children, and marriage that man discovers his better nature. The former abandon the present for the sake of higher, farther-reaching ambitions — they are more heroically inclined; while those who place their stock in children seem more intimately connected with the life and goals of a community, and with the everyday issues. There were, to be sure, men like Dante or Shakespeare, who valued both. It is also useful to point out that the more dramatic pictures of the world, where powerful wills contended — in short, a world of emulation — were conceived by those who at one point or another committed themselves to children. Nevertheless, despite their different appeals, children and fame are both allied in representing the consolations and triumphs of historical continuity. And as such they are, strangely enough, the major obstacles to fulfillment. Dante must abandon the illusory stabilities of the city, and finally in the *Purgatorio* divest himself of the hopes of children and fame, before he can regain the spiritually dramatic world of God's grace. While Shakespeare's world is not so God-centered, still, after the break-up of the order of history, he portrays a world of tragic turbulence and mystery. Hamlet experiences orphanhood and King Lear shudders at the thing itself.

Fame, more intimately connected with Renaissance heroic humanism, would necessarily die out when those aspiring minds turned to look for more solid virtues. Children, revealing their more practical bourgeois value, would only assume greater value in the time to come — but not in literature. They would, however, make their reappearance with the Romantic sensibility, but not, as in the Renaissance, as instances of hope in succession. Peter Coveney, in his *The Image of Childhood,* sees the growth of the child in nineteenth-century literature in relation to the writer's alienation from the historical and social world: "In a world given over increasingly to utilitarian values and the Machine, the child could become the symbol of Imagination and Sensibility, a symbol of Nature set against the forces abroad in society actively de-naturing humanity." [5] The Romantic image of childhood returns to the pre-Renaissance conception of the child, but its emphasis on sensibility and imagination differs from the Christian moral goodness that Dante sought to recover. Still more does it differ from the intervening hope in children, there being profound differences between the notions of children and of childhood (differences which are underlined when we substitute "progeny" for "children"). The one looks to the future with hope; its vision is prospective and historical, and it finds its consolation in continuity. Its concern is with the race. The Romantic appreciation of childhood implies none of these. Where history is alien, succession itself is closed. One does not look forward to one's posterity, but rather backward to one's past, the Garden once again being opposed to time. Yet within this self-enclosed world, man can pass beyond consolation toward fulfillment by discovering the necessity from which he sprang.

In short, what we bring out when sketching in the epilogue to the Renaissance faith in succession, children, and fame, is that in the modern, post-Renaissance world, such faiths are hardly possible. One contemporary social psychologist, while writing of post–World War II "protean man," could just as well be describing the historical aftermath of this study:

> Perhaps the central impairment here is that of symbolic immortality — of the universal need for imagery of connection predating and extending beyond the individual life span, whether the idiom of this immortality is biological (living on through children and grandchildren), theological (through a life after death), natural (in nature itself which outlasts all) or creative (through what man makes and does). I have suggested elsewhere that this sense of immortality is a fundamental component of ordinary psychic life, and that it is now being profoundly threatened: by simple historical velocity, which subverts the idioms (notably the theological) in which it has been traditionally maintained; and, of particular importance to protean man, by the existence of nuclear weapons, which, even without being used, call into question all modes of immortality. (Who can be certain of living on through children and grandchildren, through teachings or kindnesses?)[6]

But it must also be remembered that the Renaissance, too, knew its isolation and alienation, that the faiths in succession and history did not pass unchallenged, and that pestilence could terribly threaten hope in the future, just as the H-bomb presumably does now.

Time is a theme with forward directions in the Renaissance. Countries that did not move into the modern world, like Italy or Spain, either lost or never developed the Renaissance sense of time. Our study, which began with the late thirteenth and early fourteenth centuries, when, over a spectrum of developments, Europe began to separate itself from the rest of the world, ends with the seventeenth century, when the forces that had been previously released somehow only found their fullest development in the northern countries of Europe. Italy, at the forefront of developments until the sixteenth century, seemed to lose that position when humanism itself was superseded. There are other indications: "Interestingly enough, Italy, which had been a leading country in matters of horology during the Middle Ages, did not develop any great centre of clock and watchmaking in the modern age." [7] Spain, for that matter, appears never to have developed in any significant way a Renaissance sense of time. In Otis Green's *Spain and the Western Tradition,* with sections on "Time and Mutability" and "Hope" there is only one example, Gracian's *El Criticón,* which could be called "Renaissance" in its attitude toward time.[8] It is not surprising, then, to read in Green that "the transition from a sacramental to a secular view of nature and of events was not accomplished in Spain during our period." (IV, p. 9) Yet this was precisely the accomplishment of Shakespeare's second tetralogy, where time figures so prominently. There, if anywhere, we witness the drama of transition from a sacramental and ceremonial view of nature and the kingship, represented by Richard II, to a more secular, realistic view of power, represented by Bolingbroke and his son. Implicit in the agony of Richard II is another struggle which Shakespeare represented more profoundly in the tragedies. In the preface to his fourth volume, Professor Green asks, "How long were the Spaniards able to retain a world view built on the conviction of the inevitability and desirability of permanence . . . in the face of the opposing world view that rested on the idea of organic change as the law of life?" (p. v) His answer, however tentative, seems to place the change as late as the nineteenth century. But it was in the Renaissance, particularly in the tragedies of Shakespeare, that the desire for permanence was confronted with the evidence of change. Out of that agony arose the cry of the tragic hero. From the sacramental to the secular, from permanence to change, these are the alterations, deeply involved with time, that prepared the modern temper. Yet, after the agony, Shakespeare, like Montaigne, was able to describe worlds where an order did persist even within change.

If anything, the burgeoning time world of the Renaissance succeeded too well. It resulted in a temporal scheduling that had all the fire removed and in which only dire somberness and priggishness remained. Benjamin Franklin has been regarded as the most representative figure of the Protestant ethic and the spirit of capitalism — those developments of modern society which seem most to have carried on the temporal achievements of the Renaissance. But a more intermediary figure is in Daniel Defoe's *Robinson Crusoe.* Defoe's story is the great myth of the modern world, and his Robinson is the Odysseus of commercial bourgeois civilization. It is the middle-class book *par excellence,* showing the dearest values of the middle class in the process of formation. While taking his risks and leaving the secure, middling comforts of his father's home, Robinson Crusoe brings little discovery to his new station or to his return. The end result of his efforts is to endorse the values of the civilization he left behind, and to implant those very values in the new world he discovered. Essential to the order he imports is the calculation and scheduling of time: "After I had been there ten or twelve days, it came into my thoughts that I should lose my reckoning of time for want of books, and pen and ink, and should even forget the sabbath days from the working days." One would hardly expect the festival spirit on a deserted island, but such trepidation lest the division of work days and sabbath be neglected is remarkable. Upon a post he indicates the time of his arrival ("I came on shore here on the 30th of September, 1659"), and by notches keeps a calendar, with extra-long slits marking the seventh day of the week and the first day of the month: "and thus I kept my calendar, or weekly, monthly, and yearly reckoning of time." [9]

In typical accounting fashion, a kind of double entry bookkeeping, Robinson Crusoe lists the credits and debits of his condition, and concludes that on balance his lot is not so bad. The same kind of rational schematism goes into the inevitable *emploi du temps,* although here, certainly, such scheduling does not derive from an overplus of things to do and ambition to get them done. His diary entry of November 4: "This morning I began to order my times of work, of going out with my gun, time of sleep, and time of diversion; viz., every morning I walked out with my gun for two or three hours, if it did not rain; then employed myself to work till about eleven o'clock; then ate what I had to live on; and from twelve to two I lay down to sleep, the weather being excessive hot; and then, in the evening, to work again." (p. 75) There is no death-wish in Robinson Crusoe, no overreaching ambition; unseemly moments of hysteria, fear, and retching are blandly ignored or repressed from his account. Defoe has created the prototypic character fit to cut through nature, shear off mountains, settle the plains, and establish habitable communities amid the hostile elements. Perhaps his virtues were necessary under the circumstances into which he was thrown, but one must also admit that he displayed them with unremitting zeal. The great problem of time in the modern world is here revealed.

Once the hostile elements have been tamed, is not greater ease to be allowed, and more of the May Day spirit permitted that existed before the iron glove of Puritanism:

> Puritanism, in its marriage of convenience with industrial capitalism, was the agent which converted men to new valuations of time; which taught children even in their infancy to improve each shining hour; and which saturated men's minds with the equation, time is money. One recurrent form of revolt, whether bohemian or beatnik, has often taken the form of flouting the urgency of respectable time-values. And the interesting question arises: if Puritanism was a necessary part of the work-ethos which enabled the industrialized world to break out of the poverty-stricken economies of the past, will the Puritan valuation of time begin to decompose as the pressures of poverty relax? Is it decomposing already? Will men begin to lose that restless urgency, that desire to consume time purposively, which most people carry just as they carry a watch on their wrists? [10]

In two ways, then, the major writers of the Renaissance covered in this study anticipate the modern sense of time. While they participated actively in the distinguishing marks of the Renaissance, they also recoiled — in art at its most prophetic — from the implications of the time-world they foresaw. Throughout our study we witnessed this reaction in secular writers like Shakespeare and Montaigne, as well as more religious writers like Dante and Milton. As *Antony and Cleopatra* dramatizes, the requirements of imperial control had become too restrictive; the organizational powers of an Octavius precluded too many of the virtues of an Antony. More explicitly economic, Dante repudiates the forward pressures of an acquisitive society in terms of the stabilities of a higher spiritual order. He stood at the headwaters and saw far into future developments; Milton stood in the midst of the world that Dante prophetically deplored. Against the stern rigors of Puritanical consciousness and relentless high seriousness he suggests the virtues of small talk, easiness, the casual moments of pleasure, the unimplored visits of the Muse. These attempts to relax severity are part of a more fundamental vision, at the very core of his major works, that literally stands in opposition to the temporal pressures of the modern world, pressures, he felt, which would force man to abdicate his spiritual nature.

In the former, more casual manifestations of this spirit, Milton can be startlingly modern, and can be allied with some expected — and unexpected — successors. Jean-Jacques Rousseau, for one, performed a

profoundly symbolic act, one fraught with consequences for modern literature, when he discarded his watch upon abandoning Geneva, where
the supervision of time and the production of watches were paramount.
His defiance gave every indication of the new time values in the currents
of thought he was to initiate. It is more reasonable, however, to align
Milton with Wordsworth, both of whom appreciated the creative possibilities of a wise passiveness. Especially in relation to the growth of the
imagination, Wordsworth resisted the educational programming that
originated in the Renaissance and which only seemed more pronounced
in his day.[11] Thomas Wedgwood was the proponent of an educational
method that would by rigorous control reduce the number of hours normally wasted in idleness: "Let us suppose ourselves in possession of a
detailed statement of the first twenty years of the life of some extraordinary genius; what a chaos of perceptions! . . . How many hours, days,
months have been prodigally wasted in unproductive occupations." [12]
"Through a fixed habit of earnest thought," Wedgwood's project would
govern the aimless reverie and increase "the powers and produce of the
mind." (p. 433) For actual superintendents in his system, he had considered Coleridge and Wordsworth. It is thought that Wordsworth responded to these notions in parts of the *Prelude,* where indeed he recalls
some of the highest wisdom of Renaissance literature.

In unflattering terms Wordsworth describes the high projects of the
new educational engineers:

> Great feats have been performed, a smooth high-way,
> So they assert, has lately overbridged
> The random chaos of futurity,
> Hence all our steps are firm, and we are made
> Strong in the power of knowledge.

He scorns the presumptuous masters of such a program, "watchful men"

> And skillful in the usury of time,
> Sages who in their prescience would coerce
> All accidents, and tracing in their map
> The way we ought to tread, would chain us down
> Like engines, when will they be taught
> That in the unreasoning progress of the world
> A wiser Spirit is at work for us . . .
> Even in what seem our most unfruitful hours? [13]

What Hamlet had to learn, with more foreboding and in circumstances more menacing, Wordsworth advocates: greater allowance must be made for the unknown and the unchartable, not only in the growth of the child, but in the life of the man as well. But this comparison also reveals essential differences. Succession for Hamlet was normally quite princely and acceptable, involving tradition and community. His passage to a higher wisdom was consequently forced and involuntary. But these processes had become transformed and mechanized, so that if Wordsworth were to reach the highest wisdom of that play he must voluntarily abandon the restrictive society around him. The society represented by Claudius was criminal; the processes from which Wordsworth withdrew, while not dark, were deforming. The powers of control — his examples are largely taken from mechanics ("would chain us down / Like engines" and "lately overbridged / The random chaos of futurity") — chalk too clearly the ways that men must travel and rob the individual of new and creative organizations of experience. Against the regimentation of the mind (and its surprises), Wordsworth urges resistance in order to allow for more genial thoughts, and to encourage man's more spiritual nature.

If there has been one clear direction to the modern world since the Renaissance, it has been toward man's increased capacity to stabilize and control nature and events. This has been the result of those early attempts to limit risk, to seize the day, to make oneself the master of all things. In the Renaissance such incitements were fervent and such realizations necessary. In more recent periods of history we have come to painful awareness of the harm produced by their total success. Through the growth in the order of society, success has been negated by being prepaved. Formerly, as in the case of Prince Hal, acceptance of the terms of society led to identity and some fulfillment; in the modern world it seems to lead to dissatisfaction and a haunting sense of nothingness. By entering his father's world, Hal reintegrated a fragmented personality. But it is from the world that his father has created that modern "protean man" has been formed. By dropping out, he tries to heal his wounds and recover his wholeness. In the Renaissance, the sense of time was still human, dramatic, and mortal. But those qualities have been replaced by the clock and its corollary of a super-organized society. By removing his watch, and trying to regain a more natural sense of the time of his life, the young person of today actually returns to the Renaissance conception. Instead of an imposed, superficial order, he tries to gather up his life into a real order. Like Milton's young Christ, he searches for significance and some deliberation:

> How to begin, how to accomplish best
> His end of being on earth and mission high.

To set his own lands in order he must reject a society that presents him only with amenities and suffocating domesticity — although the sixties brought out the costly underside of that suburban pleasantness.

Milton's (and the Renaissance's) problem of the two fathers is still with us. Prolifically now, sons of middle-class fathers defect from their world in order to take the risks of a higher calling they feel within. This rebellion takes strange-seeming forms and is widespread. College teachers still are hard put to explain the unusual phenomenon of students whose tastes are almost naturally liberal, democratic, and romantic finding such fascination with the *Waste Land,* and a poet whose professions were avowedly catholic, royalist, and classical. What sense of sin and squalor, drama and significance, grace and love possesses our natures, unsatisfied by all the obvious modern decencies? As Lionel Trilling has made it his thesis in *The Liberal Imagination* and a recent essay, "The Fate of Pleasure," this is the modern version of the older theme of time and being.[14] Man needs to go beyond the pleasure principle, and like Dante and Shakespeare and Milton, or the Renaissance itself in its greatest talents and creations, take the risk of setting out, of overreaching, of getting lost in the desert, for the benefit of a more significant understanding and a richer return.

Notes

1. The Setting

1. *Europe in Transition: 1300–1520* (Boston: Houghton Mifflin, 1962); the earlier monograph appeared in the Berkshire Studies in European History (New York: Holt, 1940).

2. *La Société féodale* (Paris: Michel, 1940), I, 116–120.

3. See Carlo M. Cipolla, *Clocks and Culture: 1300–1700* (New York: Walker, 1967), for this and subsequent information.

4. "Au moyen âge: Temps de l'église et temps du marchand," *Annales, E.S.C.,* 15 (1960), 425. See also his "Le Temps du travail dans la 'crise' du XIVᵉ siècle: Du temps medieval au temps moderne," *Le Moyen Age,* 69 (1963), 597.

5. See LeGoff, "Au moyen âge," pp. 424–425, for the list of causes and the quotation.

6. Stuttgart, 1892, p. 162.

7. Trans. W. L. Luetkens (London: Kegan Paul, Trench, Trubner, 1944), p. 15.

8. Quoted in Marvin B. Becker's *Florence in Transition,* vol. 1, *The Decline of the Commune* (Baltimore, Md.: Johns Hopkins Press, 1967), p. 38.

9. *Painting in Florence and Siena after the Black Death* (Princeton, N.J.: Princeton University Press, 1951), p. 60.

10. LeGoff, "Le temps du travail," p. 611.

11. Becker, *Florence in Transition,* I, 90.

12. This maxim (no. 255) and subsequent ones come from Alfredo Schiaffini's edition, *Libro di Buoni Costumi* (Florence: Monnier, 1945), to which the parenthetical numbers in the text refer.

13. Cavalca was born in the Vico Pisano around 1270. He died in 1342, having spent most of his life in the monastery of St. Catherine in Pisa. I quote from the *Disciplina,* ed. G. Bottari (Rome, 1757).

14. For this "new time" concept as an important part of the Renaissance consciousness, see Herbert Weisinger, "The Self-Awareness of the Renaissance as a Criterion of the Renaissance," *Papers of the Michigan Academy of Science, Arts and Literature,* 29 (1944), 561; and "Who Began the Revival of Learning? The Renaissance Point of View," *ibid.,* 30 (1944), 625. For the new "periodization" involved, see Theodor E. Mommsen, "Petrarch's Conception of the 'Dark Ages,'" in *Medieval and Renaissance Studies,* ed. Eugene F. Rice, Jr. (Ithaca, N.Y.: Cornell University Press, 1959), p. 106. Both arguments are utilized by Joseph A. Mazzeo, *Renaissance and Revolution* (New York: Random House, 1965), pp. 38–41.

15. Hans Baron, "A Sociological Interpretation of the Early Renaissance in Florence," *The South Atlantic Quarterly,* 38 (1939), 437. This article is valuable for its insight into the intermingling of cultural and economic motives toward time.

16. Vittore Branca, *Boccaccio medievale* (Florence: Sansoni, 1956), esp. pp. 71–99.

17. Arthur Golding's translation of the *Metamorphoses,* XV.199–205, *Shakespeare's Ovid,* ed. W. H. D. Rouse (1904; rpt. Carbondale, Ill.: University of Southern Illinois Press, 1961). Ovid's descriptions of time were early incorporated into the *Roman de la Rose* and from there into Chaucer's translation of the *Roman,* XI.361–391, and the Host's speech, *Canterbury Tales,* Frag. II.19–32.

18. *The Consolation of Philosophy,* V.vi. Chaucer's translation: "Eternite, thanne, is parfit possessioun and altogidre of lif interminable." The "I.T." translation (1609) in the Loeb Classical Library *Boethius* (Cambridge, Mass.: Harvard University Press, 1962) differs little: "Eternity therefore is a perfect possession altogether of an endless life."

19. *St. Augustine's Confessions,* trans. William Watts, Loeb Classical Library (Cambridge, Mass.: Harvard University Press, 1951), II.237, with minor alterations.

20. Surprisingly enough it was F. H. Brabant, in his valuable study *Time and Eternity in Christian Thought* (London: Longmans, 1937), who considered the passage in question to be an indication of Augustine's "Plotinian conception of the eternal present." (p. 60) In the J. G. Pilkington translation of the *Confessions, A Select Library of the Nicene and Post-Nicene Fathers,* ed. Philip Schaff (New York, 1886), vol. I, the quotation from the Psalms is enclosed in inverted commas.

21. Two modern commentators, Maurice Pontet, *L'exégèse de S. Augustin prédicateur* (Paris: Aubier, 1945), and H.-I. Marrou, *L'Ambivalence du temps de l'histoire chez saint Augustin* (Montreal: Institute d'Etudes médiévales, 1950), pp. 43–46, quite accurately emphasize this destructive process in Augustine's conception of time. "Le temps est un effritement progressif" — Pontet. Each rejects the imputations of Bergsonianism to Augustine's temporal considerations, specifically those advanced by Jean Guitton, *Le Temps et l'éternité chez Plotin et saint Augustin* (1933; rpt., rev. Paris: Vrin, 1959). It is noteworthy that both Bergson and Guitton figure in Brabant's reading. This division is not a casual one and will be met again when modern critics, emphasizing the forward-looking, the dynamic, will neglect the older inheritance of Renaissance writers. See also the discussion by Gerhart B. Ladner, *The Idea of Reform* (Cambridge, Mass.: Harvard University Press, 1959), p. 209, n28.

22. The translation used in the Loeb Classical Library edition; see n19 above.

23. In my Ph.D. dissertation, "Views of Time in Shakespeare," (Harvard University, 1963), and in three articles, " 'Lineal Honour' and Augmentative Time in Shakespeare's Treatment of the Bolingbroke Line," *Topic: 7,*

4 (1964), 12; "Views of Time in Shakespeare," *Journal of the History of Ideas,* 26 (1965), 327; and "Time in Dante and Shakespeare," *Symposium,* 22 (1968), 261.

24. These two aspects of time are discussed, though with slightly different terminology, by Georges Poulet in the first volume of his *Etudes sur le temps humain,* translated under the title *Studies in Human Time* by Elliott Coleman (Baltimore, Md.: Johns Hopkins Press, 1956). "The [medieval] world was a world of abiding things." These things coexisted on different orders of duration, all sustained by God and forming a stable hierarchy. "Nevertheless," Poulet correctly adds, "within him and around him, [the Christian of the Middle Ages] was unable to keep from seeing change. If he felt sure of his own permanence he was at the same time constrained to notice a profound lack of permanence. Paradoxically, he felt himself to be a permanent being, a being who never changed and a being who always changed." (pp. 3–4) My own notions and even my terminology derive from Gerhart B. Ladner's splendid essay, "*Homo Viator:* Medieval Ideas on Alienation and Order," *Speculum,* 42 (1967), 233.

25. *Time in Greek Tragedy* (Ithaca, N.Y.: Cornell University Press, 1968), p. 5.

26. *Laws,* 721B.

27. "On the Originality of the Renaissance," *JHI,* 4 (1943), 51.

28. *Painting in Florence and Siena,* p. 61.

29. Trans. Robert Baldick (New York: Knopf, 1962), p. 33.

30. Similar phrasing occurs in the *Convivio,* IV, xxix, where Dante paraphrases Juvenal's eighth satire: "Che fanno queste onoranze che rimangono da li antichi, se per colui che di quelle si vuole ammantare male si vive?" ("What is the importance of ancient honors if he who wishes to mantle himself with them lives badly?") Satire VIII is behind Dante's long-standing thoughts about name and virtue: "nobilitas sola est atque unica virtus." (l. 20)

31. PL 36.419; trans. in Schaff, vol. 8, *Saint Augustine: Expositions on the Book of Psalms,* ed. A. Cleveland Coxe (1888), 114.

32. From the *Metalogicon,* trans. Daniel D. McGarry (Berkeley, Calif.: University of California Press, 1955), II.10. See also R. L. Poole, *Illustrations of the History of Medieval Thought and Learning,* 2nd ed., rev. (New York: Macmillan, 1920), pp. 176–186, for a translation of and commentary upon the passage. It is worthwhile to note, given the relations of the time-conscious bourgeoisie and Seneca, that John of Salisbury accuses Cornificius of invoking Seneca to support his reforms (*Met.* I.22).

33. *Familiarum rerum libri,* ed. V. Rossi *et al.,* 4 vols. (Florence: Sansoni, 1933–1942), XVI.11.

34. *Centuries of Childhood,* p. 149.

35. *The Civilization of the Renaissance in Italy,* trans. S. G. C. Middlemore (London: Phaidon, 1955), p. 87, and the section on "glory," pp. 87–93. Parenthetical page references are to this edition.

36. "The Ambiguity of Fame," *The Hudson Review,* 18 (1965), 171. The

French original, "Désir et horreur de la gloire," is part of a book which is very valuable for our subject, *La Chute dans le temps* (Paris: Gallimard, 1964), p. 100.

37. Quoted in Buckley's *The Triumph of Time* (Cambridge, Mass.: Harvard University Press, 1966), p. 65.

38. This very suggestive phrase is taken from John H. Finley's *Four Stages of Greek Thought* (Stanford, Calif.: Stanford University Press, 1966).

2. Dante

1. All quotations from Dante's *Commedia* conform to the critical edition of the Società Dantesca Italiana (1921; rev., Milan: Hoepli, 1955). The English renderings are from J. D. Sinclair's *The Divine Comedy,* 3 vols. (New York: Oxford University Press, 1939).

2. *St. Augustine: The City of God against the Pagans,* 7 vols., Loeb Classical Library (Cambridge, Mass.: Harvard University Press, 1966), vol. 4, trans. Philip Levine.

3. My article "Time in Dante and Shakespeare," *Symposium,* 22 (1968) gives fuller coverage of the extent of emulation's operation in the *Commedia.* See n23 of the preceding chapter.

4. In Milton, too, the myth will recur, with a clear Augustinian basis. In fact, from *Beowulf* to Joseph Conrad's *The Secret Sharer,* the Cain-Abel theme has valuable literary ramifications. It is the dread destructiveness of the feud, in *Beowulf,* reaching back to Cain, that shatters any secular ideal. This is the importance of the Cain-Abel myth for Augustine, Dante, and Milton, and the basis of their search for more religious solutions to the problem of the human will. Shakespeare confronts the same human dynamism and antagonisms, but his faith, at least until the tragedies, lies in the function of the powerful monarchy to restrain and redirect energies. While unrelated etymologically, feud happily suggests feudal, and, in fact, it was the spirit and arrogance of the aristocratic warrior cult that precipitated the feuds that Dante and Shakespeare tried to resolve or transcend. If time in its functioning is emulative, it is clear why the feud, as its social corollary, should have a key position in this study. In so far as the feud is transcended, so is time. If time is a bourgeois concern and the feud is an aristocratic liability, we can see why the new Renaissance sense of time, calling forth qualities of management and modesty, in more ways than one ran counter to the feudal understanding of time.

5. Throughout the Renaissance, the pressures of contemporary challenge to the older Christian or, at least, established edifice that had been built on the ruins of man's first Fall will be regarded as a second Fall, distinct from, but following the pattern of the original lapse. This is the meaning of the defoliation of the Tree of Life in the earthly paradise. (*Purg.* XXXIII) After being revived by the touch of the Griffon-Christ, it is beset by a series of historical incidents, all summarizing the historical confusion between church and state. Now the Tree is "due volte dirubata" ("twice-robbed"), the first time through Adam's offense, the second through the related series of his-

torical events, taken in sum. In Spenser, as we shall see, this concept will be figured by Mutabilitie; in Donne, by the death of Elizabeth Drury; and in *Richard II*, the Queen will actually reprove the Gardener for bringing her the news of Richard's deposition, news amounting to a "second fall." (III. iv.75)

6. "*Homo Viator:* Mediaeval Ideas on Alienation and Order," *Speculum,* 42 (1967), 244.

7. This thought comes from the profundity of classical reflection, Biblical and Homeric. In the *Iliad,* Apollo shows his scorn for the race of men, "who are as leaves." (XXI.464) A more immediate connection is provided by Horace's *Ars poetica,* 60–62, where language is again the subject. Dante himself, in the *Convivio* (II.xiii.10), specifically quotes adjacent lines from Horace (70–71) when he discusses the comings and goings of language. For another interpretation of Nimrod, however, see *Inf.* XXXI.77–78.

8. Raffaello Ramat sympathetically addresses "il mito dantesco di Firenze," yet realistically appraises its anti-historic tendencies. The Florence that Dante deplored, "antiroman, cuore della lega contro Arrigo VII," was on its way to becoming, if it had not already become, "la città più modernamente intelligente d'Europa." From the loathed "genti nove" were emerging Giotto, Petrarch, Boccaccio, and the founders of modern law. The "subiti guadagni" were preparing the splendid age of the merchants, which was civic in its broadest sense: the necessary foundation to humanism and the Renaissance. *Il mito dantesco di Firenze* (Florence, 1964), pp. 10–11. Taking myth in its broadest Aristotelian sense, as motivating idea, Ramat's essay comprehends the true unity of the *Commedia.*

9. See Giuseppe Boffito, "Dove e quando potè Dante vedere gli orologi meccanici che descrive in *Par.* X, 139; XXIV, 13; XXXIII, 144?" *Giornale dantesco* 39 (1938), 45, and the brief but informed discussion in Lynn White's *Medieval Technology and Social Change* (New York: Oxford University Press, 1962), p. 124 and n3. See also Lynn Thorndike's "Invention of the Mechanical Clock about 1271 A.D.," *Speculum* 16 (1941), 242.

10. Trans. Carley Dawson and Elliott Coleman (Baltimore, Md.: Johns Hopkins University Press, 1966), p. xi.

11. See his "Figura," *Scenes from the Drama of European Literature* (New York: Meridian, 1959), p. 11, and the essay of practical application, "St. Francis of Assisi in Dante's *Commedia,*" esp. pp. 95–98.

12. See Rossiter's *Angel with Horns,* ed. Graham Storey (London: Longmans, 1961), p. 37.

13. For indications of the amount of Dante's personality in Ulysses, see Petrarch's contemporary account below, chapter 3, pp. 122 and 129. For further elaboration of this notion of self-identification, see Giorgio Padoan, "Ulisse 'fandi fictor' e le vie della sapienza," *Studi danteschi,* 37 (1960), 21; Giorgio Petrocchi, "Itinerari nella *Commedia,*" *Studi danteschi,* 41 (1964), 70–73.

14. Loeb Classical Library (Cambridge, Mass.: Harvard University Press, 1963), vol. 2, trans. William H. Green.

15. In more ways than his hostility to papal policy for Italy (see his *History of Florence*), Machiavelli is a nationalistic heir of the Ghibelline spirit. He echoes the sentiments of the Cardinal when he writes to Francesco Vettori (April 16, 1527), "I love Messer Francesco Guicciardini; I love my native city more than my soul." *The Letters of Machiavelli: A Selection*, ed. and trans. Allan Gilbert (New York: Capricorn, 1961).

16. I say this fully conscious that there is no consistent pattern of capitalization in reference to fortune throughout the *Commedia*.

17. There are exceptions at both ends of the *Inferno* to this general trend. Filippo Argenti in Canto VIII makes no request to have his name remembered. Virgil tells Dante that his soul was so filled with violence and arrogance that "bontà non è che sua memoria fregi" ("no good there is to adorn his memory"), and therefore is he so furious in hell. Fame is, however, still valuable, since its absence causes such pain. (*Inf.* VIII.46–48) In the lower reaches of hell, among the fraudulent, the uses of fame continue (1) as a personal need for recognition (Mosca, XXVIII.106, Capocchio, XXIX.133–135), (2) as the simple request that word be brought back to earth concerning them (Piero da Medicina, XXVIII.70–75; Bertran de Born, XXVIII.133–134), and (3) as the device by appeal to which Dante and Virgil are able to solicit information or a service (XXVIII.91–93, XXIX.103–106, XXXI.125–127). In the last instance, Virgil is attempting to persuade the giant Antaeus to lower him and Dante to the region of Cocytus. Antaeus, of all the giants, seems to be deserving of Virgil's honorific address, since he did not participate in the assault on the heavens, and he alone is unfettered. But when we proceed to the last section of hell, the very bottom of the abyss, then even these highly qualified expressions of human longing are silenced.

18. Nor, even, does it simulate that line of poetic descent celebrated in the *Purgatorio* (see below, p. 93), where Virgil, himself in the dark, acts as lantern for those spiritual sons who follow, Statius and Dante.

19. The thought is that of DeSanctis in his essay, "L'Ugolino di Dante," *Saggi critici,* ed. Luigi Russo (Bari: Laterza, 1952), p. 33.

20. In Guido del Duca's and in Cacciaguida's accounts we can witness Dante's own "bourgeois" version of the Fall of Princes and the *ubi sunt* motif. For background, see Etienne Gilson's essay, "De la Bible à François Villon" in *Les Idées et les lettres* (Paris: Vrin, 1955), p. 9; and Italo Siciliano, *François Villon et les thèmes poétiques du Moyen Age* (Paris: Colin, 1934), pp. 256–261.

21. The importance of this ascetic ideal in Dante has been recently stressed by Giorgio Petrocchi, "Dante and Thirteenth Century Asceticism," in *From Time to Eternity,* ed. Thomas G. Bergin (New Haven, Conn.: Yale University Press, 1967).

22. See below p. 83 for similar verbs of "undoing," and the introductory matter concerning Augustine, p. 14. In contrast to such "unleaving," or defoliation (which even affects the historical Tree of Life on Mount Purgatory), there is the spiritual tree which "frutta sempre e mai non perde foglia" ("is always in fruit and never sheds its leaves," *Par.* XVIII.30)

23. For even fuller applicability of Kierkegaard's theory of character evolution, see chapter 3, Petrarch, p. 135 and chapter 8, Shakespeare's Histories, p. 326. Although the dilemma in these later writers is more critical than in Dante's *Purgatorio,* nevertheless at this study's first use of the terms "aesthetic" and "ethical," I shall fill in Kierkegaard's own ideas. They too are part of the argument of time, where with some urgency an experienced voice exhorts critical choice and the need to forge multiple facets of personality into identity and to convert activity of thought into earnestness of spirit. The following quotation from *Either/Or,* trans. Walter Lowrie, vol. 3 (1944; rev. Howard A. Johnson, Garden City, N.Y.: Anchor, 1959), will reveal Kierkegaard's meaning: "Do you not know that there comes a midnight hour when everyone has to throw off his mask? . . . Do you think you can slip away a little before midnight in order to avoid this? Or are you not terrified by it? . . . Or can you think of anything more frightful than that it might end with your nature being resolved into multiplicity, that you really might become many, become, like those unhappy demoniacs, a legion, and you would thus have lost the inmost and holiest thing of all in man, the unifying power of personality. . . . The inner drift of the personality leaves no time for thought experiments. . . . [The person is like the navigator on a ship that is always moving ahead — at some point he must decide.] If he forgets to take account of the headway, there comes at last an instant where there no longer is any question of an either/or, not because he has chosen but because he has neglected to choose, which is equivalent to saying, because others have chosen for him, because he has lost his self." (pp. 164, 167–168) This quotation also indicates the temporal pressures that help to work conversion from the aesthetic to the ethical, and while they have supreme application to Petrarch, they are not without importance for Dante's purgatorial process, especially when Kierkegaard, like Dante, invokes the shade of Cato: "So, like a Cato I shout at you my either/ or, and yet not like a Cato, for my soul has not yet acquired the resigned coldness which he possessed. But I know that only this incantation, if I have the strength for it, will be capable of rousing you, not to an activity of thought, for of that you have no lack, but to an earnestness of spirit. Perhaps you will succeed without that in accomplishing much, perhaps even in astonishing the world . . . and yet you will miss the highest thing, the only thing which truly gives meaning to life; perhaps you will gain the whole world and lose your own self." (pp. 171–172)

24. In Mario E. Cosenza's *Petrarch's Letters to Classical Authors* (Chicago, Ill.: University of Chicago Press, 1910), pp. 156–157.

25. Quoted by Carol L. Marks in "Traherne and Hermes Trismegistus," *Renaissance News* 19 (1966), 131.

26. See J. W. Mackail *The Springs of Helicon* (London: Longmans, Green, 1909), pp. xvi, 12–18.

27. In a sense this is T. S. Eliot's interpretation in "Virgil and the Christian World," *On Poetry and Poets* (New York: Farrar, Straus, 1957).

28. Recently there have been good discussions of the earthly paradise

motif in Dante and the later Renaissance. See Poggioli, "Dante *Poco Tempo Silvano*: Or a 'Pastoral Oasis' in the *Commedia*," Dante Society Annual Report, 80 (1962), 1; A. Bartlett Giamatti, *The Earthly Paradise and the Renaissance Epic* (Princeton, N.J.: Princeton University Press, 1966), pp. 94–122; and Harry Levin, *The Myth of the Golden Age in the Renaissance* (Bloomington, Ind.: Indiana University Press, 1969), Appendix A, "Paradises, Heavenly and Earthly."

29. Sinclair's extra-textual translation: "O my own blood! O grace of God poured forth above measure! To whom as to thee was heaven's gate ever opened twice?" Although the language is Dante's own, the *Aeneid,* of course, bears the suggestion for the thought (cf. VI.133–135; 687–689) without the notion of grace abounding.

30. There are other indications of Dante's paradisal reaffirmation of fame. The men who share the cross with Cacciaguida are all worthy; together they form in fact Dante's Nine Worthies. Their fame is duly recorded:

> spiriti son beati, che giù, prima
> che venissero al ciel, fuor di gran voce,
> sì ch'ogni musa ne sarebbe opima.

> [they are] blessed spirits which below, before they came to
> heaven, were of so great fame that every muse would be
> enriched by them. (XVIII.31–33)

31. That the tree is an image of the world's disorder is the point, I gather, of Phillip Damon's article, "Geryon, Cacciaguida and the Y of Pythagoras," *Dante Studies* 85 (1967), 25–30, esp. 27. His more personal reading of the inverted tree seems to me to be transcended by John D. Sinclair's larger social interpretation, which I quote. The tree represents the possibility of earthly life; again, after Sinclair, it is a "symbol of all righteous order in the earthly life." Dante's commitment to the earthly city is re-evidenced by the well-nigh sacred function he attributes to the operation of justice and order in human society. "For the whole subject of the *Purgatorio* is the perfecting, by penitence, and fellowship and prayer, of the life of man among men." (See Sinclair's fine commentary on Cantos XXXII and XXXIII.)

32. *The Pursuit of the Millennium* (1957; rev. London: Temple Smith, 1970).

33. A paraphrase from Cullmann's *Christ and Time,* trans. Floyd V. Filson (Philadelphia: Westminister, 1964), p. 91.

3. Petrarch

1. *Familiarum rerum libri,* ed. V. Rossi *et al.*, 4 vols. (Florence: Sansoni, 1933–1942). This is my basic source for the familiar letters. For the *Epistolae seniles* I have had to use, in the absence of a modern critical edition, two

sources: *Epistolae rerum senilium* in *Francisci Petrarchae opera omnia,* 3 vols. (Basel: 1554), vol. 2; and G. Fracassetti's Italian translation, *Lettere senili di Francesco Petrarca,* 2 vols. (Florence: 1869–1870). The translations I use here are from Morris Bishop's *Letters from Petrarch* (Bloomington, Ind.: Indiana University Press, 1966), with the indication "Bishop" followed by the page number; or M. E. Cosenza, *Petrarch's Letters to Classical Authors,* essentially *Fam.* XXIV.3–12, with copious commentary. As in the former case, my references there will be indicated in the text by "Cosenza," followed by page number. Where no translation is extant the renderings have been my own, with no references.

2. *Studi sul canzoniere del Petrarca* (Rome: Editrice Studium, 1958), p. 62. There is a chapter on Petrarch's sense of time and transience in Umberto Bosco's *Francesco Petrarca* 2nd ed. (Bari: Laterza, 1961), pp. 54–67. The poet Giuseppe Ungaretti in an essay "Il poeta dell'oblio," *Primato,* 4 (1943), has written of time and memory in the *Rime* (rpt. in *Civiltà letteraria d'Italia,* eds. Vittore Branca and Cesare Galimberti, 2 vols. (Florence: Sansoni, 1962), I, 359–362. See also C. Calcaterra, *Nella selva del Petrarca* (Bologna: Cappelli, 1942).

3. Chicago, Ill.: University of Chicago Press, 1961, p. v.

4. I quote Petrarch's poetry from the *Rime, Trionfi e poesie latine,* ed. F. Neri *et al.* (Milan and Naples: Ricciardi, 1951).

5. Among the *Rerum memorandum libri* Petrarch records that Plato died when he was exactly eighty-one years of age: "mira res dictu, ipso suo natali die" ("strange to say, [his death occurred] on the very date of his birth"). Petrarch then quotes Seneca's observation that Plato had perfectly completed his life since the number of his years at death was the product of nine squared. *Rerum,* ed. G. Billanovich (Florence: Sansoni, 1945), p. 31. For contractions of a more tragic bent see below, chapter 9: Shakespeare's Tragedies, p. 363.

6. Trans. by Hans Nachod in *The Renaissance Philosophy of Man,* ed. E. Cassirer *et al.* (Chicago, Ill.: University of Chicago Press, 1948), pp. 47–133. The Basel edition of the *Opera* (1554) is the justification for printing the letter (*Sen.* XIII.5) before the text of the treatise.

7. *An Essay on the Development of Christian Doctrine,* quoted by Buckley, *The Triumph of Time,* p. 23.

8. I.iv.9, trans. Jacob Zeitlin (Urbana, Ill.: University of Illinois Press, 1924), pp. 150–151.

9. Petrarch was evidently the first to divide history into three cultural epochs, the period of classical antiquity, the intervening period of neglect and little accomplishment, and the present age of renascence. See Mommsen, "Petrarch's Conception of the 'Dark Ages,'" chapter 1, n14, above. See also the bulk of the letters in Book XXIV, where Petrach complains about time, but also about the sloth of the preceding age.

10. See J. B. Trapp's "Owl's Ivy and the Poet's Bays: An Inquiry into Poetic Garlands," *Journal of the Warburg and Courtauld Institutes,* 21 (1958), 227. See also Wilkins, *Life,* pp. 24–29.

11. "Petrarch's 'Coronation Oration,' " trans. Ernest H. Wilkins, *PMLA*, 68 (1953), 1245. All further quotations from the "Oration" will refer to this version.

12. *Life*, p. 29.

13. This letter is, surprisingly, as yet untranslated into English. A Latin text, together with Fracassetti's Italian version, is contained in *Francesco Petrarca: Prose*, ed. G. Martellotti *et al.* (Milan and Naples: Ricciardi, 1955). Hereafter all references to the contents of this edition will occur in the text as *Prose*.

14. In the 1554 edition this letter is numbered XIV.4. In the earlier editions 1501 and 1503 it is XV.3. Fracassetti and Wilkins follow the earlier numeration. For the discrepancies in numbering between the various editions see Wilkins, *The Prose Letters of Petrarch: A Manual* (New York: Vanni, 1951), pp. 6–10.

15. Both lives are reprinted and translated in C. A. Dinsmore, *Aids to the Study of Dante* (Boston, Mass. 1903).

16. (1955; rpt. rev., Princeton, N.J.: Princeton University Press, 1966). See the section "The Crisis in Civic Conduct and Outlook," pp. 315–331, and also p. 110 for a discussion of Salutati's reversal of Petrarch's stand on marriage.

17. Giovanni di Pagolo Morelli, *Ricordi,* ed. V. Branca (Florence: Monnier, 1956).

18. A great exception is the prologue to the second book of the *De remediis,* where Petrarch discourses on the Heraclitean struggle of opposites, "Lis omnibus una est: nilque non secundum litem sit." See Marcel Françon's valuable article, "Petrarch, Disciple of Heraclitus," *Speculum,* 11 (1936), esp. pp. 265–268. While the evidence is impressive, especially if we remember the conflict of opposites in Petrarch's love poetry (for example, sonnet 134, "Pace non trovo e non ò da far guerra"), still, even here it is an internal conflict, not one that focuses on competitive social ambitions and human wills, those energies that play so formidable part in Dante's or Shakespeare's more dramatic conceptions of the world.

19. In his "Oration," p. 1248, Petrarch declares that "the laurel tree is shady and affords a resting place for those who labor." He also quotes two passages from Horace in support of this interpretation. For Christian material relating shade to the protection afforded by the tree of the cross, see Stanley Stewart, *The Enclosed Garden* (Madison, Wis.: University of Wisconsin Press, 1966), "Shade," pp. 60–96.

20. Sonnet 16, sestina 22, and canzone 50 are a few of them.

21. Panofsky, in his article "Father Time," has shown how Petrarch's sense of the destructive, even predatory power of time influenced Renaissance iconography. Petrarch's poetic reflections upon mutability and upon the power of poetry to counteract oblivion had a demonstrable impact on later poets like DuBellay and Spenser. In yet another area, one of Petrarch's major bequests to humanism was his vigorous (and scheduled) exploitation of all available hours. In the course of this study we shall return to these

areas of influence in their appropriate places. It is an interesting question, however, whether, setting historical influence aside, Petrarch was even the first poet to develop these areas of temporal consciousness. From *Inf.* XXIV.46–54 we recall Virgil's exhortation (quoted in the general introduction) that Dante put away all sloth if he hopes to achieve fame, without which man's life is as so much froth. And, at the outset of *Par.* XVI, Dante warns that nobility must be added to day by day, otherwise it will be cut away by the shears of time — certainly an indication that time had acquired a hostile and menacing image before Petrarch. In the *Purgatorio* time is precious, and references to the shortness of the remaining hours are many, all pointing to the need for active and diligent effort. Finally, Dante even senses some tragic possibilities in time: the promising Henry VII came to rule before Italy was ready ("ch'a drizzare Italia / verrà prima ch'ella sia disposta," *Par.* XXX.137–138).

22. To mention only a few instances, poems 269, 283, 317, and 323 of the *Rime* all betray this sensitivity to the suddenness of death. And, as these examples suggest, the terror is increased by the blighting of a life's work. Milton also, in *Lycidas,* will dramatize the horror of premature death, before life's high ideals could be realized.

23. See LeGoff, "Le Temps du travail," p. 611, and E. P. Thompson, "Time, Work-discipline and Industrial Capitalism," *Past and Present,* 38 (1967), 86–89, for the image of time as currency.

24. *The Merchant of Prato* (London: Jonathan Cape, 1967), p. 13.

25. *Ad Lucilium epistulae morales,* 3 vols., trans. Richard M. Gummere, Loeb Classical Library (Cambridge, Mass.: Harvard University Press, 1917), I.5.

26. *Prose,* 56; and also "Dilata parumper solutionis dies, sed non cassa ratio est" ("The day of settlement might be deferred, but the reckoning is not cancelled," p. 194).

27. For the various meanings of the mirror in relation to time see Panofsky, "Father Time," p. 82, n50. For the *miroir* of death, see also Siciliano, *François Villon,* p. 254 and notes.

28. Incidentally, variations on the word *blind,* indicating deluded sight, occur 23 times in the *Rime* and 13 times in the *Trionfi.*

29. Miss Fredelle Bruser is alert to the Christian form of the *carpe diem* motif in her "*Comus* and the Rose Song," *SP,* 64 (1947), 630–633. She quotes from Jeremy Taylor's *Holy Dying:* "This instant will never return again, and yet it may be this instant will declare, or secure the fortune of a whole eternity. The old Greeks and Romans taught us the prudence of this rule; but Christianity teaches us the Religion of it." The distinction is thus clear between the two uses of the same motif. Petrarch, for instance, in addition to using the stern warnings of Cicero and Horace, repeats the classical "Collige, virgo, rosas" to religious ends in *Fam.* I.3.

30. In the *Africa* the same arguments are used. Fame is consistently attacked for its inanity, its shadowiness. "Sed nomine vivere nil est." Then, too, simple geographic and temporal limitations confine the extent of fame.

The differences of people, in language and customs, suggest further how little of the world is actually available to renown. Man's fame will suffer even more from time: death takes away those men with whom he spent his life; the successive generations of men overwhelm the preceding (this being one of the few areas where Petrarch recognizes the emulative processes); and envy works against great accomplishments, detraction, we shall be told later, not suffering honor. Tomb monuments themselves will crumble and this will be a kind of second death. A third death (and both of these instances are given in the *Africa*) occurs when the books themselves by which we would like to be remembered also perish. These purgatorial arguments can be compared with Dante's *Purg.* XI, and derive from the philosophic tradition of Cicero's *Somnium Scipionis,* Macrobius' commentary thereon, and Boethius' *Consolation,* esp. II.7, in which form they probably had their greatest influence on fourteenth-century poets.

31. There are other areas of importance which might be mentioned here. Not only did Augustine lay the foundations for the concept of eternity, but his eschatological framework, as Patrides has shown, is the essential one for the Christian sense of history, and as such will recur from Dante through Milton. But, at the same time, as Marrou and Pontet have observed, Augustine had a vivid sense of the perishability of the flesh and of time as a process of "undoing." In J. A. Mazzeo's *Renaissance and Revolution* (New York: Random House, 1965), Augustine is linked with Dante and Machiavelli in their "anthropology of desire," their senses of insatiable cupidity (see pp. 75–77, 85). Petrarch was not directly open to the communal, historic Augustine his mentor was more the author of the *Confessions,* where emphasis is on personal conversion.

32. *Ad Lucilium,* I.325.

33. For other early *emplois du temps* see LeGoff, "Le Temps du travail," p. 612 and n53.

34. "Time Perception in Children: Psychological Time," rpt. in *Voices of Time,* ed. J. T. Fraser (New York: Braziller, 1966), pp. 211–212.

35. In the pictorial arts, as Millard Meiss informs us in his superb study, *Painting in Florence and Siena after the Black Death,* the story of Job, "rarely if ever represented in earlier Tuscan panels and frescoes," became relevant. For the Sienese, laid low by economic collapse, pestilence, and marauding bands, "the story of Job, an old paradigm of trial and affliction, acquired a specially poignant meaning. Not only did Job suffer from a disease whose outward symptoms were like those of the plague; his cattle were driven off and his children killed." (p. 68, n36, n37)

36. *Being and Time,* trans. John Macquarrie and Edward Robinson (New York: Harper, 1962), p. 392.

37. "The Evolution of Petrarch's Thought: Reflections on the State of Petrarch Studies," *Bibliothèque d'Humanisme et Renaissance,* 61 (1963), 25. See also the summary statement on p. 40. This essay has been reprinted in Baron's *From Petrarch to Leonardo Bruni: Studies in Humanistic and Political Literature* (Chicago, Ill.: University of Chicago Press, 1968).

Another valuable essay, like Baron's indicating discernible stages in Petrarch's intellectual evolution, is Guido Martellotti's introduction to his collaborative edition of the *Prose.*

38. *Of His Own Ignorance,* trans. Hans Nachod, p. 104. See n6, above.

39. *Ad Lucilium,* I.321.

40. *Culture and Anarchy,* ed. J. Dover Wilson (Cambridge: Cambridge University Press, 1932), p. 142.

41. *Ad Lucilium,* I.323.

4. The Backgrounds of History and Tragedy in Sixteenth-Century Thought

1. *The Crisis of the Early Italian Renaissance* (1955; rpt. rev. Princeton, N.J.: Princeton University Press, 1966). In the summary that follows I rely greatly on this seminal work.

2. For evidence of these changes taking place before the period discussed by Baron, see Marvin B. Becker, "Popular Government and the Stern Paideia," *The Decline of the Commune,* vol. I of *Florence in Transition* and Gene A. Brucker, *Florentine Politics and Society, 1343–1378* (Princeton, N.J.: Princeton University Press, 1962), pp. 48, 72–73, 136, 242, 294, 390, and 396.

3. "The Humanist Concept of the Prince and *The Prince* of Machiavelli," *Journal of Modern History,* 11 (1939), 449.

4. *Tutte le opere di Niccolò Machiavelli,* ed. Francesco Flora and Carlo Cordiè, 2 vols. (1949; 2nd ed. Milan: Mondadori, 1968), I.119, 409.

5. *Machiavelli and Guicciardini: Politics and History in Sixteenth-Century Florence* (Princeton, N.J.: Princeton University Press, 1965), pp. 192 and 198. Professor Gilbert's "sense" of Machiavelli is excellent, pp. 192–200.

6. For the alteration of the Christian historical picture see C. A. Patrides, *The Phoenix and the Ladder: the Rise and Decline of the Christian View of History,* University of California English Studies, 29 (Berkeley and Los Angeles, Calif.: University of California Press, 1964), pp. 36–37.

7. Gilbert, *Machiavelli and Guicciardini,* p. 200.

8. *The Complete Plays of Christopher Marlowe,* ed. Irving Ribner (New York: Odyssey, 1963), to which all quotations from Marlowe's plays conform.

9. For a fuller discussion of these differing contexts see J. G. A. Pocock's review article, " 'The Onely Politician': Machiavelli, Harrington and Felix Raab," *Historical Studies: Australia and New Zealand,* 12 (1966), where he writes that English adoption of Machiavelli's thought "is never a response to the naked dictatorship of Fortune; it is a complex humanist response to what could be recognized and diagnosed . . . as a complex historical situation." (p. 284) Further, Machiavelli "did not see politics as the complex structure of properties and privileges, liberties and rights, which one could get to know only by living in a comprehensive and ex-

haustively described system of private and public law." (p. 280) Although Pocock is writing of seventeenth-century English political theorists, what he writes of them could also be said of Shakespeare's own sense of a complex network of legal and historical relationships into which change must be fitted.

10. Gilbert, *Machiavelli and Guicciardini,* pp. 267–270.

11. Trans. Mario Domandi (New York; Harper Torchbook, 1964), to which all quotations in the text refer.

12. Edited by Raffaele Spongano (Florence: Sansoni, 1951); my quotations refer to the recent translation by Mario Domandi, called *Maxims and Reflections of a Renaissance Statesman* (New York: Harper Torchbook, 1965).

13. See Enid Welsford, *The Fool: His Social and Literary History* (London: Faber and Faber, 1935); Walter Kaiser, *Praisers of Folly,* Harvard Studies in Comparative Literature, 25 (Cambridge, Mass.: Harvard University Press, 1963); Michel Foucault, *Madness and Civilization,* trans. Richard Howard (New York: Random House, 1965), chap. I, "Stultifera Navis"; and a brilliant essay by the late Robert Klein, "Un Aspect de l'hermeneutique a l'age de l'humanisme: Le theme du fou et l'ironie humaniste," *Archivio di Filosofia* (Padua, 1963), p. 12.

14. Samuel Daniel, *Poems and a Defense of Ryme,* ed. Arthur Colby Sprague (Cambridge, Mass.: Harvard University Press, 1930).

5. Rabelais

1. *Gargantua and Pantagruel* 2 vols., Everyman's Library (London: Dent & Sons, 1929), I, 162–165. The translation is that of Sir Thomas Urquhart. Since Rabelais' chapters are brief, there is no need of textual reference other than to book and chapter. The French in the text conforms to the standard *Oeuvres de François Rabelais,* edition critique, ed. Abel Lefranc *et al.,* 6 vols. (Geneva: Droz, 1913–1955).

2. Trans. Sears Reynolds Jayne, *The University of Missouri Studies,* 19 (1944), 202–203.

3. Trans. Benjamin Jowett, 2nd ed., rev., The Library of Liberal Arts (Indianapolis, Ind.: Bobbs-Merrill, 1956), p. 50.

4. *Vittorino da Feltre and Other Humanist Educators,* Classics in Education, 18 (1897; rpt. New York: Columbia University Teachers College Bureau of Publications, 1963), 2.

5. Woodward, *Vittorino da Feltre,* p. 62.

6. See Woodward's description in *Studies in Education during the Age of the Renaissance: 1400–1600* (Cambridge: Cambridge University Press, 1906), p. 108. Erasmus is a focal point representing the concentration of Petrarchan and fifteenth-century humanistic ideals and serving also as the conduit for their more Northern and international distribution. In him the interests of time, education, and children merge. In all of these areas he

is the "great transmitter"; see Paul Oskar Kristeller, "Erasmus from an Italian Perspective," *Renaissance Quarterly,* 23 (1970), esp. 13–14.

7. Reprinted in Woodward, *Vittorino da Feltre,* pp. 96–118 and Eugenio Garin's *L'educazione umanistica in Italia,* 4th ed. (Bari: Laterza, 1964), pp. 57–112. I use Woodward's somewhat free version. Of the *De ingenius* (1392), Woodward writes that Vergerius therein "lays down tentatively, but with clear conviction, the basis upon which Humanist education was presently to be built up." (p. 14)

8. Garin, *L'educazione,* p. 98.

9. *I libri della famiglia* in vol. 1, *Opere volgari,* ed. Cecil Grayson, Scrittori d'Italia, 218 (Bari: Laterza, 1960), 169, to which all future page citations refer.

10. Woodward, *Erasmus,* p. 221.

11. From the *De tradendis disciplinis* (1523), translated by Foster Watson as *Vives: On Education* (Cambridge: Cambridge University Press, 1913), p. 45.

12. Woodward, *Vittorino da Feltre,* pp. 175–176.

13. Woodward also speaks of the humanistic combination of a "strict method of study" with "an enthusiastic adaptation of the past to the needs of the present" (*Vittorino da Feltre,* p. 38); and Garin refers to the paradoxical translation of the sense of liberation into program (*L'educazione in Europa: 1400–1600,* 2nd ed. (Bari: Laterza, 1966), p. 72.

14. In Garin, *L'educazione umanistica,* p. 128.

15. Matteo Palmieri reveals the Renaissance sense of energy and love of variety at the base of this practice, "The nature of our mind universalizes beyond each thing and so quickly observes every part that not only is it capable of doing more than one thing in a day, but at the very same time it can perform several exercises." (Garin, *L'educazione umanistica,* p. 125)

16. See A. Chapuis, *De horologiis in arte* (Lausanne: Scriptar, 1954), p. 22, and pp. 15, 38, and 40 for the portraits refered to below.

17. Cipolla, *Clocks and Culture,* p. 104. See A. Franklin, *La Mèsure du temps,* vol. 4 of *La Vie privée d'autrefois* (Paris: 1888), p. 139.

18. Lucien Febvre, *Le Problème de l'incroyance au XVIᵉ siècle* (Paris: Albin Michel, 1947), pp. 426–434.

19. Walter Kaiser, in *Praisers of Folly,* pp. 160–161, writes well of this predicament.

20. See n2 of the next chapter for text and notations here used.

6. Montaigne

1. The phrase "choose en soy" (thing in itself) resonantly and memorably echoed by King Lear (III.iv.108–111), occurs in "Of diversion" (Fr. 633–634/Th. 932): "Our thoughts are always elsewhere; the hope of a better life stays and supports us, or the hope of our children's worth, or the future glory of our name. [Montaigne then gives illustrations from

antiquity and concludes:] These and other such circumstances occupy, divert, and distract us from consideration of the thing in itself."

2. As in n1 above, quotations from Montaigne's *Essais* will be followed by notations referring first to an English translation, Donald Frame's *The Complete Works of Montaigne* (Stanford, Calif.: Stanford University Press, 1957), and secondly to the French original, as contained in Albert Thibaudet's edition, *Essais de Michel de Montaigne,* Pléiade (Paris: Gallimard, 1958). Thus, the passage from "Of Vanity" should have been followed by (Fr. 764/Th. 1120).

3. *BHR*, 27 (1965), 361.

4. *Mimesis,* trans. Willard Trask (Princeton, N.J.: Princeton University Press, 1953), pp. 322–329.

5. George Santayana, *Three Philosophical Poets,* Harvard Studies in Comparative Literature, 1 (Cambridge, Mass.: Harvard University Press, 1910), 79.

6. "On the Dissemination of Realism," *Proceedings of the Vth Congress of the International Comparative Literature Assoc.* (Amsterdam: Swets and Zeitlinger, 1969), pp. 233–234.

7. *The Modern Theme,* trans. James Cleugh (New York: Norton, 1933), pp. 69–70.

8. *Montaigne: A Biography* (New York: Harcourt, Brace, 1965), esp. pp. 63–84.

9. Le Roy's *De la vicissitude ou variété des choses en l'univers* first appeared in 1575. This work was translated into English by R(obert) A(shley), *Of the Interchangeable Course, or Variety of Things in the Whole World* (London, 1594) and inspired John Norden's *Vicissitudo Rerum* (1600) Shakespeare Assoc. Facsimiles no. 4 (London: Oxford University Press, 1931). This connection has been studied by K. Koller, "Two Elizabethan Expressions of the Idea of Mutability," *SP*, 35 (1938), 228. Werner L. Gundersheimer has recently devoted a monograph to *The Life and Works of Louis Le Roy,* Travaux d'Humanisme et Renaissance, 82 (Geneva: Droz, 1966). Le Roy's evolution is interesting in the light of Cassirer's notions, and Gundersheimer finally labels him a "despairing optimist." (p. 127) Le Roy also was impressed by the role of opposites ("all things in the universe are tempered and conserved by contraries and opposites"), and he too makes use of Heraclitus (see Gundersheimer, p. 97).

10. Florio's slightly more detailed version of this passage betrays the Elizabethan's tendency to elaborate on mutability: "The flower of age dieth, fadeth and fleeth, when age comes upon us, and youth endeth in the flower of a full growne mans age: Child-hood in youth, and the first age, dieth in infancie: and yesterday endeth in this day, and to day shall die in to morrow. And nothing remaineth or ever continueth in one state." What we have here, as *Hamlet* or *King Lear* will make more manifest, is a philosophy of tragedy, predicated on a profound sense of change, a change that overrules all objects of human care. It has been held that Sophocles' philosopher was Heraclitus (see J. C. Kamerbeek, "Sophocle et Heraclite, quelques

observations sur leurs rapports," *Studia Vollgraff* [1948]). In this light there is more than passing significance in the fact that Shakespeare moved from history to tragedy at the time of Montaigne's introduction into England.

11. For the literature of the Golden Age, see Levin's *The Myth of the Golden Age in the Renaissance,* esp. pp. 74–83 for Montaigne's relation to the growing "primitivism"; and Henri Baudet's *Paradise on Earth,* trans. Elizabeth Wentholt (New Haven, Conn.: Yale University Press, 1965). There are two highly useful anthologies dealing with Utopian thought: *The Quest for Utopia: An Anthology of Imaginary Societies,* eds. Glenn Negley and J. Max Patrick (New York: H. Schuman, 1952), and "Utopia," *Daedalus,* Spring, 1965. An article by Renato Poggioli, "Definizione dell' Utopia," *Inventario,* 1 (1946–1947), is luminous.

12. *L'ideale eroico,* vol. 2, *Diffusione europea e tramonto,* pp. 15, 66.

13. Montaigne's complacency is really a tribute to the fecundity of France. The conditions over which he was optimistic continue to bewilder modern historians: "The economic history of France in the two centuries 1550 to 1750 is an intriguing puzzle to the economic and social historian. To the distant observer the country seems always on the verge of a final collapse and all odds seem to be against any possible recovery. Yet as the legendary phoenix, consumed in fire by her own acts, France always managed to rise in youthful freshness from her own ashes. An incredible amount of robust human energies must have been constantly fermenting under the troubled surface." (Cipolla, *Clocks,* p. 74)

14. Auerbach, *Mimesis,* p. 310.

15. *L'Influence du voyage de Montaigne sur les "Essais,"* (Princeton, N.J.: Princeton University Press, 1946).

16. *Montaigne,* ed. Floyd Gray (Paris: Gallimard, 1963), p. 191.

17. From the poem "Brother and Sister," quoted in Buckley, *The Triumph of Time,* p. 172, n5.

18. Paul Reyher, *Essai sur les idées dans l'oeuvre de Shakespeare* (Paris: Didier, 1947), p. 412.

19. Frame, *Montaigne: A Biography,* p. 83.

20. The concept of fox-historiography is taken, of course, from Isaiah Berlin's *The Hedgehog and the Fox: An Essay on Tolstoy's View of History* (New York: Simon and Shuster, 1953), where Montaigne is indeed listed among the foxes (see p. 2).

21. I consider this material a quite specific refutation, in Montaigne's own words, of some of Poulet's ideas in his first volume of *Studies in Human Time,* translated by Elliott Coleman. This book has many good things to say (in the chapter on Montaigne the material is excellent, especially the idea of "prise" — the intellectual understanding that makes material one's own); yet, on one side it overlooks some important parts of Montaigne's development. Poulet describes Montaigne's notions: "Each new occasion is an occasion of making a new use of oneself or of possessing oneself in another fashion. . . . Thus time now appears as the infinite pos-

sibility of all the moments out of which in its diversity life is produced and possessed. To live in time . . . is to live conscious of moving forward into a possession of oneself which is inexhaustible. The essential thing is to be ready all the time to receive the successive gifts of these possible selves." (pp. 46–47) Now certainly Poulet, in his construction of the moral patterns of Montaigne's thought, can adduce substantial evidence to support his notions. I do not disagree with his statements, merely with their insufficiency to describe the full development of Montaigne. Here, perhaps, a study based upon moral-philosophical pattern that neglects personal evolution and historical change reveals some of its inherent defects. The passage to which this note is keyed quite simply reveals different concerns in Montaigne's later thought. In the same essay, Montaigne can also write, "I am no longer headed for any great change or inclined to plunge into a new and untried way of life, not even a better one. It is too late to become other than I am." (Fr. 772/Th. 1132) Even if we recall that kind of thought which most supports Poulet's arguments, the thought of Montaigne *en voyage*, the open comedy of discovery and renewal, still Poulet's thought needs to be modified. Montaigne is not driving toward some open future; rather the future is closed — the curtain of *chorismos* has fallen — and it is for this reason that Montaigne preoccupies himself primarily with the present thing. Montaigne's message is not that of modern vitalism or mobilism. The modern filiations of Poulet's thought emerge when he writes that Montaigne has the "constant need to find himself again, like Gide, fresh and free, when confronting the object he has to seize and judge." (p. 48) And behind Gide is, of course, Bergson. The conclusions we are forced to draw are similar to those of chapter 1, n21, where reference was made to the older inheritance in relation to modern reinterpretations of Augustine, again deriving from Bergson. Certainly in viewing the Renaissance reaction to time, one must, if only from natural sympathy, emphasize the creative possibilities and the freedom. But the greatness of Renaissance temporal reflection does not exist in the avoidance of history but in its transcendence through participation. The Renaissance sense of energy and freedom encounters life's lessons of limitation, and only through such encounter does a new, more mature and more profound notion of the individual life — its achievements and its journey — emerge. Finally, one is not tempted to go forward, but rather to gather up the sense of a life, as it has been formed, and recognize the richness in its own necessities.

22. See Jean Starobinski's "Montaigne: Des morts exemplaires à la vie sans example," *Critique*, 24 (1968), 923.

23. "Of physiognomy" makes this clear: "But it seems to me that death is indeed the end ("le bout"), but not therefore the goal ("le but"), of life; it is its finish, its extremity, but not therefore its object." (Fr. 805/Th. 1180) For a record of the change see Frame, *Montaigne: A Biography*, pp. 299–300.

24. Of course Montaigne's actual words are here only roughly approx-

imated. He in fact wrote, "Quand je dance, je dance; quand je dors, je dors." Elsewhere he did express his preference for "une société et familiarité forte et virile, une amitié qui se flatte en l'aspreté et vigueur de son commerce, comme l'amour, és morsures et esgratigneures sanglantes" ("I like a strong, manly fellowship and familiarity, a friendship that delights in sharpness and vigor of its intercourse, as does love in bites and scratches that draw blood," Th. 1034/Fr. 705).

25. "Sur la structure d'un essai de Montaigne (III,13: De l'expérience)," *BHR*, 23 (1961), 281. Poulet reaches a similar conclusion in *Studies in Human Time*: "By dint of portraying passage, Montaigne obtains communication with being." (p. 49)

7. Spenser

1. All my quotations conform to the standard *The Works of Edmund Spenser: A Variorum Edition,* ed. Edwin Greenlaw, C. G. Osgood, F. M. Padelford, *et al.,* 11 vols. (Baltimore, Md.: Johns Hopkins Press, 1932–1957).

2. See pp. 197–210, *L'ideale eroico del rinascimento*: II. *Diffusione europea e tramonto* (Naples: Edizione Scientifiche italiane, 1965). While recognizing the complexity of the case, Weise can still clearly affirm the lexical presence of heroic humanism in Spenser, p. 202.

3. In his commentary E.K. himself provides the reader with the Ovidian and Horatian sources of this vaunt. Very similar expressions in Ronsard and Du Bellay are provided in Sidney Lee's *The French Renaissance in England* (New York, 1910), p. 277. For a Shakespearean similarity (sonnet 55) see the same author's "Ovid and Shakespeare," *The Quarterly Review*, 210 (1909), 462.

4. See especially *Delia,* sonnet 37, and Shakespeare's sonnet 64. Miss Scott is correct in her assertion that "Du Bellay's *Antiquitez de Rome,* translated by Spenser in his *Ruines of Rome,* had furnished material for philosophical and poetic meditation to an entire generation. The themes that Daniel treated before Shakespeare are part of petrarchism and as such are to be met throughout the Renaissance." *Les Sonnets élizabethains* (Paris: H. Campion, 1929), p. 250.

5. Following Elton (p. 57), Mr. Leishman sees the importance of Spenser's *The Ruines of Time,* wherein "he was the first English poet to treat memorably the topic [poetic immortality] with which we are concerned. [He then traces the derivations of the poem through Du Bellay back to Petrarch.] It was no doubt out of Spenser's long preoccupation with these in many ways thoroughly medieval notions on the Triumph of Time that the much more notable *Ruines of Time* emerged." *Themes and Variations in Shakespeare's Sonnets* (London: Hutchinson, 1961), p. 70. Of course, as we have seen in the *Ruines of Rome,* there is more to time than ruin — there is also the challenge of response and the possibility of enduring cul-

tural achievement. Nevertheless, the emphasis on the Petrarchan foundation to the large meditations on time in French and English poetry is accurate — no matter what reading, medieval or Renaissance, one gives to the content.

6. See the introductory remarks to Camden's *Britain,* trans. P. Holland (Hertfordshire, 1610). Spenser used the *Britannia* of 1590. For the presence of Camden in the poem see the commentary on *The Minor Poems,* vol. 2 (Baltimore, Md.: Johns Hopkins Press, 1957).

7. Spenser's encomium of Camden memorializes a real link between history and poetry in the English Renaissance. In major works, writers of prime importance were concerned to express their inspired sense of the connection between the past and the present. We have only to think of the *Faerie Queene,* Daniel's *The Civil Wars,* Drayton's *Poly-Olbion,* Shakespeare's history plays, and even Milton's *History of Britain.* Noteworthy is Mme. de Romilly's comment that in fifth-century Greece the discovery of history, of the relationship between past and present, was coincidental with the discovery of time (*Time in Greek Tragedy,* p. 11).

8. My discussion here was anticipated by A. Bartlett Giamatti, *The Earthly Paradise and the Renaissance Epic* (Princeton, N.J.: Princeton University Press, 1966); "The essential difference between the two places is the fact of time. This is what the Bower pretends to do without and what the Garden embodies." (p. 285) The notion of "trial" (for which see the next section) was also anticipated in pages 240–242. I believe, however, that in my argument these areas have their own point, context, and development.

9. The bibliography here is ample. John Addington Symonds "The Pathos of the Rose in Poetry," *Essays Speculative and Suggestive* (London and New York: 1907), and Fredelle Bruser, "*Comus* and the Rose Song," *SP,* 44 (1947), 625, are both very helpful, the latter in substantive discussion of crucial problems, rather than a mere listing. See also Leishman, *Themes and Variations,* pp. 66–69, 81–82; Scott, *Les Sonnets,* pp. 122–124, 241–243; Laumonier, *Ronsard, poète lyrique,* (Paris: Hachette, 1932), pp. 578–591; John E. Matzke, "On the Source of the Italian and English Idioms Meaning 'To Take Time by the Forelock,' with Special Reference to Bojardo's *Orlando Innamorato,* Book X, Cantos VII–IX," *PMLA,* 8 (1893), 303; George L. Kittredge, "'To Take Time by the Forelock,'" *MLN,* 8 (1893), 459; Rudolf Wittkower, "Chance, Time, and Virtue," *Journal of the Warburg Institute,* 1 (1937–38), 38; Panofsky, "Father Time," and Stürzl, *Der Zeitbegriff,* "Die Locke des Kairos," p. 160, and "*Carpe diem,*" p. 428.

10. See Bruser on this point, pp. 628–633, and my discussion of Petrarch, Chapter 3, n29.

11. Although one might have expected it, there is no indication of dramatic irony in Samuel Daniel's several uses of the *carpe florem* motif in his *Delia,* 31 and 32. As our next section will show, Spenser's *Amoretti* 70 is

no exception, since it is contained in the larger picture of religious sanction, marriage, and progeny.

12. Not unexpectedly, the theme of time to which Spenser so heroically responds, and which evinces his own abhorrence of bestial oblivion, does not dispose him favorably to the developing primitivism of the Renaissance (or for that matter of the modern world). In this, as in other regards, he stands almost diametrically opposed to the more resilient, unheroic wisdom of Montaigne. See Harry Levin's *The Myth of the Golden Age in the Renaissance,* pp. 81–83, for attention to the Grylle passage in the context of Renaissance primitivism.

13. Philip Larkin in "Poetry of Departures," *The Less Deceived* (Hessle, East Yorkshire: Marvell Press, 1955).

14. My sense of Spenser here — if not his terminology — is somewhat akin to that of C. S. Lewis, *English Literature in the Sixteenth Century* (Oxford: Clarendon Press, 1954), pp. 391–393.

15. For other expressions of this qualitative sense of time and of the human capacity to forget all past troubles, see also *An Hymne in Honour of Love,* 239–244, 294–300; and the *Epithalamion,* 31–33.

16. From the famous poem, LXI in the Loeb Classical Library *Catullus, Tibullus and Pervigilium Veneris* (1913; rev. London: Heinemann, 1931), trans. F. W. Cornish.

17. In the same LXI, see 217–221.

18. *Shakespeare's Festive Comedy* (Princeton, N.J.: Princeton University Press, 1959), pp. 3–15, esp. 10.

19. Clearly in this discussion I have ignored the number symbolism seen in the *Epithalamion* by A. Kent Hieatt, *Short Time's Endless Monument* (New York: Columbia University Press, 1960). While I am generally suspicious of the interpretive value of such numerology, still it was somewhat astonishing to learn that during the summer solstice in southern Ireland the number of daylight hours is sixteen and a fraction and that in Spenser's poem night arrives at the fifth line of the seventeenth stanza. For an intelligent analysis of the value and the problems of Hieatt's approach see Enid Welsford's *Spenser: Fowre Hymnes, Epithalamion* (New York: Barnes and Noble, 1967), Appendix II, "Number Symbolism in *Epithalamion.*" More ambitious in his use of number symbolism is Alastair Fowler, *Spenser and the Numbers of Time* (London: Routledge and Kegan Paul, 1964); see William Nelson's review in *Renaissance News,* 18 (1965), 52.

Two articles that Harry Berger, Jr., included in his *Spenser, A Collection of Critical Essays* (Englewood Cliffs, N.J.: Prentice Hall Spectrum, 1968) are relevant here: M. L. Wine's "Spenser's 'Sweete Themmes': Of Time and the River," p. 40, and Richard Neuse's "The Triumph over Hasty Accidents: A Note on the Symbolic Mode of the *Epithalamion,*" p. 47.

20. This notion of decline is not new with Spenser. In the proem to Book V of the *Faerie Queene,* the world "growes daily wourse and wourse." Here, too, the transvaluation of values is attributed to mutability:

> For that which all men then did vertue call,
>> Is now cald vice; and that which vice was hight,
>> Is now hight vertue, and so us'd of all:
>> Right now is wrong, and wrong that was is right,
>> As all things else in time are chaunged quight.
>
> (4)

While Spenser in the body of his epic will represent the established view of order, in this proem he announces fears that the *Cantos of Mutabilitie* will more forcefully dramatize. The dissolution is cosmic, as the formerly immutable heavens themselves experience alteration (with harmful consequences for directionless man). See Douglas Bush's *Science and English Poetry* (New York: Oxford University Press, 1950), pp. 22–25.

21. See my chapter on Dante, p. 32, for an earlier use of the "second fall" idea.

22. See Raymond Jenkins, "Spenser and Ireland," *ELH*, 19 (1952), from which I quote this suggestive paragraph: "In the cantos of *Mutabilitie* Spenser's joy in his home seems haunted by the fear that an Irish raid will in a moment reduce the work of a lifetime to ruins. This consciousness makes the poetry of these cantos so suggestive of the instability of life. . . . In Ireland, at least, it seemed that lawlessness had become omnipotent, that endless restlessness had triumphed over endless peace. Though he avers that Mutabilitie ministers to an ultimate perfection wherein there shall be no charge, we feel that this reconciliation is not clear to his heart. It is only achieved by will; it is an act of faith. The last stanzas of the *Faerie Queene* are therefore the voice of a spirit utterly wearied by the vicissitudes of Ireland . . . so constant in her inconstancy." (p. 142)

23. Dean Church in his imaginative *Spenser* (New York: 1879), pp. 176–177, repeats the romantic legend of Spenser that the hardheaded Ben Jonson did much to propagate.

24. Esp. pp. 86–96.

25. *The Works of Edmund Spenser*, IX.52.

26. *The Problem of Order* (Chapel Hill, N.C.: University of North Carolina Press, 1962), pp. 55–56, 116–117.

27. Trans. A. J. Ungersma (Richmond, Va.: John Knox Press, 1964), p. 22.

8. Shakespeare's Histories

1. Line citations refer to *The Complete Works of Shakespeare*, ed. George Lyman Kittredge (Boston: Ginn, 1936), to which the quotations conform.

2. This speech, while out of step with the more challenging and dramatic nature of time in Shakespeare's historical — and natural — world, has much in common with Lucrece's tirades, especially her antelapsarian account of time's more beneficent functionings (936–959):

> Time's office is to fine the hate of foes,
>> To eat up errors by opinion bred,
>> Not spend the dowry of a lawful bed.
>
> .   .   .   .   .
>
> To show the beldame daughters of her daughter,
> To make the child a man, the man a child,
> To slay the tiger that doth live by slaughter,
> To tame the unicorn and lion wild,
> To mock the subtle in themselves beguil'd,
>> To cheer the ploughman with increaseful crops
>> And waste huge stones with little waterdrops.

Time's operations are decidedly moral in Lucrece's expectations. Even, in this section, where some hostility is suggested, time is rather about its business of conferring honorable *vetustas* upon ancient things. Dislodged from this happier time, Lucrece plunges to the opposite extreme, and makes time an agent of dark and insidious intent, makes it, in fact, the immoral counterpart of the benevolent time she had previously envisioned:

> Misshapen Time, copesmate of ugly Night,
> Swift subtle post, carrier of grisly care,
> Eater of youth, false slave to false delight,
> Base watch of woes, sin's packhorse, virtue's snare!
> Thou nursest all, and murth'rest all that are.
>> O, hear me then, injurious, shifting Time!
>> Be guilty of my death, since of my crime.
>>
>> (925–931)

This section of her address, in fact, anticipates the several invocations to a malevolent nature, to which Lady Macbeth and Macbeth turn for assistance.

The true historical dimensions of this poem are revealed near its end, when Brutus, in contrast to his later namesake, decides to give blows instead of words. After Lucrece takes her life, out of shame at her defilement, her husband Collatine and her father Lucretius join in a melodramatic duet of mournful exclamation. Brutus, who was only feignedly mad, like several other characters plotting revenge, gives them a lesson in historical action:

> Why, Collatine, is woe the cure for woe?
> Do wounds help wounds, or grief help grievous deeds?
> Is it revenge to give thyself a blow
> For his foul act by whom thy fair wife bleeds?
> Such childish humour from weak minds proceeds.
>> Thy wretched wife mistook the matter so,
>> To slay herself that should have slain her foe.
>>
>> (1821–1827)

Rather than weakening their resolve, in the manner of Richard II, with the "relenting dew of lamentation," he urges them to form instead a compact, and pray to the Roman gods that they might suffer Tarquin to be banished "by our strong arms." The difference between words and arms, so persistent in Shakespeare's vision, is here shown in embryo. This "revenge tragedy," like all revenge tragedies, is misnamed; since it urges effective action, it shares the ethic of the history plays.

3. I have already referred to the Ovidian source for this passage (*Met.* XV.199–205 in chapter 1, n17.

4. IV.i, available in *Elizabethan Plays,* ed. Hazelton Spencer (Boston: Heath, 1933).

5. My references are to Irving Ribner's valuable edition, *The Complete Plays of Christopher Marlowe* (New York: Odyssey, 1963).

6. John Choker, in his article, "Le Temps psychologique," *Journal de Psychologie,* 53 (1956), 303, 288. This entire number is devoted to the problem of time.

7. *Time in Greek Tragedy,* p. 9.

8. On this point see Cassirer, *The Platonic Renaissance in England,* trans., James P. Pettegrove (London: Nelson, 1953), pp. 8–24 and 104 ff.

9. Throughout this study, I shall be quoting from the 1560 edition, reprinted as *Wilson's Arte of Rhetorique,* ed. G. H. Mair (Oxford: Clarendon Press, 1909).

10. Some of the epistle's history is revealing here. Written in 1498 as a rhetorical example of persuasive argument for Lord Mountjoy, the letter was included in Erasmus' *De conscribendis epistolis* (1522). It entered into English Reform politics when it was translated by Richard Taverner and addressed to Thomas Cromwell, "A Ryght Frutefull Epystle / devysed by the moste excellent clerk Erasmus / in laude and prayse of matrymony" (1531–1532). In the prefatory letter to Cromwell, Taverner explains that, seeking to recommend himself for some service, he came upon the letter of Erasmus. He found it "expedient" to translate, and under Cromwell's protection to communicate it to the people, especially so "when he considered the blynd superstition of men and women which cease not day by day to profess and vow perpetual chastity before they sufficiently know themselves and the infirmitie of their nature, which thing (in my opinion) hath been and is yet unto this day the root and very cause original of innumerable mischiefs. I pray our lord Jesus of his infinite goodness to provide some speedy reformation, when it shall be his pleasure." E. J. Devereux, in his *A Bibliography of English Translations of Erasmus to 1700* (D.Phil., Oxford, 1967), writes, "In 1532 there began what can only be described as a *campaign* of publication and translation, much of it of Erasmus, aimed at achieving a combined religious and political reformation in England by persuading readers to support religious change, the Royal Supremacy, and the break with the Papacy." (p. xviii) "Taverner's translation of the *Encomium Matrimonii* marks the beginning of the campaign by its clear implication

that *adiaphora* [things indifferent to salvation] such as clerical celibacy could be attacked with relative impunity." (p. xxi) See also J. K. McConica, *English Humanists and Reformation Politics under Henry VII and Edward VI* (Oxford: Clarendon Press, 1965), pp. 116–118. In the letter's reliance on the language of growth, the doctrine of use and production, it obviously fits into the political — and economic — requirements of an emergent nation.

Stürzl, "Die Unsterblichkeit durch das Kind," p. 433, gives other instances of the use of "progeny" as a literary theme. More important for its significant discussion of the meaning of generation and "increase" for the Elizabethans and for Shakespeare is J. W. Lever's *The Elizabethan Love Sonnet* (London: Methuen, 1956), pp. 189–201. Mr. Lever rightly notes the importance of Erasmus' letter, and to his mention of it my own discussion is indebted.

11. *Before the Armada: The Growth of English Foreign Policy 1485– 1588* (London: Jonathan Cape, 1966), p. 16.

12. I have used the text in *Chief Pre-Shakespearean Dramas,* ed. Joseph Quincy Adams (Boston, Mass.: Houghton Mifflin, 1924).

13. For "husbandry" see Lever, *The Elizabethan Love Sonnet,* p. 194 and Wilson, *The Arte of Rhetorique,* p. 53.

14. (1935; rpt. Boston, Mass.: Beacon, 1958), p. 222.

15. See Geoffrey Bullough, *Narrative and Dramatic Sources of Shakespeare,* esp. vol. 3 (New York: Columbia University Press, 1960), where perhaps it is only the theme of time that might be suggested from Holinshed's account. After the Welsh forces dispersed, the chronicles can conclude that "the kings lingering of time before his coming over, gave opportunitie to the duke." (p. 400) But nowhere do these themes have anything like the dramatic forms given them by Shakespeare.

16. In a country as lush and green as England, gardening is naturally a national sport. And in Shakespeare's great tetralogies, where he is most intent on exemplifying his country's historical values and ideals, it is only fitting that the demands and the rewards of the garden should figure so prominently as standards of judgment. So, in the one English work that enjoys so special a relationship with the second tetralogy, Thomas Elyot's *The Governour,* a more prosaic but essentially anglicized education of the prince, the wisdom of gardening informs his concern both with the growth of the child and with the commonwealth. In a chapter of special relevance for *Richard II* (Book III, chap. xxx — that in matters of advice the general good ought always to outweigh the private) Elyot for not the first time uses the analogy from the garden. "For who commendeth those gardeners that will put all their diligence in trimming or keeping delicately one knot or bed of herbs, suffering all the remnant of their garden to be subverted with a great number of moles, and do attend at no time for the taking and destroying of them, until the herbs, wherein they have employed all their labours, be also turned up and perished, and the moles increased in so infinite numbers that no industry or labor may suffice to consume them, whereby the la-

bor is frustrate and all the garden made unprofitable and also unpleasant? In this similitude to the garden may also be resembled the public weal." *The Governour*, 2 vols., ed. Henry H. S. Croft (London: 1880), II.433–445.

But it is in Erasmus' epistle that the entire network of values functioning in the second tetralogy — the importance of children, the garden and the public order — is brought together. He lists examples from the animal world of the affection borne to their young by parents: "And this they call the law of Nature, the which as it is of most strength and force, so it spreadeth abroad most largely. Therefore, he is counted no good Gardener, that being content with things present, doth diligently prune his old Trees, and hath either no regard to imp or graft young Sets: because the self same Orchard (though it be never so well trimmed) must needs decay in time, and all the Trees die within few years: so he is not to be counted half a diligent citizen, that being content with the present multitude, hath no regard to increase the number." Wilson, p. 48.

17. Hugh MacLean, "Time and Horsemanship in Shakespeare's Histories," *UTQ*, 35 (1960), 229, rightly perceives the relationship between temporal mastery and horsemanship. See this article for the many additional references, although the author does not mention the prototypic speech of Tamburlaine. It should be further pointed out that Faustus, in his desperate antagonism toward time, is not being cavalier when he recalls Ovid, "O lente, lente currite noctis equi." Iconographically, this merger of time and horsemanship is rich. Several works depicting Temperance, equipped with clock and halter, are reproduced in Chapuis, pp. 2, 3. George Whitney's *Choice of Emblemes* (1586), ed. Henry Green (London: 1866) is illustrative. "Temeritas," p. 6, is depicted by an incompetent horseman being cast headlong. The fierce horses with "stomach stout" represent the will, which needs to be bridled. Another, "Non locus virum, sed vir locum ornat" — dedicated to Sir Philip Sidney — reveals the better guide who is capable of mastering the steed's fierce courage, concluding, "And eke such horse, the fool should not bestride."

18. Considering Richard's childlessness, his failures at honorable husbandry, and his obvious incapacity in governing his land, it is remarkable how many times figures of childbirth or of begetting enter into his speeches and those of his queen. Too little attention has been paid to Richard's wife: she is his spokeswoman and sets the pattern for his reaction and address (Coleridge's reference to Richard's "intellectual feminineness" is very appropriate). It is through her that we get the royal party's first reaction to the news of Bolingbroke's return. Before the news arrives, she is filled with fearful premonitions. Some sorrow, ripe in fortune's womb, is coming toward her. To Bushy's rational explanation of this sorrow, the queen replies that her sorrow is not the usual conceit:

> Conceit is still deriv'd
> From some forefather grief. Mine is not so,

> For nothing hath begot my something grief,
> Or something hath the nothing that I grieve.
>   (II.ii.35–38)

Green enters bringing the adverse report of Bolingbroke's arrival and the supporters he has gained. The queen's reply contains the third meaningful reference to childbearing in this short scene:

> So, Green, thou art the midwife to my woe,
> And Bolingbroke my sorrow's dismal heir.
> Now hath my soul brought forth her prodigy;
> And I, a gasping new-deliver'd mother,
> Have woe to woe, sorrow to sorrow join'd.
>   (61–65)

When we recall that both the king's and queen's language of childbirth is related to nothingness, we also should think that hysteria was a mother.

19. Paul A. Jorgensen, in " 'Redeeming time' in *Henry IV*," *Redeeming Shakespeare's Words* (Berkeley and Los Angeles, Calif.: University of California Press, 1962), p. 54, makes the statement that "The concept of time remains external to the play [*RII*]." For other treatments of time in Shakespeare's histories, see Benjamin T. Spencer, "*2 Henry IV* and the Theme of Time," *UTQ*, 13 (1944), 394; Peter Seng, "Songs, Time, and the Rejection of Falstaff," *Shakespeare's Survey*, 15 (1962), 31; Harold E. Toliver, "Falstaff, the Prince, and the History Play," *SQ*, 16 (1965), 63; MacLean's article mentioned in n17; and several of my own essays. For related material, see Tom Driver's *The Sense of History in Greek and Shakespearean Drama* (New York: Columbia University Press, 1960); Toliver's "Shakespeare and the Abyss of Time," *JEGP*, 64 (1965), 234; *Shakespearean Research and Opportunities*, ed. W. R. Elton, indicates the growing number of theses, books, and articles either completed or projected that deal with time in Shakespeare.

20. For a discussion of the various levels of plot, see Harry Levin's, "The Shakespearean Overplot," *Renaissance Drama*, 8 (1965), 63.

21. For another application of this notion, see Romilly's *La Crainte et l'angoisse dans le theatre d'Eschyle* (Paris: "Les belles Lettres," 1958).

22. *The Civil Wars*, ed. Laurence Michel (New Haven, Conn.: Yale University Press, 1958), I.21. The notion is an ancient one, and, in the English tradition, could properly be called Boethian. The point of adversity is so that man does not wax proud by long "welefulnesse" — in Chaucer's rendering.

23. *The Presentation of Time in the Elizabethan Drama*, Yale Studies in English, 44 (New York: Holt, 1912), 91 and 103–104.

24. J. Dover Wilson, *The Fortunes of Falstaff* (Cambridge: Cambridge University Press, 1943), pp. 39–40.

25. See the chapter "Character versus Action in Shakespeare," *The Poetry of Experience* (New York: Random House, 1957), p. 160.

26. "J. Dover Wilson on Falstaff," in *Classics and Commercials* (New York: Farrar, Straus, 1950), pp. 166–167.

27. "At Stratford-on-Avon," *Essays and Introductions* (New York: Macmillan, 1961), p. 105. A. C. Bradley's essay "On Falstaff," was printed in his *Oxford Lectures on Poetry*, 2nd ed. (London: Macmillan, 1950).

28. See his edition of *I Henry IV* (Cambridge: Cambridge University Press, 1946), p. 188.

29. Printed in *The Renaissance*, ed. Tinsley Helton (Madison, Wis.: University of Wisconsin Press, 1961), p. 148; reprinted in *Refractions* (New York: Oxford University Press, 1966).

30. *Shakespeare's History Plays* (New York: Macmillan, 1947), p. 315. Other useful ideas of *Macbeth* and time are in J. Middleton Murry's *Shakespeare* (New York: Harcourt, Brace, 1936); Roy Walker, *The Time Is Free: A Study of "Macbeth"* (London: Drakers, 1949); and Tom Driver, *The Sense of History in Greek and Shakespearean Drama.*

31. Quoted in the New Arden *Macbeth*, ed. Kenneth Muir, 9th ed., rev. (Cambridge, Mass.: Harvard University Press, 1962), p. 159.

9. Shakespeare's Tragedies

1. *The Poetics,* trans. S. H. Butcher, rpt. in *Criticism: The Foundations of Modern Judgment,* ed. Mark Schorer *et al.* (New York: Harcourt, Brace, 1948), p. 202.

2. Suggested by a valuable chapter, "The Structure of Tragedy," some of whose thoughts I here have paraphrased, in T. R. Henn's *The Harvest of Tragedy* (London: Methuen, 1956), esp. p. 32. The suggestiveness of this book is rich throughout. My temporal notion of "contraction" is supported by Professor Henn's awareness that tragedy possesses "a compression and energy that is found in no other form." (p. xii)

3. *Science and the Modern World* (Cambridge: Cambridge University Press, 1926), p. 13.

4. 1944; rpt. Gloucester, Mass.: P. Smith, 1968, p. 89.

5. The phrase is Harley Granville-Barker's, in his *Prefaces to Shakespeare,* 2 vols. (Princeton, N.J.: Princeton University Press, 1946–1947), II, 350.

6. From Camden's *The History of the Most Renowned and Victorious Princess Elizabeth, Late Queen of England,* trans. Robert Norton (1630), rpt. in *The Age of Elizabeth: Selected Source Materials in Elizabethan Social and Literary History* (Boston, Mass.: Houghton Mifflin, 1960), p. 19.

7. From "Carnival," *Soliloquies in England and Later Soliloquies* (New York: Scribner's, 1922), p. 142.

8. H. B. Charlton's discussion of the experimental nature of *Romeo and Juliet* is useful: *Shakespearian Tragedy* (Cambridge: Cambridge University Press, 1949).

9. The New Arden *Antony and Cleopatra,* ed. M. R. Ridley, 9th ed., rev. (Cambridge, Mass.: Harvard University Press, 1954), Appendix V, 258–285, carries the relevant parts of the North-Plutarch text.

10. New York: Macmillan, 1942, p. 174.

11. *Prefaces to Renaissance Literature,* p. 90.

12. *Beyond Tragedy* (New York: Scribner's, 1937), pp. 28–30.

13. *Essai sur les idées dans l'oeuvre de Shakespeare,* p. 412.

14. For this and other parallel passages, see John M. Robertson's classic study, *Montaigne and Shakespeare* (London: 1909), pp. 42–43.

15. For probably the best exposition of the notion of Christian tragedy see A. S. P. Woodhouse, "Tragic Effect in *Samson Agonistes,*" *UTQ,* 28 (1958–1959), 205.

16. I quote from Douglas Bush's *The Complete Poetical Works of John Milton* (Boston, Mass.: Houghton Mifflin, 1965).

17. Princeton, N.J.: Princeton University Press, 1929, p. 72.

18. " 'We Came Crying Hither': An Essay on Some Characteristics of *King Lear,*" *The Yale Review,* 54 (1964), 170.

19. "Character and Society in *King Lear,*" rpt. *Shakespeare: The Tragedies,* ed. Alfred Harbage (Englewood Cliffs, N.J.: Prentice-Hall Spectrum, 1964), p. 146.

10. Shakespeare's Comedies and Last Plays

1. Evanthius, an ancient critic, succinctly describes the nature of comedy: "The moral of tragedy is that life should be rejected; of comedy, that it should be embraced." Translated by J. V. Cunningham in *Woe or Wonder: The Emotional Effect of Shakespearean Tragedy,* collected in *Tradition and Poetic Structure* (Denver: Swallow, 1960), p. 164 and note p. 259.

2. *Shakespeare's Comedies* (Oxford: Clarendon Press, 1960).

3. *Shakespeare's Happy Comedies* (London: Faber and Faber, 1962), p. 73.

4. Like all other writers on comedy in general and on the nature of Shakespearean comedy in particular, I have benefitted from the ideas of Northrop Frye in such essays as "The Argument of Comedy," *English Institute Essays,* 1948 (New York: Columbia University Press, 1949); and those of C. L. Barber in *Shakespeare's Festive Comedy.*

5. For a summary of this motif and the numerical variants thereof, see S. C. Chew's *The Pilgrimage of Life* (New Haven: Yale University Press, 1962), pp. 153–173.

6. This same notion has been expressed by Frederick Turner in an Oxford University B.Litt. dissertation, "Shakespeare and the Nature of Time" (1967), p. 31.

11. Milton

1. This data is given by David Masson in his *The Life of John Milton* (1859–1880), I (rev. ed., 1881), 152–153 and 232–236.

2. All quotations of Milton's poetry are taken from Douglas Bush's *The Complete Poetical Works of John Milton* (Boston: Houghton Mifflin, 1965); the prose is taken from *The Works of John Milton*, 18 vols. (New York: Columbia University Press, 1931–1938), shortened to *Works* in the text, with volume number and page reference following.

3. Two of Milton's ablest modern editors, Merritt Y. Hughes and, after him, Douglas Bush, in the light of this verse from Isaiah, regard the offspring not as physical progeny but as spiritual reward.

4. I say "in effect," since Milton did not strictly disinherit them; he merely left them the money due him from Mr. Powell, his first wife's father: "They shall have no other benefit of my estate than the said portion, and what I have besides done for them; they having been very undutiful to me [20 July 1674]." (*Works*, XVIII.424)

5. See *The Student's Milton*, ed., Frank Allen Patterson (New York: Appleton-Century-Crofts, rev. 1933), pp. xxii, xxv (from which I quote); and *The Early Lives of Milton*, ed. Helen Darbishire (London: Constable, 1932), pp. 10, 6.

6. Patterson, xvii, xxiii; Darbishire, 24, 12.

7. From the instructive note by Donald Dorian, the Yale *Complete Prose of John Milton* (New Haven: Yale University Press, 1959), II, 371–372. On the issue of Puritanism and holidays see Christopher Hill, "The Uses of Sabbatarianism," in *Society and Puritanism in Pre-Revolutionary England* (London: Secker and Warburg, 1964): "Protestants and especially Puritans elevated the Sabbath, the *regular* day of rest and meditation suited to the regular and continuous rhythms of modern industrial society: they attacked the very numerous and irregular festivals which had hitherto marked out the seasons. To celebrate a hundred or more saints' days in a year was all very well in an agricultural society like that of medieval England, or the more primitive pre-Christian societies whose festivals the saints' days so often preserve. Agricultural labour is spasmodic, very intense for brief periods. But an industrialized society, such as England was becoming in the sixteenth century, needs regular disciplined labour." (p. 146) I do not need to mention how Mr. Hill's emphasis on the need for regularity and discipline of labor coincides with many of the Renaissance concerns with time that this study has been following. Certainly Milton, in his way and on his different plane, shares these modern attempts to systematize work habits. But in his later, most serious works, values of ease, patience, and divine trust assume greater importance.

8. Andrew Bongiorno astutely observes that if logic is somewhat reluctantly readmitted into the young man's curriculum, "metaphysics is banished once and for all and is never so much as named again." "Tendencies in Milton's *Of Education*," *Journal of General Education*, 4 (1949), 109 ff. As Professor Bongiorno points out, this tendency is fully anticipated in the *Third Prolusion*, "Against the Scholastic Philosophy" (see *Works*, XII.165, 167, 169). "And found no end, in wand'ring mazes lost" — this passage, from *Paradise Lost* (II.555–565), shows the strong continuity of the anti-metaphysical bias in Milton.

9. Italian would be learned at odd hours, but Hebrew at set times.

10. In *The Reason* Milton wrote that he "might perhaps leave something so written to aftertimes as they should not willingly let it die." (*Works,* III.i.236) In *Areopagitica* he values those who value learning for itself, and for no other end "but the service of God and of truth, and perhaps that lasting fame and perpetuity of praise which God and good men have consented shall be the reward of those whose published labors advance the good of mankind." (IV.323–324) While qualified, these are nevertheless stirring assertions, testimony of his intense humanistic faith. There is an index to the Columbia edition of the works of Milton where many references to fame are listed. In his poetry, his "On Shakespeare. 1630" is a memorial comment to Shakespeare's power and lastingness, "Dear son of memory, great heir of fame." Even the loose chronoligical distinctions that we have been making are blurred by *When the assault was intended to the city* (Sonnet VIII, "Captain or colonel . . ."), which evidences a conventional belief in the poet's power to bestow fame. We can have recourse to Bush's headnote, which is accurate in its judgment: "It is a quite impersonal consideration, amidst the violence of war, of the value of poetry, in terms of its "eternizing" power, as ancient and Renaissance poets often wrote of it." Benjamin refers to it as a "rather peculiar sonnet." (p. 83) See Chapter 12, n4 below.

11. In this regard, see also sonnet IX, "Lady that in the prime . . ."

12. In the highly serious, anonymous *Life of Milton* it is even clear that industriousness and full use of his talent were considered attributes of Milton's character. Reporting the very brief courtship of Mary Powell — the marriage took place after only a month's time — the biographer adds parenthetically that this was "according to [Milton's] practice of not wasting that precious talent." (Patterson, p. xviii, Darbishire, p. 22) In an earlier passage he sums up the young poet's continental journey this way: "He had by this time laid in a great stock of knowledge, which as he designed not for the purchase of wealth, so neither intended he it, as a miser's hoard, to lie useless." (Patterson, p. xvii, Darbishire, p. 21) But as these poems show, in Milton's most serious utterances when it comes to higher issues, the parable of the talents and the doctrine of use are of clearly subordinate value. In sonnet IX, Milton praises the young woman for having chosen "The better part with Mary and with Ruth," where we remember that Mary chose to return to Jesus rather than join her sister Martha in housework. (Luke, 10.42) Comus, tempting the Lady, resorts to the argument of use: "Beauty is Nature's coin, must not be hoarded, / But must be current." (739–740)

13. Joseph H. Summers, *The Muses' Method* (London: Chatto and Windus, 1962), pp. 13–14.

14. In *Surprised by Sin* (New York: St. Martin's, 1967), Stanley Fish acknowledges that his own work was anticipated by Summers, see p. 2, n1.

15. On the theme of truth being the daughter of time, see the classic essay by Fritz Saxl, "Veritas filia temporis," *Philosophy and History: The Ernst Cassirer Festschrift* (Oxford: Clarendon Press, 1936), p. 197; the

section "Temporis filia veritas," in Stürzl's *Der Zeitbegriff*, and also briefly Gertrud Bing's "*Nugae circa veritatem:* Notes on Anton Francesco Doni," *Journal of the Warburg Institute*, 1 (1937–1938), 306, 309, n3, n5. The young Milton of course endorsed the creative potential implied in this concept. In the *Seventh Prolusion, Of Education,* and especially the *Areopagitica*, it is the fundamental faith, asserted or not, of Milton's program. But like Dante in the *Purgatorio* and the *Paradiso*, Milton in *Paradise Lost* is impressed more by man's falling off than by his progress. "So all shall turn degenerate, all depraved." (XI.806). If in his *Naturam non pati senium* Milton lined up on the side of Hakewill in the celebrated controversy, in his later poetry he seems clearly on the side of Goodman. See Victor Harris, *All Coherence Gone* (Chicago: University of Chicago Pres, 1949).

16. Christopher Hill, in a discussion of the new developing work discipline ("The Industrious Sort of People") asserts that "In *Paradise Lost* Milton twice went out of his way to emphasize that Adam and Eve worked *before* the Fall." (*Puritanism and Society*, p. 128) What "out of his way" means is not entirely clear. Yet in a more fundamental sense the passage is misleading, since while Adam and Eve worked, their labor was not enforced: it was still part of their free will and spirit. This is an important difference, because certainly after the Fall, labor, as a product of sin, is onerous and objectionable. Milton's own proclivity for study and earlier his advocacy of long hours (which however was later relaxed to an easier regimen) pose no contradiction here, since presumably this was a free expression of man's higher possibilities, in which he could delight.

17. "Time and Space in Milton," *From Shakespeare to Joyce* (Garden City, N. Y.: Doubleday, 1944), p. 416. This essay was a portion of "Criticisms Criticized," *JEGP*, 41 (1942), where Stoll's emphasis on time is part of a larger critique of Marjorie Nicolson's article, "Milton and the Telescope," included in her *Science and Imagination* (Ithaca, N.Y.: Great Seal Books, 1956). It was Miss Nicolson who quoted David Masson's remark and attempted to substantiate it by discussing time in Shakespeare and space in Milton. The thought does not appear in Masson's writings; it was attributed to him by William Allen Nielson, who heard Masson's lectures at Edinburgh. (See *Science and Imagination*, p. 9, n31.) Modern scholars, undeterred by the neatness of Masson's position, have continued to discuss the great prominence of time in Milton's thought, and have formed, in so doing, the best bibliography on time devoted to any of the writers covered in this study. In addition to the work of Patrides, see Laurence Stapleton, "Milton's Conception of Time in *The Christian Doctrine, Harvard Theological Review*, 57 (1964), 9; "Perspectives of Time in *Paradise Lost*," *PQ*, 45 (1960), 734; a doctoral dissertation by Laury Zwicky, "Milton's Use of Time: Image and Principle," (University of Oklahoma, 1959); Summers' "Grateful Vicissitude" in *Paradise Lost*," *PMLA*, 69 (1954), 251, rpt. in *The Muse's Method*; Rosalie L. Colie, "Time and Eternity: Paradox and Structure in *Paradise Lost*," *Journal of the Warburg and Courtauld Institutes*, 23 (1960), 127, rpt. in *Paradoxia Epidemica* (Princeton, N.J.: Princeton University Press, 1966). See also Arnold Williams' "Renaissance Commentaries on

Genesis and Some Elements of the Theology of *Paradise Lost*," *PMLA*, 56 (1941), 151; Albert R. Cirillo, "Noon-Midnight and the Temporal Structure of *Paradise Lost*," *ELH*, 29 (1962), 372, and " 'Hail Holy Light' and the Divine Time in *Paradise Lost*," *JEGP*, 68 (1969), 45, in addition to the sections of books referred to in n25.

18. Reprinted in *Prefaces to Renaissance Literature*. See p. 66.

19. See "Ascending by Degrees Magnificent: The Christian View of History" and "Till Time Stand Fixed: The Eschata of History," in the second.

20. *Milton and the Christian Tradition*, p. 259.

21. "*Paradise Lost*: The Hill of History," *The Huntington Library Quarterly*, 31 (1967), 44. See also his bibliography covering the fully warranted recent attention paid to the merits of Books XI and XII, and reflecting the increased modern awareness of historiography. George Williamson's article "The Education of Adam," *MP*, 61 (1963), 96, reprinted in *Milton: Modern Essays in Criticism*, ed. Arthur E. Barker (New York: Oxford Galaxy, 1965), should also be added. Barker contributes bibliographical notes, pp. 307, 356.

22. Panofsky's article is of course fundamental. Edmund Reiss deals with the problem in "An Instance of Milton's Use of Time," *MLN*, 72 (1957), 410, but does not make use of Panofsky's historical clarification.

23. Patrides, *Milton and the Christian Tradition*, p. 222.

24. W. B. C. Watkins, *An Anatomy of Milton's Verse* (Baton Rouge, La.: Louisiana State University Press, 1955), p. 44.

25. "*Figura*" *Scenes from the Drama of European Literature* (New York: Meridian, 1959), pp. 58–59. I could of course have quoted from the excellent work of recent Milton scholars. For discussions of the disruption of normal time sequences in *Paradise Lost*, and of the temporal implications of myth and typology, see Isabel MacCaffrey's "*Paradise Lost*" *as Myth* (Cambridge, Mass.: Harvard University Press, 1959); Helen Gardner's *A Reading of "Paradise Lost"* (New York: Oxford University Press, 1965), pp. 35–51; William G. Madsen's *From Shadowy Types to Truth: Studies in Milton's Symbolism* (New Haven, Conn.: Yale University Press, 1968); and Fish's *Surprised by Sin*, pp. 30–37.

25. *From Shakespeare to Joyce*, p. 416.

27. Of *Paradise Regained*, Edward Phillips writes in his biography, "It is generally censured to be much inferior to the other [*Paradise Lost*], though he could not hear with patience any such thing when related to him." (Patterson, xliii; Darbishire, 75–76)

28. "Theme and Pattern in *Paradise Regained*," *UTQ*, 25 (1955–1956), 176.

29. "*Kairos* in *Paradise Regained*: the Divine Plan," *ELH*, 31 (1964), 271; and the same author's doctoral dissertation, "Milton's Use of Time: Image and Principle," (University Microfilm, 1961).

30. As Mr. Zwicky does in "*Kairos*," p. 274.

31. See Richard Ellmann, *James Joyce* (New York: Oxford University Press, 1959), pp. 430, 449.

12. Summary and Epilogue

1. "Le Temps du travail," p. 611.

2. Trans. F. Hopman (London: E. Arnold, 1924), p. 70. The full representation of this complex problem is given in the late Maria Rosa Lida de Malkiel's *L'Idée de la gloire dans la tradition occidentale,* trans. Sylvia Roubaud (Paris: Klincksieck, 1968), the translated title of which might give a better idea of its scope than the Spanish original, *La idea de la fama en la Edad Media Castellana* (Mexico: Fondo de Cultura Economica, 1952). There she discusses many of the affirmative and negative positions that men have held in regard to fame from classical antiquity through the Christian middle ages. Her thesis is similar to Huizinga's: that one needs to qualify the innovative character of the Renaissance devotion to fame. While maintaining that "dans ses grandes lignes" there is a decisive difference (p. vii), and that in the Renaissance the affirmation of fame was "plus variée et plus explicite," still she concludes, "il reste que la soif de renom qui caracterise le debut de l'Age moderne constitue l'aboutissement d'une evolution continue tout au long du Moyen Age, et non point un retour a l'Antiquité sans lien avec le proche passé medieval." (p. 285) Primarily the connection indicated is with the profane spheres of chivalric and courtly literatures. But here, as I argue in my text, the code of honor involves incontestable verities of social rank and personal valor. One must do nothing to disgrace or belittle such status. To maintain the honor of one's lady has, of course, nothing to do with fame; and the honor of battle is not a long-lasting achievement. Honor here exists in a close network of known relations: its extent is spatial, geographic — whereas Renaissance fame is temporal, extending to unknown posterity. Still there are striking examples of posterior fame (see p. 115). The most interesting examples come from the lettered class, and their veneration of the book, which was to them coextensive with knowledge. The belief in the lastingness of the written word definitely looks forward to Renaissance hopes. See pp. 148–150, esp. the valuable passage from Richard of Bury's *Philobiblon,* where man is at war with time, a Saturn who devours his children.

3. "Literary Fame," p. 65.

4. "Fame, Poetry, and the Order of History in the Literature of the English Renaissance," *Studies in the Renaissance,* 6 (1959), 84. Other evidence testifies to the great changes brought about in these matters by the seventeenth century. For Herbert Read, Cartesianism removed personal and poetic values from a scientific universe — *The Sense of Glory* (Cambridge: Cambridge University Press, 1929), pp. 57 ff. For Whitehead, whom Read quotes, "the real concomitant of Cartesianism is Puritanism." (p. 72) Looking beyond religion and philosophy to society, M. Ariès indicates other areas of consideration, "In the second half of the seventeenth century, the genres born of Erasmus's 'civility' and Castiglione's 'courtier' underwent some significant changes. The Renaissance ideal of ambition and elevation disap-

peared at the same time as the courtier was replaced by the *honnête homme* and the court by society." (p. 388)

5. 1957; rev. rpt., Baltimore: Penguin Peregrine, 1967, p. 31.

6. Robert Jay Lifton, "Protean Man," *History and Human Survival* (New York: Random House, 1970), pp. 329–330.

7. From Cipolla, *Clocks and Culture,* pp. 53–54.

8. Vol. 4 (Madison, Wis.: University of Wisconsin Press, 1966), p. 36. There were of course sonnets with *carpe diem* exhortations, i.e., Gongora's "Mientras por competir con tu cabello." See B. Escandon, *Los temas de "Carpe diem" y la brevedad de la rosa en la poesia española* (Barcelona, 1938).

9. New York: Washington Square Press, 1963, p. 66.

10. E. P. Thompson, "Time, Work-discipline, and Industrial Capitalism," *Past and Present,* 38 (1967), 95. However, one can also wonder, given the material of this study, if Mr. Thompson is correct in declaring that "Puritanism . . . was the agent which converted men to new valuations of time." Do we not have earlier indications of such new valuations, of which even Puritanism was a product? That it did intensify developments already under way, there is no doubt.

11. In his conclusion Philippe Ariès writes of the "Victorian gravity" that settled on the education of children: "The solicitude of family, church, moralists and administrators deprived the child of the freedom he had hitherto enjoyed among adults. It inflicted on him the birch, the prison-cell, in a word, the punishments usually reserved for convicts from the lowest strata of society. But this severity was the expression of a very different feeling from the old indifference: an obsessive love which was to dominate society from the eighteenth century on." (p. 413) It is no accident, then, given this background, that *Great Expectations* should open with a child and a convict meeting in a cemetery, nor that writers should look back to a period of childhood spontaneity, before the rigorous hands seized their youth, nor that Wordsworth should have pervaded nineteenth-century literature like the smell of fresh grass.

12. Quoted by David V. Erdman in Part I of an extremely interesting two-part article,"Coleridge,Wordsworth, and the Wedgwood Fund," *Bulletin of the New York Public Library,* 60 (1956), 430.

13. This draft version can be had in *The Poetical Works of William Wordsworth,* vol. 5, ed. Ernest de Selincourt and Helen Darbishire (Oxford: Clarendon Press, 1949), pp. 345–346. Revisions were made in the 1805–6 and 1850 versions, for which see *Wordsworth's Prelude,* ed. Selincourt, 2nd ed. rev. by Darbishire (Oxford: Clarendon Press, 1959), pp. 156–157.

14. The essay is contained in *Romanticism Reconsidered,* Selected Papers from the English Institute, ed. Northrop Frye (New York: Columbia University Press, 1963).

Index

Harvard Studies in Comparative Literature

* Out of print